Monographs in Theoretical Computer Science
An EATCS Series

More information about this series at http://www.springer.com/series/776

Kenichi Morita

Theory of Reversible Computing

 Springer

Kenichi Morita
Professor Emeritus, Hiroshima University
Hiroshima, Japan

Series Editors
Monika Henzinger
Faculty of Science
Universität Wien
Wien, Austria

Mogens Nielsen
Department of Computer Science
Aarhus Universitet
Aarhus, Denmark

Arto Salomaa
Turku Centre of Computer Science
Turku, Finland

Juraj Hromkovič
ETH Zentrum
Department of Computer Science
Swiss Federal Institute of Technology
Zürich, Switzerland

Grzegorz Rozenberg
Leiden Centre of Advanced
Computer Science
Leiden University
Leiden, The Netherlands

ISSN 1431-2654   ISSN 2193-2069   (electronic)
Monographs in Theoretical Computer Science. An EATCS Series
ISBN 978-4-431-56832-2   ISBN 978-4-431-56606-9   (eBook)
DOI 10.1007/978-4-431-56606-9

Printed on acid-free paper

This Springer imprint is published by Springer Nature
The registered company is Springer Japan KK
The registered company address is: Chiyoda First Bldg. East, 8-1 Nishi-Kanda Chiyoda-ku, 101-0065 Tokyo, Japan

To my parents, my wife, my children, and my grandchildren

Preface

A reversible computing system is a "backward deterministic" system such that every state of the system has at most one predecessor. Hence, there is no pair of distinct states that go to the same state. Though its definition is so simple, it is closely related to physical reversibility. The study of reversible computing originated from an investigation of energy dissipation in reversible and irreversible computing systems. Rolf Landauer investigated the relation between reversibility in computing and reversibility in physics in his paper "Irreversibility and heat generation in the computing process" (IBM J. Res. Dev., Vol. 5, pp. 183–191, 1961). He pointed out that an irreversible logical operation inevitably causes energy dissipation in the computing system. Since then, reversible computing has been studied in relation to physical reversibility. Besides the problem of energy dissipation in computing, it is important to know how reversibility can be effectively utilized in computing. This is because future computing devices will surely be implemented directly by physical phenomena in the nano-scale level, and reversibility is one of the fundamental microscopic physical laws of Nature. For this purpose, various models of reversible computing have been proposed and investigated till now.

In this book, reversible computing is studied from the standpoint of the theory of automata and computing. We deal with various reversible computing models belonging to several different levels, which range from a microscopic level to a macroscopic one. They are reversible physical models, reversible logic elements, reversible functional modules composed of logic elements, reversible computing systems such as Turing machines, cellular automata, and others. The purpose of this book is to clarify how computation can be carried out efficiently and elegantly in these reversible computing models. We shall see that even very simple reversible systems have computational universality in spite of the constraint of reversibility. We shall also see various reversible systems in different levels are related each other, i.e., a reversible system in a higher level can be constructed out of those in a lower level. Moreover, the construction methods are often very unique and different from those in the traditional methods. Thus, these computing models as well as the designing methods will give us new insights for future computing systems.

This book is not a comprehensive textbook on reversible computing, but describes mainly the results shown in the papers by myself and my colleagues, which were published between 1989 and 2017. In this book, readers will see how the world of reversible computing works, how reversible computing systems are constructed out of simple reversible primitives, how they are different from the traditional computing systems, and how they can be computationally universal. In fact, we shall see even very simple reversible systems have high capability of computing, and thus reversibility is not a constraint, but a useful property for computing.

This book consists of 14 chapters. Chapter 1 is an introduction. In Chaps. 2–4, reversible logic elements for constructing reversible machines are investigated. In Chaps. 5–8, reversible Turing machines, a standard model of reversible computing systems, are studied. In Chap. 9, some other reversible computing models are investigated. In Chaps. 10–14, reversible cellular automata, a spatiotemporal model of reversible dynamical systems, are studied.

There is no prerequisite knowledge to read this book besides some basics on logic, discrete mathematics and formal languages. But, it is preferable to have some knowledge on the theories of automata and computing. Fortunately, the framework of reversible computing itself is very simple. Therefore, in many cases, readers can easily understand the basic function and the structure of each such system. However, its behavior can be very complex even if the structure of the system is simple. Hence, sometimes, it becomes quite difficult to follow its behavior by using only paper and pencil. In some of these cases, readers can find files in the References that contain computer simulation results of such reversible systems.

More than 50 years have passed since Landauer's paper appeared. Thus, the history of reversible computing is relatively long. But, it is still developing, and there remain many problems to be investigated. Also, even at present, it is not so clear which results will become practically useful in the future. However, the world of reversible computing will lead readers to the new ways of thinking that cannot be found in the traditional design methodologies for computing systems. I hope the theory of reversible computing will stimulate readers' interest, and open new vistas for future computing systems.

Acknowledgments. This work would not have been accomplished without the help and encouragement given by many people in many countries. I would express my highest gratitude to all of them. In particular, I would express my special thanks to Prof. Toshio Mitsui and Prof. Kazuhiro Sugata who guided me in the early days of my research career in Osaka University. Frequent discussions with them led me to the research fields of automata theory, cellular automata, and finally reversible computing. Since then, I had many good colleagues and students in Hiroshima University, Yamagata University, Osaka University, and other places in the world. Working with them was a great pleasure for me. I am grateful to them, especially, Susumu Adachi, Andrew Adamatzky, Artiom Alhazov, Yoichi Fujii, Yoshifumi Gono, Masateru Harao, Takahiro Hori, Katsunobu Imai, Teijiro Isokawa, Chuzo Iwamoto, Atsushi Kanno, Hiroko Kato, Jia Lee, Maurice Margenstern, Genaro J. Martinez, Mitsuya Morimoto, Yuta Mukai, Noritaka Nishihara, Masanori Ogino,

Tsuyoshi Ogiro, Ferdinand Peper, Akihiko Shirasaki, Rei Suyama, Keiji Tanaka, Tsuyoshi Tanizawa, Yasuyuki Tojima, Ryoichi Ueno, Satoshi Ueno, Hiroshi Umeo, Yoshikazu Yamaguchi, and Yasunori Yamamoto for their helpful discussions, cooperation, and coauthoring the papers on reversible computing and related fields.

I also express my cordial thanks to the anonymous reviewer for his/her very careful reading and valuable comments. The manuscript was greatly improved by the detailed comments.

This work on reversible computing was supported by JSPS KAKENHI Grant Number JP15K00019.

September 2017   *Kenichi Morita*

Contents

Acronyms

CA	cellular automaton
CM	counter machine
CTS	cyclic tag system
CTSH	cyclic tag system with halting condition
ECA	elementary cellular automaton
ETPCA	elementary triangular partitioned cellular automaton
GoL	Game of Life
ID	instantaneous description
IDTM	irreversible deterministic Turing machine
INTM	irreversible nondeterministic Turing machine
$\mathscr{L}(\mathscr{A})$	class of languages accepted by the class of automata $\mathscr{A}$
LBA	linear-bounded automaton
MFA	multi-head finite automaton
m-TS	m-tag system
PCA	partitioned cellular automaton
RCA	reversible cellular automaton
RCM	reversible counter machine
RDTM	reversible deterministic Turing machine
RE	rotary element
RETPCA	reversible elementary triangular partitioned cellular automaton
RLEM	reversible logic element with memory
RMFA	reversible multi-head finite automaton
RNTM	reversible nondeterministic Turing machine
RPCA	reversible partitioned cellular automaton
RSM	reversible sequential machine
RTM	reversible Turing machine
SM	sequential machine
TM	Turing machine
TM($S(n)$)	$S(n)$ space-bounded Turing machine
UTM	universal Turing machine
URTM	universal reversible Turing machine

Chapter 1
Introduction

Abstract Reversible computing is a paradigm that has a close relation to physical reversibility. Since microscopic physical laws are reversible, and future computing devices will surely be implemented directly by physical phenomena in the nano-scale level, it is an important problem to know how reversibility can be effectively utilized in computing. Reversible computing systems are defined as systems for which each of their computational configurations has at most one predecessor. Hence, they are "backward deterministic" systems. Though the definition is thus rather simple, these systems reflect physical reversibility very well, and they are suited for investigating how computing systems can be realized in reversible physical environments. In this chapter, we argue reversibility in physics and computing, the significance of reversible computing, and the scope of this volume. Various models of reversible computing ranging from a microscopic level to a macroscopic one are dealt with from the viewpoint of the theory of automata and computing. Terminologies and notations on logic, mathematics, and formal languages used in this volume are also summarized.

Keywords reversibility in computing, reversibility in physics, reversible computing machine, reversible cellular automaton, reversible logic element

1.1 Reversibility in Physics and Computing

Reversibility is a notion that was argued originally in physics. It is known that microscopic physical laws are reversible in the sense that they are invariant under the time-reversal operation. For example, in classical mechanics, the same law holds for both positive and negative directions of time. It is also the case in quantum mechanics, where an evolution of a quantum system is described by a unitary operator. Since physical reversibility is thus one of the fundamental microscopic properties of Nature, it is an important problem to know how such a property can be effectively utilized in computing. This is because future computing devices will surely be implemented directly by physical phenomena in the nano-scale level.

Reversibility in computing is an analogous notion to physical reversibility, but its definition is rather simple. Reversible computing systems are systems for which each of their computational configurations has at most one predecessor. Hence, every computing process can be traced backward uniquely from the end to the start. In other words, they are backward deterministic systems. Though its definition is thus simple, we shall see later that these systems reflect physical reversibility very well.

Landauer [37] first argued the relation between reversibility in computing and reversibility in physics. He proposed *Landauer's principle* stating that any irreversible logical operation, such as erasure of a piece of information from memory, or a merge of two paths in a program, is associated with physical irreversibility in the macroscopic level, and hence it necessarily causes heat generation in the computing system. In particular, if one bit of information is completely erased in the system, at least $kT \ln 2$ of energy will be dissipated, where k is the Boltzmann constant, and T is the absolute temperature. If the computing system is reversible, then no such lower bound on energy consumption exists, and hence it leads to a possibility of dissipation-less computing system.

Today's computers are composed of electronic devices, and logical operations are realized by controlling the average behavior of a very large number of electrons. Thus, generally, they consume much more energy than $kT \ln 2$ per each primitive operation, even for reversible logical operations. They also require considerable amounts of energy for giving clock signals to the electronic circuits. Therefore, at present, $kT \ln 2$ is a negligible amount of energy in them. However, computing devices will be implemented in a much more microscopic level in the future. At that time, the lower bound $kT \ln 2$ will become critical. In addition, besides the problem of energy consumption, for the purpose of further miniaturization of computing systems, we have to find a way of directly utilizing microscopic physical phenomena for logical operations, where reversibility is one of the key features. Thus, investigating effective methods for using such properties of Nature in computing will give us a new insight into constructing future computers.

1.2 Significance of Reversible Computing

Reversible computing is a paradigm in which reversible computers are hierarchically constructed based on reversible physical phenomena and reversible operations. In the theory of reversible computing, there are several levels of computing models ranging from a microscopic level to a macroscopic one. In the bottom (i.e., microscopic) level, there are reversible physical models. Reversible logic elements are in the next level. Then, there are reversible logic circuits that work as functional modules in reversible systems. In the top level, there are various models of reversible computers. In this hierarchy, each system in a higher level can be constructed from systems in a lower level.

The objective of the study of reversible computing is to clarify how computation can be performed efficiently in reversible computers, how elegantly higher level reversible systems can be constructed from those in the lower level, and which kind of simple reversible primitives are universal and useful for constructing reversible computers. As we shall see in the following chapters, many reversible systems have high computing capability in spite of the strong constraint of reversibility. Furthermore, universal reversible computers can be composed of very simple reversible logic elements. In addition, some of the models are constructed in a very unique way, which cannot be seen in the traditional design theory of computing systems made of logic gates and memories.

A Turing machine (TM) is a standard model in the traditional theory of computing. A reversible Turing machine (RTM) is a backward deterministic TM, and is also useful in the theory of reversible computing. Lecerf first studied RTMs in the paper [40], where the halting problem and some other related decision problems on them were shown to be unsolvable like the case of general (i.e., irreversible) TMs. Later, Bennett [7] studied RTMs from the viewpoint of Landauer's principle. Note that it is easy to simulate an irreversible TM by an RTM by recording all the movements in a history tape. But, when the computation terminates, they are left as "garbage" information. Disposal of the garbage information is actually equivalent to erasure of the information, and hence it leads to energy dissipation. Bennett showed that it is possible to construct an RTM that simulates a given TM and leaves no garbage information on its tape when it halts (see Sect. 5.2.3). This result is important, because any computation can be performed in an efficient way with respect to energy consumption in an ideal situation.

After the work of Bennett, various reversible computing models ranging from microscopic to macroscopic ones have been proposed and investigated. In particular, reversible cellular automata, reversible logic elements and circuits, reversible physical models, and others were studied, and their relation to physical reversibility was argued.

A cellular automaton (CA) is a framework that can deal with spatiotemporal phenomena, and thus a reversible CA is an abstract model of a reversible spatial dynamical system. A CA is a system composed of an infinite number of identical finite automata called cells, which are placed and connected uniformly in a space. Hence, it is also suited for studying how complex phenomena appear from simple functions. Toffoli [63] investigated the relation between irreversible CAs and reversible CAs, and showed that an irreversible k-dimensional CA can be simulated by a $(k+1)$-dimensional reversible CA, and thus two-dimensional reversible CAs are computationally universal. Later, Margolus [41] proposed a very simple universal two-dimensional reversible CA. On the other hand, Morita and Harao [49] proved that reversible CAs can be universal even in the one-dimensional case. After that, it has been shown that there are various simple one- and two-dimensional universal reversible CAs (see Chaps. 11–13). Therefore, computational universality emerges even from a very primitive function of a cell.

Reversible logic elements are those whose operations are described by an injective (i.e., one-to-one) functions. An early study on reversible logic gates is found in the paper of Petri [55]. Later, Toffoli [64, 65] studied them in the relation to physical reversibility. In particular, he proposed a universal reversible logic gate called a Toffoli gate. Then, Fredkin and Toffoli [25] introduced another universal reversible gate called a Fredkin gate, and showed that any logical function can be realized by a garbage-less circuit composed of it. On the other hand, Morita [45] proposed a reversible logic element with one-bit memory called a *rotary element* (RE) and showed any RTM can be concisely constructed by it in a very unique method (see Sect. 6.1). Thus, besides reversible gates, a reversible logic element with memory (RLEM), a kind of reversible sequential machine (RSM), is also useful in reversible computing. Note that today's computers are designed based on the well-known logic elements such as AND, OR, NOT, and some others. These operations, in particular, AND, OR and NOT, have been known since the era of ancient Greece (see e.g., [13]), and thus have a very long history. Since they were obtained from the analysis of thinking and reasoning processes performed by humans, it is easy for us to understand and use them. However, to investigate future computing systems, we should not be tied to old traditions, and we have to look for new bases and methods that are directly related to microscopic physical phenomena.

As for physical models of reversible computing, Fredkin and Toffoli [25] proposed an interesting model called the billiard ball model (BBM). It consists of idealized balls and reflectors. Logical operations are simulated by elastic collisions of moving balls. They showed any reversible logic circuit composed of Fredkin gates can be embedded in BBM. Of course, it can work only in an idealized situation, since it requires infinite precision on the sizes, positions and velocities of balls. However, it is a very insightful model for considering the relation between physical reversibility and computational reversibility.

As seen above, various interesting ideas have been proposed so far, and they opened new vistas in the theory of reversible computing. However, to understand it more deeply, we still have to find and develop new methodologies for it, which do not exist in the world of traditional computing. In order to do so, it is important not to consider reversibility as a "constraint", but to find a way of using it positively as a "useful property".

1.3 Scope of This Volume

In this volume, reversible computing is studied from the viewpoint of the theory of automata and computing. It mainly describes the results shown in the past studies by the author of this volume, his colleagues, and his former students. But, of course, other researchers' results related to them are also cited for completeness. Thus, it is not a very comprehensive book on reversible computing. Instead, it investigates various aspects of computational universality in reversible systems in detail.

This volume studies, in particular, the problems of how reversible machines can be designed, how computing can be carried out in a reversible machine, how simple universal reversible computers can be, which universal reversible logic elements are useful for constructing reversible computers elegantly, and so on. The following chapters will give answers to these problems obtained so far. Although some of them may be improved in future research, they will provide good insights into reversible computing.

1.3.1 Organization of this book

The following chapters can be divided into three parts. The first part consists of Chaps. 2–4, in which reversible logic elements and circuits are studied. It also investigates the relation between reversible logic elements and a reversible physical model. The second part consists of Chaps. 5–9, in which reversible Turing machines (RTMs) and related models are studied. Thus, it deals with several reversible computing systems in the macroscopic level. But, it also argues how RTMs can be constructed out of reversible logic elements. The third part consists of Chaps. 10–14, in which reversible cellular automata (RCAs) are studied. Here, the problem of how complex phenomena, such as computational universality, appear from simple reversible operations is investigated. Hence, the framework of RCAs itself also connects between the microscopic and macroscopic levels. The details of each chapter are as follows.

In Chap. 2, a reversible logic element called a rotary element (RE) is given. Different from a reversible logic gate, it is defined as a two-state reversible sequential machine (RSM) with four input symbols and four output symbols. It is shown that any RSM can be compactly implemented by an RE. In this sense it is a universal logic element for constructing reversible machines. It is also shown that RE is simply realized in the billiard ball model (BBM), a kind of reversible physical model. In Chap. 3, two-state RLEMs are classified, and their universality is investigated. It is remarkable that *all* the non-degenerate RLEMs except only four two-symbol RLEMs are universal. In addition, three two-symbol RLEMs among four are proved to be non-universal. A systematic realization method of four-symbol RLEMs in the BBM is also shown. In Chap. 4, reversible logic gates and their circuits are studied. In particular, the Fredkin gate and its circuits are dealt with. Their basic properties, and their relation to RE are given. Furthermore, a method of constructing a garbage-less circuit out of Fredkin gates that simulates a given RSM is shown.

In Chap. 5, a reversible Turing machine (RTM) is defined, and its basic properties are shown. First, universality of a garbage-less RTM proved by Bennett [7] is explained. Then, simplification methods of RTMs, i.e., reducing the numbers of tapes, symbols, and states of an RTM, are shown. In Chap. 6, constructing methods of RTMs out of reversible logic elements are studied. It is shown that any RTM can be realized concisely as a circuit composed only of REs, or other two-state RLEMs. The methods are very different from the conventional ones that use logic gates and memory elements. In Chap. 7, universal RTMs (URTMs), which are RTMs that can simulate any TM, are studied. Here, it is investigated how we can obtain URTMs with small numbers of states and symbols. By simulating cyclic tag systems, a kind of universal string rewriting systems proposed by Cook [14], several small URTMs are constructed. In Chap. 8, memory limited computing in RTMs is studied. In particular, it is argued how reversibility and determinism affect the computational power of space-bounded TMs. In Chap. 9, several models of reversible machines other than RTMs are studied. It is shown that a reversible counter machine with only two counters is computationally universal. Equivalence of a reversible two-way multi-head finite automaton and an irreversible one with the same number of heads is also proved.

In Chap. 10, reversible cellular automata (RCAs) are studied. Basic properties of RCAs and design methods are shown. Here, the framework of partitioned CAs (PCAs) is given for making it easy to design RCAs. In Chap. 11, universality of one-dimensional RCAs is investigated, and several RCAs that simulate RTMs and cyclic tag systems are constructed. In Chap. 12, two models of universal two-dimensional 16-state RCAs that can simulate Fredkin gates are given. A universal 81-state RCA in which any reversible two-counter machine can be simulated by their *finite* configurations is also shown. In Chap. 13, CAs on the triangular tessellation called the elementary triangular partitioned cellular automata (ETPCAs) are studied. There are 256 ETPCAs, and among them there are 36 reversible ETPCAs. In spite of the extreme simplicity of their local transition functions, they have very rich computing capabilities, and it is shown that ten reversible ETPCAs are computationally universal. In Chap. 14, self-reproduction in RCAs is studied. Self-reproducing CAs were first studied by von Neumann [51]. Later, Langton [39] proposed a simplified framework for self-reproducing CAs. Here, it is shown that self-reproduction of Langton's type is possible in two- and three-dimensional RCAs.

1.3.2 Related studies and references

Here, we give some remarks on related studies and references of reversible computing, though they are not exhaustive.

As described in Sect. 1.1, Landauer [37] investigated the relation between physical reversibility and logical reversibility. After that, several studies on reversible computing from the physical or thermodynamic viewpoint appeared [7, 8, 9, 11, 31]. Feynman also argued reversible computing from the standpoint of physics [21, 22], and his idea opened the way to quantum computing [19, 20]. Since evolution of a quantum computing system is described by a unitary operator, reversible computing is closely related to quantum computing (see, e.g., [27]). Various models of quantum computing, such as quantum Turing machines [6, 12, 17, 53], quantum finite automata [32], and quantum cellular automata [4, 5, 68], have been proposed. These quantum computing systems can be considered as generalizations of reversible ones. Both reversible computing and quantum computing are research fields where we are looking for microscopic phenomena that can be directly used as primitive operations for computing. DNA computing and molecular computing (e.g., [1, 57, 70, 71]) also have the same objectives on such a point.

So far, many kinds of reversible computing models were proposed and their properties were investigated. Bennett [10] studied time/space trade-offs in reversible Turing machines (RTMs), which is related to garbage generation and its reversible erasure in RTMs. On the other hand, Lange, McKenzie and Tapp [38] showed that any irreversible TM can be simulated by an RTM without increasing the memory space, though its computing time grows exponentially. Note that a simpler simulation method is given in Sect. 8.2.2. There are also studies on one-way reversible finite automata [3, 56], two-way reversible finite automata [32], reversible pushdown automata [33], one-way reversible multi-head finite automata [34], and so on. In Chap. 9, reversible counter machines, and two-way reversible multi-head finite automata will be investigated. The paper by Vitányi [67] gives a survey on reversible computing based on RTMs.

As for the study on cellular automata (CAs), there is a classical literature [51] on von Neumann's works that investigate construction-universality as well as computational universality of CAs. The reference [30] is a general survey on CAs, and [18, 52] are on universality of CAs. Reversible CAs (RCAs) have been studied since the early stage of their history [28, 44, 50, 59], but they were called *injective CAs* at that time. There are survey papers by Kari [29], Toffoli and Margolus [66], and Morita [46, 47, 48] on RCAs and related topics.

We now give an additional remark on reversibility in computing. It is known that microscopic physical laws are time-reversal-symmetric (see, e.g., [36]), and thus the same laws hold also for the negative direction of time. But, since reversible computing systems are simply defined as backward deterministic ones, the backward transition rules may not be the same as the forward ones. Gajardo, Kari and Moreira [26] introduced the notion of time-symmetry on CAs. It is an interesting property, and is much closer to physical reversibility. This notion is also defined for other machines by Kutrib and Worsch [35]. However, here we do not use this definition because of the following reason. In many cases, reversible computing machines are constructed hierarchically. Namely, reversible machines are implemented as a reversible logic circuit consisting of reversible logic elements, and the elements are realized in a reversible physical model. In this hierarchy, only the physical model is given as a system whose evolution is time-reversal-symmetric. Therefore, the whole computing system can be embedded in a time-reversal-symmetric system in the bottom level, even if it is not so in the higher level.

Since this volume investigates reversible systems from the standpoint of theory of computing, there are topics that are not dealt with. Among them, it is an important problem how a reversible computer can be realized in hardware. So far, there have been several interesting attempts such as implementation of reversible logic circuits as electrically controlled switches [42], c-MOS implementation of reversible logic gates and circuits [16], and adiabatic circuits for reversible computer [23, 24]. Also, recently, studies on synthesis of reversible and quantum logic circuits have been extensively done [2, 15, 43, 58, 60, 61, 62, 69]. However, ultimately, reversible logic elements and computing systems should be implemented at the atomic or molecular level. Although finding such solutions is very difficult, it is a challenging problem left for future investigations. Studies on more practical architectures for reversible computers, and on reversible programming languages are also interesting subjects that are not dealt with in this volume. On reversible programming languages and software, see, e.g., [54, 72, 73]. In the research field of reversible computing, there will still be many interesting problems to study, and therefore unique ideas and novel methodologies are sought.

1.4 Terminology and Notations

In this section, we explain basic terminology and notations on logic, mathematics, and formal languages used in this book.

First, we give notations on logic. Here, P, P_1 and P_2 are propositions, x is a variable, and $P(x)$ is a predicate with a free variable x.

$\neg P$ Negation of P
$P_1 \vee P_2$ Disjunction (logical OR) of P_1 and P_2
$P_1 \wedge P_2$ Conjunction (logical AND) of P_1 and P_2
$P_1 \Rightarrow P_2$ P_1 implies P_2
$P_1 \Leftrightarrow P_2$ P_1 if and only if P_2
$\forall x (P(x))$ For all x, $P(x)$ holds
$\exists x (P(x))$ There exists x such that $P(x)$ holds

When describing logical functions of logic gates, and combinatorial logic circuits, operations of NOT (negation), logical OR, and logical AND are expressed by $\bar{a}$, $a + b$, and $a \cdot b$, respectively, instead of $\neg$, $\vee$, and $\wedge$. Exclusive OR (XOR) is denoted by $a \oplus b$. Here, a and b are Boolean variables with a value 0 (false) or 1 (true).

Notations and symbols on set theory are as follows, where S, S_1 and S_2 are sets, a is an object, x is a variable, and $P(x)$ is a predicate with a free variable x.

$\emptyset$ The empty set
$a \in S$ a is an element of S
$S_1 \subseteq S_2$ S_1 is a subset (not necessarily a proper subset) of S_2
$S_1 \subset S_2$ S_1 is a proper subset of S_2
$S_1 \cup S_2$ The union of S_1 and S_2
$S_1 \cap S_2$ The intersection of S_1 and S_2
$S_1 - S_2$ The difference of S_1 and S_2
$S_1 \times S_2$ The Cartesian product of S_1 and S_2 (note that $S \times S$ is denoted by S^2)
2^S The power set of S
$|S|$ The number of elements in S
$\mathbb{N}$ The set of all natural numbers (including 0)
$\mathbb{Z}$ The set of all integers
$\mathbb{Z}_+$ The set of all positive integers
$\mathbb{R}$ The set of all real numbers
$\{x \mid P(x)\}$ The set of all elements x that satisfy $P(x)$

A *singleton* is a set that has exactly one element.

Next, terminology on relations and mappings (functions) is given. Let S_1 and S_2 be sets. If $R \subseteq S_1 \times S_2$, then R is called a *(binary) relation*. Generally, let $S_1, \ldots, S_n$ be sets, and if $R \subseteq S_1 \times \cdots \times S_n$, then R is called an *n-ary relation*. For the case $R \subseteq S \times S \ (= S^2)$, we define $R^n \ (n \in \mathbb{N})$ recursively as follows: $R^0 = \{(x,x) \mid x \in S\}$, and $R^{i+1} = \{(x,y) \mid \exists z \in S \ ((x,z) \in R \ \wedge \ (z,y) \in R^i)\} \ (i \in \mathbb{N})$. Then, R^* and R^+ are defined below.

R^* The *reflexive and transitive closure* of the relation R, i.e., $R^* = \bigcup_{i=0}^{\infty} R^i$

R^+ The *transitive closure* of the relation R, i.e., $R^+ = \bigcup_{i=1}^{\infty} R^i$

A relation $f \subseteq S_1 \times S_2$ is called a *partial mapping* (or *partial function*) from S_1 to S_2, if it satisfies

$$\forall x \in S_1 \ \forall y_1, y_2 \in S_2 \ (((x,y_1) \in f) \wedge ((x,y_2) \in f) \Rightarrow (y_1 = y_2)),$$

which means that for each $x \in S_1$ there exists at most one $y \in S_2$ such that $(x,y) \in f$. A partial mapping f is called a *mapping* (or *function*) from S_1 to S_2, if it further satisfies

$$\forall x \in S_1 \ \exists y \in S_2 \ ((x,y) \in f).$$

It is also called a *total mapping* (or *total function*). A partial mapping f from S_1 to S_2 is denoted by $f : S_1 \to S_2$, where the sets S_1 and S_2 are called the *domain* and the *codomain* of f, respectively. As usual, $(x,y) \in f$ is denoted by $y = f(x)$. Note that if $(x,y) \notin f$ for all $y \in S_2$, then $f(x)$ is undefined. The notation $x \mapsto f(x)$ indicates x maps to $f(x)$.

Let f and g be total mappings such that $f : A_1 \to B$, $g : A_2 \to B$, and $A_1 \subseteq A_2$. If $\forall x \in A_1 (g(x) = f(x))$ holds, then g is called an *extension* of f, and f is called a *restriction* of g to A_1, which is denoted by $g|_{A_1}$.

A partial mapping $f : S_1 \to S_2$ is called *injective* if

$$\forall x_1, x_2 \in S_1 \ \forall y \in S_2 \ ((f(x_1) = y) \wedge (f(x_2) = y) \Rightarrow (x_1 = x_2)).$$

A partial mapping $f : S_1 \to S_2$ is called *surjective* if

$$\forall y \in S_2 \ \exists x \in S_1 \ (f(x) = y).$$

A partial mapping $f : S_1 \to S_2$ that is both injective and surjective is called *bijective*. If a total mapping $f : S_1 \to S_2$ is injective (surjective, or bijective, respectively), then it is called an *injection* (*surjection*, or *bijection*).

Let $f : S_1 \to S_2$ be an injection. The *inverse partial mapping* of f is denoted by $f^{-1} : S_2 \to S_1$, and is defined as follows.

$$\forall x \in S_1 \ \forall y \in S_2 \ (f(x) = y \ \Leftrightarrow \ f^{-1}(y) = x)$$

Hence, $f^{-1}(f(x)) = x$ holds for all $x \in S_1$, and f^{-1} is an injective partial mapping. Note that, for $y_0 \in S_2$, if there is no $x \in S_1$ such that $f(x) = y_0$, then $f^{-1}(y_0)$ is undefined. If f is a bijection, then f^{-1} is totally defined, and thus called the *inverse mapping* of f, which is also a bijection.

Notations on formal languages are given below. A nonempty finite set of symbols is called an *alphabet*. Let Σ be an alphabet. A finite sequence of symbols $a_1 \cdots a_n$ ($n \in \mathbb{N}$) taken from Σ is called a *string* (or *word*) over the alphabet Σ. The *concatenation* of strings w_1 and w_2 is denoted by $w_1 \cdot w_2$ (usually $\cdot$ is omitted). The length of a string w is denoted by $|w|$. Hence, if $w = a_1 \cdots a_n$, then $|w| = n$. We denote the *empty string* (i.e., the string of length 0) by λ. The *reversal* of a string w is denoted by w^R. Thus, if $w = a_1 \cdots a_n$, then $w^R = a_n \cdots a_1$. For a symbol a, we use a^n to denote the string consisting of n repetitions of a ($n \in \mathbb{N}$). We define the set of strings Σ^n ($n \in \mathbb{N}$) recursively as follows: $\Sigma^0 = \{\lambda\}$, and $\Sigma^{i+1} = \{aw \mid a \in \Sigma \wedge w \in \Sigma^i\}$ ($i \in \mathbb{N}$). Then, Σ^* and Σ^+ are defined below.

Σ^* The set of all strings over Σ including λ, i.e., $\Sigma^* = \bigcup_{i=0}^{\infty} \Sigma^i$

Σ^+ The set of all strings over Σ of positive length, i.e., $\Sigma^+ = \bigcup_{i=1}^{\infty} \Sigma^i$

Let Σ_1 and Σ_2 be alphabets. A *string homomorphism* is a mapping $\varphi : \Sigma_1^* \rightarrow \Sigma_2^*$ that satisfy the following: $\varphi(\lambda) = \lambda$, $\varphi(a) \in \Sigma_2^*$ for all $a \in \Sigma_1$, and $\varphi(aw) = \varphi(a)\varphi(w)$ for all $a \in \Sigma_1$ and $w \in \Sigma_1^*$.

A subset of Σ^* is called a *(formal) language* over the alphabet Σ. Let L, L_1 and L_2 be languages over Σ. The *concatenation* of L_1 and L_2 is defined by $L_1 \cdot L_2 = \{w_1 w_2 \mid w_1 \in L_1 \wedge w_2 \in L_2\}$. We define the language L^n recursively in a similar manner as in Σ^n: $L^0 = \{\lambda\}$, and $L^{i+1} = L \cdot L^i$ ($i \in \mathbb{N}$). Then, L^* and L^+ are as follows: $L^* = \bigcup_{i=0}^{\infty} L^i$, and $L^+ = \bigcup_{i=1}^{\infty} L^i$.

In the later chapters, we define some automata as acceptors of languages to investigate their capability. For this purpose, we use the notation $\mathscr{L}(\mathscr{A})$ to denote the *class of languages* accepted by the class of automata $\mathscr{A}$, i.e., $\mathscr{L}(\mathscr{A}) = \{L \mid L \text{ is accepted by some } A \in \mathscr{A}\}$ (see, e.g., Sect. 8.1.4).

References

1. Adleman, L.M.: Molecular computation of solutions to combinatorial problems. Science **266**, 1021–1024 (1994). doi:10.1126/science.7973651
2. Al-Rabadi, A.N.: Reversible Logic Synthesis. Springer (2004). doi:10.1007/978-3-642-18853-4
3. Angluin, D.: Inference of reversible languages. J. ACM **29**, 741–765 (1982). doi:10.1145/322326.322334
4. Arrighi, P., Grattage, J.: Intrinsically universal n-dimensional quantum cellular automata. J. Comput. Syst. Sci. **78**, 1883–1898 (2012). doi:10.1016/j.jcss.2011.12.008
5. Arrighi, P., Grattage, J.: Partitioned quantum cellular automata are intrinsically universal. Natural Computing **11**, 13–22 (2012). doi:10.1007/s11047-011-9277-6
6. Benioff, P.: The computer as a physical system: A microscopic quantum mechanical Hamiltonian model of computers as represented by Turing machines. J. Statist. Phys. **22**, 563–591 (1980). doi:10.1007/BF01011339
7. Bennett, C.H.: Logical reversibility of computation. IBM J. Res. Dev. **17**, 525–532 (1973). doi:10.1147/rd.176.0525

8. Bennett, C.H.: The thermodynamics of computation — a review. Int. J. Theoret. Phys. **21**, 905–940 (1982). doi:10.1007/BF02084158

9. Bennett, C.H.: Notes on the history of reversible computation. IBM J. Res. Dev. **32**, 16–23 (1988). doi:10.1147/rd.321.0016

10. Bennett, C.H.: Time/space trade-offs for reversible computation. SIAM J. Comput. **18**, 766–776 (1989). doi:10.1137/0218053

11. Bennett, C.H., Landauer, R.: The fundamental physical limits of computation. Sci. Am. **253**, 38–46 (1985). doi:10.1038/scientificamerican0785-48

12. Bernstein, E., Vazirani, U.V.: Quantum complexity theory. SIAM J. Comput. **26**, 1411–1473 (1997). doi:10.1137/S0097539796300921

13. Bocheński, J.M.: Ancient Formal Logic. North-Holland, Amsterdam (1951)

14. Cook, M.: Universality in elementary cellular automata. Complex Syst. **15**, 1–40 (2004)

15. De Vos, A.: Reversible Computing: Fundamentals, Quantum Computing, and Applications. Wiley-VCH (2010). doi:10.1002/9783527633999

16. De Vos, A., Desoete, B., Adamski, A., Pietrzak, P., Sibinski, M., Widerski, T.: Design of reversible logic circuits by means of control gates. In: Proc. PATMOS 2000 (eds. D. Soudris, P. Pirsch, E. Barke), LNCS 1918, pp. 255–264 (2000). doi:10.1007/3-540-45373-3_27

17. Deutsch, D.: Quantum theory, the Church-Turing principle and the universal quantum computer. Proc. R. Soc. Lond. A **400**, 97–117 (1985). doi:10.1098/rspa.1985.0070

18. Durand-Lose, J.O.: Cellular automata, universality of. In: Encyclopedia of Complexity and Systems Science (eds. R.A. Meyers, et al.), pp. 901–913. Springer (2009). doi:10.1007/978-0-387-30440-3_59

19. Feynman, R.P.: Simulating physics with computers. Int. J. Theoret. Phys. **21**, 467–488 (1982). doi:10.1007/BF02650179

20. Feynman, R.P.: Quantum mechanical computers. Opt. News **11**, 11–46 (1985). doi:10.1364/ON.11.2.000011

21. Feynman, R.P.: Feynman lectures on computation (eds., A.J.G. Hey and R.W. Allen). Perseus Books, Reading, Massachusetts (1996)

22. Feynman, R.P.: The computing machines in the future (Nishina Memorial Lecture in Tokyo, 1985). In: Lect. Notes Phys. **746**, pp. 99–113 (2008). doi:10.1007/978-4-431-77056-5_6

23. Frank, M.P.: Reversibility for efficient computing. Ph.D. thesis, MIT (1999)

24. Frank, M.P., Vieri, C., Ammer, M.J., Love, N., Margolus, N.H., Knight, T.E.: A scalable reversible computer in silicon. In: Unconventional Models of Computation (eds. C.S. Calude, J. Casti and M.J. Dinneen), pp. 183–200. Springer (1998)

25. Fredkin, E., Toffoli, T.: Conservative logic. Int. J. Theoret. Phys. **21**, 219–253 (1982). doi:10.1007/BF01857727

26. Gajardo, A., Kari, J., Moreira, M.: On time-symmetry in cellular automata. J. Comput. Syst. Sci. **78**, 1115–1126 (2012). doi:10.1016/j.jcss.2012.01.006

27. Gruska, J.: Quantum Computing. McGraw-Hill, London (1999)

28. Hedlund, G.A.: Endomorphisms and automorphisms of the shift dynamical system. Math. Syst. Theory **3**, 320–375 (1969). doi:10.1007/BF01691062

29. Kari, J.: Reversible cellular automata. In: Proc. DLT 2005 (eds. C. de Felice, A. Restivo), LNCS 3572, pp. 57–68 (2005). doi:10.1007/11505877_5

30. Kari, J.: Theory of cellular automata: a survey. Theoret. Comput. Sci. **334**, 3–33 (2005). doi:10.1016/j.tcs.2004.11.021

31. Keyes, R.W., Landauer, R.: Minimal energy dissipation in logic. IBM J. Res. Dev. **14**, 152–157 (1970). doi:10.1147/rd.142.0152

32. Kondacs, A., Watrous, J.: On the power of quantum finite state automata. In: Proc. 36th FOCS, pp. 66–75. IEEE (1997). doi:10.1109/SFCS.1997.646094

33. Kutrib, M., Malcher, A.: Reversible pushdown automata. J. Comput. Syst. Sci. **78**, 1814–1827 (2012). doi:10.1016/j.jcss.2011.12.004

34. Kutrib, M., Malcher, A.: One-way reversible multi-head finite automata. In: Proc. RC 2012 (eds. R. Glück, T. Yokoyama), LNCS 7581, pp. 14–28 (2013). doi:10.1007/978-3-642-36315-3_2

35. Kutrib, M., Worsch, T.: Time-symmetric machines. In: Proc. RC 2013 (eds. G.W. Dueck, D.M. Miller), LNCS 7948, pp. 168–181 (2013). doi:10.1007/978-3-642-38986-3_14
36. Lamb, J., Roberts, J.: Time-reversal symmetry in dynamical systems: A survey. Physica D **112**, 1–39 (1998). doi:10.1016/S0167-2789(97)00199-1
37. Landauer, R.: Irreversibility and heat generation in the computing process. IBM J. Res. Dev. **5**, 183–191 (1961). doi:10.1147/rd.53.0183
38. Lange, K.J., McKenzie, P., Tapp, A.: Reversible space equals deterministic space. J. Comput. Syst. Sci. **60**, 354–367 (2000). doi:10.1006/jcss.1999.1672
39. Langton, C.G.: Self-reproduction in cellular automata. Physica D **10**, 135–144 (1984). doi:10.1016/0167-2789(84)90256-2
40. Lecerf, Y.: Machines de Turing réversibles — récursive insolubilité en $n \in N$ de l'équation $u = \theta^n u$, où θ est un isomorphisme de codes. Comptes Rendus Hebdomadaires des Séances de L'académie des Sciences **257**, 2597–2600 (1963)
41. Margolus, N.: Physics-like model of computation. Physica D **10**, 81–95 (1984). doi:10.1016/0167-2789(84)90252-5
42. Merkle, R.C.: Reversible electronic logic using switches. Nanotechnology **4**, 20–41 (1993). doi:10.1088/0957-4484/4/1/002
43. Miller, D.M., Maslov, D., Dueck, G.W.: A transformation based algorithm for reversible logic synthesis. In: Proc. Design Automation Conference, pp. 318–323 (2003). doi:10.1109/DAC.2003.1219016
44. Moore, E.F.: Machine models of self-reproduction. Proc. Symposia in Applied Mathematics, Am. Math. Soc. **14**, 17–33 (1962). doi:10.1090/psapm/014/9961
45. Morita, K.: A simple reversible logic element and cellular automata for reversible computing. In: Proc. MCU 2001 (eds. M. Margenstern, Y. Rogozhin), LNCS 2055, pp. 102–113 (2001). doi:10.1007/3-540-45132-3_6
46. Morita, K.: Reversible computing and cellular automata — A survey. Theoret. Comput. Sci. **395**, 101–131 (2008). doi:10.1016/j.tcs.2008.01.041
47. Morita, K.: Computation in reversible cellular automata. Int. J. of General Systems **41**, 569–581 (2012). doi:10.1080/03081079.2012.695897
48. Morita, K.: Reversible cellular automata. In: Handbook of Natural Computing (eds. G. Rozenberg, T. Bäck, J.N. Kok), pp. 231–257. Springer (2012). doi:10.1007/978-3-540-92910-9_7
49. Morita, K., Harao, M.: Computation universality of one-dimensional reversible (injective) cellular automata. Trans. IEICE Japan **E72**, 758–762 (1989)
50. Myhill, J.: The converse of Moore's Garden-of-Eden theorem. Proc. Am. Math. Soc. **14**, 658–686 (1963). doi:10.2307/2034301
51. von Neumann, J.: Theory of Self-reproducing Automata (ed. A.W. Burks). The University of Illinois Press, Urbana (1966)
52. Ollinger, N.: Universalities in cellular automata. In: Handbook of Natural Computing, pp. 189–229. Springer (2012). doi:10.1007/978-3-540-92910-9_6
53. Peres, A.: Reversible logic and quantum computers. Phys. Rev. A **32**, 3266–3276 (1985). doi:10.1103/PhysRevA.32.3266
54. Perumalla, K.S.: Introduction to Reversible Computing. CRC Press (2014)
55. Petri, C.A.: Grundsätzliches zur Beschreibung diskreter Prozesse. In: Proc. 3rd Colloquium über Automatentheorie (eds. W. Händler, E. Peschl, H. Unger), Birkhäuser Verlag, pp. 121–140 (1967). doi:10.1007/978-3-0348-5879-3_10
56. Pin, J.E.: On reversible automata. In: Proc. LATIN '92 (ed. I. Simon), LNCS 583, pp. 401–416 (1992). doi:10.1007/BFb0023844
57. Păun, G., Rozenberg, G., Salomaa, A.: DNA Computing. Springer (1998). doi:10.1007/978-3-662-03563-4
58. Rice, J.E.: An introduction to reversible latches. The Computer J. **51**, 700–709 (2008). doi:10.1093/comjnl/bxm116
59. Richardson, D.: Tessellations with local transformations. J. Comput. Syst. Sci. **6**, 373–388 (1972). doi:10.1016/S0022-0000(72)80009-6
60. Saeedi, M., Markov, I.L.: Synthesis and optimization of reversible circuits - a survey. ACM Comput. Surv. **45**, 21 (2013). doi:10.1145/2431211.2431220

61. Shende, V.V., Prasad, A.K., Markov, I.L., Hayes, J.P.: Synthesis of reversible logic circuits. IEEE Trans. Computer-Aided Design of Integrated Circuits and Systems **22**, 710–722 (2003). doi:10.1109/TCAD.2003.811448

62. Thapliyal, H., Ranganathan, N.: Design of reversible sequential circuits optimizing quantum cost, delay, and garbage outputs. ACM Journal on Emerging Technologies in Computing Systems **6**, 14:1–14:31 (2010). doi:10.1145/1877745.1877748

63. Toffoli, T.: Computation and construction universality of reversible cellular automata. J. Comput. Syst. Sci. **15**, 213–231 (1977). doi:10.1016/S0022-0000(77)80007-X

64. Toffoli, T.: Reversible computing. In: Automata, Languages and Programming (eds. J.W. de Bakker, J. van Leeuwen), LNCS 85, pp. 632–644 (1980). doi:10.1007/3-540-10003-2_104

65. Toffoli, T.: Bicontinuous extensions of invertible combinatorial functions. Math. Syst. Theory **14**, 12–23 (1981). doi:10.1007/BF01752388

66. Toffoli, T., Margolus, N.: Invertible cellular automata: a review. Physica D **45**, 229–253 (1990). doi:10.1016/0167-2789(90)90185-R

67. Vitányi, P.M.B.: Time, space, and energy in reversible computing. In: Conf. Computing Frontiers, pp. 435–444 (2005). doi:10.1145/1062261.1062335

68. Watrous, J.: On one-dimensional quantum cellular automata. In: Proc. FOCS, pp. 528–537 (1995). doi:10.1109/SFCS.1995.492583

69. Wille, R., Drechsler, R.: Towards a Design Flow for Reversible Logic. Springer (2010). doi:10.1007/978-90-481-9579-4

70. Winfree, E.: Self-healing tile sets. In: Nanotechnology: Science and Computation, pp. 55–78. Springer (2006). doi:10.1007/3-540-30296-4_4

71. Winfree, E., Liu, F., Wenzler, L.A., Seeman, N.C.: Design and self-assembly of two-dimensional DNA crystals. Nature **394**, 539–544 (1998). doi:10.1038/28998

72. Yokoyama, T.: Reversible computation and reversible programming languages. Electron. Notes in Theoret. Comput. Sci. **253**, 71–81 (2010). doi:10.1016/j.entcs.2010.02.007

73. Yokoyama, T., Axelsen, H.B., Glück, R.: Fundamentals of reversible flowchart languages. Theoret. Comput. Sci. (2015). doi:10.1016/j.tcs.2015.07.046

Chapter 2
Reversible Logic Elements with Memory

Abstract A reversible logic element with memory (RLEM) is presented as a logical primitive for constructing reversible computing systems. In the conventional design theory of logic circuits, logic gates, which are elements without memory, are mainly used as logical primitives. On the other hand, in the case of reversible computing, RLEMs are also useful as logical primitives. This is because reversible machines can be constructed easily and concisely by a simple RLEM. In addition, the design method using RLEMs is very different from those in the traditional theory of logic circuits based on logic gates. Thus RLEMs give new vistas and suggest various possibilities in the theory of reversible computing. Here, we present a typical 2-state 4-symbol RLEM called a rotary element (RE), and investigate how it is realized in the billiard ball model, a reversible physical model of computing, and how reversible sequential machines can be constructed from it.

Keywords reversible logic element with memory, rotary element, reversible sequential machine, billiard ball model

2.1 Logical Primitives for Reversible Computers

A *logic element* is a primitive for composing logic circuits by which computing systems are implemented. There are two types of logic elements: one without memory, which is usually called a *logic gate*, and one with memory. In the traditional design theory of logic circuits, logic gates such as AND, OR, NOT, NAND, and others are used as primitives, and thus logic gates are dealt with separately from memory elements such as flip-flops. In the theory of reversible logic circuits, also, logic gates have been treated as the main primitives for circuit design, and there has been much research on them. However, as we shall see in the following sections and chapters, a *reversible logic element with memory* (RLEM) is also useful for composing various models of reversible computing systems. In particular, we shall see that even very simple RLEMs have universality, and we can compose reversible se-

15

quential machines, reversible Turing machines, and others rather easily from them. In addition, these machines are constructed in a very different manner from those in the traditional design theory of logic circuits. Since RLEMs thus give new vistas and suggest various possibilities in the theory of reversible computing, we mainly discuss RLEMs in this book.

A reversible logic element is one whose operation is described by an injection. For example, a NOT gate is reversible, since it realizes the injective logical function $f_{\text{NOT}} : \{0,1\} \to \{0,1\}$ where $f_{\text{NOT}}(0) = 1$ and $f_{\text{NOT}}(1) = 0$. On the other hand, NAND is irreversible, since it realizes the non-injective logical function $f_{\text{NAND}} : \{0,1\}^2 \to \{0,1\}$ where $f_{\text{NAND}}(0,0) = 1$, $f_{\text{NAND}}(0,1) = 1$, $f_{\text{NAND}}(1,0) = 1$, and $f_{\text{NAND}}(1,1) = 0$. It is, of course, possible to implement reversible computing models, such as reversible Turing machines, by irreversible logic elements like NAND gates and flip-flops. But, such an implementation is almost meaningless because of the following reason. One of the objectives of the study of reversible computing is to find an efficient method of implementing reversible machines by reversible logic elements, and to find an elegant way of realizing reversible logic elements by physically reversible phenomena. Hence, our final goal is to realize a reversible computer in a reversible physical system in an efficient way. Therefore, the important point of the study of reversible logic elements is to find a key element that lies in the intermediate level between the levels of abstract machines and physical systems. Namely, the problem is which reversible logic element is useful for constructing reversible machines, and is easily realizable in a reversible physical system. We investigate this problem based mainly on RLEMs in this book. In fact, there are several interesting RLEMs from which reversible machines are constructed very simply. We shall also see that they are concisely implemented in the billiard ball model, a kind of a reversible physical model of computing.

In this chapter, we introduce a particular reversible logic element with 1-bit memory called a *rotary element* (RE) [5], since its operation is very easily understood. We shall see that the RE can be concisely realized in the billiard ball model, and it is powerful enough for constructing reversible sequential machines.

2.2 Reversible Logic Element with Memory (RLEM)

We first define a sequential machine (SM) and its reversible version, since a reversible logic element with memory (RLEM) is a kind of reversible sequential machine (RSM). An SM given here is a finite automaton with an output port as well as an input port, which is often called an SM of Mealy type.

Definition 2.1. A *sequential machine* (SM) is a system defined by $M = (Q, \Sigma, \Gamma, \delta)$, where Q is a finite set of internal states, Σ and Γ are finite sets of input and output symbols, and $\delta : Q \times \Sigma \to Q \times \Gamma$ is a move function. If δ is injective, M is called a *reversible sequential machine* (RSM). Note that if M is reversible, then $|\Sigma| \leq |\Gamma|$ must hold. It is also called a $|Q|$-state $|\Gamma|$-symbol RSM.

A reversible logic element with memory is an RSM having the same numbers of input and output symbols defined below.

Definition 2.2. A *reversible logic element with memory* (RLEM) is an RSM $M = (Q, \Sigma, \Gamma, \delta)$ such that $|\Sigma| = |\Gamma|$. It is also called a $|Q|$-state $|\Gamma|$-symbol RLEM.

The move function δ of an SM M gives the next state of M and the output symbol from the present state and the input symbol deterministically, and thus M is a *deterministic* SM. If the present state is p, the input symbol is a_i, and $\delta(p, a_i) = (q, s_j)$ holds, then the next state is q and the output is s_j as shown in Fig. 2.1 **(a)**. To use an SM as a logic element for composing a logic circuit, we interpret the SM as a machine having "decoded" input ports and output ports as in Fig. 2.1 **(b)**. Namely, for each input symbol, there is a unique input port, to which a particle (or token) can be given. Likewise, for each output symbol, there is a unique output port, from which a particle can appear. Note that particles should not be given to two or more input ports at the same time. The operations of the SM M is undefined for the case that particles are given to two or more input ports simultaneously. Thus, an SM as a logic element is completely different from a logic gate in this respect.

When making a logic circuit using such SMs, we assume the following: Each output port of an SM can be connected to only one input port of another (maybe the same) SM. Thus, fan-out of an output is not allowed. In the following, we consider only RLEMs with two or more states, and two or more symbols, since 1-state or 1-symbol RLEMs are trivial ones.

Fig. 2.1 (a) A sequential machine $M = (Q, \{a_1, \ldots, a_m\}, \{s_1, \ldots, s_n\}, \delta)$ such that $\delta(p, a_i) = (q, s_j)$, and **(b)** an interpretation of a sequential machine as a module having decoded input ports and output ports for utilizing it as a building module of a logic circuit

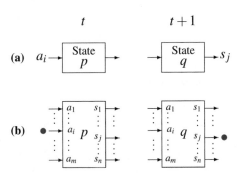

2.2.1 Rotary element (RE), a typical RLEM

There are infinitely many kinds of RLEMs if we do not bound the number of states or the number of symbols. But, here we consider a particular 2-state RLEM called a rotary element (RE) [5], since it is a typical RLEM whose operation is very easily understood by an intuitive interpretation.

Definition 2.3. A *rotary element* (RE) is a 2-state 4-symbol RLEM $M_{RE} = (\{V, H\}, \{n, e, s, w\}, \{n', e', s', w'\}, \delta_{RE})$, where δ_{RE} is given in Table 2.1.

Table 2.1 The move function δ_{RE} of a rotary element (RE)

Present state	Input			
	n	e	s	w
V	V s'	H n'	V n'	H s'
H	V w'	H w'	V e'	H e'

In Table 2.1, each of eight items gives a next state and an output for a present state and an input. For example, if the present state is H and the input is n, then the next state is V and the output is w', and hence $\delta_{RE}(H, n) = (V, w')$. It is easily verified that δ_{RE} is injective.

An RE has the following interpretation on its operation. It is depicted by a square box containing a rotatable bar inside (Fig. 2.2). The states V and H are represented by the direction of the bar that is either vertical or horizontal. There are four input lines and four output lines corresponding to the sets of input symbols $\{n, e, s, w\}$ and output symbols $\{n', e', s', w'\}$.

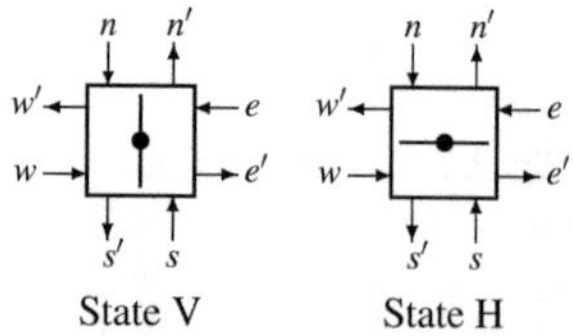

Fig. 2.2 Two states of a rotary element (RE)

The rotatable bar controls the moving direction of a particle coming to the element. When no particle exists, nothing happens on the RE. If a particle comes from the direction parallel to the rotatable bar, then it goes out from the output port of the opposite side without affecting the direction of the bar (Fig. 2.3 **(a)**). If a particle comes from the direction orthogonal to the bar, then it makes a right turn, and rotates the bar by 90 degrees (Fig. 2.3 **(b)**).

We assume at most one particle is inputted to an RE at a time. Thus, its movement is undefined for the case two or more particles are given. The definition could be extended so that it can also operate in such a case. However, we do not do so. The reason is that, even without such an extension, an RE is shown to be "universal" in the sense that any RSM is realized by a circuit composed only of REs (Sect. 2.3). In addition, it is desirable to keep the definition of RLEMs as simple as possible for clarifying the frontier between universal and non-universal RLEMs, and for investigating the relation between RLEMs and a reversible physical system.

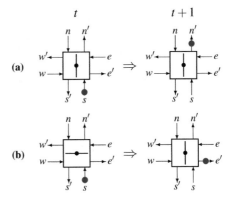

Fig. 2.3 Operations of RE:
(a) the parallel case, and (b)
the orthogonal case

2.2.2 Circuit composed of REs

We now compose reversible logic circuits out of REs.

Definition 2.4. An *RE-circuit* is a system composed of a finite number of copies of RE, which are connected to each other under the following constraint.

1. Each output port of an RE can be connected to at most one input port of another (or may be the same) RE, i.e., fan-out of an output is inhibited.
2. Two or more output ports should not be connected to one input port, i.e., merging of outputs is inhibited.

Some input ports (output ports, respectively) of REs that are not connected to any other ports are specified as input ports (output ports) of the whole circuit. When we use RE-circuits, the following condition must be satisfied.

3. An input particle can be given at most one input port of the circuit at a time only when no particle exists in the circuit.

The above conditions will be defined more precisely and generally in Definitions 3.4 and 3.5 in Sect. 3.5.1. Note that in Sect. 4.2.1, the condition 3 is changed so that two or more particles can be given to an RE-circuit at a time to simulate reversible logic gates. But, even in that case, the number of particles given to each RE in the circuit must be at most one at a time.

Let C be an RE-circuit composed of m copies of RE that has the sets of input ports $\Sigma = \{a_1, \ldots, a_k\}$ and output ports $\Gamma = \{s_1, \ldots, s_l\}$. Note that k need not be equal to l, since some open input/output ports of REs may not be specified as input/output ports of the whole circuit. Here, each state of C is represented by $\mathbf{x} = (x_1, \ldots, x_m) \in \{V, H\}^m$. Then, C realizes an RSM $M = (\{V, H\}^m, \Sigma, \Gamma, \delta)$, where δ is defined as follows. Assume C is in the state $\mathbf{x} \in \{V, H\}^m$ and a particle is given to the port $a_i \in \Sigma$. If the particle finally goes out from the port $s_j \in \Gamma$ and the state of C at that time is $\mathbf{x}' \in \{V, H\}^m$, then $\delta(\mathbf{x}, a_i) = (\mathbf{x}', s_j)$.

Example 2.1. Let C_1 be an RE-circuit shown in Fig. 2.4. Note that C_1 is identical to the RE-column of degree 2, which will be defined in Sect. 2.3, except that the latter has neither the input port c nor the output port t. The RSM realized by C_1 is $M_1 = (\{V,H\}^3, \Sigma, \Gamma, \delta_1)$, where $\Sigma = \{a_1, a_2, b_1, b_2, c\}$, $\Gamma = \{r_1, r_2, s_1, s_2, t\}$, and δ_1 is given in Table 2.2. Four cases of computing processes of C_1 among 40 cases in Table 2.2 are shown in Fig. 2.5.

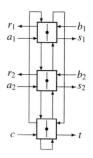

Fig. 2.4 An example of an
RE-circuit C_1

Table 2.2 The move function δ_1 of the RSM M_1 realized by the RE-circuit C_1

Present state	Input				
	a_1	a_2	b_1	b_2	c
(V,V,V)	(V,V,V) s_1	(V,V,V) s_2	(V,V,H) s_1	(V,V,H) s_2	(V,V,V) t
(V,V,H)	(V,V,V) r_1	(V,V,V) r_2	(V,V,H) r_1	(V,V,H) r_2	(V,V,H) t
(V,H,V)	(H,V,V) r_2	(V,H,V) s_2	(H,V,H) s_2	(V,H,V) r_2	(V,H,V) t
(V,H,H)	(H,V,H) r_2	(V,H,H) s_2	(V,H,H) r_1	(V,H,H) r_2	(V,H,H) t
(H,V,V)	(H,V,V) s_1	(H,V,V) s_2	(H,V,V) r_1	(V,H,V) s_1	(H,V,V) t
(H,V,H)	(H,V,H) s_1	(V,H,V) r_1	(H,V,H) r_1	(V,H,H) s_1	(H,V,H) t
(H,H,V)	(H,H,V) s_1	(H,H,V) s_2	(H,H,V) r_1	(H,H,V) r_2	(H,H,V) t
(H,H,H)	(H,H,H) s_1	(H,H,H) s_2	(H,H,H) r_1	(H,H,H) r_2	(H,H,H) t

The state-transition diagram obtained from Table 2.2 is shown in Fig. 2.6. In this figure, the label x/y attached to a directed edge shows an input-output relation where x is an input symbol, and y is an output symbol. In Fig. 2.6, i stands for 1 and 2, and thus, e.g., a_i/s_i indicates a_1/s_1 and a_2/s_2. From the diagram, we can observe there are four connected components of states: $\{(V,V,V),(V,V,H)\}$, $\{(V,H,V),(V,H,H),(H,V,H),(H,V,V)\}$, $\{(H,H,H)\}$, and $\{(H,H,V)\}$. Thus, it is seen that the states (H,H,H) and (H,H,V) are useless, since from each of these the states, M_1 cannot go to other states. Also note that, from Table 2.2, we can see that the input and output ports c and t are useless, since c does not change the state of M_1 at all, and in this case the output is always t.   □

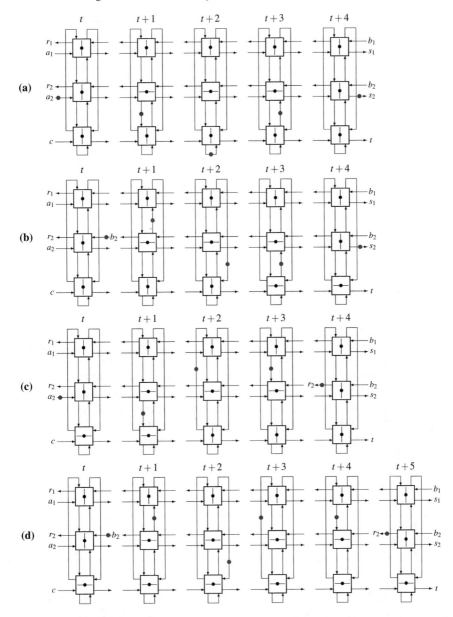

Fig. 2.5 Four cases of the computing processes of the RE-circuit C_1 that realizes the RSM M_1 with the move function δ_1: **(a)** $\delta_1((V,V,V),a_2) = ((V,V,V),s_2)$, **(b)** $\delta_1((V,V,V),b_2) = ((V,V,H),s_2)$, **(c)** $\delta_1((V,V,H),a_2) = ((V,V,V),r_2)$, and **(d)** $\delta_1((V,V,H),b_2) = ((V,V,H),r_2)$

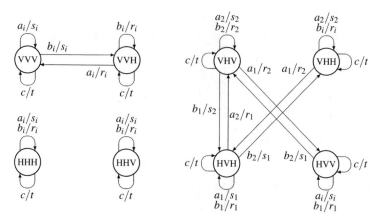

Fig. 2.6 State-transition diagram of the RSM M_1

2.2.3 Realizing RE in the billiard ball model

In this section, we consider the problem how an RE can be realized in a reversible physical system. In our present technology, it is difficult to implement a reversible logic element in a reversible physical system in the nano-scale level. However, some thought experiments in an idealized circumstance suggest a possibility of realizing it. The *billiard ball model* (BBM), is a physical model of computing proposed by Fredkin and Toffoli [3]. It is an idealized mechanical model consisting of balls and reflectors. Balls can collide with other balls or reflectors. It is assumed that collisions are elastic, and there is no friction. Figure 2.7 shows a process where a ball bounces at a reflector.

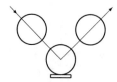

Fig. 2.7 A ball and a reflector in the billiard ball model (BBM)

Fredkin and Toffoli [3] showed that a *Fredkin gate*, which is a kind of universal reversible logic gate, can be realized in this model by appropriately placing reflectors and moving balls (see Sect. 4.1.5). As will be shown in Sect. 4.2.2, an RE can be constructed out of Fredkin gates. Therefore, it is in principle possible to realize it in BBM. However, if we employ this method, the resulting configuration of BBM will be very complex, since 12 copies of Fredkin gates are needed to simulate an RE. Instead, we show here a direct and compact realization of an RE given in [7].

Figure 2.8 gives a configuration of BBM that can simulate an RE in the two-dimensional Euclidian space $\mathbb{R}^2$. A stationary ball called a *state-ball* is put at the

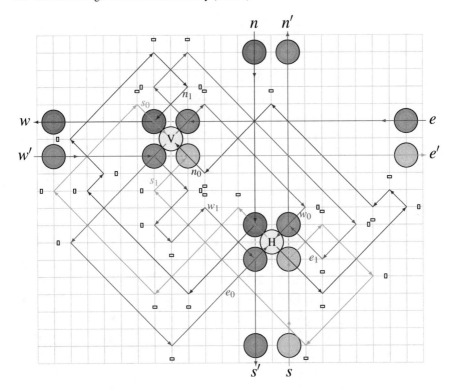

Fig. 2.8 Rotary element (RE) realized in BBM

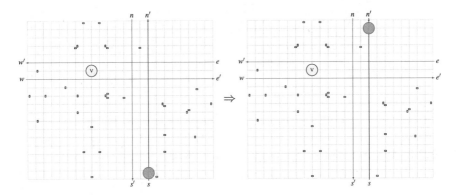

Fig. 2.9 The process of simulating $\delta_{RE}(V,s) = (V,n')$ of RE

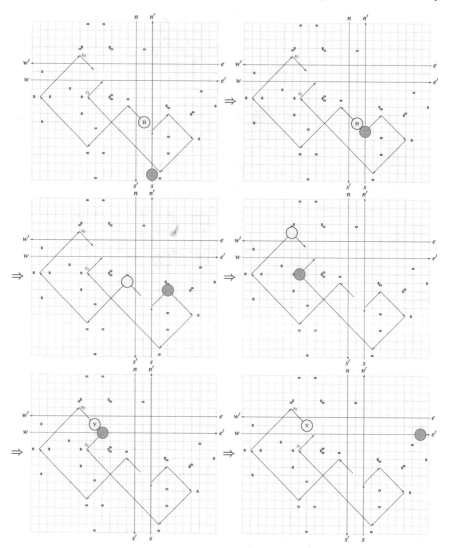

Fig. 2.10 The process of simulating $\delta_{\mathrm{RE}}(\mathrm{H}, s) = (\mathrm{V}, e')$ of RE

position H or V in the figure, whose center has integer coordinates. These positions H and V correspond to the states H and V of the RE. The radius of the ball is assumed to be $\sqrt{2}$. Small rectangles in Fig. 2.8 are reflectors for balls, and they are placed so that balls change their direction at integer coordinates. A moving ball called a *signal-ball* can be given to any one of the input ports n, e, s, and w. We assume balls can move in eight directions: north, north-east, east, south-east, south, south-west, west, and north-west. In Fig. 2.8 all the trajectories of balls are written

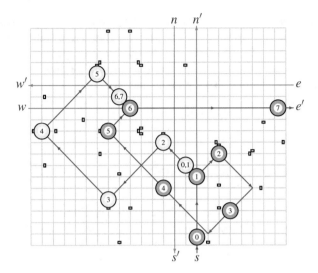

Fig. 2.11 The same process as in Fig. 2.10 that simulates $\delta_{RE}(H,s) = (V,e')$ of RE

in one figure, and thus it may look complicated. But, the essential idea is simple as explained below.

Figure 2.9 shows the case that the RE is in the state V and a signal-ball is given to s (it is the case of Fig. 2.3 **(a)**). In this case, the signal-ball (dark one) simply goes straight ahead interacting neither with the state-ball (pale one) nor with reflectors, and finally comes out from the output port n'. This is a trivial case.

Figure 2.10 shows the case that the RE is in the state H and a signal-ball is given to s (it is the case of Fig. 2.3 **(b)**). The dark ball collides with the pale ball, and they travel along the trajectories s_0 and s_1 (in Fig. 2.8), respectively. Then the balls again collide. By the second collision, the pale one stops at the position V, while the dark one continues to travel rightward and finally goes out from the port e'. Note that the second collision is a reverse process of the first collision. Figure 2.11 shows the same process as in Fig. 2.10, but it is drawn in one figure. If all the collisions are elastic, and there is no friction, then the speed of the dark ball at the output port is the same as that at the input port. Hence, there is no dissipation of energy in this operation.

An advantage of this method is that, in an idle state, the state-ball is stationary. Therefore, a signal-ball can be given at any moment and with any speed, hence there is no need to synchronize the two balls. On the other hand, if we try to implement a logic gate, such as a NAND gate, in a physical system, then some synchronization mechanism is necessary. In the current technology for digital circuits, a clock signal is used to synchronize two or more data signals. Also in the case of the BBM realization of a Fredkin gate [3] many balls must be synchronized precisely, and must have exactly the same velocity, and it is indeed extremely difficult.

One may think it is still impossible to implement an RE by a real mechanical hardware of BBM. However, considering the role of the stationary ball in this method, it need not be a movable particle, but can be a state of some stationary object, such as a quantum state of an atom or similar. The incoming ball can be a moving particle, something like a photon, and there may be no need to adjust the arrival timing. So, this method suggests a possibility of implementing an RE in a real physical system with reversibility.

2.3 Making Reversible Sequential Machines (RSMs) from RE

In this section, we prove any reversible sequential machine (RSM) can be implemented as a reversible logic circuit composed only of REs. It is shown based on the method given in [6].

2.3.1 RE-column, a building module for RSMs

We first prepare a building module called an *RE-column*. Figure 2.12 shows an RE-column of degree n, which consists of $n+1$ copies of REs. The circuit C_1 in Example 2.1 (Fig. 2.4) was an RE-column of degree 2 (but the input and output ports c and t are removed here). Let

$$M_{\text{REC}_n} = (\{V,H\}^{n+1}, \{a_1,\ldots,a_n,b_1,\ldots,b_n\}, \{r_1,\ldots,r_n,s_1,\ldots,s_n\}, \delta_{\text{REC}_n})$$

be the RSM realized by the RE-column of degree n. Though M_{REC_n} has 2^{n+1} states, we consider only the states $(V,\ldots,V,V)$ and $(V,\ldots,V,H)$, i.e., all the REs except the bottom one are in the state V. The states $(V,\ldots,V,V)$ and $(V,\ldots,V,H)$ are called an *unmarked state*, and a *marked state*, respectively. The move function δ_{REC_n} for these states is described in Table 2.3. Note that Fig. 2.5 shows examples of computing processes in the RE-column of degree 2.

Table 2.3 The move function δ_{REC_n} of the RE-column for the unmarked and marked states ($i \in \{1,\ldots,n\}$)

Present state	Input	
	a_i	b_i
Unmarked: $(V,\ldots,V,V)$	$(V,\ldots,V,V)\,s_i$	$(V,\ldots,V,H)\,s_i$
Marked: $(V,\ldots,V,H)$	$(V,\ldots,V,V)\,r_i$	$(V,\ldots,V,H)\,r_i$

Fig. 2.12 An RE-column of degree n

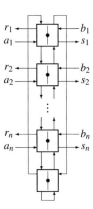

2.3.2 Composing reversible sequential machines by RE-columns

When simulating an m-state n-symbol RSM, m copies of an RE-column of degree n will be placed and connected in a row. From Table 2.3, we can observe the following facts. If an RE-column is in the unmarked state and the input is a_i, then the state remains unchanged and the output is s_i. This operation is used to go through (i.e., ignore) an unmarked RE-column. On the other hand, if the RE-column is in the marked state and the input is a_i, then the state changes to the unmarked one, and the output is r_i. This operation is used to find a marked RE-column. If an RE-column is in the unmarked state and the input is b_i, then the state changes to the marked one, and the output is s_i. This operation is used to set an RE-column to be marked.

Theorem 2.1. *[6] Every RSM can be realized by an RE-circuit.*

Proof. We first explain the construction method of an RE-circuit that simulates a given RSM by an example. Let $M_2 = (\{q_1, q_2, q_3\}, \{a_1, a_2, a_3\}, \{s_1, s_2, s_3\}, \delta_2)$ be a 3-state 3-symbol RSM, where δ_2 is described in Table 2.4.

Table 2.4 The move function δ_2 of an RSM M_2

	Input		
Present state	a_1	a_2	a_3
q_1	$q_2\,s_2$	$q_3\,s_1$	$q_1\,s_2$
q_2	$q_3\,s_2$	$q_2\,s_1$	$q_1\,s_3$
q_3	$q_3\,s_3$	$q_2\,s_3$	$q_1\,s_1$

We prepare three copies of RE-columns of degree 3, and connect them as shown in Fig. 2.13. It is a "framework circuit" for composing any 3-state 3-symbol RSM. There are 12 REs arranged in four rows and in three columns. The REs in the i-th row correspond to the input symbol a_i and the output symbol s_i of M_2 ($i \in \{1, 2, 3\}$).

The REs in the j-th column correspond to the state q_j of M_2 ($j \in \{1,2,3\}$). The RE that is in the i-th row of the j-th column is denoted by (i, j)-RE. We assume only one RE-column is in the marked state in the circuit. In Fig. 2.13, the third column is set to the marked state. This means the simulated RSM M_2 is in the state q_3.

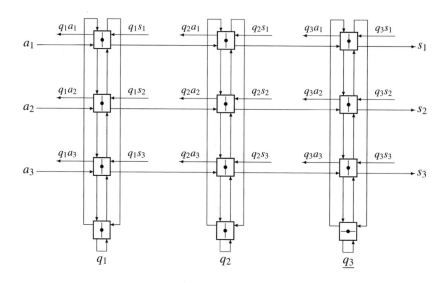

Fig. 2.13 The framework circuit for implementing a 3-state 3-symbol RSM. Here, the third RE-column is marked, i.e., its bottom RE is in the state H

Assume, for example, a particle is given to the input port a_2. Then, since the first and the second RE-columns are in the unmarked state, the particle goes through these columns without changing their state, and arrives at the third column. Since the third column is in the marked state, the particle makes it in the unmarked state, and then goes out from the west output port of the $(2,3)$-RE (labeled by $q_3 a_2$). By this, the crossing point of the third column and the second row, which corresponds to the combination of q_3 and a_2, is found.

Since $\delta_2(q_3, a_2) = (q_2, s_3)$, the west output port of the $(2,3)$-RE is connected to the east input port of the $(3,2)$-RE (labeled by $q_2 s_3$). By this, the particle sets the second column to the marked state, and travels rightward along the line in the third row. Since the third column is in the unmarked state, the particle goes through it, and finally comes out from the output port s_3. By above, the movement $\delta_2(q_3, a_2) = (q_2, s_3)$ is simulated. Giving such connection lines appropriately for all the combinations of q_j ($j \in \{1,2,3\}$) and a_i ($i \in \{1,2,3\}$), we obtain a circuit shown in Fig. 2.14 that simulates M_2.

It is easy to extend the above construction method to the general case. Let $M = (\{q_1,\ldots,q_m\}, \{a_1,\ldots,a_{n'}\}, \{s_1,\ldots,s_n\}, \delta)$ be an m-state n-symbol RSM, where $n' \leq n$. Then, prepare m copies of the RE-column of degree n, and connect them

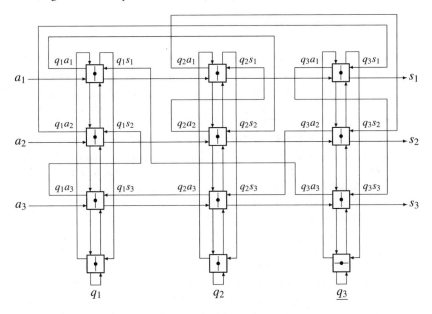

Fig. 2.14 The RSM M_2 realized by an RE-circuit. Here, M_2 is in the state q_3

like in Fig. 2.13. For each $i \in \{1,\dots,n'\}$ and $j \in \{1,\dots,m\}$, if $\delta(q_j,a_i) = (q_l,s_k)$, then connect the west output port of the (i,j)-RE to the east input port of the (k,l)-RE. Since M is an RSM, line connections are made consistently, i.e., no merge of output lines occurs. In the case $n' < n$, only n' ports are used as input ports of the whole circuit. By above, we obtain an RE-circuit consisting of $m(n+1)$ copies of RE that simulates M.   □

The above RE-circuit that simulates an RSM uses only one particle in its computing process, and thus never produces useless signals. In this sense, it is a "garbage-less" logic circuit. As we shall see in Sect. 4.1, garbage information is sometimes generated, when we use a reversible combinatorial logic circuit composed of reversible logic gate. Since discarding the garbage information is an irreversible process, we should give garbage-less logic circuits like the ones in Theorem 2.1.

We define the notion of universality of an RLEM as follows.

Definition 2.5. An RLEM is called *universal* if any RSM is realized by a circuit composed only of copies of the RLEM. An RLEM is called *non-universal* if it is not universal.

The above definition is justified by the fact that a finite state control and a memory cell of a reversible Turing machine (RTM) are defined as RSMs (Sect. 6.1), and that an RTM is computationally universal [1]. By Theorem 2.1 we have the following.

Corollary 2.1. *RE is universal.*

2.4 Concluding Remarks

We introduced a reversible logic element with memory (RLEM), and showed how
it is used as a logical primitive for reversible computing. In the conventional design
theory of logic circuits, logic gates, which are elements without memory, are mainly
used as primitives (but, in the study of asynchronous circuits, logic elements with
memory are sometimes used [2, 4]). On the other hand, in the case of reversible
computing, it turned out that RLEMs are also useful as logical primitives. Here, we
presented a typical 2-state 4-symbol RLEM called a rotary element (RE) [5], and
showed that it has a simple and direct realization in the billiard ball model (BBM),
and that it is universal in the sense any RSM can be composed only of it.

Another advantage of using RLEMs is that there is no need to synchronize incoming signals at the element. In the case of a logic gate, like a 2-input NAND gate,
two input signals come from places apart from the gate position. These signals must
arrive at the gate simultaneously. Otherwise, we cannot obtain a correct output. In
the current technology for electronic circuits, synchronization of signals is implemented by a clock signal supplied to the whole circuit. On the other hand, in the
case of an RLEM, an incoming signal interacts with the state of the RLEM. Hence,
the state can be regarded as a kind of stationary signal that is always at the element's
position. Therefore, the input signal can be given at any moment, and the operation
of the RLEM is triggered by it. This fact is well understood by the BBM realization
of RE shown in Sect. 2.2.3. In this sense, an RLEM has an *asynchronous* nature.

In this chapter, we considered only an RE as an RLEM. But, there are still infinitely many kinds of RLEMs even if we consider only 2-state ones. In the next
chapter, 2-state RLEMs are classified, and it is clarified which RLEMs are universal
and which are not. In Chap. 6, it is shown that any reversible Turing machine can be
constructed by RE very simply.

References

1. Bennett, C.H.: Logical reversibility of computation. IBM J. Res. Dev. **17**, 525–532 (1973).
   doi:10.1147/rd.176.0525
2. Büning, H.K., Priese, L.: Universal asynchronous iterative arrays of Mealy automata. Acta
   Informatica **13**, 269–285 (1980). doi:10.1007/BF00288646
3. Fredkin, E., Toffoli, T.: Conservative logic. Int. J. Theoret. Phys. **21**, 219–253 (1982).
   doi:10.1007/BF01857727
4. Keller, R.M.: Towards a theory of universal speed-independent modules. IEEE Trans. Computers **C-23**, 21–33 (1974). doi:10.1109/T-C.1974.223773
5. Morita, K.: A simple reversible logic element and cellular automata for reversible computing.
   In: Proc. MCU 2001 (eds. M. Margenstern, Y. Rogozhin), LNCS 2055, pp. 102–113 (2001).
   doi:10.1007/3-540-45132-3_6
6. Morita, K.: A new universal logic element for reversible computing. In: Grammars and Automata for String Processing (eds. C. Martin-Vide, and V. Mitrana), pp. 285–294. Taylor &
   Francis, London (2003). doi:10.1201/9780203009642.ch28
7. Morita, K.: Reversible computing and cellular automata — A survey. Theoret. Comput. Sci.
   395, 101–131 (2008). doi:10.1016/j.tcs.2008.01.041

Chapter 3
Classification of Reversible Logic Elements with Memory and Their Universality

Abstract A reversible logic element with memory (RLEM) is a logical primitive useful for composing reversible machines. It is a kind of reversible sequential machine (RSM), and thus has finite numbers of states and input/output symbols. First, we prove that *every* non-degenerate 2-state k-symbol RLEM is universal if $k > 2$. Hence, any RSM can be constructed by such a universal RLEM. On the other hand, it is shown that RLEMs Nos. 2-2, 2-3 and 2-4 among the four non-degenerate 2-state 2-symbol RLEMs are non-universal, and thus we obtain a simple hierarchy among 2-state RLEMs. We then show that there is a compact realization method of RSMs by RLEM 4-31 or RLEM 3-7. Hence, these RLEMs are useful for constructing reversible machines, as well as rotary element (RE), a typical 2-state 4-symbol RLEM. We also give a simple and systematic method of realizing a reversible 4-symbol RLEM with arbitrary number of states in the billiard ball model (BBM), a reversible physical model of computing.

Keywords reversible logic element with memory, universality, reversible sequential machine, billiard ball model

3.1 Classification of RLEMs

In Chap. 2, we introduced a particular reversible logic element with memory (RLEM) called a rotary element (RE), and showed that it is universal in the sense that any reversible sequential machine can be constructed by it (Theorem 2.1). Besides RE, there are infinitely many kinds of RLEMs if we do not limit the number of states or symbols. Thus, it is important to know which RLEMs are universal and which are not. In this chapter, we investigate 2-state k-symbol RLEMs ($k > 1$), and show that *all* non-degenerate 2-state RLEMs are universal except only four 2-symbol RLEMs (Theorem 3.1). We prove that three RLEMs among four kinds of 2-symbol RLEMs are non-universal (Theorem 3.2), though it is still open whether the remaining one is universal. From these results, we obtain a simple hierarchy

31

among 2-state RLEMs (Fig. 3.29). We also show that any 4-symbol RLEM can be realized in the billiard ball model in a systematic way (Theorem 3.4).

In this section, we make several preparations for the above. We first introduce a graphical representation of a 2-state RLEM so that we can recognize its behavior intuitively. We then define an equivalence relation among 2-state k-symbol RLEMs to reduce the total number of RLEMs to be investigated. We also define the notion of "degeneracy" of an RLEM. By this, without loss of generality, we can consider only non-degenerate RLEMs. Based on the above notions, we classify 2-state k-symbol RLEMs.

3.1.1 Graphical representation of RLEMs

Here, we give a graphical representation of a 2-state RLEM to express its move function pictorially, and to draw a circuit composed of it. Consider a 2-state 4-symbol RLEM $M_{4\text{-}312} = (\{0,1\}, \{a,b,c,d\}, \{s,t,u,v\}, \delta_{4\text{-}312})$ as an example, which has an identification number 4-312 (the numbering method will be given later). Its move function $\delta_{4\text{-}312}$ is given in Table 3.1. The graphical representation of $M_{4\text{-}312}$ is shown in Fig. 3.1. Each of the two states is represented by a rectangle having input and output ports. The relation between input and output is indicated by solid and dotted lines. We assume a particle is given to at most one input port at a time as in the case of RE. If a particle is given to some input port, it travels along the line connected to the input port, and goes out from the output port connected to it. If a particle goes through a dotted line, the state does not change (Fig. 3.2 **(a)**). On the other hand, if it goes through a solid line, the state changes to the other (Fig. 3.2 **(b)**).

Table 3.1 The move function $\delta_{4\text{-}312}$ of the 2-state RLEM 4-312

	Input			
Present state	a	b	c	d
State 0	$0\,s$	$0\,t$	$1\,s$	$1\,u$
State 1	$0\,u$	$0\,v$	$1\,t$	$1\,v$

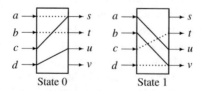

Fig. 3.1 A graphical representation of the 2-state RLEM 4-312

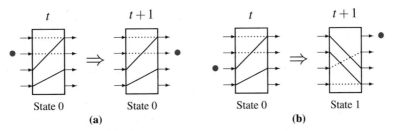

t	$t+1$	t	$t+1$
State 0	State 0	State 0	State 1
(a)		**(b)**	

Fig. 3.2 Examples of operations of the 2-state RLEM 4-312. **(a)** If a particle passes a dotted line, then the state remains to be the same. **(b)** If a particle passes a solid line, then the state changes to the other

We now give a formal definition of a graphical representation.

Definition 3.1. Let $M = (\{0,1\}, \{a_1, \ldots, a_k\}, \{s_1, \ldots, s_k\}, \delta)$ be a 2-state k-symbol RLEM. A labeled graph $G_M = (V, E, f)$ defined as follows is called a *graphical representation* of M, where V and E are sets of vertices and edges, and $f : E \to \{\text{dot}, \text{sol}\}$ is a label function. Note that "dot" and "sol" correspond to a dotted line and a solid line, respectively. The graph G_M consists of two subgraphs $G_M^q = (V_q, E_q, f_q)$ ($q \in \{0,1\}$), where V_q, E_q, and f_q are defined as follows.

$$V_q = \{a_1^q, \ldots, a_k^q\} \cup \{s_1^q, \ldots, s_k^q\}$$
$$E_q = \{(a_i^q, s_j^q) \mid \exists q' \in \{0,1\} \ (\delta(q, a_i) = (q', s_j))\}$$
$$f_q(a_i^q, s_j^q) = \begin{cases} \text{dot if } \delta(q, a_i) = (q, s_j) \\ \text{sol if } \delta(q, a_i) = (1 - q, s_j) \end{cases}$$

Hence, $V = V_0 \cup V_1$, $V_0 \cap V_1 = \emptyset$, $E = E_0 \cup E_1$, $E_0 \cap E_1 = \emptyset$, and $f_q = f|_{E_q}$. An edge (a_i^q, s_j^q) is called a *solid edge* if $f(a_i^q, s_j^q) = \text{sol}$, and called a *dotted edge* if $f(a_i^q, s_j^q) = \text{dot}$.

When drawing a figure of G_M, we usually omit to write the superscript q of a_i^q and s_j^q by indicating the state q at each subgraph G_M^q as in Fig. 3.1.

The following lemma shows some properties of a graphical representation [3]. It is derived from the fact that the move function of an RLEM is bijective.

Lemma 3.1. *For any 2-state k-symbol RLEM $M = (\{0,1\}, \{a_1, \ldots, a_k\}, \{s_1, \ldots, s_k\}, \delta)$ and its graphical representation $G_M = (V, E, f)$, the following properties hold.*

(1) For any $i \in \{1, \ldots, k\}$ and $q \in \{0,1\}$ there is exactly one edge that has a_i^q as a start point. Hence, $|E_q| = k$.

(2) For any $j \in \{1, \ldots, k\}$ there are exactly two edges that have s_j^0 or s_j^1 as end points. If one edge has s_j^0, and the other has s_j^1 as endpoints, then the labels of these edges must be the same. If the both edges have s_j^0 (or s_j^1) as endpoints, then the labels of these edges must be different, and they are called merging edges.

(3) The number of edges with the label "sol" in G_M^0 is the same as that in G_M^1.

(4) If G_M^0 has merging edges, then G_M^1 also has them, and vice versa.

Proof. (1) From the definition of the set of edges E_q, it is clear that there is at least one edge that has a_i^q as a start point. Next we assume, on the contrary, there exist two distinct edges $(a_i^q, s_j^q) \in E_q$, and $(a_i^q, s_{j'}^q) \in E_q$ for some $i, j, j' \in \{1, \ldots, k\}$ $(j \neq j')$, and $q \in \{0, 1\}$. Then, by the definition of G_M, $\delta(q, a_i) = (q', s_j)$ and $\delta(q, a_i) = (q'', s_{j'})$ hold for some $q', q'' \in \{0, 1\}$. It contradicts the fact M is deterministic (i.e., δ is a mapping from $\{0, 1\} \times \{a_1, \ldots, a_k\}$ to $\{0, 1\} \times \{s_1, \ldots, s_k\}$).

(2) Since M is reversible, δ is a bijection from $\{0, 1\} \times \{a_1, \ldots, a_k\}$ to $\{0, 1\} \times \{s_1, \ldots, s_k\}$. Therefore, for each $j \in \{1, \ldots, k\}$, there exists a unique pair $(q_0, a_{i_0}) \in \{0, 1\} \times \{a_1, \ldots, a_k\}$ such that $\delta(q_0, a_{i_0}) = (0, s_j)$. Likewise, for each $j \in \{1, \ldots, k\}$, there exists a unique pair $(q_1, a_{i_1}) \in \{0, 1\} \times \{a_1, \ldots, a_k\}$ such that $\delta(q_1, a_{i_1}) = (1, s_j)$ and $(q_0, a_{i_0}) \neq (q_1, a_{i_1})$. Hence, there are exactly two edges in E that have s_j^0 or s_j^1 as end points.

There are four cases: (i) If $q_0 = q_1 = 0$, then, by the definition of G_M, $(a_{i_0}^0, s_j^0) \in E_0$, $f(a_{i_0}^0, s_j^0) = $ dot, $(a_{i_1}^0, s_j^0) \in E_0$, and $f(a_{i_1}^0, s_j^0) = $ sol. The edges $(a_{i_0}^0, s_j^0)$ and $(a_{i_1}^0, s_j^0)$ are merging edges. For example, in Fig. 3.1 the edges (a, s) and (c, s) in the state 0 are the merging edges of this case. (ii) If $q_0 = 0$ and $q_1 = 1$, then $(a_{i_0}^0, s_j^0) \in E_0$, $f(a_{i_0}^0, s_j^0) = $ dot, $(a_{i_1}^1, s_j^1) \in E_1$, and $f(a_{i_1}^1, s_j^1) = $ dot. They are both dotted edges. In Fig. 3.1, (b, t) in the state 0 and (c, t) in the state 1 are the dotted edges of this case. (iii) If $q_0 = 1$ and $q_1 = 0$, then $(a_{i_0}^1, s_j^1) \in E_1$, $f(a_{i_0}^1, s_j^1) = $ sol, $(a_{i_1}^0, s_j^0) \in E_0$, and $f(a_{i_1}^0, s_j^0) = $ sol. They are both solid edges. In Fig. 3.1, (d, u) in the state 0 and (a, u) in the state 1 are the solid edges of this case. (iv) If $q_0 = q_1 = 1$, then $(a_{i_0}^1, s_j^1) \in E_1$, $f(a_{i_0}^1, s_j^1) = $ sol, $(a_{i_1}^1, s_j^1) \in E_1$, and $f(a_{i_1}^1, s_j^1) = $ dot. They are merging edges. In Fig. 3.1, (d, v) and (d, v) in the state 1 are the merging edges of this case.

(3) Let n_q be the number of solid edges in G_M^q $(q \in \{0, 1\})$. Assume, on the contrary, $n_0 \neq n_1$. We consider only $n_0 > n_1$, since the case $n_0 < n_1$ is similar. Let A_0 and A_1 be as follows.

$$A_0 = \{(0, a_i) \mid \exists j \in \{1, \ldots, k\} \ (\delta(0, a_i) = (1, s_j))\}$$
$$A_1 = \{(1, a_i) \mid \exists j \in \{1, \ldots, k\} \ (\delta(1, a_i) = (1, s_j))\}$$

Then, $|A_0| = n_0$ and $|A_1| = k - n_1$ hold. Hence, $|A_0 \cup A_1| = n_0 + (k - n_1) > k$. Therefore, there exist $j_0 \in \{1, \ldots, k\}$ and $(q_1, a_{i_1}), (q_2, a_{i_2}) \in A_0 \cup A_1$ such that $(q_1, a_{i_1}) \neq (q_2, a_{i_2})$ and $\delta(q_1, a_{i_1}) = \delta(q_2, a_{i_2}) = (1, s_{j_0})$. This contradicts the fact δ is injective.

(4) Assume, on the contrary, G_M^0 has merging edges, but G_M^1 does not (the other case is similarly proved). Let $(a_{i_1}^0, s_{j_0}^0)$ and $(a_{i_2}^0, s_{j_0}^0)$ be merging edges in G_M^0. Then, by (2), $(a_j^1, s_{j_0}^1) \notin E_1$ for any $j \in \{1, \ldots, k\}$. Since there is no merging edges in G_M^1, $|E_1| < k$ holds. But, it contradicts (1). □

3.1.2 Equivalence in RLEMs

We define an equivalence relation among 2-state RLEMs. Let $M = (Q, \Sigma, \Gamma, \delta)$ be a 2-state k-symbol RLEM. Since $\delta : Q \times \Sigma \rightarrow Q \times \Gamma$ is a bijection and $|Q \times \Gamma| = 2k$, there are $(2k)!$ kinds of 2-state k-symbol RLEMs. However, among them there are many equivalent RLEMs, which can be obtained from another by renaming states and/or the input/output symbols (see Definition 3.2 below). Hence, the total number of essentially different 2-state k-symbol RLEMs decreases considerably. Also, among 2-state k-symbol RLEMs, there are "degenerate" RLEMs, each of which is further equivalent to either a 2-state k'-symbol RLEM such that $k' < k$, or a 1-state RLEM (Definition 3.3). Hence, only non-degenerate RLEMs are the proper 2-state k-symbol ones that should be investigated. Surprisingly, it will be proved that "all" non-degenerate 2-state RLEMs are universal except only four 2-symbol RLEMs (Theorem 3.1).

We now give an *identification number* to each of 2-state RLEMs, and then classify them. Let

$$M = (\{0,1\}, \{a_1, \ldots, a_k\}, \{s_1, \ldots, s_k\}, \delta)$$

be a 2-state k-symbol RLEM. Since the move function δ is a bijection, it can be specified by a permutation of the set $\{0,1\} \times \{s_1, \ldots, s_k\}$, and thus there are $(2k)!$ kinds of move functions. Hence, 2-state k-symbol RLEMs and their move functions are numbered by $0, \ldots, (2k)! - 1$ in the lexicographic order of permutations. An identification number is obtained by attaching "k-" to the serial number, e.g., 4-312. Thus the 4-symbol RLEM with the identification number 4-312 is denoted by RLEM 4-312.

Example 3.1. In the 2-state 2-symbol case, there are 24 RLEMs. Each of them is denoted by RLEM 2-n, and is defined by $M_{2\text{-}n} = (\{0,1\}, \{a_1, a_2\}, \{s_1, s_2\}, \delta_{2\text{-}n})$ ($n \in \{0, \ldots, 23\}$). Their move functions are given in Table 3.2. □

We regard two sequential machines (SMs) are "equivalent" if one can be obtained by renaming the states and the input/output symbols of the other. This notion is formalized as follows.

Definition 3.2. Let $M_1 = (Q_1, \Sigma_1, \Gamma_1, \delta_1)$ and $M_2 = (Q_2, \Sigma_2, \Gamma_2, \delta_2)$ be two SMs (or RLEMs) such that $|Q_1| = |Q_2|$, $|\Sigma_1| = |\Sigma_2|$, and $|\Gamma_1| = |\Gamma_2|$. The SMs M_1 and M_2 are called *equivalent* and denoted by $M_1 \sim M_2$, if there exist bijections $f : Q_1 \rightarrow Q_2$, $g : \Sigma_1 \rightarrow \Sigma_2$, and $h : \Gamma_1 \rightarrow \Gamma_2$ that satisfy

$$\forall q \in Q_1, \ \forall a \in \Sigma_1 \ (\delta_1(q,a) = \psi(\delta_2(f(q), g(a)))), \tag{3.1}$$

where $\psi : Q_2 \times \Gamma_2 \rightarrow Q_1 \times \Gamma_1$ is defined as follows.

$$\forall q \in Q_2, \ \forall s \in \Gamma_2 \ (\psi(q,s) = (f^{-1}(q), h^{-1}(s))) \tag{3.2}$$

It is easy to verify that the relation "$\sim$" is an equivalence relation, i.e., it is reflexive, symmetric, and transitive. If $M_1 \sim M_2$ and M_1 and M_2 are 2-state RLEMs with identification numbers k-n_1 and k-n_2, we also write RLEM k-$n_1 \sim$ RLEM k-n_2.

Table 3.2 The move function $\delta_{2\text{-}n}$ of the 2-state 2-symbol RLEM $M_{2\text{-}n}$ ($n \in \{0,\ldots,23\}$)

n	$\delta_{2\text{-}n}(0,a_1)$	$\delta_{2\text{-}n}(0,a_2)$	$\delta_{2\text{-}n}(1,a_1)$	$\delta_{2\text{-}n}(1,a_2)$
0	$(0,s_1)$	$(0,s_2)$	$(1,s_1)$	$(1,s_2)$
1	$(0,s_1)$	$(0,s_2)$	$(1,s_2)$	$(1,s_1)$
2	$(0,s_1)$	$(1,s_1)$	$(0,s_2)$	$(1,s_2)$
3	$(0,s_1)$	$(1,s_1)$	$(1,s_2)$	$(0,s_2)$
4	$(0,s_1)$	$(1,s_2)$	$(0,s_2)$	$(1,s_1)$
5	$(0,s_1)$	$(1,s_2)$	$(1,s_1)$	$(0,s_2)$
6	$(0,s_2)$	$(0,s_1)$	$(1,s_1)$	$(1,s_2)$
7	$(0,s_2)$	$(0,s_1)$	$(1,s_2)$	$(1,s_1)$
8	$(0,s_2)$	$(1,s_1)$	$(0,s_1)$	$(1,s_2)$
9	$(0,s_2)$	$(1,s_1)$	$(1,s_2)$	$(0,s_1)$
10	$(0,s_2)$	$(1,s_2)$	$(0,s_1)$	$(1,s_1)$
11	$(0,s_2)$	$(1,s_2)$	$(1,s_1)$	$(0,s_1)$
12	$(1,s_1)$	$(0,s_1)$	$(0,s_2)$	$(1,s_2)$
13	$(1,s_1)$	$(0,s_1)$	$(1,s_2)$	$(0,s_2)$
14	$(1,s_1)$	$(0,s_2)$	$(0,s_1)$	$(1,s_2)$
15	$(1,s_1)$	$(0,s_2)$	$(1,s_2)$	$(0,s_1)$
16	$(1,s_1)$	$(1,s_2)$	$(0,s_1)$	$(0,s_2)$
17	$(1,s_1)$	$(1,s_2)$	$(0,s_2)$	$(0,s_1)$
18	$(1,s_2)$	$(0,s_1)$	$(0,s_2)$	$(1,s_1)$
19	$(1,s_2)$	$(0,s_1)$	$(1,s_1)$	$(0,s_2)$
20	$(1,s_2)$	$(0,s_2)$	$(0,s_1)$	$(1,s_1)$
21	$(1,s_2)$	$(0,s_2)$	$(1,s_1)$	$(0,s_1)$
22	$(1,s_2)$	$(1,s_1)$	$(0,s_1)$	$(0,s_2)$
23	$(1,s_2)$	$(1,s_1)$	$(0,s_2)$	$(0,s_1)$

Example 3.2. Consider the 24 kinds of 2-state 2-symbol RLEMs, whose move functions are given in Table 3.2. Then, we can show the following, and thus there are eight equivalence classes.

$$M_{2\text{-}0} \sim M_{2\text{-}7}$$
$$M_{2\text{-}1} \sim M_{2\text{-}6}$$
$$M_{2\text{-}2} \sim M_{2\text{-}10} \sim M_{2\text{-}13} \sim M_{2\text{-}21}$$
$$M_{2\text{-}3} \sim M_{2\text{-}11} \sim M_{2\text{-}12} \sim M_{2\text{-}20}$$
$$M_{2\text{-}4} \sim M_{2\text{-}8} \sim M_{2\text{-}15} \sim M_{2\text{-}19}$$
$$M_{2\text{-}5} \sim M_{2\text{-}9} \sim M_{2\text{-}14} \sim M_{2\text{-}18}$$
$$M_{2\text{-}16} \sim M_{2\text{-}23}$$
$$M_{2\text{-}17} \sim M_{2\text{-}22}$$

For example, $M_{2\text{-}3} \sim M_{2\text{-}20}$ is shown as follows. Here, $M_{2\text{-}3} = (\{0,1\}, \{a_1,a_2\}, \{s_1,s_2\}, \delta_{2\text{-}3})$, and $M_{2\text{-}20} = (\{0',1'\}, \{a'_1,a'_2\}, \{s'_1,s'_2\}, \delta_{2\text{-}20})$, and their move functions are given in Table 3.3 (see also Table 3.2). Note that the states and symbols of $M_{2\text{-}20}$ have a prime ($'$) so that we do not confuse them with those of $M_{2\text{-}3}$.

Table 3.3 The move functions $\delta_{2\text{-}3}$ and $\delta_{2\text{-}20}$ of 2-state 2-symbol RLEMs 2-3 and 2-20

Present state	Input a_1	a_2
0	$0\,s_1$	$1\,s_1$
1	$1\,s_2$	$0\,s_2$
$\delta_{2\text{-}3}$ of RLEM 2-3		

Present state	Input a_1'	a_2'
$0'$	$1'\,s_2'$	$0'\,s_2'$
$1'$	$0'\,s_1'$	$1'\,s_1'$
$\delta_{2\text{-}20}$ of RLEM 2-20		

Let $f : \{0,1\} \to \{0',1'\}$, $g : \{a_1,a_2\} \to \{a_1',a_2'\}$, and $h : \{s_1,s_2\} \to \{s_1',s_2'\}$ be bijections defined as follows.

$$f(0) = 0', \quad f(1) = 1'$$
$$g(a_1) = a_2', \quad g(a_2) = a_1'$$
$$h(s_1) = s_2', \quad h(s_2) = s_1'$$

Thus, $\psi : \{0',1'\} \times \{s_1',s_2'\} \to \{0,1\} \times \{s_1,s_2\}$ defined by Eq. 3.2 is as below.

$$\psi(0',s_1') = (0,s_2), \ \psi(0',s_2') = (0,s_1), \ \psi(1',s_1') = (1,s_2), \ \psi(1',s_2') = (1,s_1).$$

We can verify Eq. (3.1) as follows, and thus $M_{2\text{-}3} \sim M_{2\text{-}20}$.

$$\psi(\delta_{2\text{-}20}(f(0),g(a_1))) = \psi(\delta_{2\text{-}20}(0',a_2')) = \psi(0',s_2') = (0,s_1) = \delta_{2\text{-}3}(0,a_1)$$
$$\psi(\delta_{2\text{-}20}(f(0),g(a_2))) = \psi(\delta_{2\text{-}20}(0',a_1')) = \psi(1',s_2') = (1,s_1) = \delta_{2\text{-}3}(0,a_2)$$
$$\psi(\delta_{2\text{-}20}(f(1),g(a_1))) = \psi(\delta_{2\text{-}20}(1',a_2')) = \psi(1',s_1') = (1,s_2) = \delta_{2\text{-}3}(1,a_1)$$
$$\psi(\delta_{2\text{-}20}(f(1),g(a_2))) = \psi(\delta_{2\text{-}20}(1',a_1')) = \psi(0',s_1') = (0,s_2) = \delta_{2\text{-}3}(1,a_2)$$

$\square$

Example 3.3. Consider the RLEM $M_{4\text{-}289} = (\{0,1\}, \{a_1,a_2,a_3,a_4\}, \{s_1,s_2,s_3,s_4\}, \delta_{4\text{-}289})$, where $\delta_{4\text{-}289}$ is given in Table 3.4.

Table 3.4 The move function $\delta_{4\text{-}289}$ of the 2-state RLEM 4-289

Present state	Input a_1	a_2	a_3	a_4
State 0	$0\,s_1$	$0\,s_2$	$1\,s_1$	$1\,s_2$
State 1	$0\,s_3$	$0\,s_4$	$1\,s_4$	$1\,s_3$

We can see that RE (Table 2.1 in Sect. 2.2.1) and $M_{4\text{-}289}$ are equivalent, and hence $M_{RE} \sim M_{4\text{-}289}$, under the bijections f, g, and h defined below.

$$f(H) = 0, \quad f(V) = 1$$
$$g(n) = a_3, \quad g(s) = a_4, \quad g(e) = a_1, \quad g(w) = a_2$$
$$h(n') = s_3, \quad h(s') = s_4, \quad h(e') = s_2, \quad h(w') = s_1$$

$\square$

The total numbers of different 2-state 2-, 3- and 4-symbol RLEMs are 24, 720, and 40320, respectively. However, the number of equivalence classes is considerably smaller than the total number in each case. It has been shown that the numbers of equivalence classes of 2-state 2-, 3- and 4-symbol RLEMs are 8, 24, and 82, respectively [4]. Figures 3.3–3.5 show all representative RLEMs in the equivalence classes of 2-, 3- and 4-symbol RLEMs. Each representative is chosen so that it has the smallest identification number in the class.

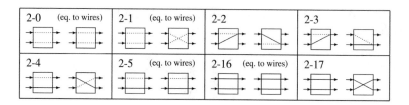

Fig. 3.3 Representatives of eight equivalence classes of 2-state 2-symbol RLEMs, where the two states 0 and 1 of an RLEM are given in each box

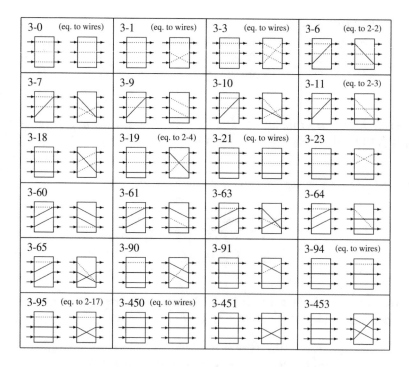

Fig. 3.4 Representatives of 24 equivalence classes of 2-state 3-symbol RLEMs

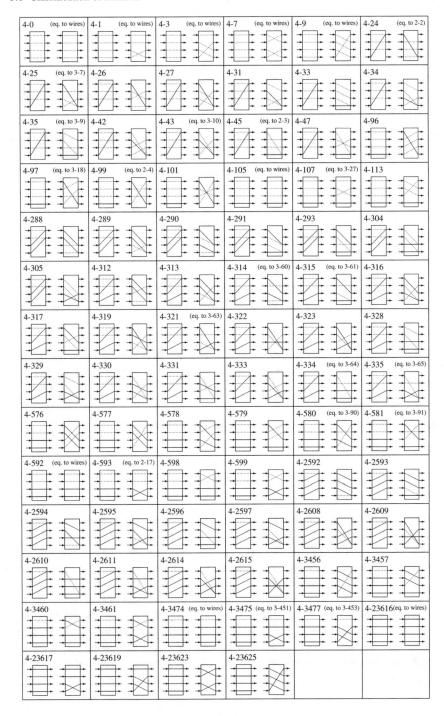

Fig. 3.5 Representatives of 82 equivalence classes of 2-state 4-symbol RLEMs

3.1.3 Degeneracy in RLEMs

Among RLEMs there are some "degenerate" ones that are further equivalent to connecting wires, or equivalent to a simpler element with fewer symbols. In Figs. 3.3–3.5, they are indicated at the upper-right corner of each box. Here, we give a precise definition of a degenerate RLEM.

Definition 3.3. Let $M = (\{0,1\}, \{a_1, \ldots, a_k\}, \{s_1, \ldots, s_k\}, \delta)$ be a 2-state k-symbol RLEM and $G_M = (V, E, f)$ be its graphical representation. If one of the following conditions (i) – (iii) holds, M is called a *degenerate* RLEM.

(i) $\forall i, j \in \{1, \ldots, k\}, \ \forall q \in \{0, 1\} \ ((a_i^q, s_j^q) \in E \ \Rightarrow \ f(a_i^q, s_j^q) = \text{dot})$
   In this case there is no input that makes a state change (e.g., RLEM 3-3 in Fig. 3.4), i.e., two states are disconnected in its state-transition diagram. Thus, M is nothing but a collection of connecting wires.

(ii) $\forall i, j \in \{1, \ldots, k\} \ ((a_i^0, s_j^0) \in E_0 \ \Rightarrow \ (a_i^1, s_j^1) \in E_1 \ \wedge \ f(a_i^0, s_j^0) = f(a_i^1, s_j^1))$
   The relation between inputs and outputs, and the state change are exactly the same in the states 0 and 1 (e.g., RLEM 3-450 in Fig. 3.4). Thus, M is equivalent to a 1-state RLEM. Hence, again, M can be regarded as a collection of simple connecting wires.

(iii) $\exists i, j \in \{1, \ldots, k\} \ (f(a_i^0, s_j^0) = f(a_i^1, s_j^1) = \text{dot})$
   It means that, both in the states 0 and 1, the input a_i gives the output s_j without changing the state (e.g., a_2 and s_2 in RLEM 3-6 in Fig. 3.4). Thus, we can see a_i and s_j play only a role of a simple wire. Hence, if we remove a_i and s_j from M, it becomes equivalent to some $(k-1)$-symbol RLEM.

The RLEM M is called a *non-degenerate* RLEM, if it is not degenerate.

3.1.4 Classification of 2-, 3- and 4-symbol RLEMs

Table 3.5 shows a classification result based on Definition 3.3 [4]. It should be noted that the conditions (i) – (iii) in Definition 3.3 are not disjoint. For example, there is a degenerate RLEM that satisfies both (ii) and (iii), e.g., RLEM 3-94 in Fig. 3.4. Therefore, when counting the number of degenerate ones of type (ii), those of type (i) are excluded. Likewise, when counting ones of type (iii), those of type (i) and (ii) are excluded. The total numbers of equivalence classes of non-degenerate 2-, 3- and 4-symbol RLEMs are 4, 14, and 55, respectively, and they are the important ones.

   Taking a finite number of copies of RLEMs, and connecting them appropriately, we can compose an RLEM-circuit. When connecting RLEMs, essentially the same conditions given in Definition 2.4 must be satisfied. A more precise definition of an RLEM-circuit will be given in Definition 3.4.

Table 3.5 Numbers of representatives of degenerate and non-degenerate k-symbol RLEMs ($k = 2, 3, 4$)

k	Representatives	Degenerate RLEMs			Non-degenerate RLEMs
		Type (i)	Type (ii)	Type (iii)	
2	8	2	2	0	4
3	24	3	3	4	14
4	82	5	4	18	55

3.2 Universality of All Non-degenerate 2-State RLEMs with Three or More Symbols

In this section, it is shown that every non-degenerate 2-state RLEMs with three or more symbols is universal. To prove it, we first show that each of 14 non-degenerate 2-state 3-symbol RLEMs is universal in Sect. 3.2.1. Then, in Sect. 3.2.2, it is shown that from each of non-degenerate k-symbol RLEM, we can obtain a non-degenerate $(k-1)$-symbol RLEM ($k > 2$).

3.2.1 Realizing RE using non-degenerate 3-symbol RLEMs

We first show RE can be simulated by a circuit made of RLEM 3-10, and thus RLEM 3-10 is universal. It was first shown in [1]. Later, the circuit was simplified in [3].

Lemma 3.2. *[1, 3] RE can be realized by a circuit composed of RLEM 3-10.*

Proof. Figure 3.6 gives a circuit composed of RLEM 3-10 that realizes RE [3]. Figure 3.8 shows a simulation process for the case where the initial state is H and the input is n. At time $t = 10$, the circuit becomes the state corresponding to the state V and a particle goes out from the output port w'. We can see, in the case where the initial state is H and the input is w, the state of the circuit remains unchanged, and output is obtained from the port e' at $t = 2$. It is easy for readers to verify other cases (see also Table 2.1 and Fig. 2.3). Hence, the circuit simulates RE correctly.   □

Note that in [1], RLEM 3-10 was called a "coding-decoding module". There, RE was realized by a circuit composed of 12 copies of the coding-decoding module.

The next lemma states that RLEM 3-10 can be simulated by a circuit made of one RLEM 2-3 and one RLEM 2-4 [1]. In [1], RLEMS 2-3 and 2-4 are called a "reading toggle" and an "inverse reading toggle", respectively. By this lemma, we can see the set of RLEMS {2-3, 2-4} is universal, i.e., any RSM can be constructed using a finite number of copies of RLEMs 2-3 and 2-4.

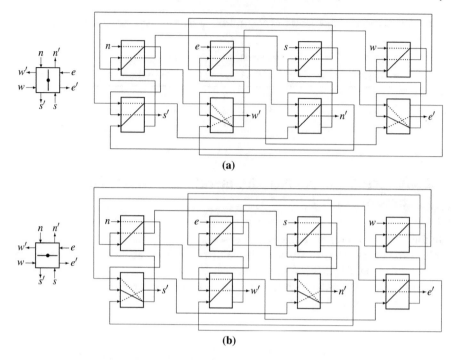

(a)

(b)

Fig. 3.6 A circuit made of RLEMs 3-10 that simulates RE. **(a)** The state V, and **(b)** the state H

Lemma 3.3. *[1] RLEM 3-10 can be realized by a circuit composed of RLEMs 2-3 and 2-4.*

Proof. Figure 3.7 shows a method of realizing 3-10 by 2-3 and 2-4 [1]. It is easy to verify that the circuit correctly simulates RLEM 3-10.   □

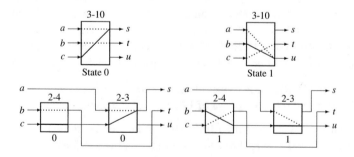

Fig. 3.7 Realizing a 3-symbol RLEM 3-10 by 2-symbol RLEMs 2-4 and 2-3

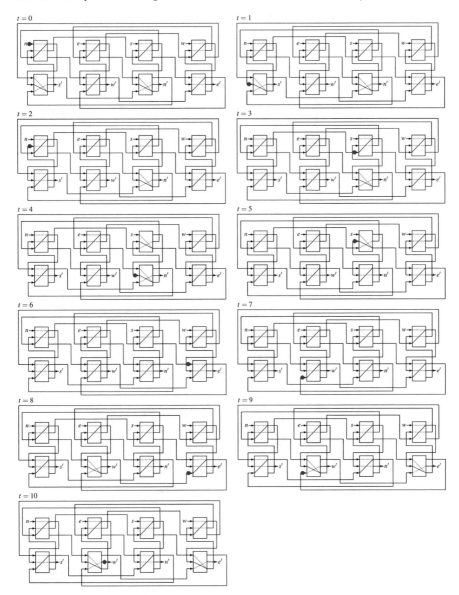

Fig. 3.8 A simulation process of $\delta_{RE}(H,n) = (V,w')$ of RE by a circuit made of RLEM 3-10. At time 0 the circuit is in the state corresponding to the state H of RE, and a particle is given to the input port n. At time 10 it becomes the state corresponding to the state V, and a particle goes out from the output port w'

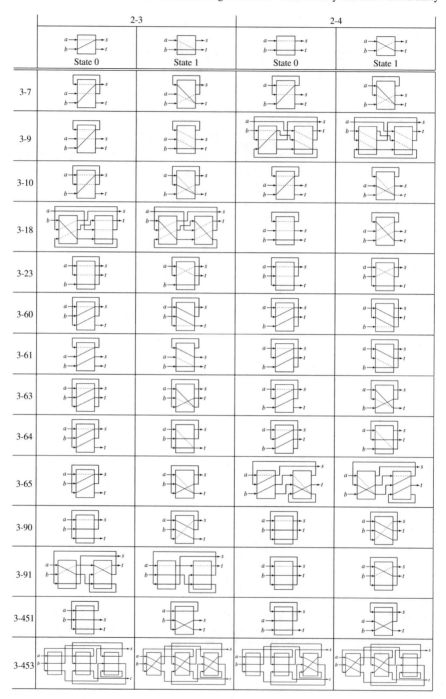

Fig. 3.9 Realizing 2-symbol RLEMs 2-3 and 2-4 by each of 14 kinds of non-degenerate 3-symbol RLEMs

Lemma 3.4. *[3] Each of RLEMs 2-3 and 2-4 can be realized by a circuit composed of any one of 14 non-degenerate 2-state 3-symbol RLEM.*

Proof. The 28 circuits that simulate RLEMs 2-3 and 2-4 composed of each of 14 non-degenerate 3-symbol RLEMs is given in Fig. 3.9. In most cases, 2-3 and 2-4 are obtained by adding a feed-back loop (i.e., connecting some output port to some input port) to a 3-symbol RLEM. But, for 6 cases, two or three 3-symbol RLEMs are needed to realize 2-3 or 2-4.   □

From Corollary 2.1 and Lemmas 3.2–3.4 we have the following lemma.

Lemma 3.5. *[3] Every non-degenerate 2-state 3-symbol RLEM is universal.*

3.2.2 Making a non-degenerate $(k-1)$-symbol RLEM from a non-degenerate k-symbol RLEMs

In this section we prove the next lemma.

Lemma 3.6. *Let M_k be an arbitrary non-degenerate k-symbol RLEM such that $k > 2$. Then, there exists a non-degenerate $(k-1)$-symbol RLEM M_{k-1} that can be simulated by M_k.*

Proof. Let $M_k = (\{0,1\}, \{a_1, \ldots, a_k\}, \{s_1, \ldots, s_k\}, \delta)$ be a given k-symbol RLEM, and $G_{M_k} = (V, E, f)$ be the graphical representation of M_k defined in Definition 3.1. Let α_1 and α_2 be conditions defined as follows, where $i, i', j \in \{1, \ldots, k\}$.

$$\alpha_1 = \exists\, i, j\ (f(a_i^0, s_j^0) = f(a_i^1, s_j^1) = \text{sol})$$
$$\alpha_2 = \exists\, i, i', j\ (f(a_i^0, s_j^0) = \text{sol} \ \wedge\ f(a_{i'}^0, s_j^0) = \text{dot})$$

The condition α_1 means there exist two solid edges at the same position of $G_{M_k}^0$ and $G_{M_k}^1$, while α_2 means there are merging edges in in $G_{M_k}^0$ (hence merging edges also exist in $G_{M_k}^1$ by Lemma 3.1 (4)). We consider the following three cases.

(1) α_1: The case where two solid edges exist at the same position of $G_{M_k}^0$ and $G_{M_k}^1$.
(2) $\neg\alpha_1 \wedge \alpha_2$: The case where α_1 does not hold, and merging edges exist in G_{M_k}.
(3) $\neg\alpha_1 \wedge \neg\alpha_2$: The case where α_1 does not hold, and no merging edge exists.

We use a method of adding a "feedback loop" that connects some output port to some input port of M_k. Apparently, we obtain a $(k-1)$-symbol RLEM by this, but it may be a degenerate one, if a feedback is given inappropriately. However, we shall show that it is always possible to obtain a non-degenerate $(k-1)$-symbol RLEM M_{k-1}, if a feedback is appropriately given. The three cases (1) – (3) are further classified into subcases below. Methods of adding feedback loops for the subcases are illustrated in Fig. 3.10. In the following, we assume $i, i', i'', j, j', j'' \in \{1, \ldots, k\}$.

First consider the case (1). This is further classified into the subcase (1a) where there exists a solid edge other than (a_i^0, s_j^0) and (a_i^1, s_j^1), and the subcase (1b) where there is no other solid edge.

Case	k-symbol RLEM with a feedback	Resulting $(k-1)$-symbol RLEM

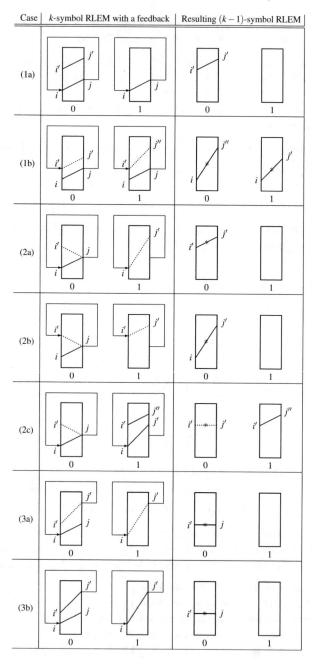

Fig. 3.10 Seven subcases for reducing a non-degenerate k-symbol RLEM to a non-degenerate $(k-1)$-symbol RLEM. By giving a feedback loop to each k-symbol RLEM as shown in the figure, all the edges connecting to it are removed, and edges with $*$ are newly created. Note that, here, only indices such as i and j are written instead of writing a_i^q and s_j^q

(1a) This is the subcase where there is a solid edge other than (a_i^0, s_j^0), and (a_i^1, s_j^1). Then, by Lemma 3.1 (3), both $G_{M_k}^0$ and $G_{M_k}^1$ contain extra solid edges. We can thus assume the following statement instead of α_1:

$$\exists \, i, i', j, j'$$
$$(i \neq i' \wedge j \neq j'$$
$$\wedge \, f(a_i^0, s_j^0) = f(a_i^1, s_j^1) = f(a_{i'}^0, s_{j'}^0) = \text{sol}).$$

Note that, by Lemma 3.1 (2), $j = j'$ is not possible. In this subcase, a feedback loop connecting s_j to a_i is added as shown in Fig. 3.10 (1a). Then, in the resulting $(k-1)$-symbol RLEM M_{k-1}, the vertices a_i^0, s_j^0, a_i^1, and s_j^1 are deleted, and hence the solid edges (a_i^0, s_j^0), and (a_i^1, s_j^1) are also removed. But, no new edge is created here. We can see M_{k-1} is non-degenerate by the following reasons. The condition (i) of Definition 3.3 does not hold, because there remains a solid edge $(a_{i'}^0, s_{j'}^0)$ in M_{k-1}. The condition (ii) does not hold, since only the edges $(a_i^0, s_j^0), (a_i^1, s_j^1)$ are removed, and M_k is non-degenerate. Finally, since M_k is non-degenerate and no new edge is created in M_{k-1}, the condition (iii) does not hold for M_{k-1}. Hence, M_{k-1} is non-degenerate.

(1b) This is the subcase where only dotted edges exist other than (a_i^0, s_j^0) and (a_i^1, s_j^1). Then, by the fact that M_k is non-degenerate there are dotted edges $(a_{i'}^0, s_{j'}^0)$ and $(a_{i'}^1, s_{j''}^1)$ such that $j' \neq j''$. Thus the following statement holds instead of α_1:

$$\exists \, i, i', j, j', j''$$
$$(i \neq i' \wedge j \neq j' \wedge j' \neq j'' \wedge j \neq j''$$
$$\wedge \, f(a_i^0, s_j^0) = f(a_i^1, s_j^1) = \text{sol} \wedge f(a_{i'}^0, s_{j'}^0) = f(a_{i'}^1, s_{j''}^1) = \text{dot}).$$

Note that, by Lemma 3.1 (2), neither $j = j'$ nor $j = j''$ is possible. Furthermore, since M_k is non-degenerate, $j' = j''$ is not possible. In this subcase, a feedback loop connecting s_j to $a_{i'}$ is added as shown in Fig. 3.10 (1b). Then, in M_{k-1}, the vertices $a_{i'}^0, s_j^0, a_{i'}^1$, and s_j^1 are deleted, and hence the edges $(a_i^0, s_j^0), (a_i^1, s_j^1), (a_{i'}^0, s_{j'}^0)$ and $(a_{i'}^1, s_{j''}^1)$ are removed. If we give a particle to the input port a_i in the state 0, the state changes to 1, and the particle finally goes out from the output port $s_{j''}$. Therefore, a new solid edge $(a_i^0, s_{j''}^0)$ is created. Likewise, a solid edge $(a_i^1, s_{j'}^1)$ is also created. We can see M_{k-1} is non-degenerate because of the following reason. The conditions (i) and (ii) of Definition 3.3 do not hold, because two solid edges $(a_i^0, s_{j''}^0)$, and $(a_i^1, s_{j'}^1)$ such that $j' \neq j''$ are added. The condition (iii) does not hold, since M_k is non-degenerate and no new dotted edge is added. Hence, M_{k-1} is non-degenerate.

Next, consider the case (2). Here, $\neg \alpha_1$ holds, and there are merging edges in $G_{M_k}^0$, i.e., a solid edge (a_i^0, s_j^0) and a dotted edge $(a_{i'}^0, s_j^0)$. It is further classified into the subcase (2a) where there is a dotted edge $(a_i^1, s_{j'}^1)$, the subcase (2b) where there is a dotted edge $(a_{i'}^1, s_{j'}^1)$, and the subcase (2c) where there are two solid edges $(a_i^1, s_{j'}^1)$ and $(a_{i'}^1, s_{j''}^1)$. We can see there is no other subcase in (2).

(2a) This is the subcase where there is a dotted edge $(a_i^1, s_{j'}^1)$ besides the merging edges. Hence, the following statement holds in addition to $\neg \alpha_1$:

$$\exists\, i, i', j, j'$$
$$(i \neq i' \wedge j \neq j'$$
$$\wedge f(a_i^0, s_j^0) = \mathrm{sol} \wedge f(a_{i'}^0, s_j^0) = f(a_i^1, s_{j'}^1) = \mathrm{dot}).$$

Note that, by Lemma 3.1 (2), $j = j'$ is impossible. In this subcase, a feedback loop connecting s_j to a_i is added as shown in Fig. 3.10 (2a). Then, in M_{k-1}, the vertices a_i^0, s_j^0, a_i^1 and s_j^1, and the edges (a_i^0, s_j^0), $(a_{i'}^0, s_j^0)$ and $(a_i^1, s_{j'}^1)$ are removed. If we give a particle to the input port $a_{i'}$ in the state 0, the state changes to 1, and the particle finally goes out from the output port $s_{j'}$, and thus a new solid edge $(a_{i'}^0, s_{j'}^0)$ is created. We can see M_{k-1} is non-degenerate by the following reasons. The condition (i) of Definition 3.3 does not hold, because a solid edge $(a_{i'}^0, s_{j'}^0)$ is added. Next, we assume, on the contrary, the condition (ii) holds. Then, since $k > 2$ there must be i'' and j'' such that $i'' \neq i$, $i'' \neq i'$, $j'' \neq j$, $j'' \neq j'$, $(a_{i''}^0, s_{j''}^0), (a_{i''}^1, s_{j''}^1) \in E$, and $f(a_{i''}^0, s_{j''}^0) = f(a_{i''}^1, s_{j''}^1)$. Since M_k is non-degenerate, these edges cannot be dotted ones. But, we here assume $\neg \alpha_1$ holds, and hence $f(a_{i''}^0, s_{j''}^0) = f(a_{i''}^1, s_{j''}^1) = \mathrm{sol}$ is also impossible. Therefore the condition (ii) does not hold. Finally, since M_k is non-degenerate and no new dotted edge is added, the condition (iii) does not hold.

(2b) This is the subcase where there is a dotted edge $(a_{i'}^1, s_{j'}^1)$ besides the merging edges. Hence, the following statement holds in addition to $\neg \alpha_1$:

$$\exists\, i, i', j, j'$$
$$(i \neq i' \wedge j \neq j'$$
$$\wedge f(a_i^0, s_j^0) = \mathrm{sol} \wedge f(a_{i'}^0, s_j^0) = f(a_{i'}^1, s_{j'}^1) = \mathrm{dot}).$$

Note that $j = j'$ is impossible by Lemma 3.1 (2). In this subcase, a feedback loop connecting s_j to $a_{i'}$ is added as shown in Fig. 3.10 (2b). Then, in M_{k-1}, the vertices $a_{i'}^0, s_j^0, a_{i'}^1$ and s_j^1, and the edges (a_i^0, s_j^0), $(a_{i'}^0, s_j^0)$ and $(a_{i'}^1, s_{j'}^1)$ are removed. If we give a particle to the input port a_i in the state 0, the state changes to 1, and the particle finally goes out from the output port $s_{j'}$, and thus a new solid edge $(a_i^0, s_{j'}^0)$ is created. We can see M_{k-1} is non-degenerate by the same reason as in the subcase (2a).

(2c) This is the subcase where there are solid edges $(a_i^1, s_{j'}^1)$ and $(a_{i'}^1, s_{j''}^1)$ besides the merging edges. Hence, the following statement holds in addition to $\neg \alpha_1$:

$$\exists\, i, i', j, j', j''$$
$$(i \neq i' \wedge j \neq j' \wedge j' \neq j'' \wedge j \neq j''$$
$$\wedge f(a_i^0, s_j^0) = f(a_i^1, s_{j'}^1) = f(a_{i'}^1, s_{j''}^1) = \mathrm{sol} \wedge f(a_{i'}^0, s_j^0) = \mathrm{dot}).$$

Note that, by Lemma 3.1 (2), none of $j = j'$, $j = j''$, and $j' = j''$ is possible. In this subcase, a feedback connecting s_j to a_i is added as in Fig. 3.10 (2c). Then, in M_{k-1}, the vertices a_i^0, s_j^0, a_i^1 and s_j^1, and the edges $(a_i^0, s_j^0), (a_{i'}^0, s_j^0)$ and $(a_i^1, s_{j''}^1)$ are removed. If we give a particle to the input port $a_{i'}$ in the state 0, the state changes from 0 to 1, and then from 1 to 0. The particle finally goes out from the output port $s_{j'}$. Thus a new dotted edge $(a_{i'}^0, s_{j'}^0)$ is newly created. We can see M_{k-1} is non-degenerate by the following reasons. The conditions (i) of Definition 3.3 does not hold, because the solid edge $(a_i^1, s_{j''}^1)$ is not deleted. In M_{k-1} a new dotted edge $(a_{i'}^0, s_{j'}^0)$ is added, but no dotted edge $(a_{i'}^1, s_{j'}^1)$ can exist, since there is a solid edge $(a_i^1, s_{j''}^1)$. Therefore, neither the condition (ii) nor (iii) holds.

Finally, consider the case (3) where no merging edge exists, and $\neg\alpha_1$ holds. Since M_k is non-degenerate, there is at least one solid edge (a_i^0, s_j^0). This case is further classified into the subcase (3a) where a dotted edge $(a_i^1, s_{j'}^1)$ exists, and the subcase (3b) where a solid edge $(a_i^1, s_{j'}^1)$ exists. In both subcases $j \neq j'$ holds, because of Lemma 3.1 (2) for the subcase (3a), and because of the assumption $\neg\alpha_1$ for the subcase (3b).

(3a) This is the subcase where a solid edge (a_i^0, s_j^0) and a dotted edge $(a_i^1, s_{j'}^1)$ exist. Then, there is a dotted edge $(a_{i'}^0, s_{j'}^0)$ since we assume there are no merging edges. Hence, the next statement holds in addition to $\neg\alpha_1 \wedge \neg\alpha_2$:

$$\exists i, i', j, j'$$
$$(i \neq i' \wedge j \neq j'$$
$$\wedge f(a_i^0, s_j^0) = \text{sol} \wedge f(a_{i'}^0, s_{j'}^0) = f(a_i^1, s_{j'}^1) = \text{dot}).$$

In this subcase, a feedback connecting $s_{j'}$ to a_i is added as in Fig. 3.10 (3a). Then, in M_{k-1}, the vertices $a_i^0, s_{j'}^0, a_i^1$ and $s_{j'}^1$, and the edges (a_i^0, s_j^0), $(a_{i'}^0, s_{j'}^0)$ and $(a_i^1, s_{j'}^1)$ are removed. If we give a particle to the input port $a_{i'}$ in the state 0, the state changes to 1, and the particle finally goes out from the output port s_j, and thus a new solid edge $(a_{i'}^0, s_j^0)$ is created. We can see M_{k-1} is non-degenerate by the same reason as in the subcase (2a).

(3b) This is the subcase where solid edges (a_i^0, s_j^0) and $(a_i^1, s_{j'}^1)$ exist. Then, there is also a solid edge $(a_{i'}^0, s_{j'}^0)$ since we assume there are no merging edges. Hence, the following statement holds in addition to $\neg\alpha_1 \wedge \neg\alpha_2$:

$$\exists i, i', j, j'$$
$$(i \neq i' \wedge j \neq j'$$
$$\wedge f(a_i^0, s_j^0) = f(a_{i'}^0, s_{j'}^0) = f(a_i^1, s_{j'}^1) = \text{sol}).$$

In this subcase, a feedback loop connecting $s_{j'}$ to a_i is added as shown in Fig. 3.10 (3a). Then, in M_{k-1}, the vertices $a_i^0, s_{j'}^0, a_i^1$ and $s_{j'}^1$, and the edges $(a_i^0, s_j^0), (a_{i'}^0, s_{j'}^0)$ and $(a_i^1, s_{j'}^1)$ are removed. If we give a particle to the input port $a_{i'}$ in the state 0, the state changes from 0 to 1, from 1 to 0, and from 0 to 1, three times. The particle finally goes out from the output port s_j, and thus a new solid edge $(a_{i'}^0, s_j^0)$ is created. We can see M_{k-1} is non-degenerate by the same reason as in the subcase (2a).

By above, we can always obtain a non-degenerate $(k-1)$-symbol RLEM from any non-degenerate k-symbol RLEM for $k > 2$. This completes the proof.   □

Example 3.4. In Fig. 3.11, examples of realizing non-degenerate 3-symbol RLEMs from 4-symbol RLEMs 4-26, 4-23617, and 4-23623 based on the procedure given in Lemma 3.6 are shown. By applying the procedure (2a) to 4-26, (1a) to 4-23617, and (3b) to 4-23623, we can obtain non-degenerate 3-symbol RLEMs 3-23, 3-451, and 3-451, respectively. Note that $\neg\alpha_1$ is assumed in the procedures (2) and (3) in Lemma 3.6. Therefore, (3b) should not be applied to 4-23617, since (1a) is applicable to it. Otherwise, a degenerate 3-symbol RLEM 3-450 is derived.   □

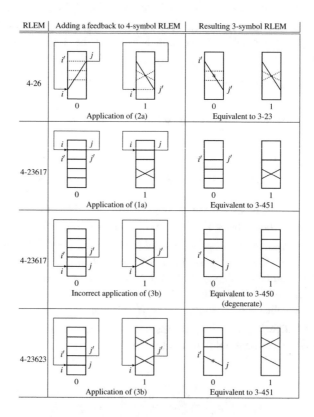

Fig. 3.11 Application examples of the procedure given in Lemma 3.6 to some 4-symbol RLEMs. Edges with ∗ are newly created

From Lemmas 3.5 and 3.6, the following theorem is derived.

Theorem 3.1. *Every non-degenerate 2-state k-symbol RLEM is universal, if $k > 2$.*

3.3 Systematic Construction of RSMs out of Universal RLEMs

In Sect. 2.3, a method of composing RSMs by RE is given (Theorem 2.1). Here, we explain the methods shown in Sects. 3.2.1 and 3.2.2 can be applied for constructing RSMs from a given universal RLEM. In the next example, we take RLEM 4-26, and show how RSMs can be realized as a circuit composed of it. It is also possible to construct RSMs by other RLEMs in a similar manner.

Example 3.5. We consider RLEM 4-26. Figure 3.12 shows the graphical representation of RLEM 4-26. To obtain a non-degenerate 3-symbol RLEM from it, we use the method of Lemma 3.6. The procedure (2a) in Lemma 3.6 can be applied to RLEM 4-26, and we have RLEM 3-23 as shown in Fig. 3.13 (see also Fig. 3.11 in Example 3.4). Further adding feedback loops to the circuit in Fig. 3.13 by the method of Lemma 3.4, we have circuits that realize RLEMs 2-3 and 2-4 as in Figs. 3.14 and 3.15. Connecting these circuits in the manner shown in Fig. 3.7 of Lemma 3.3, a circuit that simulates RLEM 3-10 is obtained (Fig. 3.16). Substituting each occurrence of RLEM 3-10 in Fig. 3.6 of Lemma 3.2 by the circuit given in Fig. 3.16, we finally obtain a circuit composed of RLEM 4-26 that realizes RE (but, here we omit to write the resulting circuit). In Theorem 2.1 a construction method of a circuit made of RE that realizes a given RSM is given. Hence, replacing each RE in it by the circuit that realizes RE, we have a circuit composed of copies of RLEM 4-26 that realizes the RSM. If it is an m-state n-symbol RSM, then the circuit has $16m(n+1)$ copies of RLEM 4-26. $\qquad\square$

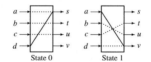

Fig. 3.12 RLEM 4-26

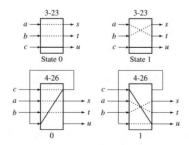

Fig. 3.13 Adding a feedback loop to RLEM 4-26 by the method of Lemma 3.6, we obtain RLEM 3-23, a non-degenerate one

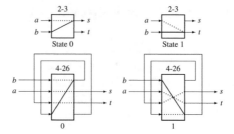

Fig. 3.14 RLEM 2-3 is obtained from RLEM 4-26 further adding a feedback loop by the method of Lemma 3.4

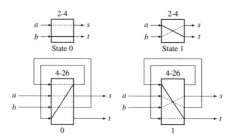

Fig. 3.15 RLEM 2-4 is obtained from RLEM 4-26 further adding a feedback loop by the method of Lemma 3.4

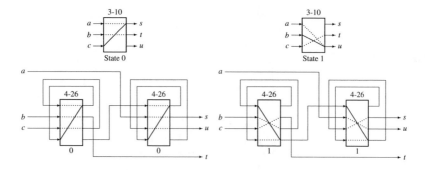

Fig. 3.16 Connecting the circuits in Figs. 3.14 and 3.15 by the method of Lemma 3.3, we have a circuit that realizes RLEM 3-10

By the above method, we can systematically construct a circuit that realizes a given RSM from *any* universal RLEM. However, we need a larger number of copies of the RLEM than the case of RE. By Lemmas 3.2–3.4 (see also Figs. 3.6, 3.7 and 3.9), we can see that the number of copies of 3-symbol RLEM required to simulate an RE is as follows:

  8 if we use RLEM 3-10
  16 if we use RLEM 3-7, 3-23, 3-60, 3-61, 3-63, 3-64, 3-90, or 3-451
  24 if we use RLEM 3-9, 3-18, 3-65, or 3-91
  48 if we use RLEM 3-453

By Lemma 3.6, we can obtain a non-degenerate 3-symbol RLEM from any non-degenerate k-symbol RLEM ($k > 3$) by adding feedback loops to it. Thus, the above numbers also give the number of copies of the k-symbol RLEM to simulate an RE, depending on which 3-symbol RLEM is obtained from the k-symbol RLEM.

    Lemmas 3.2–3.4, and 3.6 are, of course, for the purpose of proving universality of non-degenerate k-symbol RLEMs ($k > 2$), and thus the methods shown there are not suited for realizing an RSM compactly. In the next section, we give efficient methods of constructing RSMs by particular RLEMs 4-31 and 3-7.

3.4 Compact Realization of RSMs Using RLEMs 4-31 and 3-7

We first consider the problem of realizing RSMs compactly by RLEM 4-31, which is shown in Fig. 3.17. We define a circuit module called a *column of RLEM 4-31 of degree n*, or *4-31-column of degree n* for short, which is made of n copies of RLEM 4-31 [2]. Figure 3.18 shows a 4-31-column of degree 3. Though 4-31-column of degree n has 2^n states in total, we consider only two macroscopic states **0** and **1**, here **0** (**1**, respectively) is the state such that all the elements are in the state 0 (1). Then, the behavior of 4-31-column of degree 3 in Fig. 3.18 is described by a 2-state 6-symbol RLEM shown in Fig. 3.19. Let $\delta_{4\text{-}31\text{-}n}$ be the move function of 4-31-column of degree n. Then, $\delta_{4\text{-}31\text{-}n}$ is described by Table 3.6. It is seen that it is the same as the move function of RE-column of degree n shown in Table 2.3, except that the output is shifted upward or downward by one row when the state changes.

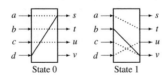

Fig. 3.17 RLEM 4-31

    We take again the example of the 3-state 3-symbol RSM M_2 whose move function δ_2 is given in Table 2.4. As in Sect. 2.3, we first prepare a "framework circuit" consisting of three rows and three columns of RLEM 4-31 shown in Fig. 3.20. Generally, for an m-state n-symbol RSM, we prepare an $n \times m$ array of RLEM 4-31. As in the case of Fig. 2.13, the j-th column corresponds to the state q_j of M_2 ($j \in \{1,2,3\}$). If M_2's state is q_j, then all the RLEMs of the j-th column is set to the state 1. All other RLEMs are set to the state 0. In Fig. 3.20, it is in the state q_2. The

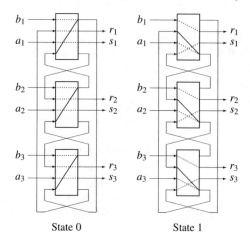

Fig. 3.18 4-31-column of degree 3

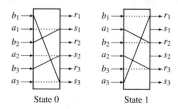

Fig. 3.19 Macroscopic behavior of 4-31-column of degree 3

Table 3.6 The move function $\delta_{4\text{-}31\text{-}n}$ of the 4-31-column of degree n for the states **0** and **1** ($i \in \{1,\ldots,n\}$). Here, addition (+) and subtraction (−) are in mod n

	Input	
Present state	a_i	b_i
0	**0** s_i	**1** s_{i-1}
1	**0** r_{i+1}	**1** r_i

RLEMs of the i-th row corresponds to the input symbol a_i as well as the output symbol s_i ($i \in \{1,2,3\}$). If a particle is given to an input port e.g. a_1 of Fig. 3.20, then after setting the all RLEMs of the second column to the state 0, the particle finally comes out from the port "$q_2 a_1$". Hence, the crossing point of the second column and the first row is found, though the port "$q_2 a_1$" is shifted downward by one row cyclically. Since $\delta_0(q_2, a_1) = (q_3, s_2)$, the RLEMs of the third column should be set to the state 1, and the particle must go out from the port s_2. This can be performed by giving a particle to the line "$q_3 s_2$". Again, the port "$q_3 s_2$" is shifted downward by one row. Connecting all the lines appropriately according to δ_2, we finally obtain the circuit composed of RLEM 4-31 shown in Fig. 3.21 that simulates M_2.

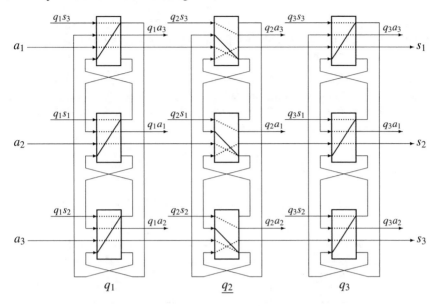

Fig. 3.20 The framework circuit for implementing a 3-state 3-symbol RSM

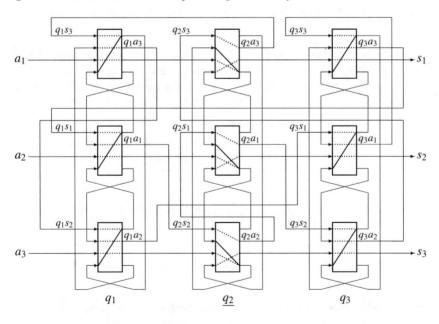

Fig. 3.21 The circuit composed of RLEM 4-31 that simulates the RSM M_2 whose move function is given in Table 2.4. Here, M_2 is in the state q_2, since the second column is in the state **1**

Note that, similar to the case of the RE-circuit in Theorem 2.1 the above circuit is garbage-less, since it uses only one particle in its computing process, and never produces useless signals.

Next, we consider the problem of constructing RSMs by RLEM 3-7. It is easily done, since RLEM 4-31 is implemented by a circuit consisting only two copies of RLEM 3-7 as shown in Fig. 3.22 [2]. By this method, an m-state n-symbol RSM can be constructed using $2mn$ copies of RLEM 3-7.

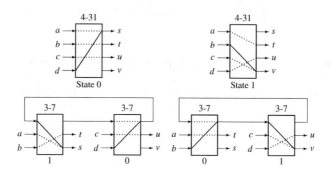

Fig. 3.22 RLEM 4-31 can be realized by a circuit composed of two copies of RLEM 3-7

The number of elements required for realizing an m-state n-symbol RSM by RLEMs 4-289 (RE), 4-31, and 3-7 are shown in Table 3.7. So far, however, it has not yet been well clarified which RLEMs are useful for compact realization of RSMs, and which are not.

Table 3.7 The number of elements needed for realizing an m-state n-symbol RSM

RLEM	Number of elements
4-289 (RE)	$m(n+1)$
4-31	mn
3-7	$2mn$

3.5 Frontier Between Universal and Non-universal RLEMs

In this section, we investigate universality of the four non-degenerate 2-state 2-symbol RLEMs to clarify the frontier between universal and non-universal RLEMs. The four RLEMs are shown in Fig. 3.23. It will be proved that RLEMs 2-2, 2-3 and 2-4 are non-universal, and that RLEM 2-2 is the weakest one in the class of non-degenerate 2-state RLEMs. By this, we obtain a simple hierarchy among 2-state RLEMs. However, it is left open whether RLEM 2-17 is universal or not.

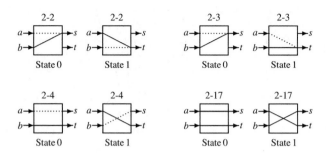

Fig. 3.23 The four non-degenerate 2-state 2-symbol RLEMs

3.5.1 Definitions on RLEM-circuits

We now give a precise definition of a reversible circuit composed of RLEMs (i.e., RLEM-circuit) and of a notion of simulation to prove non-universality of three 2-symbol RLEMs.

Definition 3.4. A *reversible logic circuit* composed of 2-state RLEMs (or *RLEM-circuit* for short) is defined by $C = ((M_1, \ldots, M_m), \Sigma, \Gamma, f)$, where each M_i ($i = 1, \ldots, m$) is an RLEM such that $M_i = (\{0,1\}, \Sigma_i, \Gamma_i, \delta_i)$. Here, $\delta_i : \{0,1\} \times \Sigma_i \to \{0,1\} \times \Gamma_i$ is a move function of M_i, and $\Sigma, \Sigma_1, \ldots, \Sigma_m, \Gamma, \Gamma_1, \ldots, \Gamma_m$ are mutually disjoint. The items Σ and Γ are sets of input ports and output ports of C, respectively, which satisfy $|\Sigma| \leq |\Gamma|$. The function $f : \bigcup_{i=1}^{m} \Gamma_i \cup \Sigma \to \bigcup_{i=1}^{m} \Sigma_i \cup \Gamma$ is an injection called a *connection function*.

Next, an RSM realized by a reversible logic circuit is defined.

Definition 3.5. Let $C = ((M_1, \ldots, M_m), \Sigma, \Gamma, f)$ be an RLEM-circuit. A *state of an RLEM-circuit* of C is an m-tuple $\mathbf{x} = (x_1, \ldots, x_m) \in \{0,1\}^m$. A *configuration of an RLEM-circuit* of C is a pair $(\mathbf{x}, p) \in \{0,1\}^m \times (\bigcup_{i=1}^{m} (\Sigma_i \cup \Gamma_i) \cup \Sigma \cup \Gamma)$, which means the i-th RLEM M_i is in the state x_i ($i = 1, \ldots, m$), and a particle is at the position p. A *transition relation* $\vdash_C$ between configurations of C is defined as follows.

$$((x_1, \ldots, x_m), p) \vdash_C ((x_1, \ldots, x_m), p') \text{ if } p \in \bigcup_{i=1}^{m} \Gamma_i \cup \Sigma \wedge f(p) = p'$$
$$((x_1, \ldots, x_i, \ldots, x_m), p) \vdash_C ((x_1, \ldots, x_i', \ldots, x_m), p')$$
$$\text{if } p \in \Sigma_i \wedge \delta_i(x_i, p) = (x_i', p')$$

Reflexive and transitive closure of $\vdash_C$ is denoted by $\vdash_C^*$. The RSM M^C realized by C is given as below.

$$M^C = (\{0,1\}^m, \Sigma, \Gamma, \delta^C)$$
$$\delta^C(\mathbf{x}, p) = (\mathbf{x}', p') \text{ if } \mathbf{x}, \mathbf{x}' \in \{0,1\}^m, \ p \in \Sigma, \ p' \in \Gamma \wedge (\mathbf{x}, p) \vdash^*_C (\mathbf{x}', p')$$

Note that, since f and δ_i $(i = 1, \ldots, m)$ are injective functions, there exists at most one $(\mathbf{x}', p')$ (or $(\mathbf{x}, p)$, respectively) such that $(\mathbf{x}, p) \vdash_C (\mathbf{x}', p')$ for any $(\mathbf{x}, p) \in \{0,1\}^m \times (\bigcup_{i=1}^m (\Sigma_i \cup \Gamma_i) \cup \Sigma \cup \Gamma)$ (or $(\mathbf{x}', p')$). We can also see that, for any $(\mathbf{x}, p) \in \{0,1\}^m \times \Sigma$, there is exactly one $(\mathbf{x}', p') \in \{0,1\}^m \times \Gamma$ such that $\delta^C(\mathbf{x}, p) = (\mathbf{x}', p')$. We now define the notion of simulation of an RSM by another RSM.

Definition 3.6. Let $M_1 = (Q_1, \Sigma, \Gamma, \delta_1)$ and $M_2 = (Q_2, \Sigma, \Gamma, \delta_2)$ be two RSMs. We say M_1 is *simulated* by M_2 under a *state-mapping* φ, if $\varphi : Q_1 \to (2^{Q_2} - \emptyset)$ is a function such that $\forall q, q' \in Q_1 (q \neq q' \Rightarrow \varphi(q) \cap \varphi(q') = \emptyset)$, and satisfies the following condition.

$$\forall q_1, q_1' \in Q_1, \ \forall a \in \Sigma, \ \forall s \in \Gamma :$$
$$\delta_1(q_1, a) = (q_1', s) \Rightarrow \forall q_2 \in \varphi(q_1), \exists q_2' \in \varphi(q_1') \ (\delta_2(q_2, a) = (q_2', s))$$

If M_2 is realized by a reversible logic circuit C, then we also say that M_1 is *simulated* by C under the state-mapping φ.

Note that, in general, each state q of M_1 is simulated by many states in $\varphi(q)$ of M_2. Also note that, in the case the number of states of M_1 is not minimized, its behavior may be mimicked by M_2 having a smaller number of states. However, we employ the above definition, since we only consider the case of simulating non-degenerate 2-state RLEMs hereafter.

Example 3.6. Consider a reversible logic circuit C shown in Fig. 3.24 (C is the same circuit given in Fig. 3.7). It is formalized as follows.

$$C = ((M_1, M_2), \{a, b, c\}, \{s, t, u\}, f)$$
$$M_1 = (\{0,1\}, \{a_1, b_1\}, \{s_1, t_1\}, \delta_1)$$
$$M_2 = (\{0,1\}, \{a_2, b_2\}, \{s_2, t_2\}, \delta_2)$$

The connection function f of C, and the move functions δ_1 and δ_2 of M_1 and M_2 are given in Table 3.8. Here, M_1 and M_2 are RLEMS 2-4 and 2-3, respectively.

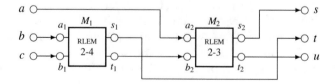

Fig. 3.24 An example of a reversible logic circuit C composed of RLEMs 2-4 and 2-3

The RSM M^C realized by C is

$$M^C = (\{0,1\}^2, \{a, b, c\}, \{s, t, u\}, \delta^C),$$

where the move function δ^C is given in Table 3.9 (a). The following is an example of a computation process in C.

$$((0,0),c) \vdash_{\overline{C}} ((0,0),b_1) \vdash_{\overline{C}} ((1,0),t_1) \vdash_{\overline{C}} ((1,0),b_2) \vdash_{\overline{C}} ((1,1),s_2) \vdash_{\overline{C}} ((1,1),s)$$

This process is shown in Fig. 3.25. Hence, $\delta^C((0,0),c) = ((1,1),s)$. We can see that M^C simulates RLEM 3-10, whose move function is shown in Table 3.9 (b). The state-mapping φ is given by $\varphi(0) = \{(0,0)\}$ and $\varphi(1) = \{(1,1)\}$. □

Table 3.8 (a) The connection function f of the circuit C, (b) the move function δ_1 of M_1, and (c) the move function δ_2 of M_2

p	$f(p)$
a	a_2
b	a_1
c	b_1
s_1	t
t_1	b_2
s_2	s
t_2	u

(a)

δ_1	Input	
Present state	a_1	b_1
0	$0\ s_1$	$1\ t_1$
1	$0\ t_1$	$1\ s_1$

(b)

δ_2	Input	
Present state	a_2	b_2
0	$0\ s_2$	$1\ s_2$
1	$1\ t_2$	$0\ t_2$

(c)

Table 3.9 (a) The move function δ^C of the RSM M^C realized by C, and (b) the move function of RLEM 3-10

Present state	Input		
	a	b	c
$(0,0)$	$(0,0)\ s$	$(0,0)\ t$	$(1,1)\ s$
$(0,1)$	$(0,1)\ u$	$(0,1)\ t$	$(1,0)\ u$
$(1,0)$	$(1,0)\ s$	$(0,1)\ s$	$(1,0)\ t$
$(1,1)$	$(1,1)\ u$	$(0,0)\ u$	$(1,1)\ t$

(a)

Present state	Input		
	a	b	c
0	$0\ s$	$0\ t$	$1\ s$
1	$1\ u$	$0\ u$	$1\ t$

(b)

Note that, if a circuit C is given as a diagram like Fig. 3.24, it is easy to describe C and M^C formally, though the descriptions may be lengthy. Therefore, in the following constructions, we only give circuit diagrams.

We now define the notion of simulation among RLEMs based on Definition 3.6.

Definition 3.7. Let M_1 and M_2 be two RLEMs. We say M_1 is *simulated* by M_2, if there exists a circuit C composed only of M_2 such that M_1 is simulated by C.

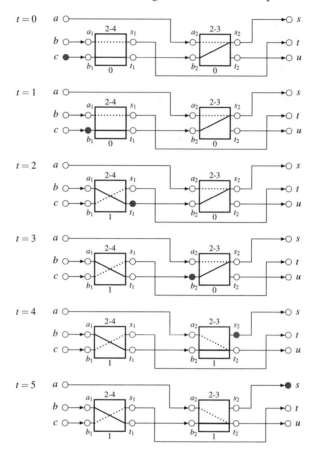

Fig. 3.25 An example of a computing process of the circuit C composed of RLEMs 2-4 and 2-3

3.5.2 Non-universality of three kinds of 2-state 2-symbol RLEMs

Here, we show that among four non-degenerate 2-state 2-symbol RLEMs (Fig. 3.23), three RLEMs are non-universal. They are RLEMs 2-2, 2-3, and 2-4. However, until now, it is not known whether RLEM 2-17 is universal or not. In the following, we show for each of RLEMs 2-2, 2-3, and 2-4, there are some other 2-symbol RLEMs that cannot be simulated by the RLEM. By this, we obtain a relationship among 2-symbol RLEMs as well as their non-universality.

Lemma 3.7. *[6] RLEM 2-2 can simulate neither RLEM 2-3, 2-4, nor 2-17.*

Proof. Assume, on the contrary, RLEM 2-3 (proofs for 2-4 and 2-17 are similar) is simulated by a circuit $C = ((M_1, \ldots, M_m), \{a, b\}, \{s, t\}, f)$ composed only of RLEM 2-2, i.e., $M_i = (\{0, 1\}, \{a_i, b_i\}, \{s_i, t_i\}, \delta^{2\text{-}2})$ $(i = 1, \ldots, m)$, where $\delta^{2\text{-}2}$ is the move function of RLEM 2-2 (see Fig. 3.23). Let $U = \{a, b\} \cup \{s_i, t_i \mid i \in \{1, \ldots, m\}\}$, and

$V = \{s,t\} \cup \{a_i, b_i \mid i \in \{1, \ldots, m\}\}$ be sets of vertices in C. The connecting function $f : U \to V$ is a bijection here, since $|U| = |V|$. We now define a set of vertices W as the smallest set that satisfies (i) $a \in W$, (ii) $x \in U \cap W \Rightarrow f(x) \in W$, (iii) $a_i \in V \cap W \Rightarrow s_i \in W$, and (iv) $b_i \in V \cap W \Rightarrow t_i \in W$. Let $\overline{W} = (U \cup V) - W$. Figure 3.26 shows an example of C, where vertices in W are indicated by $\bullet$, while those in $\overline{W}$ are by $\circ$. Note that the set W is determined only by the connection function f, not by the states of the RLEMs. We observe that $b \in \overline{W}$, and $|\{s,t\} \cap W| = 1 \wedge |\{s,t\} \cap \overline{W}| = 1$, since f is a bijection. Next, sets of RLEMs $E_W, E_{\overline{W}}, E_{W,\overline{W}} \subseteq \{1, \ldots, m\}$ are given as follows: $E_W = \{i \mid a_i \in W \wedge b_i \in W\}$, $E_{\overline{W}} = \{i \mid a_i \in \overline{W} \wedge b_i \in \overline{W}\}$, and $E_{W,\overline{W}} = \{1, \ldots, m\} - (E_W \cup E_{\overline{W}})$. In Fig. 3.26, $E_W = \{1,2\}$, $E_{\overline{W}} = \{5,6\}$, and $E_{W,\overline{W}} = \{3,4\}$.

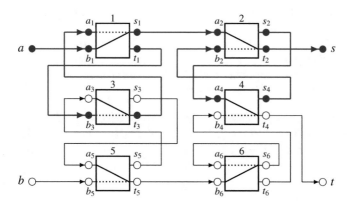

Fig. 3.26 An example of a circuit C composed of six copies of RLEM 2-2

Assume an input particle is given to the port a or b of the circuit C. Then, the particle visits vertices in C one after another according to the transition relation $\vdash_C$. By the definitions of RLEM 2-2, W, $\overline{W}$, E_W, $E_{\overline{W}}$, and $E_{W,\overline{W}}$, we can easily see the following claims hold.

1. A particle can move from a vertex in W to a vertex in $\overline{W}$, or from a vertex in $\overline{W}$ to a vertex in W only at an RLEM in $E_{W,\overline{W}}$.
2. Assume $i \in E_{W,\overline{W}}$, and $a_i \in W$. If the element i is in the state 0, then a particle at $a_i \in W$ or at $b_i \in \overline{W}$ will go to $s_i \in W$. Thus it is not possible to go from W to $\overline{W}$ at the element i in the state 0. On the other hand, if the element i is in the state 1, then a particle at $a_i \in W$ or at $b_i \in \overline{W}$ will go to $t_i \in \overline{W}$, and thus it is not possible to go from $\overline{W}$ to W. The case $b_i \in W$ is also similar.
3. Assume $i \in E_{W,\overline{W}}$. If a particle moves from a vertex in W to that in $\overline{W}$, or from $\overline{W}$ to W at the element i, then the element i changes its state, and vice versa.
4. Let $o_1 \in \{s,t\} \cap W$ and $o_2 \in \{s,t\} \cap \overline{W}$. Starting from some initial state of the circuit C, if a particle travels from $a \in W$ to $o_2 \in \overline{W}$, then the number of times that the particle goes from W to $\overline{W}$ is equal to that from $\overline{W}$ to W plus 1. The case where a particle travels from $b \in \overline{W}$ to $o_1 \in W$ is also similar.

By above, each time a particle travels from $a \in W$ to $o_2 \in \overline{W}$ (or from $b \in \overline{W}$ to $o_1 \in W$, respectively), the number of elements in $E_{W,\overline{W}}$ in the state that can make a particle move from W to $\overline{W}$ (from $\overline{W}$ to W) decreases by 1. Note that, if a particle travels from $a \in W$ to $o_1 \in W$, or from $b \in \overline{W}$ to $o_2 \in \overline{W}$, the above number does not change.

Consider RLEM 2-3 (see Fig. 3.23). Starting from the state 0, we give an input sequence $(bb)^n$ $(n = 1, 2, \ldots)$ to the RLEM 2-3. Then, it produces an output sequence $(st)^n$. By the assumption, the circuit C composed of RLEMs 2-2 performs this behavior. In either case of $s \in W \wedge t \in \overline{W}$ or $s \in \overline{W} \wedge t \in W$, the number of elements in $E_{W,\overline{W}}$ in the state that can make a particle move from $\overline{W}$ to W decreases indefinitely as n grows large, since the input is always $b \in \overline{W}$. But, this contradicts the assumption that C is composed of m RLEMs 2-2, and thus $E_{W,\overline{W}}$ is finite. Hence, the circuit C cannot simulate RLEM 2-3.

For RLEM 2-4, if we give an input sequence $(ba)^n$, it produces $(tt)^n$. For RLEM 2-17, if we give $(bb)^n$, it produces $(st)^n$. By a similar argument as above, it is impossible for a circuit composed of RLEMs 2-2 to do such behavior, and thus RLEM 2-2 can simulate neither RLEM 2-4 nor 2-17.   □

Let $M = (Q, \Sigma, \Gamma, \delta)$ be an SM. From δ, we define $\delta_{\text{state}} : Q \times \Sigma \to Q$, and $\delta_{\text{output}} : Q \times \Sigma \to \Gamma$ as follows: $\forall p, q \in Q, \forall a \in \Sigma, \forall s \in \Gamma$ $(\delta_{\text{state}}(p,a) = q \wedge \delta_{\text{output}}(p,a) = s \Leftrightarrow \delta(p,a) = (q,s))$. Then, we extend δ_{state}, δ_{output}, and δ to δ^*_{state}, δ^*_{output}, and δ^* as below, where λ denotes the empty string.

$$\forall q \in Q, \forall a \in \Sigma, \forall \sigma \in \Sigma^* :$$
$$\delta^*_{\text{state}}(q, \lambda) = q$$
$$\delta^*_{\text{state}}(q, \sigma a) = \delta_{\text{state}}(\delta^*_{\text{state}}(q, \sigma), a)$$
$$\delta^*_{\text{output}}(q, \lambda) = \lambda$$
$$\delta^*_{\text{output}}(q, \sigma a) = \delta^*_{\text{output}}(q, \sigma) \cdot \delta_{\text{output}}(\delta^*_{\text{state}}(q, \sigma), a)$$
$$\delta^*(q, \sigma) = (\delta^*_{\text{state}}(q, \sigma), \delta^*_{\text{output}}(q, \sigma))$$

It is easy to see that δ^* is injective iff δ is injective. Hereafter, we denote δ^*_{state}, δ^*_{output}, and δ^* by δ_{state}, δ_{output}, and δ, since no confusion will occur.

Lemma 3.8. *[6] Let $M = (Q, \Sigma, \Gamma, \delta)$ be an RSM. Then, for any $q \in Q$, $\sigma \in \Sigma^+$, and $\gamma \in \Gamma^+$ such that $|\sigma| = |\gamma|$, the following holds:* $\forall n \in \mathbb{N}$ $(\delta_{\text{output}}(q, \sigma^n) = \gamma^n) \Rightarrow \exists k > 0$ $(\delta_{\text{state}}(q, \sigma^k) = q)$.

Proof. Assume, on the contrary, there is no such k. Since Q is finite, there are i, j $(0 < i < j)$ that satisfy $\delta_{\text{state}}(q, \sigma^i) = \delta_{\text{state}}(q, \sigma^j)$. Let i_0, j_0 be a pair where i_0 is the least one among such i, j. Then, $\delta_{\text{state}}(q, \sigma^{i_0-1}) \neq \delta_{\text{state}}(q, \sigma^{j_0-1})$. But, $\delta(\delta_{\text{state}}(q, \sigma^{i_0-1}), \sigma) = \delta(\delta_{\text{state}}(q, \sigma^{j_0-1}), \sigma)$ holds. This contradicts the assumption M is reversible, and the lemma is proved.   □

Lemma 3.9. *[6] RLEM 2-3 can simulate neither RLEM 2-4, nor 2-17.*

Proof. Assume, on the contrary, RLEM 2-4 is simulated by a circuit $C = ((M_1, \ldots, M_m), \{a,b\}, \{s,t\}, f)$ composed only of RLEM 2-3 under a state-mapping φ. Here,

$M_i = (\{0,1\}, \{a_i, b_i\}, \{s_i, t_i\}, \delta^{2\text{-}3})$ $(i = 1, \ldots, m)$. We can observe that the following arguments also hold for the case of simulating 2-17 only replacing "2-4" by "2-17". Let $U = \{a, b\} \cup \{s_i, t_i \mid i \in \{1, \ldots, m\}\}$, and $V = \{s, t\} \cup \{a_i, b_i \mid i \in \{1, \ldots, m\}\}$ be sets of vertices in C. Then, the connection function $f : U \to V$ is a bijection here. Let M^C be the RSM realized by C, and δ^C be the move function of it. Let $\delta^{2\text{-}4}$ be the move function of RLEM 2-4 (see Fig. 3.23). Then, $\delta^{2\text{-}4}_{\text{output}}(0, (ba)^n) = (tt)^n$ holds for all $n \in \mathbb{N}$. Assume $q_0^C \in \varphi(0)$, i.e., it is one of the states of C that correspond to the state 0 of RLEM 2-4. Note that there may be many states of C that correspond to 0 of RLEM 2-4. Thus q_0^C can be chosen arbitrarily from them. Since C simulates RLEM 2-4, $\delta^C_{\text{output}}(q_0^C, (ba)^n) = (tt)^n$ also holds for all $n \in \mathbb{N}$. By Lemma 3.8, there exists a positive integer k such that $\delta^C_{\text{state}}(q_0^C, (ba)^k) = q_0^C$.

Here, we analyze the following process of C: Starting from q_0^C, the circuit C receives the particle sequence $(ba)^k$, gives the output sequence $(tt)^k$, and finally comes back to the state q_0^C. Let $W (\subset U \cup V)$ be the set of vertices where a particle visits at least once in this process. Since $\forall u \in U (u \in W \Leftrightarrow f(u) \in W)$, and f is a bijection, we can see $|U \cap W| = |V \cap W|$. On the other hand, we observe $a, b \in U \cap W$ and $t \in V \cap W$, but $s \notin V \cap W$. Therefore, $|\{s_i, t_i \mid i \in \{1, \ldots, m\}\} \cap W| + 1 = |\{a_i, b_i \mid i \in \{1, \ldots, m\}\} \cap W|$, and thus there exists some $i \in \{1, \ldots, m\}$ such that $|\{a_i, b_i\} \cap W| > |\{s_i, t_i\} \cap W|$ holds. Here, $|\{a_i, b_i\} \cap W| > 0 \wedge |\{s_i, t_i\} \cap W| = 0$ is impossible, since it means a particle disappears in this element. Hence, $|\{a_i, b_i\} \cap W| = 2 \wedge |\{s_i, t_i\} \cap W| = 1$ must hold. Since $|\{a_i, b_i\} \cap W| = 2$, the i-th RLEM 2-3 receives a particle at b_i at some time, which causes a state change of this element by the move function of RLEM 2-3. However, the i-th RLEM must change its state even times, because C will finally go back to the state q_0^C. Hence, the i-th RLEM must receive a particle at b_i again, since only b_i makes a state change of RLEM 2-3. But, we can see, from the move function of RLEM 2-3, the input b_i gives the output s_i in the state 0, while the same input b_i gives the other output t_i in the state 1. It contradicts $|\{s_i, t_i\} \cap W| = 1$. By above, we can conclude that the lemma holds. $\square$

Since the move function $\delta^{2\text{-}4}$ of RLEM 2-4 is an "inverse" of the move function $\delta^{2\text{-}3}$ of RLEM 2-3 (i.e., $\delta^{2\text{-}4}$ is isomorphic to $(\delta^{2\text{-}3})^{-1}$), the following lemma is proved by a symmetric manner to that in Lemma 3.9.

Lemma 3.10. *[6] RLEM 2-4 can simulate neither RLEM 2-3, nor 2-17.*

Proof. Assume, on the contrary, RLEM 2-3 is simulated by a circuit $C = ((M_1, \ldots, M_m), \{a, b\}, \{s, t\}, f)$ composed only of RLEM 2-4 under a state-mapping φ. Here, $M_i = (\{0,1\}, \{a_i, b_i\}, \{s_i, t_i\}, \delta^{2\text{-}4})$ $(i = 1, \ldots, m)$. We can observe that the following arguments also hold for the case of simulating 2-17 only replacing "2-3" by "2-17", and "(st)" by "(ts)". Let $U = \{a, b\} \cup \{s_i, t_i \mid i \in \{1, \ldots, m\}\}$, and $V = \{s, t\} \cup \{a_i, b_i \mid i \in \{1, \ldots, m\}\}$ be sets of vertices in C. The connection function $f : U \to V$ is a bijection here. Let M^C be the RSM realized by C, and δ^C be the move function of it. Let $\delta^{2\text{-}3}$ be the move function of RLEM 2-3. Then, $\delta^{2\text{-}3}_{\text{output}}(0, (bb)^n) = (st)^n$ holds for all $n \in \mathbb{N}$. Assume $q_0^C \in \varphi(0)$, i.e., it is one of the states of C that correspond to the state 0 of RLEM 2-3. Since C simulates RLEM

2-3, $\delta^C_{\text{output}}(q_0^C,(bb)^n) = (st)^n$ holds for all $n \in \mathbb{N}$. By Lemma 3.8, there exists a positive integer k such that $\delta^C_{\text{state}}(q_0^C,(bb)^k) = q_0^C$.

We analyze the following process of C: Starting from q_0^C, the circuit C receives the particle sequence $(bb)^k$, gives the output sequence $(st)^k$, and finally comes back to the state q_0^C. Let $W(\subset U \cup V)$ be the set of vertices where a particle visits at least once in this process. Since $\forall u \in U(u \in W \Leftrightarrow f(u) \in W)$, and f is a bijection, we can see $|U \cap W| = |V \cap W|$. On the other hand, we observe $b \in U \cap W$ and $s,t \in V \cap W$, but $a \notin U \cap W$. Therefore, $|\{s_i,t_i \mid i \in \{1,\ldots,m\}\} \cap W| = |\{a_i,b_i \mid i \in \{1,\ldots,m\}\} \cap W| + 1$, and thus there exists some $i \in \{1,\ldots,m\}$ such that $|\{a_i,b_i\} \cap W| < |\{s_i,t_i\} \cap W|$ holds. Here, $|\{a_i,b_i\} \cap W| = 0 \wedge |\{s_i,t_i\} \cap W| > 0$ is impossible, since it means a particle is suddenly created at this element. Hence, $|\{a_i,b_i\} \cap W| = 1 \wedge |\{s_i,t_i\} \cap W| = 2$ must hold. Since $|\{s_i,t_i\} \cap W| = 2$, the i-th RLEM 2-4 gives a particle to t_i at some time in this process, which accompanies a state change of this element by the move function of RLEM 2-4. However, the i-th RLEM must change its state even times, because C will finally goes back to the state q_0^C. Hence, the i-th RLEM must give a particle to t_i again, since RLEM 2-4 can change its state only when it gives the output t_i. But, we can see, from the move function of RLEM 2-4, the output t_i can be obtained by the input b_i in the state 0, while the same output t_i can be obtained by the input a_i in the state 1. It contradicts $|\{a_i,b_i\} \cap W| = 1$. By above, we can conclude that the lemma holds. □

By Lemmas 3.7, 3.9, and 3.10, we have the following theorem.

Theorem 3.2. *[6] RLEMs 2-2, 2-3, and 2-4 are non-universal.*

The following lemma says RLEM 2-2 is the weakest one among non-degenerate 2-state RLEMs. Note that RLEM 2-2 is equivalent to "half rotary element" shown in Fig. 3.27.

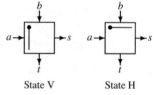

Fig. 3.27 A half rotary element, which is equivalent to RLEM 2-2

Lemma 3.11. *[6] RLEM 2-2 can be simulated by any one of RLEMs 2-3, 2-4, and 2-17.*

Proof. It is proved by the three circuits $C_{2\text{-}3}$, $C_{2\text{-}4}$, and $C_{2\text{-}17}$ that simulate RLEM 2-2 shown in Fig. 3.28. They were found by an exhaustive search by computer.

The circuit $C_{2\text{-}3}$ composed of RLEM 2-3 (Fig. 3.28 **(a)**) simulates RLEM 2-2 under the state-mapping $\varphi_{2\text{-}3}$ such that $\varphi_{2\text{-}3}(0) = \{(0,1,1,1)\}$ and $\varphi_{2\text{-}3}(1) = \{(1,1,1,0)\}$. Transitions of configurations in $C_{2\text{-}3}$ are as follows, and thus it simulates RLEM 2-2 correctly.

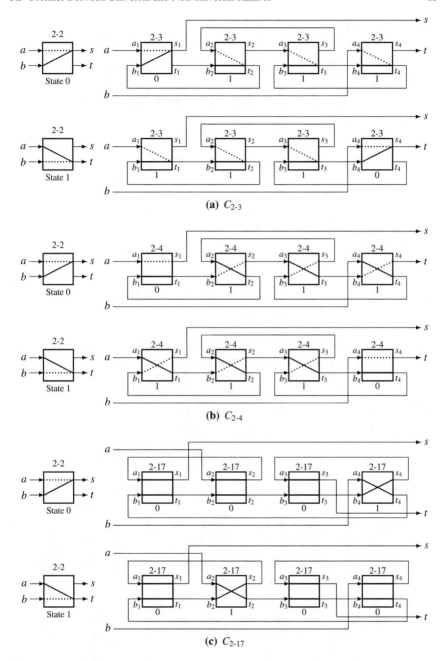

Fig. 3.28 Circuits (**a**) $C_{2\text{-}3}$, (**b**) $C_{2\text{-}4}$, and (**c**) $C_{2\text{-}17}$, which are composed of RLEMs 2-3, 2-4, and 2-17, respectively, and simulate RLEM 2-2

$((0,1,1,1),a) \vdash^*_{C_{2\text{-}3}} ((0,1,1,1),s).$
$((0,1,1,1),b) \vdash^*_{C_{2\text{-}3}} ((0,1,1,1),b_3) \vdash^*_{C_{2\text{-}3}} ((0,1,0,1),b_4) \vdash^*_{C_{2\text{-}3}} ((0,1,0,0),b_3)$
$\qquad \vdash^*_{C_{2\text{-}3}} ((0,1,1,0),a_2) \vdash^*_{C_{2\text{-}3}} ((0,1,1,0),b_1) \vdash^*_{C_{2\text{-}3}} ((1,1,1,0),s).$
$((1,1,1,0),a) \vdash^*_{C_{2\text{-}3}} ((1,1,1,0),b_2) \vdash^*_{C_{2\text{-}3}} ((1,0,1,0),b_1) \vdash^*_{C_{2\text{-}3}} ((0,0,1,0),b_2)$
$\qquad \vdash^*_{C_{2\text{-}3}} ((0,1,1,0),a_3) \vdash^*_{C_{2\text{-}3}} ((0,1,1,0),b_4) \vdash^*_{C_{2\text{-}3}} ((0,1,1,1),t).$
$((1,1,1,0),b) \vdash^*_{C_{2\text{-}3}} ((1,1,1,0),t).$

The circuit $C_{2\text{-}4}$ composed of RLEM 2-4 (Fig. 3.28 **(b)**) simulates RLEM 2-2 under the state-mapping $\varphi_{2\text{-}4}$ such that $\varphi_{2\text{-}4}(0) = \{(0,1,1,1)\}$ and $\varphi_{2\text{-}4}(1) = \{(1,1,1,0)\}$. Transitions of configurations in $C_{2\text{-}4}$ are as follows, and thus it simulates RLEM 2-2 correctly.

$((0,1,1,1),a) \vdash^*_{C_{2\text{-}4}} ((0,1,1,1),s).$
$((0,1,1,1),b) \vdash^*_{C_{2\text{-}4}} ((0,1,1,0),b_3) \vdash^*_{C_{2\text{-}4}} ((0,1,1,0),a_2) \vdash^*_{C_{2\text{-}4}} ((0,0,1,0),b_1)$
$\qquad \vdash^*_{C_{2\text{-}4}} ((1,0,1,0),b_2) \vdash^*_{C_{2\text{-}4}} ((1,1,1,0),b_1) \vdash^*_{C_{2\text{-}4}} ((1,1,1,0),s).$
$((1,1,1,0),a) \vdash^*_{C_{2\text{-}4}} ((0,1,1,0),b_2) \vdash^*_{C_{2\text{-}4}} ((0,1,1,0),a_3) \vdash^*_{C_{2\text{-}4}} ((0,1,0,0),b_4)$
$\qquad \vdash^*_{C_{2\text{-}4}} ((0,1,0,1),b_3) \vdash^*_{C_{2\text{-}4}} ((0,1,1,1),b_4) \vdash^*_{C_{2\text{-}4}} ((0,1,1,1),t).$
$((1,1,1,0),b) \vdash^*_{C_{2\text{-}4}} ((1,1,1,0),t).$

The circuit $C_{2\text{-}17}$ composed of RLEM 2-17 (Fig. 3.28 **(c)**) simulates RLEM 2-2 under the state-mapping $\varphi_{2\text{-}17}$, where $\varphi_{2\text{-}17}(0) = \{(0,0,0,1),(1,1,0,1)\}$ and $\varphi_{2\text{-}17}(1) = \{(0,1,0,0),(0,1,1,1)\}$. Transitions of configurations in $C_{2\text{-}17}$ are as follows. Note that to each state of RLEM 2-2, there correspond two states of $C_{2\text{-}17}$, and all the four states are used to simulate RLEM 2-2.

$((0,0,0,1),a) \vdash^*_{C_{2\text{-}17}} ((0,1,0,1),a_1) \vdash^*_{C_{2\text{-}17}} ((1,1,0,1),s).$
$((0,0,0,1),b) \vdash^*_{C_{2\text{-}17}} ((0,0,0,0),b_1) \vdash^*_{C_{2\text{-}17}} ((1,0,0,0),b_2) \vdash^*_{C_{2\text{-}17}} ((1,1,0,0),b_3)$
$\qquad \vdash^*_{C_{2\text{-}17}} ((1,1,1,0),b_4) \vdash^*_{C_{2\text{-}17}} ((1,1,1,1),b_1) \vdash^*_{C_{2\text{-}17}} ((0,1,1,1),s).$
$((1,1,0,1),a) \vdash^*_{C_{2\text{-}17}} ((1,0,0,1),b_3) \vdash^*_{C_{2\text{-}17}} ((1,0,1,1),b_4) \vdash^*_{C_{2\text{-}17}} ((1,0,1,0),a_3)$
$\qquad \vdash^*_{C_{2\text{-}17}} ((1,0,0,0),b_4) \vdash^*_{C_{2\text{-}17}} ((1,0,0,1),b_1) \vdash^*_{C_{2\text{-}17}} ((0,0,0,1),s).$
$((1,1,0,1),b) \vdash^*_{C_{2\text{-}17}} ((1,1,0,0),b_1) \vdash^*_{C_{2\text{-}17}} ((0,1,0,0),s).$
$((0,1,0,0),a) \vdash^*_{C_{2\text{-}17}} ((0,0,0,0),b_3) \vdash^*_{C_{2\text{-}17}} ((0,0,1,0),b_4) \vdash^*_{C_{2\text{-}17}} ((0,0,1,1),b_1)$
$\qquad \vdash^*_{C_{2\text{-}17}} ((1,0,1,1),b_2) \vdash^*_{C_{2\text{-}17}} ((1,1,1,1),b_3) \vdash^*_{C_{2\text{-}17}} ((1,1,0,1),t).$
$((0,1,0,0),b) \vdash^*_{C_{2\text{-}17}} ((0,1,0,1),a_3) \vdash^*_{C_{2\text{-}17}} ((0,1,1,1),t).$
$((0,1,1,1),a) \vdash^*_{C_{2\text{-}17}} ((0,0,1,1),b_3) \vdash^*_{C_{2\text{-}17}} ((0,0,0,1),t).$
$((0,1,1,1),b) \vdash^*_{C_{2\text{-}17}} ((0,1,1,0),b_1) \vdash^*_{C_{2\text{-}17}} ((1,1,1,0),b_2) \vdash^*_{C_{2\text{-}17}} ((1,0,1,0),a_1)$
$\qquad \vdash^*_{C_{2\text{-}17}} ((0,0,1,0),b_2) \vdash^*_{C_{2\text{-}17}} ((0,1,1,0),b_3) \vdash^*_{C_{2\text{-}17}} ((0,1,0,0),t).$

$\square$

From the above results we can obtain a simple hierarchy among 2-state RLEMs shown in Fig. 3.29. However, it is not known whether RLEM 2-17 is universal.

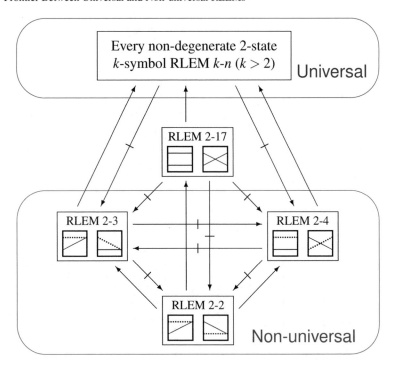

Fig. 3.29 A hierarchy among non-degenerate 2-state RLEMs. Here, $A \rightarrow B$ ($A \not\rightarrow B$, respectively) indicates that A can (cannot) be simulated by B

3.5.3 Universality of combinations of 2-state 2-symbol RLEMs

Although each of RLEMs 2-3 and 2-4 is non-universal, we can construct a circuit composed of RLEMs 2-3 and 2-4 that simulates RE, a universal RLEM, by Lemmas 3.2 and 3.3. Therefore, the combination of RLEMs 2-3 and 2-4 is universal. In the following, we shall show that the combinations of RLEMs 2-3 and 2-17, and RLEMs 2-4 and 2-17 are also universal. However, at present, it is not known whether RLEM 2-17 is universal. Therefore, this result is meaningful only if RLEM 2-17 is non-universal.

Definition 3.8. Let S be a finite set of RLEMs. the set S is called *universal* if any RSM can be simulated by a circuit composed of copies of RLEMs taken from S.

Lemma 3.12. *[6] RLEM 2-3 can be simulated by a circuit composed of RLEMs 2-4 and 2-17. RLEM 2-4 can be simulated by a circuit composed of RLEMs 2-3 and 2-17.*

Proof. It is proved by giving two circuits $C_{2\text{-}4,17}$, and $C_{2\text{-}3,17}$ that simulate RLEMs 2-3, and 2-4, respectively, shown in Fig. 3.30. They were also found by an exhaustive search by computer as in the case of Lemma 3.11.

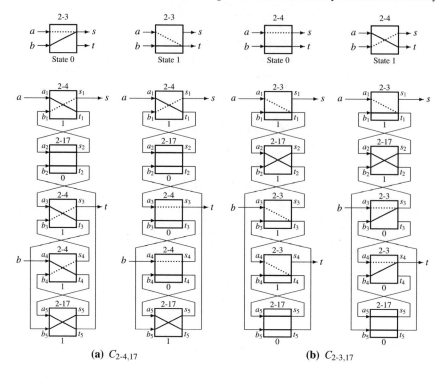

Fig. 3.30 Circuits (a) $C_{2\text{-}4,17}$, and (b) $C_{2\text{-}3,17}$, which are composed of RLEMs 2-4 and 2-17, and RLEMs 2-3 and 2-17, and simulate RLEMs 2-3, and 2-4, respectively

The circuit $C_{2\text{-}4,17}$ composed of RLEMs 2-4 and 2-17 (Fig. 3.30 (a)) simulates RLEM 2-3 under the state-mapping $\varphi_{2\text{-}4,17}(0) = \{(1,0,1,1,1)\}$ and $\varphi_{2\text{-}4,17}(1) = \{(1,0,0,0,1)\}$. Transitions of configurations in $C_{2\text{-}4,17}$ are as follows, and thus it simulates RLEM 2-3 correctly.

$$((1,0,1,1,1),a) \vdash^{*}_{C_{2\text{-}4,17}} ((0,0,1,1,1),a_2) \vdash^{*}_{C_{2\text{-}4,17}} ((0,1,1,1,1),b_1)$$
$$\vdash^{*}_{C_{2\text{-}4,17}} ((1,1,1,1,1),a_2) \vdash^{*}_{C_{2\text{-}4,17}} ((1,0,1,1,1),a_3)$$
$$\vdash^{*}_{C_{2\text{-}4,17}} ((1,0,0,1,1),b_5) \vdash^{*}_{C_{2\text{-}4,17}} ((1,0,0,1,0),b_4)$$
$$\vdash^{*}_{C_{2\text{-}4,17}} ((1,0,0,1,0),b_3) \vdash^{*}_{C_{2\text{-}4,17}} ((1,0,1,1,0),b_5)$$
$$\vdash^{*}_{C_{2\text{-}4,17}} ((1,0,1,1,1),b_2) \vdash^{*}_{C_{2\text{-}4,17}} ((1,1,1,1,1),a_3)$$
$$\vdash^{*}_{C_{2\text{-}4,17}} ((1,1,0,1,1),b_5) \vdash^{*}_{C_{2\text{-}4,17}} ((1,1,0,1,0),b_4)$$
$$\vdash^{*}_{C_{2\text{-}4,17}} ((1,1,0,1,0),b_3) \vdash^{*}_{C_{2\text{-}4,17}} ((1,1,1,1,0),b_5)$$
$$\vdash^{*}_{C_{2\text{-}4,17}} ((1,1,1,1,1),b_2) \vdash^{*}_{C_{2\text{-}4,17}} ((1,0,1,1,1),b_1)$$
$$\vdash^{*}_{C_{2\text{-}4,17}} ((1,0,1,1,1),s).$$

$$((1,0,1,1,1),b) \vdash^*_{C_{2\text{-}4,17}} ((1,0,1,0,1),a_5) \vdash^*_{C_{2\text{-}4,17}} ((1,0,1,0,0),b_2)$$
$$\vdash^*_{C_{2\text{-}4,17}} ((1,1,1,0,0),a_3) \vdash^*_{C_{2\text{-}4,17}} ((1,1,0,0,0),b_5)$$
$$\vdash^*_{C_{2\text{-}4,17}} ((1,1,0,0,1),b_2) \vdash^*_{C_{2\text{-}4,17}} ((1,0,0,0,1),b_1)$$
$$\vdash^*_{C_{2\text{-}4,17}} ((1,0,0,0,1),s).$$

$$((1,0,0,0,1),a) \vdash^*_{C_{2\text{-}4,17}} ((0,0,0,0,1),a_2) \vdash^*_{C_{2\text{-}4,17}} ((0,1,0,0,1),b_1)$$
$$\vdash^*_{C_{2\text{-}4,17}} ((1,1,0,0,1),a_2) \vdash^*_{C_{2\text{-}4,17}} ((1,0,0,0,1),a_3)$$
$$\vdash^*_{C_{2\text{-}4,17}} ((1,0,0,0,1),t).$$

$$((1,0,0,0,1),b) \vdash^*_{C_{2\text{-}4,17}} ((1,0,0,0,1),b_3) \vdash^*_{C_{2\text{-}4,17}} ((1,0,1,0,1),b_5)$$
$$\vdash^*_{C_{2\text{-}4,17}} ((1,0,1,0,0),b_4) \vdash^*_{C_{2\text{-}4,17}} ((1,0,1,1,0),a_5)$$
$$\vdash^*_{C_{2\text{-}4,17}} ((1,0,1,1,1),b_4) \vdash^*_{C_{2\text{-}4,17}} ((1,0,1,1,1),b_3)$$
$$\vdash^*_{C_{2\text{-}4,17}} ((1,0,1,1,1),t).$$

The circuit $C_{2\text{-}3,17}$ composed of RLEMs 2-3 and 2-17 (Fig. 3.30 **(b)**) simulates RLEM 2-4 under the state-mapping $\varphi_{2\text{-}3,17}(0) = \{(1,1,1,1,0)\}$ and $\varphi_{2\text{-}3,17}(1) = \{(1,1,0,0,0)\}$. Transitions of configurations in $C_{2\text{-}3,17}$ are as follows.

$$((1,1,1,1,0),a) \vdash^*_{C_{2\text{-}3,17}} ((1,1,1,1,0),a_2) \vdash^*_{C_{2\text{-}3,17}} ((1,0,1,1,0),b_5)$$
$$\vdash^*_{C_{2\text{-}3,17}} ((1,0,1,1,1),b_3) \vdash^*_{C_{2\text{-}3,17}} ((1,0,0,1,1),a_4)$$
$$\vdash^*_{C_{2\text{-}3,17}} ((1,0,0,1,1),a_5) \vdash^*_{C_{2\text{-}3,17}} ((1,0,0,1,0),b_3)$$
$$\vdash^*_{C_{2\text{-}3,17}} ((1,0,1,1,0),b_2) \vdash^*_{C_{2\text{-}3,17}} ((1,1,1,1,0),b_5)$$
$$\vdash^*_{C_{2\text{-}3,17}} ((1,1,1,1,1),b_3) \vdash^*_{C_{2\text{-}3,17}} ((1,1,0,1,1),a_4)$$
$$\vdash^*_{C_{2\text{-}3,17}} ((1,1,0,1,1),a_5) \vdash^*_{C_{2\text{-}3,17}} ((1,1,0,1,0),b_3)$$
$$\vdash^*_{C_{2\text{-}3,17}} ((1,1,1,1,0),b_2) \vdash^*_{C_{2\text{-}3,17}} ((1,0,1,1,0),b_1)$$
$$\vdash^*_{C_{2\text{-}3,17}} ((0,0,1,1,0),a_2) \vdash^*_{C_{2\text{-}3,17}} ((0,1,1,1,0),b_1)$$
$$\vdash^*_{C_{2\text{-}3,17}} ((1,1,1,1,0),s).$$

$$((1,1,1,1,0),b) \vdash^*_{C_{2\text{-}3,17}} ((1,1,1,1,0),a_4) \vdash^*_{C_{2\text{-}3,17}} ((1,1,1,1,0),a_5)$$
$$\vdash^*_{C_{2\text{-}3,17}} ((1,1,1,1,1),b_4) \vdash^*_{C_{2\text{-}3,17}} ((1,1,1,0,1),a_5)$$
$$\vdash^*_{C_{2\text{-}3,17}} ((1,1,1,0,0),b_3) \vdash^*_{C_{2\text{-}3,17}} ((1,1,0,0,0),a_4)$$
$$\vdash^*_{C_{2\text{-}3,17}} ((1,1,0,0,0),t).$$

$$((1,1,0,0,0),a) \vdash^*_{C_{2\text{-}3,17}} ((1,1,0,0,0),a_2) \vdash^*_{C_{2\text{-}3,17}} ((1,0,0,0,0),b_5)$$
$$\vdash^*_{C_{2\text{-}3,17}} ((1,0,0,0,1),b_3) \vdash^*_{C_{2\text{-}3,17}} ((1,0,1,0,1),b_2)$$
$$\vdash^*_{C_{2\text{-}3,17}} ((1,1,1,0,1),b_5) \vdash^*_{C_{2\text{-}3,17}} ((1,1,1,0,0),b_4)$$
$$\vdash^*_{C_{2\text{-}3,17}} ((1,1,1,1,0),t).$$

$$((1,1,0,0,0),b) \vdash^*_{C_{2\text{-}3,17}} ((1,1,0,0,0),b_2) \vdash^*_{C_{2\text{-}3,17}} ((1,0,0,0,0),b_1)$$
$$\vdash^*_{C_{2\text{-}3,17}} ((0,0,0,0,0),a_2) \vdash^*_{C_{2\text{-}3,17}} ((0,1,0,0,0),b_1)$$
$$\vdash^*_{C_{2\text{-}3,17}} ((1,1,0,0,0),s).$$

$\square$

From Corollary 2.1, and Lemmas 3.2, 3.3 and 3.12, we have the following theorem stating that any two combination taken from the three RLEMs 2-3, 2-4 and 2-17 is universal.

Theorem 3.3. *[1, 6] The sets of RLEMs {RLEM 2-3, RLEM 2-4}, {RLEM 2-3, RLEM 2-17}, and {RLEM 2-4, RLEM 2-17} are universal.*

3.6 Realizing 4-Symbol RLEMs in the Billiard Ball Model

In Sect. 2.2.3 it is shown that RE can be realized in the billiard ball model (BBM), a reversible physical model of computing, where only two balls called a state-ball, and a signal-ball are used. Since any RLEM can be composed of RE, it is also realizable in BBM. However, the resulting BBM configuration obtained by this method will become complex, and many state-balls are required. Here, we show there is a simple and systematic method of realizing any 4-symbol RLEM in BBM.

Theorem 3.4. *[5] Any m-state 4-symbol RLEM can be realized in the billiard ball model (m ∈ {2, 3, . . .}). There, one state-ball for keeping the state, and one signal-ball for giving input/output are used to simulate the RLEM.*

Proof. Let $M = (\{0, \ldots, m-1\}, \{a, b, c, d\}, \{s, t, u, v\}, \delta)$ be a given m-state 4-symbol RLEM ($m \in \{2, 3, \ldots\}$). We design a configuration (i.e., placement of reflectors and balls) of BBM that can simulate M. Here, we assume balls can move eight directions as in the case of RE in Sect. 2.2.3, i.e., north, east, south, west, north-east, south-east, south-west, and north-west in the Euclidean space $\mathbb{R}^2$. We also use two kinds of balls called a state-ball, and a signal-ball. The diameter of the balls is assumed to be 1. Reflectors for balls should be placed so that balls can change their moving direction only at integer coordinates.

We first introduce a *basic BBM module* for m-state 4-symbol RLEMs. Figure 3.31 shows a basic BBM module for $m = 4$. Four circles numbered by $0, \ldots, 3$ are possible positions of placing a state-ball, which correspond to the states $0, \ldots, 3$ of M, respectively. For example, if a state-ball is put stationarily at the position 2, then we assume M is in the state 2. The lines with the labels a, b, c and d are the ones for giving a signal-ball as an input. Likewise, the lines with s, t, u and v are the ones where the signal-ball will appear as an output. A signal-ball can move along solid lines, while a state-ball can move along a dotted line after colliding with the signal-ball. Thus, these lines indicate possible trajectories of the balls. In this figure, we omitted to write reflectors for simplifying the figure, but their positions can be easily identified from the possible trajectories.

We now explain how the operations of M can be simulated using RLEM 4-31 as an example. The move function $\delta_{4\text{-}31}$ of RLEM 4-31 is given in Table 3.10 (see also Fig. 3.17). Figure 3.32 **(a)** shows an implementation of $\delta_{4\text{-}31}(0, d) = (1, s)$ in the basic BBM module for 2-state 4-symbol RLEMs.

Assume a state-ball is placed stationarily at the position 0. If a signal-ball comes along the line d, then it collides with the state-ball at the position 0. Immediately

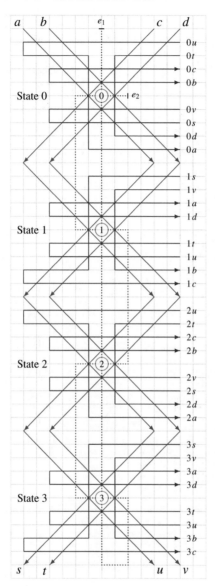

Fig. 3.31 The basic BBM module for 4-state 4-symbol RLEMs

Table 3.10 The move function $\delta_{4\text{-}31}$ of RLEM 4-31

	Input			
Present state	a	b	c	d
0	$0s$	$0t$	$0u$	$1s$
1	$1t$	$0v$	$1v$	$1u$

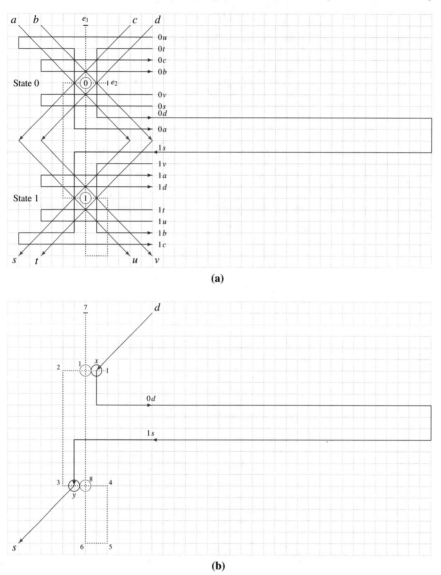

Fig. 3.32 (a) Realizing $\delta_{4\text{-}31}(0,d) = (1,s)$ in the basic BBM module for 2-state 4-symbol RLEMs. (b) Trajectories of two balls. The signal-ball travels as follows: $d \to x \to y \to s$. While the signal-ball goes from x to y, the state-ball moves along the dotted line, and visits the points in the following order: $1 \to 2 \to 3 \to 4 \to 5 \to 6 \to 7 \to 6 \to 5 \to 4 \to 8$. The lengths of the paths of two balls between two collisions must be the same (in this case, the length is 72)

after the collision, the signal-ball moves south, and then goes east along the line labeled $0d$. On the other hand, the state-ball starts to move along the dotted line to the west.

The dotted line has several left/right turns by 90 degrees. It also has turns by 180 degrees at the both ends (indicated by e_1 and e_2), and thus a state-ball can move both directions along the dotted line. Furthermore, it has crossings at the positions of circles. Therefore, the ball can move in 4 directions, i.e., north, east, south, and west, at the crossings. Consider the crossing point corresponding to the state 1. Assume a state-ball is coming along the dotted line from the east, and a signal-ball is coming from the line labeled by $1s$ at a right timing. Then, the state-ball stops at the crossing point, and the signal ball eventually goes out from the line labeled s. This is essentially the reverse process of the first collision. Hence, by connecting the port $0d$ to the port $1s$ appropriately, we can simulate the movement $\delta_{4\text{-}31}(0,d) = (1,s)$ of $M_{4\text{-}31}$. But, we must consider the timing of the second collision at the crossing point corresponding to the state 1. Since the output is s, the state-ball on the dotted line must come from the east when colliding with the signal-ball. Hence, the trajectory of the state-ball should be $1 \to 2 \to 3 \to 4 \to 5 \to 6 \to 7 \to 6 \to 5 \to 4 \to 8$ in Fig. 3.32 **(b)**. The total length of the trajectory of solid line, which corresponds to the delay of the signal-ball, between two collision points (i.e., from x to y in Fig. 3.32 **(b)**) must be adjusted to be the same as that of the dotted line. This is easily done by adjusting the length of the eastward path in this figure (in this case the length is 72).

Figure 3.33 gives the whole configuration realizing the RLEM 4-31 in BBM. It is easy to generalize the above method to many-state 4-symbol RLEMs. Thus, we can see that any RLEM with 4 symbols and with arbitrary number of states can be realized in BBM using only one state-ball. In addition, it is also possible to realize any RLEM with less than four symbols in this way by simply removing irrelevant lines from such a figure. □

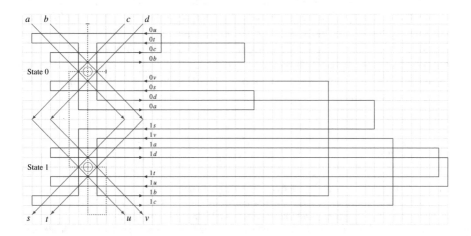

Fig. 3.33 RLEM 4-31 realized in BBM

3.7 Concluding Remarks

In Sect. 2.2.1, rotary element (RE), a specific type of reversible logic elements with memory (RLEMs), was presented. On the other hand, there are infinitely many kinds of RLEMs besides RE. Thus, it is important to know which RLEMs are universal, and which RLEMs are useful for constructing reversible machines.

In this chapter, we first introduced an equivalence relation and the notion of degeneracy in 2-state k-symbol RLEMs, and classified them. Then, we investigated their universality. Among the results we have obtained, it is remarkable that *every* non-degenerate k-symbol RLEM is universal if $k > 2$ (Theorem 3.1). Hence, any reversible sequential machine (RSM) can be constructed by such a universal RLEM. As we shall see in Chap. 6, we can construct a reversible Turing machine from a universal RLEM. On the other hand, it is also shown that RLEMs 2-2, 2-3 and 2-4 among the four non-degenerate 2-symbol RLEMs are non-universal (Theorem 3.2). From these results, we obtain a simple hierarchy among 2-state RLEMs as shown in Fig. 3.29. But, it is an open problem whether RLEM 2-17 is universal or not.

In Sect. 2.3, it was shown that any RSM can be composed of RE very simply (Theorem 2.1). In Sect. 3.4, we investigated which RLEMs are useful besides RE for composing RSMs. We showed that there is a compact realization method of RSMs by RLEM 4-31 or RLEM 3-7. However, so far, it has not yet been well clarified which RLEMs are useful for composing reversible machines, and thus it is left for the future study.

In Sect. 3.6, we gave a systematic method of realizing any reversible 4-symbol RLEM with arbitrary number of states in the billiard ball model (BBM). As in the method of realizing RE in BBM shown in Sect. 2.2.3, only one state-ball is required for each RLEM, and a signal-ball can be given at any moment and in any speed. Hence, in this case there is no need to synchronize many balls at all, while in the case of realizing reversible logic gates in BBM, speed and timing of many balls should be exactly adjusted. Of course, even in the case of RLEM, it is impossible to actually implement it as a mechanical system, since it requires infinite precision. However, considering the role of the stationary ball in this method, it need not be a movable particle, but can be a state of some stationary object, such as a quantum state of an atom or like that. Hence, this method suggests a possibility to implement RLEMs in a real physical system with reversibility, and thus may lead highly miniaturized computing systems.

References

1. Lee, J., Peper, F., Adachi, S., Morita, K.: An asynchronous cellular automaton implementing 2-state 2-input 2-output reversed-twin reversible elements. In: Proc. ACRI 2008 (eds. H. Umeo, et al.), LNCS 5191, pp. 67–76 (2008). doi:10.1007/978-3-540-79992-4_9
2. Morita, K., Ogiro, T.: How can we construct reversible machines out of reversible logic element with memory? In: Computing with New Resources (eds. C.S. Calude et al.), LNCS 8808, pp. 352–366. Springer (2014). doi:10.1007/978-3-319-13350-8_26

3. Morita, K., Ogiro, T., Alhazov, A., Tanizawa, T.: Non-degenerate 2-state reversible logic elements with three or more symbols are all universal. J. Multiple-Valued Logic and Soft Computing **18**, 37–54 (2012)
4. Morita, K., Ogiro, T., Tanaka, K., Kato, H.: Classification and universality of reversible logic elements with one-bit memory. In: Proc. MCU 2004 (ed. M. Margenstern), LNCS 3354, pp. 245–256 (2005). doi:10.1007/978-3-540-31834-7_20
5. Mukai, Y., Morita, K.: Realizing reversible logic elements with memory in the billiard ball model. Int. J. Unconventional Computing **8**, 47–59 (2012)
6. Mukai, Y., Ogiro, T., Morita, K.: Universality problems on reversible logic elements with 1-bit memory. Int. J. Unconventional Computing **10**, 353–373 (2014)

Chapter 4
Reversible Logic Gates

Abstract A reversible logic gate is a memory-less logic element that realizes an injective logical function. Fredkin gate, Toffoli gate, interaction gate, and switch gate are typical ones. Here, we investigate basic properties of reversible logic gates and circuits, which are needed in the following chapters. First, logical universality of them is discussed. Then, a construction method of an almost garbage-less reversible combinatorial logic circuit is explained. Reducing the total amount of garbage signals is an important problem in designing reversible logic circuits. Finally, relations among Fredkin gate, reversible logic elements with 1-bit memory (RLEMs), and reversible sequential machines (RSM) are studied. In particular, it is shown that we can construct a completely garbage-less circuit out of Fredkin gates and delay elements that simulates a given RSM. This result will be used to show universality of reversible cellular automata in the later chapters.

Keywords reversible logic gate, Fredkin gate, garbage-less circuit, rotary element, reversible sequential machine

4.1 Reversible Logic Gates and Circuits

In Chaps. 2 and 3, we presented reversible logic elements with memory (RLEMs), and studied their universality and how to use them. There, we gave a systematic method of composing reversible sequential machines (RSMs) out of them. In this chapter, we study reversible logic elements without memory, which are usually called reversible logic gates, and circuits made of them. We first introduce typical reversible logic gates, in particular, Fredkin gate, Toffoli gate and others, and investigate their logical universality. Next, we explain how a "garbage-less" circuit can be constructed from them that realizes a given (not necessarily injective) logical function. In the design theory of circuits composed of reversible logic gates, it is an important problem to reduce the amount of garbage signals produced in the circuit. This is because production of garbage information leads inevitable power dissipation in the computing system [2, 5]. In Sect. 4.2, we consider the relationship among reversible logic gates, rotary element (RE), and RSMs. In particular, we shall show that RE and RSMs can be realized by completely garbage-less circuits composed of Fredkin gates and delay elements. In Chap. 6, a garbage-less construction method of reversible Turing machines (RTMs) out of REs is shown. Hence, it is also possible to realize RTMs as garbage-less circuit composed of Fredkin gates and delay elements. In Sects. 12.3, 13.2 and 13.3, these results will be used to design computationally universal reversible cellular automata having very simple local transition rules, in which any circuit composed of Fredkin gates can be embedded.

4.1.1 Reversible logic gates

We define a logical function, a logic gate, and a reversible logic gate as follows.

Definition 4.1. A function $f : B^m \to B^n$ is called a *logical function* or a *Boolean function* $(m, n \in \{1, 2, \ldots\})$, if $B = \{0, 1\}$, where 0 and 1 stand for the truth values "false" and "true", respectively. An element that realizes the function f is called an *m-input n-output logic gate*. If the function f is injective, then the gate that realizes f is called a *reversible logic gate*. Note that, in this case, $m \leq n$ must hold.

Early study on reversible logic gates was made by Petri [11]. Then, Toffoli [16, 17], and Fredkin and Toffoli [5] investigated them in connection with physical reversibility. We first introduce typical examples of reversible logic gates.

Fredkin gate proposed by Fredkin and Toffoli [5] is one that realizes the logical function $f_F : \{0, 1\}^3 \to \{0, 1\}^3$ such that $f_F : (c, p, q) \mapsto (c, c \cdot p + \overline{c} \cdot q, c \cdot q + \overline{c} \cdot p)$, where $\cdot$, $+$, and $\overline{}$ stand for logical product, logical sum, and negation, respectively. Here, we depict it as in Fig. 4.1 **(a)**, which is the original representation given in [5]. There are also other representations shown in Fig. 4.1 **(b)** and **(c)**. In the design theory of quantum logic circuits, Fig. 4.1 **(b)** or **(c)** is often used.

As in Fig. 4.2, the input c controls how to connect the other two input lines to the output lines. The truth table of the Fredkin gate is given in Table 4.1, from which injectivity of f_F is easily verified.

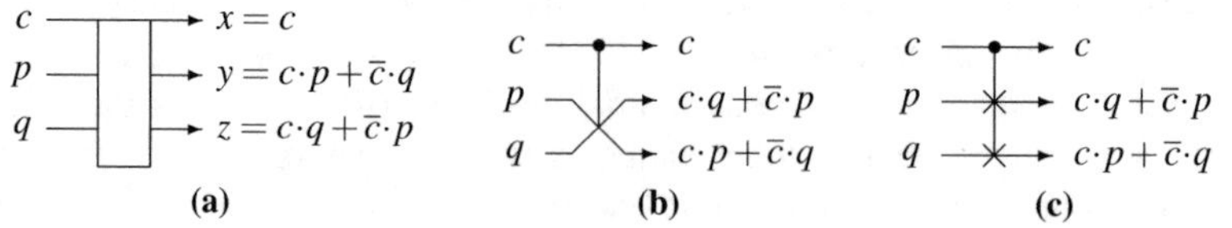

(a)   (b)   (c)

Fig. 4.1 Pictorial representations of Fredkin gate. The representation **(a)** is the original one given in [5], while **(b)** or **(c)** is often used in the design theory of quantum logic circuits. Note that the positions of the second and the third outputs of **(b)** and **(c)** differ from those of **(a)**

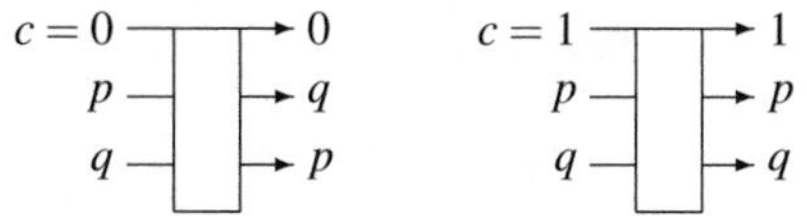

Fig. 4.2 Operations of Fredkin gate

Table 4.1 The truth table of the logical function $f_F : (c,p,q) \mapsto (x,y,z)$ of Fredkin gate

c p q	x y z
0 0 0	0 0 0
0 0 1	0 1 0
0 1 0	0 0 1
0 1 1	0 1 1
1 0 0	1 0 0
1 0 1	1 0 1
1 1 0	1 1 0
1 1 1	1 1 1

Fredkin gate has another property that is related to the conservation law in physics. A logical function $f : \{0,1\}^m \to \{0,1\}^n$ is called *bit-conserving*, if the following condition holds.

$$\forall \mathbf{x} = (x_1,\ldots,x_m) \in \{0,1\}^m, \forall \mathbf{y} = (y_1,\ldots,y_n) \in \{0,1\}^n$$
$$(f(\mathbf{x}) = \mathbf{y} \Rightarrow (|\{i \mid x_i = 1 \wedge i \in \{1,\ldots,m\}\}| = |\{i \mid y_i = 1 \wedge i \in \{1,\ldots,n\}\}|))$$

Namely, the number of 1's in the input is always the same as the number of 1's in the output. If the signals 0 and 1 are represented by absence and presence of a particle, some amount of energy, or something like them in a physical system, then this property corresponds to the conservation law of mass, energy, or other physical quantity. From Table 4.1 we can see Fredkin gate is a bit-conserving gate.

The *generalized AND/NAND gate* proposed by Toffoli [16] is the gate that realizes the function $\theta^{(n)} : (x_1,x_2,\ldots,x_{n-1},x_n) \mapsto (x_1,x_2\ldots,x_{n-1},(x_1 \cdot x_2 \cdots x_{n-1}) \oplus x_n)$, where $\oplus$ is the operation of exclusive OR. It controls the input x_n by the logical product of $x_1,x_2,\ldots,x_{n-1}$, i.e., if $x_1 \cdot x_2 \cdots x_{n-1} = 0$ then the n-th output is x_n, and if $x_1 \cdot x_2 \cdots x_{n-1} = 1$ then it is $\bar{x}_n$. The functions $\theta^{(2)}$ and $\theta^{(3)}$ are called the *controlled NOT* (CNOT) and the *Toffoli gate*, respectively. The logical function realized by the Toffoli gate is thus $f_T : (x_1,x_2,x_3) \mapsto (x_1,x_2,(x_1 \cdot x_2) \oplus x_3)$. The Toffoli gate is depicted as in Fig. 4.3, and the truth table of f_T is given in Table 4.2.

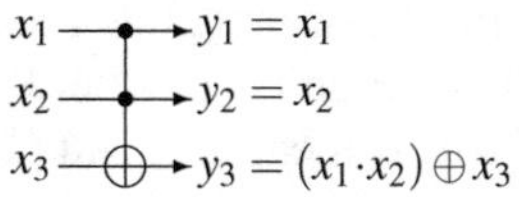

Fig. 4.3 Toffoli gate

Table 4.2 The truth table of the logical function $f_T : (x_1, x_2, x_3) \mapsto (y_1, y_2, y_3)$ of Toffoli gate

x_1 x_2 x_3	y_1 y_2 y_3
0 0 0	0 0 0
0 0 1	0 0 1
0 1 0	0 1 0
0 1 1	0 1 1
1 0 0	1 0 0
1 0 1	1 0 1
1 1 0	1 1 1
1 1 1	1 1 0

4.1.2 Reversible combinatorial logic circuits

Connecting reversible logic gates, we can compose a logic circuit. We introduce a reversible combinatorial logic circuit that realizes an injective logical function.

Definition 4.2. Let S be a finite set of reversible logic gates. A *reversible combinatorial logic circuit* Φ over S is a system composed of a finite number of copies of reversible logic gates taken from S, which are connected each other under the following constraint.

1. Each output of a gate can be connected to at most one input of some other gate, i.e., fan-out of an output is inhibited.
2. Two or more outputs should not be connected to one input port of some other gate, i.e., merging of outputs is inhibited.
3. The circuit should not contain a closed path, i.e., no feedback loop is allowed.

Note that, in the above definition, fan-out (copying) of an output is not allowed in 1. There are several reasons to put this restriction. The first reason is as follows. In the traditional technique for (irreversible) logic circuits, fan-out is implemented at the cost of supplying some amount of energy. Since energy consumption is an important problem in reversible computing, fan-out should be inhibited, and such an operation must be treated explicitly in a logic circuit. Secondly, a quantum circuit, which is a circuit model in quantum computing, can be viewed as an extension of a reversible logic circuit. In a quantum circuit, signals have values of quantum bits rather than classical bits (i.e., 0 or 1). In quantum physics, "no-cloning theorem" for quantum bits has been proved [4, 19]. Hence, a signal in a quantum circuit cannot be copied. Since reversible logic circuits are often used as parts of quantum circuits, fan-out is inhibited also in these circuits. The third reason is that we sometimes use an "inverse" circuit of a given reversible circuit (see Sect. 4.1.4). If the original circuit contains fan-out, then the inverse circuit will have a merge of two or more outputs, and thus there arises a problem to define its behavior.

Let Φ be a reversible combinatorial logic circuit. The input ports of gates that are not connected to other gates are the input ports of the entire circuit Φ. Likewise, the output ports of gates that are not connected to other gates are the output ports of Φ. Obviously, if we supply truth values to the input ports of Φ, then it gives output values from those output ports. Thus, the whole circuit Φ implements some injective logical function. However, here, we use the following technique to "embed" a non-injective logical function in Φ. The set of input ports of Φ are partitioned into a set $X = \{x_1, \ldots, x_m\}$ of *actual inputs*, and a set $C = \{c_1, \ldots, c_k\}$ of *constant inputs*. The set of output ports of Φ are partitioned into a set $Y = \{y_1, \ldots, y_n\}$ of *actual outputs*, and a set $G = \{g_1, \ldots, g_l\}$ of *garbage outputs* (Fig. 4.4). Note that we also use the symbols $x_1, \ldots, x_m, c_1, \ldots, c_k, y_1, \ldots, y_n$, and $g_1, \ldots, g_l$ to represent the truth value at the corresponding ports. Furthermore, the logical function realized by the whole circuit is written by the same symbol Φ. Hence, $\Phi(c_1, \ldots, c_k, x_1, \ldots, x_m) = (g_1, \ldots, g_l, y_1, \ldots, y_n)$.

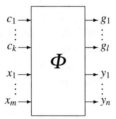

Fig. 4.4 Embedding a logical function $f : (x_1, \ldots, x_m) \mapsto (y_1, \ldots, y_n)$ in a reversible combinatorial logic circuit Φ. It has constant inputs $c_1, \ldots, c_k$, and garbage outputs $g_1, \ldots, g_l$, besides actual inputs $x_1, \ldots, x_m$, and actual outputs $y_1, \ldots, y_n$

Definition 4.3. Let $f : \{0,1\}^m \to \{0,1\}^n$ be a logical function, and Φ be an injective logical function with the sets of actual inputs $X = \{x_1, \ldots, x_m\}$, constant inputs $C = \{c_1, \ldots, c_k\}$, actual outputs $Y = \{y_1, \ldots, y_n\}$, and garbage outputs $G = \{g_1, \ldots, g_l\}$. We say f is *embedded* in Φ, if the following condition holds.

$$\exists (c_1, \ldots, c_k) \in \{0,1\}^k,$$
$$\forall (x_1, \ldots, x_m) \in \{0,1\}^m, \ \forall (y_1, \ldots, y_n) \in \{0,1\}^n,$$
$$\exists (g_1, \ldots, g_l) \in \{0,1\}^l$$
$$(f(x_1, \ldots, x_m) = (y_1, \ldots, y_n) \Rightarrow \Phi(c_1, \ldots, c_k, x_1, \ldots, x_m) = (g_1, \ldots, g_l, y_1, \ldots, y_n))$$

This condition says that by allowing to supply appropriate constant values to $c_1, \ldots, c_k$, and to generate garbage outputs from $g_1, \ldots, g_l$, the circuit Φ computes the logical function f (even if it is non-injective).

4.1.3 Logical universality of reversible logic gates

Logical universality of a reversible logic gate, and a set of reversible logic gates is defined as follows.

Definition 4.4. Let S be a finite set of reversible logic gates. If any logical function f is embedded in a reversible combinatorial logic circuit over S, then the set S is called *logically universal*, or *functionally complete*. If a set S is logically universal, and S is a singleton, i.e., $S = \{s\}$ for some reversible logic gate s, then the the gate s is also called *logically universal*.

   In the case of traditional (irreversible) logic gates and circuits (in this case there is no notion of garbage outputs), it is well known that the set $\{$AND, NOT$\}$ is logically universal. To prove universality of a given set S of reversible logic gates, it is sufficient to show each of the functions AND, NOT, and fan-out can be embedded in a circuit constructed from gates taken from S.

   In [5] it is shown that Fredkin gate is logically universal. Figure 4.5 gives circuits that embed AND, NOT, and fan-out. Note that each of these circuits consists of one Fredkin gate. Thus, any logical function can be embedded in a circuit composed only of Fredkin gates. Toffoli gate is also logically universal [16]. Figure 4.6 gives circuits that embed AND, NOT, and fan-out.

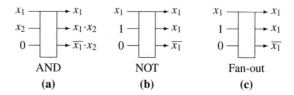

Fig. 4.5 Logical universality of Fredkin gate. **(a)** AND, **(b)** NOT, and **(c)** fan-out are embedded in the circuits by allowing constant inputs and garbage outputs

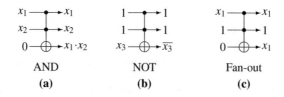

Fig. 4.6 Logical universality of Toffoli gate. **(a)** AND, **(b)** NOT, and **(c)** fan-out are embedded in the circuits

Fredkin gate and Toffoli gate are 3-input 3-output gates. Besides them, there are many logically universal ones. The total number of 3-input 3-output reversible logic gates is $8! = 40320$, and most of them are logically universal. In fact, it is known that 38976 gates among them are universal [3]. On the other hand, there is no logically universal n-input n-output reversible logic gate, if $n < 3$ [3]. Hence, Fredkin gate, Toffoli gate, and other universal 3-input 3-output gates are the minimal universal reversible ones for the case that the numbers of inputs and outputs are the same. However, if we consider the case such that the number of outputs is larger than that of inputs, then there are slightly simpler logically universal ones.

Switch gate [5] is a 2-input 3-output reversible logic gate shown in Fig. 4.7 **(a)**. The truth table of the logical function f_{sw} realized by the switch gate is given in Table 4.3. It is a bit-conserving gate. The input c controls the connection between the input x and the output y_2 or y_3, i.e., if $c = 1$ then x is connected to y_2, and if $c = 0$ then x is connected to y_3. We can see that AND is embedded in the circuit of Fig. 4.7 **(a)**, and NOT and fan-out are embedded in Fig. 4.7 **(b)**. Hence, the switch gate is logically universal.

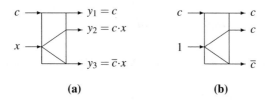

(a)   **(b)**

Fig. 4.7 Switch gate and its logical universality. **(a)** Here, AND is obtained from y_2. **(b)** Giving constant 1 to the input x, NOT and fan-out are obtained

Table 4.3 The truth table of the logical function $f_{sw} : (c,x) \mapsto (y_1, y_2, y_3)$ of switch gate

c x	y_1 y_2 y_3
0 0	0 0 0
0 1	0 0 1
1 0	1 0 0
1 1	1 1 0

Interaction gate [5] is a 2-input 4-output reversible and bit-conserving logic gate shown in Fig. 4.8 **(a)**, which is sometimes called a *collision gate*. The truth table of the logical function f_{int} realized by the interaction gate is given in Table 4.4. We can see that AND is embedded in the circuit of Fig. 4.8 **(a)**, and NOT and fan-out are embedded in Fig. 4.8 **(b)**. Hence, the interaction gate is also logically universal.

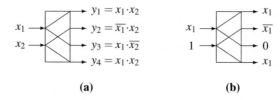

(a)   **(b)**

Fig. 4.8 Interaction gate and its logical universality. **(a)** Here, AND is obtained from y_1 and y_4. **(b)** Giving constant 1 to the input x_2, NOT and fan-out are obtained

Table 4.4 The truth table of the logical function $f_{\text{int}} : (x_1, x_2) \mapsto (y_1, y_2, y_3, y_4)$ of interaction gate

x_1 x_2	y_1 y_2 y_3 y_4
0 0	0 0 0 0
0 1	0 1 0 0
1 0	0 0 1 0
1 1	1 0 0 1

4.1.4 Clearing garbage information

As we saw in the previous subsection, *any* logical function can be embedded in a circuit composed of universal reversible logic gates by allowing to supply constant inputs to the circuit, and to produce garbage outputs from it (see also Fig. 4.4). However, discarding the garbage outputs is an irreversible process, since it is a kind of erasure of information. Thus, garbage signals should be minimized by designing the circuit appropriately. Here, we explain the method of reducing the amount of garbage information given by Fredkin and Toffoli [5].

We first introduce the notions of an inverse reversible logic gate, and an inverse reversible combinatorial logic circuit.

Definition 4.5. Let $f : \{0,1\}^m \to \{0,1\}^n$ be an injective logical function $(m \leq n)$, and s be the m-input n-output reversible logic gate that realizes f. The *inverse logic gate* of s is an n-input m-output logic gate that realizes the partial logical function f^{-1}, the inverse of f.

Inverse switch gate is a 3-input 2-output logic gate depicted as in Fig. 4.9 **(a)**. It realizes the partial logical function $f_{\text{sw}}^{-1} : \{0,1\}^3 \to \{0,1\}^2$, which is defined only on the set $\{(0,0,0),(0,0,1),(1,0,0),(1,1,0)\}$ as shown in in Table 4.5 **(a)**. Hence, for example, $(1,1,1)$ should not be given as its input.

Inverse interaction gate is a 4-input 2-output logic gate given in Fig. 4.9 **(b)**. It realizes the partial logical function $f_{\text{int}}^{-1} : \{0,1\}^4 \to \{0,1\}^2$, which is defined only on the set $\{(0,0,0,0),(0,1,0,0),(0,0,1,0),(1,0,0,1)\}$ as shown in Table 4.5 **(b)**.

Since the inverse switch gate (inverse interaction gate, respectively) realizes a partial function, it is usually used together with the switch gate (interaction gate).

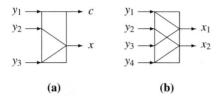

Fig. 4.9 (a) Inverse switch gate, and (b) inverse interaction gate

Table 4.5 The truth tables of the partial logical functions (a) $f_{sw}^{-1} : (y_1, y_2, y_3) \mapsto (c, x)$ of inverse switch gate, and (b) $f_{int}^{-1} : (y_1, y_2, y_3, y_4) \mapsto (x_1, x_2)$ of inverse interaction gate

y_1 y_2 y_3	c x
0 0 0	0 0
0 0 1	0 1
1 0 0	1 0
1 1 0	1 1

(a)

y_1 y_2 y_3 y_4	x_1 x_2
0 0 0 0	0 0
0 1 0 0	0 1
0 0 1 0	1 0
1 0 0 1	1 1

(b)

From Table 4.1, we can see that the *inverse Fredkin gate* is the Fredkin gate itself. Therefore, it has the same pictorial representation. Likewise, from Table 4.2, we can see that the *inverse Toffoli gate* is the Toffoli gate itself.

Definition 4.6. Let Φ be a reversible combinatorial logic circuit. The *inverse reversible combinatorial logic circuit* Φ^{-1} is one obtained from Φ by replacing each occurrence of a reversible logic gate by its inverse reversible logic gate, and thus its inputs and outputs are exchanged.

We also use Φ to denote the logical function $\Phi : \{0,1\}^m \to \{0,1\}^n$ $(m < n)$ realized by Φ. Then, the logical function realized by the circuit Φ^{-1} is the partial logical function $\Phi^{-1} : \{0,1\}^n \to \{0,1\}^m$. Therefore, $\Phi^{-1}(\Phi(\mathbf{x})) = \mathbf{x}$ holds for all $\mathbf{x} \in \{0,1\}^m$. We omit its formal proof, since it is clear from the construction of Φ^{-1}. In fact, it is apparent from the following examples.

Figure 4.10 **(a)** shows an example of a reversible combinatorial logic circuit composed of switch gates. Its inverse circuit is obtained by taking a "mirror image" of it, and exchanging inputs and outputs as shown in Fig. 4.10 **(b)**. Figure 4.11 **(a)** is an example of a circuit composed of Fredkin gates. Its inverse circuit is given in Fig. 4.11 **(b)**.

As explained in Sect. 4.1.3, any logical function can be embedded in some reversible logic circuit Φ by allowing to give constant inputs, and to generate garbage outputs (see also Fig. 4.4). If we connect Φ and Φ^{-1} serially as in Fig. 4.12, we can erase all the garbage information reversibly, and get a "clean" constant $\mathbf{c}$ that can be reused. But, since this circuit also changes the actual output $\mathbf{y}$ to the actual input $\mathbf{x}$, we must insert fan-out circuits between Φ and Φ^{-1} to copy $\mathbf{y}$ as shown in Fig. 4.13. By this method, the actual output $\mathbf{y}$ is obtained without generating garbage information $\mathbf{g}$. This circuit also gives the actual input $\mathbf{x}$ and the complement of the actual

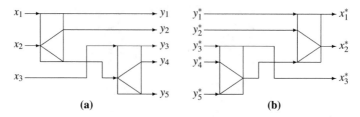

Fig. 4.10 (**a**) A circuit composed of switch gates, and (**b**) its inverse circuit

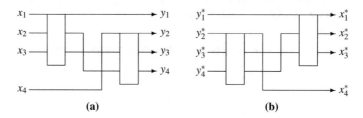

Fig. 4.11 (**a**) A circuit composed of Fredkin gates, and (**b**) its inverse circuit

output $\overline{\mathbf{y}}$, which are another kind of garbage information. However, since the number of bits of garbage $\mathbf{g}$ can be an exponential function of that of $\mathbf{x}$, the total number of bits of $\mathbf{x}$ and $\overline{\mathbf{y}}$ is generally much less than that of $\mathbf{g}$. In this sense, a circuit of the form in Fig. 4.13 is an *almost garbage-less logic circuit*, and we have the following proposition (again its formal proof is omitted).

Proposition 4.1. *Let s be a logically universal reversible logic gate. Then, for any logical function f, there is an almost garbage-less reversible combinatorial logic circuit composed of s and its inverse logic gate in which f is embedded.*

We consider an example of a reversible combinatorial logic circuit composed of switch gates that realizes the logical function $\overline{x_1 \oplus x_2}$ shown in Fig. 4.14. Combining this circuit, its inverse circuit, and a fan-out circuit (Fig. 4.7 (**b**)), we obtain an almost garbage-less circuit that computes $\overline{x_1 \oplus x_2}$ given in Fig. 4.15.

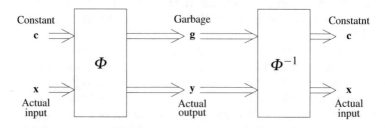

Fig. 4.12 Cleanup of the garbage information by a reversible combinatorial logic circuit Φ and its inverse Φ^{-1}

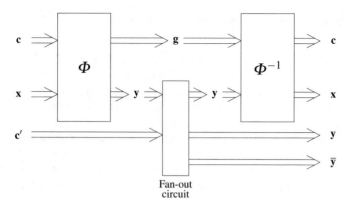

Fig. 4.13 Construction of an "almost garbage-less" reversible combinatorial logic circuit that computes a non-injective logical function [5]

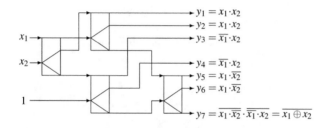

Fig. 4.14 A circuit composed of switch gates that computes the logical function $\overline{x_1 \oplus x_2}$. This circuit produces many garbage outputs

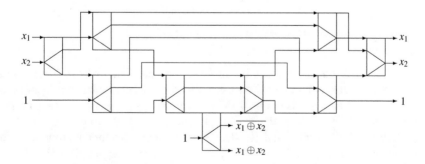

Fig. 4.15 An almost garbage-less circuit composed of switch gates and inverse switch gates that computes the logical function $\overline{x_1 \oplus x_2}$

4.1.5 Realization in the billiard ball model

Fredkin and Toffoli [5] first proposed the *billiard ball model* (BBM), and showed that Fredkin gate is simulated in it. As explained in Sect. 2.2.3, BBM is a reversible physical model of computing consisting of ideal balls and reflectors. Collisions of balls with other balls and reflectors are elastic, and there is no friction.

Interaction gate and switch gate, which are simpler than Fredkin gate, are implemented in BBM. Interaction gate is realized by the collision of two moving balls as shown in Fig. 4.16 [5]. This is the reason why the gate is also called a collision gate. Switch gate is realized as in Fig. 4.17 [5]. Inverse interaction gate and inverse switch gate are obtained by simply inverting the moving directions of balls.

Fig. 4.16   Realization of interaction gate in the billiard ball model [5]

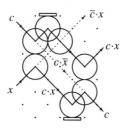

Fig. 4.17   Realization of switch gate in the billiard ball model [5]

There are two methods of constructing Fredkin gate. The first one is shown in Fig. 4.18 in which three interaction gates, and three inverse interaction gates are used [5]. The second one is in Fig. 4.19 in which two switch gates, and two inverse switch gates are used. Note that, in [5], it is written that the circuit in Fig. 4.19 was designed by Feynman and Ressler. Thus, placing reflectors appropriately so that the circuit of Fig. 4.18 or 4.19 is implemented, Fredkin gate is realized as a configuration in BBM.

By above, we see any reversible combinatorial logic circuit can also be implemented in BBM. Since the circuits in Figs. 4.18 and 4.19 have neither constant inputs nor garbage outputs, there is no need to use a ball corresponding to them in the BBM. However, if we construct the almost garbage-less reversible combinato-

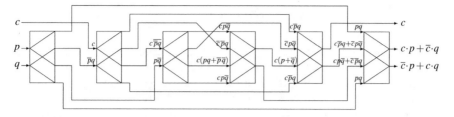

Fig. 4.18 Composing Fredkin gate by three collision gates and three inverse collision gates [5]

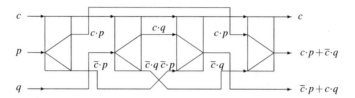

Fig. 4.19 Composing Fredkin gate by two switch gates and two inverse switch gates [5]

rial logic circuit by the method discussed in Sect. 4.1.4 (Fig. 4.13), some amount of constant supply and garbage generation occur in the BBM realization. If such a circuit is used to compose a computing system like a Turing machine, then it operates repeatedly, and thus the total amount of garbage grows considerably. Since supply of constants and disposal of garbage correspond to supply and dissipation of energy, respectively, it is desirable if we can obtain a completely garbage-less circuit. In Sect. 2.3, we designed a circuit composed of rotary elements (REs) that simulates a given reversible sequential machine (RSM), and produces no garbage at all. In Sect. 4.2.3, we shall show that it is also possible to design a completely garbage-less circuit made of Fredkin gates and delay elements that simulates a given RSM, and is completely garbage-less.

4.2 Relation Between Reversible Logic Gates and Reversible Sequential Machines

In this section, we investigate the relation among reversible logic gates, reversible logic elements with memory (RLEMs), and reversible sequential machines (RSMs). In particular, we give a method of realizing an RSM as a completely garbage-less circuit composed of reversible logic gates.

4.2.1 Making Fredkin gate from RE

Fredkin gate is simulated by an RE-circuit, a circuit composed of rotary elements (REs) [9]. Input signals 0 and 1 in Fredkin gate are represented by absence and presence of a particle in the RE-circuit. Since Fredkin gate has three input lines at which signals arrive at the same time, we allow to give two or more particles to the RE-circuit at the same time. But, they should not arrive at each RE simultaneously. Thus, we use a *delay element* shown in Fig. 4.20 to adjust operation timings of each RE in the RE-circuit. Note that RE itself has a unit time delay.

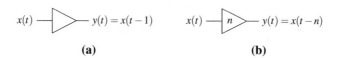

(a)   (b)

Fig. 4.20 (a) A delay element with a unit time delay, and (b) that of n units of time

Figure 4.21 shows RE-circuits (with delay elements) that realize switch gate, and inverse switch gate. Operations of the RE-circuit for switch gate in the case $c = x = 1$ is given in Fig. 4.22 (it is easy to verify its operations in other cases). Combining the circuits for switch gate and inverse switch gate as given in Fig. 4.19, we obtain an RE-circuit shown in Fig. 4.23 that simulates Fredkin gate.

In an RE-circuit that simulates a reversible logic gate, the time delay between input and output must be constant for all the combination of inputs. Otherwise, there arises a problem to connect many logic gates implemented as RE-circuits. The time delay of the RE-circuit for switch gate given in Fig. 4.21 is 7 units of time if $c = 0, x = 1$, while 5 units of time in other cases. Therefore, a delay element of 2 units of time should be inserted at the output line $c \cdot x$ to meet this condition. In the RE-circuit for Fredkin gate (Fig. 4.23) the delay time is adjusted to be always 20 units of time as a whole.

In [10] it is shown that we can construct a circuit that simulates Fredkin gate not only by RE but also by any of the 14 non-degenerate 2-state 3-symbol RLEMs (but we do not give here the circuits).

Although Fredkin gate can be simulated by an RE-circuit as shown in Fig. 4.23, it is *not* a good usage of RE. First, eight copies of RE are required to simulate only one Fredkin gate. Second, as we have already seen in Sect. 2.3, any RSM can be simulated by an RE-circuit with a simple structure. Therefore, if our objective is to construct reversible computing systems, we should look for a direct and efficient method of composing them by RE and by other RLEMs.

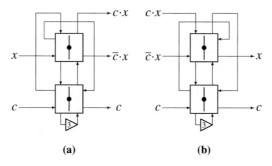

Fig. 4.21 Realization of (**a**) switch gate, and (**b**) inverse switch gate as RE-circuits

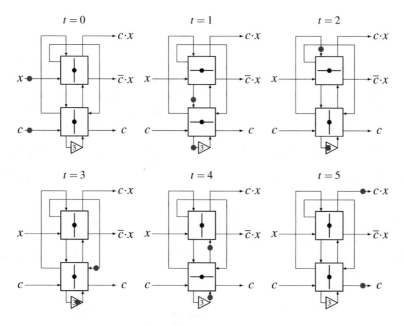

Fig. 4.22 Simulation process of a switch gate by a circuit composed of rotary elements and a delay element in the case $c = x = 1$

4.2.2 Making RE from Fredkin gate

We consider the problem how rotary element (RE) can be simulated by a circuit composed of Fredkin gates and delay elements. In the next subsection we shall show a systematic implementation method of an RSM as a completely garbage-less circuit composed of Fredkin gates and delay elements. Although RE is a kind of an RSM, we give here a particular design of a circuit that simulates RE. It is simpler than the one obtained by the method of the next subsection.

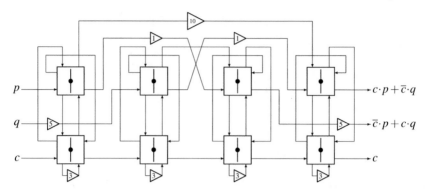

Fig. 4.23 Realization of Fredkin gate by rotary elements and delay elements [9]

Since Fredkin gate itself has no memory, a circuit composed of Fredkin gates that simulates RE must have loops and delay elements in it. The states of RE must be distinguished by circulating a signal "1" in the circuit in different ways.

A circuit that simulates RE is given in Fig. 4.24 that consists of 12 Fredkin gates and many delay elements [8]. Here, we assume that every connecting line between two Fredkin gates has some delay, and thus a delay element is inserted in it. In fact, if Fredkin gate is implemented in a physical system like BBM (Sect. 4.1.5), transmission delay of signals is inevitable. Here, signal "1" in this circuit is represented by a particle in the following figures.

The circuit shown in Fig. 4.24 is in the state H of RE, since a particle exists at the position of "State H". If no other particle exists, then it travels along the bold line, and goes back to the same position after eight units of time. Likewise, if a particle is put at the position of "State V", then it means the circuit is in the state V. Also in this case, the particle travels along a similar loop, and goes back to the same position after eight steps.

If an input particle is given at the port n, s, e, or w when the circulating particle is at the position of "State H" or "State V", then the circuit starts to simulate the operation of RE. Figures 4.25 and 4.26 show the case that the state is H and the input is s, the orthogonal case of Fig. 2.3 **(b)**. As shown in Fig. 4.26 ($t = 8$), it finally goes to the state V and gives the output e', and thus $\delta_{RE}(H, s) = (V, e')$ is correctly simulated. The four Fredkin gates in the leftmost column checks if the orthogonal case occurs. If it is the case, the particle circulating in a loop is moved to another loop by one of the four Fredkin gate in the center column. Then, by the gates in the rightmost column, the other particle goes out from the specified output port. It is easy to follow the operation of the circuit for the parallel case (Fig. 2.3 **(a)**), since two particles do not interact at the same Fredkin gate.

It should be noted that this circuit is a completely garbage-less logic circuit, i.e., it never produces garbage information at all, since the values of the four constant input lines and the four output lines are all 0's. In fact, these four output lines can be connected to the four input lines.

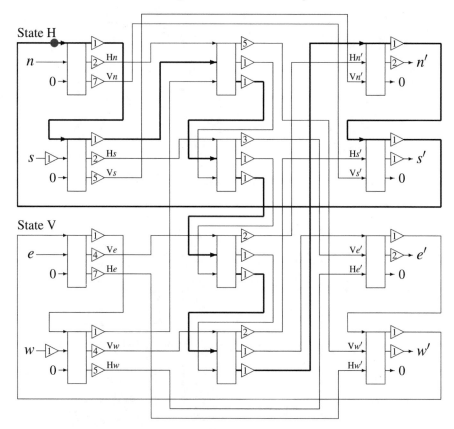

Fig. 4.24 Realization of rotary element by a completely garbage-less circuit composed of Fredkin gates and delay elements [8]. In this figure, the state is H, which is kept by a signal "1" represented by a particle ● that moves along the loop indicated by the bold line

4.2.3 Making reversible sequential machines from Fredkin gate

In the previous subsection, we presented a completely garbage-less circuit composed of Fredkin gates and delay elements that simulates RE. We can, of course, use this circuit to construct RSMs by the method given in Sect. 2.3. Replacing each occurrence of RE of an RE-circuit, e.g., shown in Fig. 2.14, by the circuit of Fig. 4.24, we obtain a circuit that simulates a given RSM. In this subsection, however, we show a direct and systematic method of composing a completely garbage-less circuit out of Fredkin gates and delay elements that simulates an RSM [7].

We first design several building modules, and then they are combined to make a larger circuit that simulates an RSM. To represent a symbol or a state of an RSM in a circuit, we use a "bundle" of decoded lines. That is, for a set of symbols (or states) $X = \{x_1, \ldots, x_n\}$, we prepare a bundle of n signal lines in the circuit. The

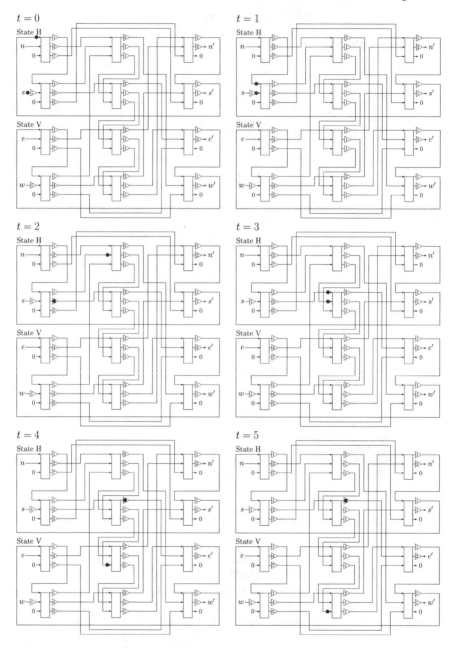

Fig. 4.25 Simulation process of rotary element (RE) by a circuit composed of Fredkin gates and delay elements for the case $\delta_{RE}(H, s) = (V, e')$

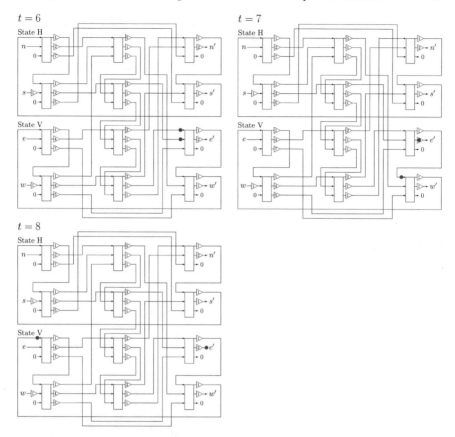

Fig. 4.26 Simulation process of rotary element (RE) by a circuit composed of Fredkin gates and delay elements for the case $\delta_{RE}(H,s) = (V,e')$ (continued)

i-th line in the bundle uniquely corresponds to x_i, and it is also denoted by x_i. If the value of the i-th line is 1, we regard x_i is occurring in the RSM. Hence, just one of the lines $x_1, \ldots, x_n$ must have the value 1. The building modules designed here are as follows. Essentially, they are reversible combinatorial logic circuit that realize injective logical functions. However, they contain delay elements in the circuits, since they will be combined, and feedback loop will be added.

1. Switch module: SWITCH(n)

   It is a building module that branches the input bundle $a_1, \ldots, a_n$ to the output bundle $q \cdot a_1, \ldots, q \cdot a_n$ or $\bar{q} \cdot a_1, \ldots, \bar{q} \cdot a_n$ according to the value of the input q. It is schematically represented by the Fig. 4.27. Here, we pose the following constraints to the inputs.

   (i) If $q = 1$, then just one of the inputs $a_1, \ldots, a_n$ is 1.

   (ii) $q \cdot b = 0$.

   The circuit for SWITCH(3) is given in Fig. 4.28. It is easily verified that this circuit has the desired function. It is also easy to draw the circuit of SWITCH(n) for general n. The total delay between input and output of this module is $2n$.

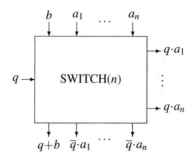

Fig. 4.27 Schematic representation of a switch module SWITCH(n). It is used under the following constraint: If $q = 1$ then just one of $a_1, \ldots, a_n$ is 1, and $q \cdot b = 0$

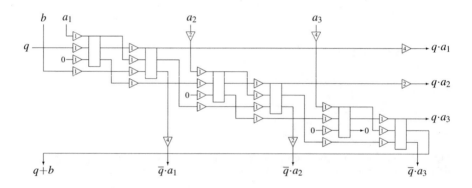

Fig. 4.28 The circuit of SWITCH(3) composed of Fredkin gates and delay elements [7]

2. Delay module: d-DELAY(n)
   The delay module d-DELAY(n) simply consists of n delay elements of d units of time as shown in Fig. 4.29.
3. Decoder module: DECODER(m,n)
   It decodes the combination of values of two input bundles with m and n lines, which are $q_1, \ldots, q_m$, and $a_1, \ldots, a_n$. The decoded result is put to the bundle with mn lines $q_1 \cdot a_1, \ldots, q_m \cdot a_n$. The schematic representation is in Fig. 4.30. It is used under the constraint that exactly one of $q_1, \ldots, q_m$ is 1, and exactly one of $a_1, \ldots, a_n$ is 1. If $q_h = 1$ and $a_i = 1$, then the module will finally give $q_h \cdot a_i = 1$ and $r = 1$. This module is built from switch modules and delay modules as shown in Fig. 4.31. It is clear that this circuit works as above because of the function of SWITCH(n). The delay between input and output of this module is $2mn$. In the following, we also use the inverse circuit of the decoder

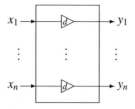

Fig. 4.29 A delay module d-DELAY(n)

module, i.e., DECODER$(m,n)^{-1}$, which is composed of SWITCH$(n)^{-1}$ and d-DELAY$(n)^{-1}$. Although these circuits contain delay elements besides Fredkin gates, their inverse are obtained in a similar manner as in Sect. 4.1.4. For example, SWITCH$(3)^{-1}$ is given in Fig. 4.32. Note that d-DELAY$(n)^{-1}$ is identical with d-DELAY(n).

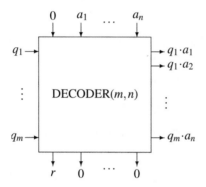

Fig. 4.30 Schematic representation of a decoder module DECODER(m,n). It is used under the following constraint: Exactly one of $a_1,\ldots,a_n$ is 1, and exactly one of $q_1,\ldots,q_m$ is 1

4. Permutation module: PERM(f)
   Let $f : \{1,\ldots,n\} \to \{1,\ldots,n\}$ be a bijection (i.e., permutation over $\{1,\ldots,n\}$). The circuit PERM(f) realizes this permutation as shown in Fig. 4.33.

   We now show a construction method of RSMs using the building modules described above. Let $M = (Q,\Sigma,\Gamma,\delta)$ be a given RSM. We first consider the case $|\Sigma| = |\Gamma|$. The case $|\Sigma| < |\Gamma|$ will be discussed later. We assume $Q = \{q_1,\ldots,q_m\}$, $\Sigma = \{a_1,\ldots,a_n\}$, and $\Gamma = \{s_1,\ldots,s_n\}$. Let $f^\delta : \{1,\ldots,mn\} \to \{1,\ldots,mn\}$ be a mapping defined as follows.

$$\forall q_h, q_j \in Q, \forall a_i \in \Sigma, \forall s_k \in \Gamma (f^\delta((h-1)n+i) = (j-1)n+k \Leftrightarrow \delta(q_h,a_i) = (q_j,s_k))$$

Since δ is a bijection, f^δ is also so, and thus it is a permutation over $\{1,\ldots,mn\}$. Then, the RSM M is realized as a circuit given in Fig. 4.34.

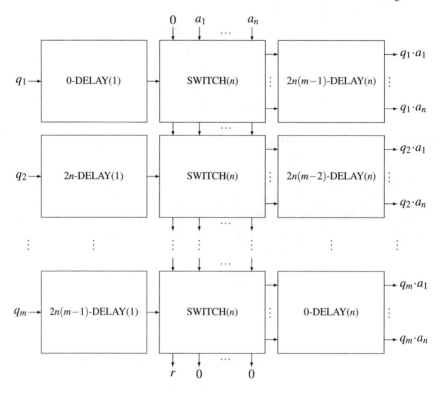

Fig. 4.31 Composing DECODER(m,n) from switch modules and delay modules

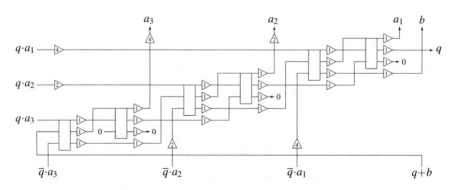

Fig. 4.32 The circuit of the inverse switch module SWITCH$(3)^{-1}$ [7]. It is an inverse circuit of the one shown in Fig. 4.28

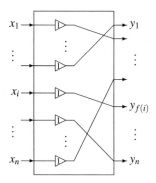

Fig. 4.33 A permutation module PERM(f)

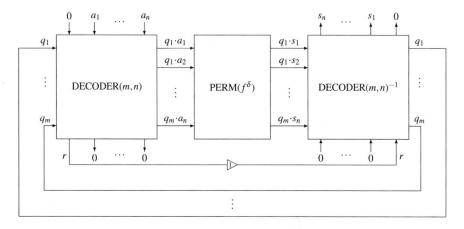

Fig. 4.34 The circuit composed of Fredkin gates and delay elements that simulates the reversible sequential machine $M = (\{q_1, \ldots, q_m\}, \{a_1, \ldots, a_n\}, \{s_1, \ldots, s_n\}, \delta)$ [7]

Assume the present state of M is q_h and the current input symbol is a_i. Then, signals 1's are put on the line q_h and a_i in Fig. 4.34. All other lines have signal 0's. By the function of DECODER(m, n), the combination of q_h and a_i is found, and a signal 1 will appear on the line $q_h \cdot a_i$. If $\delta(q_h, a_i) = (q_j, s_k)$, then the module PERM($f^\delta$) gives a signal 1 on the line $q_j \cdot s_k$. Finally, DECODER(m, n)$^{-1}$ separates the signal on the line $q_j \cdot s_k$ into q_j and s_k, and thus the next state and the output is correctly given. The total delay between input and output is $4mn + 1$, and thus input signal should be given every $4mn + 1$ steps.

Next, we consider the case that the given RSM $M = (Q, \Sigma, \Gamma, \delta)$ is one such that $|\Sigma| < |\Gamma|$. Hence, we assume $\Sigma = \{a_1, \ldots, a_{n_0}\}$, $\Gamma = \{s_1, \ldots, s_n\}$, and $n_0 < n$. In this case, we prepare "dummy" input symbols $a_{n_0+1}, \ldots, a_n$, and let $\Sigma' = \{a_1, \ldots, a_{n_0}, a_{n_0+1}, \ldots, a_n\}$. Since $\delta : Q \times \Sigma \to Q \times \Gamma$ is an injection, and $|Q \times \Sigma'| = |Q \times \Gamma|$, we can effectively find a bijection $\delta' : Q \times \Sigma' \to Q \times \Gamma$ that is an extension of δ, i.e., $\delta'(q_h, a_i) = \delta(q_h, a_i)$ holds for all $q_h \in Q$ and $a_i \in \Sigma$. Thus, replacing the module PERM(f^{δ}) by PERM($f^{\delta'}$) in Fig. 4.34, we obtain a circuit that simulates M. Here, the input lines $a_{n_0+1}, \ldots, a_n$ are not used.

By above, we obtain the following theorem.

Theorem 4.1. *[7] For any RSM M we can construct a completely garbage-less logic circuit composed of Fredkin gates and delay elements that simulates M.*

Combining this method and the one given in Sect. 4.1.5, we can compose a configuration of BBM that simulates a given RSM with only two balls.

4.3 Concluding Remarks

In this chapter, we studied basic properties of reversible logic gates and circuits, in particular, logical universality, garbage-less logic circuits, implementation in the billiard ball model, and the relations to reversible logic elements with memory (RLEMs) and reversible sequential machines (RSMs). There are infinitely many kinds of reversible logic gates, but here we focused on several typical ones, i.e., the Fredkin gate, the Toffoli gate, the interaction gate, and the switch gate.

In Sect. 4.2.3, it was shown that any RSM can be simulated by a completely garbage-less logic circuit composed of Fredkin gates and delay elements. Though the circuit constructed from rotary elements (REs) given in Sect. 2.3 is simpler than the above one for simulating an RSM, this result is useful for designing a computationally universal two-dimensional reversible cellular automaton with a small number of states. This is because the Fredkin gate is further decomposed into interaction gates and inverse interaction gates, or switch gates and inverse switch gates, which are simpler than the Fredkin gate, as in Figs. 4.18 and 4.19. In fact, the switch gate and its inverse can be embedded in a very simple two-dimensional reversible cellular automata (Sects. 12.3, 13.2 and 13.3).

Here, we presented only the topics that will be used in the following chapters, but did not investigate others, especially practical design methods of logic circuits composed of reversible logic gates. Recently, studies on efficient implementation of reversible and quantum logic circuits have been done extensively. On this topic, see, e.g., [1, 3, 6, 12, 13, 14, 15, 18].

References

1. Al-Rabadi, A.N.: Reversible Logic Synthesis. Springer (2004). doi:10.1007/978-3-642-18853-4
2. Bennett, C.H.: Logical reversibility of computation. IBM J. Res. Dev. **17**, 525–532 (1973). doi:10.1147/rd.176.0525
3. De Vos, A.: Reversible Computing: Fundamentals, Quantum Computing, and Applications. Wiley-VCH (2010). doi:10.1002/9783527633999
4. Dieks, D.: Communication by EPR devices. Physics Letters A **92**, 271–272 (1982). doi:10.1016/0375-9601(82)90084-6

5. Fredkin, E., Toffoli, T.: Conservative logic. Int. J. Theoret. Phys. **21**, 219–253 (1982). doi:10.1007/BF01857727
6. Miller, D.M., Maslov, D., Dueck, G.W.: A transformation based algorithm for reversible logic synthesis. In: Proc. Design Automation Conference, pp. 318–323 (2003). doi:10.1109/DAC.2003.1219016
7. Morita, K.: A simple construction method of a reversible finite automaton out of Fredkin gates, and its related problem. Trans. IEICE Japan **E-73**, 978–984 (1990)
8. Morita, K.: Reversible Computing (in Japanese). Kindai Kagaku-sha Co., Ltd., Tokyo, ISBN978-4-7649-0422-4 (2012)
9. Morita, K., Ogiro, T., Tanaka, K., Kato, H.: Classification and universality of reversible logic elements with one-bit memory. In: Proc. MCU 2004 (ed. M. Margenstern), LNCS 3354, pp. 245–256 (2005). doi:10.1007/978-3-540-31834-7_20
10. Ogiro, T., Kanno, A., Tanaka, K., Kato, H., Morita, K.: Nondegenerate 2-state 3-symbol reversible logic elements are all universal. Int. J. Unconventional Comput. **1**, 47–67 (2005)
11. Petri, C.A.: Grundsätzliches zur Beschreibung diskreter Prozesse. In: Proc. 3rd Colloquium über Automatentheorie (eds. W. Händler, E. Peschl, H. Unger), Birkhäuser Verlag, pp. 121–140 (1967). doi:10.1007/978-3-0348-5879-3_10
12. Rice, J.E.: An introduction to reversible latches. The Computer J. **51**, 700–709 (2008). doi:10.1093/comjnl/bxm116
13. Saeedi, M., Markov, I.L.: Synthesis and optimization of reversible circuits - a survey. ACM Comput. Surv. **45**, 21 (2013). doi:10.1145/2431211.2431220
14. Shende, V.V., Prasad, A.K., Markov, I.L., Hayes, J.P.: Synthesis of reversible logic circuits. IEEE Trans. Computer-Aided Design of Integrated Circuits and Systems **22**, 710–722 (2003). doi:10.1109/TCAD.2003.811448
15. Thapliyal, H., Ranganathan, N.: Design of reversible sequential circuits optimizing quantum cost, delay, and garbage outputs. ACM Journal on Emerging Technologies in Computing Systems **6**, 14:1–14:31 (2010). doi:10.1145/1877745.1877748
16. Toffoli, T.: Reversible computing. In: Automata, Languages and Programming (eds. J.W. de Bakker, J. van Leeuwen), LNCS 85, pp. 632–644 (1980). doi:10.1007/3-540-10003-2_104
17. Toffoli, T.: Bicontinuous extensions of invertible combinatorial functions. Math. Syst. Theory **14**, 12–23 (1981). doi:10.1007/BF01752388
18. Wille, R., Drechsler, R.: Towards a Design Flow for Reversible Logic. Springer (2010). doi:10.1007/978-90-481-9579-4
19. Wootters, W.K., Zurek, W.H.: A single quantum cannot be cloned. Nature **299**, 802–803 (1982). doi:10.1038/299802a0

Chapter 5
Reversible Turing Machines

Abstract A reversible Turing machine (RTM) is a basic model for studying computational universality, and computational complexity in reversible computing. In this chapter, after giving definitions on RTMs, we explain the method of Bennett for constructing a three-tape RTM that simulates a given irreversible TM. By this, computational universality of the class of three-tape RTMs is derived. We then clarify basic properties of RTMs, and study several variations of RTMs. In particular, we give simplification methods for RTMs. They are methods for reducing the number of tapes, the number of tape symbols, and the number of states of RTMs. From them, the computational universality of one-tape two-symbol RTMs with one-way infinite tape, and one-tape three state RTMs is derived. These results are useful for showing the computational universality of other reversible systems, and for composing reversible computing machines out of reversible logic elements.

Keywords reversible Turing machine, quadruple formulation, quintuple formulation, computational universality, simplification of Turing machine

5.1 Turing Machines and Reversibility

A Turing machine (TM) is a standard model of computing in the traditional theory of computing. According to the Church-Turing thesis [4, 15], the intuitive notion of "effective computability" is characterized by a TM. In this sense, the class of TMs is computationally universal. Since a TM has a simple structure, it is also convenient to make use of a reversible version of a TM as a standard model in the theory of reversible computing. In fact, we shall see that a TM still keeps computational universality even if reversibility constraint is added (Sect. 5.2).

Lecerf [8] first investigated reversible Turing machines (RTMs), and showed the unsolvability of the halting problem and some related problems on them. Bennett [1, 2, 3] studied them from the standpoint of thermodynamics of computing. He showed that every one-tape irreversible TM is simulated by a three-tape RTM without leaving garbage information on the tapes when it halts [1], and thus the latter RTM is computationally universal.

In this chapter, we study basic properties of RTMs. We first give definitions on RTMs, in particular, the reversibility condition for a TM (Sect. 5.1). We shall see that reversibility is defined symmetrically with determinism, and thus an RTM can be regarded as a "backward deterministic" TM. Then, we explain the method of Bennett that converts a given one-tape irreversible TM into a three-tape RTM (Sect. 5.2). Next, we give several variations of RTMs, and show that RTMs can be converted into restricted types of RTMs. In particular, we show methods of converting two-way infinite tapes into one-way infinite ones, and reducing the numbers of tapes, tape symbols, and states (Sect. 5.3). Hence, some restricted classes of RTMs such as one-tape two-symbol RTMs, and one-tape three-state RTMs are also computationally universal. These results are useful for proving the computational universality of other reversible systems, and for giving universal reversible Turing machines (Chap. 7). It should also be noted that if a TM satisfies the reversibility condition, then it is realized as a garbage-less circuit composed only of reversible logic elements as will be shown in Chap. 6, and thus it is further realized in the billiard ball model (see Sect. 2.2.3).

5.1.1 Basic definitions on reversible Turing machines (RTMs)

Here, we define TMs in the quadruple and quintuple forms, and then give the notions of determinism and reversibility, instantaneous descriptions, and transition relations.

5.1.1.1 One-tape TMs in the quadruple and quintuple forms

We give two kinds of formulations on TMs, i.e., the quadruple formulation, and the quintuple formulation. In the quadruple form, the operations of read-write and head-shift are separated. If we use this formulation, we can easily obtain an "inverse" RTM of a given RTM. By this, a garbage-less RTM that simulates a given irreversible TM was designed in [1]. On the other hand, the quintuple form is convenient for describing RTMs concisely, since the operations of read-write and head-shift are combined. In the following, we mainly use the quintuple form. However, we sometimes use the quadruple form depending on the purpose.

A one-tape Turing machine (TM) consists of a finite control, a read-write head, and a two-way infinite tape divided into squares in which symbols are written (Fig. 5.1). Formal definitions of a TM in the quadruple form and in the quintuple form are given below.

Definition 5.1. A *one-tape Turing machine (TM) in the quadruple form* is defined by

$$T = (Q, S, q_0, F, s_0, \delta),$$

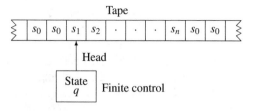

Fig. 5.1 A one-tape Turing machine (TM)

where Q is a non-empty finite set of states, S is a non-empty finite set of tape symbols, q_0 is an *initial state* $(q_0 \in Q)$, F is a set of *final states* $(F \subseteq Q)$, and s_0 is a special *blank symbol* $(s_0 \in S)$. The sixth item δ is a move relation, which is a subset of $(Q \times S \times S \times Q) \cup (Q \times \{/\} \times \{-1, 0, +1\} \times Q)$. The symbol "/" means that T does not read a tape symbol. The symbols "-1", "0", and "$+1$" are *shift directions* of the head, which stand for "left-shift", "zero-shift", and "right-shift", respectively. Each element of δ is a *quadruple* of the form $[p, s, s', q] \in (Q \times S \times S \times Q)$, or $[p, /, d, q] \in (Q \times \{/\} \times \{-1, 0, +1\} \times Q)$. A quadruple is a kind of an *instruction* for T, which can be regarded as an imperative statement to T. The quadruple $[p, s, s', q]$ is called a *read-write quadruple* or a *read-write rule*. It means if T reads the symbol s in the state p, then write s', and go to the state q. The quadruple $[p, /, d, q]$ is called a *shift quadruple* or a *shift rule*. It means if T is in the state p, then shift the head to the direction d, and go to the state q. We assume each state $q_f \in F$ is a *halting state*, i.e., there is no quadruple of the form $[q_f, x, y, q]$ in δ.

Note that, since a shift direction of the head is represented by $d \in \{-1, 0, +1\}$, the inverse of the direction d can be simply represented by $-d$. But, in the following, we also use "$-$" and "$+$" instead of "-1", and "$+1$" for simplicity.

Also note that a final state in F is an "answering state" that gives an output for a given input on the tape. Final states are important when we formulate a TM as an acceptor of a formal language (see Sect. 8.1.1). In such a case, a final state is considered as an *accepting state* for a given input word. On the other hand, there is also a case where a set F of final states is not specified. In particular, when we investigate a problem of reducing the number of states of TMs, F is not specified (see Sects. 5.3.4, 5.3.5, and Chap. 7).

Definition 5.2. A *one-tape Turing machine (TM) in the quintuple form* is defined by

$$T = (Q, S, q_0, F, s_0, \delta),$$

where Q, S, q_0, F and s_0 are the same as in Definition 5.1. Here, δ is a move relation, which is a subset of $(Q \times S \times S \times \{-1, 0, +1\} \times Q)$. The symbols "$-1$", "$0$", and "$+1$" are also the same as in Definition 5.1. Each element of δ is a *quintuple* of the form $[p, s, s', d, q]$, which is called a *rule* of T. It means if T reads the symbol s in the state p, then write s', shift the head to the direction d, and go to the state q.

5.1.1.2 Determinism and reversibility of one-tape TMs

Next, determinism and reversibility of TMs are defined. Although we study mainly
deterministic TMs in this book (but in Sect. 8.1 nondeterministic TMs are also investigated), δ is given as a "relation" rather than a "function". This is because determinism and reversibility can be defined symmetrically by this formulation. Thus,
we can see reversible TMs are "backward deterministic" ones.

Definition 5.3. Let $T = (Q, S, q_0, F, s_0, \delta)$ be a TM in the quadruple form. We call
T a *deterministic TM*, if the following holds for any pair of distinct quadruples
$[p_1, x_1, y_1, q_1]$ and $[p_2, x_2, y_2, q_2]$ in δ.

$$(p_1 = p_2) \;\Rightarrow\; (x_1 \neq / \;\wedge\; x_2 \neq / \;\wedge\; x_1 \neq x_2)$$

It means that for any pair of distinct rules, if the present states are the same, then
they are both read-write rules, and the read symbols are different.

We call T a *reversible TM* (RTM), if the following holds for any pair of distinct
quadruples $[p_1, x_1, y_1, q_1]$ and $[p_2, x_2, y_2, q_2]$ in δ.

$$(q_1 = q_2) \;\Rightarrow\; (x_1 \neq / \;\wedge\; x_2 \neq / \;\wedge\; y_1 \neq y_2)$$

It means that for any pair of distinct rules, if the next states are the same, then they
are both read-write rules, and the written symbols are different. The above is called
the *reversibility condition* for TMs in the quadruple form.

Definition 5.4. Let $T = (Q, S, q_0, F, s_0, \delta)$ be a TM in the quintuple form. We call
T a *deterministic TM*, if the following holds for any pair of distinct quintuples
$[p_1, s_1, t_1, d_1, q_1]$ and $[p_2, s_2, t_2, d_2, q_2]$ in δ.

$$(p_1 = p_2) \;\Rightarrow\; (s_1 \neq s_2)$$

It means that for any pair of distinct rules, if the present states are the same, then the
read symbols are different.

We call T a *reversible TM* (RTM), if the following holds for any pair of distinct
quintuples $[p_1, s_1, t_1, d_1, q_1]$ and $[p_2, s_2, t_2, d_2, q_2]$ in δ.

$$(q_1 = q_2) \;\Rightarrow\; (d_1 = d_2 \;\wedge\; t_1 \neq t_2)$$

It means that for any pair of distinct rules, if the next states are the same, then the
shift directions are the same, and the written symbols are different. The above is
called the *reversibility condition* for TMs in the quintuple form.

In the following, we consider mainly deterministic TMs, and thus the word "deterministic" is omitted. Hence, by a "reversible TM" (RTM), we mean a deterministic reversible TM. Note that, however, in Sect. 8.1 nondeterministic TMs are also
studied, and thus a different terminology will be used only there.

5.1.1.3 Instantaneous descriptions of TMs and transition relation on them

An instantaneous description (ID) of a TM is an expression to denote its computational configuration (i.e., a whole state) [6].

Definition 5.5. Let $T = (Q, S, q_0, F, s_0, \delta)$ be a one-tape TM. We assume $Q \cap S = \emptyset$ (otherwise, rename some elements in Q or S). An *instantaneous description* (ID) of T is a string of the form $\alpha q \beta$ such that $q \in Q$ and $\alpha, \beta \in S^*$. The set of all IDs of T is denoted by $\mathrm{ID}(T)$, i.e., $\mathrm{ID}(T) = \{\alpha q \beta \mid \alpha \in S^* \wedge \beta \in S^* \wedge q \in Q\}$. The ID $\alpha q \beta$ describes the *computational configuration* (i.e., the whole state) of T such that the content of the tape is $\alpha\beta$ (the remaining part of the tape contains only blank symbols), and T is reading the leftmost symbol of β (if $\beta \neq \lambda$) or s_0 (if $\beta = \lambda$) in the state q. An ID $\alpha q \beta$ is called a *standard form ID* if $\alpha \in (S - \{s_0\})S^* \cup \{\lambda\}$, and $\beta \in S^*(S - \{s_0\}) \cup \{\lambda\}$. Namely, a standard form ID is obtained from a general ID by removing superfluous blank symbols from the left and the right ends. An ID $\alpha q_0 \beta$ is called an *initial ID*. An ID $\alpha q \beta$ is called a *final ID* if $q \in F$.

We now define the transition relation $\vdash_{\overline{T}}$ on $\mathrm{ID}(T)$ in Definitions 5.6 and 5.7. Note that, actually, this relation is defined on the set of standard form IDs. The relation $\vdash_{\overline{T}}$ describes the transition between a pair of computational configurations of T. In the following definitions, we also define the notions of "applicability" and "reverse applicability" of a rule to an ID.

Definition 5.6. Let $T = (Q, S, q_0, F, s_0, \delta)$ be a TM in the quadruple form. The *transition relation* $\vdash_{\overline{T}}$ on $\mathrm{ID}(T)$ is defined as the one that satisfies the following: For every $p, q \in Q$, $\alpha \in (S - \{s_0\})S^* \cup \{\lambda\}$, $\beta \in S^*(S - \{s_0\}) \cup \{\lambda\}$, and $s, s', t \in S$, the relations (1) – (16) holds.

$$(1) \quad \alpha p s \beta \vdash_{\overline{T}} \alpha q s' \beta \quad \text{if } [p, s, s', q] \in \delta \wedge \beta \neq \lambda.$$
$$(2) \quad \alpha p s \vdash_{\overline{T}} \alpha q s' \quad \text{if } [p, s, s', q] \in \delta \wedge s' \neq s_0.$$
$$(3) \quad \alpha p s \vdash_{\overline{T}} \alpha q \quad \text{if } [p, s, s_0, q] \in \delta.$$
$$(4) \quad \alpha p \vdash_{\overline{T}} \alpha q s' \quad \text{if } [p, s_0, s', q] \in \delta \wedge s' \neq s_0.$$
$$(5) \quad \alpha p \vdash_{\overline{T}} \alpha q \quad \text{if } [p, s_0, s_0, q] \in \delta.$$
$$(6) \quad \alpha p s \beta \vdash_{\overline{T}} \alpha s q \beta \quad \text{if } [p, /, +, q] \in \delta \wedge \alpha \neq \lambda.$$
$$(7) \quad p s \beta \vdash_{\overline{T}} s q \beta \quad \text{if } [p, /, +, q] \in \delta \wedge s \neq s_0.$$
$$(8) \quad p s_0 \beta \vdash_{\overline{T}} q \beta \quad \text{if } [p, /, +, q] \in \delta.$$
$$(9) \quad \alpha p \vdash_{\overline{T}} \alpha s_0 q \quad \text{if } [p, /, +, q] \in \delta \wedge \alpha \neq \lambda.$$
$$(10) \quad p \vdash_{\overline{T}} q \quad \text{if } [p, /, +, q] \in \delta.$$
$$(11) \quad \alpha p \beta \vdash_{\overline{T}} \alpha q \beta \quad \text{if } [p, /, 0, q] \in \delta.$$
$$(12) \quad \alpha t p \beta \vdash_{\overline{T}} \alpha q t \beta \quad \text{if } [p, /, -, q] \in \delta \wedge \beta \neq \lambda.$$
$$(13) \quad \alpha t p \vdash_{\overline{T}} \alpha q t \quad \text{if } [p, /, -, q] \in \delta \wedge t \neq s_0.$$
$$(14) \quad \alpha s_0 p \vdash_{\overline{T}} \alpha q \quad \text{if } [p, /, -, q] \in \delta.$$
$$(15) \quad p \beta \vdash_{\overline{T}} q s_0 \beta \quad \text{if } [p, /, -, q] \in \delta \wedge \beta \neq \lambda.$$
$$(16) \quad p \vdash_{\overline{T}} q \quad \text{if } [p, /, -, q] \in \delta.$$

Here, we assume there is no other case than (1) – (16), in which $\alpha p \beta \vdash_{\overline{T}} \alpha' q \beta'$ holds for some $\alpha, \alpha', \beta, \beta' \in S^*$ and $p, q \in Q$. Each rule in (1) – (16) are called *applicable* to the ID of the left-hand side of $\vdash_T$. By applying the rule to it, the ID of the right-hand side is obtained. Likewise, each rule in (1) – (16) are also called *reversely applicable* to the ID of the right-hand side of $\vdash_T$. By reversely applying the rule to it, the ID of the left-hand side is obtained.

Definition 5.7. Let $T = (Q, S, q_0, F, s_0, \delta)$ be a TM in the quintuple form. The *transition relation* $\vdash_T$ on $\mathrm{ID}(T)$ is defined as the one that satisfies the following: For every $p, q \in Q$, $\alpha \in (S - \{s_0\})S^* \cup \{\lambda\}$, $\beta \in S^*(S - \{s_0\}) \cup \{\lambda\}$, and $s, s', t \in S$, the relations (1) – (20) holds.

$$
\begin{aligned}
&(1)\ \ \alpha p s \beta \vdash_T \alpha s' q \beta && \text{if } [p, s, s', +, q] \in \delta \wedge \alpha \neq \lambda. \\
&(2)\ \ p s \beta \vdash_T s' q \beta && \text{if } [p, s, s', +, q] \in \delta \wedge s' \neq s_0. \\
&(3)\ \ p s \beta \vdash_T q \beta && \text{if } [p, s, s_0, +, q] \in \delta. \\
&(4)\ \ \alpha p \vdash_T \alpha s' q && \text{if } [p, s_0, s', +, q] \in \delta \wedge \alpha \neq \lambda. \\
&(5)\ \ p \vdash_T s' q && \text{if } [p, s_0, s', +, q] \in \delta \wedge s' \neq s_0. \\
&(6)\ \ p \vdash_T q && \text{if } [p, s_0, s_0, +, q] \in \delta. \\
&(7)\ \ \alpha p s \beta \vdash_T \alpha q s' \beta && \text{if } [p, s, s', 0, q] \in \delta \wedge \beta \neq \lambda. \\
&(8)\ \ \alpha p s \vdash_T \alpha q s' && \text{if } [p, s, s', 0, q] \in \delta \wedge s' \neq s_0. \\
&(9)\ \ \alpha p s \vdash_T \alpha q && \text{if } [p, s, s_0, 0, q] \in \delta. \\
&(10)\ \ \alpha p \vdash_T \alpha q s' && \text{if } [p, s_0, s', 0, q] \in \delta \wedge s' \neq s_0. \\
&(11)\ \ \alpha p \vdash_T \alpha q && \text{if } [p, s_0, s_0, 0, q] \in \delta. \\
&(12)\ \ \alpha t p s \beta \vdash_T \alpha q t s' \beta && \text{if } [p, s, s', -, q] \in \delta \wedge \beta \neq \lambda. \\
&(13)\ \ \alpha t p s \vdash_T \alpha q t s' && \text{if } [p, s, s', -, q] \in \delta \wedge s' \neq s_0. \\
&(14)\ \ p s \beta \vdash_T q s_0 s' \beta && \text{if } [p, s, s', -, q] \in \delta \wedge \beta \neq \lambda. \\
&(15)\ \ p s \vdash_T q s_0 s' && \text{if } [p, s, s', -, q] \in \delta \wedge s' \neq s_0. \\
&(16)\ \ p s \vdash_T q && \text{if } [p, s, s_0, -, q] \in \delta. \\
&(17)\ \ \alpha t p \vdash_T \alpha q t s' && \text{if } [p, s_0, s', -, q] \in \delta \wedge s' \neq s_0. \\
&(18)\ \ \alpha t p \vdash_T \alpha q t && \text{if } [p, s_0, s_0, -, q] \in \delta. \\
&(19)\ \ p \vdash_T q s_0 s' && \text{if } [p, s_0, s', -, q] \in \delta \wedge s' \neq s_0. \\
&(20)\ \ p \vdash_T q && \text{if } [p, s_0, s_0, -, q] \in \delta.
\end{aligned}
$$

We assume there is no other case than (1) – (20), in which $\alpha p \beta \vdash_T \alpha' q \beta'$ holds for some $\alpha, \alpha', \beta, \beta' \in S^*$ and $p, q \in Q$. The notions of *applicability* and *reverse applicability* of a rule to an ID are defined similarly as in Definition 5.6.

The above definitions of the relation $\vdash_T$ on $\mathrm{ID}(T)$ are slightly complex, since there are many cases to consider. However, they are for removing superfluous blank symbols from IDs. In fact, the notion of transition among IDs itself is rather straightforward.

Let $T = (Q, S, q_0, F, s_0, \delta)$ be a TM, and $\vdash_T$ be the transition relation on $\mathrm{ID}(T)$. The reflexive and transitive closure of $\vdash_T$ is denoted by $\vdash_T^*$. The transitive closure is denoted by $\vdash_T^+$. The relation of n-step transition is denoted by $\vdash_T^n$. Let γ be an ID of T. We say γ is a *halting ID*, if there is no ID γ' such that $\gamma \vdash_T \gamma'$. Let $\alpha_i, \beta_i \in S^*$, and $p_i \in Q$ $(n \in \mathbb{N}, i = 0, 1, \ldots, n)$. We say $\alpha_0 p_0 \beta_0 \vdash_T \alpha_1 p_1 \beta_1 \vdash_T \cdots \vdash_T \alpha_n p_n \beta_n$ is a *complete computing process* of T starting from $\alpha_0 p_0 \beta_0$, if $\alpha_0 p_0 \beta_0$ is an initial ID (i.e., $p_0 = q_0$), and $\alpha_n p_n \beta_n$ is a halting ID.

We now give a simple example of an RTM.

Example 5.1. Consider the RTM T_{copy} in the quintuple form:

$$T_{\text{copy}} = (Q_{\text{copy}}, \{0, 1, a, m\}, q_{\text{start}}, \{q_{\text{final}}\}, 0, \delta_{\text{copy}}).$$

Here, $Q_{\text{copy}} = \{q_{\text{start}}, q_{\text{find0}}, q_{\text{next0}}, q_{\text{return}}, q_{\text{final}}\}$, and δ_{copy} is as follows.

$$\delta_{\text{copy}} = \{\ [q_{\text{start}}, 1, m, +, q_{\text{find0}}],\quad [q_{\text{start}}, a, a, 0, q_{\text{final}}],\quad [q_{\text{find0}}, 0, 1, +, q_{\text{next0}}],$$
$$[q_{\text{find0}}, 1, 1, +, q_{\text{find0}}],\quad [q_{\text{find0}}, a, a, +, q_{\text{find0}}],\quad [q_{\text{next0}}, 0, 0, -, q_{\text{return}}],$$
$$[q_{\text{return}}, 1, 1, -, q_{\text{return}}],\quad [q_{\text{return}}, a, a, -, q_{\text{return}}],\quad [q_{\text{return}}, m, 1, +, q_{\text{start}}]\ \}$$

We can also describe δ_{copy} in a tabular form as in Table 5.1. It is easy to see that T_{copy} is deterministic and reversible. Reversibility of T_{copy} is verified in the following manner. Consider, for example, a pair of quintuples $[q_{\text{start}}, 1, m, +, q_{\text{find0}}]$ and $[q_{\text{find0}}, 1, 1, +, q_{\text{find0}}]$. They have the same next state q_{find0}, and the same shift direction $+$, but have different tape symbols m and 1 to be written. Hence, this pair satisfies the reversibility condition in Definition 5.4. Checking all the pairs of quintuples in δ_{copy} in a similar manner, we can verify that T_{copy} is reversible.

Table 5.1 The move relation δ_{copy} of the RTM T_{copy} in the quintuple form described in the tabular form

	0	1	a	m
q_{start}		$m, +, q_{\text{find0}}$	$a, 0, q_{\text{final}}$	
q_{find0}	$1, +, q_{\text{next0}}$	$1, +, q_{\text{find0}}$	$a, +, q_{\text{find0}}$	
q_{next0}	$0, -, q_{\text{return}}$			
q_{return}		$1, -, q_{\text{return}}$	$a, -, q_{\text{return}}$	$1, +, q_{\text{start}}$
q_{final}				

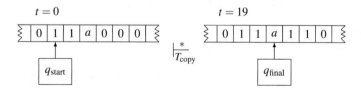

Fig. 5.2 An RTM T_{copy} that copies a given unary number

Given a unary expression 1^n of a natural number n, T_{copy} copies it to the right of the delimiter a as shown in Fig. 5.2. More precisely, the complete computing process of T_{copy} for $n = 2$ is described below, where $11 q_{\text{final}} a 1 1$ is a halting ID.

$$
\begin{aligned}
& q_{start}\,1\,1\,a && \vdash_{T_{copy}} m\,q_{find0}\,1\,a && \vdash_{T_{copy}} m\,1\,q_{find0}\,a && \vdash_{T_{copy}} m\,1\,a\,q_{find0} \\
& \vdash_{T_{copy}} m\,1\,a\,1\,q_{next0} && \vdash_{T_{copy}} m\,1\,a\,q_{return}\,1 && \vdash_{T_{copy}} m\,1\,q_{return}\,a\,1 && \vdash_{T_{copy}} m\,q_{return}\,1\,a\,1 \\
& \vdash_{T_{copy}} q_{return}\,m\,1\,a\,1 && \vdash_{T_{copy}} 1\,q_{start}\,1\,a\,1 && \vdash_{T_{copy}} 1\,m\,q_{find0}\,a\,1 && \vdash_{T_{copy}} 1\,m\,a\,q_{find0}\,1 \\
& \vdash_{T_{copy}} 1\,m\,a\,1\,q_{find0} && \vdash_{T_{copy}} 1\,m\,a\,1\,1\,q_{next0} && \vdash_{T_{copy}} 1\,m\,a\,1\,q_{return}\,1 && \vdash_{T_{copy}} 1\,m\,a\,q_{return}\,1\,1 \\
& \vdash_{T_{copy}} 1\,m\,q_{return}\,a\,1\,1 && \vdash_{T_{copy}} 1\,q_{return}\,m\,a\,1\,1 && \vdash_{T_{copy}} 1\,1\,q_{start}\,a\,1\,1 && \vdash_{T_{copy}} 1\,1\,q_{final}\,a\,1\,1
\end{aligned}
$$

The RTM T_{copy} starts from the initial state q_{start} reading the leftmost symbol 1 of the given unary expression. The state q_{start} is the one to find the symbol 1 to be copied, and to mark it by m. If it is the case, T_{copy} goes to the state q_{find0} to find the symbol 0 to the right. When T_{copy} finds 0, it rewrites the symbol 0 into 1. By this, one symbol 1 is copied. Then, it further shifts its head to the right, and goes to q_{next0} to read the next 0. After that, T_{copy} goes back to the marked position by the state q_{return} to repeat the above process of copying a single symbol 1. If T_{copy} reads the delimiter a in the state q_{start}, then it enters the state q_{final}, and halts. Thus, the following relation holds for all $n \in \mathbb{Z}_+$.

$$ q_{start}\,1^n\,a \;\vdash^{*}_{T_{copy}}\; 1^n\,q_{final}\,a\,1^n $$

Note that, in the construction of the RTM T_{copy}, the state q_{next0} is necessary to make it reversible. If we remove the state q_{next0}, and replace the quintuple $[q_{find0}, 0, 1, +, q_{next0}]$ by $[q_{find0}, 0, 1, -, q_{return}]$, then the pair $[q_{find0}, 0, 1, -, q_{return}]$ and $[q_{return}, 1, 1, -, q_{return}]$ violates the reversibility condition, though it still works as an irreversible TM that copies a unary number.   □

The next lemma shows that if a TM T is deterministic (reversible, respectively), then every computational configuration of T has at most one successor (predecessor) configuration. Although the proof of the lemma is rather straightforward, it has the following meaning. If T is deterministic, then the transition relation $\vdash_{T}$ among configuration becomes a partial function. Furthermore, if T is deterministic and reversible, then the partial function $\vdash_{T}$ becomes injective. Namely, these "global" properties on configurations are determined by the "local" properties (i.e., determinism and reversibility) of a TM. On the other hand, as we shall see in Sect. 10.3.1, this is not the case in (traditional) cellular automata.

Lemma 5.1. *The following statements hold for any TM $T = (Q, S, q_0, F, s_0, \delta)$ (in the quadruple form or in the quintuple form).*

1. *If T is deterministic, then for any standard form ID γ of T, there is at most one standard form ID γ' such that $\gamma \vdash_{T} \gamma'$.*
2. *If T is reversible, then for any standard form ID γ of T, there is at most one standard form ID γ' such that $\gamma' \vdash_{T} \gamma$.*

Proof. 1. Assume T is deterministic, and the ID γ is written as $\gamma = \alpha p \beta$ for some $\alpha, \beta \in S^*$ and $p \in Q$. Let b be the leftmost symbol of β (if $\beta = \lambda$, then s_0). In the case of quadruple form, applicable rules are of the form $[p, /, d, p']$ or $[p, b, s, p']$ by Definition 5.6. In the case of quintuple form, applicable rules are of the form $[p, b, s, d, p']$ by Definition 5.7. Since T satisfies the condition for determinism in

Definition 5.3 or 5.4, there is at most one rule in δ applicable to $\alpha p\beta$. Hence, there is at most one ID γ' such that $\gamma \vdash_{T} \gamma'$.

2. Assume T is reversible, and the ID γ is written as $\gamma = \alpha p\beta$ for some $\alpha, \beta \in S^*$ and $p \in Q$. Let a be the rightmost symbol of α (if $\alpha = \lambda$, then s_0), b be the leftmost symbol of β (if $\beta = \lambda$, then s_0), and b' be the second symbol of β from the left (if $|\beta| < 2$, then s_0). First, consider the case of the quadruple form. Then, reversely applicable rules are of the form $[p', /, d, p]$ or $[p', s, b, p]$ by Definition 5.6. Since T satisfies the condition for reversibility in Definition 5.3, there is at most one rule in δ reversely applicable to $\alpha p\beta$. Second, consider the case of the quintuple form. Then, reversely applicable rules are of the form $[p', s, a, +, p]$, $[p', s, b, 0, p]$, or $[p', s, b', -, p]$ by Definition 5.7. Since T satisfies the reversibility condition in Definition 5.4, there is at most one rule in δ reversely applicable to $\alpha p\beta$. Hence, in both cases, there is at most one ID γ' such that $\gamma' \vdash_{T} \gamma$. □

5.1.2 Notion of simulation and computational universality

Since we often construct a TM that simulates another TM, we define the notion of simulation according to the definition by Rogozhin [13].

Definition 5.8. For any deterministic TM T, let $\psi_T : \mathrm{ID}(T) \to \mathrm{ID}(T)$ be a partial recursive function defined as follows.

$$\forall \alpha, \beta \in \mathrm{ID}(T) \ (\psi_T(\alpha) = \beta \ \Leftrightarrow \ (\alpha \vdash_{T}^{*} \beta \wedge \beta \text{ is a halting ID}))$$

Namely, $\psi_T(\alpha)$ is the halting ID reachable from α, if T eventually halts. Otherwise, it is undefined.

Let T and $\tilde{T}$ be TMs. If there exist total recursive functions $c : \mathrm{ID}(T) \to \mathrm{ID}(\tilde{T})$, and $d : \mathrm{ID}(\tilde{T}) \to (\mathrm{ID}(T) \cup \{\bot\})$ that satisfy the following, then we say $\tilde{T}$ simulates T. Note that $d(\tilde{\alpha}) = \bot$ for an ID $\tilde{\alpha}$ of $\tilde{T}$ means there is no ID α of T that corresponds to $\tilde{\alpha}$. Here, c and d are called an *encoding function*, and a *decoding function*, respectively. (For the theory of recursive functions, see, e.g., [7, 9].)

$$\forall \alpha \in \mathrm{ID}(T)$$
$$((\psi_T(\alpha) \text{ is defined} \ \Rightarrow \ d(\psi_{\tilde{T}}(c(\alpha))) = \psi_T(\alpha)) \wedge$$
$$(\psi_T(\alpha) \text{ is undefined} \ \Rightarrow \ \psi_{\tilde{T}}(c(\alpha)) \text{ is undefined}))$$

When we construct a TM $\tilde{T}$ that simulates a given TM T below, we do not give exact descriptions of the functions c and d, since they are usually clear from the construction method of $\tilde{T}$, though their precise description may be lengthy.

In the following chapters, we also deal with computing systems other than Turing machines such as counter machines (Sect. 9.2), cellular automata (Chaps. 10–13), and others. In many cases, the notion of simulation are similarly defined as above: Definition 9.5 is for counter machines, and Definitions 11.2 and 12.2 are for cellular automata. Note that, when simulating an acceptor of a formal language, only an answer of yes or no is required, and thus the notion of simulation should be modified (see Theorems 8.2, 8.3 and 9.3).

Next, we define computational universality of a class $\mathscr{S}$ of computing systems based on TMs. Here, $\mathscr{S}$ can be any class of computing systems provided that the notion of simulation is defined appropriately for the systems in $\mathscr{S}$. In this chapter, however, we consider only the cases such that $\mathscr{S}$ is some restricted class of RTMs, e.g., the class of one-tape two-symbol RTMs.

Definition 5.9. A class $\mathscr{S}$ of computing systems is called *computationally univer-sal* (or *Turing universal*) if for each one-tape TM there exists a system in $\mathscr{S}$ that simulates the TM.

It is known that for any partial recursive function, there is a one-tape Turing machine that computes it, and vice versa (see e.g., [9]). Therefore, we can also define the notion of computational universality based on partial recursive functions.

The above notion of universality is basically for a "class" of computing systems, and in this chapter, we show that various subclasses of RTMs are computationally universal. On the other hand, as we shall see in Chap. 7, there is an RTM that can simulate *any* one-tape TM, which is called a universal RTM (Definition 7.1). We also call such a specific RTM computationally universal.

In Chaps. 11–13 we study computational universality of cellular automata (CAs). There, the term "Turing universality" will be used as the synonym of computa-tional universality, since there is another universality called "intrinsic universality" (Sect. 12.5).

5.1.3 Conversion between the quadruple and quintuple forms

We show that any RTM in the quadruple form can be converted into an RTM in the quintuple form, and vice versa.

Lemma 5.2. *For any RTM $T = (Q, S, q_0, F, s_0, \delta)$ in the quadruple form, we can construct an RTM $\hat{T} = (Q, S, q_0, F, s_0, \hat{\delta})$ in the quintuple form that satisfies the fol-lowing.*

$$\forall \alpha_1, \alpha_2, \beta_1, \beta_2 \in S^* \ \forall q_1, q_2 \in Q$$
$$((\alpha_1 q_1 \beta_1 \ \vdash_{\overline{T}} \ \alpha_2 q_2 \beta_2) \Leftrightarrow (\alpha_1 q_1 \beta_1 \ \vdash_{\overline{\hat{T}}} \ \alpha_2 q_2 \beta_2))$$

Proof. The set $\hat{\delta}$ of quintuples is defined as follows.

$$\hat{\delta}_1 = \{[p, s, t, 0, q] \mid [p, s, t, q] \in \delta \ \wedge \ s, t \in S\}$$
$$\hat{\delta}_2 = \{[p, s, s, d, q] \mid [p, /, d, q] \in \delta \ \wedge \ s \in S\}$$
$$\hat{\delta} = \hat{\delta}_1 \cup \hat{\delta}_2$$

From Definitions 5.6 and 5.7, it is easy to see that each quintuple in $\hat{\delta}_1$ and $\hat{\delta}_2$ directly simulates the original quadruple. Hence, $((\alpha_1 q_1 \beta_1 \ \vdash_{\overline{T}} \ \alpha_2 q_2 \beta_2) \Leftrightarrow (\alpha_1 q_1 \beta_1 \ \vdash_{\overline{\hat{T}}} \ \alpha_2 q_2 \beta_2))$ holds for all $\alpha_1, \alpha_2, \beta_1, \beta_2 \in S^*$ and $q_1, q_2 \in Q$.

Reversibility of $\hat{T}$ is verified by checking all the pairs of distinct quintuples $r_1 = [p_1, s_1, t_1, d_1, q_1]$ and $r_2 = [p_2, s_2, t_2, d_2, q_2]$ in $\hat{\delta}$ satisfy the reversibility condition, i.e., if we assume $q_1 = q_2$, then $d_1 = d_2$ and $t_1 \neq t_2$ hold. There are following three cases. The first case is $r_1, r_2 \in \hat{\delta}_1$. In this case, $d_1 = d_2 = 0$, and there are distinct quadruples $[p_1, s_1, t_1, q_1]$ and $[p_2, s_2, t_2, q_2]$ in δ such that $q_1 = q_2$. Since T is reversible, $t_1 \neq t_2$ holds. Thus, the pair r_1 and r_2 satisfies the reversibility condition. The second case is $r_1, r_2 \in \hat{\delta}_2$. Since T is reversible, there is no distinct pair of quadruples $[p_1, /, d_1, q_1]$ and $[p_2, /, d_2, q_2]$ such that $q_1 = q_2$. Hence, if $q_1 = q_2$ in r_1 and r_2, then $p_1 = p_2$ and $d_1 = d_2$ hold. From the definition of $\hat{\delta}_2$, if $p_1 = p_2$, $d_1 = d_2$, $q_1 = q_2$ and $r_1 \neq r_2$, then $t_1 \neq t_2$. Therefore, the pair r_1 and r_2 satisfies the reversibility condition. The third case is $r_1 \in \hat{\delta}_1$ and $r_2 \in \hat{\delta}_2$ (since the case $r_1 \in \hat{\delta}_2$ and $r_2 \in \hat{\delta}_1$ is similar, it is omitted). Then, there are quadruples $[p_1, s_1, t_1, q_1]$ and $[p_2, /, d_2, q_2]$ in δ such that $q_1 = q_2$. But, this contradicts the assumption that T is reversible. Hence, this case cannot occur. By above, we conclude $\hat{T}$ is reversible. □

In the RTM $\hat{T}$ in Lemma 5.2 each quintuple in $\hat{\delta}$ simulates only one quadruple in δ. But, if there are two quadruples, say, $[p, s, t, q']$ and $[q', /, d, q]$ in δ, they can be simulated by a single quintuple $[p, s, t, d, q]$. However, we do not go into the details of this conversion method here.

Lemma 5.3. *For any RTM $T = (Q, S, q_0, F, s_0, \delta)$ in the quintuple form, we can construct an RTM $\tilde{T} = (\tilde{Q}, S, q_0, F, s_0, \tilde{\delta})$ in the quadruple form for some $\tilde{Q} \ (\supset Q)$ that satisfies the following.*

$$\forall \alpha_1, \alpha_2, \beta_1, \beta_2 \in S^* \ \forall q_1, q_2 \in Q$$
$$((\alpha_1 q_1 \beta_1 \models_{T} \alpha_2 q_2 \beta_2) \Leftrightarrow (\alpha_1 q_1 \beta_1 \models_{\tilde{T}}^{2} \alpha_2 q_2 \beta_2))$$

Proof. Let $Q' = \{q' \mid q \in Q\}$. Then, the set of states of $\tilde{T}$ is $\tilde{Q} = Q \cup Q'$. The set $\tilde{\delta}$ of quadruples of $\tilde{T}$ is defined as follows.

$$\tilde{\delta} = \{[p, s, t, q'], [q', /, d, q] \mid [p, s, t, d, q] \in \delta\}$$

Since T is a reversible TM, there is no pair of quintuples $[p_1, s_1, t_1, d_1, q]$ and $[p_2, s_2, t_2, d_2, q]$ in δ such that $d_1 \neq d_2$. Thus, for each $q \in Q$, there is at most one shift rule of the form $[q', /, d, q]$ in $\tilde{\delta}$. Therefore, if $[p, s, t, q']$ is applied to an ID, then the next applicable rule is only $[q', /, d, q]$, and hence $((\alpha_1 q_1 \beta_1 \models_{T} \alpha_2 q_2 \beta_2) \Leftrightarrow (\alpha_1 q_1 \beta_1 \models_{\tilde{T}}^{2} \alpha_2 q_2 \beta_2))$ holds for all $\alpha_1, \alpha_2, \beta_1, \beta_2 \in S^*$ and $q_1, q_2 \in Q$.

Next we show $\tilde{T}$ satisfies the reversibility condition, i.e., for every pair of distinct quadruples $r_1 = [p_1, x_1, y_1, q_1]$ and $r_2 = [p_2, x_2, y_2, q_2]$ in $\tilde{\delta}$, if $q_1 = q_2$, then $x_1 \neq /$, $x_2 \neq /$, and $y_1 \neq y_2$ hold. We consider the following three cases. The first case is both r_1 and r_2 are shift rules. In this case, from $\tilde{\delta}$ defined above, if $q_1 = q_2$, then r_1 and r_2 must be as follows: $r_1 = [q', /, d_1, q]$, $r_2 = [q', /, d_2, q]$ for some $q \in Q$ and $d_1, d_2 \in \{-, 0, +\}$. But, by the argument in the previous paragraph we see $d_1 = d_2$, and thus r_1 and r_2 must be identical. Hence, this case cannot occur. The second case is r_1 is a shift rule, and r_2 is a read-write rule, i.e., $r_1 = [p_1, /, d_1, q_1]$, $r_2 = [p_2, s_2, t_2, q_2]$ for some $d_1 \in \{-,0,+\}$ and $s_2,t_2 \in S$. In this case, from the definition of $\tilde{\delta}$, $q_1 \in Q'$ and $q_2 \in Q$ must hold. Therefore, this case also cannot occur. The third case is both r_1 and r_2 are read-write rules. If we assume $q_1 = q_2$, then $r_1 = [p_1,s_1,t_1,q']$, $r_2 = [p_2,s_2,t_2,q']$ for some $t_1,t_2 \in S$ and $q' \in Q'$. Assume, on the contrary, the pair r_1 and r_2 violates the reversibility condition, i.e., $t_1 = t_2$. In this case, from $\tilde{\delta}$, and from the argument in the previous paragraph, there are $[p_1,s_1,t_1,d,q]$ and $[p_2,s_2,t_2,d,q]$ in δ for some $d \in \{-,0,+\}$. However, since T is reversible, $t_1 \neq t_2$ holds, and thus it contradicts the assumption $t_1 = t_2$. Hence, the pair r_1 and r_2 satisfies the reversibility condition. By above, we can conclude $\tilde{T}$ is reversible.   □

Example 5.2. Applying the conversion method in Lemma 5.3 to the quintuple RTM T_{copy} given in Example 5.1, we obtain the following RTM $\tilde{T}'_{\text{copy}}$ in the quadruple form that simulates T_{copy}.

$$\tilde{T}_{\text{copy}} = (\tilde{Q}_{\text{copy}}, \{0,1,a,m\}, q_{\text{start}}, \{q_{\text{final}}\}, 0, \tilde{\delta}_{\text{copy}})$$
$$\tilde{Q}_{\text{copy}} = \{\, q'_{\text{start}}, q_{\text{start}}, q'_{\text{find0}}, q_{\text{find0}}, q'_{\text{next0}}, q_{\text{next0}}, q'_{\text{return}}, q_{\text{return}}, q'_{\text{final}}, q_{\text{final}} \,\}$$
$$\tilde{\delta}_{\text{copy}} = \{\, [q'_{\text{start}}, /, +, q_{\text{start}}], \quad [q_{\text{start}}, 1, m, q'_{\text{find0}}], \quad [q_{\text{start}}, a, a, q'_{\text{final}}],$$
$$[q'_{\text{find0}}, /, +, q_{\text{find0}}], \quad [q_{\text{find0}}, 0, 1, q'_{\text{next0}}], \quad [q_{\text{find0}}, 1, 1, q'_{\text{find0}}],$$
$$[q_{\text{find0}}, a, a, q'_{\text{find0}}], \quad [q'_{\text{next0}}, /, +, q_{\text{next0}}], \quad [q_{\text{next0}}, 0, 0, q'_{\text{return}}],$$
$$[q'_{\text{return}}, /, -, q_{\text{return}}], \quad [q_{\text{return}}, 1, 1, q'_{\text{return}}], \quad [q_{\text{return}}, a, a, q'_{\text{return}}],$$
$$[q_{\text{return}}, m, 1, q'_{\text{start}}], \quad [q'_{\text{final}}, /, 0, q_{\text{final}}] \,\}$$

Table 5.2 describes $\tilde{\delta}_{\text{copy}}$ in a tabular form. The computing process of $\tilde{T}_{\text{copy}}$ for the unary input 11 is as follows, where $11 q_{\text{final}} a 11$ is a halting ID.

$$q_{\text{start}} 1 1 a \; \underset{\tilde{T}_{\text{copy}}}{\vdash} \; q'_{\text{find0}} m 1 a \; \underset{\tilde{T}_{\text{copy}}}{\vdash} \; m q_{\text{find0}} 1 a \; \underset{\tilde{T}_{\text{copy}}}{\overset{36}{\vdash}} \; 1 1 q_{\text{final}} a 1 1$$

                                                                                                                                                □

Table 5.2 The move relation $\tilde{\delta}_{\text{copy}}$ of the RTM $\tilde{T}_{\text{copy}}$ in the quadruple form converted from T_{copy} in the quintuple form in Example 5.1. The rightmost column "shift" is for the shift rules of $\tilde{T}_{\text{copy}}$

	0	1	a	m	shift
q'_{start}					$+, q_{\text{start}}$
q_{start}		m, q'_{find0}	a, q'_{final}		
q'_{find0}					$+, q_{\text{find0}}$
q_{find0}	$1, q'_{\text{next0}}$	$1, q'_{\text{find0}}$	a, q'_{find0}		
q'_{next0}					$+, q_{\text{next0}}$
q_{next0}	$0, q'_{\text{return}}$				
q'_{return}					$-, q_{\text{return}}$
q_{return}		$1, q'_{\text{return}}$	a, q'_{return}	$1, q'_{\text{start}}$	
q'_{final}				$0, q_{\text{final}}$	
q_{final}					

5.1.4 Inverse reversible Turing machines

We define the notion of an "inverse RTM" T^{-1} of a given RTM T, which "undoes" the computation performed by T. Namely, starting from a final ID β of T, the inverse RTM T^{-1} traces the computation process of T backward, and finally reaches an initial ID α of T (provided that if T starts from α, it eventually halts in β).

By above, we can see a final state of T acts as an initial state of T^{-1}, while an initial state of T acts as a final (and halting) state of T^{-1}. Consequently, in T, there must not be a rule (i.e., a quadruple or a quintuple) whose next state is the initial state of T, and the set of final states of T must be a singleton. Sometimes it is not easy to design an RTM with this property. In such a case, however, we can obtain an RTM in the following way. First, any TM can be easily converted into an irreversible TM with this property (see Definition 5.18), The latter TM can be further converted into a three-tape RTM with this property (see Theorem 5.1). It is also possible to convert it into a one-tape RTM (see Theorem 5.3).

We first consider the case of RTMs in the quadruple form. In this case, the inverse RTM is defined very simply, since, for any quadruple, its inverse quadruple can be directly given.

Definition 5.10. Let $T = (Q, S, q_0, \{q_f\}, s_0, \delta)$ be an RTM in the quadruple form. Note that we assume it has only one final state. We also assume there is no quadruple in δ whose fourth element is q_0, and thus no state in Q goes to q_0. The TM T^{-1} defined as follows is called the *inverse TM* of the RTM T.

$$T^{-1} = (\hat{Q}, S, \hat{q}_f, \{\hat{q}_0\}, s_0, \hat{\delta})$$
$$\hat{Q} = \{\hat{q} \mid q \in Q\}$$
$$\hat{\delta} = \{[\hat{q}, t, s, \hat{p}] \mid [p, s, t, q] \in \delta \wedge s, t \in S\} \cup \{[\hat{q}, /, -d, \hat{p}] \mid [p, /, d, q] \in \delta\}$$

Lemma 5.4. *Let $T = (Q, S, q_0, \{q_f\}, s_0, \delta)$ be an RTM in the quadruple form such that there is no quadruple in δ whose fourth element is q_0. Let $T^{-1} = (\hat{Q}, S, \hat{q}_f, \{\hat{q}_0\}, s_0, \hat{\delta})$ be the inverse TM of T. Then, T^{-1} is an RTM, and it satisfies the following condition.*

$$\forall \alpha_1, \alpha_2, \beta_1, \beta_2 \in S^* \; \forall p, q \in Q$$
$$((\alpha_1 p \beta_1 \vdash_T \alpha_2 q \beta_2) \Leftrightarrow (\alpha_2 \hat{q} \beta_2 \vdash_{T^{-1}} \alpha_1 \hat{p} \beta_1))$$

Proof. By Definitions 5.3 and 5.10, T^{-1} is reversible (deterministic, respectively), since T is deterministic (reversible). Hence, T^{-1} is an RTM.

By Definitions 5.6 and 5.10, it is also clear that the relation $((\alpha_1 p \beta_1 \vdash_T \alpha_2 q \beta_2) \Leftrightarrow (\alpha_2 \hat{q} \beta_2 \vdash_{T^{-1}} \alpha_1 \hat{p} \beta_1))$ holds, since $[\hat{q}, t, s, \hat{p}]$ ($[\hat{q}, /, -d, \hat{p}]$, respectively) in $\hat{\delta}$ is an "inverse quadruple" that undoes the operation by $[p, s, t, q]$ ($[p, /, d, q]$) in δ. $\square$

By Lemma 5.4, if $\alpha q_0 \beta \vdash_T \cdots \vdash_T \alpha' q_f \beta'$ is a complete computing process of T, then $\alpha' \hat{q}_f \beta' \vdash_{T^{-1}} \cdots \vdash_{T^{-1}} \alpha \hat{q}_0 \beta$ is a complete computing process of T^{-1}, where $\alpha' \hat{q}_f \beta'$ is an initial ID, and $\alpha \hat{q}_0 \beta$ is a final ID of T^{-1}.

Next, we consider the case of quintuple formulation. In this case, the definition of inverse TM is slightly complicated, since an inverse quintuple cannot be directly obtained from a given quintuple. This is because the head shift operation is after the read-write operation, and thus the "phase" is shifted at each execution step of a quintuple of the inverse RTM. An inverse TM in this case is defined under a suitable condition as in Definition 5.12. We now make some preparations for it.

Definition 5.11. Let $T = (Q, S, q_0, F, s_0, \delta)$ be a TM in the quintuple form. Let Q_-, Q_0, and Q_+ be sets of states defined as follows.

$$
\begin{aligned}
Q_- &= \{q \mid \exists p \in Q \; \exists s, t \in S \; ([p, s, t, -, q] \in \delta)\} \\
Q_0 &= \{q \mid \exists p \in Q \; \exists s, t \in S \; ([p, s, t, 0, q] \in \delta)\} \\
Q_+ &= \{q \mid \exists p \in Q \; \exists s, t \in S \; ([p, s, t, +, q] \in \delta)\}
\end{aligned}
$$

We say T has the *unique shift-direction property*, if Q_-, Q_0 and Q_+ are mutually disjoint, i.e., $Q_- \cap Q_0 = \emptyset$, $Q_0 \cap Q_+ = \emptyset$, and $Q_+ \cap Q_- = \emptyset$. In this case, we can define the function $h_{sd} : Q \to \{-, 0, +\}$ as follows.

$$
h_{sd}(q) = \begin{cases} - & \text{if } q \in Q_- \\ 0 & \text{if } q \notin Q_- \cup Q_+ \\ + & \text{if } q \in Q_+ \end{cases}
$$

$h_{sd}(q)$ is called the *shift direction associated with q*. Namely, the shift direction of the head just before entering q is $h_{sd}(q)$. Hence, if $[p, s, t, d, q] \in \delta$, then $d = h_{sd}(q)$.

Lemma 5.5. *Every RTM has the unique shift-direction property.*

Proof. This lemma directly follows from the reversibility condition in Definition 5.4.   □

Next, we define a function $\varphi_{sft} : \mathrm{ID}(T) \times \{-, 0, +\} \to \mathrm{ID}(T)$. $\varphi_{sft}(\gamma, d)$ gives the ID of T such that the head position in γ is shifted to the direction d. More precisely, it is defined as the one that satisfies the following condition: For every $q \in Q$, $\alpha \in (S - \{s_0\})S^* \cup \{\lambda\}$, $\beta \in S^*(S - \{s_0\}) \cup \{\lambda\}$, and $s, t \in S$, the following relations hold. Note that they are similar to (6) – (16) in Definition 5.6.

$$
\begin{aligned}
\varphi_{sft}(\alpha q s \beta, +) &= \alpha s q \beta && \text{if } \alpha \neq \lambda \\
\varphi_{sft}(q s \beta, +) &= s q \beta && \text{if } s \neq s_0 \\
\varphi_{sft}(q s_0 \beta, +) &= q \beta \\
\varphi_{sft}(\alpha q, +) &= \alpha s_0 q && \text{if } \alpha \neq \lambda \\
\varphi_{sft}(q, +) &= q \\
\varphi_{sft}(\alpha q \beta, 0) &= \alpha q \beta \\
\varphi_{sft}(\alpha t q \beta, -) &= \alpha q t \beta && \text{if } \beta \neq \lambda \\
\varphi_{sft}(\alpha t q, -) &= \alpha q t && \text{if } t \neq s_0 \\
\varphi_{sft}(\alpha s_0 q, -) &= \alpha q \\
\varphi_{sft}(q \beta, -) &= q s_0 \beta && \text{if } \beta \neq \lambda \\
\varphi_{sft}(q, -) &= q
\end{aligned}
$$

Definition 5.12. Let $T = (Q, S, q_0, \{q_f\}, s_0, \delta)$ be an RTM in the quintuple form. We assume there is no quintuple in δ whose fifth element is q_0. We also assume $h_{\text{sd}}(q_f) = 0$. The TM T^{-1} defined below is called the *inverse TM* of the RTM T.

$$T^{-1} = (\hat{Q}, S, \hat{q}_f, \{\hat{q}_0\}, s_0, \hat{\delta})$$
$$\hat{Q} = \{\hat{q} \mid q \in Q\}$$
$$\hat{\delta} = \{[\hat{q}, t, s, -h_{\text{sd}}(p), \hat{p}] \mid [p, s, t, h_{\text{sd}}(q), q] \in \delta\}$$

Lemma 5.6. *Let $T = (Q, S, q_0, \{q_f\}, s_0, \delta)$ be an RTM in the quintuple form. We assume that there is no quintuple in δ whose fifth element is q_0, and $h_{\text{sd}}(q_f) = 0$. Let $T^{-1} = (\hat{Q}, S, \hat{q}_f, \{\hat{q}_0\}, s_0, \hat{\delta})$ be the inverse TM of T. Then, T^{-1} is an RTM, and it satisfies the following condition.*

$$\forall \alpha_1, \alpha_2, \beta_1, \beta_2 \in S^* \; \forall p, q \in Q$$
$$((\alpha_1 p \beta_1 \vdash_{T} \alpha_2 q \beta_2) \Leftrightarrow (\varphi_{\text{sft}}(\alpha_2 \hat{q} \beta_2, -h_{\text{sd}}(q)) \vdash_{T^{-1}} \varphi_{\text{sft}}(\alpha_1 \hat{p} \beta_1, -h_{\text{sd}}(p))))$$

Proof. First, we show T^{-1} in Definition 5.12 is an RTM. Let $\hat{r}_1 = [\hat{q}_1, t_1, s_1, \hat{d}_1, \hat{p}_1]$ and $\hat{r}_2 = [\hat{q}_2, t_2, s_2, \hat{d}_2, \hat{p}_2]$ be arbitrary pair of distinct rules in $\hat{\delta}$ such that $\hat{p}_1 = \hat{p}_2$. Then there are rules $[p_1, s_1, t_1, d_1, q_1]$ and $[p_2, s_2, t_2, d_2, q_2]$ in δ. Since T is deterministic, and $p_1 = p_2$, $s_1 \neq s_2$ holds. Also $\hat{d}_1 = -h_{\text{sd}}(p_1) = -h_{\text{sd}}(p_2) = \hat{d}_2$ holds. Therefore, the pair $\hat{r}_1$ and $\hat{r}_2$ satisfies the reversibility condition.

Next, $\alpha_1 p \beta_1 \vdash_{T} \alpha_2 q \beta_2$ iff $\varphi_{\text{sft}}(\alpha_2 \hat{q} \beta_2, -h_{\text{sd}}(q)) \vdash_{T^{-1}} \varphi_{\text{sft}}(\alpha_1 \hat{p} \beta_1, -h_{\text{sd}}(p))$ is shown. We first assume $\alpha_1 p \beta_1 \vdash_{T} \alpha_2 q \beta_2$, and this transition is made by the application of a rule $[p, s, t, h_{\text{sd}}(q), q]$. Then, $\hat{r} = [\hat{q}, t, s, -h_{\text{sd}}(p), \hat{p}] \in \hat{\delta}$. We can see that in the ID $\varphi_{\text{sft}}(\alpha_2 \hat{q} \beta_2, -h_{\text{sd}}(q))$ the RTM T^{-1} is reading the symbol t. Hence, by applying the rule $\hat{r}$ to it, the ID $\varphi_{\text{sft}}(\alpha_1 \hat{p} \beta_1, -h_{\text{sd}}(p))$ is derived, since $\alpha_1 \hat{p} \beta_1$ is obtained from $\varphi_{\text{sft}}(\alpha_2 \hat{q} \beta_2, -h_{\text{sd}}(q))$ by replacing the state $\hat{q}$ by $\hat{p}$, and the symbol t, which is read by T^{-1}, by s. Therefore, $\varphi_{\text{sft}}(\alpha_2 \hat{q} \beta_2, -h_{\text{sd}}(q)) \vdash_{T^{-1}} \varphi_{\text{sft}}(\alpha_1 \hat{p} \beta_1, -h_{\text{sd}}(p))$ holds.

Second, we assume $\varphi_{\text{sft}}(\alpha_2 \hat{q} \beta_2, -h_{\text{sd}}(q)) \vdash_{T^{-1}} \varphi_{\text{sft}}(\alpha_1 \hat{p} \beta_1, -h_{\text{sd}}(p))$, and this transition is made by the application of a rule $[\hat{q}, t, s, -h_{\text{sd}}(p), \hat{p}] \in \hat{\delta}$. Then, $r = [p, s, t, h_{\text{sd}}(q), q] \in \delta$. We can see that in the ID $\alpha_1 p \beta_1$ the RTM T is reading the symbol s. Hence, by applying the rule r to it, the ID $\varphi_{\text{sft}}(\varphi_{\text{sft}}(\alpha_2 q \beta_2, -h_{\text{sd}}(q)), h_{\text{sd}}(q)) = \alpha_2 q \beta_2$ is derived, since $\varphi_{\text{sft}}(\alpha_2 q \beta_2, -h_{\text{sd}}(q))$ is obtained from $\alpha_1 p \beta_1$ by replacing the state p by q, and the symbol s, which is read by T, by t. Therefore, $\alpha_1 p \beta_1 \vdash_{T} \alpha_2 q \beta_2$ holds. By above, this lemma is proved. □

Corollary 5.1. *Let $T = (Q, S, q_0, \{q_f\}, s_0, \delta)$ be an RTM in the quintuple form. We assume that there is no quintuple in δ whose fifth element is q_0, and $h_{\text{sd}}(q_f) = 0$. Then, for the inverse TM $T^{-1} = (\hat{Q}, S, \hat{q}_f, \{\hat{q}_0\}, s_0, \hat{\delta})$, the following relation holds.*

$$\forall \alpha, \alpha', \beta, \beta' \in S^*$$
$$((\alpha q_0 \beta \vdash_{T}^{*} \alpha' q_f \beta') \Leftrightarrow (\alpha' \hat{q}_f \beta' \vdash_{T^{-1}}^{*} \alpha \hat{q}_0 \beta))$$

Proof. By Lemma 5.6, if $\alpha q_0 \beta \vdash_{T} \cdots \vdash_{T} \alpha' q_f \beta'$ is a complete computing process of T, then $\varphi_{\text{sft}}(\alpha' \hat{q}_f \beta', -h_{\text{sd}}(q_f)) \vdash_{T^{-1}} \cdots \vdash_{T^{-1}} \varphi_{\text{sft}}(\alpha \hat{q}_0 \beta, -h_{\text{sd}}(q_0))$ holds. Since

$h_{sd}(q_f) = h_{sd}(q_0) = 0$, $\varphi_{sft}(\alpha'\hat{q}_f\beta', -h_{sd}(q_f)) = \alpha'\hat{q}_f\beta'$, and $\varphi_{sft}(\alpha\hat{q}_0\beta, -h_{sd}(q_0))$ $= \alpha\hat{q}_0\beta$. Hence, $\alpha'\hat{q}_f\beta' \mid_{\overline{T^{-1}}} \cdots \mid_{\overline{T^{-1}}} \alpha\hat{q}_0\beta$ is a complete computing process of T^{-1}.

□

Example 5.3. Consider the RTM $T_{copy} = (Q_{copy}, \{0, 1, a, m\}, q_{start}, \{q_{final}\}, 0, \delta_{copy})$ given in Example 5.1. Though $h_{sd}(q_{final}) = 0$ holds in T_{copy}, δ_{copy} contains a quintuple $[q_{return}, m, 1, +, q_{start}]$ whose fifth element is the initial state, and thus T_{copy} does not meet the condition given in Lemma 5.6. Therefore, we define the following RTM $T_{copy'}$ by adding a new initial state $q_{initial}$ to T_{copy} to satisfy these conditions.

$$T_{copy'} = (Q_{copy'}, \{0, 1, a, m\}, q_{initial}, \{q_{final}\}, 0, \delta_{copy'})$$

Here, $Q_{copy'} = \{q_{initial}, q_{start}, q_{find0}, q_{next0}, q_{return}, q_{final}\}$, and $\delta_{copy'}$ is as follows.

$$\delta_{copy'} = \{ \ [q_{initial}, 0, 0, +, q_{start}],$$
$$[q_{start}, 1, m, +, q_{find0}], \quad [q_{start}, a, a, 0, q_{final}], \quad [q_{find0}, 0, 1, +, q_{next0}],$$
$$[q_{find0}, 1, 1, +, q_{find0}], \quad [q_{find0}, a, a, +, q_{find0}], \quad [q_{next0}, 0, 0, -, q_{return}],$$
$$[q_{return}, 1, 1, -, q_{return}], \quad [q_{return}, a, a, -, q_{return}], \quad [q_{return}, m, 1, +, q_{start}] \ \}$$

The following is a complete computing process of $T_{copy'}$ starting from $q_{initial} 0 1 a$.

$$q_{initial} 0 1 a \mid_{\overline{T_{copy'}}} q_{start} 1 a \mid_{\overline{T_{copy'}}} m q_{find0} a \mid_{\overline{T_{copy'}}} m a q_{find0}$$
$$\mid_{\overline{T_{copy'}}} m a 1 q_{next0} \mid_{\overline{T_{copy'}}} m a q_{return} 1 \mid_{\overline{T_{copy'}}} m q_{return} a 1 \mid_{\overline{T_{copy'}}} q_{return} m a 1$$
$$\mid_{\overline{T_{copy'}}} 1 q_{start} a 1 \mid_{\overline{T_{copy'}}} 1 q_{final} a 1$$

In general, $q_{initial} 0 1^n a \mid_{\overline{T_{copy'}}}^* 1^n q_{final} a 1^n$ holds for all $n \in \mathbb{N}$.

We can see $Q_- = \{q_{return}\}, Q_0 = \{q_{final}\}, Q_+ = \{q_{start}, q_{find0}, q_{next0}\}$, and $q_{initial} \notin Q_- \cup Q_0 \cup Q_+$. Thus, $h_{sd}(q_{initial}) = 0$, $h_{sd}(q_{start}) = +$, $h_{sd}(q_{find0}) = +$, $h_{sd}(q_{next0}) = +$, $h_{sd}(q_{return}) = -$, and $h_{sd}(q_{final}) = 0$ hold in $T_{copy'}$. We now give the inverse RTM $T_{copy'}^{-1}$ by the method described in Definition 5.12.

$$T_{copy'}^{-1} = (\hat{Q}_{copy'}, \{0, 1, a, m\}, \hat{q}_{final}, \{\hat{q}_{initial}\}, 0, \hat{\delta}_{copy'})$$
$$\hat{Q}_{copy'} = \{\hat{q}_{initial}, \hat{q}_{start}, \hat{q}_{find0}, \hat{q}_{next0}, \hat{q}_{return}, \hat{q}_{final}\}$$
$$\hat{\delta}_{copy'} = \{ \ [\hat{q}_{start}, 0, 0, 0, \hat{q}_{initial}],$$
$$[\hat{q}_{find0}, m, 1, -, \hat{q}_{start}], \quad [\hat{q}_{final}, a, a, -, \hat{q}_{start}], \quad [\hat{q}_{next0}, 1, 0, -, \hat{q}_{find0}],$$
$$[\hat{q}_{find0}, 1, 1, -, \hat{q}_{find0}], \quad [\hat{q}_{find0}, a, a, -, \hat{q}_{find0}], \quad [\hat{q}_{return}, 0, 0, -, \hat{q}_{next0}],$$
$$[\hat{q}_{return}, 1, 1, +, \hat{q}_{return}], \quad [\hat{q}_{return}, a, a, +, \hat{q}_{return}], \quad [\hat{q}_{start}, 1, m, +, \hat{q}_{return}] \ \}$$

In general, $1^n \hat{q}_{final} a 1^n \mid_{\overline{T_{copy'}^{-1}}}^* \hat{q}_{initial} 0 1^n a$ holds for all $n \in \mathbb{N}$, and thus $T_{copy'}^{-1}$ undoes the computation performed by $T_{copy'}$. The following is a complete computing process of $T_{copy'}^{-1}$ starting from $1 q_{final} a 1$.

$$1\,\hat{q}_{\text{final}}\,a\,1 \quad \underset{T_{\text{copy}'}^{-1}}{\vdash} \hat{q}_{\text{start}}\,1\,a\,1 \quad \underset{T_{\text{copy}'}^{-1}}{\vdash} m\,\hat{q}_{\text{return}}\,a\,1 \quad \underset{T_{\text{copy}'}^{-1}}{\vdash} m\,a\,\hat{q}_{\text{return}}\,1$$

$$\underset{T_{\text{copy}'}^{-1}}{\vdash} m\,a\,1\,\hat{q}_{\text{return}} \quad \underset{T_{\text{copy}'}^{-1}}{\vdash} m\,a\,\hat{q}_{\text{next0}}\,1 \quad \underset{T_{\text{copy}'}^{-1}}{\vdash} m\,\hat{q}_{\text{find0}}\,a \quad \underset{T_{\text{copy}'}^{-1}}{\vdash} \hat{q}_{\text{find0}}\,m\,a$$

$$\underset{T_{\text{copy}'}^{-1}}{\vdash} \hat{q}_{\text{start}}\,0\,1\,a \quad \underset{T_{\text{copy}'}^{-1}}{\vdash} \hat{q}_{\text{initial}}\,0\,1\,a$$

$\square$

5.2 Converting Irreversible Turing Machines to Reversible Ones

In this section we introduce the method of Bennett [1] to convert a given one-tape irreversible TM into a three-tape RTM. His method is a starting point of studying computational universality of RTMs. Note that, in Sect. 8.2 we shall show another method of converting a TM to an RTM. Here, we make a three-tape RTM that simulates a given TM without leaving garbage information on the tapes when it halts. It is constructed using an inverse RTM as a component for clearing the garbage information. In [1] the quadruple formulation was used, since an inverse RTM can be easily given. However, in this section, we use the quintuple formulation, and construct an inverse RTM based on the method shown in Definition 5.12. By this, we can describe the resulting RTM rather compactly.

5.2.1 Three-tape Turing machines

Here we consider a three-tape Turing machine, which has three tapes, three read-write heads, and a finite control (Fig. 5.3). It is defined as follows.

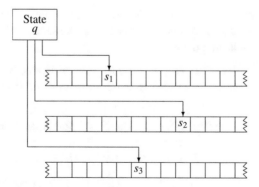

Fig. 5.3 Three-tape Turing machine

Definition 5.13. A *three-tape Turing machine in the quintuple form* is defined by

$$T = (Q, (S_1, S_2, S_3), q_0, F, (s_{0,1}, s_{0,2}, s_{0,3}), \delta),$$

where Q is a non-empty finite set of states, S_1, S_2, and S_3 are non-empty finite sets of symbols for the three tapes, q_0 is an initial state ($q_0 \in Q$), F is a set of final states ($F \subseteq Q$), $s_{0,i}$ ($i = 1, 2, 3$) is a special blank symbol of the i-th tape ($s_{0,i} \in S_i$). Let $S = (S_1 \times S_2 \times S_3)$. The item δ is a move relation, which is a subset of $(Q \times S \times S \times \{-, 0, +\}^3 \times Q)$. The symbols "$-$", "$0$", and "$+$" are the shift directions of each head. Each element of δ is a quintuple of the form $[p, [s_1, s_2, s_3], [t_1, t_2, t_3], [d_1, d_2, d_3], q] \in (Q \times S \times S \times \{-, 0, +\}^3 \times Q)$. It means if T reads the symbols s_1, s_2 and s_3 in the state p, then rewrite them into t_1, t_2 and t_3, shift the three heads to the directions d_1, d_2 and d_3, respectively, and go to the state q.

The above definition can be easily extended for a k-tape TM for general $k \in \{2, 3, \ldots\}$. Determinism and reversibility of a three-tape TM in the quintuple form are defined in a similar manner as in the case of a one-tape TM.

Definition 5.14. Let $T = (Q, (S_1, S_2, S_3), q_0, F, (s_{0,1}, s_{0,2}, s_{0,3}), \delta)$ be a three-tape TM. T is called a *deterministic TM*, if the following holds for any pair of distinct quintuples $[p, [s_1, s_2, s_3], [t_1, t_2, t_3], [d_1, d_2, d_3], q]$ and $[p', [s_1', s_2', s_3'], [t_1', t_2', t_3'], [d_1', d_2', d_3'], q']$ in δ.

$$(p = p') \;\Rightarrow\; ([s_1, s_2, s_3] \neq [s_1', s_2', s_3'])$$

It means that for any pair of distinct rules, if the present states are the same, then the combinations of the read symbols are different.

T is called a *reversible TM* (RTM), if the following holds for any pair of distinct quintuples $[p, [s_1, s_2, s_3], [t_1, t_2, t_3], [d_1, d_2, d_3], q]$ and $[p', [s_1', s_2', s_3'], [t_1', t_2', t_3'], [d_1', d_2', d_3'], q']$ in δ.

$$(q = q') \;\Rightarrow\; ([d_1, d_2, d_3] = [d_1', d_2', d_3'] \wedge [t_1, t_2, t_3] \neq [t_1', t_2', t_3'])$$

It means that for any pair of distinct rules, if the next states are the same, then the combinations of the shift directions of the heads are the same, and the combinations of the written symbols are different.

As in the case of one-tape TM, we do not consider nondeterministic three-tape TMs in this section, and thus we omit to write "deterministic" hereafter.

Definition 5.15. Let $T = (Q, (S_1, S_2, S_3), q_0, F, (s_{0,1}, s_{0,2}, s_{0,3}), \delta)$ be a three-tape TM. An *instantaneous description* (ID) of T is an expression of the form

$$((\alpha_1, \beta_1), (\alpha_2, \beta_2), (\alpha_3, \beta_3), q)$$

such that $\alpha_i, \beta_i \in S_i^*$ ($i = 1, 2, 3$), and $q \in Q$. The ID of T describes the *computational configuration* of T where the state of T is q, the content of the i-th tape is $\alpha_i \beta_i$ (the remaining part of the tape contains only blank symbols), and T is reading the leftmost symbol of β_i (if $\beta \neq \lambda$) or s_0 (if $\beta = \lambda$). An *initial ID* (*final ID*, respectively) is one such that $q = q_0$ ($q \in F$). The set of all IDs of T is denoted by ID(T).

The transition relation $\vdash_T$ on ID(T) is defined similarly as in the case of Definition 5.7, and thus we do not give its precise definition here.

5.2.2 Inverse three-tape Turing machines

We define an inverse TM for a given three-tape RTM. It is defined similarly as in Definition 5.12 by extending the function h_{sd} in Definition 5.11 suitably.

Definition 5.16. Let $T = (Q, (S_1, S_2, S_3), q_0, \{q_f\}, (s_{0,1}, s_{0,2}, s_{0,3}), \delta)$ be a three-tape RTM in the quintuple form, and let $S = S_1 \times S_2 \times S_3$. For each $d \in D = \{-, 0, +\}$, Q_d^1, Q_d^2, and Q_d^3 are defined as follows.

$$Q_d^1 = \{q \mid \exists p \in Q \ \exists s, t \in S \ \exists d_2, d_3 \in D \ ([p, s, t, [d, d_2, d_3], q] \in \delta)\}$$
$$Q_d^2 = \{q \mid \exists p \in Q \ \exists s, t \in S \ \exists d_1, d_3 \in D \ ([p, s, t, [d_1, d, d_3], q] \in \delta)\}$$
$$Q_d^3 = \{q \mid \exists p \in Q \ \exists s, t \in S \ \exists d_1, d_2 \in D \ ([p, s, t, [d_1, d_2, d], q] \in \delta)\}$$

Since T is an RTM, Q_-^i, Q_0^i and Q_+^i are mutually disjoint for each $i \ (\in \{1, 2, 3\})$, and thus we can define the function $h_{sd}^i : Q \rightarrow D$, and $h_{sd} : Q \rightarrow D^3$ as follows.

$$h_{sd}^i(q) = \begin{cases} - & \text{if } q \in Q_-^i \\ 0 & \text{if } q \notin Q_-^i \cup Q_+^i \\ + & \text{if } q \in Q_+^i \end{cases}$$
$$\mathbf{h}_{sd}(q) = [h_{sd}^1(q), h_{sd}^2(q), h_{sd}^3(q)]$$

Here, $h_{sd}^i(q)$ is called the *shift direction of the i-th head associated with q*, and $\mathbf{h}_{sd}(q)$ is called the *shift directions associated with q*.

The inverse TM of a given three-tape RTM is defined as follows.

Definition 5.17. Let $T = (Q, (S_1, S_2, S_3), q_0, \{q_f\}, (s_{0,1}, s_{0,2}, s_{0,3}), \delta)$ be a three-tape RTM in the quintuple form. We assume there is no quintuple in δ whose fifth element is q_0. We also assume $\mathbf{h}_{sd}(q_f) = [0, 0, 0]$. The TM T^{-1} defined as follows is called the *inverse three-tape TM* of the RTM T.

$$T^{-1} = (\hat{Q}, (S_1, S_2, S_3), \hat{q}_f, \{\hat{q}_0\}, (s_{0,1}, s_{0,2}, s_{0,3}), \hat{\delta})$$
$$\hat{Q} = \{\hat{q} \mid q \in Q\}$$
$$\hat{\delta} = \{[\hat{q}, \mathbf{t}, \mathbf{s}, -\mathbf{h}_{sd}(p), \hat{p}] \mid [p, \mathbf{s}, \mathbf{t}, \mathbf{h}_{sd}(q), q] \in \delta\}$$

We can show that the inverse TM T^{-1} is an RTM, and undoes every complete computing process of T. Since it is proved in a similar manner as in Lemma 5.6 and Corollary 5.1, we omit its proof. Hence, the following relation holds for all $\alpha_i, \alpha_i', \beta_i, \beta_i' \in S_i^* \ (i \in \{1, 2, 3\})$.

$$((\alpha_1, \beta_1), (\alpha_2, \beta_2), (\alpha_3, \beta_3), q_0) \vdash_T^* ((\alpha_1', \beta_1'), (\alpha_2', \beta_2'), (\alpha_3', \beta_3'), q_f)$$
$$\Leftrightarrow ((\alpha_1', \beta_1'), (\alpha_2', \beta_2'), (\alpha_3', \beta_3'), \hat{q}_f) \vdash_{T^{-1}}^* ((\alpha_1, \beta_1), (\alpha_2, \beta_2), (\alpha_3, \beta_3), \hat{q}_0)$$

5.2.3 Computational universality of three-tape RTMs

In this subsection we construct a three-tape RTM that simulates a given one-tape TM based on the method of Bennett [1]. Here, we use the quintuple formulation instead of the quadruple one used in [1]. First, we make some preparations for it.

Definition 5.18. Let $T = (Q, S, q_0, F, s_0, \delta)$ be a one-tape TM in the quintuple form. We formulate T as a *transducer* that computes a partial function f_T from the set of strings to the set of strings. Namely, if an input string is given on the tape, T will give an output string on the tape when it halts. We say a one-tape TM T is called a *transducer in the standard form*, if it satisfies the following conditions.

1. The TM T has a one-way infinite tape to the right (see also Sect. 5.3.1). If otherwise, it is achieved by the standard technique of folding a two-way infinite tape into a one-way infinite tape (see e.g., [6]).
2. There is no quintuple whose fifth element is q_0. If otherwise, we prepare a new state, say, q_0', set it as a new initial state, and add the quintuples $[q_0', s, s, 0, q_0]$ to δ for all $s \in S$.
3. The set F of final states is a singleton, i.e., $F = \{q_f\}$ for some q_f. If $F = \{q_{f_1}, \ldots, q_{f_k}\}$ for some $k > 1$, then we prepare a new state, say, q_f', set $\{q_f'\}$ as the new set of final states, and add the quintuples $[q_{f_i}, s, s, 0, q_f']$ to δ for all $i = 1, \ldots, k$ and for all $s \in S$.
4. Let $F = \{q_f\}$. We assume an input string α and an output string β are elements of $(S - \{s_0\})^+$, and they are given to T as the IDs $q_0 s_0 \alpha$ and $q_f s_0 \beta$, respectively. We also assume, in these IDs, T is scanning the leftmost square of the one-way infinite tape, whose tape symbol is s_0. If $q_0 s_0 \alpha \vdash_T^* q_f s_0 \beta$, then we say that, for the input string α, T gives the output string β, and thus $f_T(\alpha) = \beta$.
5. The TM T satisfies the unique shift-direction property in Definition 5.11. If otherwise, convert T into one with this property by the method given in Lemma 5.7 below. We also assume the shift direction associated with q_f is 0 (i.e., $h_{\text{sd}}(q_f) = 0$). If otherwise, we prepare a new state q_f', set $\{q_f'\}$ as the new set of final states, and add the quintuples $[q_f, s, s, 0, q_f']$ to δ for all $s \in S$.

The following lemma and corollary shows that, for any TM, we can construct a TM with the unique shift-direction property that simulates the former.

Lemma 5.7. *Let $T = (Q, S, q_0, \{q_f\}, s_0, \delta)$ be a one-tape TM in the quintuple form. We can construct a TM $T' = (Q', S, q_0^0, \{q_f^0\}, s_0, \delta')$ with the unique shift-direction property that satisfies the following relation. Here, $Q' = \{q^-, q^0, q^+ \mid q \in Q\}$, and $D = \{-, 0, +\}$.*

$$\forall \alpha, \alpha', \beta, \beta' \in S^* \ \forall p, q \in Q \ \forall n \in \mathbb{Z}_+$$
$$((\alpha p \beta \vdash_T^n \alpha' q \beta') \Leftrightarrow \forall d \in D \ \exists d' \in D \ (\alpha p^d \beta \vdash_{T'}^n \alpha' q^{d'} \beta'))$$

Proof. The set of quintuples δ' of T' is defined as follows.

$$\delta' = \{ [p^{d_1}, s, t, d_2, q^{d_2}] \mid [p, s, t, d_2, q] \in \delta \ \wedge \ d_1 \in D \}$$

It is easy to see T' is deterministic, since T is so. It is also easy to see that each $q^d \in Q'$ belongs only to the set Q'_d, since only quintuples of the form $[p^{d'}, s, t, d, q^d]$ exist. Hence, T' satisfies the unique shift-direction property.

We now show the relation in the lemma by an induction on n. First, consider the case $n = 1$. Assume $\alpha_0 p_0 \beta_0 \vdash_T \alpha_1 p_1 \beta_1$. Let $[p_0, s, t, d, p_1]$ be the quintuple applied in this transition. Then, by the definition of δ', there is a quintuple $[p_0^{d'}, s, t, d, p_1^d]$ for each $d' \in D$. Therefore, $\alpha_0 p_0^{d'} \beta_0 \vdash_{T'} \alpha_1 p_1^d \beta_1$ holds for all $d' \in D$. Conversely, we assume $\alpha_0 p_0^{d'} \beta_0 \vdash_{T'} \alpha_1 p_1^d \beta_1$, and let $[p_0^{d'}, s, t, d, p_1^d]$ be the quintuple applied in this transition. Then, from the definition of δ', there must be a quintuple $[p_0, s, t, d, p_1]$ in δ. Thus, $\alpha_0 p_0 \beta_0 \vdash_T \alpha_1 p_1 \beta_1$ holds.

Next, we assume the relation holds for $n < k$, and consider the case $n = k > 1$. Assume $\alpha_0 p_0 \beta_0 \vdash_T \alpha_1 p_1 \beta_1 \overset{k-1}{\vdash_T} \alpha_k p_k \beta_k$. Then, by the induction hypothesis, $\forall d_0 \in D \; \exists d_1 \in D \; (\alpha_0 p_0^{d_0} \beta_0 \vdash_{T'} \alpha_1 q^{d_1} \beta_1)$, and $\forall d_1 \in D \; \exists d_k \in D \; (\alpha_1 p^{d_1} \beta_1 \overset{k-1}{\vdash_{T'}} \alpha_k q^{d_k} \beta_k)$ hold. Hence, $\forall d_0 \in D \; \exists d_k \in D \; (\alpha_0 p^{d_0} \beta_0 \overset{k}{\vdash_{T'}} \alpha_k q^{d_k} \beta_k)$ is derived. Conversely, we assume $\forall d_0 \in D \; \exists d_k \in D \; (\alpha_0 p^{d_0} \beta_0 \overset{k}{\vdash_{T'}} \alpha_k q^{d_k} \beta_k)$. If a quintuple $[p_{i-1}^{d_{i-1}}, s, t, d_i, p_i^{d_i}] \in \delta'$ is used at the i-th step $\alpha_{i-1} p_{i-1}^{d_{i-1}} \beta_{i-1} \vdash_{T'} \alpha_i q_i^{d_i} \beta_i$ ($i \in \{1, \ldots, k\}$), then by the definition of δ', there must be a quintuple $[p_{i-1}, s, t, d_i, p_i]$ in δ, and thus $\alpha_{i-1} p_{i-1} \beta_{i-1} \vdash_T \alpha_i q_i \beta_i$. Therefore, $\alpha_0 p_0 \beta_0 \overset{k}{\vdash_T} \alpha_k p_k \beta_k$ holds.   □

Corollary 5.2. *Let $T = (Q, S, q_0, \{q_f\}, s_0, \delta)$ be a one-tape TM in the quintuple form. We assume there is no quintuple whose fifth element is q_0, and $h_{sd}(q_f) = 0$. We can construct a TM $T' = (Q', S, q_0^0, \{q_f^0\}, s_0, \delta')$ with the unique shift-direction property that satisfies the following relation, where $Q' = \{q^-, q^0, q^+ \mid q \in Q\}$.*

$$\forall \alpha, \alpha', \beta, \beta' \in S^*$$
$$((\alpha q_0 \beta \overset{*}{\vdash_T} \alpha' q_f \beta') \Leftrightarrow (\alpha q_0^0 \beta \overset{*}{\vdash_{T'}} \alpha' q_f^0 \beta'))$$

Proof. First, we assume $\alpha q_0 \beta \overset{*}{\vdash_T} \alpha' q_f \beta'$. Then, by Lemma 5.7, there is some $d \in D$ such that $\alpha q_0^0 \beta \overset{*}{\vdash_{T'}} \alpha' q_f^d \beta'$. On the other hand, by the assumption $h_{sd}(q_f) = 0$, and by the definition of δ', d must be 0. Next, we assume $\alpha q_0^0 \beta \overset{*}{\vdash_{T'}} \alpha' q_f^0 \beta'$. Then, by a similar argument as in Lemma 5.7, $\alpha q_0 \beta \overset{*}{\vdash_T} \alpha' q_f \beta'$ can be derived.   □

We now construct a three-tape RTM $T^\dagger$ that simulates a given one-tape TM T, which is a transducer in the standard form. We first explain an outline of the construction. Usage of the three tapes of $T^\dagger$ is as follows.

- 1st tape (working tape) keeps the contents of the tape of T.
- 2nd tape (history tape) keeps the "history" of the movements of T.
- 3rd tape (output tape) gives the output string of T.

The entire computation process of $T^\dagger$ is divided into three stages provided that T halts. They are the forward computing stage, the copying stage, and the backward computing stage. The RTM $T^\dagger$ consists of three sub-Turing machines $\tilde{T}$, T^c, and $\tilde{T}^{-1}$, which are used in these three stages. Each sub-Turing machine works as follows. Here, we assume that the quintuples in δ are numbered from 1 to $|\delta|$.

1. Forward computing stage:
   $\tilde{T}$ simulates T step by step using the working tape. In addition, at each step, $\tilde{T}$ writes the number assigned to the quintuple just executed on the history tape. By this method, $\tilde{T}$ can be reversible even if T is irreversible. Note that, if T does not halt, then $\tilde{T}$ also does not.
2. Copying stage:
   If $\tilde{T}$ halts in the final state, then T^c is activated. It copies the contents of the working tape to the output tape. We can design T^c so that it is reversible, and does not use the history tape.
3. Backward computing stage:
   $\tilde{T}^{-1}$ is activated, and the forward computing process is undone. By this, $T^\dagger$ goes back to essentially the same ID as the initial ID except the output tape, and hence the contents of the history tape are reversibly erased. Since $\tilde{T}^{-1}$ does not use the output tape, the output of T is kept on the tape at the end of this stage.

Note that the string left on the history tape at the end of the forward computing stage is considered as *garbage information*. However, it is reversibly erased by the inverse RTM $\tilde{T}^{-1}$. In addition, between the forward and backward computing stages, the copy stage is inserted to keep the output string of T. Thus, we obtain a *garbage-less* RTM $T^\dagger$. This idea was later used in [5] to compose a garbage-less combinatorial logic circuit (see Sect. 4.1.4 and Fig. 4.13).

Bennett [1] showed the following theorem, which states that for any given one-tape (irreversible) TM, we can construct a garbage-less three-tape RTM that simulates the former.

Theorem 5.1. *[1] Let* $T = (Q, S, q_0, \{q_f\}, s_0, \delta)$ *be a one-tape TM in the quintuple form. We assume, without loss of generality, T is a transducer in the standard form. Then, we can construct a three-tape RTM* $T^\dagger = (Q^\dagger, (S, S', S), q_0, \{\hat{q}_0\}, (s_0, s_0, s_0), \delta^\dagger)$ *that satisfies the following condition. Note that λ denotes the empty string.*

$$\forall \alpha, \beta \in (S - \{s_0\})^+$$
$$((q_0 s_0 \alpha \vdash_T^* q_f s_0 \beta)$$
$$\Leftrightarrow (((\lambda, s_0 \alpha), (\lambda, \lambda), (\lambda, \lambda), q_0) \vdash_{T^\dagger}^* ((\lambda, s_0 \alpha), (\lambda, \lambda), (\lambda, s_0 \beta), \hat{q}_0)))$$

Proof. The three-tape RTM $T^\dagger$ consists of three sub-RTMs $\tilde{T}$, T^c and $\tilde{T}^{-1}$ as its components. In the following, we construct each of them one by one, and finally combine them to make $T^\dagger$.

We first design the RTM $\tilde{T}$ from T for the forward computing stage. Let $\nu : \delta \to \{1, \ldots, |\delta|\}$ be a bijection, by which the elements in δ are numbered. Note that, since there are many such bijections, it is chosen arbitrarily. Let $S_h = \{1, \ldots, |\delta|\}$. Then, $\tilde{T}$ is defined as follows.

$$\tilde{T} = (Q, (S, S_h \cup \{s_0\}, S), q_0, \{q_f\}, (s_0, s_0, s_0), \delta')$$
$$\delta' = \{[p, [s, s_0, s_0], [t, \nu(r), s_0], [d, +, 0], q] \mid r = [p, s, t, d, q] \wedge r \in \delta \wedge q \neq q_f\} \cup$$
$$\{[p, [s, s_0, s_0], [t, \nu(r), s_0], [0, 0, 0], q_f] \mid r = [p, s, t, 0, q_f] \wedge r \in \delta\}$$

From δ', it is easily seen that $\tilde{T}$ simulates T on the working tape in a straightforward manner. The RTM $\tilde{T}$ also writes the number $v(r)$ of the quintuple r executed at each step on the history tape. Hence, the following relation holds.

$$\forall \alpha, \beta \in (S - \{s_0\})^+$$
$$((q_0 s_0 \alpha \vdash_T^* q_f s_0 \beta)$$
$$\Leftrightarrow \exists \eta \in S_h^* \ \exists h \in S_h$$
$$(((\lambda, s_0\alpha), (\lambda, \lambda), (\lambda, \lambda), q_0) \vdash_{\tilde{T}}^* ((\lambda, s_0\beta), (\eta, h), (\lambda, \lambda), q_f)))$$

Reversibility of $\tilde{T}$ is verified as follows. Let $[p, [s, s_0, s_0], [t, v(r), s_0], [d_1, d_2, 0], q]$, and $[p', [s', s_0, s_0], [t', v(r'), s_0], [d'_1, d'_2, 0], q']$ be arbitrary pair of distinct quintuples in δ'. If $q = q'$, then $d_1 = d'_1$, since T is a transducer in the standard form, and thus it has the unique shift-direction property. From the definition of δ', if $q = q'$, then $d_2 = d'_2$ also holds. Hence, if $q = q'$, then $[d_1, d_2, 0] = [d'_1, d'_2, 0]$ holds. On the other hand, $v(r)$ and $v(r')$ are the numbers of the different quintuples $r = [p, s, t, d_1, q]$ and $r' = [p', s', t', d'_1, q']$, and thus they are different. Hence, $[t, v(r), s_0] \neq [t', v(r'), s_0]$, and thus the above pair of quintuples satisfies the reversibility condition. Therefore, $\tilde{T}$ is reversible.

It is easy to see that there is no quintuple in δ' whose fifth element is q_0, since T is so. In addition, $\mathbf{h}_{sd}(q_f) = [0, 0, 0]$ in $\tilde{T}$.

Second, we design the RTM T^c for the copying stage. It is defined as follows, where $S'_h = \{v(r) \mid r = [p, s, t, 0, q_f] \ \wedge \ r \in \delta\}$.

$$T^c = (Q^c, (S, S_h \cup \{s_0\}, S), q_f, \{\hat{q}_f\}, (s_0, s_0, s_0), \delta^c)$$
$$Q^c = \{q_f, c_R, c_L, \hat{q}_f\}$$
$$\delta^c = \{[q_f, [s_0, t, s_0], [s_0, t, s_0], [+, 0, +], c_R] \mid t \in S'_h\} \cup$$
$$\quad \{[c_R, [s_0, t, s_0], [s_0, t, s_0], [-, 0, -], c_L] \mid t \in S'_h\} \cup$$
$$\quad \{[c_R, [s, t, s_0], [s, t, s], [+, 0, +], c_R] \mid s \in S - \{s_0\} \ \wedge \ t \in S'_h\} \cup$$
$$\quad \{[c_L, [s_0, t, s_0], [s_0, t, s_0], [0, 0, 0], \hat{q}_f] \mid t \in S'_h\} \cup$$
$$\quad \{[c_L, [s, t, s], [s, t, s], [-, 0, -], c_L] \mid s \in S - \{s_0\} \ \wedge \ t \in S'_h\}$$

T^c copies the non-blank part of the working tape into the output tape from left to right by the state c_R. Then, it makes the two heads go back to the left end of the tapes by the state c_L. Hence, the following relation holds.

$$\forall \alpha \in (S - \{s_0\})^+ \ \forall \eta \in S_h^* \ \forall h \in S_h$$
$$(((\lambda, s_0\alpha), (\eta, h), (\lambda, \lambda), q_f) \vdash_{T^c}^* ((\lambda, s_0\alpha), (\eta, h), (\lambda, s_0\alpha), \hat{q}_f))$$

Reversibility of T^c is easily verified by checking every pair of quintuples in δ^c.

Third, the RTM $\tilde{T}^{-1}$ for the reverse computing stage is obtained as follows according to Definition 5.17.

$$\tilde{T}^{-1} = (\hat{Q}, (S, S_h \cup \{s_0\}, S), \hat{q}_f, \{\hat{q}_0\}, (s_0, s_0, s_0), \hat{\delta}')$$
$$\hat{Q} = \{\hat{q} \mid q \in Q\}$$
$$\hat{\delta}' = \{[\hat{q}, \mathbf{t}, \mathbf{s}, -\mathbf{h}_{sd}(p), \hat{p}] \mid [p, \mathbf{s}, \mathbf{t}, \mathbf{h}_{sd}(q), q] \in \delta'\}$$

Hence, the following relation holds.

$$\forall \alpha, \beta \in (S - \{s_0\})^+ \ \forall \eta \in S_h^* \ \forall h \in S_h \ \forall \gamma, \gamma' \in S^*$$
$$(((\lambda, s_0\alpha), (\lambda, \lambda), (\gamma, \gamma'), q_0) \ \vdash^*_{\tilde{T}} \ ((\lambda, s_0\beta), (\eta, h), (\gamma, \gamma'), q_f)))$$
$$\Leftrightarrow \ (((\lambda, s_0\beta), (\eta, h), (\gamma, \gamma'), \hat{q}_f) \ \vdash^*_{\tilde{T}^{-1}} \ ((\lambda, s_0\alpha), (\lambda, \lambda), (\gamma, \gamma'), \hat{q}_0)))$$

Combining $\tilde{T}, T^c$ and $\tilde{T}^{-1}$, we obtain the three-tape RTM $T^\dagger$ that simulates the one-tape TM T. Here, we assume $Q \cap \{c_R, c_L\} = \emptyset$, and $\hat{Q} \cap \{c_R, c_L\} = \emptyset$ (if otherwise, rename some states in $Q \cup \hat{Q}$).

$$T^\dagger = (Q^\dagger, (S, S_h \cup \{s_0\}, S), q_0, \{\hat{q}_0\}, (s_0, s_0, s_0), \delta^\dagger)$$
$$Q^\dagger = Q \cup \{c_R, c_L\} \cup \hat{Q}$$
$$\delta^\dagger = \delta' \cup \delta^c \cup \hat{\delta}'$$

From the above construction of $\tilde{T}, T^c$ and $\tilde{T}^{-1}$, it is clear that $T^\dagger$ satisfies the relation given in the theorem.   □

Example 5.4. Consider the following one-tape TM T_{erase}.

$$T_{\text{erase}} = (Q_{\text{erase}}, \{0, 1, 2\}, q_0, \{q_f\}, 0, \delta_{\text{erase}})$$
$$Q_{\text{erase}} = \{q_0, q_R, q_L, q_f\}$$
$$\delta_{\text{erase}} = \{ \ [q_0, 0, 0, +, q_R], \ [q_R, 0, 0, -, q_L], \ [q_R, 1, 1, +, q_R],$$
$$[q_R, 2, 1, +, q_R], \ [q_L, 0, 0, 0, q_f], \ [q_L, 1, 1, -, q_L] \ \}$$

The TM T_{erase} is irreversible, since the pair $[q_R, 1, 1, +, q_R]$ and $[q_R, 2, 1, +, q_R]$ violates the reversibility condition. Given an input string $\alpha \in \{1, 2\}^*$, it scans α from the left to the right, and erases all occurrences of symbol 2, i.e., rewrites them into 1's. Then, it goes back to the left end of the tape, and halts (Fig. 5.4). The following is an example of a complete computation process of T_{erase}.

$$q_0 0122 \ \vdash_{T_{\text{erase}}} \ q_R 122 \ \vdash_{T_{\text{erase}}} \ 1 q_R 22 \ \vdash_{T_{\text{erase}}} \ 11 q_R 2 \ \vdash_{T_{\text{erase}}} \ 111 q_R$$
$$\vdash_{T_{\text{erase}}} \ 11 q_L 1 \ \vdash_{T_{\text{erase}}} \ 1 q_L 11 \ \vdash_{T_{\text{erase}}} \ q_L 111 \ \vdash_{T_{\text{erase}}} \ q_L 0111 \ \vdash_{T_{\text{erase}}} \ q_f 0111$$

In general, $q_0 0\alpha \ \vdash^*_{T_{\text{erase}}} \ q_f 01^{|\alpha|}$ holds for all $\alpha \in \{1, 2\}^*$. We can also see that T_{erase} is a transducer in the standard form.

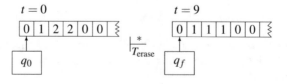

Fig. 5.4 A TM T_{erase} that erases all occurrences of symbol 2

By the method given in Theorem 5.1, we construct $\tilde{T}_{\text{erase}}, T^c_{\text{erase}}$, and $\tilde{T}^{-1}_{\text{erase}}$. Here, $S_h = \{1, \ldots, 6\}$, since $|\delta| = 6$. Let $\nu : \delta \to S_h$ be the following bijection.

$$v([q_0,0,0,+,q_R]) = 1, \ v([q_R,0,0,-,q_L]) = 2, \ v([q_R,1,1,+,q_R]) = 3,$$
$$v([q_R,2,1,+,q_R]) = 4, \ v([q_L,0,0,0,q_f]) = 5, \ v([q_L,1,1,-,q_L]) = 6$$

Then, $\tilde{T}_{\text{erase}}$ is defined as follows.

$$\tilde{T}_{\text{erase}} = (Q_{\text{erase}}, (\{0,1,2\}, \{0,1,\ldots,6\}, \{0,1,2\}), q_0, \{q_f\}, (0,0,0), \delta'_{\text{erase}})$$
$$\delta'_{\text{erase}} = \{ \ [q_0,[0,0,0],[0,1,0],[+,+,0],q_R], \ [q_R,[0,0,0],[0,2,0],[-,+,0],q_L],$$
$$[q_R,[1,0,0],[1,3,0],[+,+,0],q_R], \ [q_R,[2,0,0],[1,4,0],[+,+,0],q_R],$$
$$[q_L,[0,0,0],[0,5,0],[0,\ 0,\ 0],q_f], \ [q_L,[1,0,0],[1,6,0],[-,+,0],q_L] \ \}$$

$T_{\text{erase}}^{\text{c}}$ is given as below, since $S'_{\text{h}} = \{v(r) \mid r = [p,s,t,0,q_f] \ \wedge \ r \in \delta\} = \{5\}$.

$$T_{\text{erase}}^{\text{c}} = (Q_{\text{erase}}^{\text{c}}, (\{0,1,2\}, \{0,1,\ldots,6\}, \{0,1,2\}), q_f, \{\hat{q}_f\}, (0,0,0), \delta_{\text{erase}}^{\text{c}})$$
$$Q_{\text{erase}}^{\text{c}} = \{q_f, c_r, c_l, \hat{q}_f\}$$
$$\delta_{\text{erase}}^{\text{c}} = \{ \ [q_f,[0,5,0],[0,5,0],[+,0,+],c_R], \ [c_R,[0,5,0],[0,5,0],[-,0,-],c_L],$$
$$[c_R,[1,5,0],[1,5,1],[+,0,+],c_R], \ [c_R,[2,5,0],[2,5,2],[+,0,+],c_R],$$
$$[c_L,[0,5,0],[0,5,0],[0,0,0],\hat{q}_f], \ [c_L,[1,5,1],[1,5,1],[-,0,-],c_L],$$
$$[c_L,[2,5,2],[2,5,2],[-,0,-],c_L] \ \}$$

Finally, we give $\tilde{T}_{\text{erase}}^{-1}$. Since $\mathbf{h}_{\text{sd}}(q_0) = [0,0,0]$, $\mathbf{h}_{\text{sd}}(q_R) = [+,+,0]$, $\mathbf{h}_{\text{sd}}(q_L) = [-,+,0]$, and $\mathbf{h}_{\text{sd}}(q_f) = [0,0,0]$ hold in $\tilde{T}_{\text{erase}}$, $\tilde{T}_{\text{erase}}^{-1}$ is defined as follows.

$$\tilde{T}_{\text{erase}}^{-1} = (\hat{Q}_{\text{erase}}, (\{0,1,2\}, \{0,1,\ldots,6\}, \{0,1,2\}), \hat{q}_0, \{\hat{q}_f\}, (0,0,0), \hat{\delta}'_{\text{erase}})$$
$$\hat{Q}_{\text{erase}} = \{\hat{q}_0, \hat{q}_R, \hat{q}_L, \hat{q}_f\}$$
$$\hat{\delta}'_{\text{erase}} = \{ \ [\hat{q}_R,[0,1,0],[0,0,0],[0,\ 0,\ 0],\hat{q}_0], \ [\hat{q}_L,[0,2,0],[0,0,0],[-,-,0],\hat{q}_R],$$
$$[\hat{q}_R,[1,3,0],[1,0,0],[-,-,0],\hat{q}_R], \ [\hat{q}_R,[1,4,0],[2,0,0],[-,-,0],\hat{q}_R],$$
$$[\hat{q}_f,[0,5,0],[0,0,0],[+,-,0],\hat{q}_L], \ [\hat{q}_L,[1,6,0],[1,0,0],[+,-,0],\hat{q}_L] \ \}$$

By above, we obtain the three-tape RTM $T_{\text{erase}}^{\dagger}$ that simulates T_{erase}.

$$T_{\text{erase}}^{\dagger} = (Q_{\text{erase}}^{\dagger}, (\{0,1,2\}, \{0,1,\ldots,6\}, \{0,1,2\}), q_0, \{\hat{q}_0\}, (0,0,0), \delta_{\text{erase}}^{\dagger})$$
$$Q_{\text{erase}}^{\dagger} = \{q_0, q_R, q_L, q_f, c_R, c_L, \hat{q}_0, \hat{q}_R, \hat{q}_L, \hat{q}_f\}$$
$$\delta_{\text{erase}}^{\dagger} = \delta'_{\text{erase}} \cup \delta_{\text{erase}}^{\text{c}} \cup \hat{\delta}'_{\text{erase}}$$

The complete computing process of $T_{\text{erase}}^{\dagger}$ for the input 122 is as follows. $T_{\text{erase}}^{\dagger}$ makes 27 steps of moves.

$$((\lambda,0122),(\lambda,\lambda),(\lambda,\lambda),q_0) \qquad \vdash_{T_{\text{erase}}^{\dagger}} ((\lambda,122),(1,\lambda),(\lambda,\lambda),q_R)$$
$$\vdash_{T_{\text{erase}}^{\dagger}} ((1,22),(13,\lambda),(\lambda,\lambda),q_R) \qquad \vdash_{T_{\text{erase}}^{\dagger}} ((11,2),(134,\lambda),(\lambda,\lambda),q_R)$$
$$\vdash_{T_{\text{erase}}^{\dagger}} ((111,\lambda),(1344,\lambda),(\lambda,\lambda),q_R) \qquad \vdash_{T_{\text{erase}}^{\dagger}} ((11,1),(13442,\lambda),(\lambda,\lambda),q_L)$$
$$\vdash_{T_{\text{erase}}^{\dagger}} ((1,11),(134426,\lambda),(\lambda,\lambda),q_L) \qquad \vdash_{T_{\text{erase}}^{\dagger}} ((\lambda,111),(1344266,\lambda),(\lambda,\lambda),q_L)$$
$$\vdash_{T_{\text{erase}}^{\dagger}} ((\lambda,0111),(13442666,\lambda),(\lambda,\lambda),q_L) \qquad \vdash_{T_{\text{erase}}^{\dagger}} ((\lambda,0111),(13442666,5),(\lambda,\lambda),q_f)$$
$$\vdash_{T_{\text{erase}}^{\dagger}} ((\lambda,111),(13442666,5),(\lambda,\lambda),c_R) \qquad \vdash_{T_{\text{erase}}^{\dagger}} ((1,11),(13442666,5),(1,\lambda),c_R)$$
$$\vdash_{T_{\text{erase}}^{\dagger}} ((11,1),(13442666,5),(11,\lambda),c_R) \qquad \vdash_{T_{\text{erase}}^{\dagger}} ((111,\lambda),(13442666,5),(111,\lambda),c_R)$$
$$\vdash_{T_{\text{erase}}^{\dagger}} ((11,1),(13442666,5),(11,1),c_L) \qquad \vdash_{T_{\text{erase}}^{\dagger}} ((1,11),(13442666,5),(1,11),c_L)$$

$\vdash_{T_{\text{erase}}^{\dagger}} ((\lambda, 111), (13442666, 5), (\lambda, 111), c_L)$ $\vdash_{T_{\text{erase}}^{\dagger}} ((\lambda, 0111), (13442666, 5), (\lambda, 0111), c_L)$

$\vdash_{T_{\text{erase}}^{\dagger}} ((\lambda, 0111), (13442666, 5), (\lambda, 0111), \hat{q}_f)$ $\vdash_{T_{\text{erase}}^{\dagger}} ((\lambda, 111), (1344266, 6), (\lambda, 0111), \hat{q}_L)$

$\vdash_{T_{\text{erase}}^{\dagger}} ((1, 11), (134426, 6), (\lambda, 0111), \hat{q}_L)$ $\vdash_{T_{\text{erase}}^{\dagger}} ((11, 1), (13442, 6), (\lambda, 0111), \hat{q}_L)$

$\vdash_{T_{\text{erase}}^{\dagger}} ((111, \lambda), (1344, 2), (\lambda, 0111), \hat{q}_L)$ $\vdash_{T_{\text{erase}}^{\dagger}} ((11, 1), (134, 4), (\lambda, 0111), \hat{q}_R)$

$\vdash_{T_{\text{erase}}^{\dagger}} ((1, 12), (13, 4), (\lambda, 0111), \hat{q}_R)$ $\vdash_{T_{\text{erase}}^{\dagger}} ((\lambda, 122), (1, 3), (\lambda, 0111), \hat{q}_R)$

$\vdash_{T_{\text{erase}}^{\dagger}} ((\lambda, 0112), (\lambda, 1), (\lambda, 0111), \hat{q}_R)$ $\vdash_{T_{\text{erase}}^{\dagger}} ((\lambda, 0122), (\lambda, \lambda), (\lambda, 0111), \hat{q}_0)$

Some snapshots of the above computing process is shown in Fig. 5.5. Here, the forward computing stage is from $t = 0$ to 9, the copying stage is from $t = 9$ to 18, and the backward computing stage is from $t = 18$ to 27. $\square$

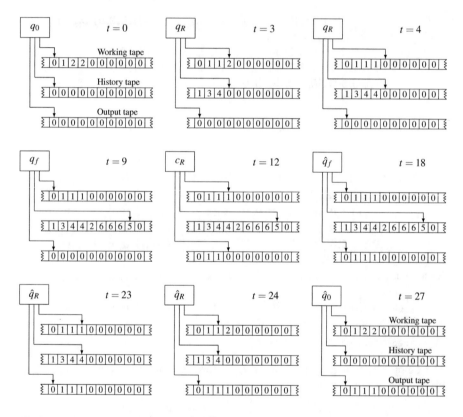

Fig. 5.5 A three-tape RTM $T_{\text{erase}}^{\dagger}$ that simulates an irreversible one-tape TM T_{erase} without leaving garbage information on the history tape

From Theorem 5.1 and Definition 5.9 we have the following corollary.

Corollary 5.3. *The class of garbage-less three-tape RTM is computationally universal.*

5.3 Variations of Reversible Turing Machines

In this section, we consider variations of RTMs, in particular, several restricted types of RTMs, and show that any RTM can be converted into the ones of the restricted forms that simulates the former. Hence, these classes of RTMs are also computationally universal. Here, we prove the following.

- RTMs with two-way infinite tapes can be converted into RTMs with one-way infinite tapes.
- Multi-tape RTMs can be converted into one-tape RTMs.
- Many-symbol RTMs can be converted into two-symbol RTMs.
- Many-state RTMs can be converted into three-state and four-state RTMs.

In the case of irreversible TMs, the corresponding results are proved relatively easily. However, in the case of RTMs, conversion methods must be carefully designed so that the produced TMs satisfy the reversibility condition. The results shown in this section will be used to show computational universality of other reversible computing systems in the following chapters. Note that all RTMs considered in this section are in the quintuple form.

5.3.1 Converting RTMs with two-way infinite tapes into RTMs with one-way infinite tapes

A *one-way infinite tape* is one that extends rightward indefinitely, but has the left end as in Fig. 5.6. If a TM goes leftward from the leftmost square, it drops off the tape, and thus it cannot make a further movement. Therefore, a TM with a one-way infinite tape should be appropriately designed so that it never drops off the tape, provided that it starts from a pre-specified "legal" initial ID. Such a TM is called a *TM with a one-way infinite tape*. Therefore, a TM with a one-way infinite tape uses only the squares whose positions are to the right of some point on the tape, even if a two-way infinite tape is given. For example, T_{copy} in Example 5.1, which starts from an initial ID of the form $q_{\text{start}} 1^n a$, is regarded as a TM with a one-way infinite tape.

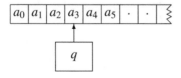

Fig. 5.6 A TM with a one-way infinite tape

We first show that any one-tape RTM with a two-way infinite tape can be converted into an RTM with a one-way infinite tape.

Theorem 5.2. *For any one-tape RTM T with a two-way infinite tape, we can construct an RTM T' with a one-way infinite tape that simulates T.*

Proof. Let $T = (Q, S, q_0, F, s_0, \delta)$. We assume T is in the quintuple form. Let h_{sd} : $Q \to \{-, 0, +\}$ be the function in Definition 5.11 such that $h_{sd}(q)$ gives the shift direction associated with $q \in Q$. Then, T' is defined as follows.

$$T' = (Q', S', q_0^+, F', [s_0, s_0], \delta')$$
$$Q' = \{q^+, q^- \mid q \in Q\}$$
$$S' = S \times (S \cup \{\triangleright\})$$
$$F' = \{q^+, q^- \mid q \in F\}$$
$$\delta_1' = \{[p^+, [s, x], [t, x], h_{sd}(q), q^+] \mid [p, s, t, h_{sd}(q), q] \in \delta \,\wedge\, x \in S\}$$
$$\delta_2' = \{[p^-, [x, s], [x, t], -h_{sd}(q), q^-] \mid [p, s, t, h_{sd}(q), q] \in \delta \,\wedge\, x \in S\}$$
$$\delta_3' = \{[p^+, [s, \triangleright], [t, \triangleright], h_{sd}(q), q^+] \mid$$
$$\qquad [p, s, t, h_{sd}(q), q] \in \delta \,\wedge\, h_{sd}(p) \neq + \,\wedge\, h_{sd}(q) \neq -\}$$
$$\delta_4' = \{[p^+, [s, \triangleright], [t, \triangleright], -h_{sd}(q), q^-] \mid$$
$$\qquad [p, s, t, h_{sd}(q), q] \in \delta \,\wedge\, h_{sd}(p) \neq + \,\wedge\, h_{sd}(q) = -\}$$
$$\delta_5' = \{[p^-, [s, \triangleright], [t, \triangleright], h_{sd}(q), q^+] \mid$$
$$\qquad [p, s, t, h_{sd}(q), q] \in \delta \,\wedge\, h_{sd}(p) = + \,\wedge\, h_{sd}(q) \neq -\}$$
$$\delta_6' = \{[p^-, [s, \triangleright], [t, \triangleright], -h_{sd}(q), q^-] \mid$$
$$\qquad [p, s, t, h_{sd}(q), q] \in \delta \,\wedge\, h_{sd}(p) = + \,\wedge\, h_{sd}(q) = -\}$$
$$\delta' = \delta_1' \cup \delta_2' \cup \delta_3' \cup \delta_4' \cup \delta_5' \cup \delta_6'$$

The tape of T' has two tracks. The right half of the tape of T is simulated by the first track of the tape of T', while the left half is simulated by the second track as shown in Fig. 5.7. Thus the two-way infinite tape is folded at the origin point. If T is scanning a square in the right half (left half, respectively) of the tape, then T' simulates T by the state of the form q^+ (q^-), and by the quintuples in δ_1' (δ_2'). In the leftmost square of the tape of T' a special symbol $\triangleright$ is written. At this square, q^+ can go to q^-, and vice versa, by the quintuples in $\delta_3' \cup \cdots \cup \delta_6'$.

Assume T starts from the initial ID

$$a_1 a_2 \cdots a_m q_0 b_1 \cdots b_n,$$

where $m, n \in \mathbb{N}$. Then, set the initial ID of T' as follows.

$$\begin{array}{ll} [a_1, \triangleright][a_2, s_0] \cdots [a_m, s_0]\, q_0^+\, [b_1, s_0][b_2, s_0] \cdots [b_n, s_0] & \text{if } m > 0 \\ q_0^+\, [b_1, \triangleright][b_2, s_0] \cdots [b_n, s_0] & \text{if } m = 0 \,\wedge\, n > 0 \\ q_0^+\, [s_0, \triangleright] & \text{if } m = 0 \,\wedge\, n = 0 \end{array}$$

From the initial ID, T' simulates T step by step by quintuples in δ'. It should be noted that the RTM T' simulates the given T in real time (i.e., exactly in the same steps), since each quintuple in δ' simulates one step of T.

Reversibility of T' is proved as follows. Let $r_1 = [p_1, u_1, v_1, d_1, q_1]$ and $r_2 = [p_2, u_2, v_2, d_2, q_2]$ be distinct quintuples in δ'. Assume $q_1 = q_2$, and they are of the form q^+ (the case of q^- is proved similarly). If both r_1 and r_2 are in δ_1', then $d_1 = h_{sd}(q_1) = h_{sd}(q_2) = d_2$, and $v_1 = [t_1, x_1]$ and $v_2 = [t_2, x_2]$ for some $t_1, t_2, x_1, x_2 \in S$.

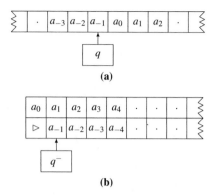

Fig. 5.7 (**a**) An RTM T with a two-way infinite tape, and (**b**) an RTM T' with a one-way infinite tape that simulates T

Since T is reversible, $t_1 \neq t_2$, and thus $v_1 \neq v_2$. Hence, r_1 and r_2 satisfies the reversibility condition. If $r_1 \in \delta_1'$ and $r_2 \in \delta_3' \cup \delta_5'$, then $d_1 = h_{sd}(q_1) = h_{sd}(q_2) = d_2$, and $v_1 \in S \times S$ and $v_2 \in \{\rhd\} \times S$. Therefore, $v_1 \neq v_2$, and thus r_1 and r_2 satisfies the reversibility condition. If $r_1, r_2 \in \delta_3' \cup \delta_5'$, then $d_1 = h_{sd}(q_1) = h_{sd}(q_2) = d_2$, and $v_1 = [t_1, \rhd]$ and $v_2 = [t_2, \rhd]$ for some $t_1, t_2 \in S$. Since T is reversible, $t_1 \neq t_2$, and thus $v_1 \neq v_2$. Hence, r_1 and r_2 satisfies the reversibility condition. By above, T' is an RTM. □

Example 5.5. Consider the following RTM T_{copyL} with a two-way infinite tape:

$$T_{copyL} = (Q_{copyL}, \{0, 1, a, m\}, q_{start}, \{q_{final}\}, 0, \delta_{copyL}).$$

Here, $Q_{copyL} = \{q_{start}, q_{find0}, q_{next0}, q_{return}, q_{final}\}$, and δ_{copyL} is as follows.

$$\delta_{copyL} = \{ \ [q_{start}, 1, m, -, q_{find0}], \quad [q_{start}, a, a, 0, q_{final}], \quad [q_{find0}, 0, 1, -, q_{next0}],$$
$$[q_{find0}, 1, 1, -, q_{find0}], \quad [q_{find0}, a, a, -, q_{find0}], \quad [q_{next0}, 0, 0, +, q_{return}],$$
$$[q_{return}, 1, 1, +, q_{return}], \quad [q_{return}, a, a, +, q_{return}], \quad [q_{return}, m, 1, -, q_{start}] \ \}$$

It is essentially the same RTM as T_{copy} in Example 5.1, but it copies the unary number to the "left" of the delimiter a for a given input $a1^n$. Namely, the following holds for all $n \in \mathbb{Z}_+$.

$$a 1^{n-1} q_{start} 1 \ |\overset{*}{\underset{T_{copyL}}{}} \ 1^n q_{final} a 1^n$$

The complete computing process of T_{copyL} for $n = 2$ is as below.

$$a 1 q_{start} 1 \quad |\overline{{}_{T_{copyL}}} \ a q_{find0} 1 m \quad |\overline{{}_{T_{copyL}}} \ q_{find0} a 1 m \quad |\overline{{}_{T_{copyL}}} \ q_{find0} 0 a 1 m$$
$$|\overline{{}_{T_{copyL}}} \ q_{next0} 0 1 a 1 m \quad |\overline{{}_{T_{copyL}}} \ q_{return} 1 a 1 m \quad |\overline{{}_{T_{copyL}}} \ 1 q_{return} a 1 m \quad |\overline{{}_{T_{copyL}}} \ 1 a q_{return} 1 m$$
$$|\overline{{}_{T_{copyL}}} \ 1 a 1 q_{return} m \quad |\overline{{}_{T_{copyL}}} \ 1 a q_{start} 1 1 \quad |\overline{{}_{T_{copyL}}} \ 1 q_{find0} a m 1 \quad |\overline{{}_{T_{copyL}}} \ q_{find0} 1 a m 1$$
$$|\overline{{}_{T_{copyL}}} \ q_{find0} 0 1 a m 1 \quad |\overline{{}_{T_{copyL}}} \ q_{next0} 0 1 1 a m 1 \quad |\overline{{}_{T_{copyL}}} \ q_{return} 1 1 a m 1 \quad |\overline{{}_{T_{copyL}}} \ 1 q_{return} 1 a m 1$$
$$|\overline{{}_{T_{copyL}}} \ 1 1 q_{return} a m 1 \quad |\overline{{}_{T_{copyL}}} \ 1 1 a q_{return} m 1 \quad |\overline{{}_{T_{copyL}}} \ 1 1 q_{start} a 1 1 \quad |\overline{{}_{T_{copyL}}} \ 1 1 q_{final} a 1 1$$

The RTM T'_{copyL} with one-way infinite tape that simulates T_{copyL} is as follows.

$T'_{copyL} = (Q'_{copyL}, S'_{copyL}, q^+_{start}, \{q^+_{final}, q^-_{final}\}, [0,0], \delta'_{copyL})$
$Q'_{copyL} = \{q^+_{start}, q^+_{find0}, q^+_{next0}, q^+_{return}, q^+_{final}, q^-_{start}, q^-_{find0}, q^-_{next0}, q^-_{return}, q^-_{final}\}$
$S'_{copyL} = \{[s_1, s_2] \mid s_1, s_2 \in \{0,1,a,m\}\} \cup \{\triangleright\}$
$\delta'_1 = \{ [q^+_{start}, [1,x], [m,x], -, q^+_{find0}], \quad [q^+_{start}, [a,x], [a,x], 0, q^+_{final}],$
$\quad [q^+_{find0}, [0,x], [1,x], -, q^+_{next0}], \quad [q^+_{find0}, [1,x], [1,x], -, q^+_{find0}],$
$\quad [q^+_{find0}, [a,x], [a,x], -, q^+_{find0}], \quad [q^+_{next0}, [0,x], [0,x], +, q^+_{return}],$
$\quad [q^+_{return}, [1,x], [1,x], +, q^+_{return}], \quad [q^+_{return}, [a,x], [a,x], +, q^+_{return}],$
$\quad [q^+_{return}, [m,x], [1,x], -, q^+_{start}] \mid x \in \{0,1,a,m\} \}$
$\delta'_2 = \{ [q^-_{start}, [x,1], [x,m], +, q^-_{find0}], \quad [q^-_{start}, [x,a], [x,a], 0, q^-_{final}],$
$\quad [q^-_{find0}, [x,0], [x,1], +, q^-_{next0}], \quad [q^-_{find0}, [x,1], [x,1], +, q^-_{find0}],$
$\quad [q^-_{find0}, [x,a], [x,a], +, q^-_{find0}], \quad [q^-_{next0}, [x,0], [x,0], -, q^-_{return}],$
$\quad [q^-_{return}, [x,1], [x,1], -, q^-_{return}], \quad [q^-_{return}, [x,a], [x,a], -, q^-_{return}],$
$\quad [q^-_{return}, [x,m], [x,1], +, q^-_{start}] \mid x \in \{0,1,a,m\} \}$
$\delta'_3 = \{ [q^+_{next0}, [0,\triangleright], [0,\triangleright], +, q^-_{return}], \quad [q^-_{start}, [a,\triangleright], [a,\triangleright], 0, q^+_{final}] \}$
$\delta'_4 = \{ [q^+_{start}, [1,\triangleright], [m,\triangleright], +, q^-_{find0}], \quad [q^-_{find0}, [0,\triangleright], [1,\triangleright], +, q^+_{next0}],$
$\quad [q^-_{find0}, [1,\triangleright], [1,\triangleright], +, q^-_{find0}], \quad [q^-_{find0}, [a,\triangleright], [a,\triangleright], +, q^-_{find0}] \}$
$\delta'_5 = \{ [q^-_{return}, [1,\triangleright], [1,\triangleright], +, q^-_{return}], \quad [q^-_{return}, [a,\triangleright], [a,\triangleright], +, q^-_{return}] \}$
$\delta'_6 = \{ [q^-_{return}, [m,\triangleright], [1,\triangleright], +, q^+_{start}] \}$
$\delta'_{copyL} = \delta'_1 \cup \delta'_2 \cup \delta'_3 \cup \delta'_4 \cup \delta'_5 \cup \delta'_6$

We can see the following holds for all $n \in \mathbb{Z}_+$.

$$[a, \triangleright][1,0]^{n-1} q^+_{start} [1,0] \vdash^*_{T'_{copyL}} q^+_{final} [a, \triangleright][1,1]^n$$

The complete computing process of T'_{copyL} for $n = 2$ is as below.

$$[a, \triangleright][1,0] q^+_{start} [1,0] \quad \vdash_{T'_{copyL}} \quad [a, \triangleright] q^+_{find0} [1,0][m,0]$$
$$\vdash_{T'_{copyL}} \quad q^+_{find0} [a, \triangleright][1,0][m,0] \quad \vdash_{T'_{copyL}} \quad [a, \triangleright] q^-_{find0} [1,0][m,0]$$
$$\vdash_{T'_{copyL}} \quad [a, \triangleright][1,1] q^+_{next0} [m,0] \quad \vdash_{T'_{copyL}} \quad [a, \triangleright] q^-_{return} [1,1][m,0]$$
$$\vdash_{T'_{copyL}} \quad q^-_{return} [a, \triangleright][1,1][m,0] \quad \vdash_{T'_{copyL}} \quad [a, \triangleright] q^+_{return} [1,1][m,0]$$
$$\vdash_{T'_{copyL}} \quad [a, \triangleright][1,1] q^+_{return} [m,0] \quad \vdash_{T'_{copyL}} \quad [a, \triangleright] q^+_{start} [1,1][1,0]$$
$$\vdash_{T'_{copyL}} \quad q^+_{find0} [a, \triangleright][m,1][1,0] \quad \vdash_{T'_{copyL}} \quad [a, \triangleright] q^-_{find0} [m,1][1,0]$$
$$\vdash_{T'_{copyL}} \quad [a, \triangleright][m,1] q^-_{find0} [1,0] \quad \vdash_{T'_{copyL}} \quad [a, \triangleright][m,1][1,1] q^+_{next0}$$
$$\vdash_{T'_{copyL}} \quad [a, \triangleright][m,1] q^-_{return} [1,1] \quad \vdash_{T'_{copyL}} \quad [a, \triangleright] q^-_{return} [m,1][1,1]$$
$$\vdash_{T'_{copyL}} \quad q^-_{return} [a, \triangleright][m,1][1,1] \quad \vdash_{T'_{copyL}} \quad [a, \triangleright] q^+_{return} [m,1][1,1]$$
$$\vdash_{T'_{copyL}} \quad q^+_{start} [a, \triangleright][1,1][1,1] \quad \vdash_{T'_{copyL}} \quad q^+_{final} [a, \triangleright][1,1][1,1]$$

We can see T'_{copyL} simulates T_{copyL} without using squares that are to the left of the square with the symbol $[a, \triangleright]$. $\square$

Theorem 5.2 can be generalized to k-tape RTM ($k \in \mathbb{Z}_+$) by applying the "folding method" in the proof of Theorem 5.2 to each of k tapes. It is, in principle, possible to apply this method to k tapes of T simultaneously. However, if we do so, we must deal with a large number of cases of combinations of positions of k heads, and thus the description of the conversion method will become quite complicated. Instead, we take a method of converting two-way infinite tapes into one-way infinite tapes "one by one".

Corollary 5.4. *For any k-tape RTM T with two-way infinite tapes ($k \in \mathbb{Z}_+$), we can construct a k-tape RTM $\tilde{T}$ with one-way infinite tapes that simulates T.*

Proof. We prove the corollary for the case of $k = 2$. Thus, we consider a two-tape RTM with two-way infinite tapes, and give a method of converting it into an RTM with one-way infinite tapes. The method is easily extended to k-tape RTMs for $k > 2$.

Let $T = (Q, (S_1, S_2), q_0, F, (s_{0,1}, s_{0,2}), \delta)$ be a two-tape RTM with two-way infinite tapes. We assume T is in the quintuple form. We first convert the first tape of T into a one-way infinite one. Let $h_{sd}^1 : Q \to \{-, 0, +\}$, and $h_{sd}^2 : Q \to \{-, 0, +\}$ be the function similarly defined in Definition 5.16 that gives the shift directions of the two heads associated with $q \in Q$. A two-tape RTM T' such that its first tape is one-way infinite, and it simulates T is defined as follows.

$$T' = (Q', (S_1', S_2), q_0^+, F', ([s_{0,1}, s_{0,1}], s_{0,2}), \delta')$$
$$Q' = \{q^+, q^- \mid q \in Q\}$$
$$S_1' = S_1 \times (S_1 \cup \{\triangleright\})$$
$$F' = \{q^+, q^- \mid q \in F\}$$
$$\delta_1' = \{[p^+, [[s_1, x_1], s_2], [[t_1, x_1], t_2], [h_{sd}^1(q), h_{sd}^2(q)], q^+] \mid$$
$$\qquad [p, [s_1, s_2], [t_1, t_2], [h_{sd}^1(q), h_{sd}^2(q)], q] \in \delta \wedge x_1 \in S_1\}$$
$$\delta_2' = \{[p^-, [[s_1, x_1], s_2], [[t_1, x_1], t_2], [-h_{sd}^1(q), h_{sd}^2(q)], q^-] \mid$$
$$\qquad [p, [s_1, s_2], [t_1, t_2], [h_{sd}^1(q), h_{sd}^2(q)], q] \in \delta \wedge x_1 \in S_1\}$$
$$\delta_3' = \{[p^+, [[s_1, \triangleright], s_2], [[t_1, \triangleright], t_2], [h_{sd}^1(q), h_{sd}^2(q)], q^+] \mid$$
$$\qquad [p, [s_1, s_2], [t_1, t_2], [h_{sd}^1(q), h_{sd}^2(q)], q] \in \delta \wedge h_{sd}^1(p) \neq + \wedge h_{sd}^1(q) \neq -\}$$
$$\delta_4' = \{[p^+, [[s_1, \triangleright], s_2], [[t_1, \triangleright], t_2], [-h_{sd}^1(q), h_{sd}^2(q)], q^-] \mid$$
$$\qquad [p, [s_1, s_2], [t_1, t_2], [h_{sd}^1(q), h_{sd}^2(q)], q] \in \delta \wedge h_{sd}^1(p) \neq + \wedge h_{sd}^1(q) = -\}$$
$$\delta_5' = \{[p^-, [[s_1, \triangleright], s_2], [[t_1, \triangleright], t_2], [h_{sd}^1(q), h_{sd}^2(q)], q^+] \mid$$
$$\qquad [p, [s_1, s_2], [t_1, t_2], [h_{sd}^1(q), h_{sd}^2(q)], q] \in \delta \wedge h_{sd}^1(p) = + \wedge h_{sd}^1(q) \neq -\}$$
$$\delta_6' = \{[p^-, [[s_1, \triangleright], s_2], [[t_1, \triangleright], t_2], [-h_{sd}^1(q), h_{sd}^2(q)], q^-] \mid$$
$$\qquad [p, [s_1, s_2], [t_1, t_2], [h_{sd}^1(q), h_{sd}^2(q)], q] \in \delta \wedge h_{sd}^1(p) = + \wedge h_{sd}^1(q) = -\}$$
$$\delta' = \delta_1' \cup \delta_2' \cup \delta_3' \cup \delta_4' \cup \delta_5' \cup \delta_6'$$

The above construction of T' is essentially the same as the one in Theorem 5.2. From δ' we can see that, operations on the second tape in T is simulated in a straightforward manner in T', i.e., exactly the same operations as those in T are performed. In this sense, conversion on the first tape does not affect the operations on the second tape at all. Reversibility of T' is verified in a similar manner as in Theorem 5.2.

Likewise, it is also possible to convert the second tape into a one-way infinite one without affecting the operations on the first tape. Combining these conversion procedures we obtain a two-tape RTM $\tilde{T}$ with one-way infinite tapes. □

5.3.2 Converting multi-tape RTMs into one-tape RTMs

We show a multi-tape RTM can be converted into an equivalent one-tape RTM based on the method given in [12].

Theorem 5.3. *For any k-tape RTM T ($k \in \mathbb{Z}_+$), we can construct a one-tape RTM T′ with a one-way infinite tape that simulates T.*

Proof. Here, we prove the theorem for $k = 2$, since it is easy to extend the construction method to the case of $k > 2$. Let $T = (Q, (S_1, S_2), q_0, F, (0,0), \delta)$ be a two-tape RTM (Fig. 5.8 **(a)**). We assume the blank symbols of the first and the second tapes are both 0 for simplicity. By Corollary 5.4 we can assume T has one-way infinite tapes. Let $h_{\mathrm{sd}}^1 : Q \to \{-, 0, +\}$, and $h_{\mathrm{sd}}^2 : Q \to \{-, 0, +\}$ be the function similarly defined in Definition 5.16 that give the shift directions of the first and the second heads associated with $q \in Q$. A one-tape RTM T' that simulates T is defined as follows.

$$
\begin{aligned}
T' =\ & (Q', S', [q_0, \mathrm{rd}_1, /, /], F', [0,0,0,0], \delta') \\
Q' =\ & \{[q, x, s_1, s_2] \mid q \in Q \ \wedge\ x \in \{\mathrm{rd}_1, \mathrm{rr}_1, \mathrm{rd}_2, \mathrm{rr}_2, \mathrm{wt}_1, \mathrm{sf}_1, \mathrm{wr}_1, \mathrm{wt}_2, \mathrm{sf}_2, \mathrm{wr}_2\} \\
& \wedge\ s_1 \in S_1 \cup \{/\} \ \wedge\ s_2 \in S_2 \cup \{/\}\} \\
S' =\ & (S_1 \times \{0,1\} \times S_2 \times \{0,1\}) \cup \{\rhd\} \\
F' =\ & \{[q, \mathrm{rd}_1, /, /] \mid q \in F\} \\
\delta'_1 =\ & \{[[p, \mathrm{rd}_1, /, /], [s_1, 0, s_2, h_2], [s_1, 0, s_2, h_2], +, [p, \mathrm{rd}_1, /, /]] \mid \\
& p \in Q - F \ \wedge\ s_1 \in S_1 \ \wedge\ s_2 \in S_2 \ \wedge\ h_2 \in \{0,1\}\} \\
\delta'_2 =\ & \{[[p, \mathrm{rd}_1, /, /], [s_1, 1, s_2, h_2], [0, 1, s_2, h_2], -, [p, \mathrm{rr}_1, s_1, /]] \mid \\
& p \in Q - F \ \wedge\ s_1 \in S_1 \ \wedge\ s_2 \in S_2 \ \wedge\ h_2 \in \{0,1\}\} \\
\delta'_3 =\ & \{[[p, \mathrm{rr}_1, a_1, /], [s_1, 0, s_2, h_2], [s_1, 0, s_2, h_2], -, [p, \mathrm{rr}_1, a_1, /]] \mid \\
& p \in Q - F \ \wedge\ a_1, s_1 \in S_1 \ \wedge\ s_2 \in S_2 \ \wedge\ h_2 \in \{0,1\}\} \\
\delta'_4 =\ & \{[[p, \mathrm{rr}_1, a_1, /], \rhd, \rhd, +, [p, \mathrm{rd}_2, a_1, /]] \mid \\
& p \in Q - F \ \wedge\ a_1 \in S_1\} \\
\delta'_5 =\ & \{[[p, \mathrm{rd}_2, a_1, /], [s_1, h_1, s_2, 0], [s_1, h_1, s_2, 0], +, [p, \mathrm{rd}_2, a_1, /]] \mid \\
& p \in Q - F \ \wedge\ a_1, s_1 \in S_1 \ \wedge\ s_2 \in S_2 \ \wedge\ h_1 \in \{0,1\}\} \\
\delta'_6 =\ & \{[[p, \mathrm{rd}_2, a_1, /], [s_1, h_1, s_2, 1], [s_1, h_1, 0, 1], -, [p, \mathrm{rr}_2, a_1, s_2]] \mid \\
& p \in Q - F \ \wedge\ a_1, s_1 \in S_1 \ \wedge\ s_2 \in S_2 \ \wedge\ h_1 \in \{0,1\}\} \\
\delta'_7 =\ & \{[[p, \mathrm{rr}_2, a_1, a_2], [s_1, h_1, s_2, 0], [s_1, h_1, s_2, 0], -, [p, \mathrm{rr}_2, a_1, a_2]] \mid \\
& p \in Q - F \ \wedge\ a_1, s_1 \in S_1 \ \wedge\ a_2, s_2 \in S_2 \ \wedge\ h_1 \in \{0,1\}\} \\
\delta'_8 =\ & \{[[p, \mathrm{rr}_2, a_1, a_2], \rhd, \rhd, +, [q, \mathrm{wt}_1, b_1, b_2]] \mid \\
& [p, [a_1, b_1], [a_2, b_2], [h_{\mathrm{sd}}^1(q), h_{\mathrm{sd}}^2(q)], q] \in \delta\} \\
\delta'_9 =\ & \{[[q, \mathrm{wt}_1, b_1, b_2], [s_1, 0, s_2, h_2], [s_1, 0, s_2, h_2], +, [q, \mathrm{wt}_1, b_1, b_2]] \mid \\
& q \in Q \ \wedge\ b_1, s_1 \in S_1 \ \wedge\ b_2, s_2 \in S_2 \ \wedge\ h_2 \in \{0,1\}\} \\
\delta'_{10} =\ & \{[[q, \mathrm{wt}_1, b_1, b_2], [0, 1, s_2, h_2], [b_1, 0, s_2, h_2], h_{\mathrm{sd}}^1(q), [q, \mathrm{sf}_1, /, b_2]] \mid \\
& q \in Q \ \wedge\ b_1 \in S_1 \ \wedge\ b_2, s_2 \in S_2 \ \wedge\ h_2 \in \{0,1\}\}
\end{aligned}
$$

$$\delta'_{11} = \{[[q, \mathrm{sf}_1, /, b_2], [s_1, 0, s_2, h_2], [s_1, 1, s_2, h_2], -, [q, \mathrm{wr}_1, /, b_2]] \mid$$
$$q \in Q \land s_1 \in S_1 \land b_2, s_2 \in S_2 \land h_2 \in \{0, 1\}\}$$
$$\delta'_{12} = \{[[q, \mathrm{wr}_1, /, b_2], [s_1, 0, s_2, h_2], [s_1, 0, s_2, h_2], -, [q, \mathrm{wr}_1, /, b_2]] \mid$$
$$q \in Q \land s_1 \in S_1 \land b_2, s_2 \in S_2 \land h_2 \in \{0, 1\}\}$$
$$\delta'_{13} = \{[[q, \mathrm{wr}_1, /, b_2], \rhd, \rhd, +, [q, \mathrm{wt}_2, /, b_2]] \mid$$
$$q \in Q \land b_2 \in S_2\}$$
$$\delta'_{14} = \{[[q, \mathrm{wt}_2, /, b_2], [s_1, h_1, s_2, 0], [s_1, h_1, s_2, 0], +, [q, \mathrm{wt}_2, /, b_2]] \mid$$
$$q \in Q \land s_1 \in S_1 \land b_2, s_2 \in S_2 \land h_1 \in \{0, 1\}\}$$
$$\delta'_{15} = \{[[q, \mathrm{wt}_2, /, b_2], [s_1, h_1, 0, 1], [s_1, h_1, b_2, 0], h^2_{\mathrm{sd}}(q), [q, \mathrm{sf}_2, /, /]] \mid$$
$$q \in Q \land s_1 \in S_1 \land b_2 \in S_2 \land h_1 \in \{0, 1\}\}$$
$$\delta'_{16} = \{[[q, \mathrm{sf}_2, /, /], [s_1, h_1, s_2, 0], [s_1, h_1, s_2, 1], -, [q, \mathrm{wr}_2, /, /]] \mid$$
$$q \in Q \land s_1 \in S_1 \land s_2 \in S_2 \land h_1 \in \{0, 1\}\}$$
$$\delta'_{17} = \{[[q, \mathrm{wr}_2, /, /], [s_1, h_1, s_2, 0], [s_1, h_1, s_2, 0], -, [q, \mathrm{wr}_2, /, /]] \mid$$
$$q \in Q \land s_1 \in S_1 \land s_2 \in S_2 \land h_1 \in \{0, 1\}\}$$
$$\delta'_{18} = \{[[q, \mathrm{wr}_2, /, /], \rhd, \rhd, +, [q, \mathrm{rd}_1, /, /]] \mid$$
$$q \in Q\}$$
$$\delta' = \delta'_1 \cup \cdots \cup \delta'_{18}$$

The RTM T' has a one-way infinite tape with four tracks (except the leftmost square where the special endmarker $\rhd$ is written) as in Fig. 5.8 **(b)**. The first and the third tracks keep the contents of the two tapes of T. In the second and the fourth tracks, the head positions of T are indicated by the symbol 1's (all other squares of these tracks contain symbol 0's). If the initial computational configuration of T is as shown in Fig. 5.8 **(a)**, then set the initial configuration of T' as in Fig. 5.8 **(b)**.

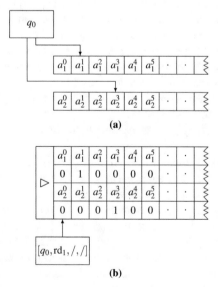

Fig. 5.8 **(a)** A two-tape RTM T, and **(b)** a one-tape RTM T' that simulates T

States of T' are of the form $[p,x,y_1,y_2]$, where $p \in Q, x \in \{\mathrm{rd}_1, \mathrm{rr}_1, \mathrm{rd}_2, \mathrm{rr}_2, \mathrm{wt}_1,$ $\mathrm{sf}_1, \mathrm{wr}_1, \mathrm{wt}_2, \mathrm{sf}_2, \mathrm{wr}_2\}, y_1 \in S_1 \cup \{/\}$, and $y_2 \in S_2 \cup \{/\}$. The symbol x indicates an operation mode of T'. Namely, rd_i is for reading a symbol on the i-th tape, rr_i is for returning to the left endmarker after the rd_i mode, wt_i is for writing a symbol on the i-th tape, sf_i is for shifting the head of the i-th tape, and wr_i is for returning to the left endmarker after the sf_i mode $(i = 1, 2)$. The symbol y_i indicates a read symbol or a symbol to be written on the i-th tape if $y_i \in S_i$ $(i = 1, 2)$.

Assume T is reading symbols a_1 and a_2 on the two tapes in the state p, and there is a quintuple $r = [p, [a_1, b_1], [a_2, b_2], [h_{\mathrm{sd}}^1(q), h_{\mathrm{sd}}^1(q)], q]$ in δ. One step of movement of T by r is simulated by a series of movements of T' in the following way. The RTM T' starts the simulation process in the state $[p, \mathrm{rd}_1, /, /]$ placing the head on the second square from the left. It goes rightward to read a tape symbol at the head position of the first track by the quintuples in δ_1'. If it reads the symbol a_1, then it is deleted and stored in the finite control by δ_2'. Hence, it becomes the state $[p, \mathrm{rr}_1, a_1, /]$, and then goes back to the left endmarker by δ_3' and δ_4'. Similarly, T' reads a tape symbol on the third track, and stores it in the finite control by δ_5', δ_6', and δ_7'. Thus, T' goes back to the left endmarker in the state $[p, \mathrm{rr}_2, a_1, a_2]$. Then, it enters the state $[q, \mathrm{wt}_1, b_1, b_2]$ by δ_8', and moves rightward to write a symbol at the head position of the first track by δ_9'. If the head position is found, then writes the tape symbol b_1 on the first track, deletes the tape symbol 1 on the second track, shifts the head to the direction $h_{\mathrm{sd}}^1(q)$, and enters the state $[q, \mathrm{sf}_1, /, b_2]$ by δ_{10}'. The RTM T' then writes the symbol 1 on the second track by δ_{11}', and goes back to the left endmarker in the state $[q, \mathrm{wr}_1, /, b_2]$ by δ_{12}' and δ_{13}'. Similarly, T' writes a tape symbol b_2 on the third track, shifts the head, and goes back to the left endmarker by $\delta_{14}', \ldots, \delta_{17}'$. It finally enters the state $[q, \mathrm{rd}_1, /, /]$, and thus one step of T by the quintuple r is simulated.

Reversibility of T' is verified by checking all the pairs of distinct quintuples $r_1 = [p_1, u_1, v_1, d_1, q_1]$ and $r_2 = [p_2, u_2, v_2, d_2, q_2]$ in δ' satisfy the reversibility condition, i.e., if $q_1 = q_2$, then $d_1 = d_2$ and $v_1 \neq v_2$ hold. Since there are many cases of combinations of r_1 and r_2, here we show only a few cases among them.

If both r_1 and r_2 are in δ_1', then $q_1 = q_2$ implies $q_1 = q_2 = [p, \mathrm{rd}_1, /, /]$ for some $p \in Q$. In this case, $d_1 = d_2 = +$. Furthermore $v_1 = [s_1^1, 0, s_2^1, h_2^1]$ and $v_2 = [s_1^2, 0, s_2^2, h_2^2]$ hold for some $s_1^1, s_1^2 \in S_1$, $s_2^1, s_2^2 \in S_2$, and $h_2^1, h_2^2 \in \{0, 1\}$. Since r_1 and r_2 are different, $s_1^1 \neq s_1^2$, $s_2^1 \neq s_2^2$, or $h_2^1 \neq h_2^2$ holds by the definition of δ_1', and thus $v_1 \neq v_2$.

If $r_1 \in \delta_2'$ and $r_2 \in \delta_3'$, then $q_1 = q_2$ implies $q_1 = [p, \mathrm{rr}_1, s_1, /], q_2 = [p, \mathrm{rr}_1, a_1, /]$ for some $p \in Q$ and $s_1, a_1 \in S_1$ such that $s_1 = a_1$. In this case, $d_1 = d_2 = +$. Furthermore $v_1 = [s_1^1, 0, s_2^1, h_2^1]$ and $v_2 = [0, 1, s_2^2, h_2^2]$ hold for some $s_1^1 \in S_1$, $s_2^1, s_2^2 \in S_2$, and $h_2^1, h_2^2 \in \{0, 1\}$. Since their second elements are different, we can see $v_1 \neq v_2$.

If both r_1 and r_2 are in δ_8', then $q_1 = [q^1, \mathrm{wt}_1, b_1^1, b_2^1]$, and $q_2 = [q^2, \mathrm{wt}_1, b_1^2, b_2^2]$ for some $q^1, q^2 \in Q$, $b_1^1, b_1^2 \in S_1$ and $b_2^1, b_2^2 \in S_2$. Since T is reversible, $(b_1^1, b_2^1) \neq (b_1^2, b_2^2)$ holds when $q^1 = q^2$. Therefore, $q_1 = q_2$ is impossible if $r_1 \neq r_2$, and thus the reversibility condition is satisfied also in this case.

In a similar manner as above, we can check all other cases. Thus, we can conclude T' is reversible. $\square$

Example 5.6. We consider a very simple two-tape RTM T_{move}, whose tapes are one-way infinite.

$$T_{\text{move}} = (\{q_0, q_f\}, (\{0, a, b\}, \{0, a, b\}), q_0, \{q_f\}, (0, 0), \delta_{\text{move}})$$
$$\delta_{\text{move}} = \{ \ [q_0, [0, 0], [0, 0], [0, 0], q_f],$$
$$[q_0, [a, 0], [0, a], [+, +], q_0], \ [q_0, [b, 0], [0, b], [+, +], q_0] \ \}$$

It moves an input string over $\{a, b\}$ given on the first tape to the second tape. Thus the following holds for all $\alpha \in \{a, b\}^+$.

$$((\lambda, \alpha), (\lambda, \lambda), q_0) \ \vdash^*_{\overline{T_{\text{move}}}} \ ((\lambda, \lambda), (\alpha, \lambda), q_f)$$

The complete computing process for the input string ab is as follows.

$$((\lambda, ab), (\lambda, \lambda), q_0) \ \vdash_{\overline{T_{\text{move}}}} \ ((\lambda, b), (a, \lambda), q_0)$$
$$\vdash_{\overline{T_{\text{move}}}} \ ((\lambda, \lambda), (ab, \lambda), q_0) \ \vdash_{\overline{T_{\text{move}}}} \ ((\lambda, \lambda), (ab, \lambda), q_f)$$

The one-tape RTM T'_{move} that simulates T_{move} obtained by the method in Theorem 5.3 is as follows.

$T'_{\text{move}} = (Q'_{\text{move}}, S'_{\text{move}}, [q_0, \text{rd}_1, /, /], F'_{\text{move}}, [0, 0, 0, 0], \delta'_{\text{move}})$

$Q'_{\text{move}} = \{ \ [q, x, s_1, s_2] \mid q \in \{q_0, q_f\} \wedge$
$\qquad\qquad x \in \{\text{rd}_1, \text{rr}_1, \text{rd}_2, \text{rr}_2, \text{wt}_1, \text{sf}_1, \text{wr}_1, \text{wt}_2, \text{sf}_2, \text{wr}_2\} \wedge s_1, s_2 \in \{0, a, b, /\} \}$

$S'_{\text{move}} = (\{0, a, b\} \times \{0, 1\} \times \{0, a, b\} \times \{0, 1\}) \cup \{\triangleright\}$

$F'_{\text{move}} = \{[q_f, \text{rd}_1, /, /]\}$

$\delta'_1 = \{[[q_0, \text{rd}_1, /, /], [s_1, 0, s_2, h_2], [s_1, 0, s_2, h_2], +, [q_0, \text{rd}_1, /, /]] \mid$
$\qquad s_1, s_2 \in \{0, a, b\} \wedge h_2 \in \{0, 1\} \}$

$\delta'_2 = \{[[q_0, \text{rd}_1, /, /], [s_1, 1, s_2, h_2], [0, 1, s_2, h_2], -, [q_0, \text{rr}_1, s_1, /]] \mid$
$\qquad s_1, s_2 \in \{0, a, b\} \wedge h_2 \in \{0, 1\} \}$

$\delta'_3 = \{[[q_0, \text{rr}_1, a_1, /], [s_1, 0, s_2, h_2], [s_1, 0, s_2, h_2], -, [q_0, \text{rr}_1, a_1, /]] \mid$
$\qquad a_1, s_1, s_2 \in \{0, a, b\} \wedge h_2 \in \{0, 1\} \}$

$\delta'_4 = \{[[q_0, \text{rr}_1, a_1, /], \triangleright, \triangleright, +, [q_0, \text{rd}_2, a_1, /]] \mid$
$\qquad a_1 \in \{0, a, b\} \}$

$\delta'_5 = \{[[q_0, \text{rd}_2, a_1, /], [s_1, h_1, s_2, 0], [s_1, h_1, s_2, 0], +, [q_0, \text{rd}_2, a_1, /]] \mid$
$\qquad a_1, s_1, s_2 \in \{0, a, b\} \wedge h_1 \in \{0, 1\} \}$

$\delta'_6 = \{[[q_0, \text{rd}_2, a_1, /], [s_1, h_1, s_2, 1], [s_1, h_1, 0, 1], -, [q_0, \text{rr}_2, a_1, s_2]] \mid$
$\qquad a_1, s_1, s_2 \in \{0, a, b\} \wedge h_1 \in \{0, 1\} \}$

$\delta'_7 = \{[[q_0, \text{rr}_2, a_1, a_2], [s_1, h_1, s_2, 0], [s_1, h_1, s_2, 0], -, [q_0, \text{rr}_2, a_1, a_2]] \mid$
$\qquad a_1, a_2, s_1, s_2 \in \{0, a, b\} \wedge h_1 \in \{0, 1\} \}$

$\delta'_8 = \{[[q_0, \text{rr}_2, 0, 0], \triangleright, \triangleright, +, [q_f, \text{wt}_1, 0, 0]], \ [[q_0, \text{rr}_2, a, 0], \triangleright, \triangleright, +, [q_0, \text{wt}_1, 0, a]],$
$\qquad [[q_0, \text{rr}_2, b, 0], \triangleright, \triangleright, +, [q_0, \text{wt}_1, 0, b]] \}$

$\delta'_9 = \{[[q, \text{wt}_1, b_1, b_2], [s_1, 0, s_2, h_2], [s_1, 0, s_2, h_2], +, [q, \text{wt}_1, b_1, b_2]] \mid$
$\qquad q \in \{q_0, q_f\} \wedge b_1, b_2, s_1, s_2 \in \{0, a, b\} \wedge h_2 \in \{0, 1\} \}$

$\delta'_{10} = \{[[q, \text{wt}_1, b_1, b_2], [0, 1, s_2, h_2], [b_1, 0, s_2, h_2], h^1_{\text{sd}}(q), [q, \text{sf}_1, /, b_2]] \mid$
$\qquad q \in \{q_0, q_f\} \wedge b_1, b_2, s_2 \in \{0, a, b\} \wedge h_2 \in \{0, 1\} \}$

$$\delta'_{11} = \{[[q,\mathrm{sf}_1,/,b_2],[s_1,0,s_2,h_2],[s_1,1,s_2,h_2],-,[q,\mathrm{wr}_1,/,b_2]] \mid$$
$$q \in \{q_0,q_f\} \wedge b_2,s_1,s_2 \in \{0,a,b\} \wedge h_2 \in \{0,1\}\}$$
$$\delta'_{12} = \{[[q,\mathrm{wr}_1,/,b_2],[s_1,0,s_2,h_2],[s_1,0,s_2,h_2],-,[q,\mathrm{wr}_1,/,b_2]] \mid$$
$$q \in \{q_0,q_f\} \wedge b_2,s_1,s_2 \in \{0,a,b\} \wedge h_2 \in \{0,1\}\}$$
$$\delta'_{13} = \{[[q,\mathrm{wr}_1,/,b_2],\triangleright,\triangleright,+,[q,\mathrm{wt}_2,/,b_2]] \mid$$
$$q \in \{q_0,q_f\} \wedge b_2 \in \{0,a,b\}\}$$
$$\delta'_{14} = \{[[q,\mathrm{wt}_2,/,b_2],[s_1,h_1,s_2,0],[s_1,h_1,s_2,0],+,[q,\mathrm{wt}_2,/,b_2]] \mid$$
$$q \in \{q_0,q_f\} \wedge b_2,s_1,s_2 \in \{0,a,b\} \wedge h_1 \in \{0,1\}\}$$
$$\delta'_{15} = \{[[q,\mathrm{wt}_2,/,b_2],[s_1,h_1,0,1],[s_1,h_1,b_2,0],h^2_{\mathrm{sd}}(q),[q,\mathrm{sf}_2,/,/]] \mid$$
$$q \in \{q_0,q_f\} \wedge b_2,s_1 \in \{0,a,b\} \wedge h_1 \in \{0,1\}\}$$
$$\delta'_{16} = \{[[q,\mathrm{sf}_2,/,/],[s_1,h_1,s_2,0],[s_1,h_1,s_2,1],-,[q,\mathrm{wr}_2,/,/]] \mid$$
$$q \in \{q_0,q_f\} \wedge s_1,s_2 \in \{0,a,b\} \wedge h_1 \in \{0,1\}\}$$
$$\delta'_{17} = \{[[q,\mathrm{wr}_2,/,/],[s_1,h_1,s_2,0],[s_1,h_1,s_2,0],-,[q,\mathrm{wr}_2,/,/]] \mid$$
$$q \in \{q_0,q_f\} \wedge s_1,s_2 \in \{0,a,b\} \wedge h_1 \in \{0,1\}\}$$
$$\delta'_{18} = \{[[q,\mathrm{wr}_2,/,/],\triangleright,\triangleright,+,[q,\mathrm{rd}_1,/,/]] \mid$$
$$q \in \{q_0,q_f\}\}$$
$$\delta'_{\mathrm{move}} = \delta'_1 \cup \cdots \cup \delta'_{18}$$

For any input string $s_1 s_2 \cdots s_n \in \{a,b\}^+$, the following relation holds.

$$\triangleright [q_0,\mathrm{rd}_1,/,/][s_1,1,0,1][s_2,0,0,0] \cdots [s_n,0,0,0]$$
$$\vdash^{*}_{T'_{\mathrm{move}}} \triangleright [q_f,\mathrm{rd}_1,/,/][0,0,s_1,0][0,0,s_2,0] \cdots [0,0,s_n,0][0,1,0,1]$$

The complete computation process T'_{move} for the input ab is as below.

$$\triangleright [q_0,\mathrm{rd}_1,/,/][a,1,0,1][b,0,0,0] \quad \vdash_{T'_{\mathrm{move}}} [q_0,\mathrm{rr}_1,a,/] \triangleright [0,1,0,1][b,0,0,0]$$
$$\vdash_{T'_{\mathrm{move}}} \triangleright [q_0,\mathrm{rd}_2,a,/][0,1,0,1][b,0,0,0] \quad \vdash_{T'_{\mathrm{move}}} [q_0,\mathrm{rr}_2,a,0] \triangleright [0,1,0,1][b,0,0,0]$$
$$\vdash_{T'_{\mathrm{move}}} \triangleright [q_0,\mathrm{wt}_1,0,a][0,1,0,1][b,0,0,0] \quad \vdash_{T'_{\mathrm{move}}} \triangleright [0,0,0,1][q_0,\mathrm{sf}_1,/,a][b,0,0,0]$$
$$\vdash_{T'_{\mathrm{move}}} \triangleright [q_0,\mathrm{wr}_1,/,a][0,0,0,1][b,1,0,0] \quad \vdash_{T'_{\mathrm{move}}} [q_0,\mathrm{wr}_1,/,a] \triangleright [0,0,0,1][b,1,0,0]$$
$$\vdash_{T'_{\mathrm{move}}} \triangleright [q_0,\mathrm{wt}_2,/,a][0,0,0,1][b,1,0,0] \quad \vdash_{T'_{\mathrm{move}}} \triangleright [0,0,a,0][q_0,\mathrm{sf}_2,/,/][b,1,0,0]$$
$$\vdash_{T'_{\mathrm{move}}} \triangleright [q_0,\mathrm{wr}_2,/,/][0,0,a,0][b,1,0,1] \quad \vdash_{T'_{\mathrm{move}}} [q_0,\mathrm{wr}_2,/,/] \triangleright [0,0,a,0][b,1,0,1]$$
$$\vdash_{T'_{\mathrm{move}}} \triangleright [q_0,\mathrm{rd}_1,/,/][0,0,a,0][b,1,0,1]$$
$$\vdash^{46}_{T'_{\mathrm{move}}} \triangleright [q_f,\mathrm{rd}_1,/,/][0,0,a,0][0,0,b,0][0,1,0,1]$$

$\square$

5.3.3 Converting many-symbol RTMs into two-symbol RTMs

We show a k-symbol RTM T ($k > 2$) can be converted into an equivalent two-symbol RTM $\tilde{T}$. Each of k symbols is encoded into a sequence over $\{0,1\}$ of length $\lceil \log_2 k \rceil$ ($\lceil x \rceil$ denotes the smallest integer not less than x), and $\tilde{T}$ deals with such codes. Although the encoding method itself is a straightforward one, $\tilde{T}$ should be carefully designed so that it satisfies the reversibility condition. The following theorem is shown based on the methods given in [11, 12]

Theorem 5.4. *For any one-tape k-symbol RTM T ($k > 2$), we can construct a one-tape two-symbol RTM $\tilde{T}$ that simulates T. Furthermore, if T is an RTM with a one-way infinite tape, then $\tilde{T}$ is also so.*

Proof. We show a method of constructing $\tilde{T}$ for the case $k = 8$. It is easy to extend the method for general k (> 2). Let $T = (Q, S_8, q_0, F, s_0, \delta)$ be a given 8-symbol RTM, where $S_8 = \{s_0, \ldots, s_7\}$. Note that, also for the case of $4 < k < 8$, we can obtain a two-symbol RTM by the following construction method. This is done by ignoring some symbols among s_5, s_6, and s_7. Let $h_{sd} : Q \to \{-, 0, +\}$ be the function defined in Definition 5.11 such that $h_{sd}(q)$ gives the shift direction associated with q in T. In $\tilde{T}$, each symbol in S_8 is encoded into a three-bit sequence over $\{0, 1\}$. Hence, the codes for $s_0, s_1, \ldots, s_7$ are $000, 001, \ldots, 111$. Here, we define three functions $c_i : S_8 \to \{0, 1\}$ ($i = 1, 2, 3$) that gives the i-th bit of the code of $s \in S_8$. Namely,

$$c_1(s_0) = c_1(s_1) = c_1(s_2) = c_1(s_3) = 0, \; c_1(s_4) = c_1(s_5) = c_1(s_6) = c_1(s_7) = 1,$$
$$c_2(s_0) = c_2(s_1) = c_2(s_4) = c_2(s_5) = 0, \; c_2(s_2) = c_2(s_3) = c_2(s_6) = c_2(s_7) = 1,$$
$$c_3(s_0) = c_3(s_2) = c_3(s_4) = c_3(s_6) = 0, \; c_3(s_1) = c_3(s_3) = c_3(s_5) = c_3(s_7) = 1.$$

Let c be the function that gives the code of a symbol in S_8, i.e., for every $s \in S_8$, $c(s) = c_1(s)c_2(s)c_3(s)$.

The two-symbol RTM $\tilde{T}$ that simulates T is given as follows.

$$
\begin{aligned}
\tilde{T} &= (\tilde{Q}, \{0, 1\}, [q_0^r], \tilde{F}, 0, \tilde{\delta}) \\
\tilde{F} &= \{ [q^r] \mid q \in F \} \\
Q^r &= \{ [q^r], [q^r, x_1], [q^r, x_1, x_2] \mid q \in Q - F \wedge x_1, x_2 \in \{0, 1\} \} \\
Q^w &= \{ [q^w, x_1], [q^w, x_1, x_2] \mid q \in Q \wedge x_1, x_2 \in \{0, 1\} \} \\
Q^s &= \{ [q^s, i] \mid q \in Q \wedge i \in \{1, 2\} \} \\
\tilde{Q} &= Q^r \cup Q^w \cup Q^s \cup \tilde{F} \\
\delta^r &= \{ [[p^r], x_1, 0, +, [p^r, x_1]], [[p^r, x_1], x_2, 0, +, [p^r, x_1, x_2]] \mid \\
&\qquad p \in Q - F \wedge x_1, x_2 \in \{0, 1\} \} \\
\delta^t &= \{ [[p^r, c_1(s), c_2(s)], c_3(s), c_3(t), -, [q^w, c_1(t), c_2(t)]] \mid \\
&\qquad [p, s, t, h_{sd}(q), q] \in \delta \} \\
\delta^w &= \{ [[q^w, x_1, x_2], 0, x_2, -, [q^w, x_1]], [[q^w, x_1], 0, x_1, h_{sd}(q), [q^s, 1]] \mid \\
&\qquad q \in Q \wedge x_1, x_2 \in \{0, 1\} \} \\
\delta^s &= \{ [[q^s, 1], x, x, h_{sd}(q), [q^s, 2]], [[q^s, 2], x, x, h_{sd}(q), [q^r]] \mid \\
&\qquad q \in Q \wedge x \in \{0, 1\} \} \\
\tilde{\delta} &= \delta^r \cup \delta^t \cup \delta^w \cup \delta^s
\end{aligned}
$$

The states in Q^r are for reading each bit of a code, those in Q^w are for writing it, and those in Q^s are for shifting the head appropriately. If the current ID of T is $a_1 \cdots a_m q b_1 \cdots b_n$, then the corresponding ID of $\tilde{T}$ is

$$c(a_1) \cdots c(a_m) [q^r] c(b_1) \cdots c(b_n).$$

By quintuples in δ^{r}, $\tilde{T}$ reads the first and the second bits of a code in the state $[q^{\mathrm{r}}]$ and $[q^{\mathrm{r}},x_1]$ in Q^{r}, respectively, and keeps the bits in its state. If it reads the third bit of a code in the state $[q^{\mathrm{r}},x_1,x_2]$, then the state transition is simulated, and the code to be written is determined by a quintuple in δ^{t}. At that time, the third bit of the code is also written. Then, $\tilde{T}$ writes the second and first bits in the state $[q^{\mathrm{w}},x_1,x_2]$ and $[q^{\mathrm{w}},x_1]$ in Q^{w} by quintuples in δ^{w}. Finally, $\tilde{T}$ shifts the head appropriately by quintuples in δ^{s} using the states $[q^{\mathrm{s}},1]$ and $[q^{\mathrm{s}},2]$. Figure 5.9 shows an example of the simulation process by $\tilde{T}$. By above, one step of T is simulated. If T halts in a final state q_f, then $\tilde{T}$ also halts in the state $[q^{\mathrm{r}}_f]$, since no quintuple for $[q^{\mathrm{r}}_f]$ is given in δ^{r}.

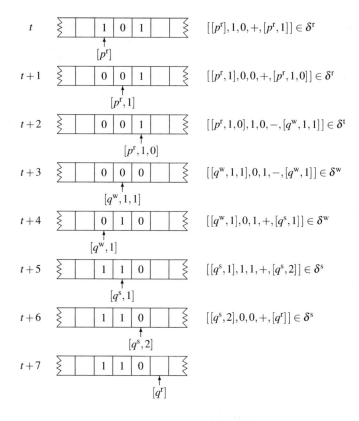

Fig. 5.9 An example of a simulation process of the quintuple $[p,s_5,s_6,+,q]$ of T by the two-symbol RTM $\tilde{T}$. The applied quintuple at each step is shown to the right of the configuration

We show $\tilde{T}$ satisfies the reversibility condition, i.e., for every pair of distinct quintuples $r_1 = [p_1,u_1,v_1,d_1,q_1]$ and $r_2 = [p_2,u_2,v_2,d_2,q_2]$ in $\tilde{\delta}$, if $q_1 = q_2$, then $d_1 = d_2$ and $v_1 \neq v_2$ hold. There are four groups δ^{r}, $\delta^{\mathrm{t}}, \delta^{\mathrm{w}}$, and δ^{s} of quintuples. We first note that, in the cases r_1 and r_2 belong to different groups (e.g., $r_1 \in \delta^{\mathrm{r}}$, and $r_2 \in \delta^{\mathrm{t}}$) the reversibility condition is trivially satisfied, since it is impossible to have

r_1 and r_2 such that $q_1 = q_2$. This is because the fifth elements are different in the quintuples belonging to different groups. Therefore, in the following, we assume r_1 and r_2 are in the same group.

In the case $r_1, r_2 \in \delta^r$, the reversibility condition is trivially satisfied, because every pair of quintuples in δ^r has the different fifth elements by the definition of δ^r.

Next, we assume $r_1, r_2 \in \delta^t$, and $q_1 = q_2$. Here, $d_1 = d_2 = -$. In this case, there must be distinct quintuples $[p'_1, s_1, t_1, h_{sd}(q), q]$ and $[p'_2, s_2, t_2, h_{sd}(q), q]$ in δ such that $q_1 = [q^w, c_1(t_1), c_2(t_1)]$, $q_2 = [q^w, c_1(t_2), c_2(t_2)]$, $c_1(t_1) = c_1(t_2)$, and $c_2(t_1) = c_2(t_2)$. But, since T is reversible, $t_1 \neq t_2$, and thus $v_1 = c_3(t_1) \neq c_3(t_2) = v_2$. Therefore, in this case, the reversibility condition is satisfied.

Consider the case $r_1, r_2 \in \delta^w$, and assume $q_1 = q_2$. There are two subcases. The first one is that there is some $q \in Q$ and $x_1 \in \{0, 1\}$ such that $q_1 = q_2 = [q^w, x_1]$. In this subcase, $d_1 = d_2 = -$, and $v_1 = 0$ and $v_2 = 1$ (or $v_1 = 1$ and $v_2 = 0$) by the definition of δ^w. The second subcase is that there is some $q \in Q$ such that $q_1 = q_2 = [q^s, 1]$. In this subcase, $d_1 = d_2 = h_{sd}(q)$, and $v_1 = 0$ and $v_2 = 1$ (or $v_1 = 1$ and $v_2 = 0$). Thus, in both of these subcases, the reversibility condition is satisfied.

Finally, consider the case $r_1, r_2 \in \delta^s$, and assume $q_1 = q_2$. Then, there is some $q \in Q$ such that $q_1 = q_2 = [q^s, 2]$ or $q_1 = q_2 = [q^r]$. In this case, $d_1 = d_2 = h_{sd}(q)$, and $v_1 = 0$ and $v_2 = 1$ (or $v_1 = 1$ and $v_2 = 0$). Thus, the reversibility condition is also satisfied. By above, we can conclude $\tilde{T}$ is reversible.

From the above method of simulating T by $\tilde{T}$, it is clear that if T is an RTM with a one-way infinite tape, then $\tilde{T}$ is also so.

In the case of $k = 16$, each symbol of T is encoded into a four-bit sequence. Thus, Q^r, Q^w, and Q^s have additional states of the forms $[q^r, x_1, x_2, x_3]$, $[q^w, x_1, x_2, x_3]$, and $[q^s, 3]$, respectively, where $x_1, x_2, x_3 \in \{0, 1\}$. Construction of $\tilde{\delta}$ is similarly done as in the case of $k = 8$. □

Example 5.7. Consider again the RTM T_{copy} in Example 5.1. Here, however, subscripts of states are abbreviated for simplicity.

$$T_{copy} = (Q_{copy}, \{0, 1, a, m\}, q_s, \{q_f\}, 0, \delta_{copy})$$
$$Q_{copy} = \{q_{st}, q_{f0}, q_{n0}, q_{rt}, q_f\}$$
$$\delta_{copy} = \{ [q_{st}, 1, m, +, q_{f0}], [q_{st}, a, a, 0, q_f], [q_{f0}, 0, 1, +, q_{n0}],$$
$$[q_{f0}, 1, 1, +, q_{f0}], [q_{f0}, a, a, +, q_{f0}], [q_{n0}, 0, 0, -, q_{rt}],$$
$$[q_{rt}, 1, 1, -, q_{rt}], [q_{rt}, a, a, -, q_{rt}], [q_{rt}, m, 1, +, q_{st}] \}$$

Since T_{copy} has four symbols, the conversion method employed here is slightly simpler than that in the proof of Theorem 5.4. The symbols $0, 1, a$, and m of T_{copy} is encoded into two-bit codes $00, 01, 10$ and 11, respectively. Hence, c_1 and c_2 are as below.

$$c_1(0) = 0, \ c_1(1) = 0, \ c_1(a) = 1, \ c_1(m) = 1$$
$$c_2(0) = 0, \ c_2(1) = 1, \ c_2(a) = 0, \ c_2(m) = 1$$

The two-symbol RTM $\tilde{T}_{copy}$ that simulates T_{copy} is defined as follows.

$$\tilde{T}_{\text{copy}} = (\tilde{Q}_{\text{copy}}, \{0,1\}, [q_{\text{s}}^{\text{r}}], \tilde{F}_{\text{copy}}, 0, \tilde{\delta}_{\text{copy}})$$

$$\tilde{F}_{\text{copy}} = \{[q_{\text{f}}^{\text{r}}]\}$$

$$Q^{\text{r}} = \{\, [q_{\text{st}}^{\text{r}}],\ [q_{\text{st}}^{\text{r}},0],\ [q_{\text{st}}^{\text{r}},1],\ [q_{\text{f0}}^{\text{r}}],\ [q_{\text{f0}}^{\text{r}},0],\ [q_{\text{f0}}^{\text{r}},1],$$
$$[q_{\text{s0}}^{\text{r}}],\ [q_{\text{s0}}^{\text{r}},0],\ [q_{\text{s0}}^{\text{r}},1],\ [q_{\text{rt}}^{\text{r}}],\ [q_{\text{rt}}^{\text{r}},0],\ [q_{\text{rt}}^{\text{r}},1],\ [q_{\text{f}}^{\text{r}}]\,\}$$

$$Q^{\text{w}} = \{\, [q_{\text{st}}^{\text{w}},0],[q_{\text{st}}^{\text{w}},1],[q_{\text{f0}}^{\text{w}},0],[q_{\text{f0}}^{\text{w}},1],[q_{\text{s0}}^{\text{w}},0],[q_{\text{s0}}^{\text{w}},1],[q_{\text{rt}}^{\text{w}},0],[q_{\text{rt}}^{\text{w}},1],[q_{\text{f}}^{\text{w}},0],[q_{\text{f}}^{\text{w}},1]\,\}$$

$$Q^{\text{s}} = \{\, [q_{\text{st}}^{\text{s}}],\ [q_{\text{f0}}^{\text{s}}],\ [q_{\text{s0}}^{\text{s}}],\ [q_{\text{rt}}^{\text{s}}],\ [q_{\text{f}}^{\text{s}}]\,\}$$

$$\tilde{Q}_{\text{copy}} = Q^{\text{r}} \cup Q^{\text{w}} \cup Q^{\text{s}} \cup \tilde{F}$$

$$\delta^{\text{r}} = \{\, [[q_{\text{st}}^{\text{r}}],0,0,+,[q_{\text{st}}^{\text{r}},0]],\ \ [[q_{\text{st}}^{\text{r}}],1,0,+,[q_{\text{st}}^{\text{r}},1]],$$
$$[[q_{\text{f0}}^{\text{r}}],0,0,+,[q_{\text{f0}}^{\text{r}},0]],\ \ [[q_{\text{f0}}^{\text{r}}],1,0,+,[q_{\text{f0}}^{\text{r}},1]],$$
$$[[q_{\text{n0}}^{\text{r}}],0,0,+,[q_{\text{n0}}^{\text{r}},0]],\ \ [[q_{\text{n0}}^{\text{r}}],1,0,+,[q_{\text{n0}}^{\text{r}},1]],$$
$$[[q_{\text{rt}}^{\text{r}}],0,0,+,[q_{\text{rt}}^{\text{r}},0]],\ \ [[q_{\text{rt}}^{\text{r}}],1,0,+,[q_{\text{rt}}^{\text{r}},1]]\,\}$$

$$\delta^{\text{t}} = \{\, [[q_{\text{st}}^{\text{r}},0],1,1,-,[q_{\text{f0}}^{\text{w}},1]],\ [[q_{\text{st}}^{\text{r}},1],0,0,-,[q_{\text{f}}^{\text{w}},1]],\ [[q_{\text{f0}}^{\text{r}},0],0,1,-,[q_{\text{n0}}^{\text{w}},0]],$$
$$[[q_{\text{f0}}^{\text{r}},0],1,1,-,[q_{\text{f0}}^{\text{w}},0]],\ [[q_{\text{f0}}^{\text{r}},1],0,0,-,[q_{\text{f0}}^{\text{w}},1]],\ [[q_{\text{n0}}^{\text{r}},0],0,0,-,[q_{\text{f0}}^{\text{w}},0]],$$
$$[[q_{\text{rt}}^{\text{r}},0],1,1,-,[q_{\text{rt}}^{\text{w}},0]],\ [[q_{\text{rt}}^{\text{r}},1],0,0,-,[q_{\text{rt}}^{\text{w}},1]],\ [[q_{\text{rt}}^{\text{r}},1],1,1,-,[q_{\text{st}}^{\text{w}},0]]\,\}$$

$$\delta^{\text{w}} = \{\, [[q_{\text{st}}^{\text{w}},0],0,0,+,[q_{\text{st}}^{\text{s}}]],\ \ [[q_{\text{st}}^{\text{w}},1],0,1,+,[q_{\text{st}}^{\text{s}}]],$$
$$[[q_{\text{f0}}^{\text{w}},0],0,0,+,[q_{\text{f0}}^{\text{s}}]],\ \ [[q_{\text{f0}}^{\text{w}},1],0,1,+,[q_{\text{f0}}^{\text{s}}]],$$
$$[[q_{\text{n0}}^{\text{w}},0],0,0,+,[q_{\text{n0}}^{\text{s}}]],\ \ [[q_{\text{n0}}^{\text{w}},1],0,1,+,[q_{\text{n0}}^{\text{s}}]],$$
$$[[q_{\text{rt}}^{\text{w}},0],0,0,-,[q_{\text{rt}}^{\text{s}}]],\ \ [[q_{\text{rt}}^{\text{w}},1],0,1,-,[q_{\text{rt}}^{\text{s}}]],$$
$$[[q_{\text{f}}^{\text{w}},0],0,0,0,[q_{\text{f}}^{\text{s}}]],\ \ \ [[q_{\text{f}}^{\text{w}},1],0,1,0,[q_{\text{f}}^{\text{s}}]]\,\}$$

$$\delta^{\text{s}} = \{\, [[q_{\text{st}}^{\text{s}}],0,0,+,[q_{\text{st}}^{\text{r}}]],\ \ [[q_{\text{st}}^{\text{s}}],1,1,+,[q_{\text{st}}^{\text{r}}]],$$
$$[[q_{\text{f0}}^{\text{s}}],0,0,+,[q_{\text{f0}}^{\text{r}}]],\ \ [[q_{\text{f0}}^{\text{s}}],1,1,+,[q_{\text{f0}}^{\text{r}}]],$$
$$[[q_{\text{n0}}^{\text{s}}],0,0,+,[q_{\text{n0}}^{\text{r}}]],\ \ [[q_{\text{n0}}^{\text{s}}],1,1,+,[q_{\text{n0}}^{\text{r}}]],$$
$$[[q_{\text{rt}}^{\text{s}}],0,0,-,[q_{\text{rt}}^{\text{r}}]],\ \ [[q_{\text{rt}}^{\text{s}}],1,1,-,[q_{\text{rt}}^{\text{r}}]],$$
$$[[q_{\text{f}}^{\text{s}}],0,0,0,[q_{\text{f}}^{\text{r}}]],\ \ \ [[q_{\text{f}}^{\text{s}}],1,1,0,[q_{\text{f}}^{\text{r}}]]\,\}$$

$$\tilde{\delta}_{\text{copy}} = \delta^{\text{r}} \cup \delta^{\text{t}} \cup \delta^{\text{w}} \cup \delta^{\text{s}}$$

A computing process $q_{\text{st}} 1^n a \ \vdash^{*}_{T_{\text{copy}}} \ 1^n q_{\text{f}} a 1^n$ of T_{copy} is simulated by

$$[q_{\text{st}}^{\text{r}}](01)^n 10 \ \vdash^{*}_{\tilde{T}_{\text{copy}}} \ (01)^n [q_{\text{f}}^{\text{r}}] 10 (01)^n$$

of $\tilde{T}_{\text{copy}}$ ($n \in \mathbb{Z}_+$). The complete computing process of the case $n = 1$ is as follows.

$[q_{\text{st}}^{\text{r}}]0110$	$\vdash_{\tilde{T}_{\text{copy}}} 0[q_{\text{st}}^{\text{r}},0]110$	$\vdash_{\tilde{T}_{\text{copy}}} [q_{\text{f0}}^{\text{w}},1]0110$	$\vdash_{\tilde{T}_{\text{copy}}} 1[q_{\text{f0}}^{\text{s}}]110$
$\vdash_{\tilde{T}_{\text{copy}}} 11[q_{\text{f0}}^{\text{r}}]10$	$\vdash_{\tilde{T}_{\text{copy}}} 110[q_{\text{f0}}^{\text{r}},1]0$	$\vdash_{\tilde{T}_{\text{copy}}} 11[q_{\text{f0}}^{\text{w}},1]00$	$\vdash_{\tilde{T}_{\text{copy}}} 111[q_{\text{f0}}^{\text{s}}]0$
$\vdash_{\tilde{T}_{\text{copy}}} 1110[q_{\text{f0}}^{\text{r}}]$	$\vdash_{\tilde{T}_{\text{copy}}} 11100[q_{\text{f0}}^{\text{r}},0]$	$\vdash_{\tilde{T}_{\text{copy}}} 1110[q_{\text{n0}}^{\text{w}},0]01$	$\vdash_{\tilde{T}_{\text{copy}}} 11100[q_{\text{n0}}^{\text{s}}]1$
$\vdash_{\tilde{T}_{\text{copy}}} 11001[q_{\text{n0}}^{\text{r}}]$	$\vdash_{\tilde{T}_{\text{copy}}} 110010[q_{\text{n0}}^{\text{r}},0]$	$\vdash_{\tilde{T}_{\text{copy}}} 11001[q_{\text{rt}}^{\text{w}},0]$	$\vdash_{\tilde{T}_{\text{copy}}} 11100[q_{\text{rt}}^{\text{s}}]1$
$\vdash_{\tilde{T}_{\text{copy}}} 1110[q_{\text{rt}}^{\text{r}}]01$	$\vdash_{\tilde{T}_{\text{copy}}} 11100[q_{\text{rt}}^{\text{r}},0]1$	$\vdash_{\tilde{T}_{\text{copy}}} 1110[q_{\text{rt}}^{\text{w}},0]01$	$\vdash_{\tilde{T}_{\text{copy}}} 111[q_{\text{rt}}^{\text{s}}]001$
$\vdash_{\tilde{T}_{\text{copy}}} 11[q_{\text{rt}}^{\text{r}}]1001$	$\vdash_{\tilde{T}_{\text{copy}}} 110[q_{\text{rt}}^{\text{r}},1]001$	$\vdash_{\tilde{T}_{\text{copy}}} 11[q_{\text{rt}}^{\text{w}},1]0001$	$\vdash_{\tilde{T}_{\text{copy}}} 1[q_{\text{rt}}^{\text{s}}]11001$
$\vdash_{\tilde{T}_{\text{copy}}} [q_{\text{rt}}^{\text{r}}]111001$	$\vdash_{\tilde{T}_{\text{copy}}} 0[q_{\text{rt}}^{\text{r}},1]11001$	$\vdash_{\tilde{T}_{\text{copy}}} [q_{\text{st}}^{\text{w}},0]011001$	$\vdash_{\tilde{T}_{\text{copy}}} 0[q_{\text{st}}^{\text{s}}]11001$
$\vdash_{\tilde{T}_{\text{copy}}} 01[q_{\text{st}}^{\text{r}}]1001$	$\vdash_{\tilde{T}_{\text{copy}}} 010[q_{\text{st}}^{\text{r}},1]001$	$\vdash_{\tilde{T}_{\text{copy}}} 01[q_{\text{f}}^{\text{w}},1]0001$	$\vdash_{\tilde{T}_{\text{copy}}} 01[q_{\text{f}}^{\text{s}}]1001$
$\vdash_{\tilde{T}_{\text{copy}}} 01[q_{\text{f}}^{\text{r}}]1001$			

$\square$

5.3.4 Converting many-state RTMs into four-state RTMs

We consider the problem of reducing the number of states of one-tape RTMs. In the next subsection, we show any RTM can be converted into a three-state RTM. However, it uses a large number of tape symbols. So, we first show a construction method of a four-state RTM, since the latter RTM uses a relatively small number of tape symbols, and it is constructed rather simply. Note that, it is not known whether we can construct a two-state RTM that simulates a given RTM till now.

Shannon [14] presented a method for converting an irreversible many-state TM into an irreversible two-state TM. We shall see that his method is also applicable to RTMs. However, the resulting RTM needs four states rather than two states. In an RTM, to each state q, there corresponds only one shift direction of the head just before it enters q, because of the unique shift-direction property of an RTM (Lemma 5.5). Therefore, two states (say, R_0 and R_1) are used to transfer an information from left to right, and for the opposite direction other two states (say, L_0 and L_1) are used.

We first prove the following lemma stating that zero-shift quintuples can be replaced by right-shift and left-shift ones, where a *zero-shift quintuple* is a quintuple of the form $[p,s,t,0,q]$.

Lemma 5.8. *For any one-tape RTM T, we can construct a one-tape RTM T' that simulates T, and has no zero-shift quintuple.*

Proof. Let $T = (Q,S,q_0,F,s_0,\delta)$, and let h_{sd} be the function that gives the shift direction of the head defined in Definition 5.11. Then T' is as follows.

$$
\begin{aligned}
T' &= (Q',S,q_0,F,s_0,\delta')\\
Q' &= Q \cup \{q' \mid h_{sd}(q) = 0\}\\
\delta'_0 &= \{[p,s,t,+,q'],\ [q',u,u,-,q] \mid [p,s,t,0,q] \in \delta \ \wedge\ u \in S\}\\
\delta'_1 &= \{[p,s,t,d,q] \mid [p,s,t,d,q] \in \delta \ \wedge\ d \in \{-,+\}\}\\
\delta' &= \delta'_0 \cup \delta'_1
\end{aligned}
$$

It is clear that $[p,s,t,0,q] \in \delta$ is simulated by a pair of quintuples $[p,s,t,+,q']$ and $[q',u,u,-,q]$ in δ' in two steps, and $[p,s,t,d,q] \in \delta$ such that $d \in \{-,+\}$ is simulated by $[p,s,t,d,q] \in \delta'$ directly. Hence, for all $\alpha_1,\alpha_2 \in S^*$, $\beta_1,\beta_2 \in S^*$, and $q_1,q_2 \in Q$, the following relation holds.

$$
\alpha_1 q_1 \beta_1 \vdash_T \alpha_2 q_2 \beta_2 \ \Leftrightarrow\ \alpha_1 q_1 \beta_1 \vdash^*_{T'} \alpha_2 q_2 \beta_2
$$

Next, we show that every pair of distinct quintuples $r_1 = [p_1,u_1,v_1,d_1,q_1]$ and $r_2 = [p_2,u_2,v_2,d_2,q_2]$ in δ' satisfies the reversibility condition, i.e., if $q_1 = q_2$ then $d_1 = d_2$ and $v_1 \neq v_2$. First consider the case $r_1 \in \delta'_0$ and $r_2 \in \delta'_1$ (or $r_1 \in \delta'_1$ and $r_2 \in \delta'_0$). In this case, $q_1 \neq q_2$ holds, since T has the unique shift-direction property, and thus the condition is satisfied. Second, consider the case $r_1, r_2 \in \delta'_0$. If $q_1 = q_2 = q'$ for some $q \in Q$, then $d_1 = d_2 = +$. Also $v_1 \neq v_2$ holds, since T is reversible. If $q_1 = q_2 = q$ for some $q \in Q$, then $d_1 = d_2 = -$, and $v_1 \neq v_2$ hold by the definition of

δ_0'. Third, consider the case $r_1, r_2 \in \delta_1'$. In this case, apparently, from reversibility of T, if $q_1 = q_2 = q$, then $d_1 = d_2 = h_{\mathrm{sd}}(q)$, and $v_1 \neq v_2$. By above, T' is an RTM. □

In Theorem 5.5 and Lemma 5.9, we assume that the given RTM has no zero-shift quintuple by Lemma 5.8.

Definition 5.19. Let $T = (Q, S, q_0, F, s_0, \delta)$ be a TM. A state $q \in Q - \{q_0\}$ is called a *useless state*, if there is no quintuple in δ such that q appears as the fifth element. Hence, q cannot be reached from any other state.

It is very easy to convert a TM into one with no useless state. It is done by removing useless states, and quintuples whose first element is a useless state.

We now show that many-state RTMs can be converted into four-state RTMs.

Theorem 5.5. *[10] For any one-tape m-state n-symbol RTM T that has no zero-shift quintuple, we can construct a one-tape four-state $(2mn + n)$-symbol RTM $\tilde{T}$ that simulates T.*

Proof. Let $T = (Q, S, p_0, s_0, \delta)$. We assume there is no useless state in Q. Note that a set of final states is not specified in T and in $\tilde{T}$, since we want to reduce the number of states here. Let Q_-, Q_0 and Q_+ be the sets of states of T defined in Definition 5.11. Since T has no zero-shift quintuple, $Q = Q_- \cup Q_+ \cup \{p_0\}$ and $Q_0 = \emptyset$ hold.

Here, we assume $Q = \{p_0, \ldots, p_{m-1}\}$, i.e., the states in Q are numbered from 0 to $m - 1$. Then, $\tilde{T}$ is given as below.

$$\tilde{T} = (\tilde{Q}, \tilde{S}, \tilde{q}_0, s_0, \tilde{\delta})$$
$$\tilde{Q} = \{L_0, L_1, R_0, R_1\}$$
$$\tilde{S} = S \cup S \times \{0^\uparrow, 1^\uparrow, \ldots, (m-1)^\uparrow\} \cup S \times \{0^\downarrow, 1^\downarrow, \ldots, (m-1)^\downarrow\}$$

Let Q_-' be defined as follows. If $p_0 \in (Q_- \cup Q_+)$, then $Q_-' = Q_-$. If $p_0 \notin (Q_- \cup Q_+)$, then $Q_-' = Q_- \cup \{p_0\}$. The initial state $\tilde{q}_0$ of $\tilde{T}$ is defined in the following manner. If $p_0 \in Q_-'$, then $\tilde{q}_0 = L_0$. If $p_0 \in Q_+$, then $\tilde{q}_0 = R_0$. The move relation $\tilde{\delta}$ of $\tilde{T}$ is defined as follows.

$$\tilde{\delta}_1 = \{ [L_0, [s, i^\uparrow], [t, j^\downarrow], +, R_0] \mid [p_i, s, t, +, p_j] \in \delta \wedge p_i \in Q_-' \}$$
$$\tilde{\delta}_2 = \{ [R_0, [s, i^\uparrow], [t, j^\downarrow], +, R_0] \mid [p_i, s, t, +, p_j] \in \delta \wedge p_i \in Q_+ \}$$
$$\tilde{\delta}_3 = \{ [R_0, u, [u, 0^\uparrow], -, L_0] \mid u \in S \}$$
$$\tilde{\delta}_4 = \{ [L_0, [t, k^\downarrow], [t, (k-1)^\downarrow], +, R_1] \mid k \in \{1, \ldots, m-1\} \wedge t \in S \}$$
$$\tilde{\delta}_5 = \{ [R_1, [u, k^\uparrow], [u, (k+1)^\uparrow], -, L_0] \mid k \in \{0, \ldots, m-2\} \wedge u \in S \}$$
$$\tilde{\delta}_6 = \{ [L_0, [t, 0^\downarrow], t, +, R_0] \mid t \in S \}$$
$$\tilde{\delta}_1' = \{ [R_0, [s, i^\uparrow], [t, j^\downarrow], -, L_0] \mid [p_i, s, t, -, p_j] \in \delta \wedge p_i \in Q_+ \}$$
$$\tilde{\delta}_2' = \{ [L_0, [s, i^\uparrow], [t, j^\downarrow], -, L_0] \mid [p_i, s, t, -, p_j] \in \delta \wedge p_i \in Q_-' \}$$
$$\tilde{\delta}_3' = \{ [L_0, u, [u, 0^\uparrow], +, R_0] \mid u \in S \}$$
$$\tilde{\delta}_4' = \{ [R_0, [t, k^\downarrow], [t, (k-1)^\downarrow], -, L_1] \mid k \in \{1, \ldots, m-1\} \wedge t \in S \}$$
$$\tilde{\delta}_5' = \{ [L_1, [u, k^\uparrow], [u, (k+1)^\uparrow], +, R_0] \mid k \in \{0, \ldots, m-2\} \wedge u \in S \}$$
$$\tilde{\delta}_6' = \{ [R_0, [t, 0^\downarrow], t, -, L_0] \mid t \in S \}$$
$$\tilde{\delta} = \tilde{\delta}_1 \cup \cdots \cup \tilde{\delta}_6 \cup \tilde{\delta}_1' \cup \cdots \cup \tilde{\delta}_6'$$

The quintuples in $\tilde{\delta}_1,\ldots,\tilde{\delta}_6$ are for simulating a right-shift quintuple of T, while those in $\tilde{\delta}_1',\ldots,\tilde{\delta}_6'$ are for a left-shift quintuple of T. Since they are given symmetrically, we explain only $\tilde{\delta}_1,\ldots,\tilde{\delta}_6$, here. The quintuples in $\tilde{\delta}_1$ and $\tilde{\delta}_2$ are for simulating a quintuple $[p_i,s,t,+,p_j]$ of T except the head-shift operation. If $\tilde{T}$ reads the symbol $[s,i^\uparrow]$ in L_0 or R_0, it writes $[t,j^\downarrow]$. By this, the read-write operation and the state-transition of T are simulated. To simulate the right-shift operation of T, the integer j must be transferred to the right-adjacent square. The quintuple in $\tilde{\delta}_3$ is for preparing this operation. Namely, the symbol u in the right-adjacent square is rewritten to $[u,0^\uparrow]$. Here, $j^\downarrow$ means the integer j will be decreased one by one until it reaches 0, and $0^\uparrow$ means that the integer 0 will be increased one by one while this square is visited by $\tilde{T}$ in the state R_1. The quintuple in $\tilde{\delta}_4$ is for decreasing the integer k, and that in $\tilde{\delta}_5$ is for increasing k. This method is based on the one in [14]. The quintuple $\tilde{\delta}_6$ is applied when the transfer of the integer j to the right-adjacent cell, which corresponds to a right-shift operation, is completed. By this, execution of the quintuple $[p_i,s,t,+,p_j]$ of T is done. The above process is shown in Fig. 5.10.

Hence, for all $p_i,p_j \in Q$, $\alpha,\alpha' \in S^*$, $\beta,\beta' \in S^*$ and $s,s' \in S$, the following relation holds.

$$\alpha\, p_i s \beta \;\vdash_{\overline{T}}\; \alpha'\, p_j s' \beta' \;\Leftrightarrow\; \alpha X_0 [s,i^\uparrow] \beta \;\vdash^{*}_{\tilde{T}}\; \alpha' Y_0 [s',j^\uparrow] \beta'$$

Here, $X_0 = L_0$ if $p_i \in Q_-'$, and $X_0 = R_0$ if $p_i \in Q_+$. Likewise, $Y_0 = L_0$ if $p_j \in Q_-'$, and $Y_0 = R_0$ if $p_j \in Q_+$.

If the initial ID of T is $\alpha\, p_0 s \beta$, then that of $\tilde{T}$ is set to $\alpha\, \tilde{q}_0 [s,0^\uparrow] \beta$. Starting from this ID, $\tilde{T}$ simulates T step by step. If T halts in the ID $\alpha'\, p_i s' \beta'$, then $\tilde{T}$ halts with the ID $\alpha' R_0 [s',i^\uparrow] \beta'$ (or $\alpha' L_0 [s',i^\uparrow] \beta'$, respectively) if $p_i \in Q_+$ ($p_i \in Q_-$). Note that, since there is no quintuple in δ applicable to $\alpha'\, p_i s' \beta'$, we can see there is no quintuple in $\tilde{\delta}$ applicable to $\alpha' R_0 [s',i^\uparrow] \beta'$ or $\alpha' L_0 [s',i^\uparrow] \beta'$ by the definitions of $\tilde{\delta}_1,\tilde{\delta}_2,\tilde{\delta}_1'$ and $\tilde{\delta}_2'$.

Though the simulation method itself is similar to the one in [14], an important point is that $\tilde{T}$ is reversible. We show every pair of distinct quintuples $r_1 = [p_1,u_1,v_1,d_1,q_1]$ and $r_2 = [p_2,u_2,v_2,d_2,q_2]$ in $\tilde{\delta}$ satisfies the reversibility condition, i.e., if $q_1 = q_2$ then $d_1 = d_2$ and $v_1 \neq v_2$. Here, we consider only the cases $q_1 = q_2 = R_0$ and $q_1 = q_2 = R_1$. The cases $q_1 = q_2 = L_0$ and $q_1 = q_2 = L_1$ are proved in a similar manner, because of the symmetric construction of $\tilde{\delta}_1,\ldots,\tilde{\delta}_6$, and $\tilde{\delta}_1',\ldots,\tilde{\delta}_6'$. We can see that if $q_1 = q_2 = R_0$ or $q_1 = q_2 = R_1$, then $d_1 = d_2 = +$. Thus, in the following, we show $v_1 \neq v_2$ if $q_1 = q_2$.

First, consider the case $q_1 = q_2 = R_0$. Then, r_1 and r_2 are contained in $\tilde{\delta}_1 \cup \tilde{\delta}_2 \cup \tilde{\delta}_6 \cup \tilde{\delta}_3' \cup \tilde{\delta}_5'$. We then consider three subcases, i.e., $r_1,r_2 \in \tilde{\delta}_1 \cup \tilde{\delta}_2$, $r_1,r_2 \in \tilde{\delta}_6$, and $r_1,r_2 \in \tilde{\delta}_3' \cup \tilde{\delta}_5'$. In all other cases, the types of symbols v_1 and v_2 are different, and thus $v_1 \neq v_2$. For example, if $r_1 \in \tilde{\delta}_1 \cup \tilde{\delta}_2$, and $r_2 \in \tilde{\delta}_6$, then $v_1 = [t,j^\downarrow]$ and $v_2 = t'$, and hence $v_1 \neq v_2$. Now consider the first subcase $r_1,r_2 \in \tilde{\delta}_1 \cup \tilde{\delta}_2$. Then, by the reversibility of T, we can see $v_1 \neq v_2$. In the second subcase $r_1,r_2 \in \tilde{\delta}_6$, it is easy to see $v_1 \neq v_2$ from the definition of $\tilde{\delta}_6$. In the third subcase $r_1,r_2 \in \tilde{\delta}_3' \cup \tilde{\delta}_5'$, we can write $v_1 = [s_1,i^\uparrow]$ and $v_2 = [s_2,j^\uparrow]$ for some $s_1,s_2 \in S$ and $i,j \in \{0,\ldots,m-1\}$. But, from the definitions of $\tilde{\delta}_3'$ and $\tilde{\delta}_5'$, we can see $i \neq j$ if $s_1 = s_2$. Hence, $v_1 \neq v_2$.

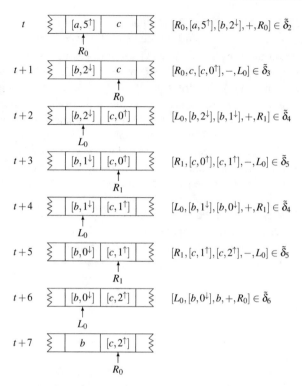

Fig. 5.10 An example of a simulation process of the quintuple $[p_5, a, b, +, p_2]$ of T by the four-state RTM $\tilde{T}$. Here, we assume $p_5 \in Q_+$

Second, consider the case $q_1 = q_2 = R_1$. Then, both r_1 and r_2 are contained in $\tilde{\delta}_4$. In this case, we can write $v_1 = [s_1, i^\downarrow]$ and $v_2 = [s_2, j^\downarrow]$ for some $s_1, s_2 \in S$ and $i, j \in \{0, \ldots, m-2\}$. But, from the definition of $\tilde{\delta}_4$, we can see $i \neq j$ if $s_1 = s_2$. Hence, $v_1 \neq v_2$. By above, we can conclude $\tilde{T}$ is reversible. $\qquad\square$

Example 5.8. We now give an example of an RTM $T_{\text{twice}} = (Q, S, p_0, \#, \delta)$, and covert it into a four-state RTM. Here, $Q = \{p_0, p_1, \ldots, p_7\}$, $S = \{\#, a\}$, and

$$\delta = \{ \ [p_0, \#, \#, +, p_1], \ [p_1, a, \#, +, p_2], \ [p_2, \#, \#, +, p_3], \ [p_2, a, a, +, p_2],$$
$$[p_3, \#, a, +, p_4], \ [p_3, a, a, +, p_3], \ [p_4, \#, a, +, p_5], \ [p_5, \#, \#, -, p_6],$$
$$[p_6, \#, \#, -, p_7], \ [p_6, a, a, -, p_6], \ [p_7, \#, a, +, p_1], \ [p_7, a, a, -, p_7] \ \}.$$

It is easy to verify T_{twice} is deterministic and reversible. The RTM T_{twice} computes the function $f(n) = 2n$, i.e., if an input word a^n is given, then it writes a^{2n} to the right of the input. For example, $p_0 \# aa \ \vdash_{T_{\text{twice}}}^{25} \ aap_1 \# aaaa$ is a complete computation process. Note that if T_{twice} starts from a legal ID of the form $p_0 \# a^n$, then it halts in the ID $a^n p_1 \# a^{2n}$, though final states are not specified.

The four-state RTM $\tilde{T}_{\text{twice}}$ obtained by the method of Theorem 5.5 is as follows.

$$\tilde{T}_{\text{twice}} = (\tilde{Q}, \tilde{S}, L_0, \#, \tilde{\delta})$$

$$\tilde{Q} = \{L_0, L_1, R_0, R_1\}$$

$$\tilde{S} = \{\#, a\} \cup \{\#, a\} \times (\{0^\uparrow, 1^\uparrow, \ldots, 7^\uparrow\} \cup \{0^\downarrow, 1^\downarrow, \ldots, 7^\downarrow\})$$

$$\tilde{\delta}_1 = \{ [L_0, [\#, 0^\uparrow], [\#, 1^\downarrow], +, R_0], [L_0, [\#, 7^\uparrow], [a, 1^\downarrow], +, R_0] \}$$

$$\tilde{\delta}_2 = \{ [R_0, [\#, 5^\uparrow], [\#, 6^\downarrow], -, L_0] \}$$

$$\tilde{\delta}_3 = \{ [R_0, \#, [\#, 0^\uparrow], -, L_0], [R_0, a, [a, 0^\uparrow], -, L_0] \}$$

$$\tilde{\delta}_4 = \{ [L_0, [\#, 1^\downarrow], [\#, 0^\downarrow], +, R_1], [L_0, [\#, 2^\downarrow], [\#, 1^\downarrow], +, R_1],$$
$$[L_0, [\#, 3^\downarrow], [\#, 2^\downarrow], +, R_1], [L_0, [\#, 4^\downarrow], [\#, 3^\downarrow], +, R_1],$$
$$[L_0, [\#, 5^\downarrow], [\#, 4^\downarrow], +, R_1], [L_0, [\#, 6^\downarrow], [\#, 5^\downarrow], +, R_1],$$
$$[L_0, [\#, 7^\downarrow], [\#, 6^\downarrow], +, R_1], [L_0, [a, 1^\downarrow], [a, 0^\downarrow], +, R_1],$$
$$[L_0, [a, 2^\downarrow], [a, 1^\downarrow], +, R_1], [L_0, [a, 3^\downarrow], [a, 2^\downarrow], +, R_1],$$
$$[L_0, [a, 4^\downarrow], [a, 3^\downarrow], +, R_1], [L_0, [a, 5^\downarrow], [a, 4^\downarrow], +, R_1],$$
$$[L_0, [a, 6^\downarrow], [a, 5^\downarrow], +, R_1], [L_0, [a, 7^\downarrow], [a, 6^\downarrow], +, R_1] \}$$

$$\tilde{\delta}_5 = \{ [R_1, [\#, 0^\uparrow], [\#, 1^\uparrow], -, L_0], [R_1, [\#, 1^\uparrow], [\#, 2^\uparrow], -, L_0],$$
$$[R_1, [\#, 2^\uparrow], [\#, 3^\uparrow], -, L_0], [R_1, [\#, 3^\uparrow], [\#, 4^\uparrow], -, L_0],$$
$$[R_1, [\#, 4^\uparrow], [\#, 5^\uparrow], -, L_0], [R_1, [\#, 5^\uparrow], [\#, 6^\uparrow], -, L_0],$$
$$[R_1, [\#, 6^\uparrow], [\#, 7^\uparrow], -, L_0], [R_1, [a, 0^\uparrow], [a, 1^\uparrow], -, L_0],$$
$$[R_1, [a, 1^\uparrow], [a, 2^\uparrow], -, L_0], [R_1, [a, 2^\uparrow], [a, 3^\uparrow], -, L_0],$$
$$[R_1, [a, 3^\uparrow], [a, 4^\uparrow], -, L_0], [R_1, [a, 4^\uparrow], [a, 5^\uparrow], -, L_0],$$
$$[R_1, [a, 5^\uparrow], [a, 6^\uparrow], -, L_0], [R_1, [a, 6^\uparrow], [a, 7^\uparrow], -, L_0] \}$$

$$\tilde{\delta}_6 = \{ [L_0, [\#, 0^\downarrow], \#, +, R_0], [L_0, [a, 0^\downarrow], a, +, R_0] \}$$

$$\tilde{\delta}'_1 = \{ [R_0, [a, 1^\uparrow], [\#, 2^\downarrow], +, R_0], [R_0, [\#, 2^\uparrow], [\#, 3^\downarrow], +, R_0],$$
$$[R_0, [a, 2^\uparrow], [a, 2^\downarrow], +, R_0], [R_0, [\#, 3^\uparrow], [a, 4^\downarrow], +, R_0],$$
$$[R_0, [a, 3^\uparrow], [a, 3^\downarrow], +, R_0], [R_0, [\#, 4^\uparrow], [a, 5^\downarrow], +, R_0] \}$$

$$\tilde{\delta}'_2 = \{ [L_0, [\#, 6^\uparrow], [\#, 7^\downarrow], -, L_0], [L_0, [a, 6^\uparrow], [a, 6^\downarrow], -, L_0],$$
$$[L_0, [a, 7^\uparrow], [a, 7^\downarrow], -, L_0] \}$$

$$\tilde{\delta}'_3 = \{ [L_0, \#, [\#, 0^\uparrow], +, R_0], [L_0, a, [a, 0^\uparrow], +, R_0] \}$$

$$\tilde{\delta}'_4 = \{ [R_0, [\#, 1^\downarrow], [\#, 0^\downarrow], -, L_1], [R_0, [\#, 2^\downarrow], [\#, 1^\downarrow], -, L_1],$$
$$[R_0, [\#, 3^\downarrow], [\#, 2^\downarrow], -, L_1], [R_0, [\#, 4^\downarrow], [\#, 3^\downarrow], -, L_1],$$
$$[R_0, [\#, 5^\downarrow], [\#, 4^\downarrow], -, L_1], [R_0, [\#, 6^\downarrow], [\#, 5^\downarrow], -, L_1],$$
$$[R_0, [\#, 7^\downarrow], [\#, 6^\downarrow], -, L_1], [R_0, [a, 1^\downarrow], [a, 0^\downarrow], -, L_1],$$
$$[R_0, [a, 2^\downarrow], [a, 1^\downarrow], -, L_1], [R_0, [a, 3^\downarrow], [a, 2^\downarrow], -, L_1],$$
$$[R_0, [a, 4^\downarrow], [a, 3^\downarrow], -, L_1], [R_0, [a, 5^\downarrow], [a, 4^\downarrow], -, L_1],$$
$$[R_0, [a, 6^\downarrow], [a, 5^\downarrow], -, L_1], [R_0, [a, 7^\downarrow], [a, 6^\downarrow], -, L_1] \}$$

$$\tilde{\delta}'_5 = \{ [L_1, [\#, 0^\uparrow], [\#, 1^\uparrow], +, R_0], [L_1, [\#, 1^\uparrow], [\#, 2^\uparrow], +, R_0],$$
$$[L_1, [\#, 2^\uparrow], [\#, 3^\uparrow], +, R_0], [L_1, [\#, 3^\uparrow], [\#, 4^\uparrow], +, R_0],$$
$$[L_1, [\#, 4^\uparrow], [\#, 5^\uparrow], +, R_0], [L_1, [\#, 5^\uparrow], [\#, 6^\uparrow], +, R_0],$$
$$[L_1, [\#, 6^\uparrow], [\#, 7^\uparrow], +, R_0], [L_1, [a, 0^\uparrow], [a, 1^\uparrow], +, R_0],$$
$$[L_1, [a, 1^\uparrow], [a, 2^\uparrow], +, R_0], [L_1, [a, 2^\uparrow], [a, 3^\uparrow], +, R_0],$$
$$[L_1, [a, 3^\uparrow], [a, 4^\uparrow], +, R_0], [L_1, [a, 4^\uparrow], [a, 5^\uparrow], +, R_0],$$
$$[L_1, [a, 5^\uparrow], [a, 6^\uparrow], +, R_0], [L_1, [a, 6^\uparrow], [a, 7^\uparrow], +, R_0] \}$$

$$\tilde{\delta}'_6 = \{ [R_0, [\#, 0^\downarrow], \#, -, L_0], [R_0, [a, 0^\downarrow], a, -, L_0] \}$$

$$\tilde{\delta} = \tilde{\delta}_1 \cup \cdots \cup \tilde{\delta}_6 \cup \tilde{\delta}'_1 \cup \cdots \cup \tilde{\delta}'_6$$

For example, the computation $p_0 \# aa \vdash_{T_{\text{twice}}} p_1 aa\# \vdash_{T_{\text{twice}}}^{24} aap_1\#aaaa$ by T_{twice} is simulated by $\tilde{T}_{\text{twice}}$ as follows.

$$L_0[\#,0^{\uparrow}]aa \qquad \vdash_{\tilde{T}_{\text{twice}}} [\#,1^{\downarrow}]R_0aa \qquad \vdash_{\tilde{T}_{\text{twice}}} L_0[\#,1^{\downarrow}][a,0^{\uparrow}]a$$

$$\vdash_{\tilde{T}_{\text{twice}}} [\#,0^{\downarrow}]R_1[a,0^{\uparrow}]a \quad \vdash_{\tilde{T}_{\text{twice}}} L_0[\#,0^{\downarrow}][a,1^{\uparrow}]a \quad \vdash_{\tilde{T}_{\text{twice}}} R_0[a,1^{\uparrow}]a\#$$

$$\vdash_{\tilde{T}_{\text{twice}}}^{286} aaR_0[\#,1^{\uparrow}]aaaa$$

All the steps of the above computing process are shown in the slide file of [10].   □

5.3.5 Converting many-state RTMs into three-state RTMs

In an RTM, an information is transferred in both directions in general, i.e., from left to right, and from right to left on the tape. Therefore, as seen in Theorem 5.5, four states are needed to simulate a given RTM by the method of Shannon. Here, we introduce a model of an RTM where the information flow is only one-way, and show that any RTM can be converted into such an RTM. We then give a method of converting it into a three-state RTM.

5.3.5.1 Converting RTMs into one-way-updating RTMs

We introduce a *one-way-updating reversible Turing machine* (1WU-RTM) as shown in Fig. 5.11, in which the information flow is one-way to the right.

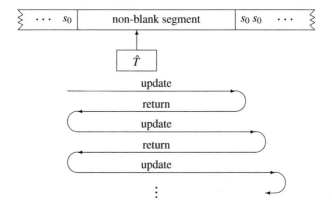

Fig. 5.11 A one-way-updating reversible Turing machine (1WU-RTM) $\hat{T}$. When it sweeps the tape from left to right, tape symbols can be rewritten to other symbols. However, when it sweeps the tape from right to left, only one specified state q_L is used, and tape symbols cannot be changed. The non-blank segment can be extended to the right at the end of each rightward sweep

Definition 5.20. [10] A *one-way-updating reversible Turing machine* (1WU-RTM) is a one-tape RTM defined by

$$\hat{T} = (\hat{Q}, \hat{S}, q_L, s_0, \hat{\delta})$$

that has no zero-shift quintuple, and satisfies the following conditions. Here, $\hat{Q}_-$ and $\hat{Q}_+$ are the set of states given in Definition 5.11.

1. The initial state q_L is the sole state of $\hat{Q}_-$:
   $\hat{Q}_- = \{q_L\}$.
2. If $\hat{T}$ reads a non-blank symbol in q_L, then it shifts the head to the left without changing the state and the symbol:
   $\forall s \in \hat{S} - \{s_0\} \ ([q_L, s, s, -, q_L) \in \hat{\delta})$.
3. If $\hat{T}$ reads a blank symbol s_0 in q_L, then it shifts the head to the right and enters a state in $\hat{Q}_+$ without changing the symbol:
   $\exists q \in \hat{Q}_+ \ ([q_L, s_0, s_0, +, q) \in \hat{\delta})$.
4. If $\hat{T}$ writes a non-blank symbol in a state in $\hat{Q}_+$, then it either enters a state in $\hat{Q}_+$ or halts:
   $\forall p \in \hat{Q}_+, \forall q \in \hat{Q}, \forall s, t \in \hat{S}, \forall d \in \{+, -\}$
   $(([p, s, t, d, q] \in \hat{\delta} \wedge t \neq s_0) \Rightarrow (d = + \wedge q \in \hat{Q}_+))$.
5. The TM $\hat{T}$ never rewrites a non-blank symbol into s_0 in a state in $\hat{Q}_+$. In addition, if it reads s_0 and leaves it unchanged, then it either enters the state q_L or halts:
   $\forall p \in \hat{Q}_+, \forall q \in \hat{Q}, \forall s \in \hat{S}, \forall d \in \{+, -\}$
   $([p, s, s_0, d, q] \in \hat{\delta} \Rightarrow (s = s_0 \wedge d = - \wedge q = q_L))$.

The next lemma shows that any RTM can be converted into a 1WU-RTM.

Lemma 5.9. *[10] For any one-tape m-state n-symbol RTM T that has no zero-shift quintuple, we can construct a one-tape $(m'n + 2n + 2)$-state $(mn^2 + n^2 + 1)$-symbol 1WU-RTM $\hat{T}$ that simulates T, where $m' = |Q_+|$.*

Proof. Let $T = (Q, S, p_0, s_0, \delta)$. We assume there is no useless state in Q. Let Q_- and Q_+ be the sets of states given in Definition 5.11. Note that $Q_0 = \emptyset$, since T has no zero-shift quintuple (see Lemma 5.8). Then, $\hat{T}$ is defined as follows.

$\hat{T} = (\hat{Q}, \hat{S}, q_L, s_0, \hat{\delta})$
$\hat{Q} = \{q_L\} \cup \{q(s) \mid s \in S \cup \{\lambda\}\} \cup \{h(s) \mid s \in S\} \cup \{q(p, s) \mid p \in Q_+, \ s \in S\}$
$\hat{S} = \{s_0\} \cup \{[s, t] \mid s, t \in S\} \cup \{[[p, s], t] \mid p \in Q, \ s, t \in S\}$
$\hat{\delta}_1 = \{[q_L, s_0, s_0, +, q(s_0)]\}$
$\hat{\delta}_2 = \{[q(s), [t, u], [s, t], +, q(u)] \mid s, t, u \in S\}$
$\hat{\delta}_3 = \{[q(s), [[p, t], u], [[p', s], t'], +, q(u)] \mid [p, t, t', -, p'] \in \delta \wedge s, u \in S \wedge$
          $\exists v \in S \ \exists d \in \{-, +\} \ \exists p'' \in Q \ ([p', s, v, d, p''] \in \delta)\}$
$\hat{\delta}_4 = \{[q(s), [[p, t], u], [[p', s], t'], +, h(u)] \mid [p, t, t', -, p'] \in \delta \wedge s, u \in S \wedge$
          $\neg \exists v \in S \ \exists d \in \{-, +\} \ \exists p'' \in Q \ ([p', s, v, d, p''] \in \delta)\}$

$$\hat{\delta}_5 = \{\, [q(s), [[p,t], u], [s,t'], +, q(p', u)] \mid [p,t,t',+,p'] \in \delta \;\wedge\; s, u \in S \,\}$$
$$\hat{\delta}_6 = \{\, [q(p', u), [s,t], [[p', u], s], +, q(t)] \mid s, t, u \in S \;\wedge\; p' \in Q_+ \;\wedge$$
$$\exists v \in S \,\exists d \in \{-,+\} \,\exists p'' \in Q \,([p', u, v, d, p''] \in \delta) \,\}$$
$$\hat{\delta}_7 = \{\, [q(p', u), [s,t], [[p', u], s], +, h(t)] \mid s, t, u \in S \;\wedge\; p' \in Q_+ \;\wedge$$
$$\neg \exists v \in S \,\exists d \in \{-,+\} \,\exists p'' \in Q \,([p', u, v, d, p''] \in \delta) \,\}$$
$$\hat{\delta}_8 = \{\, [q(s), s_0, [s, s_0], +, q(\lambda)] \mid s \in S \,\}$$
$$\hat{\delta}_9 = \{\, [q(\lambda), s_0, s_0, -, q_L] \,\}$$
$$\hat{\delta}_{10} = \{\, [q_L, [s,t], [s,t], -, q_L] \mid s, t \in S \,\}$$
$$\hat{\delta}_{11} = \{\, [q_L, [[p,s], t], [[p,s], t], -, q_L] \mid p \in Q \;\wedge\; s, t \in S \,\}$$
$$\hat{\delta}_{12} = \{\, [h(s), [t, u], [s, t], +, h(u)] \mid s, t, u \in S \,\}$$
$$\hat{\delta} = \hat{\delta}_1 \cup \cdots \cup \hat{\delta}_{12}$$

It is easy to see that $\hat{T}$ satisfies the conditions 1–5 in Definition 5.20. The condition 1 is verified from the fact that all the left-shift quintuples are in $\hat{\delta}_9, \hat{\delta}_{10}$ and $\hat{\delta}_{11}$. The condition 2 is satisfied by the quintuples in $\hat{\delta}_{10}$ and $\hat{\delta}_{11}$. The condition 3 is satisfied by the quintuple in $\hat{\delta}_1$. From $\hat{\delta}_2, \ldots, \hat{\delta}_8$, and $\hat{\delta}_{12}$ we can see the condition 4 holds. The condition 5 is satisfied by $\hat{\delta}_9$, since a quintuple that writes the symbol s_0 in a state in Q_+ is contained only in $\hat{\delta}_9$.

Let $t_1 t_2 \cdots t_{2k} \, p \, u_1 u_2 \cdots u_{2l}$ be an ID of T, where $t_i, u_j \in S \,(1 \le i \le 2k, \, 1 \le j \le 2l)$, $k \in \{0, 1, \ldots\}$, $l \in \{2, 3, \ldots\}$, and $p \in Q$. Note that, here, we allow t_1 and u_{2l} to be the blank symbol s_0, so that the lengths of $t_1 \cdots t_{2k}$ and $u_1 \cdots u_{2l}$ are even. Then the ID of $\hat{T}$ corresponding to it is:

$$q_L \, s_0 \, [t_1, t_2] \, [t_3, t_4] \, \ldots \, [t_{2k-1}, t_{2k}] \, [[p, u_1], u_2] \, [u_3, u_4] \, \ldots \, [u_{2l-1}, u_{2l}].$$

Thus, two symbols of T are packed into one square of $\hat{T}$, and the state p of T is also written in the tape of $\hat{T}$. If T has a quintuple $[p, u_1, u_1', +, p']$, then $\hat{T}$ will produce the following ID:

$$q_L \, s_0 \, [s_0, t_1] \, [t_2, t_3] \, \ldots \, [t_{2k-2}, t_{2k-1}] \, [t_{2k}, u_1'] \, [[p', u_2], u_3] \, \cdots \, [u_{2l-2}, u_{2l-1}] \, [u_{2l}, s_0].$$

On the other hand, if T has a quintuple $[p, u_1, u_1', -, p']$, then $\hat{T}$ will produce the following ID:

$$q_L \, s_0 \, [s_0, t_1] \, [t_2, t_3] \, \ldots \, [t_{2k-2}, t_{2k-1}] \, [[p', t_{2k}], u_1'] \, [u_2, u_3] \, \ldots \, [u_{2l-2}, u_{2l-1}] \, [u_{2l}, s_0].$$

Namely, each time one step of T is simulated, tape symbols of T are shifted by one place to the right. Thus, the head position of T on the tape of $\hat{T}$ is shifted to the right by two places if a right-shift quintuple is applied, and it keeps the same position if a left-shift quintuple is applied. Note that the number of non-blank symbols of the form $[s, s']$ increases by 1 each time one step of T is simulated. Generally, many non-blank symbols $[s_0, s_0]$'s will be attached in the beginning and the end of the ID.

The quintuple in $\hat{\delta}_1$ is for starting a left-to-right sweep of the tape. The quintuples in $\hat{\delta}_2$ are for shifting tape symbols of T by one position to the right in the ID. The quintuples in $\hat{\delta}_3$ and $\hat{\delta}_4$ are for simulating a left-shift quintuple of T, and shifting tape symbols of T by one position to the right. Here, the quintuples in $\hat{\delta}_3$ are for the case that T does not halt in the state p' reading the symbol s. On the other hand, the quintuples in $\hat{\delta}_4$ are for the case that T halts in the state p' reading the symbol s. The state $h(u)$ in $\hat{\delta}_4$ indicates T has halted. The quintuples in $\hat{\delta}_5$, $\hat{\delta}_6$ and $\hat{\delta}_7$ are for simulating one step movement of T by a right-shift quintuple, and shifting tape symbols of T by one position to the right. Here, the quintuples in $\hat{\delta}_6$ are for the case that T does not halt, while the quintuples in $\hat{\delta}_7$ are for the case that T halts. The quintuples in $\hat{\delta}_8$ are for extending the right end of the ID by one symbol. The quintuple in $\hat{\delta}_9$ is for turning the sweep direction at the right end of the ID. The quintuples in $\hat{\delta}_{10}$ and $\hat{\delta}_{11}$ are for going back to the left end of the ID by the state q_L. The quintuples in $\hat{\delta}_{12}$ are for going to the right end of the ID after T halted. In this case, $\hat{T}$ halts when it reads s_0 in the state $h(s_0)$.

If the initial ID of T is $t_1 t_2 \cdots t_{2k} p_0 u_1 u_2 \cdots u_{2l}$, then the initial ID of $\hat{T}$ is set to

$$q_L s_0 [t_1, t_2][t_3, t_4] \ldots [t_{2k-1}, t_{2k}] [[p_0, u_1], u_2] [u_3, u_4] \ldots [u_{2l-1}, u_{2l}].$$

The RTM $\hat{T}$ simulates T step by step as described above. One step of T is simulated by one sweep of $\hat{T}$ from left to right, and then $\hat{T}$ goes back to the left end by the state q_L. If T halts in an ID $t'_1 t'_2 \cdots t'_{2k'} p_i u'_1 u'_2 \cdots u'_{2l'}$, then $\hat{T}$ halts in the following ID.

$$[t'_1, t'_2][t'_3, t'_4] \ldots [t'_{2k'-1}, t'_{2k'}] [[p_i, u'_1], u'_2] [u'_3, u'_4] \ldots [u'_{2l'-1}, u'_{2l'}] h(s_0)$$

We show that every pair of distinct quintuples $r_1 = [p_1, a_1, b_1, d_1, q_1]$ and $r_2 = [p_2, a_2, b_2, d_2, q_2]$ in $\hat{\delta}$ satisfies the reversibility condition, i.e., if $q_1 = q_2$ then $d_1 = d_2$ and $b_1 \neq b_2$. Since $\hat{T}$ is a 1WU-RTM, if $q_1 = q_2 = q_L$ then $d_1 = d_2 = -$, and if $q_1 = q_2 \neq q_L$ then $d_1 = d_2 = +$. Hence, in the following, we show that if $q_1 = q_2$ then $b_1 \neq b_2$.

First, we consider the case $q_1 = q_2 = q_L$. Then $r_1, r_2 \in \hat{\delta}_9 \cup \hat{\delta}_{10} \cup \hat{\delta}_{11}$. In this case, it is easy to see $b_1 \neq b_2$ from the definition of $\hat{\delta}_9$, $\hat{\delta}_{10}$ and $\hat{\delta}_{11}$.

Second, we consider the case $q_1 = q_2 = q(\lambda)$. Then $r_1, r_2 \in \hat{\delta}_8$. From the definition of $\hat{\delta}_8$, it is also clear that $b_1 \neq b_2$.

Third, we consider the case $q_1 = q_2 = q(s)$ for some $s \in S$. Then $r_1, r_2 \in \hat{\delta}_1 \cup \hat{\delta}_2 \cup \hat{\delta}_3 \cup \hat{\delta}_6$. There are three subcases. The first subcase is $r_1 \in \hat{\delta}_1$. In this case, $b_1 = s_0$, and thus there is no other $r_2 \in \hat{\delta}_1 \cup \hat{\delta}_2 \cup \hat{\delta}_3 \cup \hat{\delta}_6$ such that $b_2 = s_0$. The second subcase is $r_1 \in \hat{\delta}_2$. In this case, $b_1 = [s, t]$ for some $s, t \in S$. If $r_2 \in \hat{\delta}_2$, then $b_1 \neq b_2$ by the definition of $\hat{\delta}_2$. If $r_2 \in \hat{\delta}_3 \cup \hat{\delta}_6$, then apparently $b_1 \neq b_2$ since $b_2 = [[p, s'], t']$ for some $p \in Q$ and $s', t' \in S$. The third subcase is $r_1, r_2 \in \hat{\delta}_3 \cup \hat{\delta}_6$. We must be careful in this case. If $r_1, r_2 \in \hat{\delta}_3$, then $b_1 = [[p'_1, s_1], t'_1]$ and $b_2 = [[p'_2, s_2], t'_2]$ for some $[p_1, t_1, t'_1, -, p'_1], [p_2, t_2, t'_2, -, p'_2] \in \delta$ and $s_1, s_2 \in S$. Since T is reversible, if $p'_1 = p'_2$, then $t'_1 \neq t'_2$, and thus $b_1 \neq b_2$ holds. If $r_1, r_2 \in \hat{\delta}_6$, then $b_1 = [[p'_1, u_1], s_1]$ and $b_2 = [[p'_2, u_2], s_2]$ for some $p'_1, p'_2 \in Q$ and $s_1, s_2, u_1, u_2 \in S$. In this case, from the definition of $\hat{\delta}_6$, $b_1 \neq b_2$ holds. If $r_1 \in \hat{\delta}_3$ and $r_2 \in \hat{\delta}_6$, then $b_1 = [[p'_1, s_1], t'_1]$ and $b_2 = [[p'_2, u_2], s_2]$ for some $[p_1, t_1, t'_1, -, p'_1] \in \delta$, $p'_2 \in Q_+$, and $s_1, s_2, u_2 \in S$. Since $p'_1 \in Q_-$ and $p'_2 \in Q_+$, we can conclude $b_1 \neq b_2$.

Fourth, we consider the case $q_1 = q_2 = h(s)$ for some $s \in S$. Then $r_1, r_2 \in \hat{\delta}_4 \cup \hat{\delta}_7 \cup \hat{\delta}_{12}$. There are two subcases. The first subcase is $r_1 \in \hat{\delta}_{12}$. In this case, $b_1 = [s,t]$ for some $s,t \in S$. If $r_2 \in \hat{\delta}_{12}$, then $b_1 \neq b_2$ by the definition of $\hat{\delta}_{12}$. If $r_2 \in \hat{\delta}_4 \cup \hat{\delta}_7$, then apparently $b_1 \neq b_2$. The second subcase is $r_1, r_2 \in \hat{\delta}_4 \cup \hat{\delta}_7$. This case is similar to the third subcase of the third case above. If $r_1, r_2 \in \hat{\delta}_4$, then $b_1 = [[p'_1, s_1], t'_1]$ and $b_2 = [[p'_2, s_2], t'_2]$ for some $[p_1, t_1, t'_1, -, p'_1], [p_2, t_2, t'_2, -, p'_2] \in \delta$ and $s_1, s_2 \in S$. Since T is reversible, if $p'_1 = p'_2$, then $t'_1 \neq t'_2$, and thus $b_1 \neq b_2$ holds. If $r_1, r_2 \in \hat{\delta}_7$, then $b_1 = [[p'_1, u_1], s_1]$ and $b_2 = [[p'_2, u_2], s_2]$ for some $p'_1, p'_2 \in Q$ and $s_1, s_2, u_1, u_2 \in S$. In this case, from the definition of $\hat{\delta}_7$, $b_1 \neq b_2$ holds. If $r_1 \in \hat{\delta}_4$ and $r_2 \in \hat{\delta}_7$, then $b_1 = [[p'_1, s_1], t'_1]$ and $b_2 = [[p'_2, u_2], s_2]$ for some $[p_1, t_1, t'_1, -, p'_1] \in \delta$, $p'_2 \in Q_+$, and $s_1, s_2, u_2 \in S$. Since $p'_1 \in Q_-$ and $p'_2 \in Q_+$, we can conclude $b_1 \neq b_2$.

Fifth, consider the case $q_1 = q_2 = q(p', u)$ for some $p' \in Q$ and $u \in S$. Then, $r_1, r_2 \in \hat{\delta}_5$. Thus, $b_1 = [s_1, t'_1]$ and $b_2 = [s_2, t'_2]$ for some $s_1, s_2 \in S$ and $[p_1, t_1, t'_1, +, p']$, $[p_2, t_2, t'_2, +, p'] \in \delta$. Since T is reversible, $b_1 \neq b_2$. By above, we can conclude $\hat{T}$ is reversible.   □

Example 5.9. Let $T_{\text{twice}} = (Q, S, p_0, \#, \delta)$ be the RTM in Example 5.8. We convert T_{twice} into a 1WU-RTM $\hat{T}_{\text{twice}} = (\hat{Q}, \hat{S}, q_L, \#, \hat{\delta})$ by the method of Lemma 5.9. Here, $\hat{Q}$, and $\hat{S}$ are as follows, where $Q = \{p_0, p_1, p_2, p_3, p_4, p_5, p_6, p_7\}$, $Q_- = \{p_6, p_7\}$, and $Q_+ = \{p_1, p_2, p_3, p_4, p_5\}$.

$$\hat{Q} = \{q_L\} \cup \{q(s) \mid s \in \{\#, a, \lambda\}\} \cup \{h(s) \mid s \in \{\#, a\}\} \cup$$
$$\{q(p, s) \mid p \in Q_+, s \in \{\#, a\}\}$$
$$\hat{S} = \{\#\} \cup \{[s, t] \mid s, t \in \{\#, a\}\} \cup \{[[p, s], t] \mid p \in Q, s, t \in \{\#, a\}\}$$

Thus, $|\hat{Q}| = 16$, and $|\hat{S}| = 37$. We do not describe $\hat{\delta}$, since it contains 144 quintuples. A computation process

$$p_0 \# aa \vdash_{\overline{T_{\text{twice}}}} p_1 aa \vdash_{\overline{T_{\text{twice}}}}^{24} aa p_1 \# aaaa$$

by T_{twice} is simulated by $\hat{T}_{\text{twice}}$ as below.

$$
\begin{aligned}
&q_L \# [[p_0, \#], a] [a, \#] && \vdash_{\overline{\hat{T}_{\text{twice}}}} q(\#) [[p_0, \#], a] [a, \#] \\
&\vdash_{\overline{\hat{T}_{\text{twice}}}} [\#, \#] q(p_1, a) [a, \#] && \vdash_{\overline{\hat{T}_{\text{twice}}}} [\#, \#] [[p_1, a], a] q(\#) \\
&\vdash_{\overline{\hat{T}_{\text{twice}}}} [\#, \#] [[p_1, a], a] [\#, \#] q(\lambda) && \vdash_{\overline{\hat{T}_{\text{twice}}}} [\#, \#] [[p_1, a], a] q_L [\#, \#] \\
&\vdash_{\overline{\hat{T}_{\text{twice}}}} [\#, \#] q_L [[p_1, a], a] [\#, \#] && \vdash_{\overline{\hat{T}_{\text{twice}}}} q_L [\#, \#] [[p_1, a], a] [\#, \#] \\
&\vdash_{\overline{\hat{T}_{\text{twice}}}} q_L \# [\#, \#] [[p_1, a], a] [\#, \#] && \vdash_{\overline{\hat{T}_{\text{twice}}}}^{763} [\#, \#]^{13} [a, a] [[p_1, \#], a] [a, a] [a, \#] [\#, \#]^9 h(\#)
\end{aligned}
$$

All the steps of the above computing process are shown in the slide file of [10].   □

5.3.5.2 Converting one-way-updating RTMs into three-state RTMs

Since the information flow in 1WU-RTM is one-way to the right, we can obtain an equivalent three-state RTM again by the method of Shannon [14].

Lemma 5.10. *[10] For any one-tape m-state n-symbol 1WU-RTM $\hat{T}$, we can construct a one-tape three-state $(2mn - n)$-symbol RTM $T^\dagger$ that simulates $\hat{T}$.*

Proof. Let $\hat{T} = (\hat{Q}, \hat{S}, q_L, s_0, \hat{\delta})$, and let $\hat{Q}_-$ and $\hat{Q}_+$ be the sets of states given in Definition 5.11. Here we assume $\hat{Q} = \{q_L, q_1, \ldots, q_{m-1}\}$. Then, from the definition of a 1WU-RTM (Definition 5.20), $\hat{Q}_- = \{q_L\}$, and $\hat{Q}_+ = \{q_1, \ldots, q_{m-1}\}$.

The three-state RTM $T^\dagger$ is given below.

$$
\begin{aligned}
T^\dagger &= (Q^\dagger, S^\dagger, L, s_0, \delta^\dagger) \\
Q^\dagger &= \{L, R_0, R_1\} \\
S^\dagger &= \hat{S} \cup \hat{S} \times (\{1^\uparrow, 2^\uparrow, \ldots, (m-1)^\uparrow\} \cup \{1^\downarrow, 2^\downarrow, \ldots, (m-1)^\downarrow\}) \\
\delta_1^\dagger &= \{ [L, s_0, [s_0, j^\downarrow], +, R_0] \mid [q_L, s_0, s_0, +, q_j] \in \hat{\delta} \} \\
\delta_2^\dagger &= \{ [R_0, [s, i^\uparrow], [t, j^\downarrow], +, R_0] \mid [q_i, s, t, +, q_j] \in \hat{\delta} \wedge s \in \hat{S} \wedge t \in \hat{S} - \{s_0\} \} \\
\delta_3^\dagger &= \{ [R_0, u, [u, 1^\uparrow], -, L] \mid u \in \hat{S} \} \\
\delta_4^\dagger &= \{ [L, [t, k^\downarrow], [t, (k-1)^\downarrow], +, R_1] \mid k \in \{2, \ldots, m-1\} \wedge t \in \hat{S} - \{s_0\} \} \\
\delta_5^\dagger &= \{ [R_1, [u, k^\uparrow], [u, (k+1)^\uparrow], -, L] \mid k \in \{1, \ldots, m-2\} \wedge u \in \hat{S} \} \\
\delta_6^\dagger &= \{ [L, [t, 1^\downarrow], t, +, R_0] \mid t \in \hat{S} \} \\
\delta_7^\dagger &= \{ [R_0, [s_0, i^\uparrow], s_0, -, L] \mid [q_i, s_0, s_0, -, q_L] \in \hat{\delta} \} \\
\delta_8^\dagger &= \{ [L, s, s, -, L] \mid s \in \hat{S} - \{s_0\} \} \\
\delta^\dagger &= \delta_1^\dagger \cup \cdots \cup \delta_8^\dagger
\end{aligned}
$$

The quintuple in $\delta_1^\dagger$ is for simulating $[q_L, s_0, s_0, +, q_j]$ in $\hat{\delta}$. Note that there is a unique q_j, since $\hat{T}$ is deterministic. The quintuples in $\delta_2^\dagger, \ldots, \delta_6^\dagger$ are essentially the same as $\tilde{\delta}_2, \ldots, \tilde{\delta}_6$ in Theorem 5.5. By these quintuples, each right-shift quintuple of $\hat{T}$ is simulated as in Theorem 5.5. The quintuple in $\delta_7^\dagger$ is for simulating $[q_i, s_0, s_0, -, q_L]$ in $\hat{\delta}$. In this case there is a unique q_i, since $\hat{T}$ is reversible. The quintuple in $\delta_8^\dagger$ is for simulating leftward sweep operation of $\hat{T}$.

If the initial ID of $\hat{T}$ is $\alpha q_L s \beta$ for $\alpha, \beta \in (\hat{S} - \{s_0\})^*$ and $s \in \hat{S} - \{s_0\}$, then that of $T^\dagger$ is set to $\alpha L s \beta$. After that, $T^\dagger$ simulates $\hat{T}$ step by step. If $\hat{T}$ halts with an ID $\alpha' q_i s' \beta'$, then $T^\dagger$ halts with an ID $\alpha' R_0 [s', i^\uparrow] \beta'$.

It is also easy to verify that $T^\dagger$ is reversible, i.e., every pair of distinct quintuples $r_1 = [p_1, a_1, b_1, d_1, q_1]$ and $r_2 = [p_2, a_2, b_2, d_2, q_2]$ in $\delta^\dagger$ satisfies the reversibility condition, i.e., if $q_1 = q_2$ then $d_1 = d_2$ and $b_1 \neq b_2$. We can verify it for the case $q_1 = q_2 = R_0$ or $q_1 = q_2 = R_1$ in a similar manner as in Theorem 5.5, hence we omit the proof. If $q_1 = q_2 = L$, then $r_1, r_2 \in \delta_7^\dagger \cup \delta_8^\dagger$. From the definition of $\delta_7^\dagger$ and $\delta_8^\dagger$, it is also easily verified that r_1 and r_2 satisfy the reversibility condition in this case. By above, $T^\dagger$ is an RTM. $\qquad \square$

Example 5.10. Let $\hat{T}_{\text{twice}} = (\hat{Q}, \hat{S}, q_L, \#, \hat{\delta})$ be the 1WU-RTM in Example 5.9. We convert $\hat{T}_{\text{twice}}$ into a three-state RTM $T_{\text{twice}}^{\dagger} = (\{L, R_0, R_1\}, S^{\dagger}, q_L, \#, \delta^{\dagger})$ by the method of Lemma 5.10. Here, $\hat{S}$ is as follows.

$$S^{\dagger} = \hat{S} \cup \hat{S} \times (\{1^{\uparrow}, 2^{\uparrow}, \dots, 15^{\uparrow}\} \cup \{1^{\downarrow}, 2^{\downarrow}, \dots, 15^{\downarrow}\})$$

Here, $|S^{\dagger}| = 1147$. Since $\delta^{\dagger}$ contains 1254 quintuples, we do not describe it here. A computing process

$$q_L \# [[p_0, \#], a][a, \#] \mid \frac{771}{\hat{T}_{\text{twice}}} [\#, \#]^{13} [a, a][[p_1, \#], a][a, a][a, \#][\#, \#]^9 h(\#)$$

by $\hat{T}_{\text{twice}}$ is simulated by $T_{\text{twice}}^{\dagger}$ as below, where $1^{\uparrow}$ stands for the state $h(\#)$ of $\hat{T}$.

$$L \# [[p_0, \#], a][a, \#] \mid \frac{3481}{T_{\text{twice}}^{\dagger}} [\#, \#]^{13} [a, a][[p_1, \#], a][a, a][a, \#][\#, \#]^9 R_0 [\#, 1^{\uparrow}]$$

All the steps of the above computing process are shown in the slide file of [10]. □

By Definition 5.20, a 1WU-RTM can be regarded as an RTM with a one-way infinite tape. Furthermore, the three-state RTM $T^{\dagger}$ in Lemma 5.10, which simulates a 1WU-RTM $\hat{T}$, can also be regarded as an RTM with a one-way infinite tape. This is because $T^{\dagger}$ uses the same region of the tape as the one used by $\hat{T}$. From Lemmas 5.9, 5.10, and by the above fact, we can derive the following.

Theorem 5.6. *[10] For any one-tape m-state n-symbol RTM T, we can construct a one-tape three-state RTM $T^{\dagger}$ with $O(m^2 n^3)$ symbols and with a one-way infinite tape that simulates T.*

5.3.6 Computational universality of restricted classes of RTMs

From the results shown in this section, we can derive computational universality of restricted classes of RTMs. We already know that the class of garbage-less three-tape RTMs is computationally universal (Corollary 5.3). By Theorem 5.3, a k-tape RTM ($k \in \mathbb{Z}_+$) can be converted into a one-tape RTM with a one-way infinite tape, and by Theorem 5.4, it is further converted into a one-tape two-symbol RTM with a one-way infinite tape. Thus, we obtain the following result.

Theorem 5.7. *The class of one-tape two-symbol RTMs with a one-way infinite tape is computationally universal.*

On the other hand, by Theorem 5.6, a one-tape many-state RTM can be converted into a one-tape three-state RTM, and thus we can derive the following.

Theorem 5.8. *The class of one-tape three-state RTMs with a one-way infinite tape is computationally universal.*

5.4 Concluding Remarks

In this chapter, we defined reversible Turing machines (RTMs), and clarified their basic properties. We gave two formulations of RTMs. They are RTMs in the quadruple form, and those in the quintuple form, and we showed they are convertible to each other. Since each of the forms has its own advantage, we can use either of them depending on the purpose.

We then explained the method of Bennett [1] for constructing a three-tape RTM that simulates a given irreversible TM. By a tricky use of an inverse RTM as a component machine, the constructed three-tape RTM leaves no garbage information on the tape when it halts. From this, the computational universality of three-tape RTM is derived. In Sect. 8.2, another method of constructing RTM will be given.

We also introduced variations of RTMs, in particular, several kinds of restricted types of RTMs. We showed that RTMs with two-way infinite tapes can be converted into RTMs with one-way infinite tapes, multi-tape RTMs can be converted into one-tape RTMs, many-symbol RTMs can converted into two-symbol RTMs, and many-state RTMs can be converted into three-state and four-state RTMs.

From these results, we can derive the computational universality of the class of one-tape two-symbol RTMs with one-way infinite tape, and the class of one-tape three-state RTMs. However, it is not known whether the class of one-tape two-state RTMs is computationally universal. Thus, we can say that, in most cases, the computational power of TMs does not decrease even if the reversibility constraint is added. In the following chapters, these results will be used to show the computational universality of other reversible systems, and for composing reversible computing machines out of reversible logic elements.

References

1. Bennett, C.H.: Logical reversibility of computation. IBM J. Res. Dev. **17**, 525–532 (1973). doi:10.1147/rd.176.0525
2. Bennett, C.H.: The thermodynamics of computation — a review. Int. J. Theoret. Phys. **21**, 905–940 (1982). doi:10.1007/BF02084158
3. Bennett, C.H.: Notes on the history of reversible computation. IBM J. Res. Dev. **32**, 16–23 (1988). doi:10.1147/rd.321.0016
4. Church, A.: An unsolvable problem in elementary number theory. American Journal of Mathematics **58**, 345–363 (1936). doi:10.2307/2371045
5. Fredkin, E., Toffoli, T.: Conservative logic. Int. J. Theoret. Phys. **21**, 219–253 (1982). doi:10.1007/BF01857727
6. Hopcroft, J.E., Motwani, R., Ullman, J.D.: Introduction to Automata Theory, Languages and Computation. Prentice Hall (2006)
7. Kleene, S.: Introduction to Metamathematics. North-Holland (1952)
8. Lecerf, Y.: Machines de Turing réversibles — récursive insolubilité en $n \in \mathbf{N}$ de l'équation $u = \theta^n u$, où θ est un isomorphisme de codes. Comptes Rendus Hebdomadaires des Séances de L'académie des Sciences **257**, 2597–2600 (1963)
9. Minsky, M.L.: Computation: Finite and Infinite Machines. Prentice-Hall, Englewood Cliffs, NJ (1967)

10. Morita, K.: Reversible Turing machines with a small number of states. In: Proc. NCMA 2014 (eds. S. Bensch, R. Freund, F. Otto), pp. 179–190 (2014). Slides with figures of computer simulation: Hiroshima University Institutional Repository, http://ir.lib.hiroshima-u.ac.jp/00036075

11. Morita, K.: Universal reversible Turing machines with a small number of tape symbols. Fundam. Inform. **138**, 17–29 (2015). doi:10.3233/FI-2015-1195

12. Morita, K., Shirasaki, A., Gono, Y.: A 1-tape 2-symbol reversible Turing machine. Trans. IEICE Japan **E-72**, 223–228 (1989)

13. Rogozhin, Y.: Small universal Turing machines. Theoret. Comput. Sci. **168**, 215–240 (1996). doi:10.1016/S0304-3975(96)00077-1

14. Shannon, C.E.: A universal Turing machine with two internal states. In: Automata Studies, pp. 157–165. Princeton University Press, Princeton, NJ (1956)

15. Turing, A.M.: On computable numbers, with an application to the Entscheidungsproblem. Proc. London Math. Soc., Series 2 **42**, 230–265 (1936)

Chapter 6
Making Reversible Turing Machines from Reversible Primitives

Abstract The problem how we can construct reversible Turing machines (RTMs) out of reversible primitives is investigated. It is shown that any one-tape two-symbol RTM can be concisely realized as a completely garbage-less reversible logic circuit composed of a rotary element (RE), or a reversible logic element with memory RLEM 4-31. Though we deal with only one-tape two-symbol RTMs in the quintuple form for simplicity, the construction method can be generalized for any type of RTMs. Here, an RTM is decomposed into a finite control module, and memory cells. Then, they are implemented as reversible sequential machines (RSMs) using RE or RLEM 4-31. The design methods employed here are quite different from those in the traditional design theory of logic circuits based on logic gates. Furthermore, since RE and RLEM 4-31 have simple realizations in the billiard ball model (BBM), an idealized reversible physical model, the constructed RTMs are further embeddable in BBM.

Keywords reversible Turing machine, reversible logic element with memory, rotary element, reversible logic circuit

6.1 Constructing Reversible Turing Machines out of RE

In this chapter, we show reversible Turing machines (RTMs) are constructed out of reversible logic elements with memory (RLEMs), in particular from a rotary element (RE) and from RLEM 4-31. The construction method thus gives a way that connects between the lower level reversible systems and the higher level ones. Here, we make two-symbol RTMs with a one-way infinite tape, a class of computationally universal RTMs (Theorem 5.7), since any RTM can be converted into this type of RTM. Note that, it is also possible to compose any type of RTM out of these RLEMs, but the resulting circuits will become relatively complex, and thus we do not go into its details. In this section, we explain how a two-symbol RTM is realized by an RE-circuit. It was first shown in [2]. Later, the circuit was simplified in [3].

Hence we describe the latter method here. In Sect. 6.2, we shall explain how RTMs are constructed out of RLEM 4-31 based on the method given in [4].

We design two kinds of modules for constructing two-symbol RTMs: a memory cell, and a finite control module. We shall see that these modules are in fact reversible sequential machines (RSMs). In Sect. 3.2 we saw all non-degenerate 2-symbol RLEMs except only four have universal capability for constructing RSMs (Theorem 3.1). Hence, a memory cell, and a finite control module can be composed of any one of the universal RLEMs in a systematic manner. However, here, we give special methods for designing the modules so that the numbers of RLEMs become as small as possible.

6.1.1 Memory cell for two-symbol RTMs

A *memory cell* is a module that acts as one square of a tape of an RTM. Here, we design it for two-symbol RTMs with a one-way infinite tape. We take the following method of formalizing it as an RSM, though there are many possibilities of doing so. The memory cell keeps a tape symbol $s \in \{0,1\}$, and the information h whether the head of the RTM is on this cell ($h = 1$) or not ($h = 0$). Hence, its state set is $\{(h,s) \mid h,s \in \{0,1\}\}$. As a sequential machine, the memory cell has ten kinds of input symbols listed in Table 6.1, which are interpreted as instructions to the tape unit or response signals to the finite control. For each input symbol, there is a corresponding output symbol, which is indicated by one with $'$, and thus the module has ten output symbols as well as ten input symbols (Fig. 6.1). Making an infinite number of copies of it, and connecting them to form a one-way infinite array, we can obtain a *tape unit* for the RTM. We assume there is only one memory cell that has the value $h = 1$ in the initial setting. The memory cell defined here can be commonly used for *any* two-symbol RTM with a one-way infinite tape.

Table 6.1 Ten kinds of input symbols of the memory cell, and their meanings

Symbol	Instruction/Response	Meaning
W0	Write 0	Instruction of writing the tape symbol 0 at the head position. By this instruction, read operation is also performed
W1	Write 1	Instruction of writing the tape symbol 1 at the head position. By this instruction, read operation is also performed
R0	Read 0	Response signal telling the read symbol at the head is 0
R1	Read 1	Response signal telling the read symbol at the head is 1
SL	Shift-left	Instruction of shift-left operation
SLI	Shift-left immediate	Instruction of placing the head on this cell by shifting left
SLc	Shift-left completed	Response (completion) signal of shift-left operation
SR	Shift-right	Instruction of shift-right operation
SRI	Shift-right immediate	Instruction of placing the head on this cell by shifting right
SRc	Shift-right completed	Response (completion) signal of shift-right operation

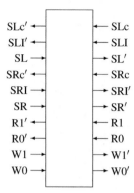

Fig. 6.1 Input and output ports of the memory cell for two-symbol RTMs. Each output is connected to the corresponding input of the neighboring memory cell, or the finite control module

The input symbol W0 or W1 is an instruction to the tape unit for writing the tape symbol 0 or 1, respectively, in the memory cell at the head position. After finishing the write operation, the output symbol R0$'$ or R1$'$ is generated as a response signal depending on the old tape symbol at the head position, and is sent to the finite control. Hence, the write instruction performs not only the write operation but also the read operation. Otherwise, reversibility of the memory cell does not hold. Assume a symbol W0 or W1 is given to a memory cell. If the tape head is not at the cell (i.e., $h = 0$), then it generates an output symbol W0$'$ or W1$'$, respectively, and sends it to the right-neighboring memory cell. If the tape head is at the cell (i.e., $h = 1$), then the cell sets its tape symbol s to 0 (if W0 is given) or 1 (if W1 is given). It also generates an output symbol R0$'$ or R1$'$ depending on the old tape symbol, and sends it to the left-neighboring memory cell.

Note that, if an RTM needs to read a tape symbol, then it is performed by the instruction W0. By this, the finite control obtains a response signal R0 or R1, and the tape symbol at the head position is cleared to 0. After that, if the RTM gives the instruction W0 or W1, then the tape symbol 0 or 1 is written at the head position, and finally the finite control receives the response signal R0.

The input symbol SL is an instruction for shifting the tape head to the left. Assume a symbol SL is given to a memory cell. If the tape head is not at the cell (i.e., $h = 0$), then it simply sends an output symbol SL$'$ to the right-neighboring cell. If the tape head is at the cell (i.e., $h = 1$), then the cell sets the value of h to 0, and sends an output symbol SLI$'$ to the left-neighboring memory cell. If the latter memory cell receives an input symbol SLI, then it sets the value of h to 1, and sends an output symbol SLc$'$ to the left. By such a process, shift-left operation is performed correctly. The input symbols SR, SRI, and SRc are similar to the symbols SL, SLI, and SLc, except that an output symbol SRI$'$ is sent to the right-neighboring cell.

Thus, the memory cell is formalized as the following 4-state 10-symbol RSM M_C, where $s \in \{0, 1\}$.

$$M_C = (Q_C, \Sigma_C, \Gamma_C, \delta_C)$$
$$Q_C = \{(h,s) \mid h,s \in \{0,1\}\}$$
$$\Sigma_C = \{\text{W0, W1, R0, R1, SL, SLI, SLc, SR, SRI, SRc}\}$$
$$\Gamma_C = \{x' \mid x \in \Sigma_C\}$$
$$\delta_C((0,s),y) = ((0,s),y') \quad (y \in \Sigma_C - \{\text{SLI, SRI}\})$$
$$\delta_C((0,s),\text{SLI}) = ((1,s),\text{SLc}')$$
$$\delta_C((0,s),\text{SRI}) = ((1,s),\text{SRc}')$$
$$\delta_C((1,0),\text{W0}) = ((1,0),\text{R0}')$$
$$\delta_C((1,1),\text{W0}) = ((1,0),\text{R1}')$$
$$\delta_C((1,0),\text{W1}) = ((1,1),\text{R0}')$$
$$\delta_C((1,1),\text{W1}) = ((1,1),\text{R1}')$$
$$\delta_C((1,s),\text{SL}) = ((0,s),\text{SLI}')$$
$$\delta_C((1,s),\text{SR}) = ((0,s),\text{SRI}')$$

It is easy to see δ_C is injective. Note that the move function δ_C is defined partially. For example, $\delta_C((1,0),\text{SRI})$ is not defined, since such a case does not occur. This is because we assume only one memory cell has the value $h = 1$ in the initial setting. To define δ_C as a total function, we should give a value of the function appropriately for the undefined cases so that it becomes an injective total function.

Here, we show the following lemma, which is proved easily.

Lemma 6.1. *Let $f : S_1 \to S_2$ be an injective partial function such that S_1 and S_2 are finite sets, and $|S_1| = |S_2|$. Let $S_1'(\subseteq S_1)$ be the set on which f is defined. Then there is a bijection $\tilde{f} : S_1 \to S_2$ that is an extension of $f|_{S_1'}$, i.e., $\tilde{f}(x) = f(x)$ for all $x \in S_1'$.*

Proof. Let $S_2' = \{f(x) \mid x \in S_1'\}$. Since f is injective, $|S_1'| = |S_2'|$ holds. Hence, there exists a bijection $g : (S_1 - S_1') \to (S_2 - S_2')$. Let $\tilde{f}$ be defined as follows.

$$\tilde{f}(x) = \begin{cases} f(x) & \text{if } x \in S_1' \\ g(x) & \text{if } x \in S_1 - S_1' \end{cases}$$

Apparently $\tilde{f}$ is a bijection.   □

Let $S(\subseteq Q_C \times \Sigma_C)$ be the set on which δ_C is defined. Since the domain and the codomain of δ_C are $Q_C \times \Sigma_C$ and $Q_C \times \Gamma_C$, respectively, and they have the same number of elements, we can apply Lemma 6.1. By this, we obtain an injective total function $\tilde{\delta}_C$, which is an extension of δ_C. Therefore, M_C with $\tilde{\delta}_C$ is an RSM. Since an injective total function is thus easily obtained, M_C with an injective partial function δ_C is also regarded as an RSM hereafter. Note that, when we deal with reversible partitioned cellular automata (RPCAs) in Chaps. 11 and 14, we shall use again Lemma 6.1 to describe them simply.

Figure 6.2 shows the RE-circuit that realizes the RSM M_C, the memory cell. It has two RE-columns, which were formalized as an RSM M_{REC_n} in Sect. 2.3. Note that if we employ the construction method of an RSM given in Theorem 2.1, we need four RE-columns, since M_C has four states. However, here, only two RE-columns are used. The left RE-column is for keeping the value h, and the right one is for the value s. Hence, if the head is at this memory cell ($h = 1$), then the bottom RE of the left column is set to the state H, and if $h = 0$, it is set to V. Likewise, if $s = 1$, then the bottom RE of the right column is set to the state H, and if $s = 0$, it is set to V. All the other REs are initially set to the state V.

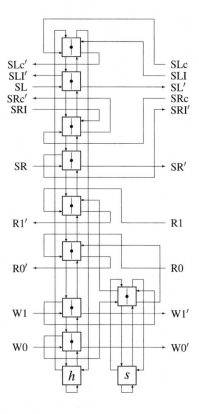

Fig. 6.2 The memory cell realized by an RE-circuit [3]

The left RE-column controls an incoming particle, which is interpreted as an input symbol to the memory cell. We can see that, if $h = 0$, then a particle given to a port other than SRI and SLI simply goes through the memory cell without affecting the state of the memory cell (see also the move function δ_{REC_n} given in Table 2.3). It is also easy to see that if $h = 0$ and either an instruction SLI or SRI is given, then h is set to 1, and the particle goes out from SLc' or SRc', respectively, showing that head-shift operation is completed. If $h = 1$ and a particle is given to W0 (or W1, respectively), then s is set to 0 (or 1), and then the particle goes out from R0 or R1 depending on the old value of s. If $h = 1$ and a particle is given to SL (or SR, respectively), then the value h is set to 0, and the particle goes out from the port SLI (or SRI). By above, M_C is correctly simulated by the RE-circuit.

6.1.2 Finite control module for two-symbol RTMs

We show a finite control of an RTM can also be realized by an RSM composed of RE. We assume the given RTM is in the quintuple form. In the RE-circuit that simulates the finite control, each quintuple is executed by producing read, write, and shift instructions successively, and sending them to the tape unit, i.e., the array of memory cells. The state of the finite control is distinguished by the states of the REs and the position of a particle in the RE-circuit. One step of the RTM is simulated in the following way. First, the W0 instruction is generated, and it is sent to the tape unit. By this, a read operation is executed. As a result, a completion signal R0 or R1 is obtained. From this information the next state of the finite control, the symbol to be written, and the shift direction are determined. Second, giving W0 or W1 instruction, a write operation is performed, and a completion signal R0 is obtained. Third, giving SL or SR instruction, shift operation is performed. Finally, it enters the next state of the RTM. The RE-circuit repeats the above procedure until it becomes a halting state.

The RE-circuit for the finite control of an RTM is designed so that the computing process is started by giving a particle from the outside, and if the RTM enters a halting state, the particle goes out from it. To activate the initial state of the RTM from the outside, we assume the RTM satisfies the following property: There is no state that goes to the initial state, i.e., there is no quintuple whose fifth element is the initial state. If otherwise, the initial state can be activated only by some state of the RTM, and thus not from the outside of the RTM. In the case of an irreversible TM it is easy to convert the RTM to satisfy this property (see Definition 5.18), but in the case of an RTM it is not trivial to do so. However, we can see that the three-tape RTM in Theorem 5.1 constructed from an irreversible TM has this property. Furthermore, it is also possible to see that the conversion methods from a multi-tape RTM to a one-tape RTM (Theorem 5.3), and from a many-symbol RTM to a two-symbol RTM (Theorem 5.4) preserves this property. Hence, we can assume, without loss of generality, a given one-tape two-symbol RTM satisfies this condition.

We consider the following example of a two-symbol RTM T_{parity}, and explain how the finite control module can be realized by an RE-circuit.

Example 6.1. Let T_{parity} be a two-symbol RTM with a one-way infinite tape defined as follows.

$$T_{\text{parity}} = (Q_{\text{parity}}, \{0, 1\}, q_0, \{q_{\text{acc}}\}, 0, \delta_{\text{parity}})$$
$$Q_{\text{parity}} = \{q_0, q_1, q_2, q_{\text{acc}}, q_{\text{rej}}\}$$
$$\delta_{\text{parity}} = \{ [\, q_0, 0, 1, +, q_1 \,], \quad [\, q_1, 0, 1, -, q_{\text{acc}} \,], \quad [\, q_1, 1, 0, +, q_2 \,],$$
$$[\, q_2, 0, 1, -, q_{\text{rej}} \,], \quad [\, q_2, 1, 0, +, q_1 \,] \}$$

It is easy to see that T_{parity} satisfies the reversibility condition, and there is no quintuple whose fifth element is q_0. T_{parity} checks if a given unary number n is even or odd. If it is even, T_{parity} halts in the accepting state q_{acc}, otherwise halts in the rejecting state q_{rej}. All the symbols read by T_{parity} are complemented. The following is a complete computing process of T_{parity} for the input "11".

$$q_0 011 \mathrel{\vdash_{T_{\text{parity}}}} 1 q_1 11 \mathrel{\vdash_{T_{\text{parity}}}} 10 q_2 1 \mathrel{\vdash_{T_{\text{parity}}}} 100 q_1 \mathrel{\vdash_{T_{\text{parity}}}} 10 q_{\text{acc}} 01$$

□

An RE-circuit for the finite control of T_{parity} is shown in Fig. 6.3. In this circuit, we lay REs in four rows. REs in the fourth (i.e., bottom) row are for the operation of reading a tape symbol. The third row is for writing a tape symbol. The second row is for the shift-right operation, and the first row is for the shift-left operation. The state transition of the RTM is performed by appropriately connecting the output lines of the REs in the fourth row to the input lines of those in the third row.

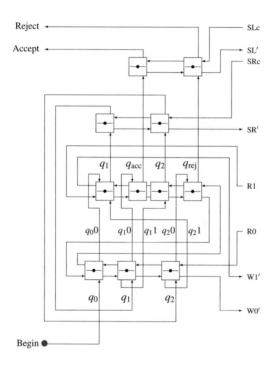

Fig. 6.3 The finite control module of the RTM T_{parity} in Example 6.1 realized by an RE-circuit [3]

In Fig. 6.3, the three REs in the fourth row correspond to q_0, q_1 and q_2, respectively. When a particle is given to the south input line of an RE in the fourth row, it sends W0 instruction to the tape unit to read the symbol at the head position. If the RE receives a signal R0 (or R1, respectively), then the particle goes out from the north (south) output line of it. By this, it determines the next state, the symbol to be written, and the shift-direction. The four REs in the third row corresponds to the next states q_1, q_{acc}, q_2, and q_{rej}, where the south input lines of the REs are for writing the symbol 0, while the north input lines are for writing the symbol 1. Thus, connections between the REs in the fourth row and those in the third row should be made appropriately according to δ_{parity}. For example, for the quintuple $[q_1, 1, 0, +, q_2]$, we make a connection line between the south output line of the RE labeled by q_1 in the fourth row to the south input line of the RE labeled by q_2 in the third row. The RE in the third row sends an instruction W0 or W1 to the tape unit. By this, write operation is performed. The RE in the third row receives a response signal R0, and thus a particle comes out from the north output line of it. Since the shift directions associated to q_1 and q_2 are both $+$, the north output lines of the REs with labels q_1 and q_2 are connected to the REs in the second row. Each RE in the second row gives an instruction SR to shift the head to the right. If it receives a completion signal SRc, then the particle goes out from its north output line. This line is thus connected to the south input line of the corresponding state in the fourth row. Likewise, since the shift directions associated to q_{acc} and q_{rej} are both $-$, the north output lines of the REs with labels q_{acc} and q_{rej} are connected to the REs in the first row. By this, shift-left operation is performed. However, since q_{acc} and q_{rej} are halting states, the north output lines of them are fed outside as output lines. On the other hand, to the south input line of the RE labeled by q_0 in the fourth row, an input line "Begin" is connected from the outside.

By above, we can see that the RE-circuit in Fig. 6.3 correctly simulates the finite control of T_{parity}, which is an RSM with 5 input symbols and 6 output symbols. It is easy to generalize this method to construct an RE-circuit that simulates a finite control of a given one-tape two-symbol RTM, though we do not describe it.

6.1.3 RE-circuit that simulates a one-tape two-symbol RTM

Figure 6.4 is the whole circuit that simulates the RTM T_{parity} in Example 6.1. It consists of the RE-circuit for the finite control, and an infinite number of copies of the memory cell circuit. Though it is an infinite circuit, it is ultimately periodic. If we give a particle to the input port "Begin" of the circuit, then it starts to compute. Finally, the particle comes out from the output port "Accept" or "Reject" depending on the parity of the given input on the tape. Note that, if the simulated RTM is garbage-less, then the constructed RE-circuit is also so. An example of its whole computing process is shown in the slide file of [3].

By above, we have the next theorem.

Theorem 6.1. *Any two-symbol RTM with a one-way infinite tape can be implemented as a garbage-less reversible logic circuit composed only of REs.*

Note that the resulting circuit is infinite, but it consists of a finite control module, and an infinite copies of a memory cell. Thus, it is an ultimately periodic circuit.

Since RE is implemented as a garbage-less circuit made of Fredkin gate as in Fig. 4.24, the whole circuit for an RTM is also realized by a garbage-less circuit composed of them. Hence, the following corollary is obtained.

Corollary 6.1. *Any two-symbol RTM with a one-way infinite tape can be implemented as a garbage-less reversible logic circuit composed of Fredkin gates and delay elements.*

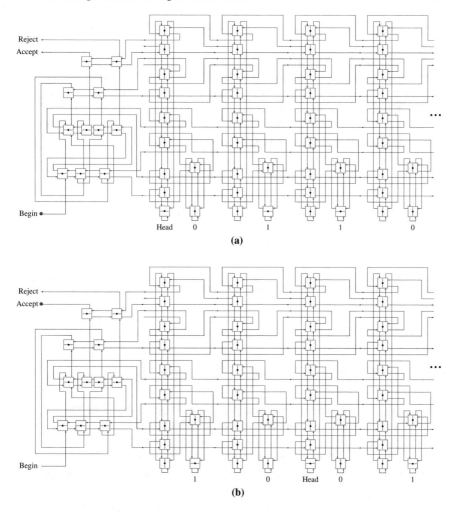

Fig. 6.4 The RE-circuit that simulates T_{parity} in Example 6.1 [3]. (**a**) The initial configuration corresponding to the ID $q_0 011$. (**b**) The final configuration corresponding to the ID $10 q_{\text{acc}} 01$

We know RE is further implemented in the billiard ball model (BBM) as shown in Fig. 2.8, we can embed the whole circuit of Fig. 6.4 in the space of BBM. It consists of infinitely many reflectors and stationary balls, but the configuration is again ultimately periodic. By giving a moving ball from the position corresponding to "Begin" input port, computing of T_{parity} is performed by collisions of balls and with reflectors. Finally a moving ball comes out from the position corresponding to "Accept" or that of "Reject". In an ideal situation, energy dissipation does not occur in this model.

6.2 Constructing Reversible Turing Machines out of RLEM 4-31

RLEM 4-31 is a 2-state 4-symbol RLEM shown in Fig. 6.5. In Sect. 3.4, a compact realization method of RSMs using RLEM 4-31 is given. It is also possible to construct RTMs out of RLEM 4-31 rather simply, and here we show its method. In Sect. 3.4, a column of RLEM 4-31 is defined (see Figs. 3.18 and 3.19), and it was used as a building module for RSMs. It is also useful for composing the memory cell, and a finite control of a one-tape two-symbol RTM.

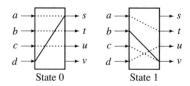

Fig. 6.5 Graphical representation of RLEM 4-31. If a signal goes through a solid line, the state changes to the other. If it goes through a dotted line, the state does not change

6.2.1 Making memory cell out of RLEM 4-31

The memory cell M_C defined in Sect. 6.1.1 is realized as shown in Fig. 6.6. The eight RLEMs except the top one form a column of RLEM 4-31. If the head is absent (present, respectively) at this cell, then the state of the column of RLEM 4-31 is set to **0** (**1**). At the top of the cell, there is a *one-bit-memory submodule* to keep a tape symbol s, which is shown in Fig. 6.7 **(a)**. Its function is as follows. If its present state is s, and the input symbol is w_t $(s,t \in \{0,1\})$, then the next state is t and the output symbol is r_s. Namely, by the input w_t the new state is set to t, and the old state s is obtained as the output r_s. This submodule is equivalent to RLEM 2-2 in Fig.6.7 **(b)**.

It is not difficult to verify that the circuit simulates M_C correctly. First, consider the case $h = 0$, i.e., the column of RLEM 4-31 is in the state **0**. If a particle is given to an input port other than SLI and SRI, then it simply goes out from the corresponding output port without affecting the state of the memory cell. If a particle is given to SLI (SRI, respectively), then the column of RLEM 4-31 is set to **1**, and the particle goes out from SLc (SRc). Second, consider the case $h = 1$. If a particle is given to W0 (W1, respectively), then the column first set to the state **0**, and the particle is sent to the w_0 (w_1) input of the one-bit-memory submodule. By this, a writing operation is performed. As a reaction of the submodule, the old state is read out, and the particle comes out from its output r_0 or r_1. Then, the column of RLEM 4-31 is again set to the state **1**, and the particle finally goes out from R0′ or R1′. If a particle is given to SL (SR, respectively), then the column is set to the state **0**, and the particle comes out from SLI (SRI).

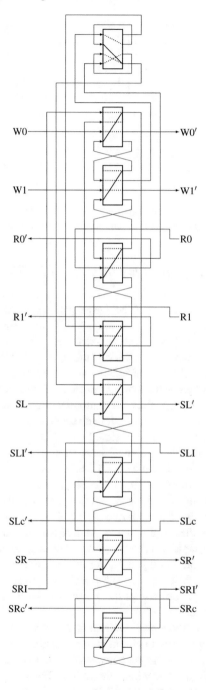

Fig. 6.6 The memory cell realized by a circuit composed of RLEM 4-31. This figure shows the case of $h = 0$ and $s = 1$ [4]

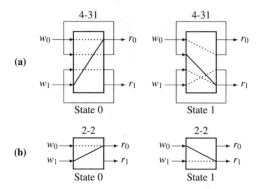

Fig. 6.7 (a) The one-bit-memory submodule composed of RLEM 4-31, which is at the top of the memory cell in Fig. 6.6. (b) RLEM 2-2, which is equivalent to the one-bit-memory submodule

6.2.2 Making finite control module out of RLEM 4-31

To construct a finite control of an RTM, we prepare a q_i-*submodule* for each state q_i of M as shown in Fig. 6.8. It has two columns of RLEM 4-31 labeled by q_i and $\hat{q}_i$. The RLEM-column labeled by $\hat{q}_i$ is used to read the tape symbol and branch the program of the RTM, i.e., it determines which quintuple $[q_i, 0, t, d, q_j]$ or $[q_i, 1, t', d', q_{j'}]$ should be applied. The column of RLEM 4-31 labeled by q_i is used to write a symbol, shift the head, and enter the state q_i. In Fig. 6.8, we assume q_i is a right-shift state. If it is a left-shift state, then the bottom RLEM of the left RLEM-column should be placed at the position of the dotted rectangle [4].

Assume M is in the state q_i. Then a signal should be given to the first input line of the second RLEM of the right column of the q_i-submodule as shown by ● in Fig. 6.8. Then, the RLEM-column enters the state **1**, and gives a signal on the command line W0′. By this, the tape symbol $s \in \{0, 1\}$ at the head position is read, and its response is obtained from Rs. Then, a signal goes out from the line labelled by $q_i s$ setting this column to state **0**. If there is a quintuple $[q_i, s, t, d, q_j]$, this line is connected to the line labelled by tdq_j of the q_j-submodule. At the q_j-submodule, after setting the left RLEM-column to the state **1**, write instruction Wt is generated. Its response must be R0, since the last instruction just before the instruction Wt was W0. Then, the q_j module executes the shift instruction Sd, and finally a signal is transferred to the second RLEM of the right column of the q_j-submodule. By above, the operation of $[q_i, s, t, d, q_j]$ is performed.

Figure 6.9 shows a finite control module of T_{parity} in Example 6.1. Note that for the initial state q_0 only the right column is necessary, and for the halting states q_{acc} and q_{rej} only the left column is necessary. Also note that lines with open ends are not used to simulate T_{parity}. The whole circuit for RTM T_{parity} is shown in Fig. 6.10. By giving a signal to the port "Begin," the circuit starts to compute. Finally the signal comes out from the output port "Accept" or "Reject." An example of its whole computing process is shown in the slide file of [4].

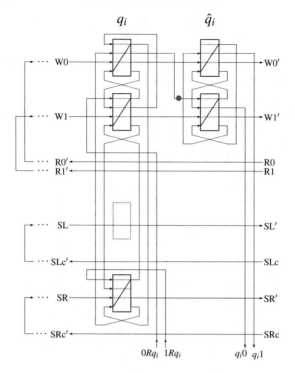

Fig. 6.8 The q_i-submodule composed of RLEM 4-31

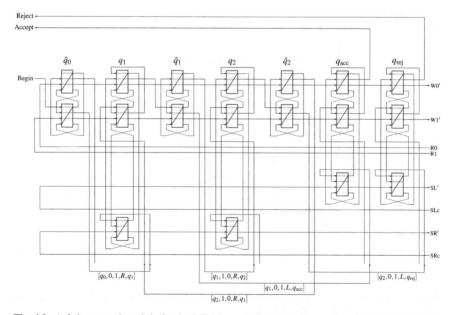

Fig. 6.9 A finite control module for the RTM T_{parity} in Example 6.1 composed of RLEM 4-31 [4]

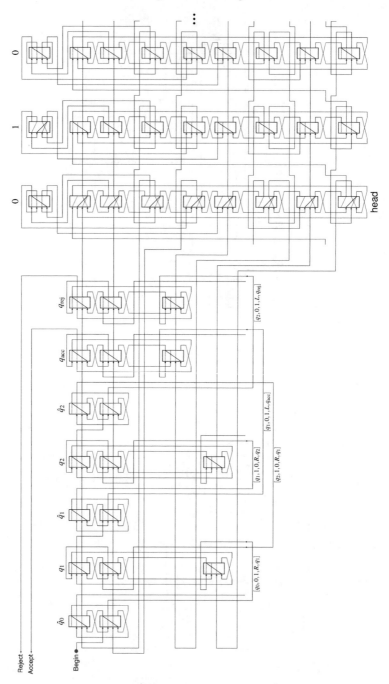

Fig. 6.10 The whole circuit composed of RLEM 4-31 that simulates the RTM T_{parity} in Example 6.1 [4]. It corresponds to the initial ID $q_0 01$

In Sect.3.6, a BBM realization of a 4-symbol RLEM is given. In particular, RLEM 4-31 is realized as in Fig. 3.33. Hence, replacing each occurrence of RLEM 4-31 in Fig. 6.10 by a BBM configuration of Fig. 3.33, we can embed the RTM in BBM.

6.3 Concluding Remarks

In this chapter, we investigated the problem how we can efficiently construct reversible Turing machines (RTMs) out of reversible primitives. It was shown that any one-tape two-symbol RTM can be concisely realized as a completely garbage-less reversible logic circuit composed of RE or RLEM 4-31. Since RLEM 4-31 is simulated by a circuit consisting of two copies of RLEM 3-7 as shown in Fig. 3.22, we also obtain a compact construction method out of RLEM 3-7. If we implement an RTM as a circuit composed of RE or RLEM 4-31, it is further embedded in the billiard ball model (BBM) easily, since RE and RLEM 4-31 have simple realizations in the BBM (Figs. 2.8 and 3.33). We can also obtain a completely garbage-less circuit made of Fredkin gate from the RE-circuit that simulates the RTM, since RE is simulated by a circuit composed of Fredkin gate (Fig. 4.24). Note that, in [1], another design method of RTMs is given using different kinds of RLEMs, in particular, RLEMs 2-3 and 2-4, which are called a reading toggle and an inverse reading toggle.

Here, we dealt with only one-tape two-symbol RTMs in the quintuple form for simplicity. However, the construction method can be generalized so that we can deal with any type of TMs, such as many-symbol RTMs, and multi-tape RTMs, though their details becomes more complex than the one-tape two-symbol case. For example, a memory cell for four-symbol RTMs can be designed as a module that has two memory bits s_1 and s_2. To each memory bit s_i $(i = 1, 2)$, it can receive a write instructions $W0_i$ or $W1_i$, and gives a response signal $R0_i$ or $R1_i$. It is also possible to construct other types of reversible machines, such as reversible counter machines and reversible multi-head finite automata, which are given in Chap. 9, out of RLEMs.

The realization method of RTMs employed here is to decompose an RTM into a finite control module, and memory cells, which are reversible sequential machines (RSMs). Although RSMs can be constructed out of any universal RLEM, It has not yet been fully investigated from which RLEMs we can construct them concisely other than RE and RLEM 4-31. Thus, it is left for the future study to find other useful RLEMs for composing RTMs and RSMs.

References

1. Lee, J., Yang, R.L., Morita, K.: Design of 1-tape 2-symbol reversible Turing machines based on reversible logic elements. Theoret. Comput. Sci. **460**, 78–88 (2012). doi:10.1016/j.tcs.2012.07.027
2. Morita, K.: A simple reversible logic element and cellular automata for reversible computing. In: Proc. MCU 2001 (eds. M. Margenstern, Y. Rogozhin), LNCS 2055, pp. 102–113 (2001). doi:10.1007/3-540-45132-3_6
3. Morita, K.: Constructing reversible Turing machines by reversible logic element with memory. In: Automata, Universality, Computation (ed. A. Adamatzky), pp. 127–138. Springer (2015). doi:10.1007/978-3-319-09039-9_6. Slides with figures of computer simulation: Hiroshima University Institutional Repository, http://ir.lib.hiroshima-u.ac.jp/00029224
4. Morita, K., Suyama, R.: Compact realization of reversible Turing machines by 2-state reversible logic elements. In: Proc. UCNC 2014 (eds. O.H. Ibarra, L. Kari, S. Kopecki), LNCS 8553, pp. 280–292 (2014). doi:10.1007/978-3-319-08123-6_23. Slides with figures of computer simulation: Hiroshima University Institutional Repository, http://ir.lib.hiroshima-u.ac.jp/00036076

Chapter 7
Universal Reversible Turing Machines

Abstract In this chapter, the problem of finding small universal Turing machines (UTMs) that satisfy the reversibility condition is studied. Such UTMs are called universal reversible Turing machines (URTMs). Let URTM(m,n) denote an m-state n-symbol URTM. We give several URTM(m,n)'s with small m and n. Here, a method of simulating cyclic tag systems (CTSs) by URTMs is employed. A CTS is a kind of a very simple string rewriting system, and is known to be computationally universal. By this method, URTM(10,8), URTM(13,7), URTM(15,6), URTM(17,5), URTM(24,4), and URTM(32,3) are obtained. On the other hand, it is generally difficult to design small reversible TMs with two symbols or with a very small number of states. For these cases, we apply general conversion methods to some of the above small URTMs, and obtain URTM(138,2), URTM(4,168), and URTM(3, 36654).

Keywords universal reversible Turing machine, small universal Turing machine, cyclic tag system

7.1 Universal Turing Machines

A universal Turing machine (UTM) U is a TM that can simulate *any* TM T. If codes (i.e., descriptions) of T and an input string w for T are given, U simulates T with w, and finally halts with a code of an output w' in the case T halts with the output w'. Note that, if T with w does not halt, then U also does not. Alan Turing himself showed it is possible to construct such a machine [16]. Of course, it is not difficult (but maybe tedious) for us to simulate a computing process of T with the input w by hand using paper and pencil. Thus, we can construct a TM that mimics this process on its tape. In this way, we can obtain a kind of a UTM that simulates other TMs directly. However, there are many other methods to construct UTMs, and thus there arise problems in which way we can construct UTMs, and how simple they can be.

We first define a UTM formally based on the definition given by Rogozhin [15]. Here, we consider the class of all one-tape TMs, and assume some Gödel numbering is given on them (for the notions of Gödel numbering, and recursive functions, see, e.g., [5, 7]). The TM with Gödel number n is denoted by T_n. Let I be the set of all instantaneous descriptions (IDs) of all one-tape TMs, i.e., $I = \bigcup_{n \in \mathbb{N}} \mathrm{ID}(T_n)$. Let $\psi_T : \mathrm{ID}(T) \to \mathrm{ID}(T)$ be the partial recursive function defined by

$$\forall \alpha, \beta \in \mathrm{ID}(T) \; (\psi_T(\alpha) = \beta \; \Leftrightarrow \; (\alpha \vdash_T^* \beta \land \beta \text{ is a halting ID})),$$

which was given in Definition 5.8.

Definition 7.1. A one-tape TM U is called a *universal Turing machine* (UTM), if the following holds. There exist total recursive functions $c : \mathbb{N} \times I \to \mathrm{ID}(U)$, and $d : \mathrm{ID}(U) \to (I \cup \{\bot\})$ that satisfy

$$\forall n \in \mathbb{N}, \; \forall \alpha \in \mathrm{ID}(T_n)$$
$$((\psi_{T_n}(\alpha) \text{ is defined} \;\;\Rightarrow\; d(\psi_U(c(n, \alpha))) = \psi_{T_n}(\alpha)) \land$$
$$(\psi_{T_n}(\alpha) \text{ is undefined} \;\;\Rightarrow\; \psi_U(c(n, \alpha)) \text{ is undefined})).$$

Note that $d(\gamma) = \bot$ for $\gamma \in \mathrm{ID}(U)$ means that for all $n \in \mathbb{N}$ there exists no $\alpha \in \mathrm{ID}(T_n)$ that corresponds to γ. Here, c and d are called an *encoding function*, and a *decoding function*, respectively.

   According to the above definition, a TM that can directly simulate any TM with any initial ID is, of course, a UTM. On the other hand, there is also an indirect method of simulating other universal systems that are simpler than Turing machines. A tag system is a kind of string rewriting system originally proposed by Post [14]. Cocke and Minsky [3] showed that for any TM with any initial ID, there is a 2-tag system, a variation of a tag system, that simulates it. Minsky [7] then gave a TM U that can simulate any 2-tag systems. A 2-tag system that mimics a given TM with an initial ID itself can be regarded as a code of the TM with the initial ID. Therefore, the code of such a 2-tag system is again a code of the TM with the initial ID. Therefore, Minsky's TM U satisfies the condition in Definition 7.1 (though we omit its details), and thus it is a UTM. Note that in the following constructions of universal reversible TMs, we do not give the encoding and decoding functions c and d precisely, since it is not difficult to define them from the construction method, but their descriptions will become lengthy.

   The study of finding UTMs with small numbers of states and tape symbols has a long history, and it attracted many researchers (see, e.g., a survey [18]). If we denote an m-state n-symbol UTM by UTM(m,n), then the problem is to find UTM(m,n) with a small value of $m \times n$. In the early stage of this study, a direct simulation method of TMs was employed. As explained above, Minsky [7] presented a method of simulating 2-tag systems, and gave a very small UTM that has seven states and four symbols. After that, the indirect simulation method has mainly been used to give small UTMs. Rogozhin [15] designed small UTM(m,n)'s for many pairs of m and n that simulate 2-tag systems. They are UTM(24,2), UTM(10,3), UTM(7,4), UTM(5,5), UTM(4,6), UTM(3,10), and UTM(2,18). Some of these results were improved later. Kudlek and Rogozhin [6] gave UTM(3,9) that simulates 2-tag systems, and Neary and Woods [13] constructed UTM(15,2), UTM(9,3), UTM(6,4), and UTM(5,5) that simulate bi-tag systems.

In this chapter, we study how a small UTM can be constructed under the constraint of reversibility. Namely, a universal reversible Turing machine is a UTM that satisfies the reversibility condition (Definition 5.4).

Definition 7.2. A one-tape universal Turing machine (UTM) that satisfies the reversibility condition is called a *universal reversible Turing machine* (URTM).

Let URTM(m,n) denote an m-state n-symbol URTM. So far, several small URTMs have been designed. Morita and Yamaguchi [12] first constructed URTM(17,5) that simulates cyclic tag systems, a variation of tag systems proposed by Cook [4]. Later, URTM(10,8), URTM(13,7), URTM(15,6), URTM(24,4), and URTM(32,3), which also simulate cyclic tag systems, were given [8, 10, 11]. On the other hand, it is in general difficult to design simple URTMs with only two symbols, or with a very small number of states. To obtain a two-symbol URTM, we can use the method of converting a many-symbol RTM into a two-symbol RTM shown in Sect. 5.3.3. By this, we have URTM(138,2) [10]. Likewise, by the methods of converting a many-state RTM into a four-state, and a three-state RTM shown in Sects. 5.3.4 and 5.3.5, we have URTM(4,168) and URTM(3, 36654). Figure 7.1 shows the state-symbol plotting of these URTMs, as well as that of UTMs.

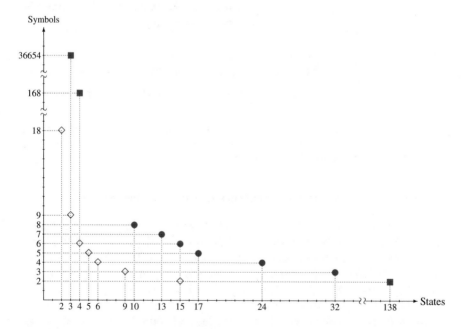

Fig. 7.1 State-symbol plotting of small URTMs and UTMs. Here, ● indicates URTMs that simulate cyclic tag systems, ■ indicates URTMs converted from other URTMs, and ◇ shows UTMs given in [6, 13, 15] that simulate 2-tag systems or bi-tag systems

In Sect. 7.2, we give basic definitions on 2-tag systems and cyclic tag systems, and show that the latter can simulate the former. Then, in Sect. 7.3, we show how we can construct simple URTMs that simulate any cyclic tag systems.

7.2 Tag Systems

In this section, we define m-tag systems and cyclic tag systems, and show some basic properties of them as preparations for constructing small URTMs in Sect. 7.3.

7.2.1 m-tag systems

An m-tag system ($m = 1, 2, \ldots$) is a kind of a string rewriting system. In this system, rewriting of strings is performed in the following way. Let $\alpha = a_1 \cdots a_n$ be a string over an alphabet A. If the system has a production rule $a_1 \to b_1 \cdots b_k$ and $n \geq m$, then we can obtain a new string $a_{m+1} \cdots a_n b_1 \cdots b_k$. Namely, if the first symbol of α is a_1 and $|\alpha| \geq m$, then remove the leftmost m symbols, and append the string $b_1 \cdots b_k$ at the right end of it as shown in Fig. 7.2. Repeating this procedure, we can obtain new strings successively. If we reach a string β to which there is no applicable production rule, or $|\beta| < m$, then the rewriting process terminates.

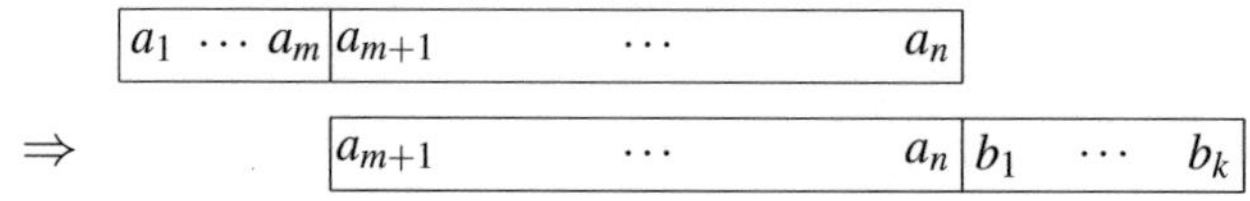

Fig. 7.2 Rewriting in an m-TS. If there is a production rule $a_1 \to b_1 \cdots b_k$ and $n \geq m$, then the first m symbols are removed, and the string $b_1 \cdots b_k$ is appended at the right end. If a_1 is a halting symbol or $n < m$, then the rewriting process terminates

We now give m-tag systems formally based on the definition by Rogozhin [15].

Definition 7.3. An m-tag system (m-TS) is defined by $T = (m, A, P)$, where m is a positive integer, A is a finite alphabet, and $P : A \to A^* \cup \{\text{halt}\}$ is a mapping that gives a set of production rules (we assume halt $\notin A$). Let $a \in A$. If $P(a) = b_1 \cdots b_k \in A^*$, we write it by $a \to b_1 \cdots b_k$, and call it a *production rule* of T. If $P(a) = \text{halt}$, then a is called a *halting symbol*. We usually write P as the set of production rules: $\{a \to P(a) \mid a \in A \land P(a) \neq \text{halt}\}$.

The *transition relation* $\underset{T}{\Rightarrow}$ on A^* is defined as follows. For any $a_1, \ldots, a_m$, $a_{m+1}, \ldots, a_n, b_1, \ldots, b_k \in A$ such that $n \geq m$,

$$a_1 \cdots a_m a_{m+1} \cdots a_n \underset{T}{\Rightarrow} a_{m+1} \cdots a_n b_1 \cdots b_k \quad \text{iff} \quad a_1 \to b_1 \cdots b_k \in P.$$

When there is no ambiguity, we use $\Rightarrow$ instead of $\underset{T}{\Rightarrow}$. Let $\alpha \in A^*$. By the above definition of $\Rightarrow$, if the first symbol of α is a halting symbol, or $|\alpha| < m$, then there is no $\alpha' \in A^*$ that satisfy $\alpha \Rightarrow \alpha'$. Such α is called a *halting string* or a *final string*. The reflexive and transitive closure of $\Rightarrow$ is denoted by $\overset{*}{\Rightarrow}$. Let $\alpha_i \in A^*$ ($i \in \{0, 1, \ldots, n\}$, $n \in \mathbb{N}$). We say $\alpha_0 \Rightarrow \alpha_1 \Rightarrow \cdots \Rightarrow \alpha_n$ is a *complete computing process* of T starting from α_0 if α_n is a halting string.

We show a simple example of a 2-TS.

Example 7.1. Consider a 2-TS $T_1 = (2, \{s, a, b, 0, 1\}, \{s \to 10, \ a \to b\})$. Here, b, 0, and 1 are halting symbols. If we give *saaaa* as an initial string, the complete computing process is as follows.

$$saaaa \ \Rightarrow \ aaa10 \ \Rightarrow \ a10b \ \Rightarrow \ 0bb$$

If the initial string is *saaaaa*, then it is as below.

$$saaaaa \ \Rightarrow \ aaaa10 \ \Rightarrow \ aa10b \ \Rightarrow \ 10bb$$

Generally, $sa^{2k+1} \overset{*}{\Rightarrow} 10b^k$ and $sa^{2k+2} \overset{*}{\Rightarrow} 0b^{k+1}$ hold for any $k \in \mathbb{N}$, where $10b^n$ and $0b^n$ are halting strings. Thus, T_1 gives the quotient and the remainder of $n/2$ for the input sa^n, i.e., the number of b's in the halting string gives the quotient, while the first symbol gives the remainder.   □

In [3, 7], it is shown any TM can be simulated by a 2-TS (here we omit its proof). Note that the notion of simulation can be similarly defined as in Definition 5.8.

Theorem 7.1. *[3, 7] For any one-tape two-symbol TM, there is a 2-TS that simulates the TM. Hence, the class of 2-TSs is computationally universal (i.e., Turing universal).*

7.2.2 Cyclic tag systems

A cyclic tag system (CTS) is a variant of a tag system proposed by Cook [4]. He used CTS to prove computational universality of the elementary cellular automaton (ECA) of rule 110 (see Example 10.3). Since CTS has two kinds of symbols, we fix its alphabet as $\{Y, N\}$. In CTS, there are k ($= 1, 2, \ldots$) production rules $Y \to w_0, Y \to w_1, \ldots, Y \to w_{k-1}$, which are used one by one cyclically in this order. More precisely, the p-th production rule $Y \to w_p$ is applicable at time t, if $p = t \bmod k$. If the first symbol of the string at time t is Y, then it is removed, and w_p is appended at the end of the string. On the other hand, if the first symbol is N, then it is removed, and nothing is appended. Hence, we can assume that the production rule $N \to \lambda$ is always applicable. Figure 7.3 shows this process. In the following, we write the set of production rules as $(w_0, \ldots, w_{k-1})$, since the left-hand side of each production rule is always Y. The systems CTSs are simpler than m-TSs because of the following reasons: They have only two kinds of symbols Y and N, production rules are used one by one in the specified order (hence there is no need of table lookup), and a string is appended only when the first symbol is Y.

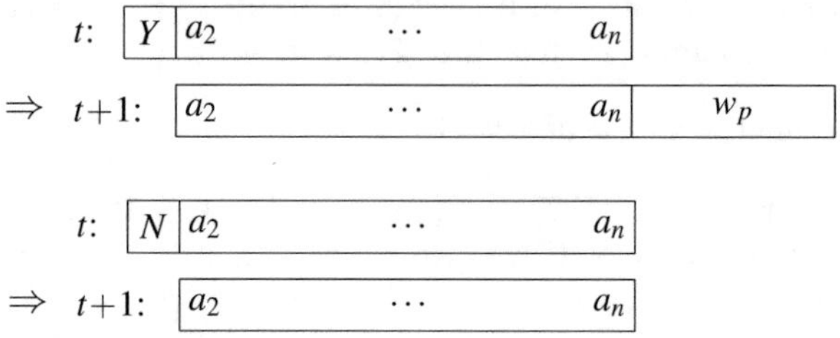

Fig. 7.3 Rewriting in a cyclic tag system at time t. Here, we assume its cycle length is k, and the p-th production rule is $y \rightarrow w_p$, where $p = t$ mod k. If the first symbol of the string at time t is Y, then it is removed, and w_p is appended at the right end. If the first symbol is N, then it is removed, and nothing is appended

CTS is formally defined as follows.

Definition 7.4. A *cyclic tag system* (CTS) is defined by

$$C = (k, (w_0, \cdots, w_{k-1})),$$

where $k \in \mathbb{Z}_+$ is the length of a cycle, and $(w_0, \cdots, w_{k-1}) \in (\{Y,N\}^*)^k$ is a k-tuple of *production rules*. A pair (v,m) is an *instantaneous description* (ID) of C, where $v \in \{Y,N\}^*$ and $m \in \{0, \cdots, k-1\}$. Here, m is called the *phase* of the ID. The *transition relation* $\underset{C}{\Rightarrow}$ is defined as follows. For any $v \in \{Y,N\}^*$, $m, m' \in \{0, \cdots, k-1\}$,

$$
\begin{aligned}
(Yv, m) &\underset{C}{\Rightarrow} (vw_m, m') && \text{iff } m' = m+1 \text{ mod } k, \\
(Nv, m) &\underset{C}{\Rightarrow} (v, m') && \text{iff } m' = m+1 \text{ mod } k.
\end{aligned}
$$

If there is no ambiguity, we use $\Rightarrow$ instead of $\underset{C}{\Rightarrow}$.

In the original definition of a CTS in [4], the notion of halting was not defined explicitly. In fact, it halts only if the ID becomes (λ, m) for some $m \in \{0, \dots, k-1\}$. Therefore, as far as we use CTS, we cannot obtain a UTM that satisfies the condition in Definition 7.1. This is because the final ID of simulated TM cannot be retrieved from the halting ID of a CTS. Therefore, when we use CTS as an intermediate system for making a UTM, then some halting mechanism should be incorporated. Though there will be several ways of defining the notion of halting, we use the method employed in [12], which is given in the following definition.

Definition 7.5. A *cyclic tag system with halting condition* (CTSH) is a system defined by

$$\hat{C} = (k, (\text{halt}, w_1, \cdots, w_{k-1})),$$

where $k \in \mathbb{Z}_+$ is the length of a cycle, and $(w_1, \cdots, w_{k-1}) \in (\{Y,N\}^*)^{k-1}$ is a $(k-1)$-tuple of *production rules*. A pair (v,m) is an *instantaneous description* (ID) of $\hat{C}$, where $v \in \{Y,N\}^*$ and $m \in \{0,\cdots,k-1\}$. m is called the *phase* of the ID. The transition relation $\underset{\hat{C}}{\Rightarrow}$ is defined below. For any $v \in \{Y,N\}^*$, $m,m' \in \{0,\cdots,k-1\}$,

$$(Yv,m) \underset{\hat{C}}{\Rightarrow} (vw_m,m') \text{ iff } (m \neq 0) \wedge (m' = m+1 \bmod k),$$
$$(Nv,m) \underset{\hat{C}}{\Rightarrow} (v,m') \quad \text{ iff } m' = m+1 \bmod k.$$

If there is no ambiguity, we use $\Rightarrow$ instead of $\underset{\hat{C}}{\Rightarrow}$. By the definition of $\Rightarrow$, we can see that, for any $v \in \{Y,N\}^*$ and $m \in \{0,\ldots,k-1\}$, IDs $(Yv,0)$ and (λ,m) have no successor ID. Hence, an ID of the form $(Yv,0)$ or (λ,m) is called a *halting ID*. Let $v_i \in \{Y,N\}^*, m_i \in \{0,\ldots,k-1\}$ $(i \in \{0,1,\ldots,n\}, n \in \mathbb{N})$. We say $(v_0,m_0) \Rightarrow (v_1,m_1) \Rightarrow \cdots \Rightarrow (v_n,m_n)$ is a *complete computing process* of $\hat{C}$ starting from an *initial string* v if $(v_0,m_0) = (v,0)$ and (v_n,m_n) is a halting ID. Here, v_n is called a *final string*. The reflexive and transitive closure of $\Rightarrow$ is denoted by $\overset{*}{\Rightarrow}$. An n-step transition is denoted by $\overset{n}{\Rightarrow}$.

Example 7.2. Consider the following CTS $C_0 = (3,(\lambda, YN, YY))$. A computing process of C_0 starting from the initial string NYY is as below.

Time t		ID	Applicable production rule
0		$(NYY,0)$	$Y \to \lambda$
1	$\underset{C_0}{\Rightarrow}$	$(YY,1)$	$Y \to YN$
2	$\underset{C_0}{\Rightarrow}$	$(YYN,2)$	$Y \to YY$
3	$\underset{C_0}{\Rightarrow}$	$(YNYY,0)$	$Y \to \lambda$
4	$\underset{C_0}{\Rightarrow}$	$(NYY,1)$	$Y \to YN$
5	$\underset{C_0}{\Rightarrow}$	$(YY,2)$	$Y \to YY$
6	$\underset{C_0}{\Rightarrow}$	$(YYY,0)$	$Y \to \lambda$
7	$\underset{C_0}{\Rightarrow}$	$(YY,1)$	$Y \to YN$
8	$\underset{C_0}{\Rightarrow}$	$\cdots$	$\cdots$

Since the IDs at time 1 and 7 are both $(YY,1)$, the process between them will be repeated infinitely after the time step 7. Thus, it does not halt.

We now modify C_0 to obtain the CTSH $\hat{C}_0 = (3,(\text{halt}, YN, YY))$. A complete computing process of $\hat{C}_0$ starting from the initial string NYY is as below.

Time t		ID	Applicable production rule
0		$(NYY,0)$	(none)
1	$\underset{\hat{C}_0}{\Rightarrow}$	$(YY,1)$	$Y \to YN$
2	$\underset{\hat{C}_0}{\Rightarrow}$	$(YYN,2)$	$Y \to YY$
3	$\underset{\hat{C}_0}{\Rightarrow}$	$(YNYY,0)$	(none)

Since $(YNYY,0)$ is a halting ID, the computing process terminates at $t = 3$. It should be noted that the computing processes of C_0 and $\hat{C}_0$ are exactly the same between $t = 0$ and $t = 3$. Hence, if we can observe the CTS C_0 from the outside of system, and can check if the ID becomes $(Yv,0)$ for some $v \in \{Y,N\}^*$, then there is no need to use CTSH. In other words, such an observation from the outside is necessary, whenever we use CTS as a system for simulating a TM.   □

We now show that any 2-TS can be simulated by a CTSH. The proof method is due to Cook [4] except that halting of CTSH is properly managed here.

Theorem 7.2. *For any 2-TS T, we can construct a CTSH $\hat{C}$ that simulates T. Hence, from Theorem 7.1, the class of CTSHs is computationally universal.*

Proof. Let $T = (2,A,P)$. We define A_N and A_H as follows: $A_N = \{a \mid P(a) \neq \text{halt}\}$ and $A_H = \{a \mid P(a) = \text{halt}\}$. They are the sets of non-halting symbols, and halting symbols, respectively. Thus, $A = A_N \cup A_H$. We denote $A_N = \{a_1,\ldots,a_n\}$ and $A_H = \{b_0,\ldots,b_{h-1}\}$. Let $k = \max\{n, \lceil \log_2 h \rceil\}$. Let $\text{bin}_k : \{0,\ldots,2^k - 1\} \to \{N,Y\}^k$ be the function that maps an integer j $(0 \le j \le 2^k - 1)$ to the k-bit binary number represented by N and Y, where N and Y stand for 0 and 1, respectively. For example, $\text{bin}_4(12) = YYNN$. Now, we define an encoding function $\varphi : A^* \to \{N,Y\}^*$. It is a string homomorphism that satisfies the following.

$$\varphi(a_i) = N^i Y N^{k-i} \quad (1 \le i \le n)$$
$$\varphi(b_i) = Y \text{bin}_k(i) \quad (0 \le i \le h-1)$$

Namely, each symbol in A is encoded into a string of length $k+1$ over $\{N,Y\}$. Now, the CTSH $\hat{C}$ that simulates T is given as follows.

$$\hat{C} = (2k+2, (\text{halt}, w_1, \ldots, w_{2k+1}))$$
$$w_i = \begin{cases} \varphi(P(a_i)) & (1 \le i \le n) \\ \lambda & (n+1 \le i \le 2k+1) \end{cases}$$

Let $s_1 \cdots s_m$ be a string over A, where $s_j \in A$ $(j \in \{1,\ldots,m\})$. In $\hat{C}$, it is represented by $(\varphi(s_1 \cdots s_m),0)$. First, consider the case $s_1 = a_i$ for some $a_i \in A_N$. Thus, in T, $s_1 \cdots s_m \underset{T}{\Rrightarrow} s_3 \cdots s_m P(a_i)$ holds. Since $\varphi(s_1 \cdots s_m) = N^i Y N^{k-i} \varphi(s_2) \varphi(s_3 \cdots s_m)$, this transition is simulated by $\hat{C}$ in $2k+2$ steps.

$$(N^i Y N^{k-i} \varphi(s_2) \varphi(s_3 \cdots s_m),0) \quad \underset{\hat{C}}{\overset{i}{\Rrightarrow}} \quad (Y N^{k-i} \varphi(s_2) \varphi(s_3 \cdots s_m),i)$$
$$\underset{\hat{C}}{\Rrightarrow} (N^{k-i} \varphi(s_2) \varphi(s_3 \cdots s_m) \varphi(P(a_i)),i+1) \quad \underset{\hat{C}}{\overset{k-i}{\Rrightarrow}} (\varphi(s_2) \varphi(s_3 \cdots s_m) \varphi(P(a_i)),k+1)$$
$$\underset{\hat{C}}{\overset{k+1}{\Rrightarrow}} (\varphi(s_3 \cdots s_m P(a_i)),0)$$

Second, consider the case $s_1 = b_i$ for some $b_i \in A_H$. In this case, $s_1 \cdots s_m$ is a halting string in T. Since $\varphi(s_1 \cdots s_m) = Y \text{bin}_k(i) \varphi(s_2 \cdots s_m)$, the ID $(Y \text{bin}_k(i) \varphi(s_2 \cdots s_m),0)$ is a halting ID also in $\hat{C}$.

By above, if

$$\alpha_0 \underset{T}{\Rrightarrow} \alpha_1 \underset{T}{\Rrightarrow} \cdots \underset{T}{\Rrightarrow} \alpha_{l-1} \underset{T}{\Rrightarrow} \alpha_l$$

is a complete computing process of T, then it is simulated by

$$(\varphi(\alpha_0),0) \overset{2k+2}{\underset{\hat{C}}{\Rightarrow}} (\varphi(\alpha_1),0) \overset{2k+2}{\underset{\hat{C}}{\Rightarrow}} \cdots \overset{2k+2}{\underset{\hat{C}}{\Rightarrow}} (\varphi(\alpha_{l-1}),0) \overset{2k+2}{\underset{\hat{C}}{\Rightarrow}} (\varphi(\alpha_l),0),$$

which is a complete computing process of $\hat{C}$. □

Example 7.3. Let $T_1 = (2, \{s,a,b,0,1\}, \{s \to 10, \ a \to b\})$ be the 2-TS in Example 7.1. We construct a CTSH $\hat{C}_1$ that simulates T_1. In T_1, the sets of non-halting and halting symbols are $A_N = \{s,a\}$, and $A_H = \{0,1,b\}$, respectively. Thus, in this case $k = 2$. We define a string homomorphism $\varphi : A^* \to \{N,Y\}^*$ as the one that satisfies the following: $\varphi(s) = NYN, \varphi(a) = NNY, \varphi(0) = YNN, \varphi(1) = YNY$, and $\varphi(b) = YYN$. Then, $\hat{C}_1 = (6, (\text{halt}, YNYYNN, YYN, \lambda, \lambda, \lambda))$. For example, a complete computing process $saa \Rightarrow a10 \Rightarrow 0b$ of T_1 is simulated in $\hat{C}_1$ as follows.

$$
\begin{array}{ll}
(NYN\ NNY\ NNY, 0) & \Rightarrow (YN\ NNY\ NNY, 1) \\
\Rightarrow (N\ NNY\ NNY\ YNY\ YNN, 2) & \Rightarrow (NNY\ NNY\ YNY\ YNN, 3) \\
\Rightarrow (NY\ NNY\ YNY\ YNN, 4) & \Rightarrow (Y\ NNY\ YNY\ YNN, 5) \\
\Rightarrow (NNY\ YNY\ YNN, 0) & \Rightarrow (NY\ YNY\ YNN, 1) \\
\Rightarrow (Y\ YNY\ YNN, 2) & \Rightarrow (YNY\ YNN\ YYN, 3) \\
\Rightarrow (NY\ YNN\ YYN, 4) & \Rightarrow (Y\ YNN\ YYN, 5) \\
\Rightarrow (YNN\ YYN, 0) &
\end{array}
$$

7.3 Small Universal Reversible Turing Machines (URTMs)

In this section, we give several small URTMs. We first construct six kinds of URTMs that can simulate any CTSH. They are URTM(10,8), URTM(13,7), URTM(15,6), URTM(17,5), URTM(24,4), and URTM(32,3). They are constructed in a similar manner, though the usage of states and tape symbols are different.

If codes of a CTSH $\hat{C}$ and an initial string $\alpha_0 \in \{Y,N\}^*$ are given, each of these URTMs simulates the rewriting process of $\hat{C}$ from the initial ID $(\alpha_0,0)$ step by step until $\hat{C}$ halts. The URTM U has a one-way infinite tape, and keeps the codes of $\hat{C}$ and an ID of $\hat{C}$ as shown in Fig. 7.4. The production rules of $\hat{C}$ are stored in the left-side segment of the tape. Initially, the segment of "removed symbols" on the tape is empty, and the initial string α_0 is kept in the segment of "current string". To indicate the border between the removed symbols and the current string, different kinds of symbols are used for the removed ones, and for the leftmost one of the current string (or, temporarily pointed by the head). Each time the leftmost symbol of the current string is removed by a rewriting in $\hat{C}$, this border is shifted to the right by one square. Thus, if the ID of $\hat{C}$ is (α,m), then α is stored in the segment of the current string. The phase m of the ID is recorded by putting a "phase marker", which is also a specified symbol of U, at the m-th production rule of $\hat{C}$ on the tape. If the first symbol of the current string is Y and $m > 0$, then the right-hand side of the m-th production rule is appended at the right end of the current string. If the first symbol is N, then nothing is appended. In both cases, the phase marker is moved to the position of the next production rule. If $\hat{C}$ enters a halting ID, then U halts.

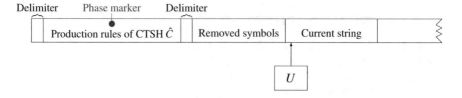

Fig. 7.4 A URTM U that simulates a CTSH $\hat{C}$

It is generally difficult to design a URTM with two symbols or with a very small number of states by the above method directly. For these cases, we use the algorithms of converting an RTM into a two-symbol RTM (Sect. 5.3.3), a four-state RTM (Sect. 5.3.4), and a three-state RTM (Sect. 5.3.5). Applying these methods to URTM(24,4), URTM(10,8), and URTM(32,3), we obtain URTM(138,2), URTM(4,168), and URTM(3, 36654), respectively.

In the following, the CTSH $\hat{C}_2$ in Example 7.4 will be used to explain how the above URTMs work.

Example 7.4. Consider a CTSH $\hat{C}_2 = (3,(\text{halt}, NY, NNY))$. A complete computing process of $\hat{C}_2$ starting from the initial string NYY is as follows: $(NYY, 0) \Rightarrow (YY, 1)$ $\Rightarrow (YNY, 2) \Rightarrow (NYNNY, 0) \Rightarrow (YNNY, 1) \Rightarrow (NNYNY, 2) \Rightarrow (NYNY, 0)$ $\Rightarrow (YNY, 1) \Rightarrow (NYNY, 2) \Rightarrow (YNY, 0)$.

7.3.1 13-state 7-symbol URTM

We first give URTM(13,7) U_{13_7} [11], since URTM(10,8) U_{10_8} in the next subsection is obtained by modifying U_{13_7}. It is defined as follows.

$$U_{13\_7} = (Q_{13\_7}, \{b, y, n, Y, N, *, \$\}, q_{\text{begin}}, b, \delta_{13\_7})$$
$$Q_{13\_7} = \{q_{\text{begin}}, q_{\text{case\_y\_1}}, q_{\text{case\_y\_2}}, q_{\text{case\_y\_n}}, q_{\text{copy\_start}}, q_{\text{copy\_y\_1}}, q_{\text{copy\_y\_2}},$$
$$q_{\text{copy\_y\_3}}, q_{\text{copy\_n\_1}}, q_{\text{copy\_n\_2}}, q_{\text{copy\_n\_3}}, q_{\text{copy\_end}}, q_{\text{cycle\_end}}\}$$

The move relation δ_{13_7} is described in Table 7.1. It contains 57 quintuples. In this table, "halt" means that the simulated CTSH halts with an ID $(Yv,0)$ for some $v \in \{Y,N\}^*$, while "null" means that it halts with an ID (λ,m) for some $m \in \mathbb{N}$. We can verify that U_{13_7} satisfies the reversibility condition by a careful inspection of δ_{13_7}. It was also verified by a computer program. Note that, if reversibility is not required, then, for example, the states $q_{\text{case\_y\_2}}$ and $q_{\text{copy\_y\_2}}$ could be merged to reduce the number of states. However, since there are quintuples $[q_{\text{case\_y\_2}}, y, y, +, q_{\text{case\_y\_2}}]$,

Table 7.1 The move relation $\delta_{13\text{-}7}$ of $U_{13\text{-}7}$

	b	y	n
q_{begin}	(null)	$Y,-,q_{\text{case\_y\_1}}$	$N,-,q_{\text{case\_y\_n}}$
$q_{\text{case\_y\_1}}$	(halt)	$y,-,q_{\text{case\_y\_1}}$	$n,-,q_{\text{case\_y\_1}}$
$q_{\text{case\_y\_2}}$		$y,+,q_{\text{case\_y\_2}}$	$n,+,q_{\text{case\_y\_2}}$
$q_{\text{case\_y\_n}}$	$*,-,q_{\text{copy\_start}}$	$y,-,q_{\text{case\_y\_n}}$	$n,-,q_{\text{case\_y\_n}}$
$q_{\text{copy\_start}}$	$b,+,q_{\text{cycle\_end}}$	$b,+,q_{\text{copy\_y\_1}}$	$b,+,q_{\text{copy\_n\_1}}$
$q_{\text{copy\_y\_1}}$	$y,+,q_{\text{copy\_y\_2}}$	$y,+,q_{\text{copy\_y\_1}}$	$n,+,q_{\text{copy\_y\_1}}$
$q_{\text{copy\_y\_2}}$	$b,-,q_{\text{copy\_y\_3}}$		
$q_{\text{copy\_y\_3}}$	$y,-,q_{\text{copy\_start}}$	$y,-,q_{\text{copy\_y\_3}}$	$n,-,q_{\text{copy\_y\_3}}$
$q_{\text{copy\_n\_1}}$	$n,+,q_{\text{copy\_n\_2}}$	$y,+,q_{\text{copy\_n\_1}}$	$n,+,q_{\text{copy\_n\_1}}$
$q_{\text{copy\_n\_2}}$	$b,-,q_{\text{copy\_n\_3}}$		
$q_{\text{copy\_n\_3}}$	$n,-,q_{\text{copy\_start}}$	$y,-,q_{\text{copy\_n\_3}}$	$n,-,q_{\text{copy\_n\_3}}$
$q_{\text{copy\_end}}$		$y,+,q_{\text{copy\_end}}$	$n,+,q_{\text{copy\_end}}$
$q_{\text{cycle\_end}}$		$y,+,q_{\text{cycle\_end}}$	$n,+,q_{\text{cycle\_end}}$

	Y	N	$*$	$\$$
q_{begin}				
$q_{\text{case\_y\_1}}$			$*,+,q_{\text{case\_y\_2}}$	$\$,-,q_{\text{case\_y\_1}}$
$q_{\text{case\_y\_2}}$	$Y,-,q_{\text{case\_y\_n}}$			$\$,+,q_{\text{case\_y\_2}}$
$q_{\text{case\_y\_n}}$			$*,-,q_{\text{case\_y\_n}}$	$\$,-,q_{\text{case\_y\_n}}$
$q_{\text{copy\_start}}$			$b,+,q_{\text{copy\_end}}$	
$q_{\text{copy\_y\_1}}$	$Y,+,q_{\text{copy\_y\_1}}$	$N,-,q_{\text{copy\_y\_3}}$	$*,+,q_{\text{copy\_y\_1}}$	$\$,+,q_{\text{copy\_y\_1}}$
$q_{\text{copy\_y\_2}}$				
$q_{\text{copy\_y\_3}}$	$Y,-,q_{\text{copy\_y\_3}}$		$*,-,q_{\text{copy\_y\_3}}$	$\$,-,q_{\text{copy\_y\_3}}$
$q_{\text{copy\_n\_1}}$	$Y,+,q_{\text{copy\_n\_1}}$	$N,-,q_{\text{copy\_n\_3}}$	$*,+,q_{\text{copy\_n\_1}}$	$\$,+,q_{\text{copy\_n\_1}}$
$q_{\text{copy\_n\_2}}$				
$q_{\text{copy\_n\_3}}$	$Y,-,q_{\text{copy\_n\_3}}$		$*,-,q_{\text{copy\_n\_3}}$	$\$,-,q_{\text{copy\_n\_3}}$
$q_{\text{copy\_end}}$	$y,+,q_{\text{begin}}$	$n,+,q_{\text{begin}}$	$*,+,q_{\text{copy\_end}}$	$\$,+,q_{\text{copy\_end}}$
$q_{\text{cycle\_end}}$			$*,+,q_{\text{cycle\_end}}$	$\$,-,q_{\text{copy\_start}}$

and $[q_{\text{copy\_y\_1}}, b, y, +, q_{\text{copy\_y\_2}}]$, they cannot be merged without violating the reversibility condition.

We now define a specific string homomorphism $\varphi_1 : \{Y,N\}^* \to \{y,n\}^*$ as follows: $\varphi_1(Y) = y$, $\varphi_1(N) = n$. Note that φ_1 is a trivial homomorphism that simply converts the uppercase Y and N into lower case y and n. But, in the following subsections, non-trivial homomorphisms will also be used. Let $\hat{C} = (k, (\text{halt}, w_1, \ldots, w_{k-1}))$ be an arbitrarily CTSH, and $v_0 \in \{Y,N\}^*$ be an initial string. Then the initial ID of $U_{13\text{-}7}$ is as follows, where $\$$ and the leftmost b are used as delimiters (see Fig. 7.4). Here, w^R denotes the reversal of the string w.

$$b \, \varphi_1(w_{k-1}^R) * \cdots * \varphi_1(w_2^R) * \varphi_1(w_1^R) * b \, \$ \, q_{\text{begin}} \, \varphi_1(v_0) \, b$$

In the case of CTSH $\hat{C}_2$ with $v_0 = NYY$ in Example 7.4, the initial ID for it is $b \, ynn * yn * b \, \$ \, q_{\text{begin}} \, nyy \, b$. Snapshots of computation of $U_{13\text{-}7}$ is as below. Here, a computational configuration is expressed by $[\alpha, q, h]$ instead of an ID, where α is a string over the tape alphabet, q is a state, and $h \in \mathbb{N}$ is the head position (the leftmost symbol is the 0-th). The head position is also indicated by the underline.

$$
\begin{aligned}
t = 0 &: [\, b\,ynn*yn*b\$\,\underline{n}yy\,b,\ q_{\text{begin}},\ 10\,] \\
7 &: [\, b\,ynn*ynb*\$\,n\underline{y}y\,b,\ q_{\text{begin}},\ 11\,] \\
8 &: [\, b\,ynn*ynb*\$\,\underline{n}Yy\,b,\ q_{\text{case\_y\_1}},\ 10\,] \\
18 &: [\, b\,ynn*y\underline{n}**\$\,nYy\,b,\ q_{\text{copy\_start}},\ 6\,] \\
19 &: [\, b\,ynn*yb\underline{*}*\$\,nYy\,b,\ q_{\text{copy\_n\_1}},\ 7\,] \\
25 &: [\, b\,ynn*yb**\$\,nYy\,\underline{b},\ q_{\text{copy\_n\_1}},\ 13\,] \\
26 &: [\, b\,ynn*yb**\$\,nYyn\,\underline{b},\ q_{\text{copy\_n\_2}},\ 14\,] \\
27 &: [\, b\,ynn*yb**\$\,nYy\underline{n}\,b,\ q_{\text{copy\_n\_3}},\ 13\,] \\
35 &: [\, b\,ynn*\underline{y}n**\$\,nYyn\,b,\ q_{\text{copy\_start}},\ 5\,] \\
36 &: [\, b\,ynn*b\underline{n}**\$\,nYyn\,b,\ q_{\text{copy\_y\_1}},\ 6\,] \\
44 &: [\, b\,ynn*bn**\$\,nYyn\,\underline{b},\ q_{\text{copy\_y\_1}},\ 14\,] \\
45 &: [\, b\,ynn*bn**\$\,nYyny\,\underline{b},\ q_{\text{copy\_y\_2}},\ 15\,] \\
46 &: [\, b\,ynn*bn**\$\,nYyn\underline{y}\,b,\ q_{\text{copy\_y\_3}},\ 14\,] \\
56 &: [\, b\,ynn\underline{*}yn**\$\,nYyny\,b,\ q_{\text{copy\_start}},\ 4\,] \\
57 &: [\, b\,ynnby\underline{n}**\$\,nYyny\,b,\ q_{\text{copy\_end}},\ 5\,] \\
64 &: [\, b\,ynnbyn**\$\,ny\underline{y}ny\,b,\ q_{\text{begin}},\ 12\,] \\
174 &: [\, \underline{b}\,ynn*yn**\$\,nyYnynny\,b,\ q_{\text{copy\_start}},\ 0\,] \\
175 &: [\, b\,y\underline{n}n*yn**\$\,nyYnynny\,b,\ q_{\text{cycle\_end}},\ 1\,] \\
184 &: [\, b\,ynn*yn*\underline{*}\$\,nyYnynny\,b,\ q_{\text{copy\_start}},\ 8\,] \\
185 &: [\, b\,ynn*yn*b\underline{\$}\,nyYnynny\,b,\ q_{\text{copy\_end}},\ 9\,] \\
291 &: [\, b\,ynnbyn**\$\,nyyny\underline{n}nyny\,b,\ q_{\text{begin}},\ 15\,] \\
292 &: [\, b\,ynnbyn**\$\,nyyny\underline{N}nyny\,b,\ q_{\text{case\_y\_n}},\ 14\,] \\
303 &: [\, b\,yn\underline{n}*yn**\$\,nyynyNnyny\,b,\ q_{\text{copy\_start}},\ 3\,] \\
315 &: [\, b\,ynb*yn**\$\,nyyny\underline{N}nyny\,b,\ q_{\text{copy\_n\_1}},\ 15\,] \\
316 &: [\, b\,ynb*yn**\$\,nyyn\underline{y}Nnyny\,b,\ q_{\text{copy\_n\_3}},\ 14\,] \\
665 &: [\, b\,ynn*yn*b\$\,nyynynnyn\underline{y}ny\,b,\ q_{\text{begin}},\ 19\,] \\
676 &: [\, b\,ynn*yn*\underline{b}\$\,nyynynnyn\underline{Y}ny\,b,\ q_{\text{case\_y\_1}},\ 8\,]
\end{aligned}
$$

We explain how U_{13_7} simulates CTSH by this example. Production rules of $\hat{C}_2$ is basically expressed by the string $ynn*yn**$. However, to indicate the phase m of an ID (v, m), the m-th $*$ from the right is altered into b (where the rightmost $*$ is the 0-th). This b is used as a "phase marker". Namely, $ynn*yn*b$, $ynn*ynb*$, and $ynnbyn**$ indicate the phase is 0, 1, and 2, respectively. Hence, in the configuration at $t = 0$, the string $ynn*yn*b$ is given on the tape. To the right of the production rules the initial string nyy is given. Between them, there is a delimiter $\$$ that is not rewritten into another symbol throughout the computation. In the state q_{begin}, the leftmost symbol of the current string is pointed by the head. Then, it is changed to the uppercase letter Y or N to indicate the leftmost position of the current string.

The state q_{begin} (appearing at time $t = 0, 7, 64, 291$, and 665) reads the first symbol y or n of the current string, and temporarily changes it into Y or N, respectively. Depending on the read symbol y or n, U_{13_7} goes to either $q_{\text{case\_y\_1}}$ ($t = 8$), or $q_{\text{case\_y\_n}}$ ($t = 292$). If the read symbol is b, U_{13_7} halts, because it means the string is null. If the symbol is y, U_{13_7} performs the following operations (the case n is explained in the next paragraph). By the state $q_{case\_y\_1}$ ($t = 8$), the URTM moves leftward to find the delimiter \$, and then visits the left-neighboring square by $q_{case\_y\_1}$. If it reads b, then it halts ($t = 676$), because the phase is 0. If otherwise, U_{13_7} returns to the delimiter \$. Then, using $q_{case\_y\_2}$, U_{13_7} goes to the state $q_{case\_y\_n}$, and moves leftward to find the phase marker b that indicates the position of the next production rule. By the state q_{copy_start} ($t = 18$, and 35) U_{13_7} starts to copy each symbol of the production rule. If U_{13_7} reads a symbol y ($t = 18$) (or n ($t = 35$), respectively), then it shifts the marker b to this position, and goes to $q_{copy\_y\_1}$ ($t = 36$) (or $q_{copy\_n\_1}$ ($t = 19$)) to attach the symbol at the end of the string to be rewritten. On the other hand, if it reads symbol $*$ in q_{copy_start} ($t = 56$), then it goes to q_{copy_end} ($t = 57$), which mean the end of execution of a production rule, and thus it starts to read the next symbol in the rewritten string ($t = 64$). Likewise, if it reads symbol b in q_{copy_start} ($t = 174$), then it goes to q_{cycle_end} ($t = 175$), which mean the end of one cycle, and thus the phase is set to 0 ($t = 185$). The state $q_{copy\_y\_1}$ is for moving rightward to find the first b that is to the right of the current string ($t = 44$), and rewrites it into y ($t = 45$). The states $q_{copy\_y\_2}$ and $q_{copy\_y\_3}$ ($t = 46$) are for returning to the marker position and for repeating the copying procedure. The states $q_{copy\_n\_1}, \ldots, q_{copy\_n\_3}$ are for copying the symbol n, which are similar to the case of y ($t = 19, 25, 26, 27$).

On the other hand, if U_{13_7} reads a symbol n in the state q_{begin} ($t = 291$), then it enters the state $q_{case\_y\_n}$ ($t = 292$), and tries to copy symbols as in the case of y. At $t = 303$ it starts to copy a symbol n in q_{copy_start}. However, since it finds a symbol N in the state $q_{copy\_n\_1}$ ($t = 315$), it enters the state $q_{copy\_n\_3}$ ($t = 316$) without attaching the symbol n at the right end. By above, the phase marker is finally shifted to the next production rule without copying the symbols of the current production rule.

Repeating the above procedure, U_{13_7} simulates a given CTSH step by step, and halts in the state $q_{case\_y\_1}$ reading the symbol b if the CTSH halts in an ID with phase 0. If the string of the CTSH becomes null, U_{13_7} halts in the state q_{begin} reading the symbol b. In the above example, U_{13_7} halts at $t = 676$, and the final string YNY of $\hat{C}_2$ is obtained at as a suffix of the string (excluding the last blank symbol b) starting from the symbol Y.

7.3.2 10-state 8-symbol URTM

Next, we give URTM(10,8) U_{10_8} [11]. It is defined as below.

$$U_{10\_8} = (Q_{10\_8}, \{b, y, n, n', Y, N, *, \$\}, q_{begin}, b, \delta_{10\_8})$$
$$Q_{10\_8} = \{q_{begin}, q_{case\_y\_1}, q_{case\_y\_2}, q_{case\_y\_n}, q_{copy\_start}, q_{copy\_y\_1}, q_{copy\_y\_2},$$
$$q_{copy\_n\_1}, q_{copy\_n\_2}, q_{copy\_end}\}$$

Table 7.2 shows the move relation δ_{10_8}. It contains 61 quintuples. The URTM U_{10_8} is constructed by modifying U_{13_7} in the previous subsection. Thus, the initial

Table 7.2 The move relation δ_{10_8} of U_{10_8}

	b	y	n	n'
q_{begin}	(null)	$y,-,q_{\text{case\_y\_1}}$	$n',-,q_{\text{case\_y\_n}}$	
$q_{\text{case\_y\_1}}$	(halt)			
$q_{\text{case\_y\_2}}$	$b,-,q_{\text{copy\_y\_2}}$	$y,-,q_{\text{case\_y\_n}}$		
$q_{\text{case\_y\_n}}$	$*,-,q_{\text{copy\_start}}$			
$q_{\text{copy\_start}}$	$b,+,q_{\text{begin}}$	$b,+,q_{\text{copy\_y\_1}}$	$b,+,q_{\text{copy\_n\_1}}$	
$q_{\text{copy\_y\_1}}$	$y,+,q_{\text{case\_y\_2}}$	$y,+,q_{\text{copy\_y\_1}}$	$n,+,q_{\text{copy\_y\_1}}$	$n',-,q_{\text{copy\_y\_2}}$
$q_{\text{copy\_y\_2}}$	$Y,-,q_{\text{copy\_start}}$	$y,-,q_{\text{copy\_y\_2}}$	$n,-,q_{\text{copy\_y\_2}}$	
$q_{\text{copy\_n\_1}}$	$n,+,q_{\text{copy\_end}}$	$y,+,q_{\text{copy\_n\_1}}$	$n,+,q_{\text{copy\_n\_1}}$	$n',-,q_{\text{copy\_n\_2}}$
$q_{\text{copy\_n\_2}}$	$N,-,q_{\text{copy\_start}}$	$y,-,q_{\text{copy\_n\_2}}$	$n,-,q_{\text{copy\_n\_2}}$	
$q_{\text{copy\_end}}$	$b,-,q_{\text{copy\_n\_2}}$	$Y,+,q_{\text{begin}}$		$N,+,q_{\text{begin}}$

	Y	N	$*$	$\$$
q_{begin}	$y,+,q_{\text{begin}}$	$n,+,q_{\text{begin}}$	$*,+,q_{\text{begin}}$	$\$,-,q_{\text{copy\_start}}$
$q_{\text{case\_y\_1}}$	$Y,-,q_{\text{case\_y\_1}}$	$N,-,q_{\text{case\_y\_1}}$	$*,+,q_{\text{case\_y\_2}}$	$\$,-,q_{\text{case\_y\_1}}$
$q_{\text{case\_y\_2}}$	$Y,+,q_{\text{case\_y\_2}}$	$N,+,q_{\text{case\_y\_2}}$		$\$,+,q_{\text{case\_y\_2}}$
$q_{\text{case\_y\_n}}$	$Y,-,q_{\text{case\_y\_n}}$	$N,-,q_{\text{case\_y\_n}}$	$*,-,q_{\text{case\_y\_n}}$	$\$,-,q_{\text{case\_y\_n}}$
$q_{\text{copy\_start}}$			$b,+,q_{\text{copy\_end}}$	
$q_{\text{copy\_y\_1}}$	$Y,+,q_{\text{copy\_y\_1}}$	$N,+,q_{\text{copy\_y\_1}}$	$*,+,q_{\text{copy\_y\_1}}$	$\$,+,q_{\text{copy\_y\_1}}$
$q_{\text{copy\_y\_2}}$	$Y,-,q_{\text{copy\_y\_2}}$	$N,-,q_{\text{copy\_y\_2}}$	$*,-,q_{\text{copy\_y\_2}}$	$\$,-,q_{\text{copy\_y\_2}}$
$q_{\text{copy\_n\_1}}$	$Y,+,q_{\text{copy\_n\_1}}$	$N,+,q_{\text{copy\_n\_1}}$	$*,+,q_{\text{copy\_n\_1}}$	$\$,+,q_{\text{copy\_n\_1}}$
$q_{\text{copy\_n\_2}}$	$Y,-,q_{\text{copy\_n\_2}}$	$N,-,q_{\text{copy\_n\_2}}$	$*,-,q_{\text{copy\_n\_2}}$	$\$,-,q_{\text{copy\_n\_2}}$
$q_{\text{copy\_end}}$	$Y,+,q_{\text{copy\_end}}$	$N,+,q_{\text{copy\_end}}$	$*,+,q_{\text{copy\_end}}$	$\$,+,q_{\text{copy\_end}}$

ID of U_{10_8} is the same as that of U_{13_7}. Furthermore, the simulation time for a given CTSH is also the same.

The difference between U_{13_7} and U_{10_8} is as follows. First, the removed symbols from the string are indicated by the uppercase letters Y and N. Second, if the leftmost symbol of the current string is n, then it is temporarily changed to n', which is a newly added symbol in U_{10_8}. Third, if the current phase is m, then the symbols of the production rules $w_1, \ldots, w_{m-1}$ are changed into the uppercase letters. By above, the states $q_{\text{copy\_y\_2}}$ and $q_{\text{case\_y\_2}}$ in U_{13_7} can be merged into one state without violating the reversibility condition. Likewise, the states $q_{\text{copy\_n\_2}}$ and $q_{\text{copy\_end}}$ in U_{13_7} can be merged into one state. Hence, in U_{10_8}, the old state $q_{\text{copy\_y\_2}}$ ($q_{\text{copy\_n\_2}}$, respectively) is removed, and the old state $q_{\text{copy\_y\_3}}$ ($q_{\text{copy\_n\_3}}$) is renamed to $q_{\text{copy\_y\_2}}$ ($q_{\text{copy\_n\_2}}$). Furthermore, the states q_{begin} and $q_{\text{cycle\_end}}$ in U_{13_7} can be merged into one state. Therefore, in U_{13_7}, $q_{\text{cycle\_end}}$ is removed. By above, the number of states of U_{10_8} is reduced to 10.

The initial ID of U_{10_8} for a given CTSH and an initial string is exactly the same as in the case of U_{13_7}. Snapshots of computation process of U_{10_8} for the CTSH $\hat{C}_2$ with the initial string NYY is as below.

$$
\begin{aligned}
t = 0 :\ & [\, b\, ynn * yn * b \,\$\, \underline{n}yy\, b,\ q_{\text{begin}},\ 10\,] \\
7 :\ & [\, b\, ynn * ynb * \,\$\, N\underline{y}y\, b,\ q_{\text{begin}},\ 11\,] \\
8 :\ & [\, b\, ynn * ynb * \,\$\, \underline{N}yy\, b,\ q_{\text{case\_y\_1}},\ 10\,] \\
18 :\ & [\, b\, ynn * y\underline{n} * * \$\, Nyy\, b,\ q_{\text{copy\_start}},\ 6\,] \\
19 :\ & [\, b\, ynn * yb\underline{*} * \$\, Nyy\, b,\ q_{\text{copy\_n\_1}},\ 7\,] \\
25 :\ & [\, b\, ynn * yb * * \$\, Nyy\, \underline{b},\ q_{\text{copy\_n\_1}},\ 13\,] \\
26 :\ & [\, b\, ynn * yb * * \$\, Nyyn\, \underline{b},\ q_{\text{copy\_end}},\ 14\,] \\
27 :\ & [\, b\, ynn * yb * * \$\, Nyy\underline{n}\, b,\ q_{\text{copy\_n\_2}},\ 13\,] \\
35 :\ & [\, b\, ynn * y\underline{N} * * \$\, Nyyn\, b,\ q_{\text{copy\_start}},\ 5\,] \\
36 :\ & [\, b\, ynn * \underline{b}\underline{N} * * \$\, Nyyn\, b,\ q_{\text{copy\_y\_1}},\ 6\,] \\
44 :\ & [\, b\, ynn * bN * * \$\, Nyyn\, \underline{b},\ q_{\text{copy\_y\_1}},\ 14\,] \\
45 :\ & [\, b\, ynn * bN * * \$\, Nyyny\, \underline{b},\ q_{\text{case\_y\_2}},\ 15\,] \\
46 :\ & [\, b\, ynn * bN * * \$\, Nyyn\underline{y}\, b,\ q_{\text{copy\_y\_2}},\ 14\,] \\
56 :\ & [\, b\, ynn\underline{*}YN * * \$\, Nyyny\, b,\ q_{\text{copy\_start}},\ 4\,] \\
57 :\ & [\, b\, ynnb\underline{Y}N * * \$\, Nyyny\, b,\ q_{\text{copy\_end}},\ 5\,] \\
64 :\ & [\, b\, ynnbYN * * \$\, N\underline{Y}yny\, b,\ q_{\text{begin}},\ 12\,] \\
174 :\ & [\, \underline{b}YNN * YN * * \$\, NYynynny\, b,\ q_{\text{copy\_start}},\ 0\,] \\
175 :\ & [\, b\underline{Y}NN * YN * * \$\, NYynynny\, b,\ q_{\text{begin}},\ 1\,] \\
184 :\ & [\, b\, ynn * yn * \underline{*}\ \$\, NYynynny\, b,\ q_{\text{copy\_start}},\ 8\,] \\
185 :\ & [\, b\, ynn * yn * b\ \underline{\$}\, NYynynny\, b,\ q_{\text{copy\_end}},\ 9\,] \\
291 :\ & [\, b\, ynnbYN * * \$\, NYYNY\underline{n}nyny\, b,\ q_{\text{begin}},\ 15\,] \\
292 :\ & [\, b\, ynnbYN * * \$\, NYYNY\underline{n}'nyny\, b,\ q_{\text{case\_y\_n}},\ 14\,] \\
303 :\ & [\, b\, yn\underline{n} * YN * * \$\, NYYNYn'nyny\, b,\ q_{\text{copy\_start}},\ 3\,] \\
315 :\ & [\, b\, ynb * YN * * \$\, NYYNY\underline{n}'nyny\, b,\ q_{\text{copy\_n\_1}},\ 15\,] \\
316 :\ & [\, b\, ynb * YN * * \$\, NYYNY\underline{n}'nyny\, b,\ q_{\text{copy\_n\_2}},\ 14\,] \\
665 :\ & [\, b\, ynn * yn * b\ \$\, NYYNYNNYN\underline{y}ny\, b,\ q_{\text{begin}},\ 19\,] \\
676 :\ & [\, b\, ynn * yn * \underline{b}\ \$\, NYYNYNNYN\underline{y}ny\, b,\ q_{\text{case\_y\_1}},\ 8\,]
\end{aligned}
$$

Comparing the above computational configurations with the ones of U_{13_7}, we can see that, e.g., at time $t = 45$ the state $q_{\text{case\_y\_2}}$ is used instead of $q_{\text{copy\_y\_2}}$, and at time $t = 175$ the state q_{begin} is used instead of $q_{\text{cycle\_end}}$. However, the essentially the same operation as in U_{13_7} is performed at each step, and thus at time $t = 676$ the final string YNY is obtained.

7.3.3 17-state 5-symbol URTM

Thirdly, we give URTM(17,5) U_{17_5} [12]. As we shall see in the following subsections, URTM(15,6), URTM(24,4), and URTM(32,3) are obtained by modifying U_{17_5}. It is defined as follows.

$$U_{17\_5} = (Q_{17\_5}, \{b, y, n, *, \$\}, q_{begin}, b, \delta_{17\_5})$$
$$Q_{17\_5} = \{q_{begin}, q_{case\_y\_1}, q_{case\_y\_2}, q_{copy\_start}, q_{copy\_y\_1}, q_{copy\_y\_2}, q_{copy\_y\_3},$$
$$q_{copy\_n\_1}, q_{copy\_n\_2}, q_{copy\_n\_3}, q_{copy\_end\_1}, q_{copy\_end\_2}, q_{cycle\_end},$$
$$q_{case\_n\_1}, q_{case\_n\_2}, q_{case\_n\_3}, q_{case\_n\_4}\}$$

Table 7.3 The move relation δ_{17_5} of U_{17_5}

	b	y	n	$*$	$\$$
q_{begin}	$\$,-,q_{case\_y\_2}$	$\$,-,q_{case\_y\_1}$	$b,-,q_{case\_n\_1}$		
$q_{case\_y\_1}$	(halt)	$y,-,q_{case\_y\_1}$	$n,-,q_{case\_y\_1}$	$*,+,q_{begin}$	$b,-,q_{case\_y\_1}$
$q_{case\_y\_2}$	$*,-,q_{copy\_start}$	$y,-,q_{case\_y\_2}$	$n,-,q_{case\_y\_2}$	$*,-,q_{case\_y\_2}$	(null)
q_{copy_start}	$b,+,q_{cycle\_end}$	$b,+,q_{copy\_y\_1}$	$b,+,q_{copy\_n\_1}$	$b,+,q_{copy\_end\_1}$	
$q_{copy\_y\_1}$	$y,+,q_{copy\_y\_2}$	$y,+,q_{copy\_y\_1}$	$n,+,q_{copy\_y\_1}$	$*,+,q_{copy\_y\_1}$	$\$,+,q_{copy\_y\_1}$
$q_{copy\_y\_2}$	$b,-,q_{copy\_y\_3}$				
$q_{copy\_y\_3}$	$y,-,q_{copy\_start}$	$y,-,q_{copy\_y\_3}$	$n,-,q_{copy\_y\_3}$	$*,-,q_{copy\_y\_3}$	$\$,-,q_{copy\_y\_3}$
$q_{copy\_n\_1}$	$n,+,q_{copy\_n\_2}$	$y,+,q_{copy\_n\_1}$	$n,+,q_{copy\_n\_1}$	$*,+,q_{copy\_n\_1}$	$\$,+,q_{copy\_n\_1}$
$q_{copy\_n\_2}$	$b,-,q_{copy\_n\_3}$				
$q_{copy\_n\_3}$	$n,-,q_{copy\_start}$	$y,-,q_{copy\_n\_3}$	$n,-,q_{copy\_n\_3}$	$*,-,q_{copy\_n\_3}$	$\$,-,q_{copy\_n\_3}$
$q_{copy\_end\_1}$		$y,+,q_{copy\_end\_1}$	$n,+,q_{copy\_end\_1}$	$*,+,q_{copy\_end\_1}$	$\$,+,q_{copy\_end\_2}$
$q_{copy\_end\_2}$		$y,+,q_{copy\_end\_2}$	$n,+,q_{copy\_end\_2}$	$*,+,q_{copy\_end\_2}$	$y,+,q_{begin}$
q_{cycle_end}		$y,+,q_{cycle\_end}$	$n,+,q_{cycle\_end}$	$*,+,q_{cycle\_end}$	$\$,-,q_{copy\_start}$
$q_{case\_n\_1}$	$*,-,q_{case\_n\_2}$	$y,-,q_{case\_n\_1}$	$n,-,q_{case\_n\_1}$	$*,-,q_{case\_n\_1}$	$\$,-,q_{case\_n\_1}$
$q_{case\_n\_2}$	$b,+,q_{case\_n\_4}$	$y,-,q_{case\_n\_2}$	$n,-,q_{case\_n\_2}$	$b,+,q_{case\_n\_3}$	
$q_{case\_n\_3}$	$n,+,q_{begin}$	$y,+,q_{case\_n\_3}$	$n,+,q_{case\_n\_3}$	$*,+,q_{case\_n\_3}$	$\$,+,q_{case\_n\_3}$
$q_{case\_n\_4}$		$y,+,q_{case\_n\_4}$	$n,+,q_{case\_n\_4}$	$*,+,q_{case\_n\_4}$	$\$,-,q_{case\_n\_2}$

The move relation δ_{17_5} is described in Table 7.3. It contains 67 quintuples. U_{17_5} has the following similarities to U_{13_7}. First, the initial ID of U_{17_5} is exactly the same as that of U_{13_7}. Second, U_{17_5} has the states with similar names (hence with similar functions) to those in U_{13_7} except the state $q_{case\_y\_n}$ in U_{13_7}. For example, q_{begin} in U_{17_5} corresponds to that in U_{13_7}, and $q_{copy\_end\_1}$ and $q_{copy\_end\_2}$ in U_{17_5} correspond to q_{copy_end} in U_{13_7}. Third, the position of a symbol being copied in a production rule is marked by b as in the case of U_{13_7} (see, e.g., the configuration at $t = 15$ below).

The main difference is the following. In U_{17_5}, after reading the first symbol of the current string in the state q_{begin}, it goes to the state $q_{case\_y\_1}$ or $q_{case\_n\_1}$ depending on the read symbol is y or n, and these two cases are managed separately. On the other hand, in U_{13_7}, after reading the symbol y or n, it goes to the state $q_{case\_y\_1}$ or $q_{case\_y\_n}$, and executes some common operations for both these cases, i.e., even in the case of n it tries to copy the symbols (see Sect. 7.3.1). In U_{17_5}, if the first symbol is n, then only the phase marker is shifted to the position of the next production rule by the states $q_{case\_n\_1}, \ldots, q_{case\_n\_4}$. The second difference is that the leftmost symbol of the current string in U_{17_5} is indicated by the symbol $\$$ or b instead of Y and N in U_{13_7} (see the configurations at $t = 8$ and $t = 1$ below). By this, the total number of symbols of U_{17_5} can be reduced to 5. Snapshots of computation process of U_{17_5} for the CTSH $\hat{C}_2$ with the initial string NYY is as follows.

$$
\begin{aligned}
t = 0 &: [\, b\, ynn * yn * b\$\, \underline{n}yy\, b,\ q_{\text{begin}},\ 10\,]\\
1 &: [\, b\, ynn * yn * b\$\, byy\, b,\ q_{\text{case\_n\_1}},\ 9\,]\\
7 &: [\, b\, ynn * ynb * \$\, nyy\, b,\ q_{\text{begin}},\ 11\,]\\
8 &: [\, b\, ynn * ynb * \$\, \underline{n}\$y\, b,\ q_{\text{case\_y\_1}},\ 10\,]\\
14 &: [\, b\, ynn * y\underline{n} * * \$\, n\$y\, b,\ q_{\text{copy\_start}},\ 6\,]\\
15 &: [\, b\, ynn * yb\underline{*} * \$\, n\$y\, b,\ q_{\text{copy\_n\_1}},\ 7\,]\\
21 &: [\, b\, ynn * yb * * \$\, n\$y\, \underline{b},\ q_{\text{copy\_n\_1}},\ 13\,]\\
22 &: [\, b\, ynn * yb * * \$\, n\$yn\, \underline{b},\ q_{\text{copy\_n\_2}},\ 14\,]\\
31 &: [\, b\, ynn * y\underline{n} * * \$\, n\$yn\, b,\ q_{\text{copy\_start}},\ 5\,]\\
32 &: [\, b\, ynn * b\underline{n} * * \$\, n\$yn\, b,\ q_{\text{copy\_y\_1}},\ 6\,]\\
40 &: [\, b\, ynn * bn * * \$\, n\$yn\, \underline{b},\ q_{\text{copy\_y\_1}},\ 14\,]\\
41 &: [\, b\, ynn * bn * * \$\, n\$yny\, \underline{b},\ q_{\text{copy\_y\_2}},\ 15\,]\\
52 &: [\, b\, ynn \underline{*} yn * * \$\, n\$yny\, b,\ q_{\text{copy\_start}},\ 4\,]\\
53 &: [\, b\, ynnb\underline{y}n * * \$\, n\$yny\, b,\ q_{\text{copy\_end\_1}},\ 5\,]\\
60 &: [\, b\, ynnbyn * * \$\, ny\underline{y}ny\, b,\ q_{\text{begin}},\ 12\,]\\
164 &: [\, \underline{b}\, ynn * yn * * \$\, ny\$nynny\, b,\ q_{\text{copy\_start}},\ 0\,]\\
165 &: [\, b\, \underline{y}nn * yn * * \$\, ny\$nynny\, b,\ q_{\text{cycle\_end}},\ 1\,]\\
174 &: [\, b\, ynn * yn * \underline{*} \$\, ny\$nynny\, b,\ q_{\text{copy\_start}},\ 8\,]\\
175 &: [\, b\, ynn * yn * b\underline{\$}\, ny\$nynny\, b,\ q_{\text{copy\_end\_1}},\ 9\,]\\
455 &: [\, b\, ynn * yn * b\$\, nyynynnynyn\underline{y}\, b,\ q_{\text{begin}},\ 19\,]\\
466 &: [\, b\, ynn * yn * \underline{bb}\, nyynynnyn\$ny\, b,\ q_{\text{case\_y\_1}},\ 8\,]
\end{aligned}
$$

We can see at time $t = 466$ the final string YNY is obtained, where the symbol $\$$ in this configuration should be read as Y (this is because the symbol y is temporarily changed to $\$$).

7.3.4 15-state 6-symbol URTM

By modifying U_{17_5} we have U_{15_6} [8]. It is defined as follows.

$$
\begin{aligned}
U_{15\_6} &= (Q_{15\_6}, \{b,y,n,*,\$,y'\}, q_{\text{begin}}, b, \delta_{15\_6})\\
Q_{15\_6} &= \{q_{\text{begin}}, q_{\text{case\_y\_1}}, q_{\text{case\_y\_2}}, q_{\text{copy\_start}}, q_{\text{copy\_y}}, q_{\text{copy\_n}},\\
&\qquad q_{\text{copy\_next\_1}}, q_{\text{copy\_next\_2}}, q_{\text{copy\_end\_1}}, q_{\text{copy\_end\_2}}, q_{\text{cycle\_end}},\\
&\qquad q_{\text{case\_n\_1}}, q_{\text{case\_n\_2}}, q_{\text{case\_n\_3}}, q_{\text{case\_n\_4}}\}
\end{aligned}
$$

The move relation δ_{15_6} is given in Table 7.4. It contains 62 quintuples. Snapshots of computation process of U_{15_6} for the CTSH $\hat{C}_2$ with the initial string NYY is as follows.

Table 7.4 The move relation δ_{15_6} of U_{15_6}

	b	y	n	$*$	$\$$	y'
q_{begin}	$\$,-,q_{\text{case\_y\_2}}$	$\$,-,q_{\text{case\_y\_1}}$	$b,-,q_{\text{case\_n\_1}}$			
$q_{\text{case\_y\_1}}$	(halt)	$y,-,q_{\text{case\_y\_1}}$	$n,-,q_{\text{case\_y\_1}}$	$*,+,q_{\text{begin}}$	$b,-,q_{\text{case\_y\_1}}$	
$q_{\text{case\_y\_2}}$	$*,-,q_{\text{copy\_start}}$	$y,-,q_{\text{case\_y\_2}}$	$n,-,q_{\text{case\_y\_2}}$	$*,-,q_{\text{case\_y\_2}}$	(null)	
$q_{\text{copy\_start}}$	$b,+,q_{\text{cycle\_end}}$	$y',+,q_{\text{copy\_y}}$	$b,+,q_{\text{copy\_n}}$	$b,+,q_{\text{copy\_end\_1}}$		
$q_{\text{copy\_y}}$	$y,+,q_{\text{copy\_next\_1}}$	$y,+,q_{\text{copy\_y}}$	$n,+,q_{\text{copy\_y}}$	$*,+,q_{\text{copy\_y}}$	$\$,+,q_{\text{copy\_y}}$	
$q_{\text{copy\_n}}$	$n,+,q_{\text{copy\_next\_1}}$	$y,+,q_{\text{copy\_n}}$	$n,+,q_{\text{copy\_n}}$	$*,+,q_{\text{copy\_n}}$	$\$,+,q_{\text{copy\_n}}$	
$q_{\text{copy\_next\_1}}$	$b,-,q_{\text{copy\_next\_2}}$					
$q_{\text{copy\_next\_2}}$	$n,-,q_{\text{copy\_start}}$	$y,-,q_{\text{copy\_next\_2}}$	$n,-,q_{\text{copy\_next\_2}}$	$*,-,q_{\text{copy\_next\_2}}$	$\$,-,q_{\text{copy\_next\_2}}$	$y,-,q_{\text{copy\_start}}$
$q_{\text{copy\_end\_1}}$		$y,+,q_{\text{copy\_end\_1}}$	$n,+,q_{\text{copy\_end\_1}}$	$*,+,q_{\text{copy\_end\_1}}$	$\$,+,q_{\text{copy\_end\_2}}$	
$q_{\text{copy\_end\_2}}$		$y,+,q_{\text{copy\_end\_2}}$	$n,+,q_{\text{copy\_end\_2}}$	$*,+,q_{\text{copy\_end\_2}}$	$y,+,q_{\text{begin}}$	
$q_{\text{cycle\_end}}$		$y,+,q_{\text{cycle\_end}}$	$n,+,q_{\text{cycle\_end}}$	$*,+,q_{\text{cycle\_end}}$	$\$,-,q_{\text{copy\_start}}$	
$q_{\text{case\_n\_1}}$	$*,-,q_{\text{case\_n\_2}}$	$y,-,q_{\text{case\_n\_1}}$	$n,-,q_{\text{case\_n\_1}}$	$*,-,q_{\text{case\_n\_1}}$	$\$,-,q_{\text{case\_n\_1}}$	
$q_{\text{case\_n\_2}}$	$b,+,q_{\text{case\_n\_4}}$	$y,-,q_{\text{case\_n\_2}}$	$n,-,q_{\text{case\_n\_2}}$	$b,+,q_{\text{case\_n\_3}}$		
$q_{\text{case\_n\_3}}$	$n,+,q_{\text{begin}}$	$y,+,q_{\text{case\_n\_3}}$	$n,+,q_{\text{case\_n\_3}}$	$*,+,q_{\text{case\_n\_3}}$	$\$,+,q_{\text{case\_n\_3}}$	
$q_{\text{case\_n\_4}}$		$y,+,q_{\text{case\_n\_4}}$	$n,+,q_{\text{case\_n\_4}}$	$*,+,q_{\text{case\_n\_4}}$	$\$,-,q_{\text{case\_n\_2}}$	

$$
\begin{aligned}
t = 0 :&\ [\, b\,ynn*yn*b\,\$\,\underline{n}yy\,b,\ q_{\text{begin}},\ 10\,] \\
1 :&\ [\, b\,ynn*yn*b\,\underline{\$}\,byy\,b,\ q_{\text{case\_n\_1}},\ 9\,] \\
7 :&\ [\, b\,ynn*ynb*\,\$\,\underline{n}yy\,b,\ q_{\text{begin}},\ 11\,] \\
8 :&\ [\, b\,ynn*ynb*\,\$\,\underline{n}\$y\,b,\ q_{\text{case\_y\_1}},\ 10\,] \\
14 :&\ [\, b\,ynn*y\underline{n}**\,\$\,n\$y\,b,\ q_{\text{copy\_start}},\ 6\,] \\
15 :&\ [\, b\,ynn*yb\underline{*}*\,\$\,n\$y\,b,\ q_{\text{copy\_n}},\ 7\,] \\
21 :&\ [\, b\,ynn*yb**\,\$\,n\$y\,\underline{b},\ q_{\text{copy\_n}},\ 13\,] \\
22 :&\ [\, b\,ynn*yb**\,\$\,n\$yn\,\underline{b},\ q_{\text{copy\_next\_1}},\ 14\,] \\
31 :&\ [\, b\,ynn*y\underline{n}**\,\$\,n\$yn\,b,\ q_{\text{copy\_start}},\ 5\,] \\
32 :&\ [\, b\,ynn*y'\underline{n}**\,\$\,n\$yn\,b,\ q_{\text{copy\_y}},\ 6\,] \\
40 :&\ [\, b\,ynn*y'n**\,\$\,n\$yn\,\underline{b},\ q_{\text{copy\_y}},\ 14\,] \\
41 :&\ [\, b\,ynn*y'n**\,\$\,n\$yny\,\underline{b},\ q_{\text{copy\_next\_1}},\ 15\,] \\
52 :&\ [\, b\,ynn\underline{*}yn**\,\$\,n\$yny\,b,\ q_{\text{copy\_start}},\ 4\,] \\
53 :&\ [\, b\,ynnbyn**\,\$\,n\$yny\,b,\ q_{\text{copy\_end\_1}},\ 5\,] \\
60 :&\ [\, b\,ynnbyn**\,\$nyyny\,b,\ q_{\text{begin}},\ 12\,] \\
164 :&\ [\, \underline{b}\,ynn*yn**\,\$\,ny\$nynny\,b,\ q_{\text{copy\_start}},\ 0\,] \\
165 :&\ [\, b\,ynn*yn**\,\$\,ny\$nynny\,b,\ q_{\text{cycle\_end}},\ 1\,] \\
174 :&\ [\, b\,ynn*yn*\underline{*}\,\$\,ny\$nynny\,b,\ q_{\text{copy\_start}},\ 8\,] \\
175 :&\ [\, b\,ynn*yn*b\,\underline{\$}\,ny\$nynny\,b,\ q_{\text{copy\_end\_1}},\ 9\,] \\
455 :&\ [\, b\,ynn*yn*b\,\$\,nyynynnyn\underline{y}ny\,b,\ q_{\text{begin}},\ 19\,] \\
466 :&\ [\, b\,ynn*yn*\underline{b}\,b\,nyynynnyn\$ny\,b,\ q_{\text{case\_y\_1}},\ 8\,]
\end{aligned}
$$

U_{15_6} has the following similarity to U_{17_5}. The initial ID of U_{15_6} is the same as that of U_{17_5}. The states of U_{15_6} whose names are similar to those in U_{17_5} also have similar functions as them. The time for simulating a CTSH in U_{15_6} is exactly the same as that in U_{17_5}.

The difference is that the position of a symbol being copied in a production rule is marked by y' or b depending on the copied symbol is y or n, where y' is a new symbol introduced in U_{15_6}. By this, after writing the symbol at the right end of the current string, it can be reversibly "forgotten", since the original symbol is kept by y' or b. Hence, $q_\text{copy\_y\_1}, q_\text{copy\_y\_2}$, and $q_\text{copy\_n\_1}, q_\text{copy\_n\_2}$ in U_{17_5} are replaced by $q_\text{copy\_next\_1}, q_\text{copy\_next\_1}$, and thus the number of states is reduced by 2.

7.3.5 24-state 4-symbol URTM

Next, URTM(24,4) U_{24_4} is given [10]. It is defined as follows.

$$U_{24\_4} = (Q_{24\_4}, \{b, y, n, *\}, q_\text{begin}, b, \delta_{24\_4})$$
$$Q_{24\_4} = \{q_\text{begin}, q_\text{case\_y\_1}, \dots, q_\text{case\_y\_3}, q_\text{copy\_start}, q_\text{copy\_y\_1}, \dots, q_\text{copy\_y\_5},$$
$$q_\text{copy\_n\_1}, \dots, q_\text{copy\_n\_5}, q_\text{copy\_end\_1}, q_\text{copy\_end\_2}, q_\text{cycle\_end},$$
$$q_\text{case\_n\_1}, \dots, q_\text{case\_n\_6}\}$$

Table 7.5 The move relation δ_{24_4} of U_{24_4}

	b	y	n	$*$
q_begin	(null)	$*,-,q_\text{case\_y\_1}$	$*,-,q_\text{case\_n\_1}$	
$q_\text{case\_y\_1}$	$b,-,q_\text{case\_y\_2}$	$y,-,q_\text{case\_y\_1}$	$n,-,q_\text{case\_y\_1}$	
$q_\text{case\_y\_2}$	(halt)			
$q_\text{case\_y\_3}$	$*,-,q_\text{copy\_start}$	$y,-,q_\text{case\_y\_3}$	$n,-,q_\text{case\_y\_3}$	$*,-,q_\text{case\_y\_3}$
$q_\text{copy\_start}$	$b,+,q_\text{cycle\_end}$	$b,+,q_\text{copy\_y\_1}$	$b,+,q_\text{copy\_n\_1}$	$b,+,q_\text{copy\_end\_1}$
$q_\text{copy\_y\_1}$	$b,+,q_\text{copy\_y\_2}$	$y,+,q_\text{copy\_y\_1}$	$n,+,q_\text{copy\_y\_1}$	$*,+,q_\text{copy\_y\_1}$
$q_\text{copy\_y\_2}$	$y,+,q_\text{copy\_y\_3}$	$y,+,q_\text{copy\_y\_2}$	$n,+,q_\text{copy\_y\_2}$	$*,+,q_\text{copy\_y\_2}$
$q_\text{copy\_y\_3}$	$b,-,q_\text{copy\_y\_4}$			
$q_\text{copy\_y\_4}$	$b,-,q_\text{copy\_y\_5}$	$y,-,q_\text{copy\_y\_4}$	$n,-,q_\text{copy\_y\_4}$	$*,-,q_\text{copy\_y\_4}$
$q_\text{copy\_y\_5}$	$y,-,q_\text{copy\_start}$	$y,-,q_\text{copy\_y\_5}$	$n,-,q_\text{copy\_y\_5}$	$*,-,q_\text{copy\_y\_5}$
$q_\text{copy\_n\_1}$	$b,+,q_\text{copy\_n\_2}$	$y,+,q_\text{copy\_n\_1}$	$n,+,q_\text{copy\_n\_1}$	$*,+,q_\text{copy\_n\_1}$
$q_\text{copy\_n\_2}$	$n,+,q_\text{copy\_n\_3}$	$y,+,q_\text{copy\_n\_2}$	$n,+,q_\text{copy\_n\_2}$	$*,+,q_\text{copy\_n\_2}$
$q_\text{copy\_n\_3}$	$b,-,q_\text{copy\_n\_4}$			
$q_\text{copy\_n\_4}$	$b,-,q_\text{copy\_n\_5}$	$y,-,q_\text{copy\_n\_4}$	$n,-,q_\text{copy\_n\_4}$	$*,-,q_\text{copy\_n\_4}$
$q_\text{copy\_n\_5}$	$n,-,q_\text{copy\_start}$	$y,-,q_\text{copy\_n\_5}$	$n,-,q_\text{copy\_n\_5}$	$*,-,q_\text{copy\_n\_5}$
$q_\text{copy\_end\_1}$	$b,+,q_\text{copy\_end\_2}$	$y,+,q_\text{copy\_end\_1}$	$n,+,q_\text{copy\_end\_1}$	$*,+,q_\text{copy\_end\_1}$
$q_\text{copy\_end\_2}$		$y,+,q_\text{copy\_end\_2}$	$n,+,q_\text{copy\_end\_2}$	$y,+,q_\text{begin}$
$q_\text{cycle\_end}$	$b,-,q_\text{copy\_start}$	$y,+,q_\text{cycle\_end}$	$n,+,q_\text{cycle\_end}$	$*,+,q_\text{cycle\_end}$
$q_\text{case\_n\_1}$	$b,-,q_\text{case\_n\_2}$	$y,-,q_\text{case\_n\_1}$	$n,-,q_\text{case\_n\_1}$	
$q_\text{case\_n\_2}$	$*,-,q_\text{case\_n\_3}$	$y,-,q_\text{case\_n\_2}$	$n,-,q_\text{case\_n\_2}$	$*,-,q_\text{case\_n\_2}$
$q_\text{case\_n\_3}$	$b,+,q_\text{case\_n\_6}$	$y,-,q_\text{case\_n\_3}$	$n,-,q_\text{case\_n\_3}$	$b,+,q_\text{case\_n\_4}$
$q_\text{case\_n\_4}$	$b,+,q_\text{case\_n\_5}$	$y,+,q_\text{case\_n\_4}$	$n,+,q_\text{case\_n\_4}$	$*,+,q_\text{case\_n\_4}$
$q_\text{case\_n\_5}$	$b,-,q_\text{case\_y\_3}$	$y,+,q_\text{case\_n\_5}$	$n,+,q_\text{case\_n\_5}$	$n,+,q_\text{begin}$
$q_\text{case\_n\_6}$	$b,-,q_\text{case\_n\_3}$	$y,+,q_\text{case\_n\_6}$	$n,+,q_\text{case\_n\_6}$	$*,+,q_\text{case\_n\_6}$

The move relation δ_{24_4} is described in Table 7.5, which has 82 quintuples. Though U_{24_4} has similarities to U_{17_5}, the initial ID is slightly different to that of U_{17_5}, since the symbol \$ cannot be used. Let $\hat{C} = (k, \{Y, N\}, (\text{halt}, w_1, \cdots, w_{k-1}))$ be a CTSH, and $v_0 \in \{Y, N\}^*$ be an initial string. Then, the initial ID for U_{24_4} is as follows, where $\varphi_1 : \{Y, N\}^* \to \{y, n\}^*$ is a homomorphism such that $\varphi_1(Y) = y, \varphi_1(N) = n)$ defined in Sect. 7.3.1.

$$b\,\varphi_1(w_{k-1}^{\text{R}}) * \cdots * \varphi_1(w_2^{\text{R}}) * \varphi_1(w_1^{\text{R}}) * b\,b\,q\_\text{begin}\,\varphi_1(v_0)\,b$$

Namely, the delimiter between the segments of production rules and removed symbols is b rather than \$. The symbol \$ used for indicating the leftmost symbol of the current string in U_{17_5} is also replaced by $*$ in U_{24_4}. Because of the above modification, we need more states than in the case of U_{17_5}. Snapshots of computation of U_{24_4} for the CTSH C_1 with $v_0 = NYY$ in Example 7.4 is as follows.

$$
\begin{aligned}
t = 0 : &\ [\,b\,ynn * yn * b\,b\,\underline{n}yy\,b,\ q_{\text{begin}},\ 10\,] \\
1 : &\ [\,b\,ynn * yn * b\,\underline{b} * yy\,b,\ q_{\text{case\_n\_1}},\ 9\,] \\
7 : &\ [\,b\,ynn * ynb * b\,n\,yy\,b,\ q_{\text{begin}},\ 11\,] \\
8 : &\ [\,b\,ynn * ynb * b\,\underline{n} * y\,b,\ q_{\text{case\_y\_1}},\ 10\,] \\
14 : &\ [\,b\,ynn * \underline{yn} * * b\,n * y\,b,\ q_{\text{copy\_start}},\ 6\,] \\
15 : &\ [\,b\,ynn * yb\,\underline{*} * b\,n * y\,b,\ q_{\text{copy\_n\_1}},\ 7\,] \\
21 : &\ [\,b\,ynn * yb * * b\,n * y\,\underline{b},\ q_{\text{copy\_n\_2}},\ 13\,] \\
22 : &\ [\,b\,ynn * yb * * b\,n * yn\,\underline{b},\ q_{\text{copy\_n\_3}},\ 14\,] \\
31 : &\ [\,b\,ynn * \underline{yn} * * b\,n * yn\,b,\ q_{\text{copy\_start}},\ 5\,] \\
32 : &\ [\,b\,ynn * b\,\underline{n} * * b\,n * yn\,b,\ q_{\text{copy\_y\_1}},\ 6\,] \\
40 : &\ [\,b\,ynn * b\,n * * b\,n * yn\,\underline{b},\ q_{\text{copy\_y\_2}},\ 14\,] \\
41 : &\ [\,b\,ynn * b\,n * * b\,n * yny\,\underline{b},\ q_{\text{copy\_y\_3}},\ 15\,] \\
52 : &\ [\,b\,ynn\underline{*}yn * * b\,n * yny\,b,\ q_{\text{copy\_start\_1}},\ 4\,] \\
53 : &\ [\,b\,ynnb\,\underline{yn} * * b\,n * yny\,b,\ q_{\text{copy\_end\_1}},\ 5\,] \\
60 : &\ [\,b\,ynnb\,yn * * b\,ny\,\underline{yn}y\,b,\ q_{\text{begin}},\ 12\,] \\
164 : &\ [\,\underline{b}\,ynn * yn * * b\,ny * nynny\,b,\ q_{\text{copy\_start}},\ 0\,] \\
165 : &\ [\,b\,\underline{yn}n * yn * * b\,ny * nynny\,b,\ q_{\text{cycle\_end}},\ 1\,] \\
174 : &\ [\,b\,ynn * yn * \underline{*}b\,ny * nynny\,b,\ q_{\text{copy\_start}},\ 8\,] \\
175 : &\ [\,b\,ynn * yn * b\,\underline{b}\,ny * nynny\,b,\ q_{\text{copy\_end\_1}},\ 9\,] \\
455 : &\ [\,b\,ynn * yn * b\,b\,nyynynnyn\,\underline{yn}y\,b,\ q_{\text{begin}},\ 19\,] \\
466 : &\ [\,b\,ynn * yn * \underline{b}\,b\,nyynynnyn * ny\,b,\ q_{\text{case\_y\_2}},\ 8\,]
\end{aligned}
$$

The URTM U_{24_4} halts at $t = 466$, and the final string YNY of $\hat{C}_2$ is obtained (here, the rightmost $*$ should be read as Y).

7.3.6 32-state 3-symbol URTM

We give URTM(32,3) U_{32_3} [10]. It is defined as follows.

$$U_{32\_3} = (Q_{24\_4}, \{b,y,n\}, q_{begin}, b, \delta_{32\_3})$$
$$Q_{32\_3} = \{q_{begin}, q_{case\_y\_1}, \ldots, q_{case\_y\_7}, q_{copy\_start\_1}, q_{copy\_start\_2}, q_{copy\_y\_1}, \ldots,$$
$$q_{copy\_y\_4}, q_{copy\_next\_1}, \ldots, q_{copy\_next\_4}, q_{copy\_n\_1}, \ldots, q_{copy\_n\_4},$$
$$q_{copy\_end\_1}, q_{copy\_end\_2}, q_{cycle\_end}, q_{case\_n\_1}, \ldots, q_{case\_n\_7}\}$$

Table 7.6 The move relation δ_{32_3} of U_{32_3}

	b	y	n
q_{begin}	(null)	$b,-,q_{case\_y\_1}$	$b,-,q_{case\_n\_1}$
$q_{case\_y\_1}$	$b,-,q_{case\_y\_2}$	$y,-,q_{case\_y\_1}$	$n,-,q_{case\_y\_1}$
$q_{case\_y\_2}$	(halt)		$n,+,q_{case\_y\_3}$
$q_{case\_y\_3}$	$b,+,q_{case\_y\_4}$		
$q_{case\_y\_4}$	$b,-,q_{case\_y\_5}$	$y,+,q_{case\_y\_4}$	$n,+,q_{case\_y\_4}$
$q_{case\_y\_5}$	$b,-,q_{case\_y\_6}$	$y,-,q_{case\_y\_5}$	$n,-,q_{case\_y\_5}$
$q_{case\_y\_6}$	$n,-,q_{case\_y\_7}$	$y,-,q_{case\_y\_6}$	$n,-,q_{case\_y\_6}$
$q_{case\_y\_7}$		$y,-,q_{copy\_start\_1}$	$n,-,q_{copy\_start\_1}$
$q_{copy\_start\_1}$	$b,+,q_{cycle\_end}$	$b,-,q_{copy\_start\_2}$	$b,+,q_{copy\_end\_1}$
$q_{copy\_start\_2}$		$y,+,q_{copy\_y\_1}$	$n,+,q_{copy\_n\_1}$
$q_{copy\_y\_1}$	$b,+,q_{copy\_y\_2}$		
$q_{copy\_y\_2}$	$b,+,q_{copy\_y\_3}$	$y,+,q_{copy\_y\_2}$	$n,+,q_{copy\_y\_2}$
$q_{copy\_y\_3}$	$b,+,q_{copy\_y\_4}$	$y,+,q_{copy\_y\_3}$	$n,+,q_{copy\_y\_3}$
$q_{copy\_y\_4}$	$y,+,q_{copy\_next\_1}$	$y,+,q_{copy\_y\_4}$	$n,+,q_{copy\_y\_4}$
$q_{copy\_next\_1}$	$b,-,q_{copy\_next\_2}$		
$q_{copy\_next\_2}$	$b,-,q_{copy\_next\_3}$	$y,-,q_{copy\_next\_2}$	$n,-,q_{copy\_next\_2}$
$q_{copy\_next\_3}$	$b,-,q_{copy\_next\_4}$	$y,-,q_{copy\_next\_3}$	$n,-,q_{copy\_next\_3}$
$q_{copy\_next\_4}$	$y,-,q_{case\_y\_7}$	$y,-,q_{copy\_next\_4}$	$n,-,q_{copy\_next\_4}$
$q_{copy\_n\_1}$	$b,+,q_{copy\_n\_2}$		
$q_{copy\_n\_2}$	$b,+,q_{copy\_n\_3}$	$y,+,q_{copy\_n\_2}$	$n,+,q_{copy\_n\_2}$
$q_{copy\_n\_3}$	$b,+,q_{copy\_n\_4}$	$y,+,q_{copy\_n\_3}$	$n,+,q_{copy\_n\_3}$
$q_{copy\_n\_4}$	$n,+,q_{copy\_next\_1}$	$y,+,q_{copy\_n\_4}$	$n,+,q_{copy\_n\_4}$
$q_{copy\_end\_1}$	$b,+,q_{copy\_end\_2}$	$y,+,q_{copy\_end\_1}$	$n,+,q_{copy\_end\_1}$
$q_{copy\_end\_2}$	$y,+,q_{begin}$	$y,+,q_{copy\_end\_2}$	$n,+,q_{copy\_end\_2}$
q_{cycle_end}	$b,-,q_{copy\_start\_1}$	$y,+,q_{cycle\_end}$	$n,+,q_{cycle\_end}$
$q_{case\_n\_1}$	$b,-,q_{case\_n\_2}$	$y,-,q_{case\_n\_1}$	$n,-,q_{case\_n\_1}$
$q_{case\_n\_2}$	$n,-,q_{case\_n\_4}$	$y,-,q_{case\_n\_2}$	$n,-,q_{case\_n\_2}$
$q_{case\_n\_3}$	$b,+,q_{case\_n\_7}$	$y,-,q_{case\_n\_4}$	$b,+,q_{case\_n\_5}$
$q_{case\_n\_4}$		$y,-,q_{case\_n\_3}$	$n,-,q_{case\_n\_3}$
$q_{case\_n\_5}$	$b,+,q_{case\_n\_6}$	$y,+,q_{case\_n\_5}$	$n,+,q_{case\_n\_5}$
$q_{case\_n\_6}$	$n,+,q_{begin}$	$y,+,q_{case\_n\_6}$	$n,+,q_{case\_n\_6}$
$q_{case\_n\_7}$	$b,-,q_{case\_n\_3}$	$y,+,q_{case\_n\_7}$	$n,+,q_{case\_n\_7}$

The move relation δ_{32_3} is given in Table 7.6. It has 82 quintuples. To specify the initial ID for U_{32_3} we use two string homomorphisms φ_1 and φ_2 such that $\varphi_1(Y) = y$, $\varphi_1(N) = n$, and $\varphi_2(Y) = yy$, $\varphi_2(N) = ny$. Let $\hat{C} = (k, \{Y, N\}, (\text{halt}, w_1, \cdots, w_{k-1}))$ be a CTSH, and $v_0 \in \{Y, N\}^*$ be an initial string. Then the initial ID for U_{32_3} is as follows.

$$b\,\varphi_2(w^R_{k-1})\,nn\,\cdots\,nn\,\varphi_2(w^R_2)\,nn\,\varphi_2(w^R_1)\,nn\,nb\,b\,q_{\text{begin}}\,\varphi_1(v_0)\,b$$

The symbols y, n, and $*$ that were used in U_{17_5} for describing production rules are here encoded by the symbol sequences yy, ny, and nn, respectively. A phase marker is represented by nb, which is obtained by changing the right symbol n of the code nn by b. Thus, to indicate the phase, the code nn at the corresponding position is replaced by nb. In the segment of the current string, the string v_0 is represented by the sequence $\varphi_1(v_0)$. Between the segment of production rules, and that of removed symbols, a delimiter b is put. If we take CTSH $\hat{C}_2$ with $v_0 = NYY$ in Example 7.4, the initial ID is: $b\,yy\,ny\,ny\,nn\,yy\,ny\,nn\,nb\,b\,q_{\text{begin}}\,nyy\,b$. Snapshots of computation of U_{32_3} from this ID is as follows. These snapshots correspond to those of U_{17_5}, U_{15_6}, and U_{24_4} in the previous subsections, though the simulation steps are different.

$$
\begin{aligned}
t = 0 :\ & [\,b\,yy\,ny\,ny\,nn\,yy\,ny\,nn\,nb\ b\underline{ny}y\,b,\ q_{\text{begin}},\ 18\,] \\
1 :\ & [\,b\,yy\,ny\,ny\,nn\,yy\,ny\,nn\,nb\ \underline{b}byy\,b,\ q_{\text{case\_n\_1}},\ 17\,] \\
9 :\ & [\,b\,yy\,ny\,ny\,nn\,yy\,ny\,nb\ nn\,b\,ny\,y\,b,\ q_{\text{begin}},\ 19\,] \\
10 :\ & [\,b\,yy\,ny\,ny\,nn\,yy\,ny\,nb\ nn\,b\underline{n}by\,b,\ q_{\text{case\_y\_1}},\ 18\,] \\
22 :\ & [\,b\,yy\,ny\,ny\,nn\,yy\,n\underline{y}\,nn\,nn\,b\,n\,by\,b,\ q_{\text{copy\_start\_1}},\ 12\,] \\
24 :\ & [\,b\,yy\,ny\,ny\,nn\,yy\,n\underline{b}\ nn\,nn\,b\,n\,by\,b,\ q_{\text{copy\_n\_1}},\ 12\,] \\
33 :\ & [\,b\,yy\,ny\,ny\,nn\,yy\,nb\ nn\,nn\,b\,n\,b\underline{y}\,b,\ q_{\text{copy\_n\_4}},\ 21\,] \\
34 :\ & [\,b\,yy\,ny\,ny\,nn\,yy\,nb\ nn\,nn\,b\,n\,byn\underline{b},\ q_{\text{copy\_next\_1}},\ 22\,] \\
46 :\ & [\,b\,yy\,ny\,ny\,nn\,\underline{yy}\,ny\,nn\,nn\,b\,n\,byn\,b,\ q_{\text{copy\_start\_1}},\ 10\,] \\
48 :\ & [\,b\,yy\,ny\,ny\,nn\,y\underline{b}\ ny\,nn\,nn\,b\,n\,byn\,b,\ q_{\text{copy\_y\_1}},\ 10\,] \\
60 :\ & [\,b\,yy\,ny\,ny\,nn\,yb\ ny\,nn\,nn\,b\,n\,byn\,\underline{b},\ q_{\text{copy\_y\_4}},\ 22\,] \\
61 :\ & [\,b\,yy\,ny\,ny\,nn\,yb\ ny\,nn\,nn\,b\,n\,byny\underline{b},\ q_{\text{copy\_next\_1}},\ 23\,] \\
76 :\ & [\,b\,yy\,ny\,ny\,n\underline{n}\,yy\,ny\,nn\,nn\,b\,n\,byny\,b,\ q_{\text{copy\_start\_1}},\ 8\,] \\
77 :\ & [\,b\,yy\,ny\,ny\,nb\ yy\,ny\,nn\,nn\,b\,n\,byny\,b,\ q_{\text{copy\_end\_1}},\ 9\,] \\
88 :\ & [\,b\,yy\,ny\,ny\,nb\ yy\,ny\,nn\,nn\,b\,ny\,\underline{y}ny\,b,\ q_{\text{begin}},\ 20\,] \\
248 :\ & [\,\underline{b}\,yy\,ny\,ny\,nn\,yy\,ny\,nn\,nn\,b\,ny\,bny\,nny\,b,\ q_{\text{copy\_start\_1}},\ 0\,] \\
249 :\ & [\,b\,yy\,ny\,ny\,nn\,yy\,ny\,nn\,nn\,b\,ny\,bny\,nny\,b,\ q_{\text{cycle\_end}},\ 1\,] \\
266 :\ & [\,b\,yy\,ny\,ny\,nn\,yy\,ny\,nn\,\underline{nn}\,b\,ny\,bny\,nny\,b,\ q_{\text{copy\_start\_1}},\ 16\,] \\
267 :\ & [\,b\,yy\,ny\,ny\,nn\,yy\,ny\,nn\,nb\ \underline{b}\,ny\,bny\,nny\,b,\ q_{\text{copy\_end\_1}},\ 17\,] \\
653 :\ & [\,b\,yy\,ny\,ny\,nn\,yy\,ny\,nn\,nb\ b\,ny\,ynynnyn\,ynyb,\ q_{\text{begin}},\ 27\,] \\
664 :\ & [\,b\,yy\,ny\,ny\,nn\,yy\,ny\,nn\,n\underline{b}\ b\,ny\,ynynnyn\,b\overline{ny}b,\ q_{\text{case\_y\_2}},\ 16\,]
\end{aligned}
$$

At $t = 664$, U_{32_3} halts, and we obtain the final string YNY of $\hat{C}_2$ at the right end of the symbol sequence, where bny should be read as YNY.

7.3.7 138-state 2-symbol URTM converted from URTM(24,4)

In the previous sections, we constructed URTM(10,8), URTM(13,7), URTM(15,6), URTM(17,5), URTM(24,4), and URTM(32,3). In each of these URTMs, the product of the numbers of states and symbols is less than 100. However, as for the 2-symbol case, it is hard to find a URTM with 50 states or less. Even if we relax the constraint on the product from 100 to, for example, 150, it seems still difficult to obtain such a URTM. If an RTM can enter a state q from different states p_1 and p_2 (i.e., a kind of "merging" in a program), then the RTM must write different symbols in p_1 and p_2 because of the reversibility condition. Hence, it becomes difficult to satisfy this condition when the machine can use only two kinds of symbols.

Table 7.7 The move relation δ_{138_2} of U_{138_2} (part 1)

	0	1
$[q^r_{begin}]$	$0,+,[q^r_{begin},0]$	$0,+,[q^r_{begin},1]$
$[q^r_{begin},0]$	(null)	$1,-,[q^w_{case\_y\_1},1]$
$[q^r_{begin},1]$	$1,-,[q^w_{case\_n\_1},1]$	
$[q^w_{begin},0]$	$0,+,[q^s_{begin}]$	
$[q^w_{begin},1]$	$1,+,[q^s_{begin}]$	
$[q^s_{begin}]$	$0,+,[q^r_{begin}]$	$1,+,[q^r_{begin}]$
$[q^r_{case\_y\_1}]$	$0,+,[q^r_{case\_y\_1},0]$	$0,+,[q^r_{case\_y\_1},1]$
$[q^r_{case\_y\_1},0]$	$0,-,[q^w_{case\_y\_2},0]$	$1,-,[q^w_{case\_y\_1},0]$
$[q^r_{case\_y\_1},1]$	$0,-,[q^w_{case\_y\_1},1]$	
$[q^w_{case\_y\_1},0]$	$0,-,[q^s_{case\_y\_1}]$	
$[q^w_{case\_y\_1},1]$	$1,-,[q^s_{case\_y\_1}]$	
$[q^s_{case\_y\_1}]$	$0,-,[q^r_{case\_y\_1}]$	$1,-,[q^r_{case\_y\_1}]$
$[q^r_{case\_y\_2}]$	(halt)	$0,+,[q^r_{case\_y\_2},1]$
$[q^r_{case\_y\_2},1]$		$1,-,[q^w_{case\_n\_5},1]$
$[q^w_{case\_y\_2},0]$	$0,-,[q^s_{case\_y\_2}]$	
$[q^s_{case\_y\_2}]$	$0,-,[q^r_{case\_y\_2}]$	$1,-,[q^r_{case\_y\_2}]$
$[q^r_{case\_y\_3}]$	$0,+,[q^r_{case\_y\_3},0]$	$0,+,[q^r_{case\_y\_3},1]$
$[q^r_{case\_y\_3},0]$	$1,-,[q^w_{copy\_start},1]$	$1,-,[q^w_{case\_y\_3},0]$
$[q^r_{case\_y\_3},1]$	$0,-,[q^w_{case\_y\_3},1]$	$1,-,[q^w_{case\_y\_3},1]$
$[q^w_{case\_y\_3},0]$	$0,-,[q^s_{case\_y\_3}]$	
$[q^w_{case\_y\_3},1]$	$1,-,[q^s_{case\_y\_3}]$	
$[q^s_{case\_y\_3}]$	$0,-,[q^r_{case\_y\_3}]$	$1,-,[q^r_{case\_y\_3}]$
$[q^r_{copy\_start}]$	$0,+,[q^r_{copy\_start},0]$	$0,+,[q^r_{copy\_start},1]$
$[q^r_{copy\_start},0]$	$0,-,[q^w_{cycle\_end},0]$	$0,-,[q^w_{copy\_y\_1},0]$
$[q^r_{copy\_start},1]$	$0,-,[q^w_{copy\_n\_1},0]$	$0,-,[q^w_{copy\_end\_1},0]$
$[q^w_{copy\_start},0]$	$0,-,[q^s_{copy\_start}]$	
$[q^w_{copy\_start},1]$	$1,-,[q^s_{copy\_start}]$	
$[q^s_{copy\_start}]$	$0,-,[q^r_{copy\_start}]$	$1,-,[q^r_{copy\_start}]$
$[q^r_{copy\_y\_1}]$	$0,+,[q^r_{copy\_y\_1},0]$	$0,+,[q^r_{copy\_y\_1},1]$
$[q^r_{copy\_y\_1},0]$	$0,-,[q^w_{copy\_y\_2},0]$	$1,-,[q^w_{copy\_y\_1},0]$
$[q^r_{copy\_y\_1},1]$	$0,-,[q^w_{copy\_y\_1},1]$	$1,-,[q^w_{copy\_y\_1},1]$
$[q^w_{copy\_y\_1},0]$	$0,+,[q^s_{copy\_y\_1}]$	
$[q^w_{copy\_y\_1},1]$	$1,+,[q^s_{copy\_y\_1}]$	
$[q^s_{copy\_y\_1}]$	$0,+,[q^r_{copy\_y\_1}]$	$1,+,[q^r_{copy\_y\_1}]$
$[q^r_{copy\_y\_2}]$	$0,+,[q^r_{copy\_y\_2},0]$	$0,+,[q^r_{copy\_y\_2},1]$
$[q^r_{copy\_y\_2},0]$	$1,-,[q^w_{copy\_y\_3},0]$	$1,-,[q^w_{copy\_y\_2},0]$
$[q^r_{copy\_y\_2},1]$	$0,-,[q^w_{copy\_y\_2},1]$	$1,-,[q^w_{copy\_y\_2},1]$
$[q^w_{copy\_y\_2},0]$	$0,+,[q^s_{copy\_y\_2}]$	
$[q^w_{copy\_y\_2},1]$	$1,+,[q^s_{copy\_y\_2}]$	
$[q^s_{copy\_y\_2}]$	$0,+,[q^r_{copy\_y\_2}]$	$1,+,[q^r_{copy\_y\_2}]$
$[q^r_{copy\_y\_3}]$	$0,+,[q^r_{copy\_y\_3},0]$	
$[q^r_{copy\_y\_3},0]$	$0,-,[q^w_{copy\_y\_4},0]$	
$[q^w_{copy\_y\_3},0]$	$0,+,[q^s_{copy\_y\_3}]$	
$[q^s_{copy\_y\_3}]$	$0,+,[q^r_{copy\_y\_3}]$	$1,+,[q^r_{copy\_y\_3}]$
$[q^r_{copy\_y\_4}]$	$0,+,[q^r_{copy\_y\_4},0]$	$0,+,[q^r_{copy\_y\_4},1]$
$[q^r_{copy\_y\_4},0]$	$0,-,[q^w_{copy\_y\_5},0]$	$1,-,[q^w_{copy\_y\_4},0]$
$[q^r_{copy\_y\_4},1]$	$0,-,[q^w_{copy\_y\_4},1]$	$1,-,[q^w_{copy\_y\_4},1]$
$[q^w_{copy\_y\_4},0]$	$0,-,[q^s_{copy\_y\_4}]$	
$[q^w_{copy\_y\_4},1]$	$1,-,[q^s_{copy\_y\_4}]$	
$[q^s_{copy\_y\_4}]$	$0,-,[q^r_{copy\_y\_4}]$	$1,-,[q^r_{copy\_y\_4}]$
$[q^r_{copy\_y\_5}]$	$0,+,[q^r_{copy\_y\_5},0]$	$0,+,[q^r_{copy\_y\_5},1]$
$[q^r_{copy\_y\_5},0]$	$1,-,[q^w_{copy\_start},0]$	$1,-,[q^w_{copy\_y\_5},0]$
$[q^r_{copy\_y\_5},1]$	$0,-,[q^w_{copy\_y\_5},1]$	$1,-,[q^w_{copy\_y\_5},1]$
$[q^w_{copy\_y\_5},0]$	$0,-,[q^s_{copy\_y\_5}]$	
$[q^w_{copy\_y\_5},1]$	$1,-,[q^s_{copy\_y\_5}]$	
$[q^s_{copy\_y\_5}]$	$0,-,[q^r_{copy\_y\_5}]$	$1,-,[q^r_{copy\_y\_5}]$
$[q^r_{copy\_n\_1}]$	$0,+,[q^r_{copy\_n\_1},0]$	$0,+,[q^r_{copy\_n\_1},1]$
$[q^r_{copy\_n\_1},0]$	$0,-,[q^w_{copy\_n\_2},0]$	$1,-,[q^w_{copy\_n\_1},0]$
$[q^r_{copy\_n\_1},1]$	$0,-,[q^w_{copy\_n\_1},1]$	$1,-,[q^w_{copy\_n\_1},1]$
$[q^w_{copy\_n\_1},0]$	$0,+,[q^s_{copy\_n\_1}]$	
$[q^w_{copy\_n\_1},1]$	$1,+,[q^s_{copy\_n\_1}]$	
$[q^s_{copy\_n\_1}]$	$0,+,[q^r_{copy\_n\_1}]$	$1,+,[q^r_{copy\_n\_1}]$
$[q^r_{copy\_n\_2}]$	$0,+,[q^r_{copy\_n\_2},0]$	$0,+,[q^r_{copy\_n\_2},1]$
$[q^r_{copy\_n\_2},0]$	$0,-,[q^w_{copy\_n\_3},1]$	$1,-,[q^w_{copy\_n\_2},0]$
$[q^r_{copy\_n\_2},1]$	$0,-,[q^w_{copy\_n\_2},1]$	$1,-,[q^w_{copy\_n\_2},1]$
$[q^w_{copy\_n\_2},0]$	$0,+,[q^s_{copy\_n\_2}]$	
$[q^w_{copy\_n\_2},1]$	$1,+,[q^s_{copy\_n\_2}]$	
$[q^s_{copy\_n\_2}]$	$0,+,[q^r_{copy\_n\_2}]$	$1,+,[q^r_{copy\_n\_2}]$

Table 7.8 The move relation δ_{138_2} of U_{138_2} (part 2)

	0	1
$[q^r_{copy\_n\_3}]$	$0,+,[q^r_{copy\_n\_3},0]$	
$[q^r_{copy\_n\_3},0]$	$0,-,[q^w_{copy\_n\_4},0]$	
$[q^w_{copy\_n\_3},1]$	$1,+,[q^s_{copy\_n\_3}]$	
$[q^s_{copy\_n\_3}]$	$0,+,[q^r_{copy\_n\_3}]$	$1,+,[q^r_{copy\_n\_3}]$
$[q^r_{copy\_n\_4}]$	$0,+,[q^r_{copy\_n\_4},0]$	$0,+,[q^r_{copy\_n\_4},1]$
$[q^r_{copy\_n\_4},0]$	$0,-,[q^w_{copy\_n\_5},0]$	$1,-,[q^w_{copy\_n\_4},0]$
$[q^r_{copy\_n\_4},1]$	$0,-,[q^w_{copy\_n\_4},1]$	$1,-,[q^w_{copy\_n\_4},1]$
$[q^w_{copy\_n\_4},0]$	$0,-,[q^s_{copy\_n\_4}]$	
$[q^w_{copy\_n\_4},1]$	$1,-,[q^s_{copy\_n\_4}]$	
$[q^s_{copy\_n\_4}]$	$0,-,[q^r_{copy\_n\_4}]$	$1,-,[q^r_{copy\_n\_4}]$
$[q^r_{copy\_n\_5}]$	$0,+,[q^r_{copy\_n\_5},0]$	$0,+,[q^r_{copy\_n\_5},1]$
$[q^r_{copy\_n\_5},0]$	$0,-,[q^r_{copy\_start},1]$	$1,-,[q^w_{copy\_n\_5},0]$
$[q^r_{copy\_n\_5},1]$	$0,-,[q^w_{copy\_n\_5},1]$	$1,-,[q^w_{copy\_n\_5},1]$
$[q^w_{copy\_n\_5},0]$	$0,-,[q^s_{copy\_n\_5}]$	
$[q^w_{copy\_n\_5},1]$	$1,-,[q^s_{copy\_n\_5}]$	
$[q^s_{copy\_n\_5}]$	$0,-,[q^r_{copy\_n\_5}]$	$1,-,[q^r_{copy\_n\_5}]$
$[q^r_{copy\_end\_1}]$	$0,+,[q^r_{copy\_end\_1},0]$	$0,+,[q^r_{copy\_end\_1},1]$
$[q^r_{copy\_end\_1},0]$	$0,-,[q^w_{copy\_end\_2},0]$	$1,-,[q^w_{copy\_end\_1},0]$
$[q^r_{copy\_end\_1},1]$	$0,-,[q^w_{copy\_end\_1},1]$	$1,-,[q^w_{copy\_end\_1},1]$
$[q^w_{copy\_end\_1},0]$	$0,+,[q^s_{copy\_end\_1}]$	
$[q^w_{copy\_end\_1},1]$	$1,+,[q^s_{copy\_end\_1}]$	
$[q^s_{copy\_end\_1}]$	$0,+,[q^r_{copy\_end\_1}]$	$1,+,[q^r_{copy\_end\_1}]$
$[q^r_{copy\_end\_2}]$	$0,+,[q^r_{copy\_end\_2},0]$	$0,+,[q^r_{copy\_end\_2},1]$
$[q^r_{copy\_end\_2},0]$		$1,-,[q^w_{copy\_end\_2},0]$
$[q^r_{copy\_end\_2},1]$	$0,-,[q^w_{copy\_end\_2},1]$	$1,-,[q^w_{begin},0]$
$[q^w_{copy\_end\_2},0]$	$0,+,[q^s_{copy\_end\_2}]$	
$[q^w_{copy\_end\_2},1]$	$1,+,[q^s_{copy\_end\_2}]$	
$[q^s_{copy\_end\_2}]$	$0,+,[q^r_{copy\_end\_2}]$	$1,+,[q^r_{copy\_end\_2}]$
$[q^r_{cycle\_end}]$	$0,+,[q^r_{cycle\_end},0]$	$0,+,[q^r_{cycle\_end},1]$
$[q^r_{cycle\_end},0]$	$0,-,[q^w_{copy\_start},0]$	$1,-,[q^w_{cycle\_end},0]$
$[q^r_{cycle\_end},1]$	$0,-,[q^w_{cycle\_end},1]$	$1,-,[q^w_{cycle\_end},1]$
$[q^w_{cycle\_end},0]$	$0,+,[q^s_{cycle\_end}]$	
$[q^w_{cycle\_end},1]$	$1,+,[q^s_{cycle\_end}]$	
$[q^s_{cycle\_end}]$	$0,+,[q^r_{cycle\_end}]$	$1,+,[q^r_{cycle\_end}]$

	0	1
$[q^r_{case\_n\_1}]$	$0,+,[q^r_{case\_n\_1},0]$	$0,+,[q^r_{case\_n\_1},1]$
$[q^r_{case\_n\_1},0]$	$0,-,[q^w_{case\_n\_2},0]$	$1,-,[q^w_{case\_n\_1},0]$
$[q^r_{case\_n\_1},1]$	$0,-,[q^w_{case\_n\_1},1]$	
$[q^w_{case\_n\_1},0]$	$0,-,[q^s_{case\_n\_1}]$	
$[q^w_{case\_n\_1},1]$	$1,-,[q^s_{case\_n\_1}]$	
$[q^s_{case\_n\_1}]$	$0,-,[q^r_{case\_n\_1}]$	$1,-,[q^r_{case\_n\_1}]$
$[q^r_{case\_n\_2}]$	$0,+,[q^r_{case\_n\_2},0]$	$0,+,[q^r_{case\_n\_2},1]$
$[q^r_{case\_n\_2},0]$	$1,-,[q^w_{case\_n\_3},1]$	$1,-,[q^w_{case\_n\_2},0]$
$[q^r_{case\_n\_2},1]$	$0,-,[q^w_{case\_n\_2},1]$	$1,-,[q^w_{case\_n\_2},1]$
$[q^w_{case\_n\_2},0]$	$0,-,[q^s_{case\_n\_2}]$	
$[q^w_{case\_n\_2},1]$	$1,-,[q^s_{case\_n\_2}]$	
$[q^s_{case\_n\_2}]$	$0,-,[q^r_{case\_n\_2}]$	$1,-,[q^r_{case\_n\_2}]$
$[q^r_{case\_n\_3}]$	$0,+,[q^r_{case\_n\_3},0]$	$0,+,[q^r_{case\_n\_3},1]$
$[q^r_{case\_n\_3},0]$	$0,-,[q^w_{case\_n\_6},0]$	$1,-,[q^w_{case\_n\_3},0]$
$[q^r_{case\_n\_3},1]$	$0,-,[q^w_{case\_n\_3},1]$	$0,-,[q^w_{case\_n\_4},0]$
$[q^w_{case\_n\_3},0]$	$0,-,[q^s_{case\_n\_3}]$	
$[q^w_{case\_n\_3},1]$	$1,-,[q^s_{case\_n\_3}]$	
$[q^s_{case\_n\_3}]$	$0,-,[q^r_{case\_n\_3}]$	$1,-,[q^r_{case\_n\_3}]$
$[q^r_{case\_n\_4}]$	$0,+,[q^r_{case\_n\_4},0]$	$0,+,[q^r_{case\_n\_4},1]$
$[q^r_{case\_n\_4},0]$	$0,-,[q^w_{case\_n\_5},0]$	$1,-,[q^w_{case\_n\_4},0]$
$[q^r_{case\_n\_4},1]$	$0,-,[q^w_{case\_n\_4},1]$	$1,-,[q^w_{case\_n\_4},1]$
$[q^w_{case\_n\_4},0]$	$0,+,[q^s_{case\_n\_4}]$	
$[q^w_{case\_n\_4},1]$	$1,+,[q^s_{case\_n\_4}]$	
$[q^s_{case\_n\_4}]$	$0,+,[q^r_{case\_n\_4}]$	$1,+,[q^r_{case\_n\_4}]$
$[q^r_{case\_n\_5}]$	$0,+,[q^r_{case\_n\_5},0]$	$0,+,[q^r_{case\_n\_5},1]$
$[q^r_{case\_n\_5},0]$	$0,-,[q^w_{case\_y\_3},1]$	$1,-,[q^w_{case\_n\_5},0]$
$[q^r_{case\_n\_5},1]$	$0,-,[q^w_{case\_n\_5},1]$	$0,-,[q^w_{begin},1]$
$[q^w_{case\_n\_5},0]$	$0,+,[q^s_{case\_n\_5}]$	
$[q^w_{case\_n\_5},1]$	$1,+,[q^s_{case\_n\_5}]$	
$[q^s_{case\_n\_5}]$	$0,+,[q^r_{case\_n\_5}]$	$1,+,[q^r_{case\_n\_5}]$
$[q^r_{case\_n\_6}]$	$0,+,[q^r_{case\_n\_6},0]$	$0,+,[q^r_{case\_n\_6},1]$
$[q^r_{case\_n\_6},0]$	$0,-,[q^w_{case\_n\_3},0]$	$1,-,[q^w_{case\_n\_6},0]$
$[q^r_{case\_n\_6},1]$	$0,-,[q^w_{case\_n\_6},1]$	$1,-,[q^w_{case\_n\_6},1]$
$[q^w_{case\_n\_6},0]$	$0,+,[q^s_{case\_n\_6}]$	
$[q^w_{case\_n\_6},1]$	$1,+,[q^s_{case\_n\_6}]$	
$[q^s_{case\_n\_6}]$	$0,+,[q^r_{case\_n\_6}]$	$1,+,[q^r_{case\_n\_6}]$

Here, we construct a 2-symbol URTM applying the method of converting a many-state RTM into a 2-symbol RTM given in Theorem 5.4. By this, from U_{24_4}, URTM(138,2) U_{138_2} is obtained [10].

$$U_{138\_2} = (Q_{138\_2}, \{0,1\}, [q^r_{begin}], 0, \delta_{138\_2})$$

The set of states Q_{138_2} and the move relation δ_{138_2} is given in Table 7.7 and 7.8. It has 220 quintuples, which were generated by a computer program. Here, the symbols $b, y, n,$ and $*$ of U_{24_4} are encoded by 00, 01, 10, and 11 in U_{138_2}, respectively. Let $\hat{C} = (k, \{Y, N\}, (halt, w_1, \cdots, w_{k-1}))$ be a CTSH, and $v_0 \in \{Y, N\}^*$ be an initial string. Let φ_1 and φ_3 be the string homomorphisms such that $\varphi_1(Y) =$

$y, \varphi_1(N) = n$, and $\varphi_3(b) = 00, \varphi_3(y) = 01, \varphi_3(n) = 10, \varphi_3(*) = 11$. Then the initial ID for U_{138_2} is as follows.

$$\varphi_3(b\,\varphi_1(w^R_{k-1}) * \cdots * \varphi_1(w^R_2) * \varphi_1(w^R_1) * b\,b)\,q^r_{\text{begin}}\,\varphi_3(\varphi_1(v_0)\,b)$$

If we take $\hat{C}_2$ in Example 7.4 as a CTSH, and YNN as an initial string v_0, the initial ID is: $0001\,10\,10\,11\,01\,10\,11\,0000\,q_{\text{begin}}\,1001\,01\,00$. The first four steps of computation of U_{138_2} from this ID is as follows.

$$
\begin{aligned}
t = 0: &\ [\,00\ 01\ 10\ 10\ 11\ 01\ 10\ 11\ 00\ 00\ \underline{10}\ 01\ 01\ 00,\ [q^r_{\text{begin}}],\ 20\,] \\
1: &\ [\,00\ 01\ 10\ 10\ 11\ 01\ 10\ 11\ 00\ 00\ \underline{00}\ 01\ 01\ 00,\ [q^r_{\text{begin}},1],\ 21\,] \\
2: &\ [\,00\ 01\ 10\ 10\ 11\ 01\ 10\ 11\ 00\ 00\ \underline{01}\ 01\ 01\ 00,\ [q^w_{\text{case\_n\_1}},1],\ 20\,] \\
3: &\ [\,00\ 01\ 10\ 10\ 11\ 01\ 10\ 11\ 00\ \underline{00}\ 11\ 01\ 01\ 00,\ [q^s_{\text{case\_n\_1}}],\ 19\,] \\
4: &\ [\,00\ 01\ 10\ 10\ 11\ 01\ 10\ 11\ 00\ \underline{00}\ 11\ 01\ 01\ 00,\ [q^r_{\text{case\_n\_1}}],\ 18\,]
\end{aligned}
$$

The above process simulates the first one step

$$
\begin{aligned}
t = 0: &\ [\,b\,ynn * yn * b\,b\,\underline{n}yy\,b,\ q_{\text{begin}},\ 10\,] \\
1: &\ [\,b\,ynn * yn * b\,\underline{b} * yy\,b,\ q_{\text{case\_n\_1}},\ 9\,]
\end{aligned}
$$

of U_{24_4}. Generally, each step of U_{24_4} is simulated by U_{138_2} in four steps. Finally, U_{138_2} halts in the following configuration.

$$t = 1864:\ [\,0001\,10\,10\,11\,01\,10\,11\,\underline{0}000\,1001\,01\,1001\,10\,1001\,10\,11\,1001\,00,\ [q^r_{\text{case\_y\_2}}],\ 16\,]$$

Since it corresponds to the final configuration

$$t = 466:\ [\,b\,ynn * yn * \underline{b}\,b\,nyynynnyn * ny\,b,\ q_{\text{case\_y\_2}},\ 8\,]$$

of U_{24_4}, the final string YNY of $\hat{C}_2$ is thus obtained by U_{138_2}.

7.3.8 4-state and 3-state URTMs converted from URTM(10,8) and URTM(32,3)

It is in general difficult to design an RTM with a small number of states. So far, no URTM with a few states and a small number of symbols has been known. Here, we use the methods of converting a many-state RTM into a four-state RTM and, a three-state RTM shown in Sects. 5.3.4 and 5.3.5.

7.3.8.1 4-state 168-symbol URTM

First, we convert U_{10_8} in Sect. 7.3.2 into a four state URTM. By this, we obtain

$$U_{4\_168} = (\{R_0, R_1, L_0, L_1\}, S_{4\_168}, R_0, b, \delta_{4\_168}),$$

which is a URTM(4,168). We describe neither S_{4_168} nor δ_{4_168} here, since δ_{4_168} has 381 quintuples (they are found in [9]). We assume the states $q_{\text{begin}}, q_{\text{case\_y\_1}}, q_{\text{case\_y\_2}}, q_{\text{case\_y\_n}}, q_{\text{copy\_start}}, q_{\text{copy\_y\_1}}, q_{\text{copy\_y\_2}}, q_{\text{copy\_n\_1}}, q_{\text{copy\_n\_2}}$, and $q_{\text{copy\_end}}$ of U_{10_8} are represented by the numbers $0, \ldots, 9$ in U_{4_168}.

Let $\hat{C} = (k, (\text{halt}, w_1, \ldots, w_{k-1}))$ be a CTSH, and $v_0 \in \{Y, N\}^+$ be an initial string, where v_0 can be written as $v_0 = s v_0'$ for $s \in \{Y, N\}$ and $v_0' \in \{Y, N\}^*$. Let φ_1 be the string homomorphism such that $\varphi_1(Y) = y$, $\varphi_1(N) = n$. Then the initial ID of U_{4_168} is as follows, where $0^\uparrow$ corresponds to the initial state q_{begin} of U_{10_8}.

$$b\ \varphi_1(w_{k-1}^R) * \cdots * \varphi_1(w_2^R) * \varphi_1(w_1^R) * b\ \$\ R_0\ [\varphi_1(s), 0^\uparrow]\ \varphi_1(v_0')\ b$$

If we take $\hat{C}_2$ in Example 7.4 as a CTSH, and YNN as an initial string, the initial ID is: $b\ ynn * yn * b\ \$\ R_0[n, 0^\uparrow]yy\ b$ The first nine steps of computing of U_{4_168} starting from this ID is as follows.

$$
\begin{aligned}
t = 0:\ & [\, b\, ynn * yn * b\, \$\, \underline{[n, 0^\uparrow]}yy\, b,\ R_0,\ 10\,] \\
1:\ & [\, b\, ynn * yn * b\, \$\, \underline{[n', 3^\downarrow]}yyb,\ L_0,\ 9\,] \\
2:\ & [\, b\, ynn * yn * b\, \underline{[\$, 0^\uparrow]}\, [n', 3^\downarrow]yyb,\ R_0,\ 10\,] \\
3:\ & [\, b\, ynn * yn * b\, \underline{[\$, 0^\uparrow]}\, [n', 2^\downarrow]yyb,\ L_1,\ 9\,] \\
4:\ & [\, b\, ynn * yn * b\, \underline{[\$, 1^\uparrow]}\, [n', 2^\downarrow]yyb,\ R_0,\ 10\,] \\
5:\ & [\, b\, ynn * yn * b\, \underline{[\$, 1^\uparrow]}\, [n', 1^\downarrow]yyb,\ L_1,\ 9\,] \\
6:\ & [\, b\, ynn * yn * b\, \underline{[\$, 2^\uparrow]}\, [n', 1^\downarrow]yyb,\ R_0,\ 10\,] \\
7:\ & [\, b\, ynn * yn * b\, \underline{[\$, 2^\uparrow]}\, [n', 0^\downarrow]yyb,\ L_1,\ 9\,] \\
8:\ & [\, b\, ynn * yn * b\, \underline{[\$, 3^\uparrow]}\, [n', 0^\downarrow]yyb,\ R_0,\ 10\,] \\
9:\ & [\, b\, ynn * yn * b\, \underline{[\$, 3^\uparrow]}\, n'yyb,\ L_0,\ 9\,]
\end{aligned}
$$

The above process simulates the first one step

$$
\begin{aligned}
t = 0:\ & [\, b\, ynn * yn * b\, \$\, \underline{n}yy\, b,\ q_{\text{begin}},\ 10\,] \\
1:\ & [\, b\, ynn * yn * b\, \$\, \underline{n}'yy\, b,\ q_{\text{case\_y\_n}},\ 9\,]
\end{aligned}
$$

of U_{10_8}, where $3^\uparrow$ corresponds to the state $q_{\text{case\_y\_n}}$. Finally, U_{4_168} halts in the following configuration.

$$t = 9630:\ [\, b\, ynn * yn * \underline{[b, 1^\uparrow]}\, \$\, NYYNYNNYNyny\, b,\ L_0,\ 8\,]$$

Since it corresponds to the final configuration

$$t = 676:\ [\, b\, ynn * yn * \underline{b}\, \$\, NYYNYNNYNyny\, b,\ q_{\text{case\_y\_1}},\ 8\,]$$

of U_{10_8}, the final string YNY of $\hat{C}_2$ is obtained by U_{4_168}.

7.3.8.2 3-state 36654-symbol URTM

Next, we make a 3-state URTM from U_{32_3}. At first, U_{32_3} is converted into a one-way-updating RTM (1WU-RTM) by the method of Lemma 5.9, and then into a 3-state RTM by the method of Lemma 5.10. By above we obtain a 3-state 36654-symbol URTM.

$$U_{3\_36654} = (\{L, R_0, R_1\}, S_{3\_36654}, L, b, \delta_{3\_36654})$$

Again, we describe neither S_{3_36654} nor δ_{3_36654} here, since δ_{3_36654} has 37936 quintuples (they are found in [9]). If we take $\hat{C}_2$ in Example 7.4 as a CTSH, and YNN as an initial string, the initial computational configuration is as follows.

$$t = 0 : [\underline{b}\,[b,y]\,[y,n]\,[y,n]\,[y,n]\,[n,y]\,[y,n]\,[y,n]\,[n,n]\,[b,b]\,[[q_{\mathrm{begin}},n],y]\,[y,b]\,[b,b]], L, 0]$$

Then, U_{3_36654} finally halts in the following configuration.

$$t = 2348492 : [\, b\,[b,b]^{332}\,[b,y]\,[y,n]\,[y,n]\,[n,y]\,[y,n]\,[y,n]\,[n,n]\,[[q_{\mathrm{case\_y\_2}},b],b] \\ [n,y]\,[y,n]\,[y,n]\,[n,y]\,[n,b]\,[n,y]\,[b,b]^{328}\,[\underline{b},1^{\uparrow}], R_0, 676]$$

Thus, U_{3_36654} correctly simulates the computing process

$$t = 0 : [\, byynynynnyynynnnb\,b\underline{n}yyb,\ q_{\mathrm{begin}},\ 18\,]$$
$$664 : [\, byynynynnyynynnn\underline{b}\,bnyynynnnyb,\ q_{\mathrm{case\_y\_2}},\ 16\,]$$

of U_{32_3}, and the final string YNY of $\hat{C}_2$ is obtained.

7.4 Concluding Remarks

In this chapter, we studied the problem of constructing small URTMs, i.e., universal TMs that satisfy the reversibility condition. From the result of Bennett [2] that any TM can be converted into an RTM, the existence of a URTM is guaranteed. However, such a URTM is not so small. Here, an m-state n-symbol URTM is denoted by URTM(m,n). To construct small URTMs, we first use a method of simulating cyclic tag systems, which are a kind of universal string rewriting systems proposed by Cook [4]. By this method, we obtain URTM(10,8), URTM(13,7), URTM(15,6), URTM(17,5), URTM(24,4), and URTM(32,3) [8, 10, 11, 12]. On the other hand, it is generally difficult to design small RTMs with two symbols or with a very small number of states. For these cases, we use general converting methods for RTMs. Applying the procedure of converting many-symbol RTMs into 2-symbol RTMs given in Sect. 5.3.3, we obtain URTM(138,2) from URTM(24,4). Also, by the procedures of converting many-state RTM into 4-state and 3-state RTMs given in Sects. 5.3.4 and 5.3.5, we obtain URTM(4,168) and URTM(3, 36654) from URTM(10,8), and URTM(32,2), respectively.

The pairs of numbers of states and symbols of these URTMs, as well as the smallest UTMs so far known, are plotted in Fig. 7.1. The products of the numbers of states and symbols of URTM(10,8), URTM(13,7), URTM(15,6), URTM(17,5), URTM(24,4), and URTM(32,3) are all less than 100, and thus relatively small. However, those of URTM(3, 36654), URTM(4,168), and URTM(URTM(138,2)), which are converted from the above ones, are very large, and it is not known whether there are much smaller URTMs. Since there has been only some research on small URTMs so far, there seems much room for improvement, and thus they are left for future study. Also, it is not known whether there is a 2-state URTM.

Woods and Neary [17] proved that cyclic tag systems, and 2-tag systems can simulate TMs in polynomial time, and thus the small UTMs of Minsky [7], Rogozhin [15], Kudlek and Rogozhin [6], Neary and Woods [13], and others can simulate TMs efficiently. It is easy to see that all the URTMs given here simulate cyclic tag systems in polynomial time. Therefore, these URTMs also simulate TMs in polynomial time. Axelsen and Glück [1] studied another type of URTM that can compute all computable injective functions, but their objective was not finding a small URTM.

In Chap. 6, a simple method for constructing 2-symbol RTMs out of a reversible logic element with memory (RLEM) was shown. Though we did not give a construction method of many-symbol RTMs, it is not difficult to do so. Hence, all the URTMs given in this chapter are, in principle, realizable as circuit composed of RLEMs. But, there is a small problem. When constructing an RTM out of RLEMs, the initial state of the RTM must not appear as the fifth element of a quintuple. Otherwise, the constructed RLEM circuit cannot be activated from the outside (see Sect. 6.1.2). All the URTMs given in this chapter do not satisfy this condition. But, as for the URTMs that directly simulate CTSH, this problem is solved by adding one more state. For example, in the case of U_{13_8}, adding the new initial state q_{init} and the quintuple $[q_{init}, \$, \$, +, q_{begin}]$, this condition is satisfied. Note that the modified URTM starts from the position of the delimiter $. Likewise, in the case of U_{24_4}, we add $[q_{init}, b, b, +, q_{begin}]$, since b is the delimiter here. Furthermore, if we obtain a 2-symbol URTM by converting this URTM(25,4), then the initial state $[q_{init}^r]$ of the 2-symbol URTM also satisfies this condition. Hence, in these cases, we can realize the modified URTMs as circuits composed of RLEMs.

Computing processes of the URTMs constructed in this chapter were simulated by a computer program. Animation-like figures of the computer simulation results, as well as description files of the URTMs, are available in [9].

References

1. Axelsen, H.B., Glück, R.: A simple and efficient universal reversible Turing machines. In: Proc. LATA 2011 (eds. A.H. Dediu, S. Inenaga, C. Martin-Vide), LNCS 6638, pp. 117–128 (2011). doi:10.1007/978-3-642-21254-3_8
2. Bennett, C.H.: Logical reversibility of computation. IBM J. Res. Dev. **17**, 525–532 (1973). doi:10.1147/rd.176.0525

3. Cocke, J., Minsky, M.: Universality of tag systems with P = 2. J. ACM **11**, 15–20 (1964). doi:10.1145/321203.321206

4. Cook, M.: Universality in elementary cellular automata. Complex Syst. **15**, 1–40 (2004)

5. Kleene, S.: Introduction to Metamathematics. North-Holland (1952)

6. Kudlek, M., Rogozhin, Y.: A universal Turing machine with 3 states and 9 symbols. In: Proc. DLT 2001 (eds. W. Kuich, G. Rozenberg, A. Salomaa), LNCS 2295, pp. 311–318 (2002). doi:10.1007/3-540-46011-X_27

7. Minsky, M.L.: Computation: Finite and Infinite Machines. Prentice-Hall, Englewood Cliffs, NJ (1967)

8. Morita, K.: Reversible computing and cellular automata — A survey. Theoret. Comput. Sci. **395**, 101–131 (2008). doi:10.1016/j.tcs.2008.01.041

9. Morita, K.: Constructing small universal reversible Turing machines (slides with figures of computer simulation). Hiroshima University Institutional Repository, http://ir.lib.hiroshima-u. ac.jp/00036736 (2015)

10. Morita, K.: Universal reversible Turing machines with a small number of tape symbols. Fundam. Inform. **138**, 17–29 (2015). doi:10.3233/FI-2015-1195

11. Morita, K.: Two small universal reversible Turing machines. In: Advances in Unconventional Computing (ed. A. Adamatzky), pp. 221–237. Springer (2017). doi:10.1007/978-3-319-33924-5_10

12. Morita, K., Yamaguchi, Y.: A universal reversible Turing machine. In: Proc. MCU 2007 (eds. J.O. Durand-Lose, M. Margenstern), LNCS 4664, pp. 90–98 (2007). doi:10.1007/978-3-540-74593-8_8

13. Neary, T., Woods, D.: Four small universal Turing machines. Fundam. Inform. **91**, 123–144 (2009). doi:10.3233/FI-2009-0036

14. Post, E.L.: Formal reductions of the general combinatorial decision problem. Am. J. Math. **65**, 197–215 (1943). doi:10.2307/2371809

15. Rogozhin, Y.: Small universal Turing machines. Theoret. Comput. Sci. **168**, 215–240 (1996). doi:10.1016/S0304-3975(96)00077-1

16. Turing, A.M.: On computable numbers, with an application to the Entscheidungsproblem. Proc. London Math. Soc., Series 2 **42**, 230–265 (1936)

17. Woods, D., Neary, T.: On the time complexity of 2-tag systems and small universal Turing machines. In: Proc. of 47th Symposium on Foundations of Computer Science, pp. 439–446 (2006). doi:10.1109/FOCS.2006.58

18. Woods, D., Neary, T.: The complexity of small universal Turing machines: a survey. Theoret. Comput. Sci. **410**, 443–450 (2009). doi:10.1016/j.tcs.2008.09.051

Chapter 8
Space-Bounded Reversible Turing Machines

Abstract In this chapter, we investigate the problem how reversibility and determinism affect language accepting capability of space-bounded Turing machines (TM). A space-bounded TM is a model whose memory space is bounded by a space function $S(n)$, where n is the input length. Here, we study the relationship among four classes of space-bounded TMs, i.e., irreversible nondeterministic (IN), irreversible deterministic (ID), reversible nondeterministic (RN), and reversible deterministic (RD) ones. We first show a very simple method of simulating an IDTM by an RDTM that uses the same numbers of storage tape symbols and storage tape squares. By a similar method, we also show that an RNTM that satisfies some condition can be simulated by an RDTM that uses the same numbers of storage tape symbols and storage tape squares. Therefore, IDTMs, RNTMs, and RDTMs with the same space function are equivalent in their language accepting powers, and thus an RDTM has relatively high capability in spite of the constraints of reversibility and determinism.

Keywords reversible Turing machine, space-bounded computation, reversibility, determinism

8.1 Reversibility and Determinism in Space-Bounded Computation

A *space-bounded Turing machine* is a model whose memory space (i.e., the total number of tape squares used in a computing process) is bounded by some function of the input length, which is called a *space function*. In this chapter, we investigate how reversibility and determinism affect the space-bounded computation. In the previous chapters, we considered only deterministic (reversible or irreversible) TMs. But, here we also investigate nondeterministic (reversible or irreversible) TMs, and thus there are four modes of computing, i.e., reversible and deterministic (RD), irreversible and deterministic (ID), reversible and nondeterministic (RN), and irreversible and nondeterministic (IN) modes. We study how computational power varies depending on these modes.

Bennett [1] showed that for any one-tape IDTM there is a three-tape RDTM that simulates the former (see Theorem 5.1). If the IDTM runs in time T and space S, then the RDTM runs in $O(T)$ with space $O(c^S)$ for some constant $c > 1$. Hence, it uses a large space, though the computing time is linear. Bennett [3] also showed that there is an RDTM that simulates a given IDTM, and runs in time $O(T^{1+\varepsilon})$ and space $O(S \log T)$ for any $\varepsilon > 0$, and thus space can be reduced considerably. On the other hand, Lange, McKenzie and Tapp [7] proved that for any IDTM we can construct an RDTM that simulates the former, and runs in time $O(c^S)$ and space $O(S)$. From these results, we can observe there is a trade-off between time and space when simulating an IDTM by an RDTM.

As for the relation between INTM and RDTM, Crescenzi and Papadimitriou [4] first showed the following result: For any INTM that runs in space S there is an RDTM that simulates it and runs in space $O(S^2)$. Since it was later shown that an IDTM with space S can be simulated by an RDTM with space $O(S)$ as stated above [7], this relation can also be derived from it and the result of Savitch [14] that an INTM with space S can be simulated by an IDTM with space $O(S^2)$.

In this chapter, we investigate the language accepting capabilities of four kinds of space-bounded TMs. Here, we define these TMs as an acceptor of languages, i.e., TMs that give only yes/no answers, for simplicity. However, it is also possible to define them as transducers, i.e., TMs that compute recursive functions, and to derive similar results. We first show a simple method for proving the equivalence of IDTMs and RDTMs with the same space function. By this, we can prove a slightly stronger result than in [7]. Namely, an IDTM can be simulated by an RDTM that uses exactly the same numbers of storage tape symbols and storage tape squares (Sect. 8.2). We then show that an RNTM that satisfies some condition can be simulated by an RDTM with the same space function using a similar technique as above (Sect. 8.3). Hence, IDTMs, RNTMs, and RDTMs with the same space function are equivalent in their language accepting capabilities.

8.1.1 Two-tape Turing machine as an acceptor of a language

We define a space-bounded TM as an acceptor of a formal language. It has two tapes as shown in Fig. 8.1. The first one is a read-only input tape, and the second one is a storage tape. An input string is given on the first tape. The storage tape is used as an auxiliary memory of the TM, and the memory space is measured by the number of squares used in a computing process. Here, we employ the quadruple formulation to define two-tape TMs, since inverse quadruples for a backward computation are easily obtained from given quadruples in this formulation. In the reversible TMs given in Theorems 8.2 and 8.3, a forward simulation and a backward simulation are very frequently switched. The quadruple formulation is suited for managing it.

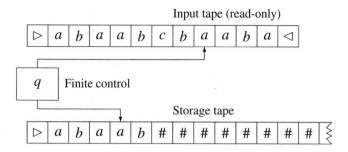

Fig. 8.1 A two-tape Turing machine as an acceptor of a language

Definition 8.1. A *two-tape Turing machine* (TM) as an *acceptor* of language consists of a finite control with two heads, a read-only input tape, and a one-way infinite storage tape, as shown in Fig. 8.1. It is defined by

$$T = (Q, \Sigma, \Gamma, \delta, \triangleright, \triangleleft, q_0, \#, A, N).$$

Here, Q is a nonempty finite set of states, Σ and Γ are nonempty finite sets of input symbols and storage tape symbols. The symbols $\triangleright$ and $\triangleleft$ are left and right endmarkers such that $\{\triangleright, \triangleleft\} \cap (\Sigma \cup \Gamma) = \emptyset$, where only $\triangleright$ is used for the storage tape. The state $q_0 (\in Q)$ is the *initial state*, $\#(\notin \Gamma)$ is a *blank symbol* of the storage tape, $A (\subset Q)$ and $N (\subset Q)$ are sets of *accepting states* and *non-accepting states* such that $A \cap N = \emptyset$. The item δ is a subset of $(Q \times (((\Sigma \cup \{\triangleright, \triangleleft\}) \times (\Gamma \cup \{\triangleright, \#\})^2) \cup \{-1, 0, +1\}^2) \times Q)$ that determines the transition relation on T's computational configurations. Note that $-1, 0$, and $+1$ stand for left-shift, no-shift, and right-shift of each head, respectively. As in Definition 5.1, we also use $-$ and $+$ instead of -1 and $+1$ for simplicity. Each element $r = [p, x, y, q] \in \delta$ is called a *rule* in the quadruple form of T, where $(x, y) = (a, (b, c)) \in ((\Sigma \cup \{\triangleright, \triangleleft\}) \times (\Gamma \cup \{\triangleright, \#\})^2)$ or $(x, y) = (d_i, d_s) \in \{-, 0, +\}^2$. A rule of the form $[p, a, [b, c], q]$ is called a *read-write rule* or a *read-write quadruple*, and means if T is in the state p and reads an input symbol a and a storage tape symbol b, then rewrites b to c and enters the state q. Here, the left endmarker $\triangleright$ of the storage tape should not be rewritten to any other symbol. A rule of the form $[p, d_i, d_s, q]$ is called a *shift rule* or a *shift quadruple*, and means if T is in the state p, then shifts the input head and the storage tape head to the directions d_i and d_s, and enters the state q. We assume each $q_h \in A \cup N$ is a *halting state*, i.e., there is no rule of the form $[q_h, x, y, p]$ in δ.

To denote a computational configuration of a two-tape TM, we use the following expression as an instantaneous description (ID). Let $w \in \Sigma^*$, $q \in Q$, $v \in (\Gamma \cup \{\#\})^*$, $h_i \in \{0, \ldots, |w| + 1\}$, and $h_s \in \{0, 1, \ldots, |v|\}$. An expression $(\triangleright w \triangleleft, \triangleright v, q, h_i, h_s)$ is called an *instantaneous description* (ID) of T with an input w, where $\triangleright v$ is an initial segment of the storage tape such that the remaining part of the tape contains only $\#$'s. The integers h_i and h_s indicate the positions of the input head and the storage tape head, where the position of $\triangleright$ is 0. Since the storage tape contains infinitely many #'s, we employ the following restriction on v to suppress unnecessary #'s: $v \in (\Gamma \cup \{\#\})^* \Gamma \vee |v| = h_s$, i.e., either the rightmost symbol of v is non-blank, or the length of v is equal to h_s.

Let S be a set of symbols. We define a partial function $s : S^+ \times \mathbb{N} \to S$ as follows, where $\mathbb{N}$ is the set of all non-negative integers. If $x = x_0 x_1 \cdots x_{n-1}$ ($x_i \in S$), then $s(x, j) = x_j$ for $j \in \{0, \ldots n-1\}$, and $s(x, j)$ is undefined for $j > n - 1$. Hence, $s(x, j)$ gives the j-th symbol of x, where the leftmost symbol is the 0-th.

We define the *transition relation* $\vdash_{T}$ between a pair of IDs $(\triangleright w \triangleleft, \triangleright v, q, h_i, h_s)$ and $(\triangleright w \triangleleft, \triangleright v', q', h_i', h_s')$ as follows.

$$(\triangleright w \triangleleft, \triangleright v, q, h_i, h_s) \vdash_{T} (\triangleright w \triangleleft, \triangleright v', q', h_i', h_s') \text{ iff (1) or (2) holds.}$$

(1) $[q, s(\triangleright w \triangleleft, h_i), [s(\triangleright v, h_s), s(\triangleright v', h_s')], q'] \in \delta \wedge (h_i', h_s') = (h_i, h_s) \wedge$
   $|v'| = |v| \wedge \forall j \, (0 \le j \le |v| \wedge j \ne h_s \Rightarrow s(\triangleright v', j) = s(\triangleright v, j))$
(2) $[q, h_i' - h_i, h_s' - h_s, q'] \in \delta \wedge$
   $(h_s' - h_s = +1 \wedge h_s = |v| \Rightarrow v' = v\#) \wedge$
   $(h_s' - h_s = -1 \wedge h_s = |v| \wedge v = v_1 \# \Rightarrow v' = v_1) \wedge$
   $(h_s' - h_s = 0 \vee h_s < |v| \vee (h_s' - h_s = -1 \wedge v \in (\Gamma \cup \{\#\})^* \Gamma) \Rightarrow v' = v)$

Note that (1) is for a read-write rule, and (2) is for a shift rule. The transitive closure, and the reflexive and transitive closure of the relation $\vdash_{T}$ is denoted by $\vdash_{T}^{+}$ and $\vdash_{T}^{*}$, respectively. When T is clear from the context, we use $\vdash$ instead of $\vdash_{T}$. An ID $(\triangleright w \triangleleft, \triangleright, q_0, 0, 0)$ is called an *initial ID* with an input $w \in \Sigma^*$. An ID C is called a *halting ID* if there is no ID C' such that $C \vdash C'$.

We say an input w is *accepted* by T if $(\triangleright w \triangleleft, \triangleright, q_0, 0, 0) \vdash_{T}^{*} (\triangleright w \triangleleft, \triangleright v, q, h_i, h_s)$ for some $q \in A$, $v \in (\Gamma \cup \{\#\})^*$, $h_i \in \{0, \ldots, |w| + 1\}$, and $h_s \in \{0, \ldots, |v|\}$. The *language accepted by* T is the set of all strings accepted by T, and denoted by $L(T)$.

$$L(T) = \{w \in \Sigma^* \mid (\triangleright w \triangleleft, \triangleright, q_0, 0, 0) \vdash_{T}^{*} (\triangleright w \triangleleft, \triangleright v, q, h_i, h_s) \text{ for some } q \in A,$$
$$v \in (\Gamma \cup \{\#\})^*, h_i \in \{0, \ldots, |w| + 1\}, \text{ and } h_s \in \{0, \ldots, |v|\}\}$$

Though the set N of non-accepting states is not used in the definition of acceptance, it is convenient to specify it for the later construction of reversible TMs.

8.1.2 Reversibility and determinism

Reversibility and determinism are defined essentially in the same way as in the case of one-tape TMs in the quadruple form (Definition 5.3), though they are slightly more complex here.

Definition 8.2. A TM $T = (Q, \Sigma, \Gamma, \delta, \triangleright, \triangleleft, q_0, \#, A, N)$ is called *deterministic*, if the following condition holds for any pair of distinct quadruples $[p, x, y, q]$ and $[p', x', y', q']$ in δ.

$$(p = p') \Rightarrow ((x,y) \notin \{-,0,+\}^2 \wedge (x',y') \notin \{-,0,+\}^2 \wedge$$
$$\forall b,c,b',c' \in \Gamma \cup \{\triangleright,\#\}(y = (b,c) \wedge y' = (b',c') \Rightarrow (x,b) \neq (x',b')))$$

It means that for any pair of distinct rules in δ, if the present states p and p' are the same, then they are both read-write rules, and the combinations of read symbols (x,b) and (x',b') are different (i.e., $x \neq x'$ or $b \neq b'$).

Definition 8.3. A TM $T = (Q,\Sigma,\Gamma,\delta,\triangleright,\triangleleft,q_0,\#,A,N)$ is called *reversible* if the following holds for any pair of distinct quadruples $[p,x,y,q]$ and $[p',x',y',q']$ in δ.

$$(q = q') \Rightarrow ((x,y) \notin \{-,0,+\}^2 \wedge (x',y') \notin \{-,0,+\}^2 \wedge$$
$$\forall b,c,b',c' \in \Gamma \cup \{\triangleright,\#\}(y = (b,c) \wedge y' = (b',c') \Rightarrow (x,c) \neq (x',c')))$$

It means that for any pair of distinct rules in δ, if the next states q and q' are the same, then they are both read-write rules and the combinations of the read input symbol and the written storage symbol (x,c) and (x',c') are different. The above condition is called a *reversibility condition* for two-tape TMs in the quadruple form.

From the Definition 8.2, it is easy to show that if T is deterministic, then for every ID C of T there is at most one ID C' such that $C \vdash_T C'$. Likewise, from the Definition 8.3, if T is reversible, then for every ID C of T there is at most one ID C' such that $C' \vdash_T C$. They are similarly proved as in Lemma 5.1 for the case of one-tape TMs.

A TM given in Definition 8.1 is generally *irreversible* and *nondeterministic* in the sense it does not necessarily satisfy the conditions in Definitions 8.2 and 8.3. Therefore, we use the notation INTM (irreversible nondeterministic TM) to denote a general TM according to the usual convention. Namely, the class of INTMs contains all TMs. Likewise, a reversible TM that is not necessarily deterministic is denoted by RNTM (reversible nondeterministic TM), and a deterministic TM that is not necessarily reversible is by IDTM (irreversible deterministic TM). A reversible and deterministic TM is denoted by RDTM. See Fig. 8.2 on their relations. Note that, commonly, an INTM and an IDTM are called a nondeterministic TM (NTM) and a deterministic TM (DTM), respectively (see, e.g., [5]).

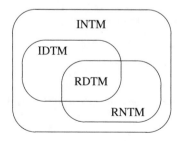

Fig. 8.2 Classes of INTM, IDTM, RNTM, and RDTM

8.1.3 Computation graph

We now define a *computation graph* of T with an input $w \in \Sigma^*$.

Definition 8.4. Let $T = (Q, \Sigma, \Gamma, \delta, \rhd, \lhd, q_0, \#, A, N)$ be a TM, and $w \in \Sigma^*$ be an input string. A *computation graph* $G_{T,w} = (V, E)$ of T with w is defined as follows. Let $\mathrm{ID}(T, w)$ be the set of all IDs of T with w, i.e.,

$$\mathrm{ID}(T,w) = \{ (\rhd w \lhd, \rhd v, q, h_i, h_s) \mid v \in (\Gamma \cup \{\#\})^* \land q \in Q \land$$
$$h_i \in \{0, \ldots, |w| + 1\} \land h_s \in \{0, \ldots, |v|\} \}.$$

The set $V (\subset \mathrm{ID}(T, w))$ of nodes is the smallest set that contains the initial ID $(\rhd w \lhd, \rhd, q_0, 0, 0)$, and satisfies the following condition:

$$\forall C_1, C_2 \in \mathrm{ID}(T, w) ((C_1 \in V \land (C_1 \mathop{\vert\!\!\!-}_T C_2 \lor C_2 \mathop{\vert\!\!\!-}_T C_1)) \Rightarrow C_2 \in V).$$

Namely, V is the set of all IDs connected to the initial ID. The set E of directed edges is: $E = \{ (C_1, C_2) \mid C_1, C_2 \in V \land C_1 \mathop{\vert\!\!\!-}_T C_2 \}$.

If T is deterministic, then outdegree of each node in V is either 0 or 1, where a node of outdegree 0 is a halting ID. On the other hand, if T is reversible, then indegree of each node in V is either 0 or 1. Figure 8.3 shows examples of computation graphs of INTM, IDTM, RNTM, and RDTM.

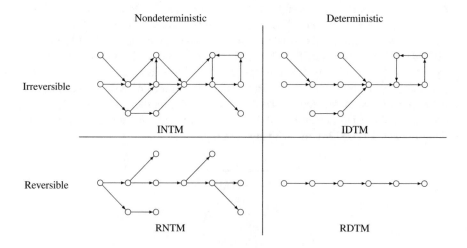

Fig. 8.3 Examples of computation graphs of INTM, IDTM, RNTM, and RDTM

8.1.4 Space-bounded TMs

Let $T = (Q, \Sigma, \Gamma, \delta, \triangleright, \triangleleft, q_0, \#, A, N)$ be a TM. We say T with $w \in \Sigma^*$ uses *bounded amount of the storage tape* if the following holds.

$$\exists m \in \mathbb{N}, \forall v \in (\Gamma \cup \{\#\})^*, \forall q \in Q, \forall h_i \in \{0, \ldots, |w|+1\}, \forall h_s \in \{0, \ldots, |v|\}$$
$$((\triangleright w \triangleleft, \triangleright, q_0, 0, 0) \vdash_T^* (\triangleright w \triangleleft, \triangleright v, q, h_i, h_s) \Rightarrow h_s \leq m)$$

It means that the number of squares of the storage tape used by T is bounded by some natural number m. Otherwise, we say T with w uses *unbounded amount of the storage tape*. Of course, if T with w eventually halts, then it uses bounded amount of the storage tape.

We now define a space-bounded TM.

Definition 8.5. Let $S : \mathbb{N} \to \mathbb{N}$ be a total function, which is called a *space function*. A TM $T = (Q, \Sigma, \Gamma, \delta, \triangleright, \triangleleft, q_0, \#, A, N)$ is called an $S(n)$-*space-bounded TM* (abbreviated by TM($S(n)$)) iff the following holds.

$$\forall w \in \Sigma^*, \forall v \in (\Gamma \cup \{\#\})^*, \forall q \in Q, \forall h_i \in \{0, \ldots, |w|+1\}, \forall h_s \in \{0, \ldots, |v|\}$$
$$((\triangleright w \triangleleft, \triangleright, q_0, 0, 0) \vdash_T^* (\triangleright w \triangleleft, \triangleright v, q, h_i, h_s) \Rightarrow h_s \leq S(|w|))$$

It means that T with w uses at most $S(|w|)$ squares of the storage tape in any computing process for any input w.

From the above definition, it is clear that if T is an $S(n)$-space-bounded TM, then T with $w \in \Sigma^*$ uses bounded amount of the storage tape for any w.

An $S(n)$-space-bounded INTM (or IDTM, RNTM, RDTM, respectively) is denoted by INTM($S(n)$) (or IDTM($S(n)$), RNTM($S(n)$), RDTM($S(n)$)). The *class of languages* accepted by the class of INTM (or INTM($S(n)$), respectively) is denoted by $\mathscr{L}$(INTM) (or $\mathscr{L}$(INTM($S(n)$))). Namely, $\mathscr{L}$(INTM) $= \{L \mid L$ is accepted by some INTM $T\}$. Similar notations are used for other classes of TMs and space-bounded TMs.

8.1.5 Normal forms for TMs

Here, we give several kinds of *normal forms* for TMs. Namely, we consider TMs that satisfy several conditions described below that are useful for showing the theorems and lemmas in the following sections. There are five conditions (C1) – (C5). We shall see that if a given TM $T = (Q, \Sigma, \Gamma, \delta, \triangleright, \triangleleft, q_0, \#, A, N)$ is an IDTM, then it can be easily converted into an equivalent TM that satisfies (C1) – (C5), and the obtained TM is again an IDTM (Lemma 8.1). This result will be used for proving Theorem 8.2. On the other hand, if a given TM is an RNTM (or RDTM), it is sometimes not easy to convert it into a normal form keeping its reversibility. However, as will be shown in Lemma 8.2 we can convert an RNTM into an equivalent RNTM that satisfies (C2) and (C3). It will be used for proving Theorem. 8.3.

(C1)   The initial state q_0 appears only in the initial ID, i.e., it does not appear as the fourth component of a rule in δ:

$$\forall [q,x,y,q'] \in \delta \ (q' \neq q_0)$$

(C2)   The TM T performs read-write and shift operations alternately. Hence, Q is written as $Q = Q_{rw} \cup Q_{sf}$ for some Q_{rw} and Q_{sf} such that $Q_{rw} \cap Q_{sf} = \emptyset$, and δ satisfies the following condition:

$$\forall [p,x,y,q] \in \delta$$
$$(((x,y) \in (\Sigma \cup \{\triangleright,\triangleleft\}) \times (\Gamma \cup \{\triangleright,\#\})^2 \ \Rightarrow \ p \in Q_{rw} \wedge q \in Q_{sf}) \wedge$$
$$((x,y) \in \{-,0,+\}^2 \ \Rightarrow \ p \in Q_{sf} \wedge q \in Q_{rw}))$$

Each element of Q_{rw} and Q_{sf} is called a *read-write state* and a *shift state*, respectively. We further assume $q_0 \in Q_{rw}$, and $A \cup N \subset Q_{sf}$, though each state in $A \cup N$ is a halting state.

(C3)   The heads of T must not go beyond the left and right endmarkers in a forward computation, and hence T does not go to an illegal ID:

$$\forall p,r \in Q_{rw}, \ \forall q \in Q_{sf},$$
$$\forall (a,(b,c)) \in (\Sigma \cup \{\triangleright,\triangleleft\}) \times (\Gamma \cup \{\triangleright,\#\})^2, \ \forall (d_i,d_s) \in \{-,0,+\}^2$$
$$([p,a,[b,c],q],[q,d_i,d_s,r] \in \delta \ \Rightarrow$$
$$(a=\triangleright \Rightarrow d_i \in \{0,+\}) \wedge (a=\triangleleft \Rightarrow d_i \in \{-,0\}) \wedge (b=\triangleright \Rightarrow d_s \in \{0,+\}))$$

Likewise, T must satisfy a similar condition in a backward computation, and hence T does not come from an illegal ID:

$$\forall p,r \in Q_{sf}, \ \forall q \in Q_{rw},$$
$$\forall (a,(b,c)) \in (\Sigma \cup \{\triangleright,\triangleleft\}) \times (\Gamma \cup \{\triangleright,\#\})^2, \ \forall (d_i,d_s) \in \{-,0,+\}^2$$
$$([r,d_i,d_s,q],[q,a,[b,c],p] \in \delta \ \Rightarrow$$
$$(a=\triangleright \Rightarrow d_i \in \{-,0\}) \wedge (a=\triangleleft \Rightarrow d_i \in \{0,+\}) \wedge (b=\triangleright \Rightarrow d_s \in \{-,0\}))$$

By this, we can deal with computation graphs that have only legal IDs.

(C4)   The TM T never erases a non-blank symbol of the storage tape. Furthermore, T does not read a blank symbol $\#$ other than the leftmost one in each ID. Namely, the following holds:

$$\forall p,r \in Q_{rw}, \ \forall q \in Q_{sf},$$
$$\forall (a,(b,c)) \in (\Sigma \cup \{\triangleright,\triangleleft\}) \times (\Gamma \cup \{\triangleright,\#\})^2, \ \forall (d_i,d_s) \in \{-,0,+\}^2$$
$$(([p,a,[b,c],q],[q,d_i,d_s,r] \in \delta \ \wedge \ c=\#) \ \Rightarrow \ (b=\# \wedge d_s \in \{-,0\}))$$

(C5)   The TM T satisfies the following condition under the assumption of (C4). It first confirms the storage tape square of the position 1 contains the blank symbol $\#$ just after starting from q_0. Furthermore, each time T rewrites $\#$ into a non-$\#$ symbol it confirms the right-neighboring symbol is $\#$. Namely, if T with an input w uses m squares of the storage tape, then T checks if these m squares initially contain $\#$'s. Note that, since T starts from $(\triangleright w \triangleleft, \triangleright, q_0, 0, 0)$, where all the squares of the storage tape except the leftmost one contain #'s, one may think this condition is useless. However, as we shall see in the proof of Theorem 8.2, it is for inhibiting the case where both IDs $(\triangleright w \triangleleft, \triangleright, q_0, 0, 0)$ and $(\triangleright w \triangleleft, \triangleright v, q_0, 0, 0)$ such that $v \in (\Gamma \cup \{\#\})^* \Gamma$ go to the same accepting ID (see also Example 8.2).

As shown in the next lemma, it is easy to convert a given IDTM into an equivalent IDTM so that it satisfies the conditions (C1) – (C5).

Lemma 8.1. *For any IDTM* $T = (Q, \Sigma, \Gamma, \delta, \triangleright, \triangleleft, q_0, \#, A, N)$, *there is an IDTM* $\tilde{T} = (\tilde{Q}, \Sigma, \tilde{\Gamma}, \tilde{\delta}, \triangleright, \triangleleft, \tilde{q}_0, \#, A, N)$ *that satisfies (C1) – (C5),* $L(T) = L(\tilde{T})$, *and* $|\tilde{\Gamma}| \leq |\Gamma| + 1$. *Furthermore, for any* $w \in \Sigma^*$, *if* T *with* w *uses* m *squares of the storage tape, then* $\tilde{T}$ *uses at most* $m + 1$ *squares of the storage tape.*

Proof. In the following, for each condition (Ci) ($i \in \{1, \ldots, 5\}$), we give a procedure for converting T into $\tilde{T}$ that satisfies (Ci). If T does not satisfy the condition (Ci), then first set $\tilde{Q} := Q$, $\tilde{\Gamma} := \Gamma$, $\tilde{\delta} := \delta$ and $\tilde{q}_0 := q_0$, and apply the "Procedure for (Ci)" to obtain $\tilde{T}$. Note that, when we apply the "Procedure for (Ci)", we assume T satisfies the conditions (Cj) for all $j \in \{1, \ldots, i-1\}$.

Procedure for (C1):   First, add the new state q_0' to $\tilde{Q}$, and set it as the initial state of $\tilde{T}$, i.e., $\tilde{q}_0 := q_0'$. Next, if there is a shift rule $[q_0, d_i, d_s, q] \in \tilde{\delta}$, then add $[q_0', d_i, d_s, q]$ to $\tilde{\delta}$. If there is a read-write rule $[q_0, \triangleright, [\triangleright, \triangleright], q] \in \tilde{\delta}$, then add $[q_0', \triangleright, [\triangleright, \triangleright], q]$ to $\tilde{\delta}$. Note that, since T is deterministic, only one of $[q_0', d_i, d_s, q]$ or $[q_0', \triangleright, [\triangleright, \triangleright], q]$ is in $\tilde{\delta}$.

Procedure for (C2):   (1) For each pair of shift rules $[p, d_i, d_s, q]$ and $[q, d_i', d_s', r]$ in $\tilde{\delta}$, add the new state q' that does not appear elsewhere in $\tilde{Q}$, and replace $[p, d_i, d_s, q]$ by the new rules $[p, d_i, d_s, q']$ and $[q', a, [b, b], q]$ for all $a \in \Sigma \cup \{\triangleright, \triangleleft\}$ and $b \in \Gamma \cup \{\triangleright, \#\}$. (2) For each pair of read-write rules $[p, a, [b, c], q]$ and $[q, a', [b', c'], r]$ in $\tilde{\delta}$, add the new state q' in $\tilde{Q}$, and replace $[p, a, [b, c], q]$ by the new rules $[p, a, [b, c], q']$ and $[q', 0, 0, q]$. As for the initial state, and the states in $A \cup N$, we do the following. (3) If q_0 is the initial state and there is a shift rule $[q_0, d_i, d_s, q]$, then add the new state q_0' to $\tilde{Q}$, set q_0' as the new initial state, and add the rule $[q_0', \triangleright, [\triangleright, \triangleright], q_0]$ to $\tilde{\delta}$. (4) For each shift rule $[p, d_i, d_s, q]$ in $\tilde{\delta}$ such that $q \in A \cup N$, add the new state q' to $\tilde{Q}$, and replace $[p, d_i, d_s, q]$ by the rules $[p, d_i, d_s, q']$ and $[q', a, [b, b], q]$ for all $a \in \Sigma \cup \{\triangleright, \triangleleft\}$ and $b \in \Gamma \cup \{\triangleright, \#\}$. By above, we can obtain Q_{rw} and Q_{sf} such that $Q = Q_{rw} \cup Q_{sf}$, $Q_{rw} \cap Q_{sf} = \emptyset$, $\tilde{q}_0 \in Q_{rw}$, and $A \cup N \subset Q_{sf}$.

Procedure for (C3):   (1) For each $q \in Q_{sf} - (A \cup N)$ execute the following. Let $[p_1, a_1, [b_1, c_1], q], \ldots, [p_m, a_m, [b_m, c_m], q]$ be all the read-write rules in $\tilde{\delta}$ whose fourth elements are q, and $[q, d, d', r]$ be the shift rule in $\tilde{\delta}$ whose first element is q. Note that, there is at most one such shift rule, since T is deterministic. For each $i \in \{1, \ldots, m\}$, if the pair $[p_i, a_i, [b_i, c_i], q]$ and $[q, d, d', r]$ violates the first condition in (C3), then remove $[p_i, a_i, [b_i, c_i], q]$ from $\tilde{\delta}$, since it makes T go to an illegal ID. (2) For each $q \in Q_{rw} - \{q_0\}$ do the following. Let $[p_1, d_1, d_1', q], \ldots, [p_m, d_m, d_m', q]$ be all the shift rules in $\tilde{\delta}$ whose fourth elements are q, and $[q, a_1, [b_1, c_1], r_1], \ldots, [q, a_n, [b_n, c_n], r_n]$ be all the read-write rules in $\tilde{\delta}$

whose first elements are q. Add the new states $q_1, \ldots, q_m$ that do not appear else-where to $\tilde{Q}$. For each $i \in \{1, \ldots, m\}$ replace the rule $[p_i, d_i, d_i', q]$ in $\tilde{\delta}$ by the rule $[p_i, d_i, d_i', q_i]$, and for each $j \in \{1, \ldots, n\}$ replace the rule $[q, a_j, [b_j, c_j], r_j]$ in $\tilde{\delta}$ by the m rules $[q_1, a_j, [b_j, c_j], r_j], \ldots, [q_m, a_j, [b_j, c_j], r_j]$. This modification does not change the language accepted by $\tilde{T}$, and it is still deterministic. Then, for each $i \in \{1, \ldots, m\}$ and $j \in \{1, \ldots, n\}$, if the pair $[p_i, d_i, d_i', q_i]$ and $[q_i, a_j, [b_j, c_j], r_j]$ vi-olates the second condition in (C3), then remove $[q_i, a_j, [b_j, c_j], r_j]$ from $\tilde{\delta}$, since it makes T go back to an illegal ID.

Procedure for (C4):   First, add a new non-blank symbol #′ to $\tilde{\Gamma}$, which simulates the role of the blank symbol #. Replace each rule $[p, a, [b, \#], q] \in \tilde{\delta}$ such that $b \in \Gamma$ by the rule $[p, a, [b, \#'], q]$. For each pair of rules $[p, a, [\#, \#], q]$ and $[q, d_i, +, r]$ in $\tilde{\delta}$, replace $[p, a, [\#, \#], q]$ by the rule $[p, a, [\#, \#'], q]$. For each rule $[p, a, [\#, c], q] \in \tilde{\delta}$ such that $c \in \Gamma$, add $[p, a, [\#', c], q]$ to $\tilde{\delta}$. For each rule $[p, a, [\#, \#], q] \in \tilde{\delta}$, add $[p, a, [\#', \#'], q]$ to $\tilde{\delta}$.

Procedure for (C5):   First, add the new states $p_1, \ldots, p_4$ that do not appear else-where to $\tilde{Q}$, and replace the rule $[q_0, \triangleright, [\triangleright, \triangleright], p] \in \tilde{\delta}$ by the following rules.

$$[q_0, \triangleright, [\triangleright, \triangleright], p_1], [p_1, 0, +, p_2], [p_2, \triangleright, [\#, \#], p_3], [p_3, 0, -, p_4], [p_4, \triangleright, [\triangleright, \triangleright], p]$$

Next, for each rule $[q, a, [\#, b], r] \in \tilde{\delta}$ such that $b \in \Gamma$, add the new states $p_1', \ldots, p_4'$ that do not appear elsewhere to $\tilde{Q}$, and replace the rule $[q, a, [\#, b], r]$ by the fol-lowing rules.

$$[q, a, [\#, b], p_1'], [p_1', 0, +, p_2'], [p_2', a, [\#, \#], p_3'], [p_3', 0, -, p_4'], [p_4', a, [b, b], r]$$

It is easy to see that the resulting $\tilde{T}$ satisfies $L(T) = L(\tilde{T})$, since $\tilde{T}$ simulates T in a straightforward manner. A new non-blank symbol #′ is added to $\tilde{\Gamma}$ only when T does not satisfy (C4). Hence, $|\tilde{\Gamma}| \leq |\Gamma| + 1$ holds. If the Procedure for (C5) is applied, then $\tilde{T}$ may scan one more storage tape square than T. Thus, for any $w \in \Sigma^*$, if T with w uses m squares of the storage tape, then $\tilde{T}$ uses at most $m + 1$ squares.   □

The following lemma shows that for any RNTM there is an equivalent RNTM that satisfies (C2) and (C3).

Lemma 8.2. *For any RNTM $T = (Q, \Sigma, \Gamma, \delta, \triangleright, \triangleleft, q_0, \#, A, N)$, there is an RNTM $\tilde{T} = (\tilde{Q}, \Sigma, \Gamma, \tilde{\delta}, \triangleright, \triangleleft, \tilde{q}_0, \#, A, N)$ that satisfies (C2), (C3), and $L(T) = L(\tilde{T})$. Fur-thermore, for any $w \in \Sigma^*$, if T with w uses m squares of the storage tape, then $\tilde{T}$ also uses m squares of the storage tape.*

Proof. For each of the conditions (C2) and (C3), we give a procedure for converting T into $\tilde{T}$. As in the proof of Lemma 8.1, if T does not satisfy the condition (C2) (or (C3), respectively) then set $\tilde{Q} := Q$, $\tilde{\Gamma} := \Gamma$, $\tilde{\delta} := \delta$ and $\tilde{q}_0 := q_0$, and apply the Procedure for (C2) (or (C3)) to obtain $\tilde{T}$.

Procedure for (C2):   (1) For each $p \in Q$, if there are shift rules $[p, d_1, d_1', q_1], \ldots,$ $[p, d_m, d_m', q_m]$ and read-write rules $[p, a_1, [b_1, c_1], r_1], \ldots, [p, a_n, [b_n, c_n], r_n]$ in $\tilde{\delta}$, then do the following. Add the state p' that does not appear elsewhere to

$\tilde{Q}$, add $[p,0,0,p']$ to $\tilde{\delta}$, and replace $[p,a_1,[b_1,c_1],r_1],\ldots,[p,a_n,[b_n,c_n],r_n]$ in $\tilde{\delta}$ by $[p',a_1,[b_1,c_1],r_1],\ldots,[p',a_n,[b_n,c_n],r_n]$. (2) For each pair of shift rules $[p,d_{\rm i},d_{\rm s},q]$ and $[q,d_{\rm i}',d_{\rm s}',r]$ in $\tilde{\delta}$, add the new state q' in $\tilde{Q}$, and replace $[p,d_{\rm i},d_{\rm s},q]$ by the new rules $[p,d_{\rm i},d_{\rm s},q']$ and $[q',a,[b,b],q]$ for all $a \in \Sigma \cup \{\triangleright,\triangleleft\}$ and $b \in \Gamma \cup \{\triangleright,\#\}$. (3) For each pair of read-write rules $[p,a,[b,c],q]$ and $[q,a',[b',c'],r]$ in $\tilde{\delta}$, add the new state q' in $\tilde{Q}$, and replace $[p,a,[b,c],q]$ by the new rules $[p,a,[b,c],q']$ and $[q',0,0,q]$. (4) If q_0 is the initial state and there is a shift rule $[q_0,d_{\rm i},d_{\rm s},q]$, then add the new state q_0' to $\tilde{Q}$, set q_0' as the new initial state, and add the rule $[q_0',\triangleright,[\triangleright,\triangleright],q_0]$ to $\tilde{\delta}$. (5) For each shift rule $[p,d_{\rm i},d_{\rm s},q]$ in $\tilde{\delta}$ such that $q \in A \cup N$, add the new state q' to $\tilde{Q}$, and replace $[p,d_{\rm i},d_{\rm s},q]$ by $[p,d_{\rm i},d_{\rm s},q']$ and $[q',a,[b,b],q]$ for all $a \in \Sigma \cup \{\triangleright,\triangleleft\}$ and $b \in \Gamma \cup \{\triangleright,\#\}$. All the above modifications (1)–(5) keep reversibility of $\tilde{T}$, since the newly added states appear nowhere else. By above, we obtain $Q_{\rm rw}$ and $Q_{\rm sf}$ such that $Q = Q_{\rm rw} \cup Q_{\rm sf}$, $Q_{\rm rw} \cap Q_{\rm sf} = \emptyset$, $\tilde{q}_0 \in Q_{\rm rw}$, and $A \cup N \subset Q_{\rm sf}$.

Procedure for (C3):   This procedure has a symmetric structure to the corresponding procedure in Lemma 8.1. (1) For each $q \in Q_{\rm sf} - (A \cup N)$ do the following. Let $[p_1,a_1,[b_1,c_1],q],\ldots,[p_m,a_m,[b_m,c_m],q]$ be all the read-write rules in $\tilde{\delta}$ whose fourth elements are q, and $[q,d_1,d_1',r_1],\ldots,[q,d_n,d_n',r_n]$ be all the shift rules in $\tilde{\delta}$ whose first elements are q. Add the new states $q_1,\ldots,q_n$ that do not appear elsewhere to $\tilde{Q}$. For each $i \in \{1,\ldots,m\}$ replace the rule $[p_i,a_i,[b_i,c_i],q]$ in $\tilde{\delta}$ by the n rules $[p_i,a_i,[b_i,c_i],q_1],\ldots,[p_i,a_i,[b_i,c_i],q_n]$, and for each $j \in \{1,\ldots,n\}$ replace the rule $[q,d_j,d_j',r_j]$ in $\tilde{\delta}$ by the rule $[q_j,d_j,d_j',r_j]$. This modification does not change the language accepted by $\tilde{T}$, and it is still reversible. For each $i \in \{1,\ldots,m\}$ and $j \in \{1,\ldots,n\}$, if the pair $[p_i,a_i,[b_i,c_i],q_j]$ and $[q_j,d_j,d_j',r_j]$ violates the first condition in (C3), then remove $[p_i,a_i,[b_i,c_i],q_j]$ from $\tilde{\delta}$, since it makes T go to an illegal ID. (2) For each $q \in Q_{\rm rw}$ do the following. Let $[p,d,d',q]$ be the shift rule in $\tilde{\delta}$ whose fourth element is q, and $[q,a_1,[b_1,c_1],r_1],\ldots,[q,a_n,[b_n,c_n],r_n]$ be all the read-write rules in $\tilde{\delta}$ whose first elements are q. Note that, there is at most one such shift rule, since T is reversible. For each $j \in \{1,\ldots,n\}$, if the pair $[p,d,d',q]$ and $[q,a_j,[b_j,c_j],r_j]$ violates the second condition in (C3), then remove $[q,a_j,[b_j,c_j],r_j]$ from $\tilde{\delta}$, since it makes T go back to an illegal ID.

It is easy to see that $L(T) = L(\tilde{T})$ holds, and $\tilde{T}$ uses the same number of storage tape squares, since $\tilde{T}$ simulates T in a straightforward manner.   □

8.2 Relation Between Irreversible Deterministic and Reversible Deterministic TMs

In this section, we investigate the relation between IDTM and RDTM. Lange, McKenzie and Tapp [7] first showed that any IDTM($S(n)$) can be simulated by an RDTM($S(n)$), and thus the classes of IDTM($S(n)$) and RDTM($S(n)$) are equivalent in their language accepting capability.

Theorem 8.1. *[7] Let $S(n)$ be a space function. For any IDTM($S(n)$) T, there is an RDTM($S(n)$) T' such that $L(T') = L(T)$.*

However, the simulation method given in [7] is rather complex. Morita [9, 10] gave a simpler method where an IDTM is simulated by an RDTM that uses exactly the same numbers of storage tape squares and storage tape symbols, and leaves no garbage information on the storage tape when it halts. Hence, it is a slightly stronger result than Theorem 8.1. In this section, we show this method.

8.2.1 Halting property of reversible space-bounded TMs

We first show the next lemma. It states that an RNTM never loops if it satisfies (C1).

Lemma 8.3. *Let $T = (Q, \Sigma, \Gamma, \delta, \triangleright, \triangleleft, q_0, \#, A, N)$ be an RNTM that satisfies (C1). Then, it never loops for any input, i.e., there is no $w \in \Sigma^*$ and no ID C such that $(\triangleright w \triangleleft, \triangleright, q_0, 0, 0) \vdash^* C \vdash^\pm C$.*

Proof. Let $C_0 \vdash C_1 \vdash C_2 \vdash \cdots$ be a computation of T starting from $C_0 = (\triangleright w \triangleleft, \triangleright, q_0, 0, 0)$. Assume, on the contrary T loops, i.e., there exists a pair of integers (i, j) such that $0 \leq i < j$ and $C_i = C_j$. Let (i_0, j_0) be the pair such that i_0 is the least integer among such (i, j)-pairs. By the condition (C1), there is no ID C_{-1} that satisfies $C_{-1} \vdash C_0$. Hence $C_0 \neq C_{i_0} = C_{j_0}$, and thus $i_0 > 0$. Therefore, $C_{i_0-1} \neq C_{j_0-1}$. But, since $C_{i_0-1} \vdash C_{i_0}$, $C_{j_0-1} \vdash C_{j_0}$, and $C_{i_0} = C_{j_0}$ hold, it contradicts the assumption T is reversible. Therefore, T never loops.   □

If an RNTM or RDTM T does not satisfy (C1), then T may loop. For example, an RDTM T_{loop} with the set of quadruples $\delta_{\text{loop}} = \{[q_0, \triangleright, [\triangleright, \triangleright], q_1], [q_1, 0, 0, q_0]\}$ loops for any input.

Corollary 8.1. *Let T be an RNTM that satisfies (C1). If T with an input $w \in \Sigma^*$ uses bounded amount of the storage tape, then it eventually halts.*

Proof. Assume, on the contrary, T with w does not halt. Then there is an infinite computation process $C_0 \vdash C_1 \vdash C_2 \vdash \cdots$, where $C_0 = (\triangleright w \triangleleft, \triangleright, q_0, 0, 0)$. Since T with w uses bounded amount of the storage tape, there are finitely many IDs reachable from C_0. Thus there are i and j ($0 < i < j$) that satisfy $C_i = C_j$. This contradicts Lemma 8.3, and the corollary is proved.   □

From Corollary 8.1, we immediately obtain the following corollary for $S(n)$-space-bounded RNTMs.

Corollary 8.2. *Let $S(n)$ be a space function, and T be an RNTM($S(n)$) that satisfies (C1). Then, it always halts for any input $w \in \Sigma^*$.*

Note that since an RDTM (or RDTM($S(n)$), respectively) is a subclass of an RNTM (or RNTM($S(n)$)) by definition, Lemma 8.3, Corollaries 8.1 and 8.2 also hold for RDTM (or RDTM($S(n)$)).

8.2.2 Space-efficient reversible simulation of irreversible TMs

We show that an IDTM can be simulated by an RDTM using exactly the same numbers of storage tape squares and the tape symbols, though the computing time may become an exponential function of the amount of the memory space. Here, we assume a given IDTM satisfies the conditions (C1) – (C5). If otherwise, we can convert it by the method given in Lemma 8.1. Note that, if it violates the condition (C4), then one more storage tape symbol should be added. Likewise, if it violates (C5), then one more storage tape square may be used. Hence, in these cases the number of storage tape symbols or squares increases by one. Here, the RDTM is so constructed that it traverses the computation graph of the IDTM in a simple way.

Theorem 8.2. *[9, 10] Let $T = (Q, \Sigma, \Gamma, \delta, \triangleright, \triangleleft, q_0, \#, A, N)$ be an IDTM. We can construct an RDTM $T^\dagger = (Q^\dagger, \Sigma, \Gamma, \delta^\dagger, \triangleright, \triangleleft, q_0, \#, \{\hat{q}_0^1\}, \{q_0^1\})$ such that the following holds.*

$$\forall w \in \Sigma^* \ (w \in L(T) \Rightarrow (\triangleright w \triangleleft, \triangleright, q_0, 0, 0) \ \underset{T^\dagger}{\overset{\pm}{\vdash}} \ (\triangleright w \triangleleft, \triangleright, \hat{q}_0^1, 0, 0))$$

$$\forall w \in \Sigma^* \ (w \notin L(T) \wedge T \text{ with } w \text{ uses bounded amount of the storage tape}$$
$$\Rightarrow (\triangleright w \triangleleft, \triangleright, q_0, 0, 0) \ \underset{T^\dagger}{\overset{\pm}{\vdash}} \ (\triangleright w \triangleleft, \triangleright, q_0^1, 0, 0))$$

$$\forall w \in \Sigma^* \ (w \notin L(T) \wedge T \text{ with } w \text{ uses unbounded amount of the storage tape}$$
$$\Rightarrow T^\dagger\text{'s computation starting from } (\triangleright w \triangleleft, \triangleright, q_0, 0, 0) \text{ does not halt})$$

Hence $L(T^\dagger) = L(T)$. Furthermore, if T uses at most m squares of the storage tape for an input w, then $T^\dagger$ with w also uses at most m squares in any of its ID in its computing process.

Proof. By Lemma 8.1 we can assume T satisfies the conditions (C1) – (C5) (but, note that the constructed RDTM $T^\dagger$ does not satisfy (C2) and (C4)). In our construction, $T^\dagger$ traverses the computation graph $G_{T,w}$ from the initial ID to find an accepting one. We first define five functions

$$\begin{aligned}
&\text{prev-rw} : Q_{\text{rw}} \to 2^{Q_{\text{sf}} \times \{-, 0, +\}^2}, \\
&\text{prev-sf} : Q_{\text{sf}} \times (\Sigma \cup \{\triangleright, \triangleleft\}) \times (\Gamma \cup \{\triangleright, \#\}) \to 2^{Q_{\text{rw}} \times (\Gamma \cup \{\triangleright, \#\})}, \\
&\text{deg}_{\text{rw}} : Q_{\text{rw}} \to \mathbb{N}, \\
&\text{deg}_{\text{sf}} : Q_{\text{sf}} \times (\Sigma \cup \{\triangleright, \triangleleft\}) \times (\Gamma \cup \{\triangleright, \#\}) \to \mathbb{N}, \text{ and} \\
&\text{deg}_{\text{max}} : Q \to \mathbb{N}
\end{aligned}$$

as follows, where Q_{rw} and Q_{sf} are the sets given in (C2).

$$\begin{aligned}
\text{prev-rw}(q) &= \{[p, d, d'] \mid p \in Q_{\text{sf}} \wedge d, d' \in \{-, 0, +\} \wedge [p, d, d', q] \in \delta\} \\
\text{prev-sf}(q, a, c) &= \{[p, b] \mid p \in Q_{\text{rw}} \wedge b \in (\Gamma \cup \{\triangleright, \#\}) \wedge [p, a, [b, c], q] \in \delta\} \\
\text{deg}_{\text{rw}}(q) &= |\text{prev-rw}(q)| \\
\text{deg}_{\text{sf}}(q, a, c) &= |\text{prev-sf}(q, a, c)| \\
\text{deg}_{\text{max}}(q) &= \begin{cases} \text{deg}_{\text{rw}}(q) & \text{if } q \in Q_{\text{rw}} \\ \max\{\text{deg}_{\text{sf}}(q, a, c) \mid a \in (\Sigma \cup \{\triangleright, \triangleleft\}) \wedge \\ \qquad c \in (\Gamma \cup \{\triangleright, \#\})\} & \text{if } q \in Q_{\text{sf}} \end{cases}
\end{aligned}$$

These functions give the information on the previous states, the previous shift directions, and the previous storage tape symbols for each ID. They are required to traverse a computation graph.

Assume T is in the ID $(\triangleright w \triangleleft, \triangleright v, q, h_i, h_s)$. If q is a read-write state (or shift state, respectively), then $\deg_{rw}(q)$ (or $\deg_{sf}(q, s(\triangleright w \triangleleft, h_i), s(\triangleright v, h_s))$) denotes the total number of previous IDs of $(\triangleright w \triangleleft, \triangleright v, q, h_i, h_s)$. Each element $[p, d, d'] \in$ prev-rw(q) (or $[p, b] \in$ prev-sf$(q, s(\triangleright w \triangleleft, h_i), s(\triangleright v, h_s))$, respectively) gives a previous state and shift directions (or a previous state and a previous storage tape symbol). We further assume the sets Q, $\{-, 0, +\}$, and $\Gamma \cup \{\triangleright, \#\}$ are totally ordered, and thus the elements of the sets prev-rw(q) and prev-sf(q, a, c) are sorted by these orders. Thus, we express prev-rw(q) and prev-sf(q, a, c) by the ordered lists as below.

$$\text{prev-rw}(q) = [[p_1, d_1, d_1'], \ldots, [p_{\deg_{rw}(q)}, d_{\deg_{rw}(q)}, d_{\deg_{rw}(q)}']]$$
$$\text{prev-sf}(q, a, c) = [[p_1, b_1], \ldots, [p_{\deg_{sf}(q,a,c)}, b_{\deg_{sf}(q,a,c)}]]$$

Furthermore, $Q^\dagger$ and $\delta^\dagger$ of $T^\dagger$ are defined as below.

$$Q^\dagger = \{q, \hat{q} \mid q \in Q\} \cup \{q^j, \hat{q}^j \mid q \in Q \wedge j \in (\{1\} \cup \{1, \ldots, \deg_{\max}(q)\})\}$$
$$\delta^\dagger = \delta_1 \cup \cdots \cup \delta_6 \cup \hat{\delta}_1 \cup \cdots \cup \hat{\delta}_5 \cup \delta_A \cup \delta_N$$
$$\delta_1 = \{[p_1, d_1, d_1', q^2], \ldots, [p_{\deg_{rw}(q)-1}, d_{\deg_{rw}(q)-1}, d_{\deg_{rw}(q)-1}', q^{\deg_{rw}(q)}],$$
$$\qquad [p_{\deg_{rw}(q)}, d_{\deg_{rw}(q)}, d_{\deg_{rw}(q)}', q] \mid q \in Q_{rw} \wedge \deg_{rw}(q) \geq 1$$
$$\qquad \wedge \text{ prev-rw}(q) = [[p_1, d_1, d_1'], \ldots, [p_{\deg_{rw}(q)}, d_{\deg_{rw}(q)}, d_{\deg_{rw}(q)}']]\}$$
$$\delta_2 = \{[p_1, a, [b_1, c], q^2], \ldots, [p_{\deg_{sf}(q,a,c)-1}, a, [b_{\deg_{sf}(q,a,c)-1}, c], q^{\deg_{sf}(q,a,c)}],$$
$$\qquad [p_{\deg_{sf}(q,a,c)}, a, [b_{\deg_{sf}(q,a,c)}, c], q] \mid q \in Q_{sf}$$
$$\qquad \wedge a \in (\Sigma \cup \{\triangleright, \triangleleft\}) \wedge c \in (\Gamma \cup \{\triangleright, \#\}) \wedge \deg_{sf}(q, a, c) \geq 1$$
$$\qquad \wedge \text{ prev-sf}(q, a, c) = [[p_1, b_1], \ldots, [p_{\deg_{sf}(q,a,c)}, b_{\deg_{sf}(q,a,c)}]]\}$$
$$\delta_3 = \{[q^1, -d_1, -d_1', p_1^1], \ldots, [q^{\deg_{rw}(q)}, -d_{\deg_{rw}(q)}, -d_{\deg_{rw}(q)}', p_{\deg_{rw}(q)}^1] \mid q \in Q_{rw}$$
$$\qquad \wedge \deg_{rw}(q) \geq 1 \wedge \text{ prev-rw}(q) = [[p_1, d_1, d_1'], \ldots, [p_{\deg_{rw}(q)}, d_{\deg_{rw}(q)}, d_{\deg_{rw}(q)}']]\}$$
$$\delta_4 = \{[q^1, a, [c, b_1], p_1^1], \ldots, [q^{\deg_{sf}(q,a,c)}, a, [c, b_{\deg_{sf}(q,a,c)}], p_{\deg_{sf}(q,a,c)}^1] \mid q \in Q_{sf}$$
$$\qquad \wedge a \in (\Sigma \cup \{\triangleright, \triangleleft\}) \wedge c \in (\Gamma \cup \{\triangleright, \#\}) \wedge \deg_{sf}(q, a, c) \geq 1$$
$$\qquad \wedge \text{ prev-sf}(q, a, c) = [[p_1, b_1], \ldots, [p_{\deg_{sf}(q,a,c)}, b_{\deg_{sf}(q,a,c)}]]\}$$
$$\delta_5 = \{[q^1, a, [c, c], q] \mid q \in Q_{sf} - (A \cup N)$$
$$\qquad \wedge a \in (\Sigma \cup \{\triangleright, \triangleleft\}) \wedge c \in (\Gamma \cup \{\triangleright, \#\}) \wedge \deg_{sf}(q, a, c) = 0\}$$
$$\hat{\delta}_i = \{[\hat{p}, x, y, \hat{q}] \mid [p, x, y, q] \in \delta_i\} \ (i = 1, \ldots, 5)$$
$$\delta_6 = \{[q, a, [b, b], q^1] \mid q \in Q_{rw} - \{q_0\}$$
$$\qquad \wedge a \in (\Sigma \cup \{\triangleright, \triangleleft\}) \wedge b \in (\Gamma \cup \{\triangleright, \#\}) \wedge \neg \exists c \exists p ([q, a, [b, c], p] \in \delta)\}$$
$$\delta_A = \{[q, 0, 0, \hat{q}^1] \mid q \in A\} \cup \{[\hat{q}, 0, 0, q^1] \mid q \in A\}$$
$$\delta_N = \{[q, 0, 0, q^1] \mid q \in N\} \cup \{[\hat{q}, 0, 0, \hat{q}^1] \mid q \in N\}$$

The number of states $|Q^\dagger|$ is estimated as follows. From the definition of $Q^\dagger$, we observe $|Q^\dagger| < 4|Q| + 2|\delta|$, since $\sum_{q \in Q} \deg_{\max}(q) \leq |\delta|$ holds. Furthermore, since $|\delta| \leq |Q|(|\Sigma| + 2)(|\Gamma| + 2)$, we have $|Q^\dagger| < (4 + 2(|\Sigma| + 2)(|\Gamma| + 2))|Q|$. Hence, the number of states of $T^\dagger$ is bounded by a linear function of that of T if the numbers of input and storage tape symbols are regarded as constants.

The set $Q^\dagger$ has four types of states. They are of the forms $q, \hat{q}, q^j$ and $\hat{q}^j$. The states without a superscript (i.e., q and $\hat{q}$) are for forward computation, while those with a superscript (i.e., q^j and $\hat{q}^j$) are for backward computation. Note that $Q^\dagger$ contains q^1 and $\hat{q}^1$ even if $\deg_{\max}(q) = 0$. The states with "^" (i.e., $\hat{q}$ and $\hat{q}^j$) are the ones indicating that an accepting ID was found in the process of traverse, while those without "^" (i.e., q and q^j) are for indicating no accepting ID has been found so far.

Using these states, $T^\dagger$ traverses a computation graph of T. Since each node of $G_{T,w}$ is identified by the ID of T of the form $(\triangleright w \triangleleft, \triangleright v, q, h_i, h_s)$, it is easy for $T^\dagger$ to keep it by the ID of $T^\dagger$ itself. If $G_{T,w}$ is a tree, $T^\dagger$ traverses it by a depth-first search (the case $G_{T,w}$ is not a tree will be explained later). In the process of depth-first search, each non-leaf node $(\triangleright w \triangleleft, \triangleright v, q, h_i, h_s)$ may be visited $\deg_{\max}(q) + 1$ times (i.e., the number of its child nodes plus 1), and thus $T^\dagger$ should keep this information in the finite control. To do so, $T^\dagger$ uses $\deg_{\max}(q) + 1$ states $q^1, \ldots, q^{\deg_{\max}(q)}$, and q for each state q of T. Here, the states $q^1, \ldots, q^{\deg_{\max}(q)}$ are used for visiting its child nodes, while q is used for visiting its parent node as shown in Fig. 8.4. In other words, the states with a superscript are for going downward in the tree (i.e., a backward simulation of T), and the state without a superscript is for going upward in the tree (i.e., a forward simulation). By "linearizing" the computation tree that contains irreversible transitions, $T^\dagger$ can traverse it reversibly. Note that the states with "^", i.e., $\hat{q}$ and $\hat{q}^j$, also have similar roles.

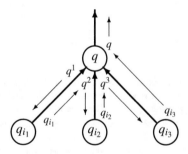

Fig. 8.4 Transitions among IDs of T, which are indicated by thick arrows. Each node represents an ID of T, though only a state of the finite control is written in a circle. Here, irreversible transitions occur at the node labeled by q (we show the case $\deg_{\max}(q) = 3$). At this node $T^\dagger$ goes back and forth using the states q^1, q^2, q^3, and q. Namely, $T^\dagger$ makes a forward transition by the state q, and backward transitions by the states q^1, q^2, and q^3, which are indicated by thin arrows

The set of rules δ_1 (or δ_2, respectively) is for simulating forward computation of T in $G_{T,w}$ for T's shift states (or read-write states). The set δ_3 (or δ_4, respectively) is for simulating backward computation of T in $G_{T,w}$ for T's read-write states (or shift states). The set δ_5 is for turning the direction of computation from backward to forward in $G_{T,w}$ for shift states (at a leaf node if $G_{T,w}$ is a tree). The set $\hat{\delta}_i$ ($i = 1, \ldots, 5$) is the set of rules for the states of the form $\hat{q}$, and is identical to δ_i except that each state has "^". The set δ_6 is for turning the direction of computation from forward to backward in $G_{T,w}$ for halting IDs with a read-write state. The set δ_A (or δ_N, respectively) is for turning the direction of computation from forward to backward for accepting (or non-accepting) states. In addition, each rule in δ_A makes $T^\dagger$ change the state from one without "^" to the corresponding one with "^".

Assume an input w is given to T, and let $G_{T,w}$ be its computation graph. Let $C = (\triangleright w \triangleleft, \triangleright v, q, h_i, h_s)$ and $C' = (\triangleright w \triangleleft, \triangleright v', q', h'_i, h'_s)$ be two IDs of T such that $C \vdash_T^{\pm} C'$, where $v, v' \in (\Gamma \cup \{\#\})^*, q, q' \in Q, h_i, h'_i \in \{0, \ldots, |w|+1\}, h_s \in \{0, \ldots, |v|\}$, and $h'_s \in \{0, \ldots, |v'|\}$. By the condition (C4), the relation $|v| \leq |v'|+1$ holds (note that $|v| = |v'|+1$ can hold only if the rightmost symbol of v is #. Therefore, for each C', the set $\{C \mid C \vdash_T^{\pm} C'\}$ is finite.

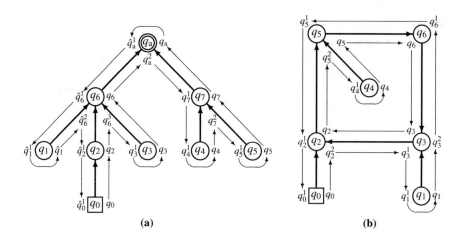

(a)   **(b)**

Fig. 8.5 Examples of computation graphs $G_{T,w}$ of an IDTM T. The node labeled by q_0 represents the initial ID of T. An RDTM $T^\dagger$ traverses these graphs along thin arrows using its IDs. **(a)** This is a case T halts in an accepting state q_a. Here, the state transition of $T^\dagger$ in the traversal of the tree is as follows: $q_0 \to q_2 \to q_6^3 \to q_3^1 \to q_3 \to q_6 \to q_a^2 \to q_7^1 \to q_4^1 \to q_4 \to q_7^2 \to q_5^1 \to q_5 \to q_7 \to q_a \to \hat{q}_a^1 \to \hat{q}_6^1 \to \hat{q}_1^1 \to \hat{q}_1 \to \hat{q}_6^2 \to \hat{q}_2^1 \to \hat{q}_0^1$. **(b)** This is a case T loops forever, but uses bounded amount of the storage tape. Here, $T^\dagger$ traverses the graph as follows: $q_0 \to q_2^2 \to q_3^1 \to q_1^1 \to q_1 \to q_3^2 \to q_6^1 \to q_5^1 \to q_2^1 \to q_0$

First, consider the case where T with w finally halts in a ID C_h. Then $G_{T,w}$ becomes a finite tree with the root C_h, since $\{C \mid C \vdash_T^{\pm} C_h\}$ is finite. Given the input w, $T^\dagger$ traverses $G_{T,w}$ by the depth-first search (Fig. 8.5 **(a)**). Note that the search starts not from the root of the tree but from the leaf node $(\triangleright w \triangleleft, \triangleright, q_0, 0, 0)$. As explained above (also see Fig. 8.4), T' goes back and forth at a node (labeled by q) where transitions of T' are irreversible. If q is a read-write state (or shift state, respectively), then rules in δ_1 and δ_3 (or δ_2 and δ_4) are used. At a leaf node $(\triangleright w \triangleleft, \triangleright v, q, h_i, h_s)$, which satisfies $\deg_{sf}(q, s(\triangleright w \triangleleft, h_i), s(\triangleright v, h_s)) = 0$, $T^\dagger$ turns the direction of computing by the rule $[q^1, s(\triangleright w \triangleleft, h_i)], [s(\triangleright v, h_s), s(\triangleright v, h_s)], q] \in \delta_5$. If $T^\dagger$ enters an accepting state of T, say q_a, which is the root of the tree while traversing the tree, then $T^\dagger$ goes to the state $\hat{q}_a^1$ by a rule in δ_A, and continues the depth-first search. After that, $T^\dagger$ uses the states of the forms $\hat{q}$ and $\hat{q}^j$ indicating that the input w should be accepted. $T^\dagger$ will eventually reach the initial ID of T by its ID $(\triangleright w\triangleleft, \triangleright, \hat{q}_0^1, 0, 0)$. Thus, $T^\dagger$ halts and accepts the input.

If $T^\dagger$ enters a halting state of T other than the accepting states, then by a rule in $\delta_N \cup \delta_6$ it continues the depth-first search without entering a state of the form $\hat{q}$. Also in this case, $T^\dagger$ will finally reach the initial ID of T by its ID $(\triangleright w\triangleleft, \triangleright, q_0^1, 0, 0)$. Thus, $T^\dagger$ halts and rejects the input.

We can see that $T^\dagger$ never halts in an ID other than $(\triangleright w\triangleleft, \triangleright, \hat{q}_0^1, 0, 0)$ and $(\triangleright w\triangleleft, \triangleright, q_0^1, 0, 0)$ by the following reasons. Firstly, $\delta^\dagger$ is so designed that $T^\dagger$ continues the traversal (and does not halt) at any node of $G_{T,w}$ such that T's state is not q_0 (as in Fig. 8.5). Secondly, since the initial ID of T is $(\triangleright w\triangleleft, \triangleright, q_0, 0, 0)$, and (C1) holds, we can assume there is no rule of the form $[q_0, a, [b, c], q]$ in δ such that $(a, (b, c)) \neq (\triangleright, (\triangleright, \triangleright))$ (if otherwise, such a rule should be removed). Therefore, $T^\dagger$ never reaches $(\triangleright w\triangleleft, \triangleright v, \hat{q}_0^1, h_i, h_s)$ or $(\triangleright w\triangleleft, \triangleright v, q_0^1, h_i, h_s)$ such that $(h_i, h_s) \neq (0, 0)$ for some $v \in (\Gamma \cup \{\#\})^*$. Thirdly, the case that $T^\dagger$ halts in $(\triangleright w\triangleleft, \triangleright v, \hat{q}_0^1, 0, 0)$ or $(\triangleright w\triangleleft, \triangleright v, q_0^1, 0, 0)$ for some $v \in (\Gamma \cup \{\#\})^*\Gamma$ is also inhibited. By the conditions (C4) and (C5), if T uses m squares of the storage tape, then initially these m squares must contain blank symbols (the case (C5) does not hold is shown in Example 8.2). Otherwise, T will halt without accepting an input. Assume T starts from the ID $(\triangleright w\triangleleft, \triangleright \#^m u, q_0, 0, 0)$ such that $u \in (\Gamma \cup \{\#\})^*\Gamma$. Then, the string u is not rewritten throughout the computation. Therefore, there is no ID C such that $(\triangleright w\triangleleft, \triangleright \#^m u, q_0, 0, 0) \vdash_{\overline{T}} C$ and $(\triangleright w\triangleleft, \triangleright, q_0, 0, 0) \vdash_{\overline{T}} C$. By above, $(\triangleright w\triangleleft, \triangleright v, q_0, 0, 0)$ with $v \in (\Gamma \cup \{\#\})^*\Gamma$ cannot be a node in $G_{T,w}$.

Next, consider the case where T eventually enters a loop of IDs $C_1 \vdash_{\overline{T}} \cdots \vdash_{\overline{T}} C_k \vdash_{\overline{T}} C_1 \vdash_{\overline{T}} \cdots$, then $G_{T,w}$ is not a tree. But, it is a finite graph, since $\{C \mid \exists i \in \{1, \ldots, k\}(C \vdash_{\overline{T}} C_i)\}$ is again finite (Fig. 8.5 (b)). In this case, since there is no accepting ID in $G_{T,w}$, $T^\dagger$ never reaches an accepting state of T no matter how $T^\dagger$ visits the nodes of $G_{T,w}$ (it may not visit all the nodes of $G_{T,w}$). Thus, $T^\dagger$ uses only the states without "^". Since T satisfies the condition (C1), $T^\dagger$ eventually halts by Corollary 8.1. By the same argument as in the case $G_{T,w}$ is a tree, $T^\dagger$ must halt in the ID $(\triangleright w\triangleleft, \triangleright, q_0^1, 0, 0)$ in this case.

Finally, consider the case where T with w uses unbounded amount of the storage tape, which implies T neither loops nor halts. In this case, $G_{T,w}$ becomes an infinite tree-like graph having no root. Thus, $T^\dagger$ traverses $G_{T,w}$ indefinitely without halting.

It is easy to see that if T uses at most m squares of the storage tape, then $T^\dagger$ also uses at most m squares. This is because the head positions and the contents of the storage tape of T is directly simulated by those of $T^\dagger$.

We can verify that $T^\dagger$ is deterministic and reversible by checking $\delta^\dagger$, though it is slightly complex (however, it is intuitively clear from Fig. 8.5). For example, consider a state $q \in Q_{rw}$. We can see that there is exactly one quadruple whose fourth element is either $q^2, \ldots, q^{\deg_{rw}(q)}$ or q, which is contained only in δ_1. Also, for each combination of $q \in Q_{rw}$, $a \in \Sigma \cup \{\triangleright, \triangleleft\}$, and $b \in \Gamma \cup \{\triangleright, \#\}$, there is at most one quadruple of the form $[p^j, a, [c, b], q^1]$ only in δ_4. Hence, the reversibility condition is satisfied for these states. Likewise, we can check it for all other states in $Q^\dagger$.

By above, we can conclude that the theorem holds. □

Example 8.1. Consider the following language.

$$L_{eq} = \{w \mid w \in \{a,b\}^* \wedge \text{ the number of } a\text{'s in } w \text{ is the same as that of } b\text{'s}\}$$

The IDTM T_{eq} defined below accepts the language L_{eq}.

$$T_{eq} = (Q, \{a,b\}, \{a,b\}, \delta, \triangleright, \triangleleft, q_0, \#, \{q_a\}, \{q_r\})$$
$$Q = \{q_0, q_1, q_2, q_3, q_4, q_5, q_6, p_1, p_2, p_3, p_4, q_a, q_r\}$$
$$\delta = \{ [q_0, \triangleright, [\triangleright, \triangleright], q_1], [q_1, +, +, q_2],$$
$$[q_2, a, [\#, a], p_1], [q_2, b, [\#, \#], q_3], [q_2, \triangleleft, [\#, \#], q_4], [q_3, +, 0, q_2],$$
$$[q_4, -, -, q_5], [q_5, a, [a, a], q_6], [q_5, a, [\triangleright, \triangleright], q_6], [q_5, b, [a, b], q_4],$$
$$[q_5, b, [\triangleright, \triangleright], q_r], [q_5, \triangleright, [a, a], q_r], [q_5, \triangleright, [\triangleright, \triangleright], q_a], [q_6, -, 0, q_5],$$
$$[p_1, 0, +, p_2], [p_2, a, [\#, \#], p_3], [p_3, 0, -, p_4], [p_4, a, [a, a], q_1] \}$$

If an input string $w \in \{a,b\}^*$ is given, T_{eq} scans it from left to right. Each time T_{eq} finds the symbol a in w, it writes a in the storage tape, and shift the head to the right. It is performed by the states q_1, q_2 and q_3. If the input head reaches $\triangleleft$, then T_{eq} changes the direction of scanning. After that, each time T_{eq} finds the symbol b in w, it rewrites the storage tape symbol a into b, and shift the head to the left using q_4, q_5 and q_6. If both of the heads reads $\triangleright$, it accepts the input. Otherwise it rejects. The states $p_1, \ldots, p_4$ are for satisfying the second half of the condition (C5). Note that T_{eq} checks the first half of the condition (C5), i.e., the storage tape square of position 1 initially contains #, by the state q_2. It is also easy to verify that T_{eq} satisfies (C1) – (C4). T_{eq} is irreversible, since the pairs $([q_1, +, +, q_2], [q_3, +, 0, q_2])$ and $([q_4, -, -, q_5], [q_6, -, 0, q_5])$ violate the reversibility condition. Examples of computing processes of T_{eq} are as below.

$$(\triangleright aabbabba\triangleleft, \triangleright, q_0, 0, 0) \vdash^{53}_{T_{eq}} (\triangleright aabbabba\triangleleft, \triangleright bbbb, q_a, 0, 0)$$

$$(\triangleright aabbabaa\triangleleft, \triangleright, q_0, 0, 0) \vdash^{57}_{T_{eq}} (\triangleright aabbabaa\triangleleft, \triangleright aabbb, q_r, 0, 2)$$

An RDTM $T_{eq}^\dagger$ that simulates T_{eq} obtained by the method in Theorem 8.2 is:

$$T_{eq}^\dagger = (Q^\dagger, \{a,b\}, \{a,b\}, \delta^\dagger, \triangleright, \triangleleft, q_0, \#, \{\hat{q}_0^1\}, \{q_0^1\})$$
$$Q^\dagger = \{q, \hat{q}, q^1, \hat{q}^1 \mid q \in Q\} \cup \{q_2^2, q_5^2, \hat{q}_2^2, \hat{q}_5^2\}$$
$$\delta^\dagger = \delta_1 \cup \cdots \cup \delta_6 \cup \hat{\delta}_1 \cup \cdots \cup \hat{\delta}_5 \cup \delta_a \cup \delta_r$$
$$\delta_1 = \{ [q_1, +, +, q_2^2], [q_3, +, 0, q_2], [q_4, -, -, q_5^2], [q_6, -, 0, q_5],$$
$$[p_1, 0, +, p_2], [p_3, 0, -, p_4] \}$$
$$\delta_2 = \{ [q_0, \triangleright, [\triangleright, \triangleright], q_1], [q_2, a, [\#, a], p_1], [q_2, b, [\#, \#], q_3], [q_2, \triangleleft, [\#, \#], q_4],$$
$$[q_5, a, [a, a], q_6], [q_5, a, [\triangleright, \triangleright], q_6], [q_5, b, [a, b], q_4], [q_5, b, [\triangleright, \triangleright], q_r],$$
$$[q_5, \triangleright, [a, a], q_r], [q_5, \triangleright, [\triangleright, \triangleright], q_a], [p_2, a, [\#, \#], p_3], [p_4, a, [a, a], q_1] \}$$
$$\delta_3 = \{ [q_2^1, -, -, q_1^1], [q_2^2, -, 0, q_3^1], [q_5^1, +, +, q_4^1], [q_5^2, +, 0, q_6^1],$$
$$[p_2^1, 0, -, p_1^1], [p_4^1, 0, +, p_3^1] \}$$

$$\delta_4 = \{\, [q_1^1, \triangleright, [\triangleright, \triangleright], q_0^1],\ [p_1^1, a, [a, \#], q_2^1],\quad [q_3^1, b, [\#, \#], q_2^1],\ [q_4^1, \triangleleft, [\#, \#], q_2^1],$$
$$[q_6^1, a, [a, a], q_5^1],\quad [q_6^1, a, [\triangleright, \triangleright], q_5^1],\ [q_4^1, b, [b, a], q_5^1],\ [q_r^1, b, [\triangleright, \triangleright], q_5^1],$$
$$[q_r^1, \triangleright, [a, a], q_5^1],\ [q_a^1, \triangleright, [\triangleright, \triangleright], q_5^1],\ [p_3^1, a, [\#, \#], p_2^1],\ [q_1^1, a, [a, a], p_4^1] \,\}$$
$$\delta_5 = \{\, [q_1^1, \triangleright, [\#, \#], q_1],\ [q_1^1, \triangleright, [a, a], q_1],\ \ldots,\ [p_3^1, \triangleleft, [b, b], p_3] \,\}$$
$$\hat{\delta}_i = \{\, [\hat{p}, x, y, \hat{q}] \mid [p, x, y, q] \in \delta_i \,\}\ (i = 1, \ldots, 5)$$
$$\delta_6 = \{\, [q_2, \triangleright, [\triangleright, \triangleright], q_2^1],\ [q_2, \triangleright, [\#, \#], q_2^1],\ \ldots,\ [p_4, \triangleleft, [b, b], p_4^1] \,\}$$
$$\delta_A = \{\, [q_a, 0, 0, \hat{q}_a^1] \,\}$$
$$\delta_N = \{\, [q_r, 0, 0, q_r^1] \,\}$$

The details of δ_5 and δ_6 are omitted here since they have 87 and 53 rules, respectively. Examples of computing processes of $T_{eq}^{\dagger}$ are as follows.

$$(\,\triangleright aabbabba\triangleleft,\ \triangleright,\ q_0,\ 0,\ 0\,) \ \vdash^{161}_{T_{eq}^{\dagger}}\ (\,\triangleright aabbabba\triangleleft,\ \triangleright,\ \hat{q}_0^1,\ 0,\ 0\,)$$

$$(\,\triangleright aabbabaa\triangleleft,\ \triangleright,\ q_0,\ 0,\ 0\,) \ \vdash^{169}_{T_{eq}^{\dagger}}\ (\,\triangleright aabbabaa\triangleleft,\ \triangleright,\ q_0^1,\ 0,\ 0\,)$$

$\square$

Next, we show an example where a given IDTM does not satisfy the condition (C5). In this case, the RDTM constructed by the method of Theorem 8.2 does not simulate the IDTM correctly.

Example 8.2. Consider the following IDTM T_1.

$$T_1 = (Q_1, \{a, b\}, \{a\}, \delta_1, \triangleright, \triangleleft, q_0, \#, \{q_a\}, \{\})$$
$$Q_1 = \{q_0, q_1, q_2, q_a\}$$
$$\delta_1 = \{\, [q_0, \triangleright, [\triangleright, \triangleright], q_1],\ [q_1, 0, +, q_2],\ [q_2, \triangleright, [\#, a], q_a],\ [q_2, \triangleright, [a, a], q_a] \,\}$$

Trivially, T_1 accepts the language $\{a, b\}^*$, since it goes to the accepting state in three steps without reading an input. It does not meet the condition (C5), because it writes the symbol a in the state q_2 without checking the tape square at the position 1 initially contains #. Namely, it writes a even if a is already written on the square.

Since $(\triangleright w \triangleleft, \triangleright, q_0, 0, 0) \vdash^3_{T_1} (\triangleright w \triangleleft, \triangleright a, q_a, 0, 1)$, any string $w \in \{a, b\}^*$ is accepted by T_1. However, since $(\triangleright w \triangleleft, \triangleright a, q_0, 0, 0) \vdash^3_{T_1} (\triangleright w \triangleleft, \triangleright a, q_a, 0, 1)$ holds, the computation tree that contains $(\triangleright w \triangleleft, \triangleright, q_0, 0, 0)$ also contains $(\triangleright w \triangleleft, \triangleright a, q_0, 0, 0)$ as its node. Hence, the RDTM $T_1^{\dagger}$ constructed by the method of Theorem 8.2 may not give a correct answer. In fact,

$$(\triangleright w \triangleleft, \triangleright, q_0, 0, 0) \vdash^3_{T_1^{\dagger}} (\triangleright w \triangleleft, \triangleright a, q_a^2, 0, 1) \vdash^3_{T_1^{\dagger}} (\triangleright w \triangleleft, \triangleright a, q_0^1, 0, 0)$$

holds, and thus w is rejected by $T_1^{\dagger}$.

$\square$

8.3 Relation Between Reversible Nondeterministic and Reversible Deterministic TMs

Here, we show that an RNTM can be simulated by an RDTM using exactly the same numbers of storage tape squares and the tape symbols provided that the RNTM satisfies (C1), and uses bounded amount of the storage tape for any input w. It is proved by a similar method as in Theorem 8.2.

Theorem 8.3. *[10] Let $T = (Q, \Sigma, \Gamma, \delta, \triangleright, \triangleleft, q_0, \#, A, N)$ be an RNTM that satisfies (C1), and uses bounded amount of the storage tape for any input $w \in \Sigma^*$. We can construct an RDTM $T^\dagger = (Q^\dagger, \Sigma, \Gamma, \delta^\dagger, \triangleright, \triangleleft, q_0^1, \#, \{\hat{q}_0\}, \{q_0\})$ such that the following holds.*

$\forall w \in \Sigma^* \ (w \in L(T) \ \Rightarrow \ (\triangleright w \triangleleft, \triangleright, q_0^1, 0, 0) \overset{+}{\underset{T^\dagger}{\vdash}} (\triangleright w \triangleleft, \triangleright, \hat{q}_0, 0, 0))$

$\forall w \in \Sigma^* \ (w \notin L(T) \ \Rightarrow \ (\triangleright w \triangleleft, \triangleright, q_0^1, 0, 0) \overset{+}{\underset{T^\dagger}{\vdash}} (\triangleright w \triangleleft, \triangleright, q_0, 0, 0))$

Hence $L(T^\dagger) = L(T)$. Furthermore, if T uses at most m squares of the storage tape for an input w, then $T^\dagger$ with w also uses at most m squares in any of its ID in its computing process.

Proof. By Lemma 8.2, we can assume T satisfies (C2) and (C3). Since T with w uses bounded amount of the storage tape, its computation graph $G_{T,w}$ becomes a finite tree by Corollary 8.2, where the initial ID $(\triangleright w \triangleleft, \triangleright, q_0, 0, 0)$ corresponds to the root of the tree (Fig. 8.6). Therefore, it can be traversed in a similar manner as in Theorem 8.2. However, since there may be two or more accepting IDs in the tree, a different technique will be used for going back to the initial ID reversibly.

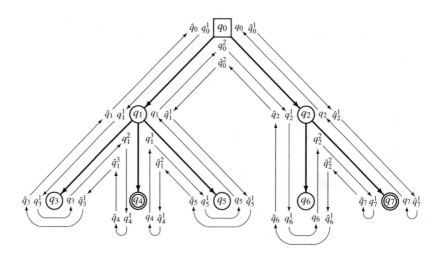

Fig. 8.6 An example of a computation tree $G_{T,w}$ of an RNTM T. The node labeled by q_0 represents the initial ID of T, while those labeled by q_4 and q_7 are accepting ones. An RDTM $T^\dagger$ traverses the tree along thin arrows. In this case, the state transition of $T^\dagger$ in the traversal is as follows: $q_0^1 \rightarrow q_1^1 \rightarrow q_3^1 \rightarrow q_3 \rightarrow q_1^2 \rightarrow q_4^1 \rightarrow \hat{q}_4 \rightarrow \hat{q}_1^3 \rightarrow \hat{q}_3^1 \rightarrow \hat{q}_3 \rightarrow \hat{q}_1 \rightarrow \hat{q}_0$

We now define five functions as follows.

$$\text{next-rw} : Q_{rw} \times (\Sigma \cup \{\triangleright, \triangleleft\}) \times (\Gamma \cup \{\triangleright, \#\}) \to 2^{(\Gamma \cup \{\triangleright, \#\}) \times Q_{sf}}$$
$$\text{next-sf} : Q_{sf} \to 2^{\{-,0,+\}^2 \times Q_{rw}}$$
$$\text{deg}_{rw} : Q_{rw} \times (\Sigma \cup \{\triangleright, \triangleleft\}) \times (\Gamma \cup \{\triangleright, \#\}) \to \mathbb{N}$$
$$\text{deg}_{sf} : Q_{sf} \to \mathbb{N}$$
$$\text{deg}_{max} : Q \to \mathbb{N}$$

$$\text{next-rw}(p,a,b) = \{[c,q] \mid q \in Q_{sf} \wedge c \in (\Gamma \cup \{\triangleright, \#\}) \wedge [p,a,[b,c],q] \in \delta\}$$
$$\text{next-sf}(p) = \{[d,d',q] \mid q \in Q_{rw} \wedge d,d' \in \{-,0,+\} \wedge [p,d,d',q] \in \delta\}$$
$$\text{deg}_{rw}(p,a,b) = |\text{next-rw}(p,a,b)|$$
$$\text{deg}_{sf}(p) = |\text{next-sf}(p)|$$
$$\text{deg}_{max}(p) = \begin{cases} \max\{\text{deg}_{rw}(p,a,b) \mid a \in (\Sigma \cup \{\triangleright, \triangleleft\}) \wedge \\ \qquad\qquad\qquad b \in (\Gamma \cup \{\triangleright, \#\})\} & \text{if } p \in Q_{rw} \\ \text{deg}_{sf}(p) & \text{if } p \in Q_{sf} \end{cases}$$

Assume T is in the ID $(\triangleright w \triangleleft, \triangleright v, p, h_i, h_s)$. If p is a read-write state (or shift state, respectively), then $\text{deg}_{rw}(p, s(\triangleright w \triangleleft, h_i), s(\triangleright v, h_s))$ (or $\text{deg}_{sf}(p)$) denotes the total number of the next IDs of $(\triangleright w \triangleleft, \triangleright v, p, h_i, h_s)$. Each element $[c,q] \in \text{next-rw}(p,a,b)$ (or $[d,d',q] \in \text{next-sf}(p)$, respectively) gives a written storage tape symbol and a next state (or shift directions and a next state). We also assume the elements of the sets $\text{next-rw}(p,a,b)$ and $\text{next-sf}(p)$ are sorted as in the proof of Theorem 8.2. Thus, $\text{prev-rw}(q)$ and $\text{prev-sf}(q,a,c)$ are expressed as below.

$$\text{next-rw}(p,a,b) = [[c_1,q_1], \ldots, [c_{\text{deg}_{rw}(p,a,b)}, q_{\text{deg}_{rw}(p,a,b)}]]$$
$$\text{next-sf}(p) = [[d_1,d_1',q_1], \ldots, [d_{\text{deg}_{sf}(p)}, d_{\text{deg}_{sf}(p)}', q_{\text{deg}_{sf}(p)}]]$$

Let $\text{next-rw}^R(p,a,b)$ and $\text{next-sf}^R(p)$ be the reversed lists of the above.
$Q^\dagger$ and $\delta^\dagger$ of $T^\dagger$ are defined as below.

$$Q^\dagger = \{q, \hat{q} \mid q \in Q\} \cup \{q^j, \hat{q}^j \mid q \in Q \wedge j \in (\{1\} \cup \{1, \ldots, \text{deg}_{max}(q)\})\}$$
$$\delta^\dagger = \delta_1 \cup \cdots \cup \delta_5 \cup \hat{\delta}_1 \cup \cdots \cup \hat{\delta}_5 \cup \delta_A \cup \delta_N$$
$$\delta_1 = \{[p^1,a,[b,c_1],q_1^1], \ldots, [p^{\text{deg}_{rw}(q,a,b)}, a, [b, c_{\text{deg}_{rw}(q,a,b)}], q_{\text{deg}_{rw}(q,a,b)}^1] \mid p \in Q_{rw}$$
$$\wedge a \in (\Sigma \cup \{\triangleright, \triangleleft\}) \wedge b \in (\Gamma \cup \{\triangleright, \#\}) \wedge \text{deg}_{rw}(p,a,b) \geq 1$$
$$\wedge \text{next-rw}(p,a,b) = [[c_1,q_1], \ldots, [c_{\text{deg}_{rw}(p,a,b)}, q_{\text{deg}_{rw}(p,a,b)}]]\}$$
$$\hat{\delta}_1 = \{[\hat{p}^1,a,[b,c_1],\hat{q}_1^1], \ldots, [\hat{p}^{\text{deg}_{rw}(q,a,b)}, a, [b, c_{\text{deg}_{rw}(q,a,b)}], \hat{q}_{\text{deg}_{rw}(q,a,b)}^1] \mid p \in Q_{rw}$$
$$\wedge a \in (\Sigma \cup \{\triangleright, \triangleleft\}) \wedge b \in (\Gamma \cup \{\triangleright, \#\}) \wedge \text{deg}_{rw}(p,a,b) \geq 1$$
$$\wedge \text{next-rw}^R(p,a,b) = [[c_1,q_1], \ldots, [c_{\text{deg}_{rw}(p,a,b)}, q_{\text{deg}_{rw}(p,a,b)}]]\}$$
$$\delta_2 = \{[p^1,d_1,d_1',q_1^1], \ldots, [p^{\text{deg}_{sf}(p)}, d_{\text{deg}_{sf}(p)}, d_{\text{deg}_{sf}(p)}', q_{\text{deg}_{sf}(q)}^1] \mid p \in Q_{sf}$$
$$\wedge \text{deg}_{sf}(p) \geq 1 \wedge \text{next-sf}(p) = [[d_1,d_1',q_1], \ldots, [d_{\text{deg}_{sf}(p)}, d_{\text{deg}_{sf}(p)}', q_{\text{deg}_{sf}(p)}]]\}$$
$$\hat{\delta}_2 = \{[\hat{p}^1,d_1,d_1',\hat{q}_1^1], \ldots, [\hat{p}^{\text{deg}_{sf}(p)}, d_{\text{deg}_{sf}(p)}, d_{\text{deg}_{sf}(p)}', \hat{q}_{\text{deg}_{sf}(q)}^1] \mid p \in Q_{sf}$$
$$\wedge \text{deg}_{sf}(p) \geq 1 \wedge \text{next-sf}^R(p) = [[d_1,d_1',q_1], \ldots, [d_{\text{deg}_{sf}(p)}, d_{\text{deg}_{sf}(p)}', q_{\text{deg}_{sf}(p)}]]\}$$

$$\delta_3 = \{\,[q_1, a, [c_1, b], p^2], \ldots, [q_{\deg_{\mathrm{rw}}(p,a,b)-1}, a, [c_{\deg_{\mathrm{rw}}(p,a,b)-1}, b], p^{\deg_{\mathrm{rw}}(p,a,b)}],$$
$$[q_{\deg_{\mathrm{rw}}(p,a,b)}, a, [c_{\deg_{\mathrm{rw}}(p,a,b)}, b], p] \mid p \in Q_{\mathrm{rw}}$$
$$\wedge\, a \in (\Sigma \cup \{\rhd, \lhd\}) \wedge b \in (\Gamma \cup \{\rhd, \#\}) \wedge \deg_{\mathrm{rw}}(p,a,b) \geq 1$$
$$\wedge\, \mathrm{next\text{-}rw}(p,a,b) = [[c_1, q_1], \ldots, [c_{\deg_{\mathrm{rw}}(p,a,b)}, q_{\deg_{\mathrm{rw}}(p,a,b)}]]\,\}$$

$$\hat{\delta}_3 = \{\,[\hat{q}_1, a, [c_1, b], \hat{p}^2], \ldots, [\hat{q}_{\deg_{\mathrm{rw}}(p,a,b)-1}, a, [c_{\deg_{\mathrm{rw}}(p,a,b)-1}, b], \hat{p}^{\deg_{\mathrm{rw}}(p,a,b)}],$$
$$[\hat{q}_{\deg_{\mathrm{rw}}(p,a,b)}, a, [c_{\deg_{\mathrm{rw}}(p,a,b)}, b], \hat{p}] \mid p \in Q_{\mathrm{rw}}$$
$$\wedge\, a \in (\Sigma \cup \{\rhd, \lhd\}) \wedge b \in (\Gamma \cup \{\rhd, \#\}) \wedge \deg_{\mathrm{rw}}(p,a,b) \geq 1$$
$$\wedge\, \mathrm{next\text{-}rw}^{\mathrm{R}}(p,a,b) = [[c_1, q_1], \ldots, [c_{\deg_{\mathrm{rw}}(p,a,b)}, q_{\deg_{\mathrm{rw}}(p,a,b)}]]\,\}$$

$$\delta_4 = \{\,[q_1, -d_1, -d_1', p^2], \ldots, [q_{\deg_{\mathrm{sf}}(p)-1}, -d_{\deg_{\mathrm{sf}}(p)-1}, -d_{\deg_{\mathrm{sf}}(p)-1}', p^{\deg_{\mathrm{sf}}(p)}],$$
$$[q_{\deg_{\mathrm{sf}}(p)}, -d_{\deg_{\mathrm{sf}}(p)}, -d_{\deg_{\mathrm{sf}}(p)}', p] \mid p \in Q_{\mathrm{sf}} \wedge \deg_{\mathrm{sf}}(p) \geq 1$$
$$\wedge\, \mathrm{next\text{-}sf}(p) = [[d_1, d_1', q_1], \ldots, [d_{\deg_{\mathrm{sf}}(p)}, d_{\deg_{\mathrm{sf}}(p)}', q_{\deg_{\mathrm{sf}}(p)}]]\,\}$$

$$\hat{\delta}_4 = \{\,[\hat{q}_1, -d_1, -d_1', \hat{p}^2], \ldots, [\hat{q}_{\deg_{\mathrm{sf}}(p)-1}, -d_{\deg_{\mathrm{sf}}(p)-1}, -d_{\deg_{\mathrm{sf}}(p)-1}', \hat{p}^{\deg_{\mathrm{sf}}(p)}],$$
$$[\hat{q}_{\deg_{\mathrm{sf}}(p)}, -d_{\deg_{\mathrm{sf}}(p)}, -d_{\deg_{\mathrm{sf}}(p)}', \hat{p}] \mid p \in Q_{\mathrm{sf}} \wedge \deg_{\mathrm{sf}}(p) \geq 1$$
$$\wedge\, \mathrm{next\text{-}sf}^{\mathrm{R}}(p) = [[d_1, d_1', q_1], \ldots, [d_{\deg_{\mathrm{sf}}(p)}, d_{\deg_{\mathrm{sf}}(p)}', q_{\deg_{\mathrm{sf}}(p)}]]\,\}$$

$$\delta_5 = \{\,[p^1, a, [b, b], p] \mid p \in Q_{\mathrm{rw}} - \{q_0\}$$
$$\wedge\, a \in (\Sigma \cup \{\rhd, \lhd\}) \wedge b \in (\Gamma \cup \{\rhd, \#\}) \wedge \deg_{\mathrm{rw}}(q,a,b) = 0\,\}$$

$$\hat{\delta}_5 = \{\,[\hat{p}, x, y, \hat{q}] \mid [p, x, y, q] \in \delta_5\,\}$$
$$\delta_A = \{\,[p^1, 0, 0, \hat{p}] \mid p \in A\} \cup \{[\hat{p}^1, 0, 0, p] \mid p \in A\}$$
$$\delta_N = \{\,[p^1, 0, 0, p] \mid p \in N\} \cup \{[\hat{p}^1, 0, 0, \hat{p}] \mid p \in N\}$$

Contrary to the case of Theorem 8.2, the states of the forms q and $\hat{q}$ are for backward computation, while those of q^j and $\hat{q}^j$ are for forward computation. If $T^\dagger$ passes an accepting ID of T, a state without "ˆ" turns to the corresponding state with "ˆ", and a state with "ˆ" turns to the one without "ˆ".

The set of rules δ_1 (or δ_2, respectively) is for simulating forward computation of T in $G_{T,w}$ for T's read-write states (or shift states). The set δ_3 (or δ_4, respectively) is for simulating backward computation of T in $G_{T,w}$ for T's read-write states (or shift states). The set δ_5 is for turning the direction of computation from forward to backward for read-write states at a leaf node. The set $\hat{\delta}_i$ $(i = 1, \ldots, 5)$ is for the states with "ˆ". Note that the traversal of the tree by the states with "ˆ" is in the opposite direction to the one by the states without "ˆ". The sets δ_A and δ_N are for turning the direction of computation from forward to backward at a leaf node. In addition, each rule in δ_A makes $T^\dagger$ to change the states without "ˆ" to those with "ˆ", and vice versa.

When traversing the tree, if $T^\dagger$ finds an accepting ID of T, it changes the direction of traversal, and goes back to the root in the state $\hat{q}_0$ (see Fig. 8.6). If there is no accepting ID in the tree, $T^\dagger$ visits all the nodes and finally goes back to the root in the state q_0.

We can verify that $T^\dagger$ is deterministic and reversible in a similar manner as in Theorem 8.2. By above, we conclude the theorem holds.   □

Example 8.3. Consider the following language.

$$L_c = \{w_1 a w_2 \mid w_1, w_2 \in \{a,b\}^* \wedge |w_1| = |w_2|\}$$

L_c is the set of all the strings of odd length whose center symbol is a. The RNTM T_c defined below accepts the language L_c.

$$T_c = (\{q_0, q_1, q_2, q_3, q_4, q_a\}, \{a,b\}, \{1\}, \delta, \triangleright, \triangleleft, q_0, \#, \{q_a\}, \{\})$$
$$\delta = \{\, [q_0, \triangleright, [\triangleright, \triangleright], q_1], \; [q_1, +, +, q_2],$$
$$[q_2, a, [\#, 1], q_1], \quad [q_2, b, [\#, 1], q_1], \quad [q_2, a, [\#, \#], q_3], \quad [q_3, +, -, q_4],$$
$$[q_4, a, [1,1], q_3], \quad [q_4, b, [1,1], q_3], \quad [q_4, \triangleleft, [\triangleright, \triangleright], q_a]\, \}$$

It is easy to see that T_c satisfies the reversibility condition. But, T_c is nondeterministic, since there is a pair of quadruples $[q_2, a, [\#, 1], q_1]$ and $[q_2, a, [\#, \#], q_3]$. It is also easy to verify that T_c satisfies (C1) – (C3). If an input string $w \in \{a,b\}^*$ is given, T_c scans it from left to right. Each time T_c reads the symbol a or b, it writes 1 in the storage tape, and shift its head to the right using the states q_1 and q_2. However, when T_c reads the symbol a in q_2, it makes a nondeterministic choice. If T_c guesses that the symbol a is at the center position, then it goes to the state q_3. Otherwise, it continues the above process using q_1 and q_2. Once T_c enters the state q_3, it does the following. Each time T_c reads a or b, it shifts the storage tape head to the left using q_3 and q_4. If T_c reads $\triangleleft$ by the input head, and reads $\triangleright$ by the storage tape head, then it halts in an accepting state. Otherwise, T_c halts without accepting w.

An example of an accepting computing process is as below.

$$(\triangleright aabababab \triangleleft, \triangleright, q_0, 0, 0) \; \vdash^{17}_{T_c} \; (\triangleright aabababab \triangleleft, \triangleright 111, q_a, 8, 0)$$

An RDTM $T_c^\dagger$ that simulates T_c obtained by the method in Theorem 8.3 is:

$$T_c^\dagger = (Q^\dagger, \{a,b\}, \{1\}, \delta^\dagger, \triangleright, \triangleleft, q_0^1, \#, \{\hat{q}_0\}, \{q_0\})$$
$$Q^\dagger = \{q, \hat{q}, q^1, \hat{q}^1 \mid q \in Q\} \cup \{q_2^2, \hat{q}_2^2\}$$
$$\delta^\dagger = \delta_1 \cup \cdots \cup \delta_6 \cup \hat{\delta}_1 \cup \cdots \cup \hat{\delta}_5 \cup \delta_a \cup \delta_r$$
$$\delta_1 = \{\, [q_0^1, \triangleright, [\triangleright, \triangleright], q_1^1], \; [q_2^1, b, [\#, 1], q_1^1], \; [q_2^1, a, [\#, 1], q_1^1], \; [q_2^2, a, [\#, \#], q_3^1],$$
$$[q_4^1, a, [1,1], q_3^1], \; [q_4^1, b, [1,1], q_3^1], \; [q_4^1, \triangleleft, [\triangleright, \triangleright], q_a^1]\, \}$$
$$\hat{\delta}_1 = \{\, [\hat{q}_0^1, \triangleright, [\triangleright, \triangleright], \hat{q}_1^1], \; [\hat{q}_2^1, b, [\#, 1], \hat{q}_1^1], \; [\hat{q}_2^1, a, [\#, \#], \hat{q}_3^1], \; [\hat{q}_2^2, a, [\#, 1], \hat{q}_1^1],$$
$$[\hat{q}_4^1, a, [1,1], \hat{q}_3^1], \; [\hat{q}_4^1, b, [1,1], \hat{q}_3^1], \; [\hat{q}_4^1, \triangleleft, [\triangleright, \triangleright], \hat{q}_a^1]\, \}$$
$$\delta_2 = \{\, [q_1^1, +, +, q_2^1], \; [q_3^1, +, -, q_4^1]\, \}$$
$$\hat{\delta}_2 = \{\, [\hat{q}_1^1, +, +, \hat{q}_2^1], \; [\hat{q}_3^1, +, -, \hat{q}_4^1]\, \}$$
$$\delta_3 = \{\, [q_1, \triangleright, [\triangleright, \triangleright], q_0], \; [q_1, b, [1, \#], q_2], \; [q_1, a, [1, \#], q_2^2], \; [q_3, a, [\#, \#], q_2],$$
$$[q_3, a, [1,1], q_4], \; [q_3, b, [1,1], q_4], \; [q_a, \triangleleft, [\triangleright, \triangleright], q_4]\, \}$$
$$\hat{\delta}_3 = \{\, [\hat{q}_1, \triangleright, [\triangleright, \triangleright], \hat{q}_0], \; [\hat{q}_1, b, [1, \#], \hat{q}_2], \; [\hat{q}_3, a, [\#, \#], \hat{q}_2^2], \; [\hat{q}_1, a, [1, \#], \hat{q}_2],$$
$$[\hat{q}_3, a, [1,1], \hat{q}_4], \; [\hat{q}_3, b, [1,1], \hat{q}_4], \; [\hat{q}_a, \triangleleft, [\triangleright, \triangleright], \hat{q}_4]\, \}$$
$$\delta_4 = \{\, [q_2, -, -, q_1], \; [q_4, -, +, q_3]\, \}$$
$$\hat{\delta}_4 = \{\, [\hat{q}_2, -, -, \hat{q}_1], \; [\hat{q}_4, -, +, \hat{q}_3]\, \}$$

$\delta_5 = \{\, [q_2^1, \triangleright, [\triangleright, \triangleright], q_2], \; [q_2^1, \triangleright, [\#, \#], q_2], \; [q_2^1, \triangleright, [1, 1], q_2], \; [q_2^1, a, [\triangleright, \triangleright], q_2],$
$\qquad [q_2^1, a, [1, 1], q_2], \; [q_2^1, b, [\triangleright, \triangleright], q_2], \; [q_2^1, b, [1, 1], q_2], \; [q_2^1, \triangleleft, [\triangleright, \triangleright], q_2],$
$\qquad [q_2^1, \triangleleft, [\#, \#], q_2], \; [q_2^1, \triangleleft, [1, 1], q_2], \; [q_4^1, \triangleright, [\triangleright, \triangleright], q_4], \; [q_4^1, \triangleright, [\#, \#], q_4],$
$\qquad [q_4^1, \triangleright, [1, 1], q_4], \; [q_4^1, a, [\triangleright, \triangleright], q_4], \; [q_4^1, a, [\#, \#], q_4], \; [q_4^1, b, [\triangleright, \triangleright], q_4],$
$\qquad [q_4^1, b, [\#, \#], q_4], \; [q_4^1, \triangleleft, [\#, \#], q_4], \; [q_4^1, \triangleleft, [1, 1], q_4] \,\}$
$\hat{\delta}_5 = \{\, [\hat{p}, x, y, \hat{q}] \mid [p, x, y, q] \in \delta_5 \,\}$
$\delta_A = \{\, [q_a^1, 0, 0, \hat{q}_a], [\hat{q}_a^1, 0, 0, q_a] \,\}$
$\delta_N = \{\, \}$

Examples of computing processes of $T_c^\dagger$ are as follows.

$$(\,\triangleright aababab \triangleleft, \; \triangleright, \; q_0^1, \, 0, 0\,) \; \left|\frac{87}{T_c^\dagger}\right. \; (\,\triangleright aababab \triangleleft, \; \triangleright, \; \hat{q}_0, \, 0, 0\,)$$

$$(\,\triangleright aabbbab \triangleleft, \; \triangleright, \; q_0^1, \, 0, 0\,) \; \left|\frac{56}{T_c^\dagger}\right. \; (\,\triangleright aabbbab \triangleleft, \; \triangleright, \; q_0, \, 0, 0\,)$$

$\square$

8.4 Concluding Remarks

We investigated how reversibility and determinism affect the language accepting capabilities of space-bounded TMs. In particular, we studied the relationship among four modes of computing in TMs, i.e., reversible and deterministic (RD), irreversible and deterministic (ID), reversible and nondeterministic (RN), and irreversible and nondeterministic (IN) modes.

Theorem 8.1 by Lange, McKenzie and Tapp [7] shows that the capability of an $S(n)$-space-bounded IDTM does not decrease even if the constraint of reversibility is added. In Theorem 8.2, by a very simple simulation method, we gave a slightly stronger result that any IDTM T can be simulated by an RDTM $T^\dagger$ that uses the same numbers of storage tape symbols and tape squares as T [9, 10] (in some cases these numbers increase only by 1). We can apply this method even if the space function $S(n)$ of the IDTM is unknown. Thus, the following relation holds for any space function $S(n)$.

$$\mathscr{L}(\text{IDTM}(S(n))) = \mathscr{L}(\text{RDTM}(S(n)))$$

A key point of the proof of Theorem 8.2 is Corollary 8.1, which states an RDTM that uses bounded amount of the storage tape and satisfies the condition (C1) eventually halts. Theorem 8.2 gives another proof of Sipser's result [15] that a space-bounded IDTM can be converted into one that always halts. In the method of Sipser, the constructed IDTM traverses a computation graph of the simulated IDTM from the node corresponding to its accepting ID. Therefore, the graph always becomes a tree, and by this the halting property is guaranteed. The method of Lange, McKenzie and Tapp [7] is also based on this idea. On the other hand, in Theorem 8.2 the computation graph is traversed from the node corresponding to the initial ID, and thus the graph may not be a tree. However, because of Corollaries 8.1 and 8.2, it is automatically guaranteed that the constructed RDTM halts even if it is not a tree provided that it uses a bounded amount of the storage tape. Hence, we only need the initial ID of the simulated IDTM, and there is no need to know the accepting ID.

On the other hand, Theorem 8.3 [10] shows that the capability of an $S(n)$-space-bounded RNTM does not decrease even if we add the constraint of determinism provided that the RNTM satisfies the condition (C1). Let $\mathrm{RNTM_{C1}}$ denote an RNTM that satisfies (C1). Thus, the following relation holds for any space function $S(n)$.

$$\mathscr{L}(\mathrm{RNTM_{C1}}(S(n))) = \mathscr{L}(\mathrm{RDTM}(S(n)))$$

This relation is proved based on a similar idea as in Theorem 8.2. Hence, any $\mathrm{RNTM_{C1}}$ T can be simulated by an RDTM $T^\dagger$ that uses the same numbers of storage tape symbols and tape squares as T. Note that if an RNTM($S(n)$) does not satisfy (C1), then it may not halt, and thus the proof technique in Theorem 8.3 cannot be applied. Empirically, in many case, we can design an RNTM so that it satisfies (C1). However, no general conversion method is known.

As for the relation between INTM and RDTM, the following is shown in [4].

$$\mathscr{L}(\mathrm{INTM}(S(n))) \subseteq \mathscr{L}(\mathrm{RDTM}((S(n))^2))$$

But, so far, it is not known whether a stronger result holds. In particular, the problem

$$\mathscr{L}(\mathrm{INTM}(S(n))) \overset{?}{=} \mathscr{L}(\mathrm{RDTM}(S(n)))$$

is a generalization of the *LBA problem*, which is a special case of $S(n) = n$, posed in [6] (LBA stands for *linear-bounded automaton*), and thus it is very hard to solve. There is also a grammar model called a *uniquely parsable grammar* [11], which has a property similar to reversibility. Namely, parsing (i.e., the backward process of derivation of words) is done deterministically. There, a grammar class that exactly characterize $\mathscr{L}(\mathrm{IDTM}(n))$ ($= \mathscr{L}(\mathrm{RDTM}(n)) = \mathscr{L}(\mathrm{RNTM_{C1}}(n))$) is given.

Besides the above four kinds of TMs, there is a *symmetric TM* (STM) proposed by Lewis and Papadimitriou [8]. In an STM the transition relation is symmetric, i.e., for every pair of IDs C_1 and C_2, $C_1 \vdash C_2$ iff $C_2 \vdash C_1$ holds. Hence, computation graphs of STMs are undirected ones as shown in Fig. 8.7. It can be defined as a TM with a set δ of quadruples such that for each quadruple r in δ, its *inverse quadruple* r^{-1} is also in δ, where $r^{-1} = [q,a,[c,b],p]$ if $r = [p,a,[b,c],q]$, and $r^{-1} = [q,-d_\mathrm{i},-d_\mathrm{s},p]$ if $r = [p,d_\mathrm{i},d_\mathrm{s},q]$. An STM can be regarded as a kind of a formulation for Brownian computation discussed in [2, 12]. In [8], it is shown that $\mathscr{L}(\mathrm{IDTM}(S(n))) \subseteq \mathscr{L}(\mathrm{STM}(S(n)))$. Hence, we can see that the capability of STM($S(n)$) is no less than $\mathrm{RNTM_{C1}}(S(n))$ and RDTM($S(n)$). On the other hand, Reingold [13] showed that if $S(n) = \log n$, an STM($\log n$) is simulated by an IDTM($\log n$) (and thus by an RDTM($\log n$)). Therefore, $\mathscr{L}(\mathrm{STM}(\log n)) = \mathscr{L}(\mathrm{IDTM}(\log n))$ holds. However, it is open for the general case whether the class of STM($S(n)$) is strictly more powerful than that of IDTM($S(n)$) or not.

Here, we formulated a TM as an acceptor. But, the techniques given in this chapter can also be applied to a TM that computes a function, i.e., a TM as a transducer.

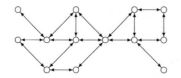 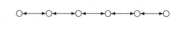

Fig. 8.7 Examples of computation graphs of STMs

By this, we can derive similar results as in Theorem 8.2 and 8.3 for space-bounded Turing machine transducers.

References

1. Bennett, C.H.: Logical reversibility of computation. IBM J. Res. Dev. **17**, 525–532 (1973). doi:10.1147/rd.176.0525
2. Bennett, C.H.: The thermodynamics of computation — a review. Int. J. Theoret. Phys. **21**, 905–940 (1982). doi:10.1007/BF02084158
3. Bennett, C.H.: Time/space trade-offs for reversible computation. SIAM J. Comput. **18**, 766–776 (1989). doi:10.1137/0218053
4. Crescenzi, P., Papadimitriou, C.H.: Reversible simulation of space-bounded computations. Theoret. Comput. Sci. **143**, 159–165 (1995). doi:10.1016/0304-3975(95)80031-4
5. Hopcroft, J.E., Motwani, R., Ullman, J.D.: Introduction to Automata Theory, Languages and Computation. Prentice Hall (2006)
6. Kuroda, S.Y.: Classes of languages and linear-bounded automata. Information and Control **7**, 207–223 (1964). doi:10.1016/S0019-9958(64)90120-2
7. Lange, K.J., McKenzie, P., Tapp, A.: Reversible space equals deterministic space. J. Comput. Syst. Sci. **60**, 354–367 (2000). doi:10.1006/jcss.1999.1672
8. Lewis, H.R., Papadimitriou, C.H.: Symmetric space-bounded computation. Theoret. Comput. Sci. **19**, 161–187 (1982). doi:10.1016/0304-3975(82)90058-5
9. Morita, K.: A deterministic two-way multi-head finite automaton can be converted into a reversible one with the same number of heads. In: Proc. RC 2012 (eds. R. Glück, T. Yokoyama), LNCS 7581, pp. 29–43 (2013). doi:10.1007/978-3-642-36315-3_3. Slides with figures of computer simulation: Hiroshima University Institutional Repository, http://ir.lib.hiroshima-u.ac.jp/00033875
10. Morita, K.: Reversibility in space-bounded computation. Int. J. of General Systems **43**, 697–712 (2014). doi:10.1080/03081079.2014.920998
11. Morita, K., Nishihara, N., Yamamoto, Y., Zhang, Z.: A hierarchy of uniquely parsable grammar classes and deterministic acceptors. Acta Inf. **34**, 389–410 (1997). doi:10.1007/s002360050091
12. Peper, F., Lee, J., Carmona, J., Cortadella, J., Morita, K.: Brownian circuits: Fundamentals. ACM J. Emerg. Technol. Comput. Syst. **9**, Article 3 (2013). doi:10.1145/2422094.2422097
13. Reingold, O.: Undirected connectivity in log-space. J. of the ACM **55**, 1–24 (2008). doi:10.1145/1391289.1391291
14. Savitch, W.J.: Relationship between nondeterministic and deterministic tape complexities. J. Comput. Syst. Sci. **4**, 177–192 (1970). doi:10.1016/S0022-0000(70)80006-X
15. Sipser, M.: Halting space-bounded computations. Theoret. Comput. Sci. **10**, 335–338 (1980). doi:10.1016/0304-3975(80)90053-5

Chapter 9
Other Models of Reversible Machines

Abstract Besides reversible Turing machines, various models of reversible machines and automata have been proposed till now. They are reversible finite automata, reversible multi-head finite automata, reversible pushdown automata, reversible counter machines, reversible cellular automata, and others. In this chapter, reversible counter machines (RCMs), and reversible multi-head finite automata (RMFAs) are studied. Reversible cellular automata will be investigated in Chaps. 10–14. A CM is a computing machine that consists of a finite control and a finite number of counters. It is shown that an RCM with only two counters is computationally universal. This result is useful for proving the universality of other reversible systems, since it is a very simple model of computing. On the other hand, an MFA is an acceptor of a language that consists of a finite control, a read-only input tape, and a finite number of input heads. It is proved that any irreversible MFA can be converted into a reversible one with the same number of heads. Hence, the language accepting power of MFAs does not decrease with the constraint of reversibility.

Keywords counter machine, reversible two-counter machine, computational universality, reversible multi-head finite automaton

9.1 Models of Reversible Automata and Machines

In the previous chapters, reversible Turing machines (RTMs) have been studied as basic models of reversible computing. There are still many other models of reversible automata and machines. They are reversible finite automata, reversible multi-head finite automata, reversible pushdown automata, reversible counter machines, reversible cellular automata, and others.

Reversible finite automata were studied by Angluin [1], and Pin [19] as acceptors of formal languages. They showed the class of reversible finite automata is less powerful than the class of irreversible finite automata. Their model can be regarded as a reversible one-way finite automaton. Kondacs and Watrous [7] studied a reversible two-way finite automaton, which consist of an input tape with endmarkers, an input head that can move in two directions, and a finite control. It was proved that the language accepting ability of reversible ones is exactly the same as irreversible finite automata [7]. Hence, reversible two-way finite automata are more powerful than reversible one-way finite automata. A reversible sequential machine (RSM), as well as a reversible logic element with memory (RLEM), discussed in Chaps. 2 and 3 is a kind of finite automaton having both input and output ports. It was proposed as a module to compose reversible computing machines, such as reversible Turing machines, rather than to study language accepting capability.

A reversible two-way multi-head finite automaton is a generalization of a reversible two-way finite automaton. It consists of an input tape, k input heads that can move in two directions ($k \in \{1, 2, \ldots\}$), and a finite control, Morita [16, 17] investigated its language accepting ability, and proved that an irreversible two-way k-head finite automaton can be simulated by a reversible one with the same number of heads. Hence, its computing power does not decrease by the constraint of reversibility. In Sect. 9.3 a procedure for converting an irreversible multi-head finite automaton into a reversible one will be described. On the other hand, Kutrib and Malcher [10] showed reversible one-way k-head finite automata are less powerful than irreversible one-way k-head finite automata.

A reversible pushdown automaton, which consists of an input tape, an input head that can move only rightward, a pushdown memory, and a finite control, was studied by Kutrib and Malcher [9]. They showed that a reversible deterministic pushdown automaton is strictly less powerful than a deterministic pushdown automaton.

A k-counter machine is a computing model consisting of a finite control and k counters. Minsky [12] showed that a two-counter machine is computationally universal. Morita [15] studied a reversible counter machine, and proved that a reversible two-counter machine is also universal. In Sect. 9.2 this result will be explained in detail. Since a reversible two-counter machine is a very simple model, it is also useful to show universality of other reversible systems (see Sect. 12.4).

A cellular automaton is a system consisting of an infinite number of identical finite automata called cells that are connected uniformly in a k-dimensional space. Each cell changes its state depending on the states of its neighboring cells by a local transition function. Applying the local function to all the cells simultaneously, the global transition function is induced, which determines how the whole system evolves. A reversible cellular automaton is one whose global function is injective, and is considered as an abstract framework for modelling reversible spatiotemporal phenomena. Topics on cellular automata will be discussed in Chaps. 10–14.

In the following sections, we investigate reversible counter machines (RCMs), and reversible multi-head finite automata (RMFAs). In Sect. 9.2, RCMs are studied. First, it is shown that any CM with k counters is simulated by a garbage-less RCM with $k + 2$ counters. Then, it is proved any RCM with k counters can be simulated by an RCM with only two counters for any k, and thus the latter is universal. In Sect. 9.3, RMFAs are studied, and it is shown that any MFA with k heads can be simulated by an RMFA with k heads using a similar technique as in the case of space-bounded RTMs (Theorem 8.2).

9.2 Reversible Counter Machines

A counter machine is a model with a finite number of counters as an auxiliary memory, each of which can keep a nonnegative integer. Its finite control can execute only the following simple operations: to increment the integer by 1, to decrement it by 1, and to test if it is zero or positive. In spite of its simplicity, it is known that a two-counter machine can simulate a Turing machine [12]. In this section, we show that any irreversible counter machine can be simulated by a reversible two-counter machine without leaving garbage information. Hence, the latter is also computationally universal.

9.2.1 Basic definitions on reversible counter machines

We define a counter machine as a kind of a multi-tape machine with a specific type of read-only tapes shown in Fig. 9.1. The tapes are one-way (rightward) infinite. The leftmost squares of the tapes contain the symbol Z's, and all other squares contain P's, where Z and P stand for "zero" and "positive". Each tape and its head act as a counter, since a non-negative integer can be kept by the position of the head (the position of the leftmost square is 0). An increment or decrement operation is done by shifting the head to the right or to the left. Testing if the integer is zero or positive is performed by reading the tape symbol at the head position.

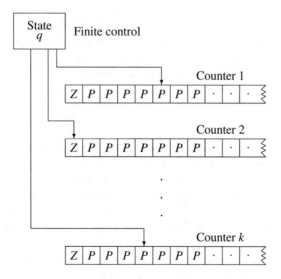

Fig. 9.1 A k-counter machine (CM(k)) formulated as a kind of a multi-tape machine

Definition 9.1. A *counter machine* (CM) is a system defined by

$$M = (Q, k, \delta, q_0, F).$$

Here, Q is a non-empty finite set of states. The integer k ($\in \{1, 2, \ldots\}$) is the number of counters (or tapes), and thus M is also called a *k-counter machine* (CM(k)). The state q_0 is an *initial state* ($q_0 \in Q$), and F is a set of *final states* ($F \subseteq Q$). The CM M uses $\{Z, P\}$ as a tape alphabet, where P is a blank symbol. The item δ is a move relation, which is a subset of $(Q \times \{1, \ldots, k\} \times \{Z, P\} \times Q) \cup (Q \times \{1, \ldots, k\} \times \{-1, 0, +1\} \times Q)$. The symbols -1, 0, and $+1$ are shift directions of the heads. As in the case of a Turing machine, -1 and $+1$ are also indicated by $-$ and $+$ for simplicity. Each element of δ is a *quadruple* (or a *rule*) of the form $[p, i, t, q] \in (Q \times \{1, \ldots, k\} \times \{Z, P\} \times Q)$, or $[p, i, d, q] \in (Q \times \{1, \ldots, k\} \times \{-, 0, +\} \times Q)$. The quadruple $[p, i, t, q]$ is called a *counter-test rule*, and means that if M is in the state p, and the head of the i-th counter reads the symbol t, then go to the state q. The quadruple $[p, i, d, q]$ is called a *count-up/down rule*, and means that if M is in the state p, then shift the i-th head to the direction d by one square, and go to the state q. We assume each state $q_f \in F$ is a *halting state*, i.e., there is no quadruple of the form $[q_f, i, x, q]$ in δ.

Determinism and reversibility of a CM is defined as follows.

Definition 9.2. Let $M = (Q, k, \delta, q_0, F)$ be a CM. M is called a *deterministic CM*, if the following condition holds for any pair of distinct quadruples $[p_1, i_1, x_1, q_1]$ and $[p_2, i_2, x_2, q_2]$ in δ, where $D = \{-, 0, +\}$.

$$(p_1 = p_2) \Rightarrow (i_1 = i_2 \wedge x_1 \notin D \wedge x_2 \notin D \wedge x_1 \neq x_2)$$

It means that for any pair of distinct rules, if the present states are the same, then they are both counter-test rules on the same counter, and the read symbols are different.

We call M a *reversible CM* (RCM), if the following holds for any pair of distinct quadruples $[p_1, i_1, x_1, q_1]$ and $[p_2, i_2, x_2, q_2]$ in δ.

$$(q_1 = q_2) \Rightarrow (i_1 = i_2 \wedge x_1 \notin D \wedge x_2 \notin D \wedge x_1 \neq x_2)$$

It means that for any pair of distinct rules, if the next states are the same, then they are both counter-test rules on the same counter, and the read symbols are different. The above is called the *reversibility condition* for CMs.

Let $\alpha = [p, i, x, q]$ be a quadruple in δ. We call α a *reversible quadruple*, if for any quadruple of the form $\beta = [p', i', x', q] \in \delta$ such that $\alpha \neq \beta$, the condition ($i = i' \wedge x \notin D \wedge x' \notin D \wedge x \neq x'$) holds. Note that, if there is no quadruple of the form β such that $\alpha \neq \beta$, then α is reversible. Also note that, if α is reversible, there is at most one quadruple of the form β in δ, since the tape alphabet is $\{Z, P\}$. On the other hand, if there is another quadruple $\gamma = [p'', i'', x'', q] \in \delta$ such that $\neg(i = i'' \wedge x \notin D \wedge x'' \notin D \wedge x \neq x'')$, then α is called an *irreversible quadruple*.

In the following, we consider only deterministic CMs, and thus the word "deterministic" will be omitted.

An instantaneous description (ID) of a CM M, and the transition relation among IDs are given in the next definition.

Definition 9.3. An *instantaneous description* (ID) of a CM $M = (Q, k, \delta, q_0, F)$ is a $(k+1)$-tuple $(q, n_1, n_2, \ldots, n_k) \in Q \times \mathbb{N}^k$. It represents M is in the state q and the i-th counter keeps n_i $(i \in \{1, \ldots, k\})$. The *transition relation* $\vdash_{M}$ over IDs of M is defined as follows. For every $q, q' \in Q$ and $n_1, \ldots, n_k, n_i' \in \mathbb{N}$,

$$(q, n_1, \ldots, n_{i-1}, n_i, n_{i+1}, \ldots, n_k) \vdash_{M} (q', n_1, \ldots, n_{i-1}, n_i', n_{i+1}, \ldots, n_k)$$

holds iff one of the following conditions (1) – (5) is satisfied.

(1) $[q, i, Z, q'] \in \delta$ and $n_i = n_i' = 0$.
(2) $[q, i, P, q'] \in \delta$ and $n_i = n_i' > 0$.
(3) $[q, i, -, q'] \in \delta$ and $n_i - 1 = n_i'$.
(4) $[q, i, 0, q'] \in \delta$ and $n_i = n_i'$.
(5) $[q, i, +, q'] \in \delta$ and $n_i + 1 = n_i'$.

Reflexive and transitive closure of $\vdash_{M}$ is denoted by $\vdash_{M}^{*}$, and n-step transition by $\vdash_{M}^{n}$ $(n = 0, 1, \ldots)$. An ID C is called a *halting ID* if there is no ID C' such that $C \vdash_{M} C'$.

Definition 9.4. Let $M = (Q, k, \delta, q_0, F)$ be a CM. We say M is in the *normal form*, if the initial state q_0 does not appear as the fourth component of any rule in δ (hence q_0 appears only at time $t = 0$), and F is a singleton.

Lemma 9.1. *For any CM $M = (Q, k, \delta, q_0, F)$, we can construct a CM M' in the normal form that simulates M.*

Proof. It is easy to construct M', since M' can be an irreversible CM. If q_0 appears as the fourth component of some rule in δ, then add a state q_0' as a new initial state and a new rule $[q_0', 1, 0, q_0]$ to M'. If F is not a singleton, say $F = \{q_{f_1}, \ldots, q_{f_n}\}$ $(n \in \{2, 3, \ldots\})$, add a new state q_f, and replace all the occurrences of q_{f_i} $(i \in \{1, \ldots, n\})$ in the rules in δ by q_f. Then, remove the states $q_{f_1}, \ldots, q_{f_n}$, and let $\{q_f\}$ be the new set of final states of M'. □

Example 9.1. Consider the following RCM(2) M_1.

$$M_1 = (\{q_0, q_1, q_2, q_3, q_4, q_5, q_6\}, 2, \delta_1, q_0, \{q_6\})$$
$$\delta_1 = \{ [q_0, 2, Z, q_1], [q_1, 2, +, q_2], [q_2, 2, +, q_3], $$
$$[q_3, 1, P, q_4], [q_3, 1, Z, q_6], [q_4, 1, -, q_5], [q_5, 2, P, q_1] \}$$

It is easy to verify that M_1 is deterministic and reversible. We can also see that M_1 is in the normal form. M_1 computes the function $f(x) = 2x + 2$. More precisely, $(q_0, x, 0) \vdash_{M_1}^{*} (q_6, 0, 2x + 2)$ holds for all $x \in \mathbb{N}$. For example, the computing process for $x = 2$ is as follows.

$$(q_0, 2, 0) \vdash_{M_1} (q_1, 2, 0) \vdash_{M_1} (q_2, 2, 1) \vdash_{M_1} (q_3, 2, 2) \vdash_{M_1} (q_4, 2, 2)$$
$$\vdash_{M_1} (q_5, 1, 2) \vdash_{M_1} (q_1, 1, 2) \vdash_{M_1} (q_2, 1, 3) \vdash_{M_1} (q_3, 1, 4) \vdash_{M_1} (q_4, 1, 4)$$
$$\vdash_{M_1} (q_5, 0, 4) \vdash_{M_1} (q_1, 0, 4) \vdash_{M_1} (q_2, 0, 5) \vdash_{M_1} (q_3, 0, 6) \vdash_{M_1} (q_6, 0, 6)$$

□

9.2.2 Simulating irreversible counter machines by reversible ones

In this subsection, we show that any (irreversible) CM can be simulated by a reversible one by adding extra counters. First, the notion of simulation in CMs is given below, which is essentially the same as Definition 5.8 for the case of Turing machines.

Definition 9.5. For any CM $M = (Q, k, \delta, q_0, F)$, define a partial recursive function $\psi_M : \mathrm{ID}(M) \to \mathrm{ID}(M)$ as follows, where $\mathrm{ID}(M)$ is the set of all IDs of M, i.e., $\mathrm{ID}(M) = Q \times \mathbb{N}^k$.

$$\forall \alpha, \beta \in \mathrm{ID}(M) \ (\psi_M(\alpha) = \beta \ \Leftrightarrow \ (\alpha \vdash^*_M \beta \wedge \beta \text{ is a halting ID}))$$

Namely, $\psi_M(\alpha)$ is the halting ID reachable from α, if M eventually halts. Otherwise, $\psi_M(\alpha)$ is undefined.

Let M and $\tilde{M}$ be CMs. If there exist total recursive functions $c : \mathrm{ID}(M) \to \mathrm{ID}(\tilde{M})$, and $d : \mathrm{ID}(\tilde{M}) \to (\mathrm{ID}(M) \cup \{\bot\})$ that satisfy the following, then we say $\tilde{M}$ *simulates* M. Note that $d(\tilde{\alpha}) = \bot$ means there is no ID α of M that corresponds to $\tilde{\alpha}$. Here, c and d are called an *encoding function*, and a *decoding function*, respectively.

$$\begin{aligned}
&\forall \alpha \in \mathrm{ID}(M) \\
&((\psi_M(\alpha) \text{ is defined} \quad \Rightarrow \ d(\psi_{\tilde{M}}(c(\alpha))) = \psi_M(\alpha)) \wedge \\
&\ (\psi_M(\alpha) \text{ is undefined} \quad \Rightarrow \ \psi_{\tilde{M}}(c(\alpha)) \text{ is undefined}))
\end{aligned}$$

In the following, we do not give precise descriptions of c and d when constructing $\tilde{M}$ that simulates M, as in the case of Turing machines.

Next, we define the notion of state-degeneration degree for CMs, and show that any CM can be converted into a CM with the state-degeneration degree 2.

Definition 9.6. Let $M = (Q, k, \delta, q_0, F)$ be a CM. A state $q \in Q$ is called *state-degenerative* if there are at least two distinct quadruples $[q_1, i_1, x_1, q]$ and $[q_2, i_2, x_2, q]$ in δ. If there are exactly m such quadruples in δ, we say that *state-degeneration degree* of q is m, and denote it by $\mathrm{sdeg}(q) = m$. That is,

$$\mathrm{sdeg}(q) = |\{[p, i, x, q] \in \delta \mid p \in Q \wedge i \in \{1, \ldots, k\} \wedge x \in \{Z, P, -, 0, +\}\}|.$$

State-degeneration degree of M is defined by

$$\mathrm{sdeg}(M) = \max\{\mathrm{sdeg}(q) \mid q \in Q\}.$$

Lemma 9.2. *[15] For any CM(k) $M = (Q, k, \delta, q_0, F)$, there is a CM(k) $M' = (Q', k, \delta', q_0, F)$ with $\mathrm{sdeg}(M') \leq 2$ and $Q \subseteq Q'$ that satisfies the following.*

$$\begin{aligned}
&\forall m_1, \ldots, m_k, n_1, \ldots, n_k \in \mathbb{N}, \forall p, q \in Q \\
&((p, m_1, \ldots, m_k) \vdash_M (q, n_1, \ldots, n_k) \ \Leftrightarrow \ (p, m_1, \ldots, m_k) \vdash^*_{M'} (q, n_1, \ldots, n_k))
\end{aligned}$$

Proof. Construction method of the CM M' is as follows. At first, set $Q' := Q$ and $\delta' := \delta$, and then do the following procedure.

Choose a state $q \in Q$ such that $\text{sdeg}(q) > 2$ (if no such q exists, we have done). If $\text{sdeg}(q) = m$ there are m quadruples

$$[q_{r_1}, i_1, x_1, q], [q_{r_2}, i_2, x_2, q], \ldots, [q_{r_m}, i_k, x_m, q].$$

In M', these m quadruples are replaced by the $2m - 2$ quadruples shown below, where $q_{s_1}, \ldots, q_{s_{m-2}}$ are new states that should be added to δ' (see Fig. 9.2).

$$
\begin{array}{llll}
[q_{r_1}, & i_1, x_1, & q_{s_1}], & [q_{r_2}, & i_2, & x_2, & q_{s_1}], \\
[q_{s_1}, & 1, 0, & q_{s_2}], & [q_{r_3}, & i_3, & x_3, & q_{s_2}], \\
& & & \vdots \\
[q_{s_{j-1}}, & 1, 0, & q_{s_j}], & [q_{r_{j+1}}, & i_{j+1}, & x_{j+1}, & q_{s_j}], \\
& & & \vdots \\
[q_{s_{m-3}}, & 1, 0, & q_{s_{m-2}}], & [q_{r_{m-1}}, & i_{m-1}, & x_{m-1}, & q_{s_{m-2}}], \\
[q_{s_{m-2}}, & 1, 0, & q], & [q_{r_m}, & i_m, & x_m, & q]
\end{array}
$$

Repeating this procedure for all $q \in Q$ such that $\text{sdeg}(q) > 2$, a CM(k) M' with $\text{sdeg}(M') \leq 2$ is obtained. It is clear that M' simulates M. □

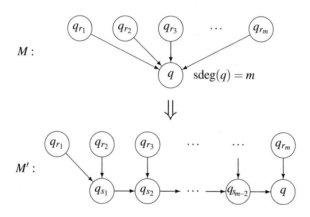

Fig. 9.2 Reducing the state-degeneration degree to 2 by adding new states $q_{s_1}, \ldots, q_{s_{m-2}}$

Note that, if M is an RCM, then $\text{sdeg}(M) \leq 2$ by the definition of reversibility of a CM (Definition 9.2).

We now show that any irreversible CM can be simulated by a reversible one by adding two extra counters to keep a "history" of a computation as in the case of constructing a reversible Turing machine by the method of Bennett [3] (see Sect. 5.2). But, here, the history is left as a garbage when it halts. A method of erasing the garbage will be given in Lemma 9.4.

Lemma 9.3. *[15] For any CM(k) $M = (Q, k, \delta, q_0, \{q_f\})$ in the normal form, there is an RCM(k+2) $M' = (Q', k+2, \delta', q_0, \{q_f\})$ in the normal form that satisfies the following.*

$$\forall m_1, \ldots, m_k, n_1, \ldots, n_k \in \mathbb{N}$$
$$((q_0, m_1, \ldots, m_k) \vdash^*_M (q_f, n_1, \ldots, n_k) \Leftrightarrow$$
$$\exists g \in \mathbb{N}((q_0, m_1, \ldots, m_k, 0, 0) \vdash^*_{M'} (q_f, n_1, \ldots, n_k, g, 0)))$$

Proof. By Lemma 9.2, we assume sdeg$(M) = 2$ (if sdeg$(M) = 1$ then M is already reversible, so we need not to consider this case). We construct CM$(k+2)$ M' that simulates M as below. M' uses k counters to simulate those of M, and keeps the history of its computation by the counter $k+1$ to make M' reversible. The counter $k+2$ is for working.

At first, set $Q' := \emptyset$ and $\delta' := \emptyset$, and then do the following procedure. By this, Q' and δ' of M' is obtained.

(1) For each reversible quadruple $[q_s, i_s, x_s, q_t]$ in δ, include the states q_s and q_t in Q', and include the following quadruple in δ'.

(1.1) $[q_s, i_s, x_s, q_t]$

(2) For each pair of irreversible quadruples $[q_r, i_r, x_r, q_t]$ and $[q_s, i_s, x_s, q_t]$ in δ, include the states $q_r, q_s, q_t, q(r,t,j), q(s,t,j), q(t,l)$ $(j = 1, \ldots, 5, \ l = 1, \ldots, 6)$ in Q', and the following quadruples in δ'.

(2.1)	$[q_r,$	$i_r,$	$x_r,$	$q(r,t,1)]$
(2.2)	$[q(r,t,1),$	$k+2,$	$Z,$	$q(r,t,2)]$
(2.3)	$[q(r,t,2),$	$k+1,$	$Z,$	$q(t,1)]$
(2.4)	$[q(r,t,2),$	$k+1,$	$P,$	$q(r,t,3)]$
(2.5)	$[q(r,t,3),$	$k+1,$	$-,$	$q(r,t,4)]$
(2.6)	$[q(r,t,4),$	$k+2,$	$+,$	$q(r,t,5)]$
(2.7)	$[q(r,t,5),$	$k+2,$	$P,$	$q(r,t,2)]$
(2.8)	$[q_s,$	$i_s,$	$x_s,$	$q(s,t,1)]$
(2.9)	$[q(s,t,1),$	$k+2,$	$Z,$	$q(s,t,2)]$
(2.10)	$[q(s,t,2),$	$k+1,$	$Z,$	$q(t,5)]$
(2.11)	$[q(s,t,2),$	$k+1,$	$P,$	$q(s,t,3)]$
(2.12)	$[q(s,t,3),$	$k+1,$	$-,$	$q(s,t,4)]$
(2.13)	$[q(s,t,4),$	$k+2,$	$+,$	$q(s,t,5)]$
(2.14)	$[q(s,t,5),$	$k+2,$	$P,$	$q(s,t,2)]$
(2.15)	$[q(t,1),$	$k+2,$	$Z,$	$q_t]$
(2.16)	$[q(t,1),$	$k+2,$	$P,$	$q(t,2)]$
(2.17)	$[q(t,2),$	$k+2,$	$-,$	$q(t,3)]$
(2.18)	$[q(t,3),$	$k+1,$	$+,$	$q(t,4)]$
(2.19)	$[q(t,4),$	$k+1,$	$P,$	$q(t,5)]$
(2.20)	$[q(t,5),$	$k+1,$	$+,$	$q(t,6)]$
(2.21)	$[q(t,6),$	$k+1,$	$P,$	$q(t,1)]$

When M executes a reversible quadruple, M' simply does so by (1.1). On the other hand, when M executes an irreversible quadruple, M' writes the information which quadruple is used into the counter $k+1$. This is done by (2.1) – (2.21). Since sdeg$(M) = 2$, there are always two possibilities of executed quadruple, say $[q_r, i_r, x_r, q_t]$ and $[q_s, i_s, x_s, q_t]$. Thus the choice sequence of quadruples (i.e., history) can be expressed in a binary number, and M' holds it in the counter $k+1$.

We first consider the case $[q_r, i_r, x_r, q_t]$ is used by M. Assume the counter $k+1$ keeps n, which represents the history up to this moment, and the counter $k+2$ keeps 0. After simulating the operation of M by (2.1), M' transfers the number n from the counter $k+1$ to the counter $k+2$ by (2.2) – (2.7). Then, using (2.15) – (2.21), M' multiplies the contents of the counter $k+2$ by 2. Thus the result $2n$ is obtained in the counter $k+1$.

Next, consider the case $[q_s, i_s, x_s, q_t]$ is used by M. Quadruples (2.8) – (2.14) acts essentially the same as (2.1) – (2.7). However, in this case, the quadruple (2.20) (rather than (2.15)) is executed first among (2.15) – (2.21). By this, the result $2n+1$ is obtained in the counter $k+1$.

Consequently, the information which quadruple was executed is kept as the least significant bit of the number in the counter $k+1$. By this operation M' becomes reversible. Indeed, it is easily verified that M' is deterministic and reversible. For example, the pairs of quadruples ((2.2), (2.7)), ((2.9), (2.14)), ((2.3), (2.21)), and ((2.10), (2.19)) satisfy the reversibility condition. It is also easy to see that M' is in the normal form.   □

Example 9.2. Consider a CM(2) $M_2 = (Q_2, 2, \delta_2, q_0, \{q_f\})$ in the normal form, where δ_2 consists of the following five quadruples.

(a) $[q_0, 1, 0, q_1]$
(b) $[q_1, 2, Z, q_f]$
(c) $[q_1, 2, P, q_2]$
(d) $[q_2, 2, -, q_3]$
(e) $[q_3, 1, +, q_1]$

The CM M_2 is irreversible, since the pair of the quadruples (a) and (e) violates the reversibility condition. Hence, these two are irreversible quadruples, while (b) – (d) are reversible ones. M_2 adds two numbers given in the counters 1 and 2, and stores the result in the counter 1. For example, $(q_0, 2, 2) \vdash^{8}_{M_2} (q_f, 4, 0)$. Since sdeg$(M_2) = 2$, we can apply the method of Lemma 9.3 to obtain RCM(4) $M'_2 = (Q'_2, 4, \delta'_2, q_0, \{q_f\})$ that simulates M_2. The set of states Q'_2 is as follows.

$$Q'_2 = Q_2 \cup \{q(0,1,j), q(3,1,j), q(1,l) \mid j \in \{1,\ldots,5\}, l \in \{1,\ldots,6\}\}$$

The set of quadruples δ'_2 is given below.

(1) Quadruples corresponding to the reversible quadruples (b) – (d).
   (1.1b) $[q_1, 2, Z, q_f]$
   (1.1c) $[q_1, 2, P, q_2]$
   (1.1d) $[q_2, 2, -, q_3]$

(2) Quadruples corresponding to the pair of irreversible quadruples (a) $[q_0, 1, 0, q_1]$ and (e) $[q_3, 1, +, q_1]$.

(2.1) $[q_0,$ $1, 0, q(0,1,1)]$
(2.2) $[q(0,1,1), 4, Z, q(0,1,2)]$
(2.3) $[q(0,1,2), 3, Z,$ $q(1,1)]$
(2.4) $[q(0,1,2), 3, P, q(0,1,3)]$
(2.5) $[q(0,1,3), 3, -, q(0,1,4)]$
(2.6) $[q(0,1,4), 4, +, q(0,1,5)]$
(2.7) $[q(0,1,5), 4, P, q(0,1,2)]$

(2.8) $[q_3,$ $1, +, q(3,1,1)]$
(2.9) $[q(3,1,1), 4, Z, q(3,1,2)]$
(2.10) $[q(3,1,2), 3, Z,$ $q(1,5)]$
(2.11) $[q(3,1,2), 3, P, q(3,1,3)]$
(2.12) $[q(3,1,3), 3, -, q(3,1,4)]$
(2.13) $[q(3,1,4), 4, +, q(3,1,5)]$
(2.14) $[q(3,1,5), 4, P, q(3,1,2)]$

(2.15) $[q(1,1), 4, Z,$ $q_1]$
(2.16) $[q(1,1), 4, P, q(1,2)]$
(2.17) $[q(1,2), 4, -, q(1,3)]$
(2.18) $[q(1,3), 3, +, q(1,4)]$
(2.19) $[q(1,4), 3, P, q(1,5)]$
(2.20) $[q(1,5), 3, +, q(1,6)]$
(2.21) $[q(1,6), 3, P, q(1,1)]$

If M_2 executes the irreversible quadruple (a), bit "0" is attached to the binary number kept in the counter 3 as the least significant bit. If M_2 executes (e), bit "1" is attached. For example, the addition 2+2 is carried out by M_2' in the following way.

$$(q_0, 2, 2, 0, 0) \vdash_{M_2'}^{4} (q_1, 2, 2, 0, 0) \vdash_{M_2'}^{1} (q_2, 2, 2, 0, 0)$$
$$\vdash_{M_2'}^{1} (q_3, 2, 1, 0, 0) \vdash_{M_2'}^{6} (q_1, 3, 1, 1, 0) \vdash_{M_2'}^{1} (q_2, 3, 1, 1, 0)$$
$$\vdash_{M_2'}^{1} (q_3, 3, 0, 1, 0) \vdash_{M_2'}^{16} (q_1, 4, 0, 3, 0) \vdash_{M_2'}^{1} (q_f, 4, 0, 3, 0)$$

□

The reversible $CM(k+2)$ M' constructed in Lemma 9.3, however, leaves a large number in the counter $k+1$ when it halts. In Lemma 9.4, a method of erasing this garbage information is shown, which is also based on the method of Bennett [3] for reversible Turing machines (see also Sect. 5.2).

Lemma 9.4. *[15] For any CM(k) $M = (Q, k, \delta, q_0, \{q_f\})$ in the normal form, there is an RCM(2k+2) $M^\dagger = (Q^\dagger, 2k+2, \delta^\dagger, q_0, \{\hat{q}_0\})$ in the normal form that satisfies the following.*

$$\forall m_1,\ldots,m_k,n_1,\ldots,n_k \in \mathbb{N}$$
$$((q_0,m_1,\ldots,m_k) \vdash^*_M (q_f,n_1,\ldots,n_k) \Leftrightarrow$$
$$(q_0,m_1,\ldots,m_k,0,0,0,\ldots,0) \vdash^*_{M^\dagger} (\hat{q}_0,m_1,\ldots,m_k,0,0,n_1,\ldots,n_k)$$

Proof. Using the method in Lemma 9.3, we first convert M to an equivalent reversible CM$(k+2)$ $M' = (Q',k+2,\delta',q_0,\{q_f\})$. We then construct $M^\dagger$ from M'. Like M', $M^\dagger$ uses the counters 1 through k for simulating those of M, and the counters $k+1$ and $k+2$ for keeping history and for working. The remaining k counters are used for storing the result of the computation. The entire computing process of $M^\dagger$ is divided into three stages as in the case of reversible Turing machines (see Theorem 5.1). They are forward computing stage, copying stage, and backward computing stage.

The set of state $Q^\dagger$ is as follows, where $\hat{Q}' = \{\hat{q} \mid q \in Q'\}$.

$$Q^\dagger = Q' \cup \hat{Q}'$$
$$\cup \{c(i,j),c(k+1,1),d(i,j') \mid i \in \{1,\ldots,k\}, j \in \{1,\ldots,4\}, j' \in \{1,\ldots,5\}\}$$

At first, set $\delta^\dagger := \emptyset$, and then do the following procedure. By this, the set of quadruples $\delta^\dagger$ of $M^\dagger$ is obtained.

1. Forward computing stage
   States and quadruples needed for this stage are exactly the same as M'. Thus, add all the quadruples in δ' to $\delta^\dagger$.

2. Copying stage
   In this stage, the contents of the counters 1 through k are copied to the counters $k+3$ through $2k+2$ using the counter $k+2$ for working.

   (1) Include the following quadruple in $\delta^\dagger$.

   (1.1) $[q_f, k+2, Z, c(1,1)]$

   (2) For each $i \in \{1,\ldots,k\}$, include the following quadruples in $\delta^\dagger$.

(2.1.i)	$[c(i,1)$,	i,	Z,	$d(i,1)]$
(2.2.i)	$[c(i,1)$,	i,	P,	$c(i,2)]$
(2.3.i)	$[c(i,2)$,	i,	$-$,	$c(i,3)]$
(2.4.i)	$[c(i,3)$,	$k+2$,	$+$,	$c(i,4)]$
(2.5.i)	$[c(i,4)$,	$k+2$,	P,	$c(i,1)]$
(2.6.i)	$[d(i,1)$,	$k+2$,	Z,	$c(i+1,1)]$
(2.7.i)	$[d(i,1)$,	$k+2$,	P,	$d(i,2)]$
(2.8.i)	$[d(i,2)$,	$k+2$,	$-$,	$d(i,3)]$
(2.9.i)	$[d(i,3)$,	i,	$+$,	$d(i,4)]$
(2.10.i)	$[d(i,4)$,	$i+k+2$,	$+$,	$d(i,5)]$
(2.11.i)	$[d(i,5)$,	i,	P,	$d(i,1)]$

   The contents of the counter i is first transferred to the counter $k+2$ by (2.1.i) – (2.5.i), and then to the both counters i and $i+k+2$ by (2.6.i) – (2.11.i). This procedure is repeated for $i = 1,\ldots,k$.

(3) Include the following quadruple in $\delta^\dagger$.

(3.1) $[c(k+1,1), k+2, Z, \hat{q}_f]$

It is easy to see that the above quadruples satisfy the reversibility condition.

3. Backward computing stage
We define x^{-1} for $x \in \{-, 0, +, Z, P\}$ as follows.

$$x^{-1} = \begin{cases} + & \text{if } x = - \\ 0 & \text{if } x = 0 \\ - & \text{if } x = + \\ Z & \text{if } x = Z \\ P & \text{if } x = P \end{cases}$$

Let $(\delta')^{-1}$ be the set of inverse quadruples obtained from δ', i.e.,

$$(\delta')^{-1} = \{ [\hat{q}, i, x^{-1}, \hat{p}] \mid [p, i, x, q] \in \delta' \}.$$

By the quadruples in $(\delta')^{-1}$, the computation performed in the forward computation stage is undone, and the contents of counter $k+1$ is erased reversibly, as in the case of reversible Turing machines. Thus, add all the quadruples in $(\delta')^{-1}$ to $\delta^\dagger$.

It is easy to see that $M^\dagger$ is in the normal form.

By $\delta^\dagger$, $M^\dagger$ performs the computations of the above three stages one by one in this order. Hence, the following holds for all $m_1, \ldots, m_k, n_1, \ldots, n_k \in \mathbb{N}$ such that $(q_0, m_1, \ldots, m_k) \vdash^*_M (q_f, n_1, \ldots, n_k)$, and for some $g \in \mathbb{N}$.

$$(q_0, m_1, \ldots, m_k, 0, 0, 0, \ldots, 0) \vdash^*_{M^\dagger} (q_f, n_1, \ldots, n_k, g, 0, 0, \ldots, 0)$$
$$\vdash^*_{M^\dagger} (\hat{q}_f, n_1, \ldots, n_k, g, 0, n_1, \ldots, n_k) \vdash^*_{M^\dagger} (\hat{q}_0, m_1, \ldots, m_k, 0, 0, n_1, \ldots, n_k)$$

Remark: In the copy stage of the above construction, all the counters 1 through k are copied. But it is of course not necessary. We can copy only needed results.   □

Example 9.3. Consider the CM(2) $M_2 = (Q_2, 2, \delta_2, q_0, \{q_f\})$, and the RCM(4) $M_2' = (Q_2', 4, \delta_2', q_0, \{q_f\})$ given in Example 9.2. We can construct a garbage-less RCM(6) $M_2^\dagger$ by the method of Lemma 9.4.

$$M_2^\dagger = (Q_2^\dagger, 6, \delta_2^\dagger, q_0, \{\hat{q}_0\})$$
$$Q_2^\dagger = Q_2' \cup \hat{Q}_2' \cup \{c(i,j), c(3,1), d(i,j') \mid i \in \{1,2\}, j \in \{1, \ldots, 4\}, j' \in \{1, \ldots, 5\}\}$$

The move relation $\delta_2^\dagger$ is the set of the following quadruples.

1. Forward computing stage (the same as δ_2')

$[q_1, \quad\quad 2, Z, \quad\quad q_f], [q_1, \quad\quad 2, P, \quad\quad q_2], [q_2, \quad\quad 2, -, \quad\quad q_3],$
$[q_0, \quad\quad 1, 0, \, q(0,1,1)], [q_3, \quad\quad 1, +, q(3,1,1)], [q(1,1), 4, Z, \quad q_1],$
$[q(0,1,1), 4, Z, q(0,1,2)], [q(3,1,1), 4, Z, q(3,1,2)], [q(1,1), 4, P, q(1,2)],$
$[q(0,1,2), 3, Z, \quad q(1,1)], [q(3,1,2), 3, Z, \quad q(1,5)], [q(1,2), 4, -, q(1,3)],$
$[q(0,1,2), 3, P, q(0,1,3)], [q(3,1,2), 3, P, q(3,1,3)], [q(1,3), 3, +, q(1,4)],$
$[q(0,1,3), 3, -, q(0,1,4)], [q(3,1,3), 3, -, q(3,1,4)], [q(1,4), 3, P, q(1,5)],$
$[q(0,1,4), 4, +, q(0,1,5)], [q(3,1,4), 4, +, q(3,1,5)], [q(1,5), 3, +, q(1,6)],$
$[q(0,1,5), 4, P, q(0,1,2)], [q(3,1,5), 4, P, q(3,1,2)], [q(1,6), 3, P, q(1,1)]$

2. Copying stage

(1.1) $[q_f, 4, Z, c(1,1)],$

(2.1.1) $[c(1,1), 1, Z, d(1,1)],$		(2.1.2) $[c(2,1), 2, Z, d(2,1)],$
(2.2.1) $[c(1,1), 1, P, \; c(1,2)],$		(2.2.2) $[c(2,1), 2, P, \; c(2,2)],$
(2.3.1) $[c(1,2), 1, -, c(1,3)],$		(2.3.2) $[c(2,2), 2, -, c(2,3)],$
(2.4.1) $[c(1,3), 4, +, c(1,4)],$		(2.4.2) $[c(2,3), 4, +, c(2,4)],$
(2.5.1) $[c(1,4), 4, P, \; c(1,1)],$		(2.5.2) $[c(2,4), 4, P, \; c(2,1)],$
(2.6.1) $[d(1,1), 4, Z, c(2,1)],$		(2.6.2) $[d(2,1), 4, Z, c(3,1)],$
(2.7.1) $[d(1,1), 4, P, d(1,2)],$		(2.7.2) $[d(2,1), 4, P, d(2,2)],$
(2.8.1) $[d(1,2), 4, -, d(1,3)],$		(2.8.2) $[d(2,2), 4, -, d(2,3)],$
(2.9.1) $[d(1,3), 1, +, d(1,4)],$		(2.9.2) $[d(2,3), 2, +, d(2,4)],$
(2.10.1) $[d(1,4), 5, +, d(1,5)],$		(2.10.2) $[d(2,4), 6, +, d(2,5)],$
(2.11.1) $[d(1,5), 1, P, d(1,1)],$		(2.11.2) $[d(2,5), 2, P, d(2,1)]$

(3.1) $[c(3,1), 4, Z, \hat{q}_f]$

3. Backward computing stage

$[\hat{q}_f, \quad\quad 2, Z, \quad\quad \hat{q}_1], [\hat{q}_2, \quad\quad 2, P, \quad\quad \hat{q}_1], [\hat{q}_3, \quad\quad 2, +, \quad\quad \hat{q}_2],$
$[\hat{q}(0,1,1), 1, 0, \quad\quad \hat{q}_0], [\hat{q}(3,1,1), 1, -, \quad\quad \hat{q}_3], [\hat{q}_1, \quad\quad 4, Z, \hat{q}(1,1)],$
$[\hat{q}(0,1,2), 4, Z, \hat{q}(0,1,1)], [\hat{q}(3,1,2), 4, Z, \hat{q}(3,1,1)], [\hat{q}(1,2), 4, P, \hat{q}(1,1)],$
$[\hat{q}(1,1), \quad 3, Z, \hat{q}(0,1,2)], [\hat{q}(1,5), \quad 3, Z, \hat{q}(3,1,2)], [\hat{q}(1,3), 4, +, \hat{q}(1,2)],$
$[\hat{q}(0,1,3), 3, P, \hat{q}(0,1,2)], [\hat{q}(3,1,3), 3, P, \hat{q}(3,1,2)], [\hat{q}(1,4), 3, -, \hat{q}(1,3)],$
$[\hat{q}(0,1,4), 3, +, \hat{q}(0,1,3)], [\hat{q}(3,1,4), 3, +, \hat{q}(3,1,3)], [\hat{q}(1,5), 3, P, \hat{q}(1,4)],$
$[\hat{q}(0,1,5), 4, -, \hat{q}(0,1,4)], [\hat{q}(3,1,5), 4, -, \hat{q}(3,1,4)], [\hat{q}(1,6), 3, -, \hat{q}(1,5)],$
$[\hat{q}(0,1,2), 4, P, \hat{q}(0,1,5)], [\hat{q}(3,1,2), 4, P, \hat{q}(3,1,5)], [\hat{q}(1,1), 3, P, \hat{q}(1,6)]$

The computing process starting from $(q_0, 2, 2, 0, 0, 0)$ is as follows.

$$(q_0, 2, 2, 0, 0, 0, 0) \vdash_{M_2^\dagger}^{31} (q_f, 4, 0, 3, 0, 0, 0)$$
$$\vdash_{M_2^\dagger}^{42} (\hat{q}_f, 4, 0, 3, 0, 4, 0) \vdash_{M_2^\dagger}^{31} (\hat{q}_0, 2, 2, 0, 0, 4, 0)$$

□

9.2.3 Universality of reversible two-counter machine

Minsky [12] showed the following result for irreversible CMs.

Lemma 9.5. *[12] For any Turing machine T there is a CM(5) M that simulates T.*

His formulation of CM is different from ours. But, it is easy to show that five counters are enough to simulate a Turing machine for our CM by an essentially the same way as shown in [12].

Minsky further showed that any k-counter machine can be simulated by a two-counter machine by a technique of using Gödel number. Namely, the contents of the k counters $n_1, \ldots, n_k$ are encoded into a single integer $p_1^{n_1} \cdots p_k^{n_k}$, where p_i is the i-th prime (i.e., $p_1 = 2$, $p_2 = 3$, $p_3 = 5, \ldots$). Thus, the contents of k counters can be packed into one counter. One more counter is necessary to perform the operations to these "virtual" counters implemented in the first counter. By this method, CM(2) is shown to be computationally universal.

Lemma 9.6. *[12] For any CM(k) M ($k \in \{3,4,\ldots\}$) there is a CM(2) M′ that simulates M.*

From Lemmas 9.5 and 9.6, universality of CM(2) is derived.

Theorem 9.1. *[12] The class of CM(2) is computationally universal.*

We show a reversible version of Theorem 9.1 below.

Lemma 9.7. *[15] For any RCM(k) M = $(Q, k, \delta, q_0, \{q_f\})$ ($k \in \{3,4,\ldots\}$) in the normal form, there is an RCM(2) $M^\dagger = (Q^\dagger, 2, \delta^\dagger, q_0, \{q_f\})$ in the normal form that satisfies the following, where p_i denotes the i-th prime number.*

$$\forall m_1, \ldots, m_k, n_1, \ldots, n_k \in \mathbb{N}$$
$$((q_0, m_1, \ldots, m_k) \vdash_M^* (q_f, n_1, \ldots, n_k) \Leftrightarrow$$
$$(q_0, p_1^{m_1} \cdots p_k^{m_k}, 0) \vdash_{M^\dagger}^* (q_f, p_1^{n_1} \cdots p_k^{n_k}, 0)$$

Proof. We first note that, in general, it cannot be assumed that a given RCM M is in the normal form (Definition 9.4), since Lemma 9.1 holds for irreversible CMs. However, if an RCM is constructed by the method given in Lemma 9.3 or 9.4, then it is in the normal form. Here, we use the method in these lemmas to have a normal form RCM M, since such an RCM can be constructed from any CM.

We now compose $M^\dagger$ from M. At first, set $Q^\dagger := \emptyset$ and $\delta^\dagger := \emptyset$, and then do the following procedure. By this, the sets $Q^\dagger$ and $\delta^\dagger$ of $M^\dagger$ are obtained.

(1) For each quadruple $[q_r, i, 0, q_s]$ in δ, add the states q_r and q_s to $Q^\dagger$, and add the same quadruple to $\delta^\dagger$.

(1.1) $[q_r, 1, 0, q_s]$

(2) For each quadruple $[q_r, i, +, q_s]$ in δ, add the states $q_r, q_s, q(r, j), q(r, 6, l)$ ($j = 1, \ldots, 7$, $l = 1, \ldots, p_i$) to $Q^\dagger$, and the following $p_i + 10$ quadruples to $\delta^\dagger$.

(2.1)	$[q_r,$	2, Z,	$q(r,1)]$
(2.2)	$[q(r,1),$	1, Z,	$q(r,5)]$
(2.3)	$[q(r,1),$	1, P,	$q(r,2)]$
(2.4)	$[q(r,2),$	1, $-$,	$q(r,3)]$
(2.5)	$[q(r,3),$	2, $+$,	$q(r,4)]$
(2.6)	$[q(r,4),$	2, P,	$q(r,1)]$
(2.7)	$[q(r,5),$	2, Z,	$q_s]$
(2.8)	$[q(r,5),$	2, P,	$q(r,6)]$
(2.9)	$[q(r,6),$	2, $-$,	$q(r,6,1)]$
(2.10.1)	$[q(r,6,1),$	1, $+$,	$q(r,6,2)]$
(2.10.2)	$[q(r,6,2),$	1, $+$,	$q(r,6,3)]$

$$\vdots$$

(2.10.p_i-1)	$[q(r,6,p_i-1),$	1, $+$,	$q(r,6,p_i)]$
(2.10.p_i)	$[q(r,6,p_i),$	1, $+$,	$q(r,7)]$
(2.11)	$[q(r,7),$	1, P,	$q(r,5)]$

By quadruples (2.1) – (2.6) the contents of the counter 1 is transferred to the counter 2. Then by (2.7) – (2.11) it is multiplied by p_i and stored in the counter 1. In this way, $[q_r, i, +, q_s]$ of M is simulated by $M^\dagger$. It is easy to verify that the above quadruples are all reversible in $\delta^\dagger$, since $[q_r, i, +, q_s]$ is reversible in δ.

(3) For each quadruple $[q_r, i, -, q_s]$ in δ, add the states $q_r, q_s, q(r, j), q(r, 5, l)$ ($j = 1, \ldots, 7$, $l = 1, \ldots, p_i$) to $Q^\dagger$, and the following $p_i + 10$ quadruples to $\delta^\dagger$.

(3.1)	$[q_r,$	2, Z,	$q(r,1)]$
(3.2)	$[q(r,1),$	1, Z,	$q(r,5)]$
(3.3)	$[q(r,1),$	1, P,	$q(r,2)]$
(3.4)	$[q(r,2),$	1, $-$,	$q(r,3)]$
(3.5)	$[q(r,3),$	2, $+$,	$q(r,4)]$
(3.6)	$[q(r,4),$	2, P,	$q(r,1)]$
(3.7)	$[q(r,5),$	2, Z,	$q_s]$
(3.8)	$[q(r,5),$	2, P,	$q(r,5,1)]$
(3.9.1)	$[q(r,5,1),$	2, $-$,	$q(r,5,2)]$
(3.9.2)	$[q(r,5,2),$	2, $-$,	$q(r,5,3)]$

$$\vdots$$

(3.9.p_i-1)	$[q(r,5,p_i-1),$	2, $-$,	$q(r,5,p_i)]$
(3.9.p_i)	$[q(r,5,p_i),$	2, $-$,	$q(r,6)]$
(3.10)	$[q(r,6),$	1, $+$,	$q(r,7)]$
(3.11)	$[q(r,7),$	1, P,	$q(r,5)]$

Quadruples (3.1) – (3.6) work just the same as (2.1) – (2.6). By (3.7) – (3.11) the contents of the counter 2 is divided by p_i and stored in the counter 1, and thus $[q_r, i, -, q_s]$ of M is simulated. It is easy to see all the quadruples are reversible.

(4) For each pair of quadruples $[q_r, i, Z, q_s]$ and $[q_r, i, P, q_t]$ in δ, add q_r, $q(r, j, 1)$, $q(r, j, 2)$ $(j = 0, \ldots, p_i)$ to $Q^\dagger$, and the following $3p_i + 3$ quadruples to $\delta^\dagger$.

(4.0)	$[q_r,$	2, Z,	$q(r, 0, 1)]$
(4.0.1)	$[q(r, 0, 1),$	1, Z,	$q'(t, 0, 1)]$
(4.0.2)	$[q(r, 0, 1),$	1, P,	$q(r, 0, 2)]$
(4.0.3)	$[q(r, 0, 2),$	1, $-,$	$q(r, 1, 1)]$
(4.1.1)	$[q(r, 1, 1),$	1, Z,	$q'(s, 1, 1)]$
(4.1.2)	$[q(r, 1, 1),$	1, P,	$q(r, 1, 2)]$
(4.1.3)	$[q(r, 1, 2),$	1, $-,$	$q(r, 2, 1)]$
(4.2.1)	$[q(r, 2, 1),$	1, Z,	$q'(s, 2, 1)]$
(4.2.2)	$[q(r, 2, 1),$	1, P,	$q(r, 2, 2)]$
(4.2.3)	$[q(r, 2, 2),$	1, $-,$	$q(r, 3, 1)]$

$$\vdots$$

$(4.p_i - 2.1)$	$[q(r, p_i - 2, 1), 1, Z, q'(s, p_i - 2, 1)]$
$(4.p_i - 2.2)$	$[q(r, p_i - 2, 1), 1, P, q(r, p_i - 2, 2)]$
$(4.p_i - 2.3)$	$[q(r, p_i - 2, 2), 1, -, q(r, p_i - 1, 1)]$
$(4.p_i - 1.1)$	$[q(r, p_i - 1, 1), 1, Z, q'(s, p_i - 1, 1)]$
$(4.p_i - 1.2)$	$[q(r, p_i - 1, 1), 1, P, q(r, p_i - 1, 2)]$
$(4.p_i - 1.3)$	$[q(r, p_i - 1, 2), 1, -, \quad q(r, p_i, 1)]$
$(4.p_i.1)$	$[q(r, p_i, 1), \quad 2, +, \quad q(r, p_i, 2)]$
$(4.p_i.2)$	$[q(r, p_i, 2), \quad 2, P, \quad q(r, 0, 1)]$

Note that, if only $[q_r, i, Z, q_s]$ exists in δ (and thus $[q_r, i, P, q_t] \notin \delta$), then $3p_i + 2$ quadruples except (4.0.1) are added to $\delta^\dagger$. On the other hand, if only $[q_r, i, P, q_t]$ exists in δ, then $2p_i + 4$ quadruples except $(4.j.1)$ $(j = 1, \ldots, p_i - 1)$ are added to $\delta^\dagger$. To test whether the contents of the counter i of M is positive or zero, $M^\dagger$ must check if the contents of the counter 1 is divisible by p_i or not. This is performed by the above quadruples. When division is completed, the contents of the counter 1 becomes 0, and the quotient is in the counter 2. Then $M^\dagger$ goes to the state $q'(t, 0, 1)$ if the remainder is 0, or $q'(s, j, 1)$ if the remainder is $j(= 1, \ldots, p_i - 1)$. Restoration of the original contents of the counter 1, and the transition to the state q_t or q_s are performed by the quadruples $(5.0.1) - (5.p_i.2)$ below.

(5) For each state q_s such that $[q, i, x, q_s]$ exists in δ for some $q \in Q$, $i \in \{1, \ldots, k\}$ and $x \in \{Z, P\}$, include $q_s, q'(s, j, 1), q'(s, j, 2)$ $(j = 0, \ldots, p_i)$ in $Q^\dagger$, and the following $2p_i + 3$ quadruples in $\delta^\dagger$. (Note that to such q_s there corresponds unique i because M is reversible.)

$$
\begin{array}{lll}
(5.0.1) & [q'(s,0,1), & 2,\,Z, & q_s] \\
(5.0.2) & [q'(s,0,1), & 2,\,P, & q'(s,0,2)] \\
(5.0.3) & [q'(s,0,2), & 2,\,-, & q'(s,p_i,1)] \\[4pt]
(5.p_i.1) & [q'(s,p_i,1), & 1,\,+, & q'(s,p_i,2)] \\
(5.p_i.2) & [q'(s,p_i,2), & 1,\,P, & q'(s,p_i-1,1)] \\[4pt]
(5.p_i-1.1) & [q'(s,p_i-1,1), & 1,\,+, & q'(s,p_i-1,2)] \\
(5.p_i-1.2) & [q'(s,p_i-1,2), & 1,\,P, & q'(s,p_i-2,1)] \\
\end{array}
$$

$$\vdots$$

$$
\begin{array}{lll}
(5.2.1) & [q'(s,2,1), & 1,\,+, & q'(s,2,2)] \\
(5.2.2) & [q'(s,2,2), & 1,\,P, & q'(s,1,1)] \\[4pt]
(5.1.1) & [q'(s,1,1), & 1,\,+, & q'(s,1,2)] \\
(5.1.2) & [q'(s,1,2), & 1,\,P, & q'(s,0,1)] \\
\end{array}
$$

We can verify that the quadruples $(4.0) - (4.p_i.2)$ and $(5.0.1) - (5.p_i.2)$ are all reversible from the fact M is reversible.

In $(1) - (5)$, each operation on a counter i of M is simulated by the set of quadruples that operate on the "virtual" counter stored in the form of $p_i^{n_i}$ in the counter 1 of $M^\dagger$. In this way, M is simulated by $M^\dagger$ step by step. □

Example 9.4. Consider an RCM(3) $M_3 = (Q_3, 3, \delta_3, q_0, \{q_f\})$ with the following quadruples as δ_3.

(a) $[q_0, 2, Z, q_1]$
(b) $[q_1, 1, Z, q_f]$
(c) $[q_1, 1, P, q_2]$
(d) $[q_2, 1, -, q_3]$
(e) $[q_3, 2, +, q_4]$
(f) $[q_4, 3, +, q_5]$
(g) $[q_5, 2, P, q_1]$

M_3 reversibly transfers the number given in the counter 1 to the counters 2 and 3. For example, $(q_0, 3, 0, 0) \vdash^{17}_{M_3} (q_f, 0, 3, 3)$. The RCM(2) $M_3^\dagger = (Q_3^\dagger, 2, \delta_3^\dagger, q_0, \{q_f\})$ constructed by the method of Lemma 9.7 has the following 93 quadruples.

1. Quadruples corresponding to (a) $[q_0, 2, Z, q_1]$:

(4.0.a)	$[q_0,\qquad 2,\ Z,\ q(0,0,1)]$
(4.0.2.a)	$[q(0,0,1),\ 1,\ P,\ q(0,0,2)]$
(4.0.3.a)	$[q(0,0,2),\ 1,\ -,\ q(0,1,1)]$
(4.1.1.a)	$[q(0,1,1),\ 1,\ Z,\ q'(1,1,1)]$
(4.1.2.a)	$[q(0,1,1),\ 1,\ P,\ q(0,1,2)]$
(4.1.3.a)	$[q(0,1,2),\ 1,\ -,\ q(0,2,1)]$
(4.2.1.a)	$[q(0,2,1),\ 1,\ Z,\ q'(1,2,1)]$
(4.2.2.a)	$[q(0,2,1),\ 1,\ P,\ q(0,2,2)]$
(4.2.3.a)	$[q(0,2,2),\ 1,\ -,\ q(0,3,1)]$
(4.3.1.a)	$[q(0,3,1),\ 2,\ +,\ q(0,3,2)]$
(4.3.2.a)	$[q(0,3,2),\ 2,\ P,\ q(0,0,1)]$

2. Quadruples corresponding to the state q_1:

(5.0.1.1)	$[q'(1,0,1),\ 2,\ Z,\qquad q_1]$
(5.0.2.1)	$[q'(1,0,1),\ 2,\ P, q'(1,0,2)]$
(5.0.3.1)	$[q'(1,0,2),\ 2,\ -, q'(1,3,1)]$
(5.3.1.1)	$[q'(1,3,1),\ 1,\ +, q'(1,3,2)]$
(5.3.2.1)	$[q'(1,3,2),\ 1,\ P, q'(1,2,1)]$
(5.2.1.1)	$[q'(1,2,1),\ 1,\ +, q'(1,2,2)]$
(5.2.2.1)	$[q'(1,2,2),\ 1,\ P, q'(1,1,1)]$
(5.1.1.1)	$[q'(1,1,1),\ 1,\ +, q'(1,1,2)]$
(5.1.2.1)	$[q'(1,1,2),\ 1,\ P, q'(1,0,1)]$

3. Quadruples corresponding to the pair (b) $[q_1, 1, Z, q_f]$ and (c) $[q_1, 1, P, q_2]$:

(4.0.bc)	$[q_1,\qquad 2,\ Z,\ q(1,0,1)]$
(4.0.1.bc)	$[q(1,0,1),\ 1,\ Z,\ q'(2,0,1)]$
(4.0.2.bc)	$[q(1,0,1),\ 1,\ P,\ q(1,0,2)]$
(4.0.3.bc)	$[q(1,0,2),\ 1,\ -,\ q(1,1,1)]$
(4.1.1.bc)	$[q(1,1,1),\ 1,\ Z,\ q'(f,1,1)]$
(4.1.2.bc)	$[q(1,1,1),\ 1,\ P,\ q(1,1,2)]$
(4.1.3.bc)	$[q(1,1,2),\ 1,\ -,\ q(1,2,1)]$
(4.2.1.bc)	$[q(1,2,1),\ 2,\ +,\ q(1,2,2)]$
(4.2.2.bc)	$[q(1,2,2),\ 2,\ P,\ q(1,0,1)]$

4. Quadruples corresponding to the state q_f:

(5.0.1.f)	$[q'(f,0,1),\ 2,\ Z,\qquad q_f]$
(5.0.2.f)	$[q'(f,0,1),\ 2,\ P, q'(f,0,2)]$
(5.0.3.f)	$[q'(f,0,2),\ 2,\ -, q'(f,2,1)]$
(5.2.1.f)	$[q'(f,2,1),\ 1,\ +, q'(f,2,2)]$
(5.2.2.f)	$[q'(f,2,2),\ 1,\ P, q'(f,1,1)]$
(5.1.1.f)	$[q'(f,1,1),\ 1,\ +, q'(f,1,2)]$
(5.1.2.f)	$[q'(f,1,2),\ 1,\ P, q'(f,0,1)]$

5. Quadruples corresponding to the state q_2:

(5.0.1.2)	$[q'(2,0,1),$	$2,$	$Z,$	$q_2]$
(5.0.2.2)	$[q'(2,0,1),$	$2,$	$P,$	$q'(2,0,2)]$
(5.0.3.2)	$[q'(2,0,2),$	$2,$	$-,$	$q'(2,2,1)]$
(5.2.1.2)	$[q'(2,2,1),$	$1,$	$+,$	$q'(2,2,2)]$
(5.2.2.2)	$[q'(2,2,2),$	$1,$	$P,$	$q'(2,1,1)]$
(5.1.1.2)	$[q'(2,1,1),$	$1,$	$+,$	$q'(2,1,2)]$
(5.1.2.2)	$[q'(2,1,2),$	$1,$	$P,$	$q'(2,0,1)]$

6. Quadruples corresponding to (d) $[q_2, 1, -, q_3]$:

(3.1.d)	$[q_2,$	$2,$	$Z,$	$q(2,1)]$
(3.2.d)	$[q(2,1),$	$1,$	$Z,$	$q(2,5)]$
(3.3.d)	$[q(2,1),$	$1,$	$P,$	$q(2,2)]$
(3.4.d)	$[q(2,2),$	$1,$	$-,$	$q(2,3)]$
(3.5.d)	$[q(2,3),$	$2,$	$+,$	$q(2,4)]$
(3.6.d)	$[q(2,4),$	$2,$	$P,$	$q(2,1)]$
(3.7.d)	$[q(2,5),$	$2,$	$Z,$	$q_3]$
(3.8.d)	$[q(2,5),$	$2,$	$P,$	$q(2,5,1)]$
(3.9.1.d)	$[q(2,5,1),$	$2,$	$-,$	$q(2,5,2)]$
(3.9.2.d)	$[q(2,5,2),$	$2,$	$-,$	$q(2,6)]$
(3.10.d)	$[q(2,6),$	$1,$	$+,$	$q(2,7)]$
(3.11.d)	$[q(2,7),$	$1,$	$P,$	$q(2,5)]$

7. Quadruples corresponding to (e) $[q_3, 2, +, q_4]$:

(2.1.e)	$[q_3,$	$2,$	$Z,$	$q(3,1)]$
(2.2.e)	$[q(3,1),$	$1,$	$Z,$	$q(3,5)]$
(2.3.e)	$[q(3,1),$	$1,$	$P,$	$q(3,2)]$
(2.4.e)	$[q(3,2),$	$1,$	$-,$	$q(3,3)]$
(2.5.e)	$[q(3,3),$	$2,$	$+,$	$q(3,4)]$
(2.6.e)	$[q(3,4),$	$2,$	$P,$	$q(3,1)]$
(2.7.e)	$[q(3,5),$	$2,$	$Z,$	$q_4]$
(2.8.e)	$[q(3,5),$	$2,$	$P,$	$q(3,6)]$
(2.9.e)	$[q(3,6),$	$2,$	$-,$	$q(3,6,1)]$
(2.10.1.e)	$[q(3,6,1),$	$1,$	$+,$	$q(3,6,2)]$
(2.10.2.e)	$[q(3,6,2),$	$1,$	$+,$	$q(3,6,3)]$
(2.10.3.e)	$[q(3,6,3),$	$1,$	$+,$	$q(3,7)]$
(2.11.e)	$[q(3,7),$	$1,$	$P,$	$q(3,5)]$

8. Quadruples corresponding to (f) $[q_4, 3, +, q_5]$:

(2.1.f)	$[q_4,\quad\quad 2, Z,\quad q(4,1)]$
(2.2.f)	$[q(4,1),\quad 1, Z,\quad q(4,5)]$
(2.3.f)	$[q(4,1),\quad 1, P,\quad q(4,2)]$
(2.4.f)	$[q(4,2),\quad 1, -,\quad q(4,3)]$
(2.5.f)	$[q(4,3),\quad 2, +,\quad q(4,4)]$
(2.6.f)	$[q(4,4),\quad 2, P,\quad q(4,1)]$
(2.7.f)	$[q(4,5),\quad 2, Z,\quad\quad q_5]$
(2.8.f)	$[q(4,5),\quad 2, P,\quad q(4,6)]$
(2.9.f)	$[q(4,6),\quad 2, -, q(4,6,1)]$
(2.10.1.f)	$[q(4,6,1), 1, +, q(4,6,2)]$
(2.10.2.f)	$[q(4,6,2), 1, +, q(4,6,3)]$
(2.10.3.f)	$[q(4,6,3), 1, +, q(4,6,4)]$
(2.10.4.f)	$[q(4,6,4), 1, +, q(4,6,5)]$
(2.10.5.f)	$[q(4,6,5), 1, +,\quad q(4,7)]$
(2.11.f)	$[q(4,7),\quad 1, P,\quad q(4,5)]$

9. Quadruples corresponding to (g) $[q_5, 2, P, q_1]$:

(4.0.g)	$[q_5,\quad\quad 2, Z, q(5,0,1)]$
(4.0.1.g)	$[q(5,0,1), 1, Z, q'(1,0,1)]$
(4.0.2.g)	$[q(5,0,1), 1, P, q(5,0,2)]$
(4.0.3.g)	$[q(5,0,2), 1, -, q(5,1,1)]$
(4.1.2.g)	$[q(5,1,1), 1, P, q(5,1,2)]$
(4.1.3.g)	$[q(5,1,2), 1, -, q(5,2,1)]$
(4.2.2.g)	$[q(5,2,1), 1, P, q(5,2,2)]$
(4.2.3.g)	$[q(5,2,2), 1, -, q(5,3,1)]$
(4.3.1.g)	$[q(5,3,1), 2, +, q(5,3,2)]$
(4.3.2.g)	$[q(5,3,2), 2, P, q(5,0,1)]$

By $\delta_3^\dagger$, $M_3^\dagger$ simulates M_3 step by step. For example, consider the following computation by M_3.

$$(q_0,1,0,0) \underset{M_3}{\vdash} (q_1,1,0,0) \underset{M_3}{\vdash} (q_2,1,0,0) \underset{M_3}{\vdash} (q_3,0,0,0)$$
$$\underset{M_3}{\vdash} (q_4,0,1,0) \underset{M_3}{\vdash} (q_5,0,1,1) \underset{M_3}{\vdash} (q_1,0,1,1) \underset{M_3}{\vdash} (q_f,0,1,1)$$

Then, $M_3^\dagger$ simulates it as follows.

$$(q_0,2^1 3^0 5^0,0) \underset{M_3^\dagger}{\vdash^{11}} (q_1,2^1 3^0 5^0,0) \underset{M_3^\dagger}{\vdash^{15}} (q_2,2^1 3^0 5^0,0) \underset{M_3^\dagger}{\vdash^{16}} (q_3,2^0 3^0 5^0,0)$$
$$\underset{M_3^\dagger}{\vdash^{13}} (q_4,2^0 3^1 5^0,0) \underset{M_3^\dagger}{\vdash^{39}} (q_5,2^0 3^1 5^1,0) \underset{M_3^\dagger}{\vdash^{83}} (q_1,2^0 3^1 5^1,0) \underset{M_3^\dagger}{\vdash^{91}} (q_f,2^0 3^1 5^1,0)$$

$\square$

From Lemmas 9.4, 9.5, and 9.7, we can conclude that RCMs with only two counters are universal.

Theorem 9.2. *[15] The class of RCM(2) is computationally universal.*

9.3 Reversible Multi-head Finite Automata

A multi-head finite automaton (MFA) is a classical model for language recognition, and has relatively high recognition capability (see [5] for the survey). Morita [16] proposed a reversible two-way multi-head finite automaton (RMFA), and investigated its properties. It is well known that the class of deterministic MFAs is characterized by the complexity class of deterministic logarithmic space. Lange, McKenzie, and Tapp [11] showed that the class of deterministic space $S(n)$ is equal to the class of reversible space $S(n)$. Hence, the class of MFAs is characterized by the class of reversible space $\log n$. Axelsen [2] showed that the class of RMFAs is also characterized by this complexity class. Then, Morita [17] proved a stronger result that any given k-head finite automaton can be converted into a reversible k-head finite automaton that simulates the former ($k = 1, 2, \dots$). Hence, an accepting power of a k-head finite automaton does not decrease even when the reversibility constraint is added. Note that, Kunc and Okhotin [8] also gave a similar result independently. In this section, we describe the simple conversion procedure given in [17]. It is based on a similar idea to convert an irreversible space-bounded Turing machine to a reversible one shown in Theorem 8.2.

9.3.1 Basic definitions on two-way multi-head finite automata

A two-way multi-head finite automaton consists of a finite control, a finite number of heads that can move in two directions, and a read-only input tape as shown in Fig. 9.3. In the following, we consider only two-way multi-head finite automata rather than one-way ones, and thus the word "two-way" will be omitted.

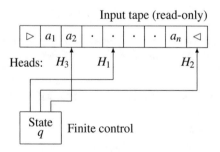

Fig. 9.3 Two-way multi-head finite automaton (MFA)

Definition 9.7. A *multi-head finite automaton* (MFA) as an *acceptor* is defined by

$$M = (Q, \Sigma, k, \delta, \triangleright, \triangleleft, q_0, A, N).$$

Here, Q is a nonempty finite set of states, and Σ is a nonempty finite set of input symbols. A positive integer $k(\in \{1,2,\dots\})$ is the number of heads, and thus M is also called a *k-head finite automaton* (MFA(k)). The symbols $\triangleright$ and $\triangleleft$ are the left and right endmarkers, respectively, such that $\{\triangleright,\triangleleft\} \cap \Sigma = \emptyset$, $q_0 (\in Q)$ is the initial state, $A (\subset Q)$ is a set of *accepting states*, and $N (\subset Q)$ is a set of *non-accepting states* such that $A \cap N = \emptyset$. The item δ is a move relation, which is a subset of $(Q \times ((\Sigma \cup \{\triangleright,\triangleleft\})^k \cup \{-1,0,+1\}^k) \times Q)$. Note that $-1, 0$, and $+1$ stand for left-shift, no-shift, and right-shift of each head, respectively. In what follows, we also use $-$ and $+$ instead of -1 and $+1$ for simplicity. Each element $r = [p,\mathbf{x},q] \in \delta$ is called a *rule* (in the triplet form) of M, where $\mathbf{x} = [s_1,\dots,s_k] \in (\Sigma \cup \{\triangleright,\triangleleft\})^k$ or $\mathbf{x} = [d_1,\dots,d_k] \in \{-,0,+\}^k$. A rule of the form $[p,[s_1,\dots,s_k],q]$ is called a *read rule*, and means if M is in the state p and reads symbols $[s_1,\dots,s_k]$ by its k heads, then go to the state q. A rule of the form $[p,[d_1,\dots,d_k],q]$ is called a *shift rule*, and means if M is in the state p then shift the heads to the directions $[d_1,\dots,d_k]$ and go to the state q. We assume each $q_h \in A \cup N$ is a *halting state*, i.e., there is no rule of the form $[q_h,\mathbf{x},p]$ in δ.

Determinism and reversibility of an MFA is defined as follows.

Definition 9.8. Let $M = (Q,\Sigma,k,\delta,\triangleright,\triangleleft,q_0,A,N)$ be an MFA. M is called a *deterministic MFA*, if the following holds for any pair of distinct rules $[p_1,\mathbf{x}_1,q_1]$ and $[p_2,\mathbf{x}_2,q_2]$ in δ.

$$(p_1 = p_2) \;\Rightarrow\; (\mathbf{x}_1 \notin \{-,0,+\}^k \wedge \mathbf{x}_2 \notin \{-,0,+\}^k \wedge \mathbf{x}_1 \neq \mathbf{x}_2)$$

It means that, if the present states are the same, then they are both read rules, and the k-tuples of read symbols $\mathbf{x}_1$ and $\mathbf{x}_2$ are different.

M is called a *reversible MFA* (RMFA), if the following holds for any pair of distinct rules $[p_1,\mathbf{x}_1,q_1]$ and $[p_2,\mathbf{x}_2,q_2]$ in δ,

$$(q_1 = q_2) \;\Rightarrow\; (\mathbf{x}_1 \notin \{-,0,+\}^k \wedge \mathbf{x}_2 \notin \{-,0,+\}^k \wedge \mathbf{x}_1 \neq \mathbf{x}_2)$$

It means that, if the next states are the same, then they are both read rules, and the k-tuples of read symbols $\mathbf{x}_1$ and $\mathbf{x}_2$ are different. The above is called the *reversibility condition*.

In the following, we consider only deterministic MFAs, and thus the word "deterministic" will be omitted.

An instantaneous description (ID) of an MFA M, and the transition relation among IDs are given in the next definition.

Definition 9.9. Let $M = (Q,\Sigma,k,\delta,\triangleright,\triangleleft,q_0,A,N)$ be an MFA. Suppose an input of the form $\triangleright w \triangleleft \in (\{\triangleright\}\Sigma^*\{\triangleleft\})$ is given to M. A triplet $(\triangleright w \triangleleft, q, (h_1,\dots,h_k))$ is called an *instantaneous description* (ID) of M with w, where $q \in Q$ and $(h_1,\dots,h_k) \in \{0,\dots,|w|+1\}^k$. It represents M is in the state q, and the i-th head is reading the h_i-th symbol of $\triangleright w \triangleleft$ ($i \in \{1,\dots,k\}$), where $\triangleright$ is the 0-th symbol.

We now define a function $s_w : \{0,\dots,|w|+1\}^k \to (\Sigma \cup \{\triangleright,\triangleleft\})^k$ as follows. If $\triangleright w \triangleleft = a_0 a_1 \cdots a_n a_{n+1}$ (hence $a_0 = \triangleright, a_{n+1} = \triangleleft$, and $w = a_1 \cdots a_n \in \Sigma^*$), and

$\mathbf{h} = (h_1, \ldots, h_k) \in \{0, \ldots, |w|+1\}^k$, then $s_w(\mathbf{h}) = (a_{h_1}, \ldots, a_{h_k})$. The function s_w gives a k-tuple of symbols in $\triangleright w \triangleleft$ read by the k heads of M at the position $\mathbf{h}$. The *transition relation* $\vdash_{M}$ over IDs of M is defined as the one that satisfies the following. For all $w \in \Sigma^*$, $q, q' \in Q$, and $\mathbf{h}, \mathbf{h}' \in \{0, \ldots, |w|+1\}$,

$$(\triangleright w \triangleleft, q, \mathbf{h}) \vdash_{M} (\triangleright w \triangleleft, q', \mathbf{h}')$$
$$\Leftrightarrow ([q, s_w(\mathbf{h}), q'] \in \delta \wedge \mathbf{h}' = \mathbf{h}) \vee$$
$$\exists \mathbf{d} \in \{-1, 0, +1\}^k ([q, \mathbf{d}, q'] \in \delta \wedge \mathbf{h}' = \mathbf{h} + \mathbf{d}).$$

The reflexive and transitive closure of the relation $\vdash_{M}$ is denoted by $\vdash_{M}^{*}$, and n-step transition by $\vdash_{M}^{n}$ ($n \in \{0, 1, \ldots\}$). An ID $(\triangleright w \triangleleft, q_0, \mathbf{0})$ is called an *initial ID* with the input w, where $\mathbf{0} = [0, \ldots, 0] \in \{0\}^k$. An ID C is called a *halting ID* if there is no ID C' such that $C \vdash_{M} C'$.

Definition 9.10. Let $M = (Q, \Sigma, k, \delta, \triangleright, \triangleleft, q_0, A, N)$ be an MFA. We say an input string $w \in \Sigma^*$ is *accepted* by M, if $(\triangleright w \triangleleft, q_0, \mathbf{0}) \vdash_{M}^{*} (\triangleright w \triangleleft, q, \mathbf{h})$ for some $q \in A$ and $\mathbf{h} \in \{0, \ldots, |w|+1\}^k$. The *language* accepted by M is the set of all words accepted by M, and is denoted by $L(M)$, i.e.,

$$L(M) = \{w \mid \exists q \in A, \exists \mathbf{h} \in \{0, \ldots, |w|+1\}^k ((\triangleright w \triangleleft, q_0, \mathbf{0}) \vdash_{M}^{*} (\triangleright w \triangleleft, q, \mathbf{h}))\}.$$

As in the case of two-tape Turing machine (Sect. 8.1.1), the set N of non-accepting states is not used in the above definition. But, it will become useful when we convert an MFA into RMFA in the next subsection.

Example 9.5. Let $L_{wcw} = \{wcw \mid w \in \{a, b\}^*\} \subset \{a, b, c\}^*$. L_{wcw} is a context-sensitive language, but is not context-free. The following RMFA(2) M_{wcw} accepts L_{wcw}.

$$M_{wcw} = (Q_{wcw}, \{a, b, c\}, 3, \delta_{wcw}, \triangleright, \triangleleft, q_0, \{q_a\}, \{\ \})$$
$$Q_{wcw} = \{q_0, q_1, q_2, q_3, q_4, q_a\}$$
$$\delta_{wcw} = \{\ [q_0, [\triangleright, \triangleright], q_1],\ [q_1, [0, +], q_2],\ [q_2, [\triangleright, a], q_1],\ [q_2, [\triangleright, b], q_1],$$
$$[q_2, [\triangleright, c], q_3],\ [q_3, [+, +], q_4],\ [q_4, [a, a], q_3],\ [q_4, [b, b], q_3],$$
$$[q_4, [c, \triangleleft], q_a]\ \}$$

It is easy to see that M_{wcw} is reversible. The input *abcab* is accepted by M_{wcw}.

$$(\triangleright abcab \triangleleft, q_0, (0,0)) \vdash_{M_{wcw}} (\triangleright abcab \triangleleft, q_1, (0,0)) \vdash_{M_{wcw}} (\triangleright abcab \triangleleft, q_2, (0,1))$$
$$\vdash_{M_{wcw}} (\triangleright abcab \triangleleft, q_1, (0,1)) \vdash_{M_{wcw}} (\triangleright abcab \triangleleft, q_2, (0,2)) \vdash_{M_{wcw}} (\triangleright abcab \triangleleft, q_1, (0,2))$$
$$\vdash_{M_{wcw}} (\triangleright abcab \triangleleft, q_2, (0,3)) \vdash_{M_{wcw}} (\triangleright abcab \triangleleft, q_3, (0,3)) \vdash_{M_{wcw}} (\triangleright abcab \triangleleft, q_4, (1,4))$$
$$\vdash_{M_{wcw}} (\triangleright abcab \triangleleft, q_3, (1,4)) \vdash_{M_{wcw}} (\triangleright abcab \triangleleft, q_4, (2,5)) \vdash_{M_{wcw}} (\triangleright abcab \triangleleft, q_3, (2,5))$$
$$\vdash_{M_{wcw}} (\triangleright abcab \triangleleft, q_4, (3,6)) \vdash_{M_{wcw}} (\triangleright abcab \triangleleft, q_a, (3,6))$$

On the other hand, the input *abcaa* is not accepted by M_{wcw}.

$(\triangleright abcaa\triangleleft, q_0, (0,0)) \underset{M_{wcw}}{\vdash} (\triangleright abcaa\triangleleft, q_1, (0,0)) \underset{M_{wcw}}{\vdash} (\triangleright abcaa\triangleleft, q_2, (0,1))$
$\underset{M_{wcw}}{\vdash} (\triangleright abcaa\triangleleft, q_1, (0,1)) \underset{M_{wcw}}{\vdash} (\triangleright abcaa\triangleleft, q_2, (0,2)) \underset{M_{wcw}}{\vdash} (\triangleright abcaa\triangleleft, q_1, (0,2))$
$\underset{M_{wcw}}{\vdash} (\triangleright abcaa\triangleleft, q_2, (0,3)) \underset{M_{wcw}}{\vdash} (\triangleright abcaa\triangleleft, q_3, (0,3)) \underset{M_{wcw}}{\vdash} (\triangleright abcaa\triangleleft, q_4, (1,4))$
$\underset{M_{wcw}}{\vdash} (\triangleright abcaa\triangleleft, q_3, (1,4)) \underset{M_{wcw}}{\vdash} (\triangleright abcaa\triangleleft, q_4, (2,5))$

Here, M_{wcw} halts without accepting the input $abcaa$, since $(\triangleright abcaa\triangleleft, q_4, (2,5))$ is a halting ID. Note that, in M_{wcw} the set of non-accepting states is empty. It is also possible to modify M_{wcw} so that it halts in the state q_r when rejecting the input, by adding 10 more rules such as $[q_4, [b,a], q_r]$ and others.   □

9.3.2 Converting a multi-head finite automaton into a reversible one with the same number of heads

Here, we introduce three kinds of *normal forms* for MFAs. In the following, we assume an MFA $M = (Q, \Sigma, k, \delta, \triangleright, \triangleleft, q_0, A, N)$ satisfies the following conditions (CM1) – (CM3). In fact, we can convert an MFA into one that satisfies these conditions in a similar manner as in Lemma 8.1 for two-tape Turing machines, where (CM1), (CM2) and (CM3) correspond to (C1), (C2) and (C3) in Lemma 8.1, respectively. Thus, we do not give its proof here.

(CM1)   The initial state q_0 does not appear as the third component of any rule in δ, and thus q_0 appears only in initial IDs:

$$\forall [q, \mathbf{x}, q'] \in \delta \ (q' \neq q_0).$$

(CM2) M performs read and shift operations alternately. Hence, Q is written as $Q = Q_{\text{read}} \cup Q_{\text{shift}}$ for some Q_{read} and Q_{shift} such that $Q_{\text{read}} \cap Q_{\text{shift}} = \emptyset$, and δ satisfies the following condition:

$$\forall [p, \mathbf{x}, q] \in \delta \ (\mathbf{x} \in (\Sigma \cup \{\triangleright, \triangleleft\})^k \Rightarrow p \in Q_{\text{read}} \wedge q \in Q_{\text{shift}}) \wedge$$
$$\forall [p, \mathbf{x}, q] \in \delta \ (\mathbf{x} \in \{-, 0, +\}^k \Rightarrow p \in Q_{\text{shift}} \wedge q \in Q_{\text{read}}).$$

It is easy to modify M so that it satisfies the above condition by adding new states to it. Each element of Q_{read} and Q_{shift} is called a *read state* and a *shift state*, respectively. We further assume $q_0 \in Q_{\text{read}}$, and $A \cup N \subset Q_{\text{shift}}$, though each state in $A \cup N$ makes no further move.

(CM3)   The heads of M must not go beyond the left and right endmarkers in a forward computation, and hence M does not go to an illegal ID:

$$\forall p, r \in Q_{\text{read}}, \ \forall q \in Q_{\text{shift}},$$
$$\forall (s_1, \ldots, s_k) \in (\Sigma \cup \{\triangleright, \triangleleft\})^k, \ \forall (d_1, \ldots, d_k) \in \{-, 0, +\}^k, \ \forall i \in \{1, \ldots, k\}$$
$$([p, [s_1, \ldots, s_k], q], [q, [d_1, \ldots, d_k], r] \in \delta$$
$$\Rightarrow (s_i = \triangleright \Rightarrow d_i \in \{0, +\}) \wedge (s_i = \triangleleft \Rightarrow d_i \in \{-, 0\})).$$

Likewise, M must satisfy a similar condition in a backward computation, and hence M does not come from an illegal ID:

$$\forall p, r \in Q_{\text{shift}}, \ \forall q \in Q_{\text{read}},$$
$$\forall (s_1, \ldots, s_k) \in (\Sigma \cup \{\triangleright, \triangleleft\})^k, \ \forall (d_1, \ldots, d_k) \in \{-, 0, +\}^k, \ \forall i \in \{1, \ldots, k\}$$
$$([r, [d_1, \ldots, d_k], q], [q, [s_1, \ldots, s_k], p] \in \delta$$
$$\Rightarrow (s_i = \triangleright \Rightarrow d_i \in \{-, 0\}) \wedge (s_i = \triangleleft \Rightarrow d_i \in \{0, +\})).$$

The following lemma shows that any RMFA eventually halts for every input, if it satisfies (CM1). It is proved in a similar manner as in Lemma 8.3. Thus, we omit its proof.

Lemma 9.8. *[16] Let $M = (Q, \Sigma, k, \delta, \triangleright, \triangleleft, q_0, A, N)$ be an RMFA that satisfies (CM1). Then it never loops for any input, i.e., there is no $w \in \Sigma^*$ and no ID C such that $(\triangleright w \triangleleft, q_0, \mathbf{0}) \vdash_{M}^{*} C \vdash_{M}^{+} C$. Therefore, M eventually halts for any input $w \in \Sigma^*$.*

We now show that for any given MFA(k) M we can construct an RMFA(k) $M^{\dagger}$ that simulates M. It is also proved in a similar manner as in Theorem 8.2 for two-tape Turing machines.

Theorem 9.3. *[17] Let $M = (Q, \Sigma, k, \delta, \triangleright, \triangleleft, q_0, A, N)$ be an MFA(k) that satisfies (CM1) – (CM3). We can construct an RMFA(k) $M^{\dagger} = (Q^{\dagger}, \Sigma, k, \delta^{\dagger}, \triangleright, \triangleleft, q_0, \{\hat{q}_0^1\}, \{q_0^1\})$ that simulates M in the following way.*

$$\forall w \in \Sigma^* \ (w \in L(M) \ \Rightarrow \ (\triangleright w \triangleleft, q_0, \mathbf{0}) \vdash_{M^{\dagger}}^{*} (\triangleright w \triangleleft, \hat{q}_0^1, \mathbf{0}))$$
$$\forall w \in \Sigma^* \ (w \notin L(M) \ \Rightarrow \ (\triangleright w \triangleleft, q_0, \mathbf{0}) \vdash_{M^{\dagger}}^{*} (\triangleright w \triangleleft, q_0^1, \mathbf{0}))$$

Proof. We first define the *computation graph* $G_{M,w} = (V, E)$ of M with an input $w \in \Sigma^*$ as follows. Let ID(M, w) be the set of all IDs of M with w, i.e., ID$(M, w) = \{(\triangleright w \triangleleft, q, \mathbf{h}) \mid q \in Q \wedge \mathbf{h} \in \{0, \ldots, |w| + 1\}^k\}$. The set $V (\subset$ ID$(M, w))$ of nodes is the smallest set that contains the initial ID $(\triangleright w \triangleleft, q_0, \mathbf{0})$, and satisfies the following condition: $\forall C_1, C_2 \in$ ID$(M, w)((C_1 \in V \wedge (C_1 \vdash_{M} C_2 \vee C_2 \vdash_{M} C_1)) \Rightarrow C_2 \in V)$. The set E of directed edges is: $E = \{(C_1, C_2) \mid C_1, C_2 \in V \wedge C_1 \vdash_{M} C_2\}$. Note that V contains only legal IDs of M because of the condition (CM3). Since $G_{M,w}$ is similarly defined as $G_{T,w}$ for a two-tape Turing machine T, see Fig. 8.5.

Apparently $G_{M,w}$ is a finite connected graph. Since M is deterministic, outdegree of each node in V is either 0 or 1, where a node of outdegree 0 corresponds to a halting ID. It is easy to see there is at most one node of outdegree 0 in $G_{M,w}$, and if there is one, then $G_{M,w}$ is a tree (Fig. 8.5 **(a)**). In this case, we identify the node of outdegree 0 as its root. Therefore, all the nodes of indegree 0 are leaves. On the other hand, if there is no node of outdegree 0, then the graph represents the computation of M having a loop, and thus it is not a tree (Fig. 8.5 **(b)**).

We make some preparations to construct $M^{\dagger}$ that traverses $G_{M,w}$. Let Q_{read} and Q_{shift} be the sets of states as described in (CM2). First, we define the following five functions: prev-read : $Q_{\text{read}} \to 2^{Q_{\text{shift}} \times \{-, 0, +\}^k}$, prev-shift : $Q_{\text{shift}} \times (\Sigma \cup \{\triangleright, \triangleleft\})^k \to$

$2^{Q_{read}}$, $\deg_r : Q_{read} \to \mathbb{N}$, $\deg_s : Q_{shift} \times (\Sigma \cup \{\triangleright, \triangleleft\})^k \to \mathbb{N}$, and $\deg_{max} : Q \to \mathbb{N}$ as follows.

$$\text{prev-read}(q) = \{[p, \mathbf{d}] \mid p \in Q_{shift} \wedge \mathbf{d} \in \{-, 0, +\}^k \wedge [p, \mathbf{d}, q] \in \delta\}$$
$$\text{prev-shift}(q, \mathbf{s}) = \{p \mid p \in Q_{read} \wedge [p, \mathbf{s}, q] \in \delta\}$$
$$\deg_r(q) = |\text{prev-read}(q)|$$
$$\deg_s(q, \mathbf{s}) = |\text{prev-shift}(q, \mathbf{s})|$$
$$\deg_{max}(q) = \begin{cases} \deg_r(q) & \text{if } q \in Q_{read} \\ \max\{\deg_s(q, \mathbf{s}) \mid \mathbf{s} \in (\Sigma \cup \{\triangleright, \triangleleft\})^k\} & \text{if } q \in Q_{shift} \end{cases}$$

Assume M is in the ID $(\triangleright w \triangleleft, q, \mathbf{h})$. If q is a read state (shift state, respectively), then $\deg_r(q)$ $(\deg_s(q, s_w(\mathbf{h})))$ denotes the total number of previous IDs of $(\triangleright w \triangleleft, q, \mathbf{h})$, and each element $[p, \mathbf{d}] \in \text{prev-read}(q)$ $(p \in \text{prev-shift}(q, s_w(\mathbf{h})))$ gives a previous state and a shift direction (a previous state). We further assume that the set Q and, of course, the set $\{-1, 0, +1\}$ are totally ordered, and thus the elements of the sets prev-read(q) and prev-shift(q, s) are sorted based on these orders. So, in the following, we denote prev-read(q) and prev-shift(q, s) by the ordered lists as below.

$$\text{prev-read}(q) = [[p_1, \mathbf{d}_1], \dots, [p_{\deg_r(q)}, \mathbf{d}_{\deg_r(q)}]]$$
$$\text{prev-shift}(q, \mathbf{s}) = [p_1, \dots, p_{\deg_s(q, \mathbf{s})}]$$

We now construct an RMFA(k) $M^\dagger$ that simulates the MFA(k) M by traversing $G_{M,w}$ for a given w. $Q^\dagger$ and $\delta^\dagger$ of $M^\dagger$ are as below, where $\mathbf{S} = (\Sigma \cup \{\triangleright, \triangleleft\})^k$.

$Q^\dagger = \{q, \hat{q} \mid q \in Q\} \cup \{q^j, \hat{q}^j \mid q \in Q \wedge j \in (\{1\} \cup \{1, \dots, \deg_{max}(q)\})\}$
$\delta^\dagger = \delta_1 \cup \dots \cup \delta_6 \cup \hat{\delta}_1 \cup \dots \cup \hat{\delta}_5 \cup \delta_a \cup \delta_r$
$\delta_1 = \{[p_1, \mathbf{d}_1, q^2], \dots, [p_{\deg_r(q)-1}, \mathbf{d}_{\deg_r(q)-1}, q^{\deg_r(q)}], [p_{\deg_r(q)}, \mathbf{d}_{\deg_r(q)}, q] \mid$
$\qquad q \in Q_{read} \wedge \deg_r(q) \geq 1 \wedge \text{prev-read}(q) = [[p_1, \mathbf{d}_1], \dots, [p_{\deg_r(q)}, \mathbf{d}_{\deg_r(q)}]]\}$
$\delta_2 = \{[p_1, \mathbf{s}, q^2], \dots, [p_{\deg_s(q, \mathbf{s})-1}, \mathbf{s}, q^{\deg_s(q, \mathbf{s})}], [p_{\deg_s(q, \mathbf{s})}, \mathbf{s}, q] \mid$
$\qquad q \in Q_{shift} \wedge \mathbf{s} \in \mathbf{S} \wedge \deg_s(q, \mathbf{s}) \geq 1 \wedge \text{prev-shift}(q, \mathbf{s}) = [p_1, \dots, p_{\deg_s(q, \mathbf{s})}]\}$
$\delta_3 = \{[q^1, -\mathbf{d}_1, p_1^1], \dots, [q^{\deg_r(q)}, -\mathbf{d}_{\deg_r(q)}, p_{\deg_r(q)}^1] \mid$
$\qquad q \in Q_{read} \wedge \deg_r(q) \geq 1 \wedge \text{prev-read}(q) = [[p_1, \mathbf{d}_1], \dots, [p_{\deg_r(q)}, \mathbf{d}_{\deg_r(q)}]]\}$
$\delta_4 = \{[q^1, \mathbf{s}, p_1^1], \dots, [q^{\deg_s(q, \mathbf{s})}, \mathbf{s}, p_{\deg_s(q, \mathbf{s})}^1] \mid$
$\qquad q \in Q_{shift} \wedge \mathbf{s} \in \mathbf{S} \wedge \deg_s(q, \mathbf{s}) \geq 1 \wedge \text{prev-shift}(q, \mathbf{s}) = [p_1, \dots, p_{\deg_s(q, \mathbf{s})}]\}$
$\delta_5 = \{[q^1, \mathbf{s}, q] \mid q \in Q_{shift} - (A \cup N) \wedge \mathbf{s} \in \mathbf{S} \wedge \deg_s(q, \mathbf{s}) = 0\}$
$\hat{\delta}_i = \{[\hat{p}, \mathbf{x}, \hat{q}] \mid [p, \mathbf{x}, q] \in \delta_i\}$ $(i = 1, \dots, 5)$
$\delta_6 = \{[q, \mathbf{s}, q^1] \mid q \in Q_{read} - \{q_0\} \wedge \mathbf{s} \in \mathbf{S} \wedge \neg \exists p ([q, \mathbf{s}, p] \in \delta)\}$
$\delta_a = \{[q, \mathbf{0}, \hat{q}^1] \mid q \in A\}$
$\delta_r = \{[q, \mathbf{0}, q^1] \mid q \in N\}$

The set of states $Q^\dagger$ has four types of states. They are of the forms $q, \hat{q}, q^j$ and $\hat{q}^j$. The states without a superscript (i.e., q and $\hat{q}$) are for forward computation, while those with a superscript (i.e., q^j and $\hat{q}^j$) are for backward computation. Note that $Q^\dagger$ contains q^1 and $\hat{q}^1$ even if $\deg_{max}(q) = 0$. The states with "$\wedge$" (i.e., $\hat{q}$ and $\hat{q}^j$) are the ones indicating that an accepting ID was found in the process of traverse, while those without "^" (i.e., q and q^j) are for indicating no accepting ID has been found so far.

The set of rules δ_1 (δ_2, respectively) is for simulating forward computation of M in $G_{M,w}$ for M's shift states (read states). The set δ_3 (δ_4, respectively) is for simulating backward computation of M in $G_{M,w}$ for M's read states (shift states). The set δ_5 is for turning the direction of computation from backward to forward in $G_{M,w}$ for shift states. The set $\hat{\delta}_i$ ($i = 1, \ldots, 5$) is the set of rules for the states of the form $\hat{q}$, and is identical to δ_i except that each state has "^". The set δ_6 is for turning the direction of computation from forward to backward in $G_{M,w}$ for halting IDs with a read state. The set δ_a (δ_r, respectively) is for turning the direction of computation from forward to backward for accepting (rejecting) states. In addition, each rule in δ_a makes $M^\dagger$ change the state from one without "^" to the corresponding one with "^". We can verify that $M^\dagger$ is deterministic and reversible by a careful inspection of $\delta^\dagger$. We can see that $M^\dagger$ also satisfies the conditions (CM1) – (CM3).

The RMFA(k) $M^\dagger$ simulates M as follows. First, consider the case $G_{M,w}$ is a tree. If an input w is given, $M^\dagger$ traverses $G_{M,w}$ by the depth-first search (Fig. 8.5 (a)). Note that the search starts not from the root of the tree but from the leaf node $(\triangleright w \triangleleft, q_0, \mathbf{0})$. Since each node of $G_{M,w}$ is identified by the ID of M of the form $(\triangleright w \triangleleft, q, \mathbf{h})$, it is easy for $M^\dagger$ to keep it by the ID of $M^\dagger$. But, if $(\triangleright w \triangleleft, q, \mathbf{h})$ is a non-leaf node, it may be visited $\deg_{\max}(q) + 1$ times (i.e., the number of its child nodes plus 1) in the process of depth-first search, and thus $M^\dagger$ should keep this information in the finite state control. To do so, $M^\dagger$ uses $\deg_{\max}(q) + 1$ states $q^1, \ldots, q^{\deg_{\max}(q)}$, and q for each state q of M. Here, the states $q^1, \ldots, q^{\deg_{\max}(q)}$ are used for visiting its child nodes, and q is used for visiting its parent node. In other words, the states with a superscript are for going downward in the tree (i.e., a backward simulation of M), and the state without a superscript is for going upward in the tree (i.e., a forward simulation). At a leaf node $(\triangleright w \triangleleft, q, \mathbf{h})$, which satisfies $\deg_s(q, s_w(\mathbf{h})) = 0$, $M^\dagger$ turns the direction of computing by the rule $[q^1, s_w(\mathbf{h}), q] \in \delta_5$.

If $M^\dagger$ enters an accepting state of M, say q_a, which is the root of the tree while traversing the tree, then $M^\dagger$ goes to the state $\hat{q}_a$, and continues the depth-first search. After that, $M^\dagger$ uses the states of the form $\hat{q}$ and $\hat{q}^j$ indicating that the input w should be accepted. $M^\dagger$ will eventually reach the initial ID of M by its ID $(\triangleright w \triangleleft, \hat{q}_0^1, \mathbf{0})$. Thus, $M^\dagger$ halts and accepts the input. Note that we can assume there is no rule of the form $[q_0, \mathbf{s}, q]$ such that $\mathbf{s} \notin \{\triangleright\}^k$ in δ, because the initial ID of M is $(\triangleright w \triangleleft, q_0, \mathbf{0})$, and (CM1) is assumed. Therefore, $M^\dagger$ never reaches an ID $(\triangleright w \triangleleft, q_0, \mathbf{h})$ of M such that $\mathbf{h} \neq \mathbf{0}$.

If $M^\dagger$ enters a halting state of M other than the accepting states, then it continues the depth-first search without entering a state of the form $\hat{q}$. Also in this case, $M^\dagger$ will finally reach the initial ID of M by its ID $(\triangleright w \triangleleft, q_0^1, \mathbf{0})$. Thus, $M^\dagger$ halts and rejects the input.

Second, consider the case $G_{M,w}$ is not a tree (see Fig. 8.5 (b)). In this case, since there is no accepting ID in $G_{M,w}$, $M^\dagger$ never enters an accepting state of M no matter how $M^\dagger$ visits the nodes of $G_{M,w}$ (it may not visit all the nodes of $G_{M,w}$). Thus, $M^\dagger$ uses only the states without "^". From $\delta^\dagger$ we can see q_0^1 is the only halting state without "^". Since M satisfies the condition (CM1), $M^\dagger$ halts with the ID $(\triangleright w \triangleleft, q_0^1, \mathbf{0})$ by Lemma 9.8, and rejects the input.

By above, we have the following relations.

$$\forall w \in \Sigma^* (w \in L(M) \Rightarrow ((\triangleright w \triangleleft, q_0, \mathbf{0}) \mathrel{\vdash^*_{M^\dagger}} (\triangleright w \triangleleft, \hat{q}_0^1, \mathbf{0})))$$

$$\forall w \in \Sigma^* (w \notin L(M) \Rightarrow ((\triangleright w \triangleleft, q_0, \mathbf{0}) \mathrel{\vdash^*_{M^\dagger}} (\triangleright w \triangleleft, q_0^1, \mathbf{0})))$$

Thus, $L(M^\dagger) = L(M)$. We can also see $M^\dagger$ is "garbage-less" in the sense it always halts with all the heads at the left endmarker.   □

Example 9.6. Let $L_p = \{w \mid \text{the length of } w \in \{1\}^* \text{ is a prime number}\}$. The following irreversible MFA(3) M_p accepts L_p.

$$M_p = (Q, \{1\}, 3, \delta, \triangleright, \triangleleft, q_0, \{q_a\}, \{\ \})$$
$$Q = \{q_0, q_1, \ldots, q_{16}, q_a\}$$
$$\begin{aligned}
\delta = \{ &[q_0, [\triangleright, \triangleright, \triangleright], q_1], \quad [q_1, [0, +, 0], q_2], \quad [q_2, [\triangleright, 1, \triangleright], q_3], \\
&[q_3, [0, +, 0], q_4], \quad [q_4, [\triangleright, 1, \triangleright], q_5], \quad [q_5, [+, -, +], q_6], \\
&[q_6, [1, 1, 1], q_5], \quad [q_6, [1, \triangleright, 1], q_7], \quad [q_6, [\triangleleft, 1, 1], q_9], \\
&[q_6, [\triangleleft, \triangleright, 1], q_9], \quad [q_7, [0, +, -], q_8], \quad [q_8, [1, 1, 1], q_7], \\
&[q_8, [1, 1, \triangleright], q_5], \quad [q_9, [0, +, -], q_{10}], \quad [q_{10}, [\triangleleft, 1, \triangleright], q_{14}], \\
&[q_{10}, [\triangleleft, 1, 1], q_{11}], \quad [q_{11}, [-, +, -], q_{13}], \quad [q_{12}, [-, 0, 0], q_{13}], \\
&[q_{13}, [1, 1, 1], q_{11}], \quad [q_{13}, [1, 1, \triangleright], q_{12}], \quad [q_{13}, [\triangleright, 1, \triangleright], q_3], \\
&[q_{14}, [0, +, 0], q_{15}], \quad [q_{15}, [\triangleleft, \triangleleft, \triangleright], q_a], \quad [q_{15}, [\triangleleft, 1, \triangleright], q_{16}], \\
&[q_{16}, [0, -, 0], q_{10}] \ \}
\end{aligned}$$

If a word $1^n \in \{1\}^*$ $(n = 2, 3, \ldots)$ is given, M_p divides n by $m = 2, 3, \ldots, n$ successively. If $m = n$ is the least integer among them that divides n, then M_p accepts 1^n. If n is not a prime, M_p halts without accepting it (in the case $n = 0$ or $n = 1$), or loops forever (in the case $n > 1$). The first head is used as a counter for carrying out a division of n by m. The second head is a counter for keeping the divisor m. The third head is an auxiliary counter for restoring m. The states q_0, q_1, and q_2 are used for initializing the algorithm. The states $q_3, \ldots, q_8$ are for dividing n by m. The states $q_9, \ldots, q_{13}$ are for checking if n is divisible by m. The states $q_{14}, \ldots, q_{17}$ are for checking if $m = n$. Note that M_p is irreversible, since e.g., the pair $[q_{11}, [-, +, -], q_{13}]$ and $[q_{12}, [-, 0, 0], q_{13}]$ violates the reversibility condition. Examples of computing processes of M_p are as below. The MFA(3) M_p accepts the input 1^7, but it loops for the input 1^6.

$$(\triangleright 1111111 \triangleleft, q_0, [0, 0, 0]) \mathrel{\vdash^{273}_{M_p}} (\triangleright 1111111 \triangleleft, q_a, [8, 8, 0])$$

$$(\triangleright 111111 \triangleleft, q_0, [0, 0, 0]) \mathrel{\vdash^{32}_{M_p}} (\triangleright 111111 \triangleleft, q_{10}, [7, 2, 0])$$

$$\mathrel{\vdash^4_{M_p}} (\triangleright 111111 \triangleleft, q_{10}, [7, 2, 0]) \mathrel{\vdash_{M_p}} \cdots$$

An RMFA(3) $M_p^\dagger$ that simulates M_p obtained by the method in Theorem 9.3 is:

$$M_p^\dagger = (Q^\dagger, \{1\}, 3, \delta^\dagger, \triangleright, \triangleleft, q_0, \{\hat{q}_0^1\}, \{q_0^1\})$$

$$Q^\dagger = \{q, \hat{q}, q^1, \hat{q}^1 \mid q \in Q\} \cup \{q_3^2, q_{10}^2, q_{13}^2, \hat{q}_3^2, \hat{q}_{10}^2, \hat{q}_{13}^2\}$$

$$\delta^\dagger = \delta_1 \cup \cdots \cup \delta_6 \cup \hat{\delta}_1 \cup \cdots \cup \hat{\delta}_5 \cup \delta_a \cup \delta_r$$

$$\delta_1 = \{\,[q_1, [0, +, 0], q_2],\quad [q_3, [0, +, 0], q_4],\quad [q_5, [+, -, +], q_6],$$
$$[q_7, [0, +, -], q_8],\quad [q_9, [0, +, -], q_{10}^2],\quad [q_{11}, [-, +, -], q_{13}^2],$$
$$[q_{12}, [-, 0, 0], q_{13}],\quad [q_{14}, [0, +, 0], q_{15}],\quad [q_{16}, [0, -, 0], q_{10}]\,\}$$

$$\delta_2 = \{\,[q_0, [\triangleright, \triangleright, \triangleright], q_1],\quad [q_2, [\triangleright, 1, \triangleright], q_3^2],\quad [q_4, [\triangleright, 1, \triangleright], q_5],$$
$$[q_6, [1, 1, 1], q_5],\quad [q_6, [1, \triangleright, 1], q_7],\quad [q_6, [\triangleleft, 1, 1], q_9],$$
$$[q_6, [\triangleleft, \triangleright, 1], q_9],\quad [q_8, [1, 1, 1], q_7],\quad [q_8, [1, 1, \triangleright], q_5],$$
$$[q_{10}, [\triangleleft, 1, \triangleright], q_{14}],\quad [q_{10}, [\triangleleft, 1, 1], q_{11}],\quad [q_{13}, [1, 1, 1], q_{11}],$$
$$[q_{13}, [1, 1, \triangleright], q_{12}],\quad [q_{13}, [\triangleright, 1, \triangleright], q_3],\quad [q_{15}, [\triangleleft, \triangleleft, \triangleright], q_a],$$
$$[q_{15}, [\triangleleft, 1, \triangleright], q_{16}]\,\}$$

$$\delta_3 = \{\,[q_2^1, [0, -, 0], q_1^1],\quad [q_4^1, [0, -, 0], q_3^1],\quad [q_6^1, [-, +, -], q_5^1],$$
$$[q_8^1, [0, -, +], q_7^1],\quad [q_{10}^1, [0, -, +], q_9^1],\quad [q_{10}^2, [0, +, 0], q_{16}^1],$$
$$[q_{13}^1, [+, -, +], q_{11}^1],\quad [q_{13}^2, [+, 0, 0], q_{12}^1],\quad [q_{15}^1, [0, -, 0], q_{14}^1]\,\}$$

$$\delta_4 = \{\,[q_1^1, [\triangleright, \triangleright, \triangleright], q_0^1],\quad [q_3^1, [\triangleright, 1, \triangleright], q_2^1],\quad [q_3^2, [\triangleright, 1, \triangleright], q_{13}^1],$$
$$[q_5^1, [\triangleright, 1, \triangleright], q_4^1],\quad [q_5^1, [1, 1, 1], q_6^1],\quad [q_5^1, [1, 1, \triangleright], q_8^1],$$
$$[q_7^1, [1, \triangleright, 1], q_6^1],\quad [q_7^1, [1, 1, 1], q_8^1],\quad [q_9^1, [\triangleleft, 1, 1], q_6^1],$$
$$[q_9^1, [\triangleleft, \triangleright, 1], q_6^1],\quad [q_{11}^1, [\triangleleft, 1, 1], q_{10}^1],\quad [q_{11}^1, [1, 1, 1], q_{13}^1],$$
$$[q_{12}^1, [1, 1, \triangleright], q_{13}^1],\quad [q_{14}^1, [\triangleleft, 1, \triangleright], q_{10}^1],\quad [q_{16}^1, [\triangleleft, 1, \triangleright], q_{15}^1],$$
$$[q_a^1, [\triangleleft, \triangleleft, \triangleright], q_{15}^1]\,\}$$

$$\delta_5 = \{\,[q_1^1, [\triangleright, \triangleright, 1], q_1],\quad [q_1^1, [\triangleright, \triangleright, \triangleleft], q_1],\quad \ldots,\quad [q_{16}^1, [\triangleleft, \triangleleft, \triangleleft], q_{16}]\,\}$$

$$\hat{\delta}_i = \{\,[\hat{p}, \mathbf{x}, \hat{q}] \mid [p, \mathbf{x}, q] \in \delta_i\,\} \; (i = 1, \ldots, 5)$$

$$\delta_6 = \{\,[q_2, [\triangleright, \triangleright, \triangleright], q_2^1],\quad [q_2, [\triangleright, \triangleright, 1], q_2^1],\quad \ldots,\quad [q_{15}, [\triangleleft, \triangleleft, \triangleleft], q_{15}^1]\,\}$$

$$\delta_a = \{\,[q_a, [0, 0, 0], \hat{q}_a^1]\,\}$$

$$\delta_r = \{\,\}$$

The details of δ_5 and δ_6 are omitted here since they have 228 and 174 rules, respectively. Examples of computing processes of $M_p^\dagger$ are as follows.

$$(\triangleright 1111111 \triangleleft, q_0, [0, 0, 0]) \;\vdash_{M_p^\dagger}^{2016}\; (\triangleright 1111111 \triangleleft, \hat{q}_0^1, [0, 0, 0])$$

$$(\triangleright 111111 \triangleleft, q_0, [0, 0, 0]) \;\vdash_{M_p^\dagger}^{118}\; (\triangleright 111111 \triangleleft, q_0^1, [0, 0, 0])$$

$\square$

9.4 Concluding Remarks

In this chapter, reversible counter machines (RCMs), and two-way reversible multi-head finite automata (RMFAs) were studied. It was shown that they have the same computing/accepting power as irreversible models even if the constraint of reversibility is added.

In Sect. 9.2, it was proved that the class of RCMs is computationally universal even if they have only two counters (Theorem 9.2). Since a reversible two-
counter machine (RCM(2)) is a simple model of reversible computing, it is also
useful to show the universality of other reversible systems. In Sect. 12.4, a simple
two-dimensional reversible cellular automaton with finite configurations that can
simulate any RCM(2) will be given.

Counter machines discussed in Sect. 9.2 were not defined as acceptors of formal
languages. It is, of course, possible to define a *counter machine acceptor* (CMA)
similar to the Turing machine acceptor in Definition 8.1. Namely, it is a model obtained from a two-tape Turing machine acceptor shown in Fig. 8.1 by replacing its
storage tape by a finite number of counters. Therefore, a CMA consists of a read-
only input tape, k counters, and a finite control. Thus, it has *read rules* and *shift rules*
for the input head besides counter-test rules and count-up/down rules. Although we
do not go into its details here, it is possible to show lemmas and theorems for CMAs
corresponding to Lemmas 9.2–9.5, 9.7, and Theorem 9.2, using similar techniques.
Hence, we can show the class of CMAs with two counters is computationally universal as acceptors of languages.

In Sect. 9.3, it was shown that any irreversible two-way k-head finite automaton (MFA(k)) is converted into a reversible one with the same number of heads
(RMFA(k)) (Theorem 9.3). Hence, the language accepting power of RMFA(k) is
exactly the same as that of MFA(k). The conversion method is similar to the case
of space-bounded TMs (Theorem 8.2). It should be noted that, in the case of space-
bounded TMs, exponential slowdown may occur by this conversion. On the other
hand, in the case of MFA, only polynomial slowdown can occur, since the total
number of IDs of an MFA is bounded by a polynomial of the input length.

The proof technique for Theorem 9.3 can be applied to some other models related
to MFA, such as a *marker automaton* studied by Blum and Hewitt [4], an *n-bounded
counter automaton* and a *rebound automaton* studied by Morita, Sugata and Umeo
[18]. Therefore, the accepting powers of these automata do not decrease even when
the reversibility constraint is added. Note that Theorem 9.3 generalizes the result
by Kondacs and Watrous [7] that a deterministic two-way finite automaton (i.e.,
MFA(1)) is simulated by a reversible two-way finite automaton (RMFA(1)).

We dealt with only reversible deterministic MFAs, and irreversible deterministic
MFAs. We can also consider reversible nondeterministic MFAs, and derive a result
that is similar to Theorem 8.3. Namely, any reversible nondeterministic MFA(k) can
be simulated by a reversible deterministic MFA(k). Thus, these three models are
equivalent in their language accepting capability.

So far, there has been much research on irreversible MFAs. Ibarra [6] proved
that MFA($k + 2$) is strictly more powerful than MFA(k), and thus there is an infinite hierarchy in their accepting power of languages with respect to the number of
heads. Later, Monien improved this result showing that MFA($k + 1$) is more powerful than MFA(k) [13], and that this relation also holds for the MFAs with a one-letter
alphabet [14]. Since RMFA(k) is equivalent to MFA(k) in their accepting ability,
RMFA($k + 1$) is strictly more powerful than RMFA(k). Furthermore, we can see

that the proof of Theorem 9.3 is independent of the alphabet size. Therefore, this hierarchy result also holds for RMFAs with a one-letter alphabet.

References

1. Angluin, D.: Inference of reversible languages.   J. ACM **29**, 741–765 (1982). doi:10.1145/322326.322334
2. Axelsen, H.B.: Reversible multi-head finite automata characterize reversible logarithmic space. In: Proc. LATA 2012 (eds. A.H. Dediu, C. Martin-Vide), LNCS 7183, pp. 95–105 (2012). doi:10.1007/978-3-642-28332-1_9
3. Bennett, C.H.: Logical reversibility of computation. IBM J. Res. Dev. **17**, 525–532 (1973). doi:10.1147/rd.176.0525
4. Blum, M., Hewitt, C.: Automata on a two-dimensional tape. In: Proc. IEEE Symp. on Switching and Automata Theory, pp. 155–160. IEEE (1967). doi:10.1109/FOCS.1967.6
5. Holzer, M., Kutrib, M., Malcher, A.: Complexity of multi-head finite automata: Origins and directions. Theoret. Comput. Sci. **412**, 83–96 (2011). doi:10.1016/j.tcs.2010.08.024
6. Ibarra, O.H.: On two-way multihead automata.   J. Comput. Syst. Sci. **7**, 28–36 (1973). doi:10.1016/S0022-0000(73)80048-0
7. Kondacs, A., Watrous, J.: On the power of quantum finite state automata. In: Proc. 36th FOCS, pp. 66–75. IEEE (1997). doi:10.1109/SFCS.1997.646094
8. Kunc, M., Okhotin, A.: Reversibility of computations in graph-walking automata. In: Proc. MFCS 2013 (eds. K. Chatterjee, J. Sgall), LNCS 8087, pp. 595–606 (2013). doi:10.1007/978-3-642-40313-2_53
9. Kutrib, M., Malcher, A.: Reversible pushdown automata. J. Comput. Syst. Sci. **78**, 1814–1827 (2012). doi:10.1016/j.jcss.2011.12.004
10. Kutrib, M., Malcher, A.: One-way reversible multi-head finite automata. In: Proc. RC 2012 (eds. R. Glück, T. Yokoyama), LNCS 7581, pp. 14–28 (2013). doi:10.1007/978-3-642-36315-3_2
11. Lange, K.J., McKenzie, P., Tapp, A.: Reversible space equals deterministic space. J. Comput. Syst. Sci. **60**, 354–367 (2000). doi:10.1006/jcss.1999.1672
12. Minsky, M.L.: Computation: Finite and Infinite Machines. Prentice-Hall, Englewood Cliffs, NJ (1967)
13. Monien, B.: Transformational methods and their application to complexity theory. Acta Inform. **6**, 95–108 (1976). doi:10.1007/BF00263746
14. Monien, B.: Two-way multihead automata over a one-letter alphabet. RAIRO Inf. Théor. **14**, 67–82 (1980)
15. Morita, K.: Universality of a reversible two-counter machine. Theoret. Comput. Sci. **168**, 303–320 (1996). doi:10.1016/S0304-3975(96)00081-3
16. Morita, K.: Two-way reversible multi-head finite automata. Fundam. Inform. **110**, 241–254 (2011). doi:10.3233/FI-2011-541
17. Morita, K.: A deterministic two-way multi-head finite automaton can be converted into a reversible one with the same number of heads. In: Proc. RC 2012 (eds. R. Glück, T. Yokoyama), LNCS 7581, pp. 29–43 (2013). doi:10.1007/978-3-642-36315-3_3. Slides with figures of computer simulation: Hiroshima University Institutional Repository, http://ir.lib.hiroshima-u.ac.jp/00033875
18. Morita, K., Sugata, K., Umeo, H.: Computational complexity of n-bounded counter automaton and multi-dimensional rebound automaton. Trans. IECE Japan **60-D**, 283–290 (1977)
19. Pin, J.E.: On reversible automata. In: Proc. LATIN '92 (ed. I. Simon), LNCS 583, pp. 401–416 (1992). doi:10.1007/BFb0023844

Chapter 10
Reversible Cellular Automata

Abstract A cellular automaton (CA) is a discrete model for a spatiotemporal phenomenon. In a CA, an infinite number of cells are placed uniformly in the space, and each cell changes its state depending on its neighboring cells by a local function. Applying the local function to all the cells in parallel, a global function is induced, by which the configuration of the cellular space evolves. A reversible CA (RCA) is one whose global function is injective. It is thus considered as an abstract model of a reversible space. We use RCAs for studying how computation and information processing are performed in a reversible space. If we use the framework of classical CAs, however, it is generally difficult to design RCAs. Instead, we use the framework of partitioned cellular automata (PCAs). Based on it, various RCAs with interesting features and/or computational universality are designed in this and in the following chapters. It is also a useful model to investigate how complex phenomena appear from a very simple reversible local function. In this chapter, after giving basic properties of RCAs, methods of simulating irreversible CAs by reversible ones, and of constructing PCAs from reversible logic elements are shown.

Keywords reversible cellular automaton, injective cellular automaton, partitioned cellular automaton, universality

10.1 Cellular Automata and Reversibility

A *cellular automaton* (CA) is a system consisting of infinitely many identical finite automata (called *cells*) placed and interconnected uniformly in a space. Each cell changes its state depending on the present states of itself and its neighboring cells according to a specified transition function called a *local function*. All the cells change their state synchronously at every discrete time. By this, the transition function of a configuration (i.e., the whole state of the CA) called a *global function* is induced. A CA was first proposed by von Neumann [38] based on the idea of Ulam [49]. von Neumann used this framework to describe his model of self-reproducing automata (see Sect. 14.1). Since then, CAs have been studied by many researchers as a dynamical system that can model various spatiotemporal phenomena, as well as a kind of parallel processing system.

A *reversible cellular automaton* (RCA) is a CA such that its global function is injective (Definition 10.4). The study of RCAs has a relatively long history. In the 1960s, Moore [26], and Myhill [35] showed the Garden-of-Eden theorem (Theorem 10.2), which gives a relation between the injectivity and surjectivity of a global function. Since then, injectivity and surjectivity have been studied extensively and more generally. But, the term "reversible CA" was not used at that time. Toffoli [44] first studied RCAs in relation to physical reversibility. Since then, the term reversible CA has been used commonly. He showed that every k-dimensional (irreversible) CA can be embedded in a $k + 1$-dimensional RCA. Since it is easy to show that Turing machines can be simulated by one-dimensional CAs, we can see a two-dimensional RCA is computationally universal. Later, a stronger result was shown in [34], i.e., even a one-dimensional RCA is computationally universal.

An RCA can be considered as an abstract model of reversible space. In fact, it is a useful framework for modeling and analyzing various reversible spatiotemporal phenomena. In particular, we can use it for studying the problem how computation and information processing are performed efficiently in physically reversible spaces. Until now, many attempts have been made to clarify the properties of RCAs, and it gradually turned out that even very simple RCAs have high computing power in spite of the constraint of reversibility.

In this chapter, we give definitions on CAs and RCAs, methods for designing RCAs, and their basic properties. In Sect. 10.2, we explain the classical framework of CAs that are in general irreversible. Examples of them are given to show how one- or two-dimensional CAs are described, and how they evolve. In Sect. 10.3, we define RCAs, and show their basic properties. We shall see that it is generally difficult to design RCAs within the framework of classical CAs. In Sect. 10.4, we give three practical methods for designing RCAs. Among them, a method that uses *partitioned cellular automata* (PCAs) will be explained in detail. In the following chapters it will be used to construct various RCAs. In Sect. 10.5, we show how irreversible CAs are simulated by RCAs. In Sect. 10.6, methods of realizing reversible PCAs by reversible logic elements are given. It connects the way from the microscopic reversibility to the macroscopic reversibility in RCAs.

10.2 Cellular Automata (CAs)

In this section, basic definitions on classical k-dimensional CAs, and some examples of them are given. So far, besides the standard framework of CAs, many interesting variants, such as asynchronous CAs (e.g., [36]), CAs in a non-Euclidean space (e.g., [19]), CAs in a space of aperiodic tiling (e.g., [39]), and so on, have been proposed and studied. However, here, we restrict CAs only to the standard ones, i.e., synchronous and deterministic CAs where cells are placed regularly in the k-dimensional Euclidean space.

10.2.1 Definitions of CAs

Definition 10.1. A *k-dimensional cellular automaton* (CA) is a system defined by

$$A = (\mathbb{Z}^k, Q, (n_1, \ldots, n_m), f, \#).$$

Here, $\mathbb{Z}$ is the set of all integers, and thus $\mathbb{Z}^k$ is the set of all k-dimensional points with integer coordinates at which *cells* are placed. The set Q is a non-empty finite set of states of each cell, and $(n_1, \ldots, n_m)$ is an element of $(\mathbb{Z}^k)^m$ called a *neighborhood* ($m \in \{1, 2, \ldots\}$). Hence, $n_i \in \mathbb{Z}^k$ ($i \in \{1, \ldots, m\}$). The positive integer m is called a *neighborhood size*. The fourth item $f : Q^m \to Q$ is a *local function*, which determines the next state of each cell from the present states of m neighboring cells. The state $\# \in Q$ is a *quiescent state* that satisfies $f(\#, \ldots, \#) = \#$. The CA A itself is sometimes called a *cellular space*. Note that we also allow a CA such that no quiescent state is specified.

If $f(q_1, \ldots, q_m) = q$ holds for $q_1, \ldots, q_m, q \in Q$, then this relation is called a *local rule* (or simply a *rule*) of the CA A. Hence, f can be described by a set of local rules.

The global function of a CA A is defined as follows.

Definition 10.2. Let $A = (\mathbb{Z}^k, Q, (n_1, \ldots, n_m), f, \#)$ be a CA. A *configuration* of A is a function $\alpha : \mathbb{Z}^k \to Q$, which assigns a state in Q to each point in $\mathbb{Z}^k$. Let $\text{Conf}(A)$ denote the set of all configurations of A, i.e., $\text{Conf}(A) = \{\alpha \mid \alpha : \mathbb{Z}^k \to Q\}$. Applying the local function f to all the cells in a configuration simultaneously, we can obtain the *global function* $F : \text{Conf}(A) \to \text{Conf}(A)$ that describes transitions among configurations of A. Namely, if α is a present configuration, $F(\alpha)$ gives the next configuration. It is defined by the following formula.

$$\forall \alpha \in \text{Conf}(A), \ x \in \mathbb{Z}^k : \ F(\alpha)(x) = f(\alpha(x + n_1), \ldots, \alpha(x + n_m))$$

The above formula says that $F(\alpha)(x)$, which is the state of the cell at the position $x \in \mathbb{Z}^k$ in the configuration $F(\alpha)$, is determined by the local function f based on the states $\alpha(x + n_1), \ldots, \alpha(x + n_m)$ of its m neighboring cells in the configuration α.

By the global function F the CA A changes its configuration step by step, and thus it induces an evolution of configurations. If $F(\alpha) = \alpha'$, then α' is called a *successor configuration* of α, and α is called a *predecessor configuration* of α'. We also express the relation $F(\alpha) = \alpha'$ by the *transition relation* $\alpha \vdash_A \alpha'$. A configuration given at time 0 is called an *initial configuration*. Let α_0 be an initial configuration of A. Then, $\alpha_0 \vdash_A F(\alpha_0) \vdash_A F^2(\alpha_0) \cdots$ (or the sequence of configurations $\alpha_0, F(\alpha_0), F^2(\alpha_0), \ldots$) is called an *evolution process* of A starting from α_0. Its finite segment $\alpha_0, F(\alpha_0), \ldots, F^n(\alpha_0)$ is also called an evolution process of A. We say a configuration α is *stable*, if $F(\alpha) = \alpha$. Thus, if a configuration becomes stable in an evolution process, then it does not change after that. A configuration $\alpha_\#$ is called a *blank configuration* if $\forall x \in \mathbb{Z}^k (\alpha_\#(x) = \#)$. Apparently $\alpha_\#$ is stable.

Let $A = (\mathbb{Z}^k, Q, (n_1, \ldots, n_m), f, \#)$ be a CA, and D be a finite subset of $\mathbb{Z}^k$. A function $p : D \to Q$ is called a *pattern* of A. Let $\alpha \in \mathrm{Conf}(A)$, and $x_0 \in \mathbb{Z}^k$. We say α *contains* the pattern p at x_0, if the following holds.

$$\forall x \in D \ (\alpha(x + x_0) = p(x))$$

We also say α *contains only* the pattern p at x_0, if

$$\forall x \in \mathbb{Z}^k ((x \in D \Rightarrow \alpha(x + x_0) = p(x)) \wedge (x \notin D \Rightarrow \alpha(x + x_0) = \#)).$$

Let α be a configuration that contains only a pattern p at some x_0. If α is stable, then p is called *stable*. Note that stability of α does not depend on the position x_0.

A configuration α is called *finite* if the set $\{x \,|\, x \in \mathbb{Z}^k \wedge \alpha(x) \neq \#\}$ is finite. Otherwise it is called *infinite*. In a finite configuration, all but a finite number of cells are in the quiescent state $\#$. Let $\mathrm{Conf}_{\mathrm{fin}}(A)$ denote the set of all finite configurations of A, i.e., $\mathrm{Conf}_{\mathrm{fin}}(A) = \{\alpha \,|\, \alpha \in \mathrm{Conf}(A) \wedge \alpha \text{ is finite}\}$. Let F_{fin} denote the restriction of F to $\mathrm{Conf}_{\mathrm{fin}}(A)$. It is easy to see that every finite configuration is mapped to a finite configuration by F, since $f(\#, \ldots, \#) = \#$. Therefore, F_{fin} defines a function $\mathrm{Conf}_{\mathrm{fin}}(A) \to \mathrm{Conf}_{\mathrm{fin}}(A)$.

A CA $A = (\mathbb{Z}^k, Q, (n_1, \ldots, n_m), f, \#)$ is also called an *m-neighbor CA*. Of course, to define the neighborhood exactly, an m-tuple of coordinates $(n_1, \ldots, n_m)$ should be given rather than m. But, we sometimes denote it by the neighborhood size when no confusion occur. Below, we show typical examples of neighborhoods that are commonly used when designing one- or two-dimensional CAs.

First, consider the two-dimensional case. Here, the cellular space is the square tessellation. The following neighborhoods N_N and N_M are called the *von Neumann neighborhood* and the *Moore neighborhood*, which are typical two-dimensional neighborhoods.

$$N_N = ((0,0), (0,1), (1,0), (0,-1), (-1,0))$$
$$N_M = ((0,0), (0,1), (1,1), (1,0), (1,-1), (0,-1), (-1,-1), (-1,0), (-1,1))$$

The von Neumann neighborhood consists of five cells. They are the cell under consideration, and the four adjacent cells to the north, east, south and west as shown in Fig. 10.1 **(a)**. Note that, hereafter, the cell under consideration, which has the relative coordinates $(0,0)$, will be called the *center cell*. The Moore neighborhood consists of the nine cells that are the center cell, and the eight adjacent cells having either a common edge or a common corner with the center cell as shown in Fig. 10.1 **(b)**. The transition relation $f(q_0, q_1, q_2, q_3, q_4) = q$ of a CA with the von Neumann neighborhood is represented pictorially as in Fig. 10.2. The case of the Moore neighborhood can be written similarly.

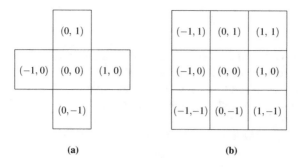

Fig. 10.1 (a) The von Neumann neighborhood, and (b) the Moore neighborhood

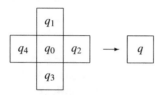

Fig. 10.2 A pictorial representation of the local rule $f(q_0, q_1, q_2, q_3, q_4) = q$ of a two-dimensional CA with the von Neumann neighborhood

Second, consider the one-dimensional case. The most commonly used neighborhood is $(-1, 0, 1)$, which consists of the left-adjacent cell, the center cell, and the right-adjacent cell. Note that, in the one-dimensional case, we use the notation like $(-1, 0, 1)$ instead of $((-1), (0), (1))$ for simplicity. In this neighborhood, the transition relation $f(q_{-1}, q_0, q_1) = q$ can be represented pictorially as in Fig. 10.3.

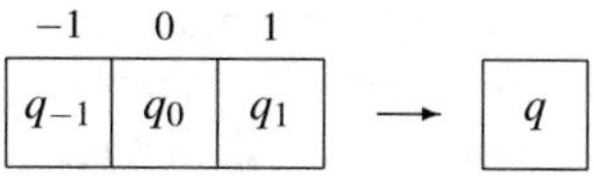

-1	0	1
q_{-1}	q_0	q_1

$\longrightarrow$ q

Fig. 10.3 A pictorial representation of the local rule $f(q_{-1}, q_0, q_1) = q$ of a one-dimensional CA with the neighborhood $(-1, 0, 1)$

Generally, we can define the neighborhood $(-r, -r+1, \ldots, 0, \ldots, r-1, r)$ for each $r \in \{1, 2, \ldots\}$. It is called the *neighborhood of radius r* for one-dimensional CAs. Hence, $(-1, 0, 1)$ is the neighborhood of radius 1. The neighborhood $(-1, 0)$ or $(0, 1)$ is called the neighborhood of radius $1/2$. In a CA with the neighborhood $(-1, 0)$ (or $(0, 1)$, respectively), information is transferred only one-way to the right (left). Therefore, it is called a *one-way CA*.

10.2.2 Examples of CAs

Example 10.1. **Game of Life (GoL).** It is a two-dimensional CA with the Moore neighborhood proposed by J.H. Conway. Since M. Gardner introduced it in *Scientific American* [13, 14], it became very popular. Although its local function is very simple, its evolution of configurations is complex, and shows life-like phenomena. Its cell has two states, which are a live state indicated by a black dot, and a dead state indicated by a blank. GoL is formally defined as follows.

$$\text{GoL} = (\mathbb{Z}^2, \{0,1\}, N_{\text{M}}, f_{\text{GoL}}, 0)$$

Here, the states 0 and 1 stand for the dead and live states, respectively. The local function f_{GoL} is as follows.

$$\forall q_0, q_1, \ldots, q_8 \in \{0,1\}:$$
$$f_{\text{GoL}}(q_0, q_1, \ldots, q_8) = \begin{cases} 1 & \text{if } q_0 = 0 \wedge (\sum_{i=1}^{8} q_i) \in \{3\} \\ 1 & \text{if } q_0 = 1 \wedge (\sum_{i=1}^{8} q_i) \in \{2,3\} \\ 0 & \text{elsewhere} \end{cases}$$

The local function f_{GoL} can also be stated by the expression "Just 3 for BIRTH, 2 or 3 for SURVIVAL" [5]. Here, "Just 3 for BIRTH" means that if the present state of the center cell is dead, and the number of live cells among the eight adjacent cells is just three, then the center cell will become live at the next time step. On the other hand, "2 or 3 for SURVIVAL" means that if the present state of the center cell is live, and the number of live cells among the eight adjacent cells is two or three, then the center cell will remain live also in the next time step. If otherwise, the next state of the center cell will be in the dead state.

Figure 10.4 shows an example of an evolution process in GoL [14]. At time $t = 0$ a configuration containing the pattern of the Cheshire Cat is given. Note that the Cheshire Cat is a cat that appears and disappears in *Alice's Adventures in Wonderland* [7]. Starting from this configuration, it evolves as shown in the figure. At $t = 7$, it becomes a configuration with a pattern called a *block*. Since the block is a stable pattern, the configuration will be the same for $t \geq 7$.

A *glider* [13] is an object shown in Fig. 10.5. After four time steps it becomes the same pattern, but shifts its position diagonally by one square. Thus, if there is no obstacle, it moves indefinitely in the cellular space. In GoL, there are many kinds of such moving objects. The glider shown in Fig. 10.5 is the smallest among them. A glider is a very useful object, since it can be used as a carrier of information. A remarkable pattern called a *glider gun*, which emits gliders periodically, was found by Gosper (see [14]). It is also known that, by colliding two gliders in an appropriate timing, various operations on them can be performed. For example, reversing the flying direction of one glider, annihilating both of the gliders, and some other operations are possible [5]. Using gliders and glider guns, as well as these techniques, we can implement logical operations AND, OR, and NOT, and thus a computer can be constructed in the space of GoL [5].

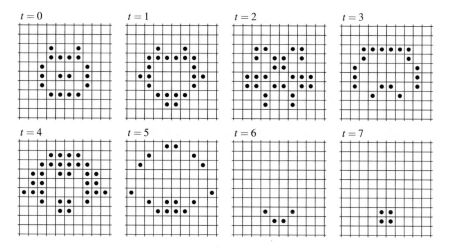

Fig. 10.4 Evolution process in GoL [14]. At $t = 0$, a configuration with the Cheshire Cat pattern is given. At $t = 7$, a configuration with a stable pattern called a block appears

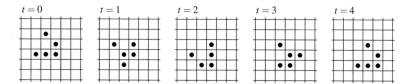

Fig. 10.5 Evolution process of configurations containing the glider pattern in GoL. This pattern moves to the south-east direction by one square in every four steps

For more details and recent developments in the study of GoL, see [2, 40]. The CA simulator *Golly* [48] is also recommended for the readers who are interested in seeing how various configurations evolve in GoL. It contains many examples of interesting configurations. Golly can simulate not only GoL, but also other CAs such as von Neumann's 29-state self-reproducing CA (see Sect. 14.1).   □

Example 10.2. **Fredkin's self-replicating CA.** It is a two-dimensional two-state CA with the von Neumann neighborhood in which any initial pattern replicates itself after certain time steps [14]. It is defined as follows.

$$SR_F = (\mathbb{Z}^2, \{0,1\}, N_N, f_F, 0)$$

As in the case of GoL, the states 0 and 1 stand for the dead and live states. The local function f_F is as follows, where $\oplus$ represents the modulo-2 addition (i.e., XOR).

$$\forall q_0, q_1, q_2, q_3, q_4 \in \{0,1\}:$$
$$f_F(q_0, q_1, q_2, q_3, q_4) = q_1 \oplus q_2 \oplus q_3 \oplus q_4$$

Namely, if the total number of live cells among the four adjacent cells is odd, then the center cell will become live at the next time step. Otherwise, it will become dead. Note that, in this CA, the next state does not depends on the present state of the center cell, though we use the von Neumann neighborhood.

Examples of evolution processes in this cellular space are shown in Figs. 10.6 and 10.7. We see that copies of the initial pattern, which is given at $t = 0$, appear at $t = 2$ in Fig. 10.6, and at $t = 8$ in Fig. 10.7. Actually, *any* finite pattern replicates itself in this cellular space. It can be easily proved using the property of modulo-2 addition, and this is left as an exercise for the readers (use the following relation, where α^t denotes the configuration at time t: $\alpha^{t+1}(x,y) = \alpha^t(x, y+1) \oplus \alpha^t(x+1, y) \oplus \alpha^t(x, y-1) \oplus \alpha^t(x-1, y)$).   □

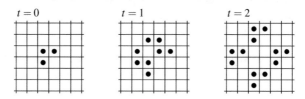

Fig. 10.6 Evolution process of the Fredkin's self-replicating CA. At $t = 2$, four copies of the pattern at $t = 0$ are created

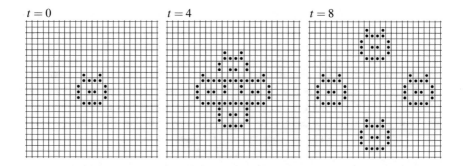

Fig. 10.7 Evolution process of the Fredkin's self-replicating CA starting from the configuration with the Cheshire Cat pattern

Example 10.3. **Elementary CA.** An *elementary cellular automaton* (ECA) [50] is a one-dimensional two-state three-neighbor CA whose neighborhood is of radius 1. There are 256 kinds of ECAs, and thus each ECA has a rule number $n \in \{0, \ldots, 255\}$. The ECA of rule n is defined as follows.

$$\text{ECA}_n = (\mathbb{Z}, \{0,1\}, (-1,0,1), f_n)$$

The rule number n is determined from f_n by the following formula.

$$n = f_n(1,1,1)\,2^7 + f_n(1,1,0)\,2^6 + \cdots + f_n(0,0,0)\,2^0$$

For example, the local function f_{110} of ECA_{110} is as below.

$$
\begin{array}{ll}
f_{110}(0,0,0) = 0 & f_{110}(0,0,1) = 1 \\
f_{110}(0,1,0) = 1 & f_{110}(0,1,1) = 1 \\
f_{110}(1,0,0) = 0 & f_{110}(1,0,1) = 1 \\
f_{110}(1,1,0) = 1 & f_{110}(1,1,1) = 0
\end{array}
$$

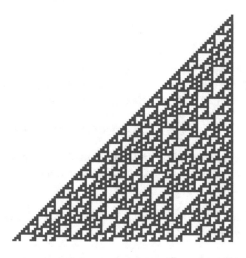

Fig. 10.8 An evolution process of the ECA rule 110. The horizontal and the vertical directions correspond to space and time, respectively. Here, downward is the positive direction of time

An example of evolution process of ECA rule 110 is shown in Fig. 10.8. Though it is a simple CA, its behavior is very complex. Wolfram [50] conjectured that it is computationally universal, i.e., any Turing machine is simulated in it. Later, Cook [8] proved it by showing that rewriting processes of cyclic tag systems (see Sect. 7.2.2) can be simulated in the cellular space of ECA rule 110. Besides the paper [8], there are many papers on ECA rule 110, e.g., [9, 22, 37].   □

10.3 Reversible Cellular Automata (RCAs)

In this section, we give definitions on reversible cellular automata (RCAs), and show basic properties on them.

10.3.1 Definitions of RCAs

We first introduce two notions related to reversibility of CAs. They are injectivity and invertibility.

Definition 10.3. Let $A = (\mathbb{Z}^k, Q, N, f)$ be a CA.

1. The CA A is called an *injective CA* if its global function F is injective.
2. The CA A is called an *invertible CA* if there exists a CA $A' = (\mathbb{Z}^k, Q, N', f')$ that satisfies the following condition:

$$\forall \alpha, \beta \in \mathrm{Conf}(A): \ F(\alpha) = \beta \text{ iff } F'(\beta) = \alpha,$$

where F and F' are the global functions of A and A', respectively. The CA A' is called the *inverse CA* of A.

It is clear from the above definition that if a CA is invertible then it is injective. Its converse also holds from the results independently proved by Hedlund [15] and Richardson [41]. This is stated by the following theorem.

Theorem 10.1. *[15, 41] Let A be a CA. The CA A is injective iff it is invertible.*

Since the notions of injectivity and invertibility in CAs are thus proved to be equivalent, we use the terminology *reversible CA* for such a CA. Hence, they are used synonymously hereafter.

Definition 10.4. Let A be a CA. We call A a *reversible CA* (RCA), if A is an injective CA (or equivalently invertible CA).

In the cases of reversible TMs (Sect. 5.1), and reversible combinatorial logic circuits (Sect. 4.1), the definitions of reversibility were much simpler than the case of RCAs. The reason is that they were defined based on their "local" properties. A reversible TM is one such that the set of their quadruples (or quintuples) satisfies the reversibility condition (Definitions 5.3 or 5.4). A reversible combinatorial logic circuit is one composed of reversible logic gates whose operations are described by injective functions (Definition 4.2). These properties can be tested in finite steps. By the above definitions, global behaviors of the systems, i.e., the transition functions of configurations of the RTMs and the logical functions of the circuits, trivially become injective. In addition, inverse RTMs (Definitions 5.10 or 5.12), and inverse reversible combinatorial logic circuits (Definition 4.6), which undo the operations of the original systems, can be obtained easily. Thus, injectivity of the system also trivially entails its invertibility. Therefore, in these systems, we can directly define reversibility without introducing the notions of global injectivity and invertibility. Note that, for a circuit composed of reversible logic elements with memory (RLEMs), it is also easy to make its inverse circuit, though we did not give it in Chap. 3.

On the other hand, it is not possible to define reversibility of CAs based on their local functions, if we use the framework of classical CAs. This is because the local function $f : Q^{|N|} \to Q$ of a CA $A = (\mathbb{Z}^k, Q, N, f)$ cannot be injective except the case where $|Q| = 1$ or $|N| = 1$. Hence, as given in Definitions 10.3 and 10.4, we must have defined based on their global functions. Because of this, testing reversibility of CAs becomes difficult. In particular, it has been shown that injectivity of two-dimensional CAs is undecidable [16] (Theorem 10.4). On the other hand, in Sect. 10.4, three methods are given to make it easy to design RCAs. There, variants or some special subclasses of standard CAs are defined so that reversibility can be tested based on their local functions.

GoL in Example 10.1 is an irreversible CA. For example, the configuration containing only one block pattern (appearing at $t = 7$ in Fig. 10.4) has two or more predecessor configurations. The configurations at $t = 6$ and $t = 7$ are such ones. Thus, the global function of GoL is not injective.

The Fredkin's self-replicating CA SR_F in Example 10.2 is also irreversible. Since there are many configurations that go to the *blank configuration*, which is the configuration such that all the cells are in the quiescent state, as shown in Fig. 10.9. Note that, actually, there are infinitely many configurations that go to the blank configuration, and it is left for readers as an exercise to show it.

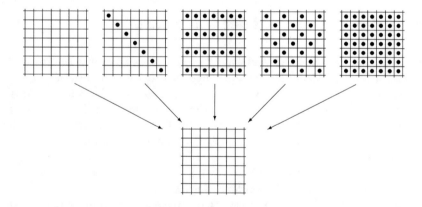

Fig. 10.9 Five examples of configurations that go to the blank configuration in the Fredkin's self-replicating CA in Example 10.2. The four configurations except the leftmost one in the upper row are the configurations in which these patterns extends infinitely in the two-dimensional space

ECA rule 110 in Example 10.3 is again irreversible. For example, both the configurations "$\cdots 000 \cdots$" and "$\cdots 111 \cdots$" (i.e., all 0's and all 1's) go to the configuration "$\cdots 000 \cdots$". Exercise: Find a pair of finite configurations that go to the same one.

Consider the following two-dimensional one-neighbor CA A_{shift}.

$$A_{\text{shift}} = (\mathbb{Z}^2, \{0,1\}, ((-1,0)), f_{\text{shift}}, 0)$$
$$f_{\text{shift}}(q) = q \text{ for all } q \in \{0,1\}$$

By the local function f_{shift}, the present state of each cell will be sent to the right neighboring cell at the next time step. Hence, every configuration shifts rightward by one square in each step (Fig. 10.10), and thus it is trivially reversible.

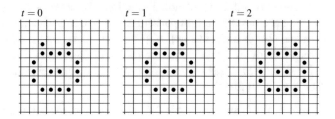

Fig. 10.10 Evolution process of A_{shift}. Here, every configuration simply shifts to the right. Thus, it is reversible, but not an interesting RCA at all

If we use the standard CAs, it is generally difficult to design nontrivial RCAs. In Sect. 10.4.3 the framework of partitioned cellular automata will be given, and in Chaps. 11–14 various RCAs will be constructed by using it.

10.3.2 Basic properties of RCAs and related CAs

Injectivity and *surjectivity* of a global function of CAs were first studied in the Garden-of-Eden problem [26, 35]. A configuration α is called a *Garden-of-Eden configuration* of a CA A if it has no predecessor configuration, i.e., $\forall \alpha' \in \text{Conf}(A)$: $F(\alpha') \neq \alpha$. A pattern p is called an *orphan* if the configuration α that contains only p is a Garden-of-Eden configuration. Existence of a Garden-of-Eden configuration is equivalent to non-surjectivity of the global function F. The *Garden-of-Eden problem* is to decide whether there is a Garden-of-Eden configuration in a given CA. As it will be stated in Theorems 10.3 and 10.4, it is decidable in the one-dimensional case, but undecidable in the higher-dimensional case.

Moore [26] first showed the proposition: If there are "erasable configurations" (which are mapped to the same configuration by the global function) then there is a Garden-of-Eden configuration (it is sometimes called Moore's Garden-of-Eden theorem). Later, Myhill [35] proved its converse. Their results are now combined and stated in the following theorem called the *Garden-of-Eden theorem*.

Theorem 10.2. *[26, 35] Let A be a CA, and F be its global function. The function F is surjective iff F_{fin} is injective.*

Since it is clear if F is injective then F_{fin} is also so, the following corollary is derived.

Corollary 10.1. *Let A be a CA. If the global function F of A is injective, then it is surjective.*

By Corollary 10.1, the global function of an RCA is bijective. A one-dimensional CA that is surjective but not injective was shown by Amoroso and Cooper [3]. The CA SR_F in Example 10.2 is also such a CA, since it is surjective by Lemma 10.1 below, and Theorem 10.2, but not injective. Thus, the converse of the above corollary does not hold.

Let F_{GoL} be the global function of GoL. Then, $(F_{GoL})_{fin}$ is not injective, since the finite configurations at time $t = 6$ and $t = 7$ in Fig. 10.4 have the same successor configuration, which is also finite. Hence, by Theorem 10.2, existence of Garden-of-Eden configurations in GoL is guaranteed. But, to find examples of such configurations, in particular orphans of small sizes, is difficult. R. Banks et al. first found an orphan in 1971, whose size is 9×33 (see [5]). Since then, various orphans were constructed by many researchers. For example, orphans of size 10×10 by M. Heule et al. (2011), of size 8×12 by S. Eker (2016), and others have been known (see "Garden of Eden" of LifeWiki: http://www.conwaylife.com/wiki/).

Next, consider the Fredkin's self-replicating CA SR_F. The following lemma says that the global function F_F of SR_F becomes injective if we restrict it on the set of finite configurations, though it is not injective in the unrestricted case (see Fig. 10.9). Therefore, by Theorem 10.2, F_F is surjective, and thus there is no Garden-of-Eden configuration in SR_F.

Lemma 10.1. *Let F_F be the global function of the Fredkin's self-replicating CA SR_F. Then, $(F_F)_{fin}$ is injective.*

Proof. We first define the binary operator $\tilde{\oplus}$ on $Conf(SR_F)$ using the XOR operator $\oplus$ on $\{0, 1\}$ as follows.

$$\forall \alpha_1, \alpha_2 \in Conf(SR_F), \ \forall x \in \mathbb{Z}^2 : (\alpha_1 \tilde{\oplus} \alpha_2)(x) = \alpha_1(x) \oplus \alpha_2(x)$$

Then, the following holds.

$$
\begin{aligned}
&F_F(\alpha_1 \tilde{\oplus} \alpha_2)(x) \\
&= (\alpha_1 \tilde{\oplus} \alpha_2)(x + (0,1)) \oplus (\alpha_1 \tilde{\oplus} \alpha_2)(x + (1,0)) \oplus \\
&\quad (\alpha_1 \tilde{\oplus} \alpha_2)(x + (0,-1)) \oplus (\alpha_1 \tilde{\oplus} \alpha_2)(x + (-1,0)) \\
&= \alpha_1(x + (0,1)) \oplus \alpha_1(x + (1,0)) \oplus \alpha_1(x + (0,-1)) \oplus \alpha_1(x + (-1,0)) \oplus \\
&\quad \alpha_2(x + (0,1)) \oplus \alpha_2(x + (1,0)) \oplus \alpha_2(x + (0,-1)) \oplus \alpha_2(x + (-1,0)) \\
&= F_F(\alpha_1)(x) \oplus F_F(\alpha_2)(x) \\
&= (F_F(\alpha_1) \tilde{\oplus} F_F(\alpha_2))(x)
\end{aligned}
$$

Hence, $F_F(\alpha_1 \tilde{\oplus} \alpha_2) = F_F(\alpha_1) \tilde{\oplus} F_F(\alpha_2)$, which means $\tilde{\oplus}$ on $Conf(SR_F)$ is a linear operator. Now assume, on the contrary, $(F_F)_{fin}$ is not injective. Then, there are two distinct finite configurations β_1 and β_2 such that $F_F(\beta_1) = F_F(\beta_2)$. Since $\beta_1 \neq \beta_2$, $\beta_1 \tilde{\oplus} \beta_2$ is a finite non-blank configuration. By the definition of the local function f_F of SR_F, it is easy to see that the following holds: If α is a finite non-blank configuration, then $F_F(\alpha)$ is also a finite non-blank configuration. Thus, $F_F(\beta_1 \tilde{\oplus} \beta_2)$ is a finite non-blank configuration. On the other hand, since $F_F(\beta_1) = F_F(\beta_2)$, $F_F(\beta_1) \tilde{\oplus} F_F(\beta_2)$ is a blank configuration. It contradicts the relation $F_F(\beta_1 \tilde{\oplus} \beta_2) = F_F(\beta_1) \tilde{\oplus} F_F(\beta_2)$ shown above. Therefore, $(F_F)_{fin}$ is injective. $\qquad \square$

After the works of Moore [26] and Myhill [35], relation among injectivity and surjectivity in unrestricted, finite, and periodic configurations have been extensively studied (see e.g., [3, 18, 23, 24, 41]).

Next, we consider decision problems on injectivity and surjectivity on CAs. For the case of one-dimensional CAs, Amoroso and Patt [4] proved that injectivity and surjectivity of the global function are both decidable.

Theorem 10.3. *[4] There is an algorithm to determine whether the global function of a given one-dimensional CA is injective (surjective) or not.*

Later, a quadratic time algorithm to determine injectivity (surjectivity) of a global function using de Bruijn graph was given by Sutner [43]. There are also several studies on enumerating all one-dimensional RCAs (e.g., [6, 27]).

For two-dimensional CAs, injectivity and surjectivity are both undecidable. Thus, they are also undecidable for the higher dimensional case. The following theorem was proved by Kari [16] by a reduction from the tiling problem, which is a well-known undecidable problem.

Theorem 10.4. *[16] The problem whether the global function of a given two-dimensional CA is injective (surjective) is undecidable.*

For each reversible CA, there is an inverse CA which undoes the operations of the former. In the two-dimensional case, we can observe the following fact on the inverse CAs [16]. Let A be an arbitrary two-dimensional reversible CA, and A' be the inverse CA of A. We cannot, in general, compute an upper-bound of the neighborhood size $|N'|$ of A' from A. If we assume, on the contrary, such an upper-bound is computable, then the total number of candidates of the inverse CA of A is also bounded. Since it is easy to test if a CA $\tilde{A}$ is the inverse of the CA A for any given $\tilde{A}$, the inverse of A can be found among the above candidates in finite steps. From this, we can design an algorithm to decide whether a given CA is reversible or not, which contradicts Theorem 10.4. It is stated in the following theorem.

Theorem 10.5. *[16] There is no computable function g such that for any two-dimensional RCA $A = (\mathbb{Z}^2, Q, N, f)$ and its inverse RCA $A' = (\mathbb{Z}^2, Q, N', f')$, the relation $|N'| \leq g(|Q|, |N|)$ holds.*

On the other hand, for the case of one-dimensional CAs, the following result has been shown by Czeizler and Kari [10].

Theorem 10.6. *[10] Let $A = (\mathbb{Z}, Q, N, f)$ be an arbitrary one-dimensional RCA, and $A' = (\mathbb{Z}, Q, N', f')$ be its inverse, where $|Q| = n$ and $|N| = m$. If N consists of m consecutive cells, then $|N'| \leq n^{m-1} - (m-1)$. Furthermore, when $m = 2$, this upper-bound is tight.*

10.4 Design Methods for RCAs

In the following chapters, we shall show that information processing capabilities of RCAs are quite high in spite of the strong constraint of reversibility. In particular, even very simple RCAs have computational universality. However, as seen in the previous section, it is generally difficult to find RCAs. In the two-dimensional case, it is not possible to test if a given CA is reversible or not by Theorem 10.4. In the case of one-dimensional CAs, there is a decision algorithm for reversibility (Theorem 10.3). But, since the decision algorithm is not so simple, it is still difficult to design RCAs with specific properties using this algorithm as an aid. Hence, we need tools for designing RCAs. So far, several methods have been proposed to make it feasible to construct RCAs. In the following, we explain three methods. They are CAs with block rules [20, 21, 47], CAs with second-order rules [20, 21, 45, 47], and partitioned CAs (PCAs) [34].

10.4.1 CAs with block rules

A local function of a standard m-neighbor CA is a function $f : Q^m \to Q$, and therefore it is impossible to make f itself be injective except the trivial case where $|Q| = 1$ or $m = 1$. Instead, if a local function is of the form $f : Q^m \to Q^m$, then it can be injective. Assume all the cells are grouped into blocks each of which consists of m cells. Such a local function maps a state of each block to a new state of the same block. If f is injective, and is applied to all the blocks in a given configuration in parallel, then the induced global function will be also injective. Of course, at the next time step, the grouping into blocks should be changed. Otherwise, interaction between blocks is impossible. Such a CA is often called a *block cellular automaton*.

Margolus [20] first proposed this type of two-dimensional CA. In his model, all the cells are grouped into blocks of size 2×2 as in Fig. 10.11 **(a)**. Its local function is specified by *block rules*, whose example is shown in Fig. 10.11 **(b)**. This CA evolves as follows: At time 0 the local function is applied to every solid line block, then at time 1 to every dotted line block, and so on, alternately. This kind of neighborhood is called the *Margolus neighborhood*. We can see that the local function defined by the block rules of Fig. 10.11 **(b)** is injective (such an injection is sometimes called a *block permutation*). Thus, the Margolus CA is reversible. He showed that the billiard ball model (BBM) (see Sect. 2.2.3) can be realized in this CA [20]. Figure 10.12 shows a reflection of a ball by a reflector in this RCA, which corresponds to the process shown in Fig. 2.7. Hence, his RCA model is computationally universal. Note that CAs with Margolus neighborhood are not conventional CAs, because each cell must know the relative position in a block and the parity of time besides its own state.

Similarly, a k-dimensional block RCA can also be defined for any k. Figure 10.13 gives a one-dimensional case of block size 2. It shows how an injective local function f is applied to blocks at each time step.

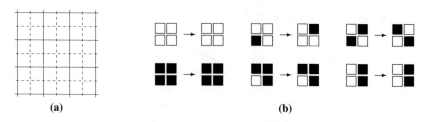

(a)   **(b)**

Fig. 10.11 The neighborhood and the rules of Margolus CA [20]. **(a)** Grouping of cells into blocks of size 2×2 by solid or dotted lines. These blocks form the Margolus neighborhood. **(b)** The block rules for the Margolus CA. Since rotation-symmetry is assumed here, rules obtained by rotating both sides of a rule are not indicated here

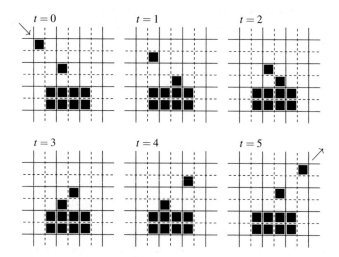

Fig. 10.12 Reflection of a ball by a reflector in the Margolus CA [20]

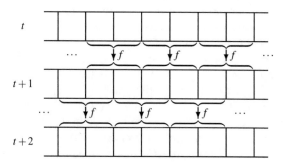

Fig. 10.13 A one-dimensional RCA with block rules defined by an injective local function f. Here the block size is 2

10.4.2 Second-order CAs

A *second-order CA* is one such that the state of a cell at time $t+1$ is determined not only by the states of the neighboring cells at time t but also by the state of the center cell at $t-1$ [20, 46, 47]. Thus, an ordinary CA is sometimes called a *first-order CA*. Margolus proposed a method of using second-order CAs to design reversible ones, and gave a specific model of a computationally universal two-dimensional three-state reversible second-order CA [20].

Let $A = (\mathbb{Z}^k, Q, (n_1, \ldots, n_m), f)$ be an arbitrary first-order (i.e., ordinary) CA. We assume a binary operator $\ominus$ is defined on the state set Q, which satisfies $a \ominus b = c$ iff $a \ominus c = b$ for all $a, b, c \in Q$. A typical example is $Q = \{0, 1, \ldots, r-1\}$ and the operation $\ominus$ is the mod-r subtraction. Let $\alpha^t \in \mathrm{Conf}(A)$ denote a configuration at time t. We define a kind of global function $\tilde{F} : (\mathrm{Conf}(A))^2 \to \mathrm{Conf}(A)$, which determines the configuration α^{t+1} from two configurations α^t and α^{t-1} as follows.

$$\forall \alpha^t, \alpha^{t-1} \in \mathrm{Conf}(A), \ \forall x \in \mathbb{Z}^k :$$
$$\tilde{F}(\alpha^t, \alpha^{t-1})(x) = f(\alpha^t(x+n_1), \ldots, \alpha^t(x+n_m)) \ominus \alpha^{t-1}(x)$$

Hence,

$$\alpha^{t+1}(x) = f(\alpha^t(x+n_1), \ldots, \alpha^t(x+n_m)) \ominus \alpha^{t-1}(x)$$

holds for all $x \in \mathbb{Z}^k$. On the other hand, by the assumption on the operator $\ominus$, the following equation also holds, which means that the state of each cell at time $t-1$ is determined by the states of the neighboring cells at t and the state of the center cell at $t+1$ by the same local function f.

$$\alpha^{t-1}(x) = f(\alpha^t(x+n_1), \ldots, \alpha^t(x+n_m)) \ominus \alpha^{t+1}(x)$$

In this sense, a second-order CA defined above is reversible for *any* function $f : Q^m \to Q$ provided that the operator $\ominus$ is appropriately given.

Behavior of such CAs, in particular, reversible second-order ECAs are investigated in [50]. There, a reversible second-order ECA of rule n is denoted by "rule nR" ($n \in \{0, \ldots, 255\}$). Relation between second-order CAs and the lattice gas model is also discussed in [45].

Example 10.4. Consider the ECA rule 90:

$$\mathrm{ECA}_{90} = (\mathbb{Z}, \{0, 1\}, (-1, 0, 1), f_{90}, 0).$$

The local function f_{90} is as below.

$f_{90}(0,0,0) = 0$	$f_{90}(0,0,1) = 1$
$f_{90}(0,1,0) = 0$	$f_{90}(0,1,1) = 1$
$f_{90}(1,0,0) = 1$	$f_{90}(1,0,1) = 0$
$f_{90}(1,1,0) = 1$	$f_{90}(1,1,1) = 0$

Alternatively, it is defined by $\forall q_{-1}, q_0, q_1 \in \{0,1\} : f_{90}(q_{-1}, q_0, q_1) = q_{-1} \oplus q_1$. It is considered as a one-dimensional version of Fredkin's self-replicating CA SR_F in Example 10.2. In fact, any finite pattern given at $t = 0$ will replicates itself as shown in Fig. 10.14. It is also easy to show the ECA rule 90 is irreversible.

We now give the reversible second-order ECA rule 90R. Here, the mod-2 subtraction $\ominus$ is identical to $\oplus$, since the set of states is $\{0,1\}$. Thus, its global function $\tilde{F}_{90}$ is as follows.

$$\forall \alpha^t, \alpha^{t-1} \in \mathrm{Conf}(\mathrm{ECA}_{90}), \ \forall x \in \mathbb{Z} :$$
$$\tilde{F}_{90}(\alpha^t, \alpha^{t-1})(x) = f_{90}(\alpha^t(x-1), \alpha^t(x), \alpha^t(x+1)) \oplus \alpha^{t-1}(x)$$
$$= \alpha^t(x-1) \oplus \alpha^t(x+1) \oplus \alpha^{t-1}(x)$$

Figure 10.15 shows examples of evolution processes of the ECA rule 90R. Though the configurations at time $t = 0$ are the same in **(a)** and **(b)**, the evolution processes are different. This is because the configurations at $t = -1$ are different.   □

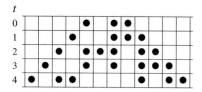

Fig. 10.14 Evolution process of the ECA rule 90. As in the case of Fredkin's self-replicating CA in Example 10.2, copies of the initial pattern are obtained at time $t = 2$ and $t = 4$

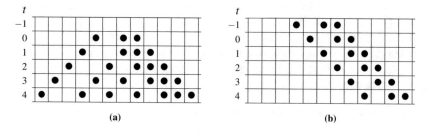

Fig. 10.15 Evolution processes of the reversible second-order ECA rule 90R. The configurations at time $t = 0$ are set to the same as in Fig. 10.14 in both **(a)** and **(b)**. But, the configurations at $t = -1$ are different. In **(a)** it is the blank configuration, and in **(b)** it is the one obtained by shifting the configuration at $t = 0$ by one square to the left

10.4.3 Partitioned CAs (PCAs) and reversible PCAs (RPCAs)

As is seen in the previous subsections, the frameworks of CAs with block rules, and second-order CAs provide methods for designing a kind of reversible cellular automata. In fact, non-trivial reversible CAs can be obtained by them even in the two-state case. However, these CAs differ from standard CAs. We now define a *partitioned cellular automaton* (PCA) as another tool for designing reversible CAs, which was first introduced in [34]. A PCA is a framework where the notion of "local reversibility" can be defined, and hence has some similarity to a CA with block rules. However, since PCAs are defined as a special subclass of standard CAs, they are in the conventional framework of CAs. In addition, flexibility of neighborhood is rather high. Thus, it is convenient to use PCAs for constructing RCAs having desired properties, in particular, computational universality. Hereafter, we mainly use this framework to design RCAs. A shortcoming of PCA is, in general, the number of states per cell becomes large.

10.4.3.1 Definition and basic properties of PCAs

Definition 10.5. A *deterministic k-dimensional m-neighbor partitioned cellular automaton (PCA)* is a system defined by

$$P = (\mathbb{Z}^k, (Q_1, \ldots, Q_m), (n_1, \ldots, n_m), f, (\#_1, \ldots, \#_m)).$$

Here, $\mathbb{Z}^k$ is the same as in the definition of a CA, and Q_i $(i = 1, \ldots, m)$ is a nonempty finite set of states of the i-th part of each cell. The state set Q of each cell is given by $Q = Q_1 \times \cdots \times Q_m$. The m-tuple $(n_1, \ldots, n_m) \in (\mathbb{Z}^k)^m$ is a *neighborhood*, and $f : Q \to Q$ is a *local function*. The state $(\#_1, \ldots, \#_m) \in Q$ is a *quiescent state* that satisfies $f(\#_1, \ldots, \#_m) = (\#_1, \ldots, \#_m)$. We also allow a PCA that has no quiescent state.

If $f(q_1, \ldots, q_m) = (q'_1, \ldots, q'_m)$ holds for $(q_1, \ldots, q_m), (q'_1, \ldots, q'_m) \in Q$, then this relation is called a *local rule* (or simply a *rule*) of the PCA P. Note that, in general, the states $\#_1, \ldots, \#_m$ may be different from each other. However, by renaming the states in each part appropriately, we can assume all the states $\#_1, \ldots, \#_m$ are the same. In the following, we employ such a convention, and write the quiescent state by $(\#, \ldots, \#)$. For a PCA P that has a quiescent state, we can define a finite and an infinite configurations in a similar manner as in CAs.

The global function induced by the local function of a PCA is defined as below.

Definition 10.6. Let $P = (\mathbb{Z}^k, (Q_1, \ldots, Q_m), (n_1, \ldots, n_m), f, (\#, \ldots, \#))$ be a PCA, and $\mathrm{pr}_i : Q \to Q_i$ be the *projection function* such that $\mathrm{pr}_i(q_1, \ldots, q_m) = q_i$ for all $(q_1, \ldots, q_m) \in Q$. The *global function* $F : \mathrm{Conf}(P) \to \mathrm{Conf}(P)$ of P is defined as the one that satisfies the following condition.

$$\forall \alpha \in \mathrm{Conf}(P), \forall x \in \mathbb{Z}^k : F(\alpha)(x) = f(\mathrm{pr}_1(\alpha(x+n_1)), \ldots, \mathrm{pr}_m(\alpha(x+n_m)))$$

It means that the next state of the cell at the position x is determined by the present states of the first part of the cell $x+n_1$, the second part of the cell $x+n_2$, $\cdots$, and the m-th part of the cell $x+n_m$.

It is easy to show that a PCA is a subclass of a standard CA.

Lemma 10.2. *Let $P = (\mathbb{Z}^k, (Q_1, \ldots, Q_m), (n_1, \ldots, n_m), f)$ be a PCA, and F be its global function. Then, there is a CA $A = (\mathbb{Z}^k, (Q_1 \times \cdots \times Q_m), (n_1, \ldots, n_m), \hat{f})$ such that $\hat{F} = F$, where $\hat{F}$ is the global function of A.*

Proof. Let $Q = Q_1 \times \cdots \times Q_m$, and $\mathrm{pr}_1, \ldots, \mathrm{pr}_m$ be the projection functions given in Definition 10.6. We define $\hat{f}$ as follows.

$$\forall q_1, \ldots, q_m \in Q : \hat{f}(q_1, \ldots, q_m) = f(\mathrm{pr}_1(q_1), \ldots, \mathrm{pr}_m(q_m))$$

Then, for any $\alpha \in \mathrm{Conf}(P)$ and $x \in \mathbb{Z}^k$,

$$\begin{aligned}
\hat{F}(\alpha)(x) &= \hat{f}(\alpha(x+n_1), \ldots, \alpha(x+n_m)) \\
&= f(\mathrm{pr}_1(\alpha(x+n_1)), \ldots, \mathrm{pr}_m(\alpha(x+n_m))) \\
&= F(\alpha)(x)
\end{aligned}$$

holds. Hence, $\hat{F} = F$.   □

We now show that, in a PCA, injectivity of the global function is equivalent to injectivity of the local function.

Lemma 10.3. *Let $P = (\mathbb{Z}^k, (Q_1, \ldots, Q_m), (n_1, \ldots, n_m), f)$ be a PCA, and F be its global function. Then, F is injective iff f is injective.*

Proof. We first show if F is injective, then f is injective. Assume, on the contrary, f is not injective. Thus, there exist $(q_1, \ldots, q_m), (q'_1, \ldots, q'_m) \in Q = (Q_1 \times \cdots \times Q_m)$ such that $f(q_1, \ldots, q_m) = f(q'_1, \ldots, q'_m)$ and $(q_1, \ldots, q_m) \neq (q'_1, \ldots, q'_m)$. Let $(\hat{q}_1, \ldots, \hat{q}_m)$ be an element arbitrarily chosen from Q. We define two configurations α and α' as below.

$$\forall i \in \{1, \ldots, m\}, \forall x \in \mathbb{Z}^k :$$
$$\mathrm{pr}_i(\alpha(x)) = \begin{cases} q_i & \text{if } x = n_i \\ \hat{q}_i & \text{elsewhere} \end{cases}$$
$$\mathrm{pr}_i(\alpha'(x)) = \begin{cases} q'_i & \text{if } x = n_i \\ \hat{q}_i & \text{elsewhere} \end{cases}$$

Since $(q_1, \ldots, q_m) \neq (q'_1, \ldots, q'_m)$, $\alpha \neq \alpha'$ holds. By the definition of F, the following holds.

$$\forall x \in \mathbb{Z}^k :$$
$$\begin{aligned}
F(\alpha)(x) &= f(\mathrm{pr}_1(\alpha(x+n_1)), \ldots, \mathrm{pr}_m(\alpha(x+n_m))) \\
&= \begin{cases} f(q_1, \ldots, q_m) & \text{if } x = (0, \ldots, 0) \\ f(\hat{q}_1, \ldots, \hat{q}_m) & \text{if } x \neq (0, \ldots, 0) \end{cases} \\
F(\alpha')(x) &= f(\mathrm{pr}_1(\alpha'(x+n_1)), \ldots, \mathrm{pr}_m(\alpha'(x+n_m))) \\
&= \begin{cases} f(q'_1, \ldots, q'_m) & \text{if } x = (0, \ldots, 0) \\ f(\hat{q}_1, \ldots, \hat{q}_m) & \text{if } x \neq (0, \ldots, 0) \end{cases}
\end{aligned}$$

But, since $f(q_1,\ldots,q_m) = f(q_1',\ldots,q_m')$, $F(\alpha) = F(\alpha')$ holds. It contradicts the assumption that F is injective.

Next, we show if f is injective, then F is injective. We assume F is not injective. Thus, there are configurations α and α' such that $F(\alpha) = F(\alpha')$ and $\alpha \neq \alpha'$. Since $\alpha \neq \alpha'$, there exist $y \in \mathbb{Z}^k$ and $j \in \{1,\ldots,m\}$ that satisfy $\mathrm{pr}_j(\alpha(y)) \neq \mathrm{pr}_j(\alpha'(y))$. Therefore, the following holds.

$$F(\alpha)(y-n_j) = f(\mathrm{pr}_1(\alpha(y-n_j+n_1)),\ldots,\mathrm{pr}_j(\alpha(y-n_j+n_j)),\ldots,$$
$$\mathrm{pr}_m(\alpha(y-n_j+n_m)))$$
$$F(\alpha')(y-n_j) = f(\mathrm{pr}_1(\alpha'(y-n_j+n_1)),\ldots,\mathrm{pr}_j(\alpha'(y-n_j+n_j)),\ldots,$$
$$\mathrm{pr}_m(\alpha'(y-n_j+n_m)))$$

From $\mathrm{pr}_j(\alpha(y-n_j+n_j)) \neq \mathrm{pr}_j(\alpha'(y-n_j+n_j))$, and the fact f is injective, $F(\alpha)(y-n_j) \neq F(\alpha')(y-n_j)$. But, it contradicts the assumption $F(\alpha) = F(\alpha')$. □

A reversible PCA is defined as follows.

Definition 10.7. Let $P = (\mathbb{Z}^k, (Q_1,\ldots,Q_m), (n_1,\ldots,n_m), f)$ be a PCA. P is called a *reversible PCA* (RPCA) if its local (or equivalently global) function is injective.

From Lemmas 10.2 and 10.3, we can see that, to obtain an RCA it suffices to give a PCA whose local function is injective. This property makes it feasible to design a large varieties of RCAs. In the case of CAs with block rules, there is non-uniformity of the neighborhood, i.e., it cyclically changes depending on time. In the case of second-order CAs, their local functions must be in a very restricted form. However, since PCA is a kind of standard CA, it is relatively easy to design it.

10.4.3.2 Neighborhoods of one- and two-dimensional PCAs

Some typical neighborhoods of one- and two-dimensional PCAs are shown below. We first give a one-dimensional three-neighbor (radius 1) PCA $P_{1d\text{-}3}$.

$$P_{1d\text{-}3} = (\mathbb{Z}, (L,C,R), (1,0,-1), f)$$

Each cell has three parts, i.e., left, center, and right parts, and their state sets are L, C, and R. The next state of a cell is determined by the present states of the left part of the right-neighboring cell, the center part of this cell, and the right part of the left-neighboring cell (not depending on the whole three parts of the three cells). Figure 10.16 shows its cellular space, and how the local function f is applied. Let $(l,c,r), (l',c',r') \in L \times C \times R$. If $f(l,c,r) = (l',c',r')$, then this equation is called a *local rule* (or simply a *rule*) of the PCA $P_{1d\text{-}3}$. It can be written in a pictorial form as shown in Fig. 10.17. Note that, in the pictorial representation, the arguments of f of the left-hand side of $f(l,c,r) = (l',c',r')$ appear in a reverse order. This is because f is a function such that $f : (L \times C \times R) \to (L \times C \times R)$, and thus the neighborhood is not $(-1,0,1)$, but $(1,0,-1)$.

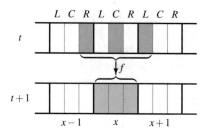

Fig. 10.16 Cellular space of a one-dimensional three-neighbor PCA $P_{1d\text{-}3}$, and its local function

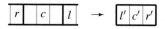

Fig. 10.17 A pictorial representation of a local rule $f(l,c,r) = (l',c',r')$ of a one-dimensional three-neighbor PCA $P_{1d\text{-}3}$

Example 10.5. Consider a simple example of a one-dimensional three-neighbor PCA $P_{1d\text{-}p}$, in which particles move and bounce off a wall.

$$P_{1d\text{-}p} = ((L,C,R),(1,0,-1),f_{1d\text{-}p},(\#,\#,\#))$$

Here, $L = R = \{\#, \bullet\}$, $C = \{\#, \blacksquare\}$, and $f_{1d\text{-}p} : (L \times C \times R) \to (L \times C \times R)$ is given in Fig. 10.18. Each of three parts has two states, and thus the cell has eight states in total. Figure 10.19 shows an example of an evolution process in $P_{1d\text{-}p}$. We can see that the state $\bullet$ in L or R acts as a moving particle, while the state $\blacksquare$ in C acts as a wall. Thus, particles move back and forth between walls. It is easy to verify $f_{1d\text{-}p}$ is injective. Hence, $P_{1d\text{-}p}$ is an RPCA, and by Lemma 10.2 it is an eight-state (standard) RCA.   □

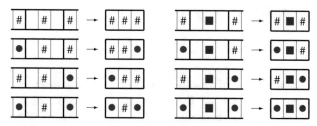

Fig. 10.18 Local rules of one-dimensional three-neighbor RPCA $P_{1d\text{-}p}$. The local function $f_{1d\text{-}p}$ of $P_{1d\text{-}p}$ is defined by these eight rules

The eight-state RPCA $P_{1d\text{-}p}$ is slightly better than the trivial RCA A_{shift} shown in Fig. 10.10. However, it is still not so interesting, since particles simply go back and forth in this cellular space. To get more interesting RPCAs, we have to increase the

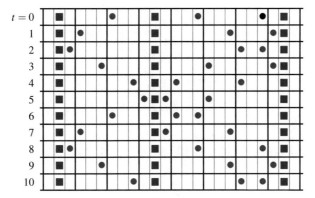

Fig. 10.19 Evolution process of one-dimensional three-neighbor RPCA P_{1d-p}. Here, the state # is represented by a blank

number of dimensions, or that of states slightly. In Chaps. 11–13 we shall design various kinds of computationally universal RCAs using the framework of PCAs. Most of these RCAs have relatively small number of states (e.g., a one-dimensional 24-state RCA, a two-dimensional eight-state RCA, and so on), and have simple local functions.

We also use one-dimensional two-neighbor (radius $1/2$) PCA P_{1d-2}.

$$P_{1d-2} = (\mathbb{Z}, (C, R), (0, -1), f)$$

Each cell has center and right parts, and their state sets are C and R, respectively. The next state of a cell is determined by the present states of the center part of this cell, and the right part of the left-neighboring cell. Figures 10.20 and 10.21 show the cellular space, and a local rule. It is a kind of a one-way CA, since information can be transferred only rightward in this cellular space. Note that P_{1d-2} is considered as a special case of P_{1d-3} where the set L of the left part states is a singleton.

We could have defined a two-neighbor PCA by $P'_{1d-2} = (\mathbb{Z}, (L, R), (1, -1), f')$, which has the left and right parts, rather than P_{1d-2}, which has the center and right parts. In P'_{1d-2}, the state of the cell at the position $x \in \mathbb{Z}$ at time t is determined by the states of the two cells at the positions $x - 1$ and $x + 1$ at time $t - 1$. Hence, the states of the cells at x and t such that $x + t$ is even (odd, respectively) do not affect the states of the cells at x' and t' such that $x' + t'$ is odd (even). Therefore, there exist two independent subsystems (but they have the same local function f') in P'_{1d-2}, each of which is equivalent to the one formulated by P_{1d-2}. Because of this, and the fact it formalizes a *one-way PCA*, we mainly use P_{1d-2} as a two-neighbor PCA.

We can observe a similarity between the a one-dimensional block CA of block size 2 (Fig. 10.13), and P_{1d-2} (Fig. 10.20). In fact, they can simulate each other in a rather straightforward manner. Again, in this case, the PCA P_{1d-2} has uniformity in its neighborhood, and thus is in the framework of standard CAs.

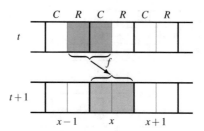

Fig. 10.20 Cellular space of a one-dimensional two-neighbor PCA $P_{\text{1d-2}}$, and its local function

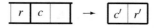

Fig. 10.21 A pictorial representation of a local rule $f(c,r) = (c',r')$ of a one-dimensional two-neighbor PCA $P_{\text{1d-2}}$

A two-dimensional five-neighbor PCA with von Neumann-like neighborhood is as follows.

$$P_{\text{2d-5}} = (\mathbb{Z}^2, (C,U,R,D,L), ((0,0),(0,-1),(-1,0),(0,1),(1,0)), f)$$

Each cell is divided into five parts. The next state of each cell is determined by the present states of the center part of the cell, the upper part of the downward neighbor, the right part of the left neighbor, the downward part of the upper neighbor, and the left part of the right neighbor. Figures 10.22 and 10.23 show the cellular space and a local rule of $P_{\text{2d-5}}$.

In addition to a five-neighbor PCA, we also use a four-neighbor PCA.

$$P_{\text{2d-4}} = (\mathbb{Z}^2, (U,R,D,L), ((0,-1),(-1,0),(0,1),(1,0)), f)$$

Figures 10.24 and 10.25 show the cellular space and a local rule of $P_{\text{2d-4}}$. It is a special case of $P_{\text{2d-5}}$ where the state set C is a singleton.

Note that, $P_{\text{2d-4}}$ has the same problem as $P'_{\text{1d-2}}$. The states of the cells at the position (x,y) and time t such that $x+y+t$ is even (odd, respectively) do not affect the states of the cells at (x',y') and t' such that $x'+y'+t'$ is odd (even). Therefore, there exist two independent subsystems in $P_{\text{2d-4}}$ that do not interact each other. However, in this case, we use $P_{\text{2d-4}}$, because it has spatial symmetry, and thus it is easier to design it.

We give a remark on the method of defining a local function of an RPCA. To obtain an RPCA $P = (\mathbb{Z}^k, (Q_1,\ldots,Q_m), (n_1,\ldots,n_m), f)$ that simulates a computing system S, we have to give an injection $f : Q \to Q$ properly, where $Q = (Q_1 \times \cdots \times Q_m)$. But, in the following, we shall define the values of f only on some subset of Q that are needed to simulate S. This is because we can always find an injection defined totally on the set Q from a partially defined injection by Lemma 6.1.

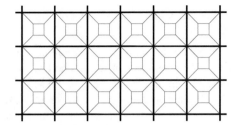

Fig. 10.22 Cellular space of a two-dimensional five-neighbor PCA P_{2d-5}, where each cell is divided into five parts

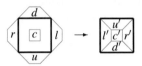

Fig. 10.23 A pictorial representation of a local rule $f(c,u,r,d,l) = (c',u',r',d',l')$ of a two-dimensional five-neighbor PCA P_{2d-5}

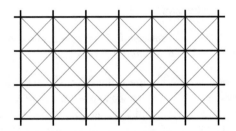

Fig. 10.24 Cellular space of a two-dimensional four-neighbor PCA P_{2d-4}

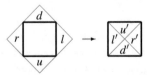

Fig. 10.25 A pictorial representation of a local rule $f(u,r,d,l) = (u',r',d',l')$ of a two-dimensional four-neighbor PCA P_{2d-4}

10.5 Simulating Irreversible CAs by Reversible CAs

In this section, we investigate the problem of simulating irreversible CAs by reversible ones. In Sect. 10.5.1, we explain the method of Toffoli [44] where a k-dimensional irreversible CA is simulated by a $(k+1)$-dimensional RCA by allowing the RCA to generate garbage signals. In Sect. 10.5.2, we show that a one-dimensional three-neighbor irreversible CA with finite configurations can be simulated by a one-dimensional three-neighbor RPCA (thus, by a three-neighbor RCA) again by allowing to produce garbage information. It is also shown that a three-neighbor RPCA can be further simulated by a one-dimensional two-neighbor RPCA. Therefore, a one-dimensional irreversible CA with an arbitrary neighborhood can be simulated by a one-dimensional two-neighbor RCA.

10.5.1 Simulating k-dimensional CA by $(k+1)$-dimensional RPCA

Toffoli [44] first showed that every irreversible CA can be simulated by an RCA by increasing the dimension by one.

Theorem 10.7. *[44] For any k-dimensional (irreversible) CA A, we can construct a $(k+1)$-dimensional RCA A' that simulates A in real time.*

Although the proof in [44] is complex, the RCA A' can be obtained rather easily if we use the framework of PCA. Here we explain it informally. Consider the case of $k = 1$. Let A be a one-dimensional three-neighbor irreversible CA that evolves as in Fig. 10.26. Then, we can construct a two-dimensional reversible PCA A' that simulates A as shown in Fig. 10.27. The configuration of A is kept in some row of A'. A state of a cell of A is stored in the left, center, and right parts of a cell in A' in triplicate. By this, each cell of A' can compute the next state of the corresponding cell of A correctly. At the same time, the previous states of the cell and the left and right neighbor cells (which were used to compute the next state) are put downward as a "garbage" signal to keep A' reversible. In other words, the additional dimension is used to record all the past history of the evolution of A. In this way, A' can simulate A reversibly. The above method is easily generalized to the case $k > 1$.

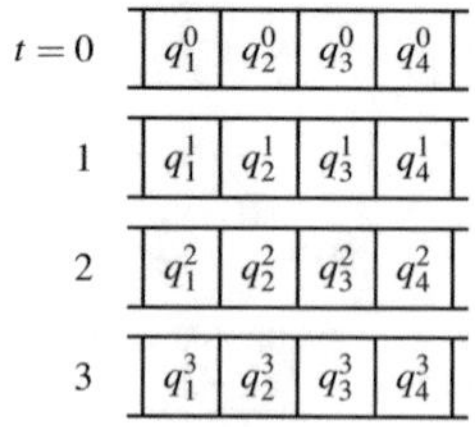

$$t = 0 \quad \boxed{q_1^0 \ \big| \ q_2^0 \ \big| \ q_3^0 \ \big| \ q_4^0}$$

$$1 \quad \boxed{q_1^1 \ \big| \ q_2^1 \ \big| \ q_3^1 \ \big| \ q_4^1}$$

$$2 \quad \boxed{q_1^2 \ \big| \ q_2^2 \ \big| \ q_3^2 \ \big| \ q_4^2}$$

$$3 \quad \boxed{q_1^3 \ \big| \ q_2^3 \ \big| \ q_3^3 \ \big| \ q_4^3}$$

Fig. 10.26 An example of an evolution process in an irreversible one-dimensional CA A

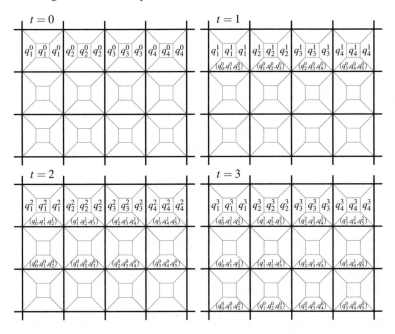

Fig. 10.27 Simulating the irreversible CA A in Fig, 10.26 by a two-dimensional RPCA A'

10.5.2 Simulating one-dimensional CA by one-dimensional RPCA

For one-dimensional CAs with finite configurations, reversible simulation is possible without increasing the dimension.

Theorem 10.8. *[30] For any one-dimensional three-neighbor (irreversible) CA A with finite configurations, we can construct a one-dimensional three-neighbor reversible CA A' with finite configurations that simulates A (but not in real time).*

Proof. Let $A = (\mathbb{Z}, Q, (-1,0,1), f, \#)$ be a given CA. Here, we assume that no non-quiescent state in Q becomes a quiescent state, i.e., $\forall q \in Q - \{\#\}$, $\forall p, r \in Q$ $(f(p,q,r) \neq \#)$ (if otherwise, such a CA can be obtained by adding a new state, say $\#'$, that plays a role of $\#$ to Q). Furthermore, we consider only configurations such that non-quiescent cells are connected.

We now construct an RPCA $A' = (\mathbb{Z}, (L, C, R), (1, 0, -1), f', (\#, \#, \#))$ that simulates A. First, L, C, and R are defined as follows, where $\tilde{Q} = \{\tilde{q} \mid q \in Q - \{\#\}\}$, $\tilde{Q}_* = \{\tilde{q}_* \mid q \in Q - \{\#\}\}$, and $* \notin Q$.

$$L = Q \cup Q^2 \cup \{\hat{\#}, *\}$$
$$C = Q$$
$$R = Q^2 \cup \tilde{Q} \cup \tilde{Q}_* \cup \{\#, *\}$$

The local function f' is defined as follows.

$$
\begin{array}{lll}
(1)\ f'(\#,p,\#) & = (\#,p,\#) & \text{if } p \in Q \\
(2)\ f'(*,p,\#) & = (p,\#,(p,\#)) & \text{if } p \in Q - \{\#\} \\
(3)\ f'(q,p,\#) & = (p,\#,(p,q)) & \text{if } p,q \in Q - \{\#\} \\
(4)\ f'(q,\#,\#) & = (\hat{\#},\#,(\#,q)) & \text{if } q \in Q - \{\#\} \ \wedge\ f(\#,\#,q) \neq \# \\
(5)\ f'(q,\#,\#) & = (\#,\#,(\#,q)) & \text{if } q \in Q - \{\#\} \ \wedge\ f(\#,\#,q) = \# \\
(6)\ f'(\hat{\#},\#,\#) & = (\#,\#,(\#,\#)) & \\
(7)\ f'((q,r),\#,(p,q)) & = ((p,q),s,\tilde{r}) & \text{if } p,q \in Q \ \wedge\ r \in Q - \{\#\} \ \wedge\ f(p,q,r) = s \\
(8)\ f'((q,\#),\#,(p,q)) & = ((p,q),s,\#) & \text{if } p \in Q \ \wedge\ q \in Q - \{\#\} \ \wedge\ f(p,q,\#) = s \\
(9)\ f'(\#,\#,(p,\#)) & = ((p,\#),s,\#) & \text{if } p \in Q - \{\#\} \ \wedge\ f(p,\#,\#) = s \\
(10)\ f'(\#,q,\tilde{r}) & = (\#,q,\tilde{r}) & \text{if } r \in Q - \{\#\} \ \wedge\ q \in Q. \\
(11)\ f'((\#,\#),\#,\#) & = (\#,\#,*) & \\
(12)\ f'((\#,r),\#,\#) & = (\#,\#,\tilde{r}_*) & \text{if } r \in Q - \{\#\} \\
(13)\ f'(\#,q,*) & = (\#,q,*) & \text{if } q \in Q - \{\#\} \\
(14)\ f'(\#,q,\tilde{r}_*) & = (\#,q,\tilde{r}_*) & \text{if } r,q \in Q - \{\#\} \\
(15)\ f'(\#,\#,*) & = (*,\#,\#) & \\
(16)\ f'(\#,\#,\tilde{r}_*) & = (*,\#,\tilde{r}) & \text{if } r \in Q - \{\#\} \\
\end{array}
$$

Let $\alpha \in \mathrm{Conf}(A)$ be an initial configuration of A. Then, A' starts from the following configuration $\alpha' \in \mathrm{Conf}(A')$.

$$
\forall i \in \mathbb{Z}: \quad \alpha'(i) = \begin{cases} (\#,\alpha(i),\#) & \text{if } \alpha(i) \neq \# \\ (*,\#,\#) & \text{if } \alpha(i) = \# \text{ and } \alpha(i-1) \neq \# \\ (\#,\#,\#) & \text{if } \alpha(i) = \# \text{ and } \alpha(i-1) = \# \end{cases}
$$

We now explain how the above rules work. In A', the state of A's cell is stored in the center part of the corresponding cell, and it is updated from right to left sequentially. This updating process is initiated by the signal "$*$" at the right end.

The rule (1) is for keeping the center part state when no other signal exists. If a non-quiescent cell of A' receives "$*$" from the right, it sends its center part state p to to the left and $(p,\#)$ to the right by the rule (2). Similarly, if a non-quiescent cell receives a state signal q from the right, it sends its center part state p to to the left and (p,q) to the right (the rule (3)). This process propagates leftward sequentially, and the rule (4) or (5) is applied at the left end. Which rule (4) or (5) is used depends on whether the *left-growing condition* $f(\#,\#,q) \neq \#$ holds or not, where q is the leftmost non-quiescent state. When the rule (4) is used, then (6) is further applied.

If a cell receives a signal (p,q) from the left and (q,r) from the right, where p,q, and r are the states of left, center, and right cells of A at this position, it becomes a new state s by the local function f, and sends (p,q) to the left and $\tilde{r}$ to the right by the rule (7). The rules (8) and (9) are for updating the states at the right end. Signals of the form $\tilde{r}$ are regarded as garbage signals generated by irreversible transitions of A, and travels towards the rightward infinite portion of the cellular space (rule (10)).

If all the cells are updated, the signal "$*$" or $\tilde{r}_*$ appears at the left end by the rule (11) or (12) (depending on whether the left-growing condition holds or not). This signal travels rightward through the non-quiescent cells by the rule (13) or (14), and then restarts the updating process by the rule (15) or (16).

An example is shown in Figs. 10.28 and 10.29. If A evolves as shown in Fig. 10.28, then A' simulates A as in Fig.10.29.

$t=0$	#	#	a	b	#	#	#
1	#	#	c	d	e	#	#
2	#	f	g	h	i	#	#

Fig. 10.28 An example of an evolution process of an irreversible CA A

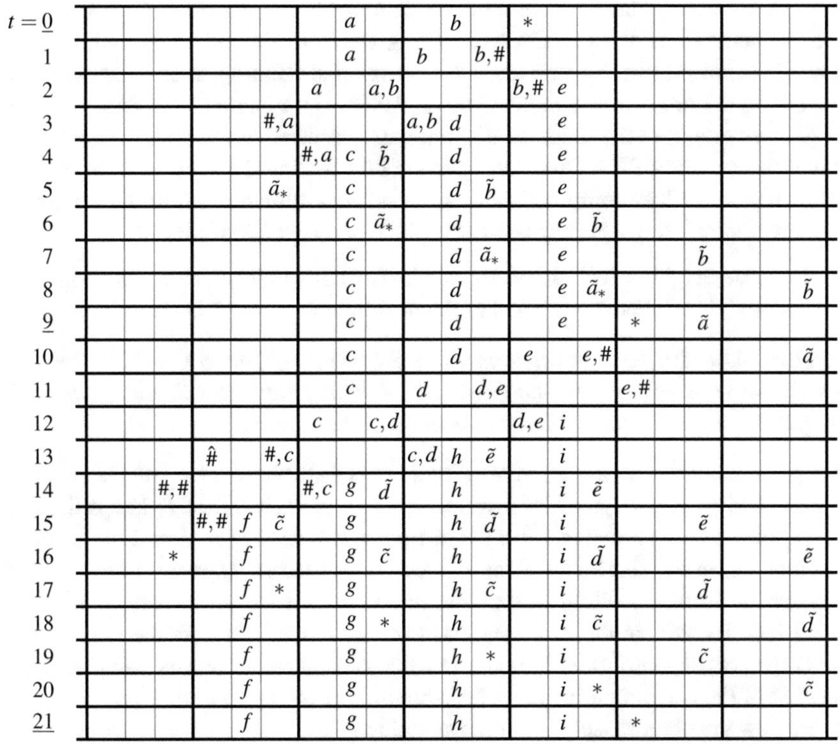

t													
0					a		b	$*$					
1					a	b	$b,\#$						
2				a	a,b		$b,\#$	e					
3			$\#,a$		a,b	d		e					
4			$\#,a$	c	$\tilde b$	d		e					
5			$\tilde a_*$	c		d	$\tilde b$	e					
6				c	$\tilde a_*$	d		e	$\tilde b$				
7				c		d	$\tilde a_*$	e			$\tilde b$		
8				c		d		e	$\tilde a_*$			$\tilde b$	
9				c		d		e		$*$	$\tilde a$		
10				c		d	e	$e,\#$			$\tilde a$		
11				c	d	d,e		$e,\#$					
12			c	c,d		d,e	i						
13		$\hat\#$	$\#,c$		c,d	h	$\tilde e$	i					
14	$\#,\#$		$\#,c$	g	$\tilde d$	h		i	$\tilde e$				
15		$\#,\#$	f	$\tilde c$	g		h	$\tilde d$	i			$\tilde e$	
16		$*$	f		g	$\tilde c$	h		i	$\tilde d$			$\tilde e$
17			f	$*$	g		h	$\tilde c$	i		$\tilde d$		
18			f		g	$*$	h		i	$\tilde c$		$\tilde d$	
19			f		g		h	$*$	i		$\tilde c$		
20			f		g		h		i	$*$		$\tilde c$	
21			f		g		h		i		$*$		

Fig. 10.29 Simulating the irreversible CA A in Fig. 10.28 by a one-dimensional RPCA A'. Configurations of A' at $t = 0,9$ and 21 correspond to those of A at $t = 0,1$ and 2. Here, the state # is indicated by a blank

The number of steps $T(n)$ to simulate one step of A by A' is calculated as follows, where n is the number of non-quiescent cells of A before transition.

$$T(n) = \begin{cases} 2n+7 \text{ if non-quiescent portion grows to the both direction} \\ 2n+6 \text{ if non-quiescent portion grows only to the left} \\ 2n+5 \text{ if non-quiescent portion grows only to the right} \\ 2n+4 \text{ if non-quiescent portion does not grow} \end{cases}$$

We can verify that every pair of distinct rules in (1) – (16) has different right-hand sides. For example, $(p, \#, (p, \#))$ and $(p, \#, (p, q))$, which are right-hand sides of the rules (2) and (3), cannot be the same, since $q \in Q - \{\#\}$. Other cases are also similarly verified. Note that, in the above construction, the local function f' is defined only on some subset of $L \times C \times R$ that are needed for simulating A. But, by Lemma 6.1, we can extend the domain of it to $L \times C \times R$, and thus obtain an injection $f' : L \times C \times R \to L \times C \times R$. Therefore, A' is an RPCA, and by Lemma 10.2 it is an RCA. If A has m states, then A' has $m^2(m^2 + m + 2)(m + 2)$ states.   □

Here, we use a standard notion of simulation, where each step of a CA is simulated by some steps of an RPCA (it will be given in Definition 11.2). But, Durand-Lose [11] showed that, by extending the notion of simulation, even a CA with infinite configurations can be simulated by an RPCA of the same dimension.

A shortcoming of the methods of simulating irreversible CAs by reversible ones is that the resulting RCAs generate garbage information. In Sect. 11.2, in order to obtain a garbage-less computationally universal one-dimensional RCA, we use the method of simulating a garbage-less reversible one-tape TM by RPCA.

The three-neighbor RPCA constructed in Theorem 10.8 can be further converted into two-neighbor RPCA as shown in the next lemma.

Lemma 10.4. *[29] For any one-dimensional three-neighbor RPCA P, we can construct a one-dimensional two-neighbor RPCA P' that simulates P. Here, finite configurations of P are encoded into finite configurations of P'.*

Proof. The intuitive idea to simulate P by P' is as follows. One step of P's transition is simulated by two steps of P'. Assume, at time $2t$, each cell of P' keeps the state (l, c, r) of the corresponding cell of P of time t, where (l, c) is stored in the center part and r is in the right part of the P''s cell (Fig. 10.30). Then, at time $2t + 1$, P' changes the storing position of the information in an appropriate way as shown in Fig. 10.30. By this, in the next step, each cell of P' can calculate the next state of the corresponding cell of P. When one cycle of this simulation is completed, the position of the corresponding cell of P' shifts rightward by one cell.

We now give P' precisely. Let P be as follows.

$$P = (\mathbb{Z}, (L, C, R), (1, 0, -1), f, (\#_L, \#_C, \#_R))$$

Note that, $\#_L, \#_C$, and $\#_R$ could be the same state, say $\#$. But here, we distinguish them each other to indicate clearly how they are managed in P'. The two-neighbor RPCA P' that simulates P is defined as below.

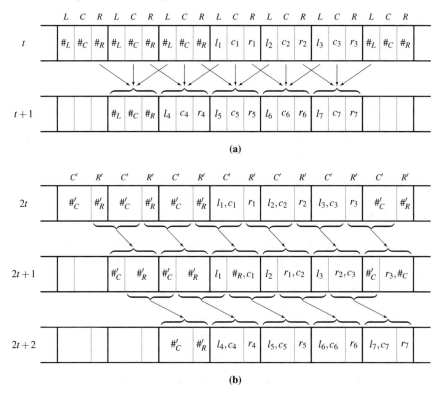

Fig. 10.30 (a) A three-neighbor RPCA P, and (b) a two-neighbor RPCA P' that simulates P. The RPCA P' needs two steps to simulate one step of P

$$P' = (\mathbb{Z}, (C', R'), (0, -1), f', (\#'_C, \#'_R))$$
$$C' = (L \times C - \{(\#_L, \#_C)\}) \cup (L - \{\#_L\}) \cup \{\#'_C\}$$
$$R' = (R - \{\#_R\}) \cup (R \times C - \{(\#_R, \#_C)\}) \cup \{\#'_R\}$$

Here, the quiescent state $\#'_C$ of the center part of P' plays a role of $(\#_L, \#_C)$ at even time step, and of $\#_L$ at odd time step. Similarly, $\#'_R$ plays a role of $\#_R$ at even time step, and of $(\#_R, \#_C)$ at odd time step. The local function f' is as follows.

(1) For each $l \in (L - \{\#_L\})$, $c \in (C - \{\#_C\})$, and $r \in (R - \{\#_R\})$, define f' as follows.

(1a) $f'((l,c),r) = (l,(r,c))$

(1b) $f'((l,\#_C),r) = (l,(r,\#_C))$

(1c) $f'((\#_L,c),r) = (\#'_C,(r,c))$

(1d) $f'(\#'_C,r) = (\#'_C,(r,\#_C))$

(1e) $f'((l,c),\#'_R) = (l,(\#_R,c))$

(1f) $f'((l,\#_C),\#'_R) = (l,\#'_R)$

(1g) $f'((\#_L,c),\#'_R) = (\#'_C,(\#_R,c))$

(1h) $f'(\#'_C,\#'_R) = (\#'_C,\#'_R)$

(2) For each $l \in (L - \{\#_L\})$, $(r,c) \in (R \times C - \{(\#_R, \#_C)\})$, $(\hat{l}, \hat{c}) \in (L \times C - \{(\#_L, \#_C)\})$, and $\hat{r} \in (R - \{\#_R\})$, define f' as follows.

(2a) $f'(l,(r,c)) = ((\hat{l}, \hat{c}), \hat{r})$ if $f(l,c,r) = (\hat{l}, \hat{c}, \hat{r})$

(2b) $f'(l,(r,c)) = ((\hat{l}, \hat{c}), \#_R')$ if $f(l,c,r) = (\hat{l}, \hat{c}, \#_R)$

(2c) $f'(l,(r,c)) = (\#_C', \hat{r})$ if $f(l,c,r) = (\#_L, \#_C, \hat{r})$

(2d) $f'(\#_C',(r,c)) = ((\hat{l}, \hat{c}), \hat{r})$ if $f(\#_L,c,r) = (\hat{l}, \hat{c}, \hat{r})$

(2e) $f'(\#_C',(r,c)) = ((\hat{l}, \hat{c}), \#_R')$ if $f(\#_L,c,r) = (\hat{l}, \hat{c}, \#_R)$

(2f) $f'(\#_C',(r,c)) = (\#_C', \hat{r})$ if $f(\#_L,c,r) = (\#_L, \#_C, \hat{r})$

(2g) $f'(l, \#_R') = ((\hat{l}, \hat{c}), \hat{r})$ if $f(l, \#, \#_R) = (\hat{l}, \hat{c}, \hat{r})$

(2h) $f'(l, \#_R') = ((\hat{l}, \hat{c}), \#_R')$ if $f(l, \#_C, \#_R) = (\hat{l}, \hat{c}, \#_R)$

(2i) $f'(l, \#_R') = (\#_C', \hat{r})$ if $f(l, \#_C, \#_R) = (\#_L, \#_C, \hat{r})$

At even time steps the rules (1a) – (1h) are used, while at odd time steps (1h) and (2a) – (2i) are used.

Let $\alpha \in \mathrm{Conf}(P)$ be an initial configuration of P. Then set the initial configuration of P' to α', which is defined as follows.

$$\forall i \in \mathbb{Z}, \text{ if } \alpha(i) = (l,c,r) \text{ then}$$

$$\alpha'(i) = \begin{cases} ((l,c),r) & \text{if } (l,c) \neq (\#_L, \#_C) \text{ and } r \neq \#_R \\ (\#_C', r) & \text{if } (l,c) = (\#_L, \#_C) \text{ and } r \neq \#_R \\ ((l,c), \#_R') & \text{if } (l,c) \neq (\#_L, \#_C) \text{ and } r = \#_R \\ (\#_C', \#_R') & \text{if } (l,c) = (\#_L, \#_C) \text{ and } r = \#_R \end{cases}$$

It is easy to verify that P' correctly simulates P step by step. It is also easy to see that finite configurations of P are simulated by finite configurations of P'.

We can verify that any pair of distinct rules of P' has different right-hand sides provided that P is reversible. First, apparently, the right-hand side of each rule in (1a) – (1h) is different from those of others. Similarly, for example, the right-hand side of a rule in (2a) has different form from others except (2d) and (2g). Also, any two rules in (2a), (2d) or (2g) must have different right-hand sides, since f is injective. It is also the case for the rules in (2b), (2e) or (2h), and for the rules in (2c), (2f) or (2i). Thus, P' is an RPCA.   □

It is easy to simulate a one-dimensional CA A of radius r by a one-dimensional (irreversible) CA A' of radius 1. It is done by keeping the states of r cells of A by one cell of A'. By Theorem 10.8, Lemmas 10.2 and 10.4, and by the above observation, we have the following corollary.

Corollary 10.2. *For any one-dimensional CA A with an arbitrary neighborhood and with finite configurations, we can construct a one-dimensional two-neighbor reversible CA A' with finite configurations that simulates A.*

10.6 Making RPCAs from Reversible Logic Elements

There is another advantage of using the framework of PCAs. That is any RPCA can be realized as a garbage-less reversible logic circuit composed of reversible logic gates or reversible logic elements with memory (RLEMs). This is because an RPCA can be regarded as a kind of a reversible sequential machine (RSM). In the one-dimensional three-neighbor case (Fig. 10.17), the states $l \in L$ and $r \in R$ are interpreted as inputs to the machine. Depending on the inputs and the internal state $c \in C$, the next internal state c', and the outputs $l' \in L$ and $r' \in R$ are determined. Note that, it has two sets of input symbols, and two sets of output symbols. In the case of two-dimensional five-neighbor PCA, it has four sets of input symbols and four sets of output symbols.

In [28] it is shown that any one-dimensional three-neighbor RPCA $P_{1d-3} = (\mathbb{Z}, (L, C, R), (1, 0, -1), f)$ can be realized by a garbage-less circuit composed of Fredkin gates and delay elements. Let $C = \{c_1, \ldots, c_k\}$, $L = \{l_1, \ldots, l_m\}$, and $R = \{r_1, \ldots, r_n\}$. Define a bijection $\hat{f} : \{1, \ldots, kmn\} \to \{1, \ldots, kmn\}$ as follows.

$$\forall c_h, c_{h'} \in C, \ \forall l_i, l_{i'} \in L, \ \forall r_j, r_{j'} \in R :$$
$$\hat{f}((h-1)mn + (i-1)n + j) = (h'-1)m'n' + (i'-1)n' + j'$$
$$\Leftrightarrow f(l_i, c_h, r_j) = (l_{i'}, c_{h'}, r_{j'})$$

Then, using the decoder module, the inverse decoder module, the permutation module, and the delay module, which were given in Sect. 4.2.3, a circuit that simulates a cell of P_{1d-3} is constructed as shown in Fig. 10.31. Putting infinitely many copies of this circuit in a line, and appropriately connecting the input and the output lines of each circuit with those of its neighboring circuits, we obtain a circuit that realizes the whole system P_{1d-3}. The delay time between the input and output ports in this circuit is $4kmn + 4km + 1$. In a similar way as above, we can construct a higher-dimensional RPCA whose neighborhood size is more than three by adding decoder modules, and inverse decoder modules.

The circuit given in Fig. 10.31 is further implemented in a billiard ball model (BBM), since Fredkin gate is realized in BBM [12] (see also Sect. 4.1.5). Thus, the framework of RPCA connects the way from a microscopic reversibility (i.e., physical reversibility) to a macroscopic reversibility (i.e., global reversibility of CAs).

It is also possible to construct an RPCA by rotary element (RE). To do so, we have to implement DECODER(m, n) and DECODER$^{-1}(m, n)$ by REs and delay elements. Figure 10.32 shows a circuit that simulates DECODER$(3, 3)$ and DECODER$^{-1}(3, 3)$. It consists of three RE-columns (see Sect. 2.3), which are initially set to the unmarked states, i.e., the bottom REs are in the state V. Since the cells of the RPCA operate synchronously, we design this module so that their delay between input and output is constant. Here, we assume each RE has a unit-time delay, and additional delay elements are inserted to adjust the total delay.

When we use this circuit as DECODER$(3, 3)$, we give two particles to the input ports a_i and b_j $(i, j \in \{1, 2, 3\})$ simultaneously. First, the particle from b_j makes

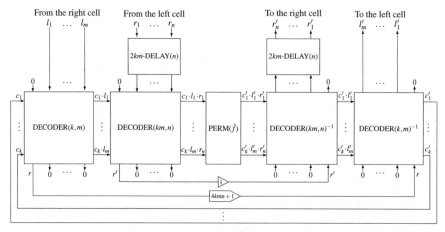

Fig. 10.31 A reversible logic circuit composed of Fredkin gates and delay elements that simulates one cell of a one-dimensional three-neighbor RPCA [28]. See also Sect. 4.2.3

the j-th column in the marked state. Note that the particle will later go out from r. Then, the particle from a_i finds the crossing point of the j-th column and the row corresponding to a_i, and goes out from the port $a_i b_j$. By this, the function of DECODER$(3,3)$ is simulated correctly. In this circuit, the total delay between input and output is 32.

When we use it as DECODER$^{-1}(3,3)$, we give two particles to the input ports $\hat{a}_i \hat{b}_j$ $(i,j \in \{1,2,3\})$ and $\hat{r}$ simultaneously. First, the particle from $\hat{a}_i \hat{b}_j$ makes the j-th column in the marked state, and it goes out from $\hat{a}_i$. Then, the particle from $\hat{r}$ finds the j-th column, and goes out from $\hat{b}_j$. Thus, the circuit correctly simulates DECODER$^{-1}(3,3)$. The delay between input and output is again 32.

Generalizing the above method, we obtain a circuit module that can simulate DECODER(m,n) and DECODER$^{-1}(m,n)$ for any m and n. By such modules, we can realize a cell of the RPCA out of REs and delay elements as in Fig. 10.31. This circuit is further embedded in BBM. But, if we employ the method shown in Fig. 2.8 to implement an RE in BBM, then the delay time of RE between input and output in the parallel case (Fig. 2.9) is different from that in the orthogonal case (Fig. 2.10). Thus, one may think it difficult to adjust the total delay time of the circuit. However, we can count the total number of transitions of the parallel case and that of the orthogonal case for each signal path in Fig. 10.32. For example, a particle on the path between a_1 and $a_1 b_2$ makes 9 transitions of the parallel case, and 5 transitions of the orthogonal case, provided that another particle is given to b_2. Hence, adjustment of the total delay is possible by inserting delay elements appropriately (its details are omitted here).

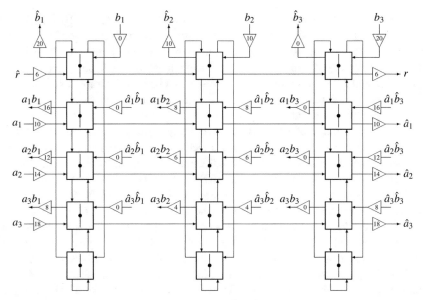

Fig. 10.32 A circuit composed of REs and delay elements that simulates DECODER$(3,3)$ and DECODER$^{-1}(3,3)$

10.7 Concluding Remarks

A reversible cellular automaton (RCA) is a tool for studying spatiotemporal phenomena in a reversible space. In particular, it provides a method for investigating how computation and information processing can be performed in a reversible environment. In this chapter, we first gave a general framework of standard (irreversible) CAs, and then defined RCAs as CAs with injective global functions (Definition 10.4). It is generally difficult to compose RCAs in the standard framework of CAs. For making it easy to design RCAs, three variants of CAs were explained. Among them, the method of using partitioned CAs (PCAs) was given in detail, since they will be used to construct computationally universal RCAs in Chaps. 11–13.

From the fact that PCAs are a subclass of standard CAs (Lemma 10.2), and the fact that injectivity of a global function is equivalent to that of a local function (Lemma 10.3), it is sufficient to design a PCA with an injective local function if we want to obtain an RCA. Thus, the framework of PCAs greatly facilitates construction of RCAs. Note that, in PCA, reversibility is easily decidable even for the two- or higher-dimensional case. But, it does not contradict the undecidability result shown in Theorem 10.4, because PCAs are a proper subclass of standard CAs.

It is known that, in the irreversible case, there is a one-dimensional three-neighbor CA with finite configurations that simulates a one-tape Turing machine. In particular, Smith [42] gave simple computationally universal one-dimensional CAs by this method. From this fact and Theorem 10.8, we have a universal one-dimensional RCA. However, the RCA constructed in Theorem 10.8 generates garbage signals, and uses many states. In Chap. 11, the universality of RCAs will be investigated in more detail, and garbage-less simple universal one-dimensional RCAs that directly simulate reversible Turing machines will be given in Theorems 11.1 and 11.2. Furthermore, in Chaps. 12 and 13, very simple universal two-dimensional RCAs that simulate reversible logic circuits, or reversible counter machines will be constructed.

Another advantage of using PCAs is that any reversible PCA can be realized as a circuit composed of reversible logic elements (Figs. 10.31 and 10.32). Since reversible logic elements such as the Fredkin gate and the rotary element are further implemented in the billiard ball model (BBM), the whole system of the reversible PCA can be embedded in the BBM. Hence, the framework of PCAs connects the way from the microscopic reversibility to the macroscopic reversibility in RCAs.

There are several survey papers and books related to RCAs that are written from different viewpoints. Toffoli and Margolus [47], and Kari [17] give good surveys on RCAs. There are also surveys on RCAs by Morita [31, 32, 33]. The paper by Kari [18], the books by Toffoli and Margolus [46], McIntosh [25], and Wolfram [50] are references on general CAs, which also contain RCAs. The book edited by Adamatzky [1] is on the topic of "collision-based computing," which also includes papers on RCAs.

References

1. Adamatzky, A. (ed.): Collision-Based Computing. Springer (2002). doi:10.1007/978-1-4471-0129-1
2. Adamatzky, A. (ed.): Game of Life Cellular Automata. Springer (2010). doi:10.1007/978-1-84996-217-9
3. Amoroso, S., Cooper, G.: The Garden of Eden theorem for finite configurations. Proc. Amer. Math. Soc. **26**, 158–164 (1970). doi:10.1090/S0002-9939-1970-0276007-5
4. Amoroso, S., Patt, Y.N.: Decision procedures for surjectivity and injectivity of parallel maps for tessellation structures. J. Comput. Syst. Sci. **6**, 448–464 (1972). doi:10.1016/S0022-0000(72)80013-8
5. Berlekamp, E., Conway, J., Guy, R.: Winning Ways for Your Mathematical Plays, Vol. 2. Academic Press, New York (1982)
6. Boykett, T.: Efficient exhaustive listings of reversible one dimensional cellular automata. Theoret. Comput. Sci. **325**, 215–247 (2004). doi:10.1016/j.tcs.2004.06.007
7. Carroll, L.: The Annotated Alice: Alice's Adventures in Wonderland and Through the Looking Glass (with an introduction and notes by Martin Gardner). Bramhall House (1960)
8. Cook, M.: Universality in elementary cellular automata. Complex Syst. **15**, 1–40 (2004)
9. Cook, M.: A concrete view of rule 110 computation. In: Proc. Complexity of Simple Programs 2008 (eds. T. Neary, D. Woods, T. Seda, N. Murphy), EPTCS 1, pp. 31–55 (2009). doi:10.4204/EPTCS.1.4
10. Czeizler, E., Kari, J.: A tight linear bound for the synchronization delay of bijective automata. Theoret. Comput. Sci. **380**, 23–36 (2007). doi:10.1016/j.tcs.2007.02.052
11. Durand-Lose, J.O.: Reversible space-time simulation of cellular automata. Theoret. Comput. Sci. **246**, 117–129 (2000). doi:10.1016/S0304-3975(99)00075-4
12. Fredkin, E., Toffoli, T.: Conservative logic. Int. J. Theoret. Phys. **21**, 219–253 (1982). doi:10.1007/BF01857727

13. Gardner, M.: Mathematical games: The fantastic combinations of John Conway's new solitaire game "Life". Sci. Am. **223 (4)**, 120–123 (1970). doi:10.1038/scientificamerican1070-120
14. Gardner, M.: Mathematical games: On cellular automata, self-reproduction, the Garden of Eden and the game "Life". Sci. Am. **224 (2)**, 112–117 (1971). doi:10.1038/scientificamerican0271-112
15. Hedlund, G.A.: Endomorphisms and automorphisms of the shift dynamical system. Math. Syst. Theory **3**, 320–375 (1969). doi:10.1007/BF01691062
16. Kari, J.: Reversibility and surjectivity problems of cellular automata. J. Comput. Syst. Sci. **48**, 149–182 (1994). doi:10.1016/S0022-0000(05)80025-X
17. Kari, J.: Reversible cellular automata. In: Proc. DLT 2005 (eds. C. de Felice, A. Restivo), LNCS 3572, pp. 57–68 (2005). doi:10.1007/11505877_5
18. Kari, J.: Theory of cellular automata: a survey. Theoret. Comput. Sci. **334**, 3–33 (2005). doi:10.1016/j.tcs.2004.11.021
19. Margenstern, M.: Cellular automata in hyperbolic spaces. In: Encyclopedia of Complexity and Systems Science (eds. R.A. Meyers, et al.), pp. 791–800. Springer (2009). doi:10.1007/978-0-387-30440-3_53
20. Margolus, N.: Physics-like model of computation. Physica D **10**, 81–95 (1984). doi:10.1016/0167-2789(84)90252-5
21. Margolus, N.: Physics and computation. Ph.D. thesis, Massachusetts Institute of Technology (1987)
22. Martinez, G.J., McIntosh, H.V., Mora, J.C.S.T.: Gliders in rule 110. Int. J. Unconventional Comput. **2**, 1–49 (2005)
23. Maruoka, A., Kimura, M.: Condition for injectivity of global maps for tessellation automata. Information and Control **32**, 158–162 (1976). doi:10.1016/S0019-9958(76)90195-9
24. Maruoka, A., Kimura, M.: Injectivity and surjectivity of parallel maps for cellular automata. J. Comput. Syst. Sci. **18**, 47–64 (1979). doi:10.1016/0022-0000(79)90051-5
25. McIntosh, H.V.: One Dimensional Cellular Automata. Luniver Press (2009)
26. Moore, E.F.: Machine models of self-reproduction. Proc. Symposia in Applied Mathematics, Am. Math. Soc. **14**, 17–33 (1962). doi:10.1090/psapm/014/9961
27. Mora, J.C.S.T., Vergara, S.V.C., Martinez, G.J., McIntosh, H.V.: Procedures for calculating reversible one-dimensional cellular automata. Physica D **202**, 134–141 (2005). doi:10.1016/j.physd.2005.01.018
28. Morita, K.: A simple construction method of a reversible finite automaton out of Fredkin gates, and its related problem. Trans. IEICE Japan **E-73**, 978–984 (1990)
29. Morita, K.: Computation-universality of one-dimensional one-way reversible cellular automata. Inform. Process. Lett. **42**(6), 325–329 (1992). doi:10.1016/0020-0190(92)90231-J
30. Morita, K.: Reversible simulation of one-dimensional irreversible cellular automata. Theoret. Comput. Sci. **148**, 157–163 (1995). doi:10.1016/0304-3975(95)00038-X
31. Morita, K.: Reversible computing and cellular automata — A survey. Theoret. Comput. Sci. **395**, 101–131 (2008). doi:10.1016/j.tcs.2008.01.041
32. Morita, K.: Computation in reversible cellular automata. Int. J. of General Systems **41**, 569–581 (2012). doi:10.1080/03081079.2012.695897
33. Morita, K.: Reversible cellular automata. In: Handbook of Natural Computing (eds. G. Rozenberg, T. Bäck, J.N. Kok), pp. 231–257. Springer (2012). doi:10.1007/978-3-540-92910-9_7
34. Morita, K., Harao, M.: Computation universality of one-dimensional reversible (injective) cellular automata. Trans. IEICE Japan **E72**, 758–762 (1989)
35. Myhill, J.: The converse of Moore's Garden-of-Eden theorem. Proc. Am. Math. Soc. **14**, 658–686 (1963). doi:10.2307/2034301
36. Nakamura, K.: Asynchronous cellular automata and their computational ability. Trans. IECE Japan **57-D**, 573–580 (1974)
37. Neary, T., Woods, D.: P-completeness of cellular automaton rule 110. In: ICALP 2006 (eds. M. Bugliesi, et al.), LNCS 4051, pp. 132–143 (2006). doi:10.1007/11786986_13
38. von Neumann, J.: Theory of Self-reproducing Automata (ed. A.W. Burks). The University of Illinois Press, Urbana (1966)

39. Owens, N., Stepney, S.: The Game of Life rules on Penrose tilings: still life and oscilla-
    tors. In: Game of Life Cellular Automata (ed. A. Adamatzky), pp. 331–378. Springer (2010).
    doi:10.1007/978-1-84996-217-9_18
40. Poundstone, W.: The Recursive Universe — Cosmic Complexity and the Limits of Scientific
    Knowledge. William Morrow & Co. (1984)
41. Richardson, D.: Tessellations with local transformations. J. Comput. Syst. Sci. **6**, 373–388
    (1972). doi:10.1016/S0022-0000(72)80009-6
42. Smith III, A.R.: Simple computation-universal cellular spaces. J. ACM **18**, 339–353 (1971).
    doi:10.1145/321650.321652
43. Sutner, K.: De Bruijn graphs and linear cellular automata. Complex Syst. **5**, 19–30 (1991)
44. Toffoli, T.: Computation and construction universality of reversible cellular automata. J. Com-
    put. Syst. Sci. **15**, 213–231 (1977). doi:10.1016/S0022-0000(77)80007-X
45. Toffoli, T., Capobianco, S., Mentrasti, P.: How to turn a second-order cellular automaton
    into a lattice gas: a new inversion scheme. Theoret. Comput. Sci. **325**, 329–344 (2004).
    doi:10.1016/j.tcs.2004.06.012
46. Toffoli, T., Margolus, N.: Cellular Automata Machines. The MIT Press (1987)
47. Toffoli, T., Margolus, N.: Invertible cellular automata: a review. Physica D **45**, 229–253
    (1990). doi:10.1016/0167-2789(90)90185-R
48. Trevorrow, A., Rokicki, T., et al.: Golly: an open source, cross-platform application for explor-
    ing Conway's Game of Life and other cellular automata. http://golly.sourceforge.net/ (2005)
49. Ulam, S.: Random processes and transformations. In: Proc. Int. Congress of Mathematicians,
    vol. 2, pp. 264–275 (1952)
50. Wolfram, S.: A New Kind of Science. Wolfram Media Inc. (2002)

Chapter 11
One-Dimensional Universal Reversible Cellular Automata

Abstract The problem of constructing Turing universal reversible one-dimensional cellular automata (RCAs) is studied. First, methods of designing three-neighbor and two-neighbor reversible partitioned CAs (RPCAs) that directly simulate a given reversible Turing machine (RTM) are shown. Since RPCAs are a subclass of RCAs, we see the class of one-dimensional RCAs is Turing universal even in the two-neighbor case. Next, the problem of finding one-dimensional RPCAs with a small number of states that can simulate any TM is investigated. The first model is a 24-state two-neighbor RPCA with ultimately periodic configurations, and the second one is a 98-state three-neighbor RPCA with finite configurations. Both of them can simulate any cyclic tag system, a kind of a universal string rewriting system. Finally, the computing power of reversible and number-conserving CAs (RNCCAs) are studied. The notion of number-conservation is a property analogous to the conservation law in physics. It is proved that there is a 96-state one-dimensional four-neighbor RNCCA that is Turing universal. Hence, the computing power of RCAs does not decrease even if the constraint of number-conservation is further added.

Keywords reversible cellular automaton, one-dimensional cellular automaton, partitioned cellular automaton, number-conserving cellular automaton, Turing universality

11.1 Universality in One-Dimensional CAs

In Chaps. 11–13, we study how we can construct RCAs that perform computing tasks. In particular, we investigate *universal* RCAs. In CAs, there are two notions of universality. They are Turing universality, and intrinsic universality. *Turing universality* is a property of a class of CAs that the whole class of Turing machines (TMs) can be simulated by them, i.e., any TM is simulated by some CA in the class. Note that a particular CA that can simulate any TM is also called Turing universal. In the previous chapters, the term *computational universality*, a synonymous term with Turing universality, was used when showing the universality of subclasses of reversible TMs or other classes of computing systems (Definition 5.9). But, here we use the term Turing universality to distinguish it clearly from intrinsic universality. On the other hand, *intrinsic universality* is a property of a CA such that *any* CA in some class of CAs is simulated by the CA (Definition 12.5). Hence, if a CA is intrinsically universal, and the simulated class of CAs is Turing universal, then the CA is Turing universal.

In this and the following chapters, various kinds of Turing universal one- and two-dimensional RCAs will be shown (intrinsic universality of some of these RCAs will be discussed in Sect. 12.5 and Chap. 13). They can simulate universal computing systems, such as reversible TMs, reversible counter machines (RCMs), cyclic tag systems (CTSs), reversible logic circuits, or other CAs. As will be given in Definitions 11.2 and 12.2, we say a CA A simulates a computing system S if each transition step of S is simulated by some steps of A, provided that every computational configuration (or ID) of S is encoded appropriately into a configuration of A. Thus, it is slightly stronger than Definition 5.8 for TMs, since in the latter case step-by-step simulation is not necessarily supposed. Note that the transition relation $\vert_{\overline{S}}$ among IDs of S in each model has been given in the previous chapters: Definitions 5.6 and 5.7 are for one-tape TMs, Definition 9.3 is for CMs, Definitions 7.4 and 7.5 are for CTSs (there, $\Rightarrow$ is used instead of $\vert\!-$), Definition 3.5 is for reversible logic circuit composed of RLEMs (though no definition has been given for circuits composed of reversible logic gates, it is possible to define it appropriately), and Definition 10.2 is for CAs.

Since a configuration of a CA is an infinite array of cells' states, there arises a problem on defining encoding and decoding functions as in the case of Definition 5.8. Here, we restrict the configurations to the class of "ultimately periodic" configurations, each of which has a finite description, for simulating other computing systems. By this, both encoding and decoding functions can be defined as total recursive functions.

11.1.1 Ultimately periodic configurations in one-dimensional CAs

We first give definitions of a periodic configuration, and an ultimately periodic configuration for a one-dimensional CA.

Definition 11.1. Let $A = (\mathbb{Z}, Q, (n_1, \ldots, n_m), f, \#)$ be a one-dimensional CA. A configuration $\alpha : \mathbb{Z} \to Q$ is called *periodic* if there is $p \in \mathbb{Z}_+$ that satisfy the following.

$$\forall x \in \mathbb{Z} \ (\alpha(x) = \alpha(x+p))$$

A configuration $\alpha : \mathbb{Z} \to Q$ is called *ultimately periodic* if there are $x_L, x_R \in \mathbb{Z}$ such that $x_L < x_R$, and $p_L, p_R \in \mathbb{Z}_+$ that satisfy the following.

$$\forall x \in \mathbb{Z} \ ((x \le x_L \Rightarrow \alpha(x - p_L) = \alpha(x)) \wedge (x \ge x_R \Rightarrow \alpha(x) = \alpha(x + p_R)))$$

The sets of all periodic configurations, and all ultimately periodic configurations of a CA A are denoted by $\text{Conf}_p(A)$, and $\text{Conf}_{up}(A)$, respectively.

A periodic configuration is one such that a finite string $a_1 \cdots a_p$ of states repeats infinitely both to the left and to the right. Thus, the positive integer p is the *period* of it. On the other hand, an ultimately periodic configuration is one that satisfies the following: (1) There are three finite strings of states $a_1 \cdots a_{p_L}$, $b_1 \cdots b_n$ and $c_1 \cdots c_{p_R}$ ($n = x_R - x_L - 1$), and (2) the string $a_1 \cdots a_{p_L}$ repeats infinitely to the left from the position x_L, the string $c_1 \cdots c_{p_R}$ repeats infinitely to the right from the position x_R, and $b_1 \cdots b_n$ lies between them. The positive integers p_L and p_R are called the *left period* and the *right period* of the configuration, respectively.

It is clear that the successor of an (ultimately) periodic configuration is also (ultimately) periodic in any CA. Note that a periodic configuration is a special case of an ultimately periodic configuration that satisfies $x_L + 1 = x_R$, and $a_1 \cdots a_{p_L} = c_1 \cdots c_{p_R}$. A finite configuration is also a special case of an ultimately periodic one that satisfies $p_L = p_R = 1$ and $a_1 = c_1 = \#$.

Note that periodic and ultimately periodic configurations for one-dimensional PCAs are also defined similarly. Thus, their precise definition are not given here.

We now give notations for a kind of *infinite strings*. Let S be a set of symbols, and $a_1 \cdots a_n \in S^+$. We denote an infinite repetition of $a_1 \cdots a_n$ to the left by $^\omega(a_1 \cdots a_n)$, and that to the right by $(a_1 \cdots a_n)^\omega$, which can be written as follows.

$$^\omega(a_1 \cdots a_n) = \cdots a_1 \cdots a_n a_1 \cdots a_n a_1 \cdots a_n$$
$$(a_1 \cdots a_n)^\omega = a_1 \cdots a_n a_1 \cdots a_n a_1 \cdots a_n \cdots$$

Now, let $\alpha : \mathbb{Z} \to Q$ be an ultimately periodic configuration with $x_L, x_R \in \mathbb{Z}$, and $p_L, p_R \in \mathbb{Z}_+$. Then it is expressed as follows using the above notations.

$$^\omega(\alpha(x_L - p_L + 1) \cdots \alpha(x_L)) \ \alpha(x_L + 1) \cdots \alpha(x_R - 1) \ (\alpha(x_R) \cdots \alpha(x_R + p_R - 1))^\omega$$

Therefore, the ultimately periodic configuration given above can be finitely described by the following triplet of strings.

$$D(\alpha) =$$
$$(\alpha(x_L - p_L + 1) \cdots \alpha(x_L), \ \alpha(x_L + 1) \cdots \alpha(x_R - 1), \ \alpha(x_R) \cdots \alpha(x_R + p_R - 1))$$

We call $D(\alpha)(\in Q^+ \times Q^* \times Q^+)$ a *description of the ultimately periodic configuration* α. If α is a finite configuration, then $D(\alpha) = (\#, \ \alpha(x_L + 1) \cdots \alpha(x_R - 1), \ \#)$, where # is the quiescent state. Furthermore, we denote the sets of all descriptions of ultimately periodic configurations, and those of finite configurations of a CA A by $D(\text{Conf}_{up}(A))$, and $D(\text{Conf}_{fin}(A))$, respectively.

$$D(\text{Conf}_{up}(A)) = \{D(\alpha) \mid \alpha \in \text{Conf}_{up}(A)\}$$
$$D(\text{Conf}_{fin}(A)) = \{D(\alpha) \mid \alpha \in \text{Conf}_{fin}(A)\}$$

11.1.2 Notion of simulation and Turing universality in one-dimensional CAs

We now define the notion of simulation of a computing system S by a one-dimensional CA. Here, we assume S is an element of a class of Turing machines, counter machines, cyclic tag systems, logic circuits, or one-dimensional CAs. However, this definition can be applied for any other suitably defined computing systems.

Definition 11.2. Let S be a computing system, and $\mathrm{ID}(S)$ be the set of all instantaneous descriptions of S. Note that, if S is a one-dimensional CA, then we use $D(\mathrm{Conf}_{\mathrm{up}}(S))$ (or $D(\mathrm{Conf}_{\mathrm{fin}}(S))$ when simulating finite configurations of S) instead of $\mathrm{ID}(S)$. Let $A = (\mathbb{Z}, Q, (n_1, \ldots, n_m), f, \#)$ be a one-dimensional CA whose global function is F_A, and let $\alpha \in \mathrm{ID}(S)$. If there exist a monotonically increasing total recursive function $\tau_\alpha : \mathbb{N} \to \mathbb{N}$, and two total recursive functions $c : \mathrm{ID}(S) \to D(\mathrm{Conf}_{\mathrm{up}}(A))$, and $d : D(\mathrm{Conf}_{\mathrm{up}}(A)) \to (\mathrm{ID}(S) \cup \{\bot\})$ that satisfy the following, then we say A *simulates* S with *ultimately periodic configurations*. Note that $d(\beta) = \bot$ for $\beta \in D(\mathrm{Conf}_{\mathrm{up}}(A))$ means there is no $\alpha \in \mathrm{ID}(S)$ that corresponds to β.

$$\forall \alpha, \alpha' \in \mathrm{ID}(S), \ \forall n \in \mathbb{N} \ (\alpha \vdash_S^n \alpha' \ \Rightarrow \ d(F_A^{\tau_\alpha(n)}(c(\alpha))) = \alpha')$$

Here, c and d are *encoding* and *decoding functions*, respectively, as in Definition 5.8. Furthermore, if c and d are total recursive functions such that $c : \mathrm{ID}(S) \to D(\mathrm{Conf}_{\mathrm{fin}}(A))$, and $d : D(\mathrm{Conf}_{\mathrm{fin}}(A)) \to (\mathrm{ID}(S) \cup \{\bot\})$, then we say A simulates S with *finite configurations*. Generally, the function τ_α depends on the initial ID α of S. However, if $\tau_\alpha = \tau_\beta$ holds for all $\alpha, \beta \in \mathrm{ID}(S)$, then we write them by τ. We say A simulates S in *real time* if $\tau(n) = n$, and in *linear time* if $\tau(n) \le kn$ for some positive constant k.

It should be noted that even if a system S is simulated by a reversible CA A with finite configurations, we do not restrict the domain of its global function to $\mathrm{Conf}_{\mathrm{fin}}(A)$ to decide its reversibility. Namely, as in Definitions 10.3 and 10.4, A is reversible iff its global function is injective on the domain $\mathrm{Conf}(A)$.

By allowing ultimately periodic configurations rather than finite ones as initial configurations, we often obtain simpler Turing universal RCAs as will be shown in Theorems 11.3 and 11.7.

Definition 11.3. A class $\mathscr{A}$ of one-dimensional CAs with finite (ultimately periodic, respectively) configurations is called *Turing universal*, if for each one-tape TM there exists a CA in $\mathscr{A}$ that can simulate the TM with finite (ultimately periodic) configurations. Likewise, a particular CA A with finite (ultimately periodic, respectively) configurations is called *Turing universal* if it can simulate *any* one-tape TM with finite (ultimately periodic) configurations.

When we design an RCA A that simulates a given system S in the following sections, we give only an informal description of encoding and decoding methods, since it is generally cumbersome to define the functions c and d precisely.

Note that, the notion of halting is defined in TMs or RTMs, while in CAs it is not. Stable configurations in CA may be a similar notion to halting IDs of TMs. However, in RCAs, it is not possible to go to a stable configuration from other configurations because of reversibility. In other words, an RCA never halts except the trivial case where the initial configuration is stable, and thus generally it cannot keep the same configuration after completing the computing process. Therefore, when we use an RCA for simulating an RTM, we should watch every configurations of it, and check if some specific pattern, which indicates an end of computation, appears in the configuration. Usually, they are defined in a simple way, e.g., the patterns that contain a final state of the TM as a "flag".

11.2 One-Dimensional RCAs That Simulate Reversible Turing Machines

In this section, we show any given one-tape RTM can be directly simulated by a one-dimensional RPCA with finite configurations, and thus by an RCA. An advantage of the method is that the constructed RCA does not generate garbage information if the RTM is garbage-less (see Corollary 5.3 and Theorem 5.3). In Sect. 11.2.1, we show an m-state n-symbol RTM is simulated by a three-neighbor RPCA with at most $(m+1)^2 n$ states (Theorem 11.1). In Sect. 11.2.2, we give a method of simulating an m-state n-symbol RTM by a two-neighbor RPCA with at most $(m+2n+1)(m+n+1)$ states (Theorem 11.2). Though the number of states of the three-neighbor RPCA is larger than that of the two-neighbor RPCA unless n is much larger than m, the simulation method of the former is simpler and easier to understand.

11.2.1 Simulating RTMs by three-neighbor RPCAs

It was first proved in [22] that a one-dimensional three-neighbor RPCA can simulate a one-tape RTM in the quadruple form, and thus the class of one-dimensional three-neighbor RCAs are Turing universal. But here, we show the method of simulating a one-tape RTM in the quintuple form by a one-dimensional RPCA given in [17, 19] to reduce the number of states of the RPCA.

Theorem 11.1. *[17, 19, 22] For any one-tape RTM T in the quintuple form, we can construct a one-dimensional three-neighbor RPCA P with finite configurations that simulates T in real time.*

Proof. Let $T = (Q, S, q_0, F, s_0, \delta)$ be a given one-tape RTM in the quintuple form (see Definition 5.2). We assume there is no state that goes to the initial state q_0, i.e., there is no quintuple whose fifth element is q_0. It is possible to assume so from the argument given in Sect. 6.1.2. We also assume that for any quintuple $[p, s, t, d, q]$ in δ the following holds: If q is a non-halting state, then $d \in \{-, +\}$, and if q is a halting state, then $d = 0$. It is easily achieved by slightly modifying the method shown in Lemma 5.8. Now, let Q_-, Q_0, and Q_+ be as follows.

$$
\begin{aligned}
Q_- &= \{q \mid \exists p \in Q \; \exists s, t \in S \left([p,s,t,-,q] \in \delta\right)\} \\
Q_0 &= \{q \mid \exists p \in Q \; \exists s, t \in S \left([p,s,t,0,q] \in \delta\right)\} \\
Q_+ &= \{q \mid \exists p \in Q \; \exists s, t \in S \left([p,s,t,+,q] \in \delta\right)\}
\end{aligned}
$$

Note that Q_-, Q_0, and Q_+ are the same as in Definition 5.11. Since T is an RTM, Q_-, Q_0, and Q_+ are mutually disjoint (Lemma 5.5). Here, Q_0 is the set of all halting states, and thus $Q_0 \supseteq F$.

A reversible PCA P that simulates T is defined as below.

$$
\begin{aligned}
P &= (\mathbb{Z}, (L, C, R), (1, 0, -1), f, (\#, s_0, \#)) \\
L &= Q_- \cup Q_0 \cup \{q_0, \#\} \\
C &= S \\
R &= Q_+ \cup Q_0 \cup \{q_0, \#\}
\end{aligned}
$$

The local function f is as below.

(1) For each $s, t \in S$, and $q \in Q - (Q_0 \cup \{q_0\})$, define f as follows.
  (1a) $f(\#, s, \#) = (\#, s, \#)$
  (1b) $f(\#, s, q_0) = (\#, s, q_0)$
  (1c) $f(q_0, s, \#) = (q_0, s, \#)$
  (1d) $f(q_0, s, q_0) = (\#, t, q)$ if $[q_0, s, t, +, q] \in \delta$
  (1e) $f(q_0, s, q_0) = (q, t, \#)$ if $[q_0, s, t, -, q] \in \delta$
(2) For each $p, q \in Q - (Q_0 \cup \{q_0\})$, and $s, t \in S$, define f as follows.
  (2a) $f(\#, s, p) = (\#, t, q)$ if $p \in Q_+ \wedge [p, s, t, +, q] \in \delta$
  (2b) $f(p, s, \#) = (\#, t, q)$ if $p \in Q_- \wedge [p, s, t, +, q] \in \delta$
  (2c) $f(\#, s, p) = (q, t, \#)$ if $p \in Q_+ \wedge [p, s, t, -, q] \in \delta$
  (2d) $f(p, s, \#) = (q, t, \#)$ if $p \in Q_- \wedge [p, s, t, -, q] \in \delta$
(3) For each $p \in Q - (Q_0 \cup \{q_0\})$, $q \in Q_0$, and $s, t \in S$, define f as follows.
  (3a) $f(\#, s, p) = (q, t, q)$ if $p \in Q_+ \wedge [p, s, t, 0, q] \in \delta$
  (3b) $f(p, s, \#) = (q, t, q)$ if $p \in Q_- \wedge [p, s, t, 0, q] \in \delta$
(4) For each $q \in Q_0$ and $s \in S$, define f as follows.
  (4a) $f(\#, s, q) = (\#, s, q)$
  (4b) $f(q, s, \#) = (q, s, \#)$

It is easy to verify that the right-hand side of each rule differs from that of any other rule, because T is reversible. Hence, by Lemma 6.1, P is reversible.

Assume the initial ID of T is

$$ t_1 \cdots t_{i-1} \, q_0 \, t_i \, t_{i+1} \cdots t_n $$

where $t_j \in S$ ($j \in \{1, \dots, n\}$). Then, set P to the following initial configuration.

$$ {}^{\omega}((\#, s_0, \#))(\#, t_1, \#) \cdots (\#, t_{i-1}, q_0)(\#, t_i, \#)(q_0, t_{i+1}, \#) \cdots (\#, t_n, \#)((\#, s_0, \#))^{\omega} $$

The rule (1a) is for keeping a symbol s such that there is no state of T in the neighboring cells. The rules (1b) and (1c) are for sending the state q_0 to the adjacent cell, which are for going back to configurations of $t < 0$. The rule (1d) or (1e) is applied where the pair of left- and right-moving signals q_0 meets at the cell containing t_i. By this a simulation process starts. After that, by the rules (2a) – (2d), P simulates T step by step in real time. If T becomes a halting state $q \ (\in Q_0)$, then two signals q's are created by the rule (3a) or (3b), and then travel leftward and rightward indefinitely by (4a) and (4b). Note that P itself cannot halt, because P is reversible. But, the final tape of T is kept unchanged in P. Termination of a simulation can be sensed from the outside of the P by observing if a final state of T appears in some cell of P's configuration as a kind of a flag. Since the initial configuration of P corresponding to an initial ID of T is finite, it is clear that P simulates T on its finite configurations. □

The number of states of P constructed in Theorem 11.1 is $(m_- + m_0 + 2)(m_+ + m_0 + 2)n$, where $m_- = |Q_-|$, $m_0 = |Q_0|$, $m_+ = |Q_+|$, and $n = |S|$. Hence, it is bounded by $(m+1)^2 n$, where $m = |Q|$.

Example 11.1. Consider the RTM $T_{copy'} = (Q_{copy'}, \{0,1,a,m\}, q_0, \{q_f\}, 0, \delta_{copy'})$ in Example 5.3. But here, the states $q_{initial}, q_{start}, q_{find0}, q_{next0}, q_{return}$, and q_{final} are renamed as q_0, q_1, q_2, q_3, q_4, and q_f, respectively, and thus $Q_{copy'} = \{q_0, \cdots, q_4, q_f\}$. The move relation $\delta_{copy'}$ is defined below.

$$\delta_{copy'} = \{ \ [q_0, 0, 0, +, q_1],$$
$$[q_1, 1, m, +, q_2], \ [q_1, a, a, 0, q_f], \ [q_2, 0, 1, +, q_3],$$
$$[q_2, 1, 1, +, q_2], \ [q_2, a, a, +, q_2], \ [q_3, 0, 0, -, q_4],$$
$$[q_4, 1, 1, -, q_4], \ [q_4, a, a, -, q_4], \ [q_4, m, 1, +, q_1] \ \}$$

Given a unary number n on the tape, $T_{copy'}$ copies it to the right of the symbol a, i.e., $q_0 01^n a \mathrel{\vdash^*_{T_{copy'}}} 1^n q_f a 1^n$ for $n \in \{0, 1, \ldots\}$. The following is a complete computing process of $T_{copy'}$ with the unary input 1.

$$q_0 01a \mathrel{\vdash_{T_{copy'}}} q_1 1a \mathrel{\vdash_{T_{copy'}}} m q_2 a \mathrel{\vdash_{T_{copy'}}} m a q_2 \mathrel{\vdash_{T_{copy'}}} m a 1 q_3$$
$$\mathrel{\vdash_{T_{copy'}}} m a q_4 1 \mathrel{\vdash_{T_{copy'}}} m q_4 a 1 \mathrel{\vdash_{T_{copy'}}} q_4 m a 1 \mathrel{\vdash_{T_{copy'}}} 1 q_1 a 1 \mathrel{\vdash_{T_{copy'}}} 1 q_f a 1$$

The RPCA $P_{copy'}$ constructed by the method of Theorem 11.1 is as follows. Note that $Q_- = \{q_4\}$, $Q_0 = \{q_f\}$, and $Q_+ = \{q_1, q_2, q_3\}$ in $T_{copy'}$.

$$P_{copy'} = (\mathbb{Z}, (L, C, R), (1, 0, -1), f, (\#, 0, \#))$$
$$L = \{q_0, q_4, q_f, \#\}$$
$$C = \{0, 1, a, m\}$$
$$R = \{q_0, q_1, q_2, q_3, q_f, \#\}$$

The local function f is defined as below.

$$
\begin{aligned}
&\text{(1a)} && f(\#,s,\#) &&= (\#,s,\#) && \text{if } s \in \{0,1,a,m\}\\
&\text{(1b)} && f(\#,s,q_0) &&= (\#,s,q_0) && \text{if } s \in \{0,1,a,m\}\\
&\text{(1c)} && f(q_0,s,\#) &&= (q_0,s,\#) && \text{if } s \in \{0,1,a,m\}\\
&\text{(1d)} && f(q_0,0,q_0) &&= (\#,0,q_1)\\
&\text{(2a)} && f(\#,1,q_1) &&= (\#,m,q_2)\\
& && f(\#,0,q_2) &&= (\#,1,q_3)\\
& && f(\#,1,q_2) &&= (\#,1,q_2)\\
& && f(\#,a,q_2) &&= (\#,a,q_2)\\
&\text{(2b)} && f(q_4,m,\#) &&= (\#,1,q_1)\\
&\text{(2c)} && f(\#,0,q_3) &&= (q_4,0,\#)\\
&\text{(2d)} && f(q_4,1,\#) &&= (q_4,1,\#)\\
& && f(q_4,a,\#) &&= (q_4,a,\#)\\
&\text{(3a)} && f(\#,a,q_1) &&= (q_f,a,q_f)\\
&\text{(4a)} && f(\#,s,q_f) &&= (\#,s,q_f) && \text{if } s \in \{0,1,a,m\}\\
&\text{(4b)} && f(q_f,s,\#) &&= (q_f,s,\#) && \text{if } s \in \{0,1,a,m\}
\end{aligned}
$$

A simulation process of $T_{\text{copy}'}$ with the unary input 1 by an RPCA $P_{\text{copy}'}$ is given in Fig. 11.1.   □

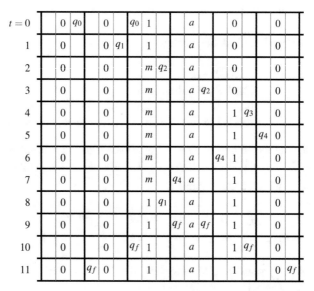

Fig. 11.1 Simulating $T_{\text{copy}'}$ by a one-dimensional three-neighbor RPCA $P_{\text{copy}'}$. The state # is indicated by a blank

11.2.2 Simulating RTMs by two-neighbor RPCAs

Next, we show a one-tape RTM can be simulated by a one-dimensional two-neighbor RPCA. Though the method is slightly more complicated than the one in Theorem 11.1, both the neighborhood size and the number of states of the RPCA are reduced.

Theorem 11.2. *[18] For any one-tape RTM T in the quintuple form, we can construct a one-dimensional two-neighbor RPCA $\tilde{P}$ with finite configurations that simulates T in real time.*

Proof. Let $T = (Q, S, q_0, F, s_0, \delta)$ be a given RTM. As in Theorem 11.1, we assume that for any quintuple $[p, s, t, d, q]$ in δ the following holds: If q is a non-halting state, then $d \in \{-, +\}$, and if q is a halting state, then $d = 0$. But, we do not require that there is no state that goes to the initial state q_0. Let Q_-, Q_0 and Q_+ be the sets in Definition 5.11 (see also Theorem 11.1). Note that Q_0 is the set of all halting states. Now, let Q'_- be as follows.

$$Q'_- = \begin{cases} Q_- & \text{if } q_0 \in Q_- \cup Q_+ \\ Q_- \cup \{q_0\} & \text{if } q_0 \notin Q_- \cup Q_+ \end{cases}$$

The RPCA $\tilde{P}$ is defined as below, where $\hat{S} = \{\hat{s} \mid s \in S\}$.

$$\tilde{P} = (\mathbb{Z}, (C, R), (0, -1), f, (s_0, s_0))$$
$$C = Q'_- \cup S \cup \hat{S} \cup \{*\}$$
$$R = Q_+ \cup Q_0 \cup S \cup \{*\}$$

The local function $f : C \times R \to C \times R$ is as follows.

(1) For each $s, t \in S$ define f as follows.
    (1a) $f(t, s) = (s, t)$
    (1b) $f(s, *) = (s, *)$
    (1c) $f(*, s) = (*, s)$
    (1d) $f(*, *) = (q_0, *)$ if $q_0 \in Q'_-$
    (1e) $f(*, *) = (*, q_0)$ if $q_0 \in Q_+$
(2) For each $p, q \in Q - Q_0$, and $s, t \in S$ define f as follows.
    (2a) $f(p, s) = (q, t)$ if $[p, s, t, -, q] \in \delta \wedge p \in Q'_-$
    (2b) $f(s, p) = (q, t)$ if $[p, s, t, -, q] \in \delta \wedge p \in Q_+$
    (2c) $f(p, s) = (t, q)$ if $[p, s, t, +, q] \in \delta \wedge p \in Q'_-$
    (2d) $f(s, p) = (t, q)$ if $[p, s, t, +, q] \in \delta \wedge p \in Q_+$
(3) For each $p \in Q - Q_0, q \in Q_0$, and $s, t \in S$ define f as follows.
    (3a) $f(p, s) = (\hat{t}, q)$ if $[p, s, t, +, q] \in \delta \wedge p \in Q'_-$
    (3b) $f(s, p) = (\hat{t}, q)$ if $[p, s, t, +, q] \in \delta \wedge p \in Q_+$
(4) For each $q \in Q_0$, and $s, t \in S$ define f as follows.
    (4a) $f(s, q) = (s, q)$
    (4b) $f(\hat{t}, s) = (\hat{s}, t)$

It is easy to verify that the right-hand sides of these rules are all different each other, because T is an RTM. Hence, we can obtain an injection f, and thus $\tilde{P}$ is an RPCA.

The initial configuration of $\tilde{P}$ is set in the following way. First, consider the case $q_0 \in Q'_-$. Assume the initial ID of T is

$$t_1 \cdots t_{2k-1} \, q_0 t_{2k} \, u_1 \cdots u_{2l}$$

where $t_i, u_j \in S$ ($i \in \{1, \ldots, 2k\}, j \in \{1, \ldots, 2l\}$). Note that t_1 and u_{2l} may be a blank symbol s_0. Then set the initial configuration of $\tilde{P}$ as follows.

$$^\omega((s_0, s_0))(t_1, t_2) \cdots (t_{2k-1}, t_{2k})(q_0, *)(u_1, u_2) \cdots (u_{2l-1}, u_{2l})((s_0, s_0))^\omega$$

Second, consider the case $q_0 \in Q_+$. Assume the initial ID of T is

$$t_1 \cdots t_{2k} \, q_0 u_1 \cdots u_{2l}$$

where $t_i, u_j \in S$ ($i \in \{1, \ldots, 2k\}, j \in \{1, \ldots, 2l\}$). Again, t_1 and u_{2l} may be a blank symbol s_0. Then set the initial configuration of $\tilde{P}$ as follows.

$$^\omega((s_0, s_0))(t_1, t_2) \cdots (t_{2k-1}, t_{2k})(*, q_0)(u_1, u_2) \cdots (u_{2l-1}, u_{2l})((s_0, s_0))^\omega$$

From the initial configuration, each step of T near the head is simulated by the rules (2a) – (2d) in real time, while the other part is by (1a) – (1c). When T enters a halting state q, the symbol of T at that position is changed to a symbol with "$\hat{\ }$" by (3a) and (3b). The halting state q acts as a right-moving signal by (4a). Though $\tilde{P}$ itself cannot halt, the final result on the tape of T is kept unchanged by (1a) – (1c), (4a), and (4b). Note that the halting position of T is marked by "$\hat{\ }$" by the rule (4b) to keep $\tilde{P}$ reversible. The rules (1b) – (1e) are for going back to configurations of $t < 0$ using the state $*$. In Theorem 11.1, the state $q_0 \in (L \cap R)$ played the role of $*$, where the collision of two q_0's initiates the computation. However, here, since the initial state q_0 of T can appear also at $t > 0$, another state $*$ is used to create an initial configuration (otherwise, q_0 will interact with other states inappropriately in $\tilde{P}$). In addition, one of the two initiation signals $*$'s cannot be erased even after their collision because of the restriction of two-neighbor PCA. Since the initial configuration of $\tilde{P}$ corresponding to an initial ID of T is finite, $\tilde{P}$ can simulate T on its finite configurations.   □

Two examples of making two-neighbor RPCAs from given RTMs by the method of Theorem 11.2 are shown below. The first one is for the case where the initial state is in Q'_-, and the second one is for the case where the initial state is in Q_+.

Example 11.2. Consider the RTM $T_{\text{copy}'}$ in Example 11.1. The RPCA $\tilde{P}_{\text{copy}'}$ constructed by the method of Theorem 11.2 is as below. Note that $Q'_- = \{q_0, q_4\}$, $Q_0 = \{q_f\}$, and $Q_+ = \{q_1, q_2, q_3\}$ in $T_{\text{copy}'}$. This the case where the initial state q_0 is in Q'_-.

$$\tilde{P}_{\text{copy}'} = (\mathbb{Z}, (C, R), (0, -1), f, (0, 0))$$
$$C = \{q_0, q_4, 0, 1, a, m, \hat{0}, \hat{1}, \hat{a}, \hat{m}, *\}$$
$$R = \{q_1, q_2, q_3, q_f, 0, 1, a, m, *\}$$

The local function f is defined as below.

(1a) $f(t,s) = (s,t)$ if $s,t \in \{0,1,a,m\}$
(1b) $f(s,*) = (s,*)$ if $s \in \{0,1,a,m\}$
(1c) $f(*,s) = (*,s)$ if $s \in \{0,1,a,m\}$
(1d) $f(*,*) = (q_0,*)$
(2a) $f(q_4,1) = (q_4,1)$
     $f(q_4,a) = (q_4,a)$
(2b) $f(0,q_3) = (q_4,0)$
(2c) $f(q_0,0) = (0,q_1)$
     $f(q_4,m) = (1,q_1)$
(2d) $f(1,q_1) = (m,q_2)$
     $f(0,q_2) = (1,q_3)$
     $f(1,q_2) = (1,q_2)$
     $f(a,q_2) = (a,q_2)$
(3b) $f(a,q_1) = (\hat{a},q_f)$
(4a) $f(s,q_f) = (s,q_f)$ if $s \in \{0,1,a,m\}$
(4b) $f(\hat{i},s) = (\hat{s},t)$ if $s,t \in \{0,1,a,m\}$

A simulation process of $T_{\text{copy}'}$ starting from the initial ID $q_0 01a$ is given in Fig. 11.2. In the configurations of $t < 0$, we can see that a right-moving signal $*$ comes from the left. When it meets another stationary $*$, the initial state q_0 is created. Then, each step of $T_{\text{copy}'}$ is simulated in real time until it reaches the final state q_f. After that, the state q_f goes rightward without affecting the tape symbols of $T_{\text{copy}'}$.   □

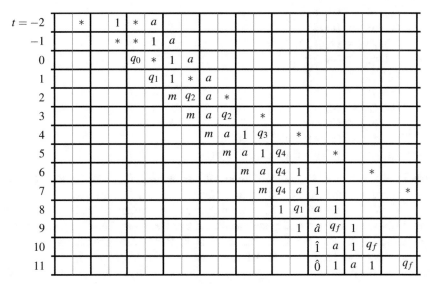

Fig. 11.2 Simulating $T_{\text{copy}'}$ by a one-dimensional two-neighbor RPCA $\tilde{P}_{\text{copy}'}$. This is the case where the initial state is in Q'_-. The state 0 is indicated by a blank

Example 11.3. Consider the RTM $T_{copy} = (Q_{copy}, \{0,1,a,m\}, q_1, \{q_f\}, 0, \delta_{copy})$ in Example 5.1. Here, its states are renamed, and thus $Q_{copy} = \{q_1, \cdots, q_4, q_f\}$. The move relation δ_{copy} is defined as follows.

$$\delta_{copy} = \{ \; [q_1,1,m,+,q_2], \; [q_1,a,a,0,q_f], \; [q_2,0,1,+,q_3],$$
$$[q_2,1,1,+,q_2], \; [q_2,a,a,+,q_2], \; [q_3,0,0,-,q_4],$$
$$[q_4,1,1,-,q_4], \; [q_4,a,a,-,q_4], \; [q_4,m,1,+,q_1] \; \}$$

It is also obtained from $T_{copy'}$ in Example 11.1 by removing the state q_0 and the quintuple $[q_0,0,0,+,q_1]$, and setting the initial state to q_1.

The RPCA $\tilde{P}_{copy}$ constructed by the method of Theorem 11.2 is as below. Note that, $Q'_- = \{q_4\}$, $Q_0 = \{q_f\}$, and $Q_+ = \{q_1,q_2,q_3\}$ in T_{copy}. This is the case where the initial state q_1 is in Q_+.

$$\tilde{P}_{copy} = (\mathbb{Z}, (C,R), (0,-1), f, (0,0))$$
$$C = \{q_4,0,1,a,m,\hat{0},\hat{1},\hat{a},\hat{m},*\}$$
$$R = \{q_1,q_2,q_3,q_f,0,1,a,m,*\}$$

The local function f is defined as below.

(1a) $f(t,s)$ $= (s,t)$ if $s,t \in \{0,1,a,m\}$
(1b) $f(s,*)$ $= (s,*)$ if $s \in \{0,1,a,m\}$
(1c) $f(*,s)$ $= (*,s)$ if $s \in \{0,1,a,m\}$
(1e) $f(*,*)$ $= (*,q_1)$
(2a) $f(q_4,1)$ $= (q_4,1)$
    $f(q_4,a)$ $= (q_4,a)$
(2b) $f(0,q_3)$ $= (q_4,0)$
(2c) $f(q_4,m)$ $= (1,q_1)$
(2d) $f(1,q_1)$ $= (m,q_2)$
    $f(0,q_2)$ $= (1,q_3)$
    $f(1,q_2)$ $= (1,q_2)$
    $f(a,q_2)$ $= (a,q_2)$
(3b) $f(a,q_1)$ $= (\hat{a},q_f)$
(4a) $f(s,q_f)$ $= (s,q_f)$ if $s \in \{0,1,a,m\}$
(4b) $f(\hat{\imath},s)$ $= (\hat{s},t)$ if $s,t \in \{0,1,a,m\}$

The local function of $\tilde{P}_{copy}$ is also almost the same as in $\tilde{P}_{copy'}$ except that the rule (1e) is used instead of (1d), and a rule in (2c) related to q_0 is removed.

A simulation process of T_{copy} starting from the initial ID $q_1 1a$ is given in Fig. 11.3. We can observe only the transition from $t = -1$ to 0 is different from that in Example 11.2. After that, evolutions of these RPCAs are essentially the same, i.e., the configuration of Fig. 11.3 at time t corresponds to that of Fig. 11.2 at $t+1$ except the positions of $*$.   □

The total number of states of the RPCA $\tilde{P}$ constructed in Theorem 11.2 is $(m'_- + 2n+1)(m_+ + m_0 + n + 1)$, where $m'_- = |Q'_-|$, $m_0 = |Q_0|$, $m_+ = |Q_+|$, and $n = |S|$. Thus, it is bounded by $(m+2n+1)(m+n+1)$, where $m = |Q|$. Converting a URTM given in Chap. 7, we can obtain a Turing universal one-dimensional RCA. Consider

$t=-2$		*		1	*	a										
-1			*	*	1	a										
0			*	q_1	1	a										
1			*		m	q_2	a									
2			*			m	a	q_2								
3			*			m	a	1	q_3							
4			*				m	a	1	q_4						
5			*					m	a	q_4	1					
6			*						m	q_4	a	1				
7			*							1	q_1	a	1			
8			*								1	$\hat{a}$	q_f	1		
9			*									$\hat{1}$	a	1	q_f	
10			*									$\hat{0}$	1	a	1	q_f

Fig. 11.3 Simulating T_{copy} by a one-dimensional two-neighbor RPCA $\tilde{P}_{copy}$. This is the case where the initial state is in Q_+. The state 0 is indicated by a blank

the 17-state 5-symbol URTM U_{17_5} given in Sect. 7.3.3. Since halting states are not included in U_{17_5}, we should add two states, say q_{halt} and q_{null}, to the state set, and also add two quintuples $[q_{case\_y\_1}, b, b, 0, q_{halt}]$ and $[q_{case\_y\_2}, \$, \$, 0, q_{null}]$ to δ_{17_5} in Table 7.3. Then, we have $|Q_-| = 7$, $|Q_0| = 2$, and $|Q_+| = 10$. By above, we obtain a 324-state Turing universal RPCA with finite configurations.

The methods given in Theorems 11.1 and 11.2 are general procedures for simulating RTMs by RCAs. Therefore, to find much simpler Turing universal RCAs, we should use some special methods for it. In the next section, one of such methods will be shown.

11.3 Simple Turing Universal One-Dimensional RPCAs

In this section, we study the problem of constructing simple Turing universal one-dimensional RCAs. Here, we employ a method of simulating cyclic tag systems (CTSs), or cyclic tag systems with halting condition (CTSHs), which are Turing universal systems (see Sect. 7.2.2). A CTS was proposed by Cook [2] to show Turing universality of the elementary cellular automaton (ECA) of rule 110. In Sect. 11.3.1, we design a two-neighbor 24-state RPCA with ultimately periodic configurations that can simulate any CTS (Theorem 11.3). In Sect. 11.3.2, we give a three-neighbor 98-state RPCA with finite configurations that can simulate any CTSH (Theorem 11.4).

11.3.1 24-state universal RPCA with ultimately periodic configurations

In [2] Cook showed that any CTS can be simulated in the ECA of rule 110 with ultimately periodic configurations. Here, we take a similar approach, and construct a one-dimensional 24-state RPCA with ultimately periodic configurations that can simulate any CTS.

Theorem 11.3. *[18] There is a 24-state one-dimensional two-neighbor RPCA P_{24} with ultimately periodic configurations that can simulate any cyclic tag system.*

Proof. The RPCA P_{24} is defined as follows.

$$P_{24} = (\mathbb{Z}, (\{Y, N, +, -\}, \{y, n, +, -, *, /\}), (0, -1), f_{24}, (Y, -))$$

The state set of each cell is $\{Y, N, +, -\} \times \{y, n, +, -, *, /\}$, and thus P_{24} has 24 states. The local function f_{24} is as below.

  (1) $f_{24}(c, r) = (c, r)$ if $c \in \{Y, N\}, r \in \{y, n, +, -, /\}$
  (2) $f_{24}(Y, *) = (+, /)$
  (3) $f_{24}(N, *) = (-, /)$
  (4) $f_{24}(-, r) = (-, r)$ if $r \in \{y, n, *\}$
  (5) $f_{24}(c, r) = (r, c)$ if $c \in \{+, -\}, r \in \{+, -\}$
  (6) $f_{24}(+, y) = (Y, *)$
  (7) $f_{24}(+, n) = (N, *)$
  (8) $f_{24}(+, /) = (+, y)$
  (9) $f_{24}(-, /) = (+, n)$
(10) $f_{24}(+, *) = (+, *)$

It is easily verified that there is no pair of distinct rules whose right-hand sides are the same. Hence, f_{24} is injective, and thus P_{24} is an RPCA.

Let $C = (k, (w_0, \ldots, w_{k-1}))$ be a CTS, and $v \in \{Y, N\}^*$ be an initial string. Let $\varphi_1 : \{Y, N\}^* \to \{(-, y), (-, n)\}^*$, and $\varphi_2 : \{Y, N\}^* \to \{(Y, -), (N, -)\}^*$ be two homomorphisms defined by $\varphi_1(Y) = (-, y)$, $\varphi_1(N) = (-, n)$, and $\varphi_2(Y) = (Y, -)$, $\varphi_2(N) = (N, -)$. Then, set the initial configuration of P_{24} as follows.

$$^{\omega}(\varphi_1(w_{k-1}^R)(-, -)(-, *) \cdots \varphi_1(w_0^R)(-, -)(-, *)) \; \varphi_2(v)(-, -) \, ((Y, -))^{\omega}$$

This is an ultimately periodic configuration. Starting from it, P_{24} simulates C with v step by step.

We explain how P_{24} simulates a CTS by the following example C_0 with an initial string NYY.

$$C_0 = (3, (Y, NN, YN))$$

The initial configuration of P_{24} is as follows (see also the first row of Fig. 11.4).

$$^{\omega}((-, n)(-, y)(-, -)(-, *) \; (-, n)(-, n)(-, -)(-, *) \; (-, y)(-, -)(-, *))$$
$$(N, -)(Y, -)(Y, -) \; (-, -) \, ((Y, -))^{\omega}$$

The production rules are given by a sequence consisting of the states $(-,y)$, $(-,n)$, $(-,*)$, and $(-,-)$ in a reverse order, where the sequence $(-,-)(-,*)$ is used as a delimiter indicating the beginning of a rule. Thus, one cycle of the rules (Y,NN,YN) is $(-,n)(-,y)(-,-)(-,*)(-,n)(-,n)(-,-)(-,*)(-,y)(-,-)(-,*)$. We should give infinite copies of this sequence to the left, since these rules are applied cyclically. We can see the right-part states $y, n, *$, and $-$ in this sequence act as right-moving signals. The initial string NYY is given to the right of it by the sequence $(N,-)(Y,-)(Y,-)(-,-)$, where $(-,-)$ is a delimiter. All the cells right to this sequence are set to $(Y,-)$.

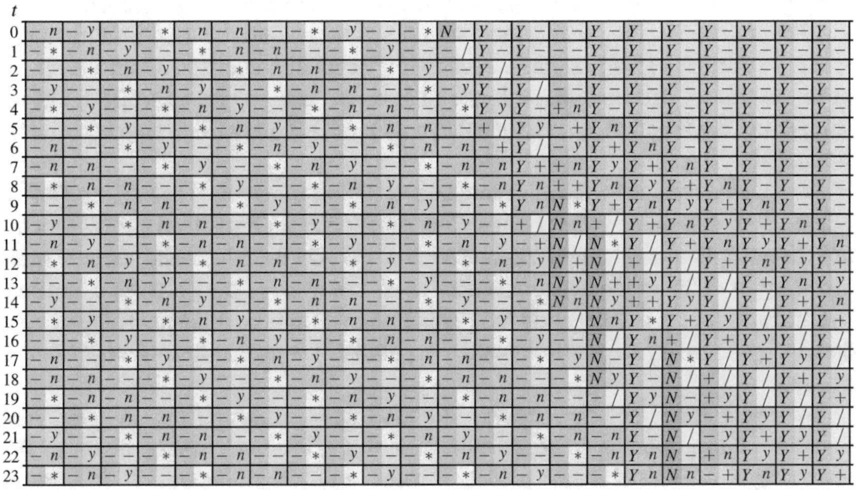

Fig. 11.4 Simulating a computing process $(NYY,0) \Rightarrow (YY,1) \Rightarrow (YNN,2) \Rightarrow (NNYN,0) \Rightarrow (NYN,1) \Rightarrow (YN,2) \Rightarrow \cdots$ of the CTS C_0 with the initial string NYY by the RPCA P_{24}

A rewriting process of C_0 is simulated as below. In P_{24}, each rewriting step of a CTS is initiated when the signal $*$ meets the head symbol Y or N of a rewritten string as shown at $t = 0, 4, 9, 14, 18, 23$ in Fig. 11.4. If the signal $*$ collides with the state Y (or N, respectively), then the signal changes Y (N) to the state $+$ $(-)$, and $*$ itself becomes $/$ by the rules (2) or (3) as shown at $t = 1, 5, 10, 15, 19$ in Fig. 11.4. The signal $/$ is sent rightward by (1), and when it meets a center state $+$ or $-$ at $t = 3, 6, 12, 18, 21$, it is changed to a signal y or n by (8) or (9) as shown at the next time step. Then the signal y or n is sent infinitely to the right by (1) as a used (garbage) signal. On the other hand, just after the collision of $*$ and Y (or N), i.e., at $t = 1, 5, 10, 15, 19$, the center-part state $+$ $(-)$ meets the signal $-$, and the former becomes a right-moving signal $+$ $(-)$, and the latter (i.e., $-$) is fixed as a center-part state at this position by (5) as shown at $t = 2, 6, 11, 16, 20$. The right-moving signal $+$ $(-)$ travels through the rewritten string consisting of Y's and N's by (1), and when it meets the center-part state $+$ or $-$ at $t = 4, 7, 13, 19, 22$, then it is fixed as a new center-part state by (5) at the next time step, which indicates the last head symbol was Y (N). Note that the old center-part state $+$ ($-$) is sent rightward as a garbage signal by (1).

Signals y's and n's, which form production rules of the CTS, go rightward through the rewritten string consisting Y's and N's by (1) until it meets $+$ or $-$. If y (n, respectively) meets $+$ as shown at $t = 8, 10, 14, 16$, then the signal becomes Y (N) and is fixed at this position by (6) or (7) (since the last head symbol was Y) at the next time step. The state $+$ is temporarily converted into a signal $*$ by (6) or (7) as shown at $t = 9, 11, 15, 17$, then further converted into the center-part state $+$ and fixed in the right-neighboring cell by (2) or (3) as shown at $t = 10, 12, 16, 18$. On the other hand, if y or n meets $-$ at $t = 5, 20$, then the signal simply goes through $-$ by (4) at the next time step, and continues to travel rightward by (1) without being fixed (since the last head symbol was N). Note that all the used information is sent rightward as garbage signals, because they cannot be deleted by the constraint of reversibility. Also note that the rule (10) is not used to simulate CTSs, but for completing the function f_{24}. By the above method, each rewriting step is correctly simulated.

We give an outline of the encoding and decoding functions c and d (see Definition 11.2) in this simulation. The encoding function c can be defined easily from the above description of an initial configuration of P_{24}. On the other hand, there is some difficulty in defining the decoding function d, because P_{24} may start to simulate a rewriting step of a CTS even if the previous step is not completed. Thus, in general, many rewriting steps are simulated in parallel. We explain below how d can be defined.

We consider a simulation process of a CTS in P_{24} starting from an initial configuration corresponding to some initial ID of a CTS. Each configuration of P_{24} appearing in such a simulation process is called a *proper configuration*. In a proper configuration, the leftmost occurrence of Y or N is the head symbol of a rewritten string unless the latter is an empty string (we will discuss this case later). A proper configuration is further called a *standard configuration*, if there is a signal $*$ in the left-neighboring cell of the head symbol. In Fig. 11.4, configurations at time $t = 0, 4, 9, 14, 18, 23$ are standard ones. Since simulation of each rewriting step of a CTS starts from a standard configuration (as already explained), we define d only for standard configurations. For other configurations d takes the value $\perp$, which means it is undefined. *Active cells* in a standard configuration are defined as follows. They are the consecutive cells that start from the cell containing the head symbol of a rewritten string, and ends at the cell containing a right-delimiter, which is either the center-part state $-$ (e.g., in the configuration at $t = 0$ in Fig. 11.4), the center-part state $+$ (e.g., $t = 4$), or the right-part state $*$ (e.g., $t = 9$).

Thus the states of active cells is one of the following forms, where $V_i \in \{Y, N\}$, and $u_i \in \{y, n, +, -, /\}$.

(i) $(V_1, u_k)(V_2, u_{k-1}) \cdots (V_k, u_1)(-, u_0)$

(ii) $(V_1, u_k)(V_2, u_{k-1}) \cdots (V_k, u_1)(+, u_0)$

(iii) $(V_1, u_k)(V_2, u_{k-1}) \cdots (V_{k-1}, u_2)(V_k, *)$

The string $V_1 V_2 \cdots V_{k-1} V_k$ forms a prefix of the rewritten string. On the other hand, the signal string (i) $-u_1 u_2 \cdots u_{k-1} u_k$, (ii) $+u_1 u_2 \cdots u_{k-1} u_k$, or (iii) $*u_2 u_3 \cdots u_{k-1} u_k$

contains an information of a suffix that is to be added to $V_1 V_2 \cdots V_{k-1} V_k$. The signal $+$ ($-$, respectively) means that subsequent occurrences of y's and n's should be (should not be) added to this prefix until next $+$ or $-$ appears. Note that, since $*$ appears temporarily just before the center-part state $+$ is created by (2), it has the same meaning as $+$. The signal $/$ is simply ignored.

Consider some examples. First, take the configuration at $t = 9$ in Fig. 11.4, where the states of active cells are $(Y,n),(N,*)$. Since the signal string is $*n$, the suffix N is attached to the prefix YN, and thus the rewritten string is YNN. Second, consider the configuration at $t = 14$, where the active cells are $(N,n),(N,y),(+,+)$. In this case, the signal string is $+yn$, and hence the rewritten string is $NNYN$. Third, consider the configuration at $t = 18$, where the active cells are $(N,y),(Y,-),(N,/),(+,/)$, and thus the signal sequence is $+/-y$. In this case, Y is not attached because there is $-$ before y, and hence the rewritten string is NYN. Finally, take a bit complex example of active cells: $(N,y),(Y,+),(Y,/),(Y,n),(N,n),(Y,-),(N,/),(N,y),(+,/)$. Since the signal string is $+y/-nn/+y$, the suffix YY is attached, and thus the rewritten string is $NYYYNYNNYY$.

The phase of an ID of a CTS that corresponds to a given standard configuration of P_{24} is easily identified by checking a fixed length of the signal sequence before the head symbol of the rewritten string. By above, we can get an ID of the CTS from a standard configuration of P_{24}, and can define the decoding function d. Using this d we can recognize whether a specific (say halting) ID of a CTS has appeared or not from the outside of the RPCA. Note that, if the rewritten string becomes an empty string, then a delimiter also disappears, and hence it is also recognizable.   □

11.3.2 98-state universal RPCA with finite configurations

Here, we investigate the problem of constructing a simple Turing universal one-dimensional RPCA with finite configurations. We show such an RPCA with 98 states that can simulate any CTSH exists.

Theorem 11.4. *[16] There is a 98-state one-dimensional three-neighbor RPCA P_{98} with finite configurations that can simulate any cyclic tag system with halting condition.*

Proof. The RPCA P_{98} is given as follows.

$$P_{98} = (\mathbb{Z},(L,C,R),(1,0,-1),f_{98},(\#,\#,\#))$$
$$L = \{\#,e\}$$
$$C = \{\#,Y,N,+,-,\bullet,Y_1\}$$
$$R = \{\#,y,n,+,-,*,e\}$$

Since $|L| = 2$ and $|C| = |R| = 7$, it has 98 states. The local function f_{98} is as below.

$$
\begin{array}{lll}
(1) & f_{98}(\#,c,\#) = (\#,c,\#) & \text{if } c \in \{\#,Y,N,+,-,\cdot,Y_1\} \\
(2) & f_{98}(\#,c,r) = (\#,c,r) & \text{if } c \in \{\#,Y,N\}, r \in \{y,n,+,-\} \\
(3) & f_{98}(\#,\cdot,r) = (\#,\cdot,r) & \text{if } r \in \{y,n,*,e\} \\
(4) & f_{98}(\#,Y,*) = (\#,\cdot,+) & \\
(5) & f_{98}(\#,N,*) = (\#,\cdot,-) & \\
(6) & f_{98}(\#,c,r) = (\#,r,c) & \text{if } c \in \{+,-\}, r \in \{+,-\} \\
(7) & f_{98}(\#,+,y) = (\#,Y,*) & \\
(8) & f_{98}(\#,+,n) = (\#,N,*) & \\
(9) & f_{98}(\#,\#,*) = (\#,+,y) & \\
(10) & f_{98}(\#,-,r) = (\#,-,r) & \text{if } r \in \{y,n\} \\
(11) & f_{98}(\#,N,e) = (e,N,\#) & \\
(12) & f_{98}(e,\cdot,\#) = (e,\cdot,\#) & \\
(13) & f_{98}(\#,Y,e) = (\#,Y_1,-) & \\
(14) & f_{98}(e,+,\#) = (\#,+,e) & \\
(15) & f_{98}(\#,+,e) = (e,+,\#) & \\
(16) & f_{98}(e,Y_1,\#) = (e,Y_1,\#) & \\
(17) & f_{98}(e,Y,\#) = (e,Y,y) & \\
(18) & f_{98}(e,N,\#) = (e,N,n) & \\
(19) & f_{98}(e,\#,\#) = (e,\#,-) & \\
(20) & f_{98}(e,+,e) = (e,+,+) & \\
(21) & f_{98}(\#,Y_1,+) = (\#,Y_1,e) & \\
(22) & f_{98}(\#,Y_1,-) = (\#,Y_1,*) & \\
(23) & f_{98}(\#,Y_1,r) = (\#,Y_1,r) & \text{if } r \in \{y,n\}
\end{array}
$$

It is easy to verify that f_{98} is injective, since there is no pair of rules whose right-hand sides are the same. Hence, P_{98} is reversible.

Let $\hat{C} = (k,(\text{halt},w_1,\ldots,w_{k-1}))$ be a CTSH, and $v \in \{Y,N\}^*$ be an initial string. Let $\hat{\varphi} : \{Y,N\}^* \rightarrow \{(\#,Y,\#),(\#,N,\#)\}^*$ be a homomorphism defined by $\hat{\varphi}(Y) = (\#,Y,\#)$, $\hat{\varphi}(N) = (\#,N,\#)$. Then, set the initial configuration of P_{98} as follows.

$$
{}^{\omega}((\#,\#,\#))\ (\#,+,e)(e,+,\#)\ \hat{\varphi}(w_{k-1}^R)(\#,\#,\#) \cdots \hat{\varphi}(w_1^R)(\#,\#,\#)
$$
$$
(\#,\#,\#)(\#,Y_1,e)\ \hat{\varphi}(v)\ (\#,-,\#)\ ((\#,\#,\#))^{\omega}
$$

Starting from this configuration, P_{98} simulates $\hat{C}$ with v step by step until $\hat{C}$ halts.

We explain how P_{98} simulates a CTHS by the following example $\hat{C}_0$ with an initial string NYY.

$$
\hat{C}_0 = (3,(\text{halt},NY,YY))
$$

The initial configuration of P_{98} is as follows (see also the first row of Fig. 11.5).

$$
{}^{\omega}((\#,\#,\#))\ (\#,+,e)(e,+,\#)\ (\#,Y,\#)(\#,Y,\#)(\#,\#,\#)\ (\#,Y,\#)(\#,N,\#)(\#,\#,\#)
$$
$$
(\#,\#,\#)(\#,Y_1,e)\ (\#,N,\#)(\#,Y,\#)(\#,Y,\#)\ (\#,-,\#)\ ((\#,\#,\#))^{\omega}
$$

From this configuration, P_{98} simulates the complete computing process $(NYY,0)$ $\Rightarrow (YY,1) \Rightarrow (YNY,2) \Rightarrow (NYYY,0) \Rightarrow (YYY,1) \Rightarrow (YYNY,2) \Rightarrow (YNYYY,0)$ as shown in Fig. 11.5.

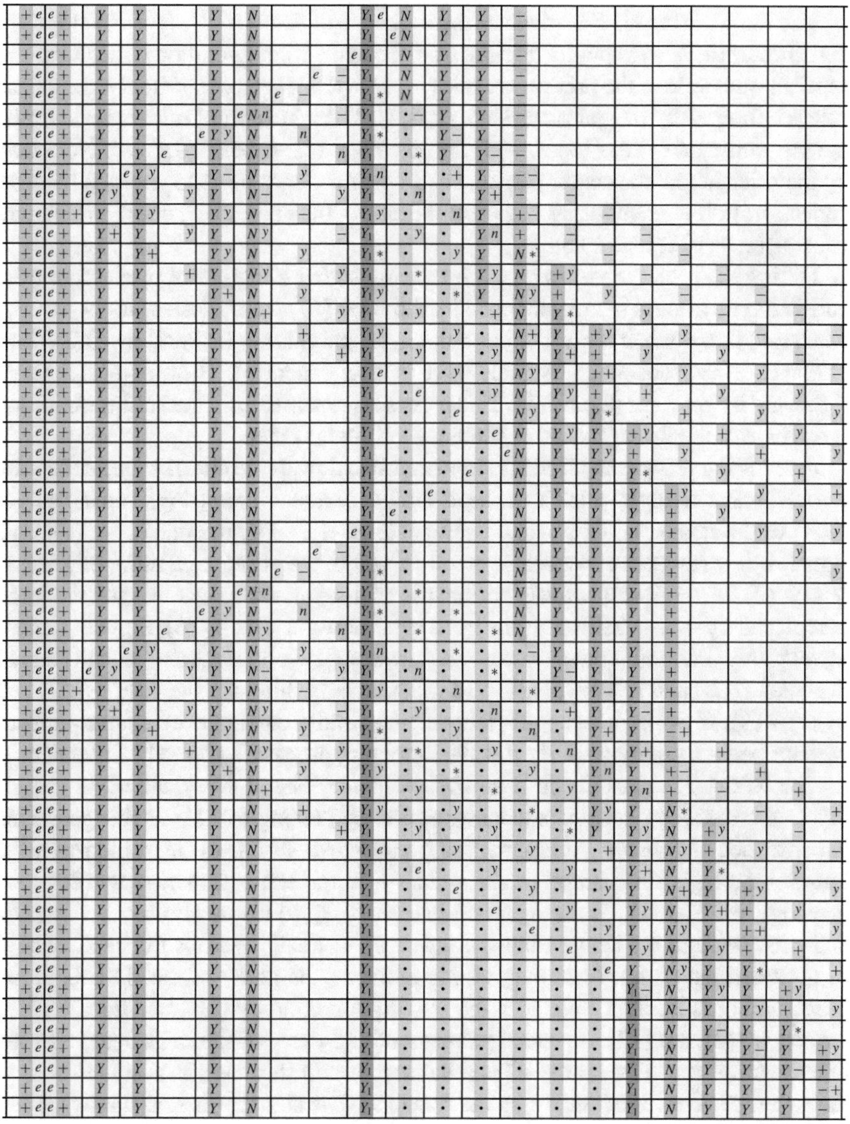

Fig. 11.5 Simulating a complete computing process of the CTSH $\hat{C}_0$ with the initial string NYY by the RPCA P_{98}. It simulates $(NYY,0) \Rightarrow (YY,1) \Rightarrow (YNY,2) \Rightarrow (NYYY,0) \Rightarrow (YYY,1) \Rightarrow (YYNY,2) \Rightarrow (YNYYY,0)$. The state # is indicated by a blank

The initial string NYY is given as the sequence of states $(\#,N,\#)(\#,Y,\#)(\#,Y,\#)$. A delimiter $(\#,-,\#)$ is put to the right of it. To make a configuration finite, a "prototype" of one cycle of the production rules is given to the left of the initial string. Each rule is delimited by the quiescent state $(\#,\#,\#)$. The whole set of rules is bounded by the left end-marker $(\#,+,e)(e,+,\#)$ and the right end-marker $(\#,Y_1,\#)$. Note that, by the rules in (1), the center part of a cell never changes its state unless it receives signals from the neighboring cells. By the rules (14) and (15), the left end-marker $(\#,+,e)(e,+,\#)$ is also stable.

Hitting the prototype rules by a left-moving signal e, signals of production rules consisting of y,n and $-$ are generated by the rules $(17)-(19)$. Later, the signal $-$ is converted into $*$ when it goes through the right end-marker $(\#,Y_1,\#)$ by (22). Thus, in this case, the sequence of signals $**ny*yy$ is generated. These signals are sent rightward by the rules (2) and (3). This process is repeated until the halting condition (i.e., ID is of the form $(Yv,0)$ for some $v \in \{Y,N\}^*$) is met.

A rewriting process in CTSH is simulated as below. If the signal $*$ meets the state Y (or N, respectively), which is the head symbol of a rewritten string, then it changes Y (N) to the state $\bullet$, and the signal itself becomes $+$ $(-)$ by the rule (4) or (5). This signal $+$ $(-$, respectively) goes rightward through the string consisting of Y's and N's by (2). If $+$ $(-$, respectively) meets the center-part state $+$ or $-$, then the latter is replaced by $+$ $(-)$ indicating the head symbol was Y (N) by (6). Signals y and n travel rightward until it meets $+$ or $-$. If y (n, respectively) meets $+$, then the signal becomes Y (N) and is fixed at this position, and $+$ is shifted to the right by one cell by $(7)-(9)$. If y or n meets $-$, then the signal simply continues to travel rightward without being fixed by (10). By this, the rewriting process is correctly simulated.

The RPCA P_{98} must check if an ID is a halting one at every end of a cycle. If this is the case, P_{98} keeps a subconfiguration containing this ID unchanged. This is performed as follows. After generating the signals of one cycle of the rules, the left-moving signal e changes to the signal $+$ at the left end-marker by (20), and goes rightward by (2). At the right end-marker $(\#,Y_1,\#)$ it again becomes e by (21), and goes through the cells of the state $(\#,\cdot,\#)$. It finally reaches the head symbol of the rewritten string. Note that, at this moment, the phase of the ID is 0. If the head symbol is N, then e changes the moving direction by (11), and goes back to the left by (2) and (12) to generate signals of one cycle of the rules again. On the other hand, if it is Y, then the ID is a halting one. In this case, Y becomes Y_1, and the signal e is converted into $-$ by the rule (13). The signal $-$ is sent rightward. By this, the halting ID is kept unchanged in the configuration of P_{98}.

The encoding and decoding functions c and d are similarly defined as in the case of Theorem 11.3. By above, we can see that any CTSH can be simulated in P_{98} with finite configurations. $\square$

11.4 Reversible and Number-Conserving CAs

The conservation law is another important property in physics besides reversibility. In most physical systems, some quantity, such as mass, energy, momentum, or others, is conserved throughout their evolution process. A number-conserving CA (NCCA) is an abstract model of such physical systems. In an NCCA, cells' states are represented by non-negative integers, and the sum of them in a configuration is kept constant even if it changes its configuration.

In this section, we study one-dimensional CAs that have both properties of reversibility and conservativeness. They are called *reversible number-conserving CAs* (RNCCAs). Although RNCCAs are a very restricted subclass of CAs, its behavior can be complex if we increase the neighborhood size and the number of states slightly. Here, we show that for any given two-neighbor s-state RPCA we can construct a four-neighbor $4s$-state RNCCA that simulates the former (Theorem 11.6). Since it was shown that a Turing universal one-dimensional two-neighbor 24-state RPCA exists (Theorem 11.3), we obtain a Turing universal one-dimensional four-neighbor 96-state RNCCA (Theorem 11.7).

11.4.1 Number-conserving CAs

In [4, 6], three kinds of number-conservation are defined. They are finite-number-conservation, periodic-number-conservation, and (general) number-conservation, which are defined for CAs with finite configurations, periodic configurations, and infinite configurations, respectively. In this section, we consider one-dimensional CAs. We assume a given CA is of the form $A = (\mathbb{Z}, Q, \{n_1, \ldots, n_m\}, f, 0)$ such that $Q = \{0, \ldots, s-1\}$ $(s \in \mathbb{Z}_+)$, and F is its global function. Note that the state 0 is assigned to the quiescent state. We denote the blank configuration by $\mathbf{0}$, i.e., $\forall x \in \mathbb{Z}$ $(\mathbf{0}(x) = 0)$.

Definition 11.4. A one-dimensional CA $A = (\mathbb{Z}, Q, \{n_1, \ldots, n_m\}, f, 0)$ is called a *finite-number-conserving CA*, if the following condition holds.

$$\forall \alpha \in \text{Conf}_{\text{fin}}(A): \sum_{x \in \mathbb{Z}} \alpha(x) = \sum_{x \in \mathbb{Z}} F(\alpha)(x)$$

Note that, since α is finite, the above summation values are always finite.

In the case of periodic configurations, it is called periodic-number-conserving if the total of the states in one period is conserved.

Definition 11.5. Let $A = (\mathbb{Z}, Q, \{n_1, \ldots, n_m\}, f, 0)$ be a one-dimensional CA, and $\text{Conf}_p(A)$ be the set of all periodic configurations of A, i.e.,

$$\text{Conf}_p(A) = \{\alpha \mid \alpha : \mathbb{Z} \to Q \wedge \exists p \in \mathbb{Z}_+ \, \forall x \in \mathbb{Z} \, (\alpha(x) = \alpha(x+p))\}.$$

Let p_α denote the period of $\alpha \in \mathrm{Conf}_\mathrm{p}(A)$. The CA A is called a *periodic-number-conserving CA*, if the following condition holds.

$$\forall \alpha \in \mathrm{Conf}_\mathrm{p}(A): \ \sum_{x=0}^{p_\alpha-1} \alpha(x) = \sum_{x=0}^{p_\alpha-1} F(\alpha)(x)$$

The notion of number-conservation is defined even for infinite configurations as in the next definition.

Definition 11.6. A one-dimensional CA $A = (\mathbb{Z}, Q, \{n_1, \ldots, n_m\}, f, 0)$ is called a *number-conserving CA*, if the following condition holds.

$$\forall \alpha \in (\mathrm{Conf}(A) - \{\mathbf{0}\}): \ \lim_{n \to \infty} \frac{\sum_{x=-n}^{n} F(\alpha)(x)}{\sum_{x=-n}^{n} \alpha(x)} = 1$$

Durand, Formenti, and Róka [4] proved that the three notions of finite-number-conservation, periodic-number-conservation, and number-conservation are all equivalent.

Theorem 11.5. *[4] Let $A = (\mathbb{Z}, Q, \{n_1, \ldots, n_m\}, f, 0)$ be a one-dimensional CA such that $Q = \{0, \ldots, s-1\}$ ($s \in \mathbb{N} - \{0\}$). Then, the following statements are equivalent.*

(1) The CA A is finite-number-conserving.
(2) The CA A is periodic-number-conserving.
(3) The CA A is number-conserving.

Hereafter, a CA that satisfies either of the conditions given in Definitions 11.4–11.6 is simply called a *number-conserving cellular automaton* (NCCA).

Note that the notion of number-conservation has a similarity to the notion of bit-conservation in Fredkin gate (Sect. 4.1.1). In fact, in a circuit composed of Fredkin gates, the total number of signal 1's is always conserved.

A reversible NCCA is one that satisfies the both conditions for reversibility and number-conservation.

Definition 11.7. Let $A = (\mathbb{Z}, Q, \{n_1, \ldots, n_m\}, f, 0)$ be an NCCA. If A is reversible, it is called a *reversible number-conserving CA* (RNCCA).

Example 11.4. Consider the elementary cellular automaton (ECA) of rule 184 (see also Example 10.3 for ECA).

$$\mathrm{ECA}_{184} = (\mathbb{Z}, \{0, 1\}, (-1, 0, 1), f_{184}, 0)$$

The local function f_{184} of ECA_{184} is as below.

$$\begin{aligned}
f_{184}(0,0,0) &= 0 & \quad f_{184}(0,0,1) &= 0 \\
f_{184}(0,1,0) &= 0 & \quad f_{184}(0,1,1) &= 1 \\
f_{184}(1,0,0) &= 1 & \quad f_{184}(1,0,1) &= 1 \\
f_{184}(1,1,0) &= 0 & \quad f_{184}(1,1,1) &= 1
\end{aligned}$$

An example of its evolution process is shown in Fig. 11.6. It is known as the simplest model of car traffic (see [24] for cellular automaton models of car traffic). The states 0 and 1 correspond to non-existence and existence of a car, respectively. Cars move rightward as a whole. The local function f_{184} can be interpreted as follows. Assume a car exists at the position x at time t. If the cell at the position $x + 1$ is vacant at time t, then the car moves to the position $x + 1$ at $t + 1$. But, if the cell at $x + 1$ is occupied by another car, then the car keeps the same position x also at time $t + 1$. By this, we can see that the total number of cars in a finite configuration is kept constant, and thus ECA$_{184}$ is an NCCA (its exact proof is found in [1]).

However, ECA$_{184}$ is not reversible, since there are distinct configurations that go to the same configuration. For example,

$$F_{184}(^{\omega}0\ 0110\ 0^{\omega}) = F_{184}(^{\omega}0\ 1010\ 0^{\omega}) = {}^{\omega}0\ 0101\ 0^{\omega}$$

holds, where F_{184} is the global function of ECA$_{184}$.   □

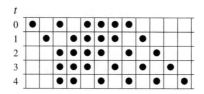

Fig. 11.6 An evolution process of the ECA rule 184. It is a simple example of an NCCA, and is known as a car traffic model. The states 0 and 1 are indicated by a blank and a dot, respectively

So far, NCCAs have been extensively studied, and various properties and characterizations of them have been given [1, 4, 6, 7, 9, 12]. In [15] Moreira investigated universality and decidability of NCCAs. As for RNCCAs, Schranko and de Oliveira [26] made an experimental study on one-dimensional RNCCAs, and showed that an s-state n-neighbor RNCCA rule can be decomposed into s-state two-neighbor RNCCA rules when s and n are very small. García-Ramos [8] proved that, in the two-neighbor case (i.e., radius 1/2), every RNCCA is a *shift-identity product cellular automaton* (SIPCA). An SIPCA is an RNCCA composed of "shift CAs" in which all signals are right-moving, and "identity CAs" in which all signals are stationary. Hence, in general, an SIPCA has both right-moving and stationary signals, but each signal is independent to others. Namely, every right-moving signal simply goes through stationary signals without affecting them. Therefore, all the two-neighbor RNCCAs show trivial behaviors in the sense that the signals do not interact each other. On the other hand, Imai, Martin and Saito [10] showed that, in the three-neighbor case (i.e., radius 1), there are RNCCAs in which some signals can interact with others, and thus they show some nontrivial behavior. However, it is not known whether there exists a Turing universal three-neighbor RNCCA.

In this section, we investigate the four-neighbor case (i.e., radius 3/2), and prove there is a Turing universal RNCCA. We first show that for any given two-neighbor

s-state RPCA, we can construct a four-neighbor $4s$-state RNCCA that simulates the former. Since there is a Turing universal two-neighbor 24-state RPCA (Theorem 11.3), we can obtain a universal four-neighbor 96-state RNCCA.

Turing universality in a variant of a one-dimensional RNCCA was studied by Morita and Imai [23], but this CA was not in the standard framework of NCCAs, because a PCA was used as an NCCA model. Though a reversible PCA is a subclass of a standard RCA, the number-conserving property of a PCA is somehow different from an NCCA, since each cell of a PCA has several parts. Namely, each cell of a usual NCCA has a single number, but that of a number-conserving PCA has a "tuple" of numbers. Theorem 11.7 in the next subsection shows there is a Turing universal RNCCA in the standard framework of an NCCA.

11.4.2 Turing universal reversible and number-conserving CA

We show any two-neighbor RPCA can be converted into a four-neighbor RNCCA. By this, we obtain a Turing universal four-neighbor RNCCA.

Theorem 11.6. *[20] For any one-dimensional two-neighbor RPCA $P = (\mathbb{Z}, (C, R)$, $(0, -1), f)$, we can construct a one-dimensional four-neighbor RNCCA A that simulates P and has $4|C| \cdot |R|$ states.*

Proof. An RNCCA A that simulates P is given as follows.

$$A = (\mathbb{Z}, \tilde{Q}, (-2, -1, 0, 1), \tilde{f}, 0),$$

where $\tilde{Q} = \{0, 1, \ldots, 4|C| \cdot |R| - 1\}$.

We need some preparations to define $\tilde{f}$. Let $\hat{C}, \check{C}, \tilde{C}, \hat{R}, \check{R}$, and $\tilde{R}$ be as follows.

$$\begin{aligned}
\hat{C} &= \{2k|R| \mid k = 0, 1, \ldots, |C| - 1\} \\
\check{C} &= \{2(k + |C|)|R| \mid k = 0, 1, \ldots, |C| - 1\} \\
\tilde{C} &= \hat{C} \cup \check{C} \\
\hat{R} &= \{k \mid k = 0, 1, \ldots, |R| - 1\} \\
\check{R} &= \{k + |R| \mid k = 0, 1, \ldots, |R| - 1\} \\
\tilde{R} &= \hat{R} \cup \check{R}
\end{aligned}$$

Each element $\tilde{c} \in \tilde{C}$ ($\tilde{r} \in \tilde{R}$, respectively) is called a *heavy* (*light*) *particle*, which is a stationary (right-moving) particle in A as explained later. The number $\tilde{c}$ ($\tilde{r}$, respectively) itself can be regarded as the mass of the heavy (light) particle. (Note that readers may think it strange that the particle of mass 0 is both heavy and light. Though the mass 0 could be considered as non-existence of a particle, we employ here the above interpretation for simplicity.) Clearly every element $\tilde{q} \in \tilde{Q}$ is uniquely decomposed into a heavy particle and a light particle, and thus the following holds.

$$\begin{aligned}
&\forall \tilde{q} \in \tilde{Q}, \exists \tilde{c} \in \tilde{C}, \exists \tilde{r} \in \tilde{R} \ (\tilde{q} = \tilde{c} + \tilde{r}) \\
&\forall \tilde{c}_1, \tilde{c}_2 \in \tilde{C}, \forall \tilde{r}_1, \tilde{r}_2 \in \tilde{R} \ (\tilde{c}_1 + \tilde{r}_1 = \tilde{c}_2 + \tilde{r}_2 \Rightarrow \tilde{c}_1 = \tilde{c}_2 \wedge \tilde{r}_1 = \tilde{r}_2)
\end{aligned}$$

We can thus regard each cell of A has a heavy particle and a light particle. We define the following functions $\tilde{p}_C : \tilde{Q} \to \tilde{C}$, and $\tilde{p}_R : \tilde{Q} \to \tilde{R}$, which give a heavy particle, and a light particle associated with a given $\tilde{q} \in \tilde{Q}$.

$$\forall \tilde{q} \in \tilde{Q}, \ \forall \tilde{c} \in \tilde{C} \ (\tilde{p}_C(\tilde{q}) = \tilde{c} \ \Leftrightarrow \ \exists \tilde{r} \in \tilde{R} \ (\tilde{q} = \tilde{c} + \tilde{r}))$$
$$\forall \tilde{q} \in \tilde{Q}, \ \forall \tilde{r} \in \tilde{R} \ (\tilde{p}_R(\tilde{q}) = \tilde{r} \ \Leftrightarrow \ \exists \tilde{c} \in \tilde{C} \ (\tilde{q} = \tilde{c} + \tilde{r}))$$

A pair of heavy particles $(\hat{c}, \check{c}) \in \hat{C} \times \check{C}$ (light particles $(\hat{r}, \check{r}) \in \hat{R} \times \check{R}$, respectively) is called a *complementary pair*, if $\hat{c} + \check{c} = 2(2|C| - 1)|R|$ ($\hat{r} + \check{r} = 2|R| - 1$). In the following, a complementary pair of heavy (light, respectively) particles is used to simulate a state in C (R). A pair of states $(\tilde{q}_1, \tilde{q}_2) \in \tilde{Q}^2$ is called *balanced with respect to heavy (light, respectively) particles* if $(\tilde{p}_C(\tilde{q}_1), \tilde{p}_C(\tilde{q}_2))$ $((\tilde{p}_R(\tilde{q}_1), \tilde{p}_R(\tilde{q}_2)))$ is a complementary pair. The set of all balanced pairs of states $(\tilde{q}_1, \tilde{q}_2)$ with respect to heavy (light, respectively) particles is denoted by B_C (B_R), i.e.,

$$B_C = \{(\tilde{q}_1, \tilde{q}_2) \in \tilde{Q}^2 \mid (\tilde{p}_C(\tilde{q}_1), \tilde{p}_C(\tilde{q}_2)) \in \hat{C} \times \check{C}$$
$$\wedge \ \tilde{p}_C(\tilde{q}_1) + \tilde{p}_C(\tilde{q}_2) = 2(2|C| - 1)|R| \},$$
$$B_R = \{(\tilde{q}_1, \tilde{q}_2) \in \tilde{Q}^2 \mid (\tilde{p}_R(\tilde{q}_1), \tilde{p}_R(\tilde{q}_2)) \in \hat{R} \times \check{R}$$
$$\wedge \ \tilde{p}_R(\tilde{q}_1) + \tilde{p}_R(\tilde{q}_2) = 2|R| - 1 \}.$$

It is easy to see that, for any $\tilde{\alpha} \in \mathrm{Conf}(A)$ and $x \in \mathbb{Z}$, the following relations hold.

$$(\tilde{\alpha}(x), \tilde{\alpha}(x+1)) \in B_C \ \Rightarrow \ (\tilde{\alpha}(x-1), \tilde{\alpha}(x)) \notin B_C \wedge (\tilde{\alpha}(x+1), \tilde{\alpha}(x+2)) \notin B_C$$
$$(\tilde{\alpha}(x), \tilde{\alpha}(x+1)) \in B_R \ \Rightarrow \ (\tilde{\alpha}(x-1), \tilde{\alpha}(x)) \notin B_R \wedge (\tilde{\alpha}(x+1), \tilde{\alpha}(x+2)) \notin B_R$$

We now choose bijections $\hat{\varphi}_C : C \to \hat{C}$, and $\hat{\varphi}_R : R \to \hat{R}$ arbitrarily, and fix them hereafter. Then define the bijections $\check{\varphi}_C : C \to \check{C}$, $\check{\varphi}_R : R \to \check{R}$, $\hat{\varphi} : C \times R \to \hat{Q}$, and $\check{\varphi} : C \times R \to \check{Q}$ as follows, where $\hat{Q} = \{\hat{c} + \hat{r} \mid \hat{c} \in \hat{C}, \hat{r} \in \hat{R}\}$, and $\check{Q} = \{\check{c} + \check{r} \mid \check{c} \in \check{C}, \check{r} \in \check{R}\}$.

$$\forall c \in C \ (\check{\varphi}_C(c) = 2(2|C| - 1)|R| - \hat{\varphi}_C(c))$$
$$\forall r \in R \ (\check{\varphi}_R(r) = 2|R| - 1 - \hat{\varphi}_R(r))$$
$$\forall c \in C, \forall r \in R \ (\hat{\varphi}(c, r) = \hat{\varphi}_C(c) + \hat{\varphi}_R(r))$$
$$\forall c \in C, \forall r \in R \ (\check{\varphi}(c, r) = \check{\varphi}_C(c) + \check{\varphi}_R(r))$$

Now, $\tilde{f} : \tilde{Q}^4 \to \tilde{Q}$ is defined as follows.

$$\tilde{f}(\tilde{q}_{-2}, \tilde{q}_{-1}, \tilde{q}_0, \tilde{q}_1) = \begin{cases} \hat{\varphi}(f(\hat{\varphi}_C^{-1}(\tilde{p}_C(\tilde{q}_0)), \hat{\varphi}_R^{-1}(\tilde{p}_R(\tilde{q}_{-1})))) \\ \quad \text{if } (\tilde{q}_{-1}, \tilde{q}_0) \in B_R \wedge (\tilde{q}_0, \tilde{q}_1) \in B_C \\ \check{\varphi}(f(\hat{\varphi}_C^{-1}(\tilde{p}_C(\tilde{q}_{-1})), \hat{\varphi}_R^{-1}(\tilde{p}_R(\tilde{q}_{-2})))) \\ \quad \text{if } (\tilde{q}_{-2}, \tilde{q}_{-1}) \in B_R \wedge (\tilde{q}_{-1}, \tilde{q}_0) \in B_C \\ \tilde{p}_C(\tilde{q}_0) + \tilde{p}_R(\tilde{q}_{-1}) \\ \quad \text{elsewhere} \end{cases} \quad (11.1)$$

Let $\tilde{F}$ be the global function induced by $\tilde{f}$. For any configuration $\tilde{\alpha} \in \mathrm{Conf}(A)$, and for any $y \in \mathbb{Z}$, the value $\tilde{F}(\tilde{\alpha})(y)$ is as follows. If $(\tilde{\alpha}(y-1), \tilde{\alpha}(y)) \in B_R \wedge (\tilde{\alpha}(y), \tilde{\alpha}(y+1)) \in B_C$, then

$$\tilde{F}(\tilde{\alpha})(y) = \hat{\phi}(f(\hat{\phi}_C^{-1}(\tilde{p}_C(\tilde{\alpha}(y))), \hat{\phi}_R^{-1}(\tilde{p}_R(\tilde{\alpha}(y-1))))), \qquad (11.2)$$

$$\tilde{F}(\tilde{\alpha})(y+1) = \check{\phi}(f(\hat{\phi}_C^{-1}(\tilde{p}_C(\tilde{\alpha}(y))), \hat{\phi}_R^{-1}(\tilde{p}_R(\tilde{\alpha}(y-1))))). \qquad (11.3)$$

It means that the complementary pairs $(\tilde{p}_R(\tilde{\alpha}(y-1)), \tilde{p}_R(\tilde{\alpha}(y)))$ and $(\tilde{p}_C(\tilde{\alpha}(y)),$ $\tilde{p}_C(\tilde{\alpha}(y+1)))$ interact each other, and the state transition of the RPCA P is simulated. Thus, the new complementary pair of heavy particles $(\tilde{p}_C(\tilde{F}(\tilde{\alpha})(y)),$ $\tilde{p}_C(\tilde{F}(\tilde{\alpha})(y+1)))$ is created at the same position as before, while the pair of light particles $(\tilde{p}_R(\tilde{F}(\tilde{\alpha})(y)), \tilde{p}_R(\tilde{F}(\tilde{\alpha})(y+1)))$ appears at the position shifted rightward by one cell. On the other hand, if $\neg((\tilde{\alpha}(y-2), \tilde{\alpha}(y-1)) \in B_R \wedge (\tilde{\alpha}(y-1),$ $\tilde{\alpha}(y)) \in B_C)) \wedge \neg((\tilde{\alpha}(y-1), \tilde{\alpha}(y)) \in B_R \wedge (\tilde{\alpha}(y), \tilde{\alpha}(y+1)) \in B_C))$, then

$$\tilde{F}(\tilde{\alpha})(y) = \tilde{p}_C(\tilde{\alpha}(y)) + \tilde{p}_R(\tilde{\alpha}(y-1)). \qquad (11.4)$$

The above means the light particle $\tilde{p}_R(\tilde{\alpha}(y-1))$ simply moves rightward without interacting with the stationary heavy particle $\tilde{p}_C(\tilde{\alpha}(y))$. From (11.2) – (11.4), it is easy to see that the following holds for all $x \in \mathbb{Z}$.

$$(\tilde{\alpha}(x), \tilde{\alpha}(x+1)) \in B_C \Leftrightarrow (\tilde{F}(\tilde{\alpha})(x), \tilde{F}(\tilde{\alpha})(x+1)) \in B_C \qquad (11.5)$$

$$(\tilde{\alpha}(x), \tilde{\alpha}(x+1)) \in B_R \Leftrightarrow (\tilde{F}(\tilde{\alpha})(x+1), \tilde{F}(\tilde{\alpha})(x+2)) \in B_R \qquad (11.6)$$

First, we show that A can simulate P correctly as described below. After that, we will show A is an RNCCA. We define an encoding function $\gamma : \mathrm{Conf}(P) \to \mathrm{Conf}(A)$ as follows, where $\alpha \in \mathrm{Conf}(P)$ and $x \in \mathbb{Z}$. Note that, in this case, γ is an encoding function defined on the set of all configurations of P rather than one of $\mathrm{Conf}_{up}(P) \to$ $\mathrm{Conf}_{up}(A)$ as in Definition 11.2.

$$\gamma(\alpha)(2x) = \hat{\phi}(\alpha(x)) \qquad (11.7)$$

$$\gamma(\alpha)(2x+1) = \check{\phi}(\alpha(x)) \qquad (11.8)$$

The configuration α in P is represented by the configuration $\gamma(\alpha)$ in A (see Fig. 11.7). Note that, by (11.7) and (11.8), the configuration $\gamma(\alpha)$ is ultimately periodic even if $\alpha \in \mathrm{Conf}(P)$ is finite. We can see $(\tilde{p}_C(\gamma(\alpha)(2x)), \tilde{p}_C(\gamma(\alpha)(2x+1))) \in$ B_C. But, $(\tilde{p}_R(\gamma(\alpha)(2x-1)), \tilde{p}_R(\gamma(\alpha)(2x))) \notin B_R$ for any $x \in \mathbb{Z}$. Therefore, by the equation (11.4) we have the following.

$$\tilde{F}(\gamma(\alpha))(2x) = \tilde{p}_C(\hat{\phi}(\alpha(x))) + \tilde{p}_R(\check{\phi}(\alpha(x-1)))$$

$$\tilde{F}(\gamma(\alpha))(2x+1) = \tilde{p}_C(\check{\phi}(\alpha(x))) + \tilde{p}_R(\hat{\phi}(\alpha(x)))$$

By above, we can observe $(\tilde{p}_C(\tilde{F}(\gamma(\alpha))(2x)), \tilde{p}_C(\tilde{F}(\gamma(\alpha))(2x+1))) \in B_C$ and $(\tilde{p}_R(\tilde{F}(\gamma(\alpha))(2x-1)), \tilde{p}_R(\tilde{F}(\gamma(\alpha))(2x))) \in B_R$, and thus the following holds by (11.2) and (11.3), where $p_C : C \times R \to C$ and $p_R : C \times R \to R$ are projection functions, and F is the global function of P.

$$\tilde{F}^2(\gamma(\alpha))(2x) = \hat{\phi}(f(\hat{\phi}_C^{-1}(\tilde{p}_C(\hat{\phi}(\alpha(x)))), \hat{\phi}_R^{-1}(\tilde{p}_R(\check{\phi}(\alpha(x-1))))))$$

$$= \hat{\phi}(f(p_C(\alpha(x)), p_R(\alpha(x-1))))$$

$$
\begin{aligned}
&= \hat{\varphi}(F(\alpha)(x)) \\
&= \gamma(F(\alpha))(2x) \\
\tilde{F}^2(\gamma(\alpha))(2x+1) &= \check{\varphi}(f(\hat{\varphi}_C^{-1}(\tilde{p}_C(\hat{\varphi}(\alpha(x)))), \hat{\varphi}_R^{-1}(\tilde{p}_R(\hat{\varphi}(\alpha(x-1)))))) \\
&= \check{\varphi}(f(p_C(\alpha(x)), p_R(\alpha(x-1)))) \\
&= \check{\varphi}(F(\alpha)(x)) \\
&= \gamma(F(\alpha))(2x+1)
\end{aligned}
$$

Thus, each evolution step of a configuration of P is correctly simulated by A in two steps under the encoding γ. Its simulation process is shown in Fig. 11.7.

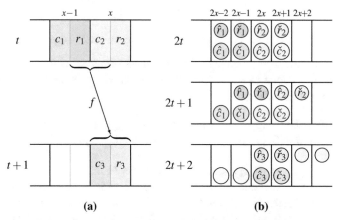

(a)   (b)

Fig. 11.7 A simulation process of **(a)** a two-neighbor RPCA P by **(b)** a four-neighbor RNCCA A. The configuration of A at time $2t$ is obtained from that of P at time t by the encoding function γ. Here, $(\hat{c}_i, \check{c}_i)$ and $(\hat{r}_i, \check{r}_i)$ $(i = 1, 2, 3)$ are complementary pairs, and thus $\hat{c}_i + \check{c}_i = 2(2|C| - 1)|R|$ and $\hat{r}_i + \check{r}_i = 2|R| - 1$

Next, we show that A is an NCCA. From the equation (11.1), we can see mass of a particle is transferred within a complementary pair, or simply shifted rightward, or does not change. Therefore, it is intuitively obvious that A is an NCCA. But, here we prove A satisfies the condition of finite-number-conservation (Definition 11.4). Let $\tilde{\alpha} \in \text{Conf}_{\text{fin}}(A)$. First, from (11.2) – (11.4), we can derive the following.

$$
\begin{aligned}
&(\tilde{\alpha}(x), \tilde{\alpha}(x+1)) \in B_C \\
&\quad \Rightarrow \tilde{p}_C(\tilde{\alpha}(x)) + \tilde{p}_C(\tilde{\alpha}(x+1)) = \tilde{p}_C(\tilde{F}(\tilde{\alpha})(x)) + \tilde{p}_C(\tilde{F}(\tilde{\alpha})(x+1)) \\
&(\tilde{\alpha}(x-1), \tilde{\alpha}(x)) \notin B_C \wedge (\tilde{\alpha}(x), \tilde{\alpha}(x+1)) \notin B_C \\
&\quad \Rightarrow \tilde{p}_C(\tilde{\alpha}(x)) = \tilde{p}_C(\tilde{F}(\tilde{\alpha})(x)) \\
&(\tilde{\alpha}(x), \tilde{\alpha}(x+1)) \in B_R \\
&\quad \Rightarrow \tilde{p}_R(\tilde{\alpha}(x)) + \tilde{p}_R(\tilde{\alpha}(x+1)) = \tilde{p}_R(\tilde{F}(\tilde{\alpha})(x+1)) + \tilde{p}_R(\tilde{F}(\tilde{\alpha})(x+2)) \\
&(\tilde{\alpha}(x-1), \tilde{\alpha}(x)) \notin B_R \wedge (\tilde{\alpha}(x), \tilde{\alpha}(x+1)) \notin B_R \\
&\quad \Rightarrow \tilde{p}_R(\tilde{\alpha}(x)) = \tilde{p}_R(\tilde{F}(\tilde{\alpha})(x+1))
\end{aligned}
$$

By above, for each n $(= 2,3,\ldots)$, there exist n_0, n_1 and n_2 such that $n_i \in \{n, n - 1\}$ $(i = 0,1,2)$, and $n_3 \in \{n-1, n-2\}$ that satisfy the following relations.

$$\sum_{x=-n_0}^{n_1} \tilde{p}_C(\tilde{\alpha}(x)) = \sum_{x=-n_0}^{n_1} \tilde{p}_C(\tilde{F}(\tilde{\alpha})(x)) \tag{11.9}$$

$$\sum_{x=-n_2}^{n_3} \tilde{p}_R(\tilde{\alpha}(x)) = \sum_{x=-n_2+1}^{n_3+1} \tilde{p}_R(\tilde{F}(\tilde{\alpha})(x)) \tag{11.10}$$

Hence, by (11.9) and (11.10) the following equation holds, since $\tilde{\alpha} \in \mathrm{Conf}_{\mathrm{fin}}(A)$.

$$\forall \tilde{\alpha} \in \mathrm{Conf}(A): \sum_{x\in\mathbb{Z}} \tilde{\alpha}(x) = \sum_{x\in\mathbb{Z}} \tilde{F}(\tilde{\alpha})(x)$$

Therefore, A is finite-number-conserving, and thus an NCCA by Theorem 11.5.

Finally, we show A is reversible. On the contrary we assume it is not. Thus, there are two configurations $\tilde{\alpha}_1, \tilde{\alpha}_2 \in \mathrm{Conf}(A)$ such that $\tilde{\alpha}_1 \neq \tilde{\alpha}_2$ and $\tilde{F}(\tilde{\alpha}_1) = \tilde{F}(\tilde{\alpha}_2)$. First, we note the following.

$$\forall x \in \mathbb{Z} \, ((\tilde{\alpha}_1(x), \tilde{\alpha}_1(x+1)) \in B_C \Leftrightarrow (\tilde{\alpha}_2(x), \tilde{\alpha}_2(x+1)) \in B_C)$$
$$\forall x \in \mathbb{Z} \, ((\tilde{\alpha}_1(x), \tilde{\alpha}_1(x+1)) \in B_R \Leftrightarrow (\tilde{\alpha}_2(x), \tilde{\alpha}_2(x+1)) \in B_R)$$

If otherwise, $\tilde{F}(\tilde{\alpha}_1) \neq \tilde{F}(\tilde{\alpha}_2)$ holds by the relations (11.5) and (11.6), and it contradicts the assumption. Since $\tilde{\alpha}_1 \neq \tilde{\alpha}_2$, there exists $x_0 \in \mathbb{Z}$ such that $\tilde{p}_C(\tilde{\alpha}_1(x_0)) \neq \tilde{p}_C(\tilde{\alpha}_2(x_0))$ or $\tilde{p}_R(\tilde{\alpha}_1(x_0)) \neq \tilde{p}_R(\tilde{\alpha}_2(x_0))$. Here, we prove it only for the case $\tilde{p}_C(\tilde{\alpha}_1(x_0)) \neq \tilde{p}_C(\tilde{\alpha}_2(x_0))$, since the case $\tilde{p}_R(\tilde{\alpha}_1(x_0)) \neq \tilde{p}_R(\tilde{\alpha}_2(x_0))$ is similarly proved. There are three subcases:

(a) $(\tilde{\alpha}_i(x_0 - 1), \tilde{\alpha}_i(x_0)) \in B_R \wedge (\tilde{\alpha}_i(x_0), \tilde{\alpha}_i(x_0 + 1)) \in B_C$ $(i = 1,2)$
(b) $(\tilde{\alpha}_i(x_0 - 2), \tilde{\alpha}_i(x_0 - 1)) \in B_R \wedge (\tilde{\alpha}_i(x_0 - 1), \tilde{\alpha}_i(x_0)) \in B_C$ $(i = 1,2)$
(c) Other than the cases (a) and (b):
  $\neg((\tilde{\alpha}_i(x_0 - 1), \tilde{\alpha}_i(x_0)) \in B_R \wedge (\tilde{\alpha}_i(x_0), \tilde{\alpha}_i(x_0 + 1)) \in B_C) \wedge$
  $\neg((\tilde{\alpha}_i(x_0 - 2), \tilde{\alpha}_i(x_0 - 1)) \in B_R \wedge (\tilde{\alpha}_i(x_0 - 1), \tilde{\alpha}_i(x_0)) \in B_C)$ $(i = 1,2)$

The case (a): By (11.2), the following relations hold.

$$\tilde{F}(\tilde{\alpha}_1)(x_0) = \hat{\varphi}(f(\hat{\varphi}_C^{-1}(\tilde{p}_C(\tilde{\alpha}_1(x_0))), \hat{\varphi}_R^{-1}(\tilde{p}_R(\tilde{\alpha}_1(x_0 - 1)))))$$
$$\tilde{F}(\tilde{\alpha}_2)(x_0) = \hat{\varphi}(f(\hat{\varphi}_C^{-1}(\tilde{p}_C(\tilde{\alpha}_2(x_0))), \hat{\varphi}_R^{-1}(\tilde{p}_R(\tilde{\alpha}_2(x_0 - 1)))))$$

From the facts $\tilde{p}_C(\tilde{\alpha}_1(x_0)) \neq \tilde{p}_C(\tilde{\alpha}_2(x_0))$, φ, φ_C and φ_R are bijections, and f is a bijection (because P is a reversible PCA), $\tilde{F}(\tilde{\alpha}_1)(x_0) \neq \tilde{F}(\tilde{\alpha}_2)(x_0)$ follows. This contradicts the assumption. The case (b): Since it is similar to the case (a), we omit the proof. The case (c): By (11.4), the following relations hold.

$$\tilde{F}(\tilde{\alpha}_1)(x_0) = \tilde{p}_C(\tilde{\alpha}_1(x_0)) + \tilde{p}_R(\tilde{\alpha}_1(x_0 - 1))$$
$$\tilde{F}(\tilde{\alpha}_2)(x_0) = \tilde{p}_C(\tilde{\alpha}_2(x_0)) + \tilde{p}_R(\tilde{\alpha}_2(x_0 - 1))$$

Again $\tilde{F}(\tilde{\alpha}_1)(x_0) \neq \tilde{F}(\tilde{\alpha}_2)(x_0)$, because $\tilde{p}_C(\tilde{\alpha}_1(x_0)) \neq \tilde{p}_C(\tilde{\alpha}_2(x_0))$, and this contradicts the assumption. By above, we can conclude that A is a reversible NCCA. This completes the proof. □

In Sect. 11.3.1, it was shown that there is a Turing universal 24-state two-neighbor RPCA with ultimately periodic configurations (Theorem 11.3). By this and Theorem 11.6, we obtain the following theorem.

Theorem 11.7. *There is a Turing universal one-dimensional four-neighbor 96-state RNCCA with ultimately periodic configurations.*

In Sect. 11.2.2, a two-neighbor RPCA that simulates a given RTM was constructed (Theorem 11.2). Hence, by Theorem 11.6, we can also obtain a four-neighbor RNCCA that directly simulates an RTM. In this case, the constructed RNCCA has ultimately periodic configurations, though the simulated RPCA has finite configurations.

11.5 Concluding Remarks

In this chapter, we studied how Turing universal one-dimensional RCAs can be designed. In Sect. 11.2, methods of constructing two- and three-neighbor RPCAs with finite configurations that directly simulate RTMs were given. If the simulated RTMs are garbage-less, then the resulting RPCAs are also garbage-less.

It should be noted that, although RTMs can be simulated by traditional CAs (rather than by PCAs), it is not possible to obtain reversible CAs by this method. Of course, global functions of such CAs can be injective if we restrict them only to the configurations that are used to simulate RTMs. But, it is not guaranteed that they are injective on the set of *all* configurations. Therefore, such CAs are useless for our purpose. Our objective is to find "structurally" reversible CAs, rather than those whose global functions are injective only on a subset of configurations. The framework of PCA is not only convenient for designing RCAs, but also suited for this purpose. In fact, it is shown RPCAs can be easily implemented by reversible logic elements (Sect. 10.6), and can be further embedded in a reversible physical space (Sect. 2.2.3).

In Sect. 11.3, the problem of finding simple Turing universal one-dimensional RCAs was studied. By this, a 24-state RPCA with ultimately periodic configurations, and a 98-state RPCA with finite configurations were given, each of which can simulate any cyclic tag system. In the case of irreversible CA, it has been shown that there is a Turing universal two-state CA with ultimately periodic configurations by Cook [2]. Thus, there will be still room for improvement in the reversible case, and it is left for the future study.

In Sect. 11.4, reversible and number-conserving CAs (RNCCAs) are studied. Conservation of mass, energy, momentum, etc. is also a basic property in physical systems, as well as reversibility. RNCCA is an abstract model having both of these properties. It was proved that any two-neighbor RPCA can be converted into a four-neighbor RNCCA (Theorem 11.6). Hence, even under such a strong constraint, a one-dimensional CA can be Turing universal.

There are other research lines on the computing capabilities of one-dimensional RCAs. Dubacq [3] gave a construction method of a one-dimensional RPCA that simulates a given TM. Since his method works even if the TM is irreversible, the number of states of the RPCA is large, i.e., $2n^2(m+1)^3$ states are required to simulate an m-state n-symbol TM. Durand-Lose [5] showed a method of constructing an intrinsically universal one-dimensional RPCA. A survey paper by Ollinger [25] deals also with the universality of reversible CAs. Sutner [27] investigates the complexity of RCAs. Formal language recognition by RCAs was studied by Kutrib and Malcher [13], and by Morita [21]. The firing squad synchronization problem (FSSP) is a well-known problem on CAs. Mazoyer [14] gave a minimal time solution for FSSP by designing a six-state (irreversible) one-dimensional CA. Imai and Morita [11] investigated this problem on RCAs, and showed that it is solved on a 99-state RPCA.

References

1. Boccara, N., Fukś, H.: Number-conserving cellular automata rules. Fundam. Inform. **52**, 1–13 (2002)
2. Cook, M.: Universality in elementary cellular automata. Complex Syst. **15**, 1–40 (2004)
3. Dubacq, J.C.: How to simulate Turing machines by invertible 1D cellular automata. Int. J. Found. Comput. Sci. **6**, 395–402 (1995). doi:10.1142/S0129054195000202
4. Durand, B., Formenti, E., Róka, Z.: Number-conserving cellular automata I: decidability. Theoret. Comput. Sci. **299**, 523–535 (2003). doi:10.1016/S0304-3975(02)00534-0
5. Durand-Lose, J.O.: Intrinsic universality of a 1-dimensional reversible cellular automaton. In: Proc. STACS 97 (eds. R. Reischuk, M. Morvan), LNCS 1200, pp. 439–450 (1997)
6. Formenti, E., Grange, A.: Number conserving cellular automata II: dynamics. Theoret. Comput. Sci. **304**, 269–290 (2003). doi:10.1016/S0304-3975(03)00134-8
7. Fukś, H., Sullivan, K.: Enumeration of number-conserving cellular automata rules with two inputs. J. Cell. Autom. **2**, 141–148 (2007)
8. García-Ramos, F.: Product decomposition for surjective 2-block NCCA. In: DMTCS Proc. on Auaomata 2011, pp. 147–158 (2011)
9. Hattori, T., Takesue, S.: Additive conserved quantities in discrete-time lattice dynamical systems. Physica D **49**, 295–322 (1991). doi:10.1016/0167-2789(91)90150-8
10. Imai, K., Martin, B., Saito, R.: On radius 1 nontrivial reversible and number-conserving cellular automata. In: Proc. Reversible Computation 2012 (eds. R. Glück, T. Yokoyama), pp. 54–60 (2012)
11. Imai, K., Morita, K.: Firing squad synchronization problem in reversible cellular automata. Theoret. Comput. Sci. **165**, 475–482 (1996). doi:10.1016/0304-3975(96)00016-3
12. Kari, J., Taati, S.: Particle displacement representation for conservative laws in two-dimensional cellular automata. In: Proc. Journées Automates Cellulaires 2008 (ed. B. Durand), pp. 65–73 (2008)
13. Kutrib, M., Malcher, A.: Fast reversible language recognition using cellular automata. Inform. Comput. **206**, 1142–1151 (2008). doi:10.1016/j.ic.2008.03.015
14. Mazoyer, J.: A six-state minimal time solution to the firing squad synchronization problem. Theoret. Comput. Sci. **50**, 183–238 (1987). doi:10.1016/0304-3975(87)90124-1

15. Moreira, A.: Universality and decidability of number-conserving cellular automata. Theoret. Comput. Sci. **292**, 711–721 (2003). doi:10.1016/S0304-3975(02)00065-8

16. Morita, K.: Simple universal one-dimensional reversible cellular automata. J. Cell. Autom. **2**, 159–166 (2007)

17. Morita, K.: Reversible computing and cellular automata — A survey. Theoret. Comput. Sci. **395**, 101–131 (2008). doi:10.1016/j.tcs.2008.01.041

18. Morita, K.: Simulating reversible Turing machines and cyclic tag systems by one-dimensional reversible cellular automata. Theoret. Comput. Sci. **412**, 3856–3865 (2011). doi:10.1016/j.tcs.2011.02.022

19. Morita, K.: Reversible cellular automata. In: Handbook of Natural Computing (eds. G. Rozenberg, T. Bäck, J.N. Kok), pp. 231–257. Springer (2012). doi:10.1007/978-3-540-92910-9_7

20. Morita, K.: Universality of one-dimensional reversible and number-conserving cellular automata. In: Proc. Automata and JAC 2012 (ed. E. Formenti), EPTCS 90, pp. 142–150 (2012). doi:10.4204/EPTCS.90.12

21. Morita, K.: Language recognition by reversible partitioned cellular automata. In: Proc. Automata 2014 (eds. T. Isokawa, et al.), LNCS 8996, pp. 106–120 (2015). doi:10.1007/978-3-319-18812-6_9

22. Morita, K., Harao, M.: Computation universality of one-dimensional reversible (injective) cellular automata. Trans. IEICE Japan **E72**, 758–762 (1989)

23. Morita, K., Imai, K.: Number-conserving reversible cellular automata and their computation-universality. Theoret. Informat. Appl. **35**, 239–258 (2001). doi:10.1051/ita:2001118

24. Nagel, K., Schreckenberg, M.: A cellular automaton model for freeway traffic. Journal de Physique I **2**, 2221–2229 (1992). doi:10.1051/jp1:1992277

25. Ollinger, N.: Universalities in cellular automata. In: Handbook of Natural Computing, pp. 189–229. Springer (2012). doi:10.1007/978-3-540-92910-9_6

26. Schranko, A., de Oliveira, P.P.B.: Derivation and representation of one-dimensional, reversible, number-conserving cellular automata rules. J. Cell. Autom. **6**, 77–89 (2010)

27. Sutner, K.: The complexity of reversible cellular automata. Theoret. Comput. Sci. **325**, 317–328 (2004). doi:10.1016/j.tcs.2004.06.011

Chapter 12
Two-Dimensional Universal Reversible Cellular Automata

Abstract The problem of finding simple universal two-dimensional reversible cellular automata (RCAs) is studied. Here, three kinds of reversible partitioned CAs (RPCAs) are designed. The first two are 16-state RPCAs in which any circuit composed of Fredkin gates and delay elements is embeddable. Since a finite control and a tape cell of a reversible Turing machine can be composed of Fredkin gates and delay elements, these RPCAs with horizontally ultimately periodic configurations are Turing universal. A cell of any two-dimensional RPCA can also be constructed out of Fredkin gates and delay elements. Hence, these two models are intrinsically universal, as well as Turing universal, in the sense that any two-dimensional RPCA can be simulated in their cellular space. The last model is an 81-state RPCA, which is again both Turing universal, and intrinsically universal. Though the number of states is larger than those of the first two, any reversible two-counter machine is embedded concisely in its finite configurations.

Keywords reversible cellular automaton, two-dimensional partitioned cellular automaton, Fredkin gate, rotary element, reversible counter machine, Turing universality, intrinsic universality

12.1 Universality in Two-Dimensional CAs

In this chapter, we give three models of simple two-dimensional RPCAs that are Turing universal, and intrinsically universal. The first and the second models S_1 and S_2 [9] are 16-state four-neighbor RPCAs on the square tessellation. We show any reversible logic circuit composed of Fredkin gate can be embedded in these RPCAs. Thus, by Corollary 6.1, any RTM can be implemented in these RPCAs with a special type of ultimately periodic configurations (Definition 12.1). The third model P_3 is an 81-state four-neighbor RPCA. Though the number of states is larger than the above two, any reversible counter machine can be concisely embedded in P_3 with finite configurations.

12.1.1 Ultimately periodic configurations in two-dimensional CAs

We give definitions of special types of a periodic configuration, and an ultimately periodic configuration for a two-dimensional CA.

Definition 12.1. Let $A = (\mathbb{Z}^2, Q, (n_1, \ldots, n_m), f, \#)$ be a two-dimensional CA. A two-dimensional configuration $\alpha : \mathbb{Z}^2 \to Q$ is called *horizontally periodic* if there are $p \in \mathbb{Z}_+$ and $y_0, y_1 \in \mathbb{Z}$ such that $y_0 < y_1$ that satisfy the following.

$$\forall (x,y) \in \mathbb{Z}^2$$
$$((y_0 \leq y \leq y_1 \;\Rightarrow\; \alpha(x,y) = \alpha(x+p,y)) \;\wedge$$
$$((y < y_0 \vee y > y_1) \;\Rightarrow\; \alpha(x,y) = \#))$$

A configuration $\alpha : \mathbb{Z}^2 \to Q$ is called *horizontally ultimately periodic* if there are $p_L, p_R \in \mathbb{Z}_+, x_L, x_R \in \mathbb{Z}$ ($x_L < x_R$), and $y_0, y_1 \in \mathbb{Z}$ ($y_0 < y_1$) that satisfy the following.

$$\forall (x,y) \in \mathbb{Z}^2$$
$$(((y_0 \leq y \leq y_1) \wedge (x \leq x_L) \;\Rightarrow\; \alpha(x - p_L, y) = \alpha(x,y)) \;\wedge$$
$$((y_0 \leq y \leq y_1) \wedge (x \geq x_R) \;\Rightarrow\; \alpha(x,y) = \alpha(x + p_R, y)) \;\wedge$$
$$((y < y_0 \vee y > y_1) \;\Rightarrow\; \alpha(x,y) = \#))$$

The sets of all horizontally periodic configurations, and all horizontally ultimately periodic configurations of a two-dimensional CA A are denoted by $\mathrm{Conf}_{hp}(A)$, and $\mathrm{Conf}_{hup}(A)$, respectively.

By the above definition, we can see that a horizontally periodic configuration is one such that a finite array of states

$$\begin{array}{ccc} a_{1,1} & \cdots & a_{1,p} \\ \vdots & & \vdots \\ a_{h,1} & \cdots & a_{h,p} \end{array}$$

repeats infinitely both to the left and to the right, where $h = y_1 - y_0 + 1$, and all the other cells are in the quiescent state #. Thus, the positive integer p is the horizontal *period* of it. Here, the term "horizontally" means that the configuration is periodic only to the horizontal direction. On the other hand, a horizontally ultimately periodic configuration is one that satisfies the following: (1) There are three finite arrays of states

$$S_L = \begin{array}{ccc} a_{1,1} & \cdots & a_{1,p_L} \\ \vdots & & \vdots \\ a_{h,1} & \cdots & a_{h,p_L} \end{array}, \quad S_C = \begin{array}{ccc} b_{1,1} & \cdots & b_{1,n} \\ \vdots & & \vdots \\ b_{h,1} & \cdots & b_{h,n} \end{array}, \quad \text{and} \quad S_R = \begin{array}{ccc} c_{1,1} & \cdots & c_{1,p_R} \\ \vdots & & \vdots \\ c_{h,1} & \cdots & c_{h,p_R} \end{array}$$

such that $h = y_1 - y_0 + 1$ and $n = x_R - x_L - 1$, (2) the array S_L repeats infinitely to the left, the array S_R repeats infinitely to the right, and the array S_C lies between them, and (3) all the other cells are in the quiescent state #. The positive integers p_L and p_R are called the *left period* and the *right period* of the configuration, respectively.

Note that a horizontally periodic configuration is a special case of a horizontally ultimately periodic configuration that satisfies $n = 0$, and $S_L = S_R$. A finite configuration is also a special case of a horizontally ultimately periodic one that satisfies $p_L = p_R = 1$ and $a_{i,1} = c_{i,1} = \#$ for all $i \in \{1, \ldots, h\}$. Horizontally periodic and ultimately periodic configurations for two-dimensional PCAs are also defined similarly. Thus, their precise definition are not given here.

Let $\alpha : \mathbb{Z}^2 \to Q$ be a horizontally ultimately periodic configuration. As in the case of one-dimensional CA (Sect. 11.1), α can be finitely described by the three arrays S_L, S_C, and S_R. We call the following $D(\alpha)$ a *description* of α.

$$D(\alpha) = (S_L, S_C, S_R)$$

If α is a finite configuration, then S_L and S_R are the arrays of size $h \times 1$ consisting only of #'s. We denote the set of all descriptions of horizontally ultimately periodic configurations of a two-dimensional CA A by $D(\text{Conf}_{\text{hup}}(A))$. The set of all descriptions of finite configurations of A is denoted by $D(\text{Conf}_{\text{fin}}(A))$.

$$D(\text{Conf}_{\text{hup}}(A)) = \{D(\alpha) \mid \alpha \in \text{Conf}_{\text{hup}}(A)\}$$
$$D(\text{Conf}_{\text{fin}}(A)) = \{D(\alpha) \mid \alpha \in \text{Conf}_{\text{fin}}(A)\}$$

12.1.2 Notion of simulation and Turing universality in two-dimensional CAs

We first define the notion of simulation in a two-dimensional CA, which is similar to Definition 11.2.

Definition 12.2. Let S be a computing system, and $\text{ID}(S)$ be the set of all instantaneous descriptions of S. Note that, if S is a two-dimensional CA, then we use $D(\text{Conf}_{\text{hup}}(S))$ (or $D(\text{Conf}_{\text{fin}}(S))$ when simulating finite configurations of S) instead of $\text{ID}(S)$. Let $A = (\mathbb{Z}^2, Q, (n_1, \ldots, n_m), f, \#)$ be a two-dimensional CA whose global function is F_A, and let $\alpha \in \text{ID}(S)$. If there exist a monotonically increasing total recursive function $\tau_\alpha : \mathbb{N} \to \mathbb{N}$, and two total recursive functions $c : \text{ID}(S) \to D(\text{Conf}_{\text{hup}}(A))$, and $d : D(\text{Conf}_{\text{hup}}(A)) \to (\text{ID}(S) \cup \{\bot\})$ that satisfy the following, then we say A *simulates* S with *horizontally ultimately periodic configurations*. Note that $d(\beta) = \bot$ for $\beta \in D(\text{Conf}_{\text{hup}}(A))$ means there is no $\alpha \in \text{ID}(S)$ that corresponds to β.

$$\forall \alpha, \alpha' \in \text{ID}(S), \ \forall n \in \mathbb{N} \ (\alpha \vdash_S^n \alpha' \ \Rightarrow \ d(F_A^{\tau_\alpha(n)}(c(\alpha))) = \alpha')$$

Here, c and d are *encoding* and *decoding functions*, respectively. Furthermore, if c and d are total recursive functions such that $c : \text{ID}(S) \to D(\text{Conf}_{\text{fin}}(A))$, and $d : D(\text{Conf}_{\text{fin}}(A)) \to (\text{ID}(S) \cup \{\bot\})$, then A *simulates* S with *finite configurations*. Generally, the function τ_α depends on the initial ID α of S. However, if $\tau_\alpha = \tau_\beta$

holds for all $\alpha, \beta \in \mathrm{ID}(S)$, then we write them by τ. We say A simulates S in *real time* if $\tau(n) = n$, and in *linear time* if $\tau(n) \le kn$ for some positive constant k.

A definition of Turing universality of a two-dimensional CA can be obtained from Definition 11.3, by simply replacing the term "ultimately periodic" by "horizontally ultimately periodic."

Definition 12.3. A class $\mathscr{A}$ of two-dimensional CAs with finite (horizontally ultimately periodic, respectively) configurations is called *Turing universal*, if for each one-tape TM there exists a CA in $\mathscr{A}$ that can simulate the TM with finite (horizontally ultimately periodic) configurations. Likewise, a specific CA A with finite (horizontally ultimately periodic, respectively) configurations is called *Turing universal* if it can simulate *any* one-tape TM with finite (horizontally ultimately periodic) configurations.

12.2 Symmetries in Two-Dimensional PCAs

Here, we define two kinds of symmetries for five-neighbor PCAs on the square grid. Since four-neighbor PCAs are a special subclass of five-neighbor PCA such that $|C| = 1$, definitions for four-neighbor PCAs are also immediately obtained.

Definition 12.4. Let P be a PCA.

$$P = (\mathbb{Z}^2, (C, U, R, D, L), ((0,0), (0,-1), (-1,0), (0,1), (1,0)), f)$$

The PCA P is called *rotation-symmetric* (or *isotropic*) if (1) and (2) hold, where $Q = C \times U \times R \times D \times L$.

(1) $U = R = D = L$
(2) $\forall (c, u, r, d, l), (c', u', r', d', l') \in Q :$
   $f(c, u, r, d, l) = (c', u', r', d', l') \implies f(c, l, u, r, d) = (c', l', u', r', d')$

P is called *reflection-symmetric* if P is rotation-symmetric and (3) holds.

(3) $\forall (c, u, r, d, l), (c', u', r', d', l') \in Q :$
   $f(c, u, r, d, l) = (c', u', r', d', l') \implies f(c, u, l, d, r) = (c', u', l', d', r')$

Rotation-symmetry means that the local function f is uniform in all the four directions. It corresponds to isotropy of a physical space in which the same physical low holds in all directions. Hence, if we express a local rule in a pictorial form as in Fig. 10.23, then for each local rule $\beta \to \gamma$ in f, there are also three local rules in f obtained from $\beta \to \gamma$ by rotating β and γ by 90°, 180°, and 270°. In other words, the set f of local rules is closed under the operation of rotating both sides of a rule by 90°.

Reflection-symmetry is the condition that the set f of local rules is closed under the operation of taking mirror images of rules. It means that even if we take the mirror image of the cellular space, it has the same local and global functions as the original one. More precisely, it is as follows. Suppose $\alpha_0 \vdash_P \alpha_1 \vdash_P \alpha_2 \vdash_P \cdots$ is an evolution process of configurations in P. If P is reflection-symmetric, then $\alpha_0^\dagger \vdash_P \alpha_1^\dagger \vdash_P \alpha_2^\dagger \vdash_P \cdots$ is also an evolution process of P, where $\alpha_i^\dagger$ denotes the mirror image of α_i with respect to either the horizontal, vertical, or $\pm 45°$ line (since it is easily proved, we omit its proof).

12.3 Simulating Reversible Logic Circuits in Simple RPCAs

We give two models of simple two-dimensional RPCAs in which any reversible logic circuit composed of Fredkin gates and delay elements is embeddable. The first model is a 16-state reflection-symmetric RPCA, and the second one is a 16-state rotation-symmetric but not reflection-symmetric RPCA.

12.3.1 16-state RPCA model S_1

The first model is a 16-state four-neighbor RPCA S_1 [9]. It is defined as follows.

$$S_1 = (\mathbb{Z}^2, (U,R,D,L), ((0,-1),(-1,0),(0,1),(1,0)), f_{S_1}, (0,0,0,0))$$
$$U = R = D = L = \{0,1\}$$

The local function f_{S_1} is given as the set of local rules shown in Fig. 12.1, where the states 0 and 1 are indicated by a blank and a dot. Since S_1 is rotation-symmetric, rotated rules are omitted in Fig. 12.1. From the local rules we can also see that S_1 is reflection symmetric. It is easy to verify that f_{S_1} is bijective, since there is no pair of rules whose right-hand sides are the same. Thus S_1 is reversible.

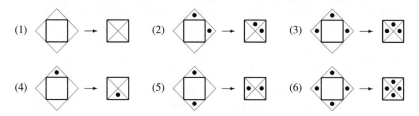

Fig. 12.1 The local rules of the 16-state four-neighbor RPCA S_1. Since S_1 is rotation-symmetric, we omit to write the rules obtained by rotating both sides of the rules by 90°, 180°, and 270°

We can see that the set of local rules of S_1 (Fig. 12.1) is essentially the same as the block rules of the Margolus CA (Fig. 10.11 **(b)**) [4]. In fact, they are isomorphic. Hence, S_1 can be viewed as a reformulation of the Margolus CA within the framework of PCA. However, the other model S_2 is different from it.

In S_1, a *signal* consists of two dots (Fig. 12.2). It moves straight ahead if no obstacle exists. A signal in S_1 corresponds to a "ball" in the billiard ball model (BBM) (Sect. 2.2.3). Collision of two balls is implemented as shown in Fig. 12.3. To construct a reflector of a ball we need a stable pattern called a *block* shown in Fig. 12.4. A *reflector* in S_1 is made of two blocks. Left-turn of a ball at a reflector is shown in Fig. 12.5. Right-turn is also possible. Using reflectors, signal routing and signal delay can be realized. Note that, in the Margolus CA, a reflector consists of 8 black squares (Fig. 10.12), and thus it is slightly different from the one in S_1.

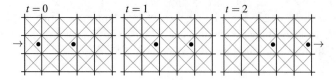

Fig. 12.2 Propagation of a signal in the RPCA S_1. A signal consists of two dots, which corresponds to a "ball" in the billiard ball model (BBM)

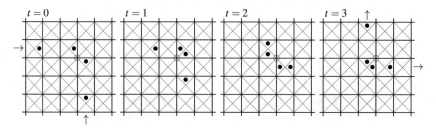

Fig. 12.3 Simulating collision of balls in BBM in the RPCA S_1. By an orthogonal collision of balls, their trajectories deviate by one cell. The virtual collision point is indicated by O

Fig. 12.4 A stable pattern called a block in the RPCA S_1

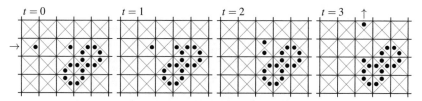

Fig. 12.5 Reflection of a ball at a reflector in the RPCA S_1

Placing reflectors in the S_1 space appropriately, we obtain a module that simulates a switch gate (Fig. 12.6). In this configuration, if $c = x = 1$, the two balls corresponding to c and x collide twice, where the collision points are indicated by $\bigcirc$ in Fig. 12.6. Hence, the delays between two collisions should be adjusted precisely. Note that, in S_1, an extra one-step delay occurs both in the collision of two balls, and in the reflection of a ball. A module that realizes an inverse switch gate can be obtained by simply exchanging the inputs and outputs of the pattern of a switch gate, since S_1 is reflection-symmetric. However, we also take a mirror image of it as shown in Fig. 12.7 for making it easy to construct a Fredkin gate.

Combining two switch gate patterns and two inverse switch gate patterns, we obtain a module that simulates a Fredkin gate (Fig. 12.8). Its size is 34×58, and the delay between inputs and outputs is 164 steps. By above, any reversible logic circuit composed of Fredkin gates and delay elements can be implemented in S_1.

12.3.2 16-state RPCA model S_2

The second model is an RPCA S_2, which is also a 16-state four-neighbor model [9]. It is defined as follows.

$$S_2 = (\mathbb{Z}^2, (U, R, D, L), ((0, -1), (-1, 0), (0, 1), (1, 0)), f_{S_2}, (0, 0, 0, 0))$$
$$U = R = D = L = \{0, 1\}$$

The local function f_{S_2} is given as the set of local rules shown in Fig. 12.9, where the states 0 and 1 are indicated by a blank and a dot, respectively. The RPCA S_2 is rotation-symmetric, but not reflection-symmetric because of the rule (3) in Fig. 12.9. It is also easy to verify that S_2 is reversible.

A *signal* (or a ball of BBM) consists of two dots also in S_2. Movement of a ball, and collision of two balls in S_2 are just the same as in S_1 (see Figs. 12.2 and 12.3). A stable pattern *block* is also the same as in S_1 (Fig. 12.4). In S_2, left-turn of a ball is implemented by a reflector consisting of a single block (Fig. 12.10). But, if we give a signal to the reflector as shown in Fig. 12.11, the reflector is broken. Thus, right-turn is not possible by a single reflector. We implement right-turn by three left-turns.

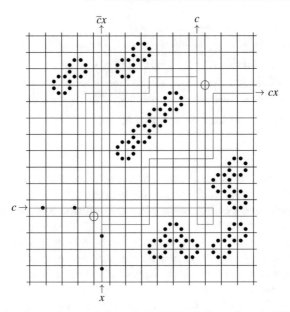

Fig. 12.6 A module that realizes a switch gate in the RPCA S_1. It simulates the BBM configuration shown in Fig. 4.17. The virtual collision points of balls are indicated by $\bigcirc$

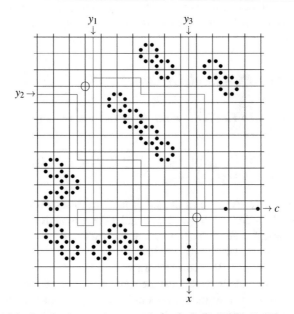

Fig. 12.7 A module that simulates an inverse switch gate in the RPCA S_1. It is a mirror image of the pattern in Fig. 12.6. It realizes the injective partial logical function $f_{sw}^{-1} : (y_1, y_2, y_3) \rightarrow (c, x)$ defined in Table 4.5. Namely, $c = y_1$ and $x = y_2 + y_3$ under the assumption of $(y_2 \Rightarrow y_1) \wedge (y_3 \Rightarrow \neg y_1)$

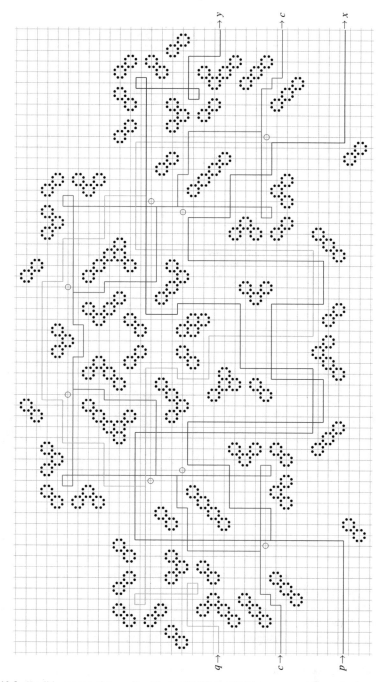

Fig. 12.8 Fredkin gate module realized in the RPCA S_1 [9]. Here, $x = cp + \bar{c}q$, and $y = cq + \bar{c}p$

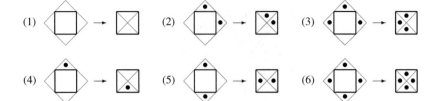

Fig. 12.9 The local rules of the 16-state four-neighbor RPCA S_2. Since S_2 is rotation-symmetric, we omit to write the rules obtained by rotating both sides of the rules by 90°, 180°, and 270°. Only the rule (3) is different from that of S_1 in Fig. 12.1

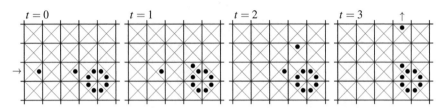

Fig. 12.10 Reflection of a ball by a reflector in the RPCA S_2. In S_2, only a left-turn of a ball is possible by a single reflector

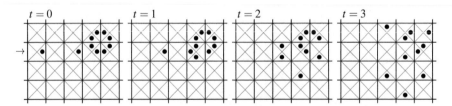

Fig. 12.11 If we give a ball to a reflector in S_2 at the position shown above, then the reflector will be broken. Hence, a right-turn is not possible by a single reflector. It is implemented by three left-turns

Figure 12.12 shows a module that simulates a switch gate. Note that, in S_2, an extra delay of one step occurs only in the collision of two balls, but not in the reflection of a ball. Fine adjustment of delays of signals must be done considering this fact. By taking a mirror image of the switch gate pattern, and exchanging the inputs and the outputs, we can get a module that simulates an inverse switch gate (Fig. 12.13). Since S_2 is not reflection-symmetric, we must apply both of the operations of taking a mirror image, and exchanging the inputs and outputs to obtain an inverse switch gate.

Combining two switch gates and two inverse switch gates, we can get a module that simulates a Fredkin gate (Fig.12.14). The size of the pattern is 30×62, and the delay between inputs and outputs is 174 steps.

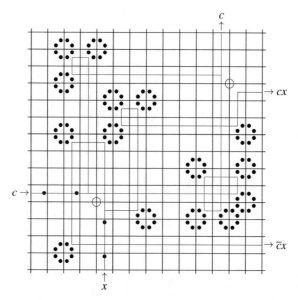

Fig. 12.12 A module that realizes a switch gate in the RPCA S_2. The virtual collision points are indicated by ○

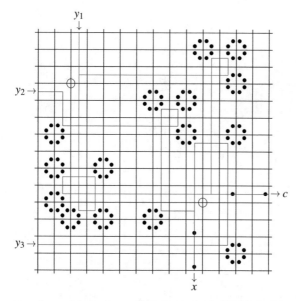

Fig. 12.13 A pattern that realizes an inverse switch gate in the RPCA S_2. Here, $c = y_1$ and $x = y_2 + y_3$ under the assumption of $(y_2 \Rightarrow y_1) \wedge (y_3 \Rightarrow \neg y_1)$. The virtual collision points are indicated by ○

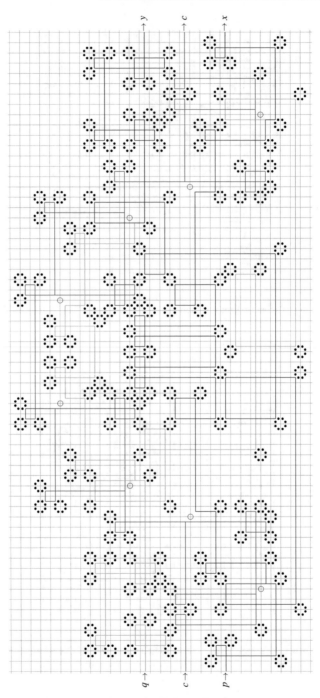

Fig. 12.14 Fredkin gate module realized in the RPCA S_2 [9]. Here, $x = cp + \bar{c}q$, and $y = cq + \bar{c}p$

12.3.3 Turing universality of the two models of 16-state RPCAs

From the results shown in Sects. 12.3.1 and 12.3.2 we shall see that the RPCAs S_1 and S_2 with horizontally ultimately periodic configurations are Turing universal. We first show the following lemma.

Lemma 12.1. *Let A be a two-dimensional RCA. If any reversible logic circuit composed of Fredkin gates and delay elements is simulated in A, then A with horizontally ultimately periodic configurations is Turing universal.*

Proof. In the previous chapters, the following results have been shown. (1) The class of one-tape two-symbol reversible Turing machines (RTMs) with a one-way infinite tape is computationally universal (Theorem 5.7). (2) Any one-tape two-symbol RTM with a one-way infinite tape can be implemented as an infinite circuit composed only of rotary elements (REs) (Theorem 6.1). (3) RE can be constructed out of Fredkin gates and delay elements (Fig. 4.24). By above, any RTM is realized as an infinite circuit made of Fredkin gates and delay elements (Corollary 6.1).

On the other hand, as shown in Fig. 6.4, the whole RE-circuit for the RTM is composed of a circuit for the finite control (Sect. 6.1.2), and an infinite number of copies of the memory cell circuit (Sect. 6.1.1). Furthermore, in the initial configuration of the whole RE-circuit (Fig. 6.4 **(a)**), all but a finite number of memory cells contain the symbol 0, and are not scanned by the head. Therefore, by appropriately implementing the RE-circuits for the finite control and the memory cell using Fredkin gates and delay elements, and then embedding them in the cellular space of A, we obtain a horizontally ultimately periodic configuration that simulates the RTM. Thus, we have the lemma.   □

Theorem 12.1. *The 16-state two-dimensional four-neighbor RPCAs S_1 and S_2 with horizontally ultimately periodic configurations are Turing universal.*

Proof. As shown in Figs. 12.8 and 12.14, Fredkin gate is implemented in S_1 and S_2. Delay time of a signal is easily adjusted by designing a signal path composed of reflectors appropriately. Thus, by Lemma 12.1 the theorem follows.   □

12.4 Simulating Reversible Counter Machines in RPCA

In Sect. 12.3, two models of simple universal two-dimensional RPCAs were given. They can simulate any reversible Turing machine (RTM) on their horizontally ultimately periodic configurations. In this section, we design an 81-state four-neighbor RPCA P_3 [8] that can simulate any reversible two-counter machine (RCM(2)) using only *finite configurations*. The RPCA P_3 is a four-neighbor one such that each part of a cell has three states. Hence, it has $3^4 = 81$ states. In P_3, rotary element (RE) (see Sect.2.2.1) is used for performing logical operations. By this, the size of a configuration that simulates an RCM(2) becomes much smaller than the case of using Fredkin gate (Fig. 12.36 is an example of such a configuration).

12.4.1 81-state RPCA model P_3

The 81-state four-neighbor two-dimensional RPCA P_3 is defined as follows.

$$P_3 = (\mathbb{Z}^2, (U, R, D, L), ((0,-1), (-1,0), (0,1), (1,0)), f_{P_3}, (0,0,0,0))$$
$$U = R = D = L = \{0, 1, 2\}$$

The local function f_{P_3} is given in Fig. 12.15. The states 0,1, and 2 are represented by a blank, $\circ$, and $\bullet$, respectively. Since P_3 is rotation-symmetric, rotated rules are not indicated in Fig. 12.15. It is not reflection-symmetric because of, e.g., rule (1). We can verify that there is no pair of rules that have the same right-hand side. Therefore, P_3 is reversible.

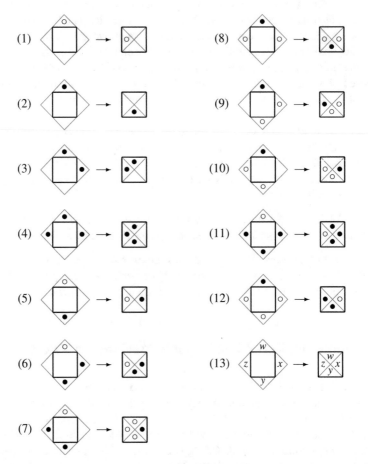

Fig. 12.15 The set of 13 rule schemes of the rotation-symmetric 81-state RPCA P_3. The rule scheme (13) represents 33 rules not specified by (1) – (12), where $w, x, y, z \in \{\text{blank}, \circ, \bullet\}$

12.4.2 Basic elements in the RPCA P_3

In P_3, a *signal* consists of a single ●. It moves straight ahead in the P_3 space unless no obstacle exists (Fig. 12.16). In order to build RCM(2)'s in the space of P_3, we first give five kinds of basic elements for processing a signal. They are shown in Fig. 12.17. The first three elements, LR-turn element, R-turn element, and reflector are for routing a signal. Rotary element will be used to implement a finite control of RCM(2) as in the case of constructing RTMs (see Sect. 6.1.2). Position marker will be used to implement counters, since it works as a kind of memory. A configuration of P_3 that simulates RCM(2) will be built only from these five kinds of elements. In the following, we explain how these five elements work.

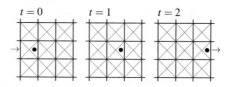

Fig. 12.16 Propagation of a signal in P_3

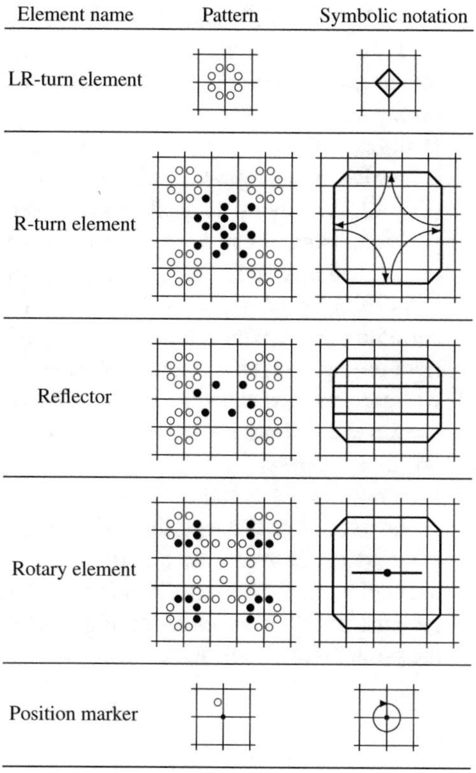

Element name	Pattern	Symbolic notation
LR-turn element		
R-turn element		
Reflector		
Rotary element		
Position marker		

Fig. 12.17 Five kinds of basic elements in P_3

1. LR-turn element

   It is a pattern that makes a signal turn leftward or rightward as in Fig. 12.18.

2. R-turn element

   This element makes an incoming signal turn only to the right (Fig.12.19). In the following construction, we sometimes use a *bidirectional signal path* on which a signal goes back and forth in both directions. We use an R-turn element as an interface between a bidirectional signal path and unidirectional signal paths as shown in Fig. 12.20. By this, the input and the output paths for a bidirectional path are separated. In addition to this function, four corners of an R-turn element act like an LR-turn element (this is also the case for the pattern of rotary element).

3. Reflector

   It is an element at which a signal changes its moving direction by 180° as shown in Fig. 12.21. Although this function can be simulated by a circuit composed of LR-turn elements and an R-turn element, it will reduce the size of the pattern that simulates an RCM(2).

4. Rotary element (RE)

   In P_3, RE is realized by the patterns shown in Fig. 12.22, where two states H and V are distinguished by the subpattern in its center. The pattern for RE is periodic, since two ○'s in its center go back and forth with period 2. Operations of RE in P_3 are expressed in a symbolic form as in Fig. 12.23 (see also Fig. 2.3). It should be noted that, in this implementation, RE has bidirectional input/output paths. Figures 12.24 and 12.25 shows the detailed simulation process of RE in P_3. Figure 12.24 is the case where a signal comes from a direction parallel to a rotatable bar, while Fig. 12.25 is the case where a signal comes from a direction orthogonal to it.

5. Position marker

   It consists of a single ○, which rotates around some point if no obstacle exists (Fig. 12.26). Giving a signal to a position marker appropriately we can move its position. Thus, it can keep a nonnegative integer by the displacement from its origin position, and is used to build a counter module. Figure 12.27 **(a)** shows a "pushing" process, while Fig. 12.27 **(b)** is a "pulling" process. Since it is a periodic pattern with the period 4, a pushing/pulling signal must be given at a right timing. But, by a single execution of the pushing operation, the right timing will shift by two steps. In Fig. 12.27 **(a)**, the phases of the position marker at $t = 1$ and $t = 4$ are the same, but the distance from the input port to the marker position increases by 1. Thus, the next right timing of giving a pushing signal becomes $t = 6 + 4i$ rather than $t = 4 + 4i$ ($i = 0, 1, \ldots$). On the other hand, by a single execution of the pulling operation, the right timing does not shift, because the distance decreases by one (Fig. 12.27 **(b)**). Since changing the input timing depending on these conditions is troublesome, we employ a method of always giving a "pair" of pushing (or pulling) signals successively. By this, we can avoid the problem of timing shift.

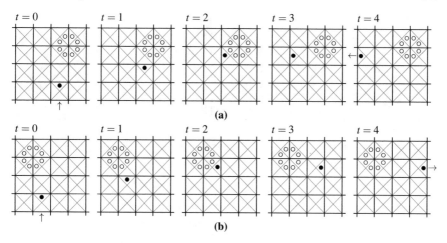

Fig. 12.18 LR-turn element in P_3. (**a**) Left-turn, and (**b**) right-turn

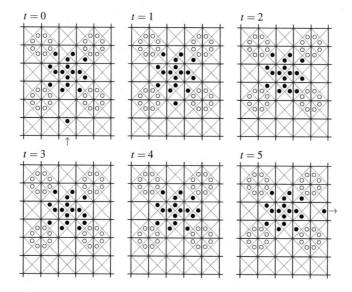

Fig. 12.19 Right-turn of a signal by R-turn element in P_3

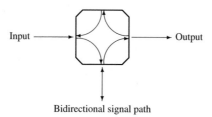

Fig. 12.20 Interface between a bidirectional signal path and unidirectional signal paths

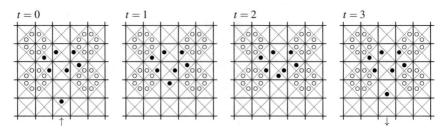

Fig. 12.21 Reflection of a signal by 180° using reflector in P_3

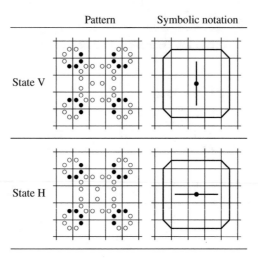

Fig. 12.22 Two states of rotary element (RE) in P_3

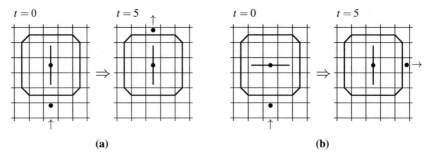

Fig. 12.23 Operations of RE in P_3 in a symbolic form. (**a**) the parallel case, and (**b**) the orthogonal case. Here, RE has bidirectional signal paths

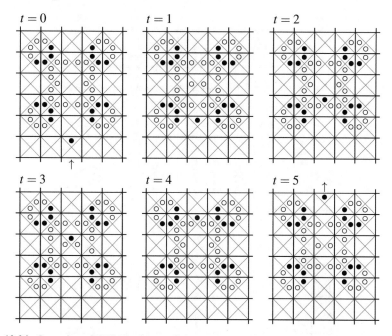

Fig. 12.24 Operation of RE in P_3: the parallel case

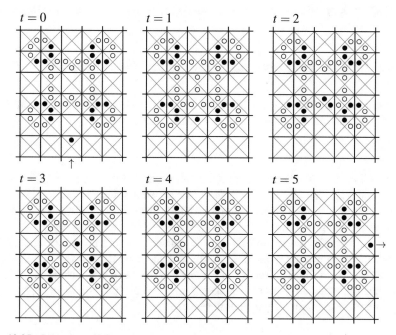

Fig. 12.25 Operation of RE in P_3: the orthogonal case

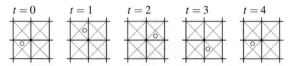

Fig. 12.26 Position marker in P_3. It rotates around some point with the period 4

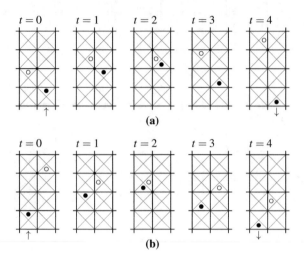

Fig. 12.27 Pushing and pulling a position marker by a signal in P_3. **(a)** Pushing, and **(b)** pulling

12.4.3 Constructing reversible counter machine in the RPCA P_3

We now show that for any given RCM(2) M, we can design a finite configuration of P_3 that simulates M using the five kinds of basic elements. Let

$$M = (Q, 2, \delta, q_0, \{q_m\})$$

be any RCM(2) in the normal form (see Definition 9.4 and Lemma 9.7). Hence, there is no state that goes to the state q_0. Here, we assume $Q = \{q_0, q_1, \cdots, q_m\}$. Thus, M has m non-final states. A configuration realizing M consists of eight kinds of *circuit modules* as shown in Fig. 12.28. During the computation, only one signal exists in the configuration, and its flow is indicated by the arrows in Fig. 12.28. In the following, we show all these modules can be built from the five kinds of basic elements. In the construction method given below, a counter module and an interconnection module are given as fixed patterns (i.e., common to all RCM(2)'s), while the other modules vary depending on M.

(1) Counter module

A counter module is a pattern for simulating a counter unit of an RCM(2) as shown in Fig. 12.29. To simulate two counters, two copies of this module are needed.

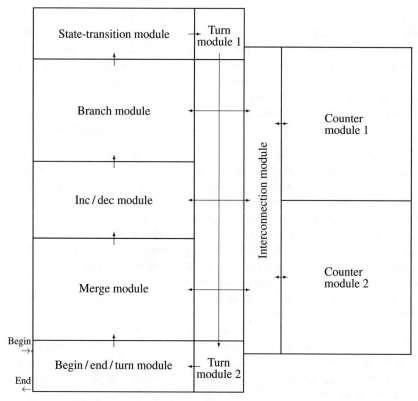

Fig. 12.28 A reversible two-counter machine composed of eight kinds of circuit modules embedded in the cellular space of P_3. Arrows show the flow of a signal

A counter machine has three kinds of operations for each counter (except a "no-operation" i.e., the quadruple of the type $[q_i, j, 0, q_k]$): (i) an increment operation to the j-th counter, (ii) a decrement operation to the j-th counter, and (iii) a conditional branch (i.e., test) operation testing whether the content of the j-th counter is zero or positive. These operations should be performed in the counter module.

In addition, a "merge operation", which is in some sense an inverse operation of a branch operation of (iii), should also be implemented in this module. The reason is as follows. When a conditional branch operation is performed, two kinds of responses, which are distinguished by the position (or path) of a returned signal, are obtained depending on the content of the counter. After making an appropriate state transition by the response, such an information should be reversibly erased. Otherwise, the signal must keep all the test results so far made by its position, and hence we must prepare unbounded number of signal paths in the configuration to distinguish such information; that is impossible. Therefore, we need a mechanism that merges two different signal paths into one, a kind of erasing operation. However, a simple erasing operation without referring any information containing the one to be erased causes an irreversible state transition, because we cannot go back to the previous state uniquely after such a simple erasure. A reversible erasure of this information can be performed by referring the contents of the counter just tested. This is explained in (f) – (h) below. In order to implement both branch and merge operations, two position markers (whose displacements from the origin are always kept equal) are used in the counter module.

To perform these operations, there are eight input/output ports in the counter module $j \in \{1,2\}$ as listed below (some of them are common in their position).

(a) I_j: Increment command/response port for the j-th counter

If a signal is given in this port, both of the position markers are pushed rightward by two cells. After that, the completion signal goes out from this port. The four REs to the right of I_j are for pushing the lower and upper markers twice.

(b) D_j: Decrement command/response port for the j-th counter

If a signal is given in this port, both of the position markers are pulled leftward by two cells. After that, the completion signal goes out from this port. The four REs to the right of D_j are for pulling the lower and upper markers twice.

(c) T_j: Test command port for the j-th counter

If a signal is given in this port, the content of the j-th counter is tested as described in (d) and (e) below.

(d) Z_j: Zero-response port for the j-th counter

If the content of the j-th counter is zero, the signal from T_j first pushes the upper position marker downward, then pushes it upward (thus restores it at the original position). This process is repeated twice to restore the phase of the position marker, and finally goes out from the port Z_j.

(e) P_j: Positive-response port for the j-th counter

If the content of the j-th counter is positive, the signal from T_j goes through this module without interacting with the markers, and finally goes out from P_j.

(f) Z'_j: Zero-state input port for the j-th counter

Z'_j, as well as P'_j and T'_j in (g) and (h), are used for the merge operation. Whenever a signal is put into the port Z'_j, the content of the j-th counter must be zero. The signal first pushes the lower position marker downward, then pushes it upward. This process is repeated twice, and finally goes out from T'_j.

(g) P'_j: Positive-state input port for the j-th counter

Whenever a signal is put into this port, the content of the j-th counter must be positive. The signal goes through this module without interacting with the position markers, and finally goes out from T'_j.

(h) T'_j: Undo-test (or merge) output port for the j-th counter

In either case of (f) or (g), a signal goes out from T'_j reversibly "undoing" the last test operation on the j-th counter (i.e., two paths coming from Z'_j and P'_j are merged into T'_j).

By above, if the position of each marker is $2n$ cells right from the origin, then we can regard that the counter keeps the integer n.

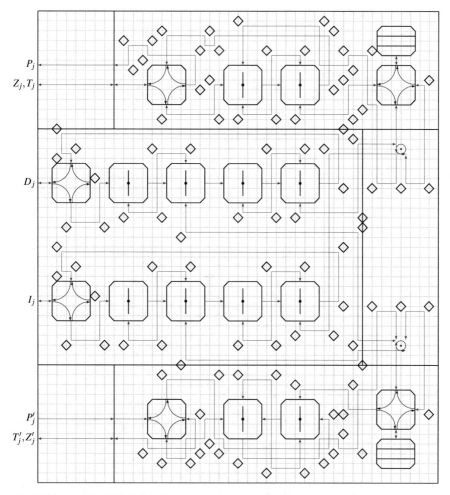

Fig. 12.29 Counter module j for the counter j in P_3. In this configuration, two position markers are at the origin showing that it keeps the integer 0

(2) Interconnection module

It is a circuit that connects between the block of counter modules, and the block of inc/dec, branch, and merge modules appropriately. Figure 12.30 shows an interconnection module with two counter modules.

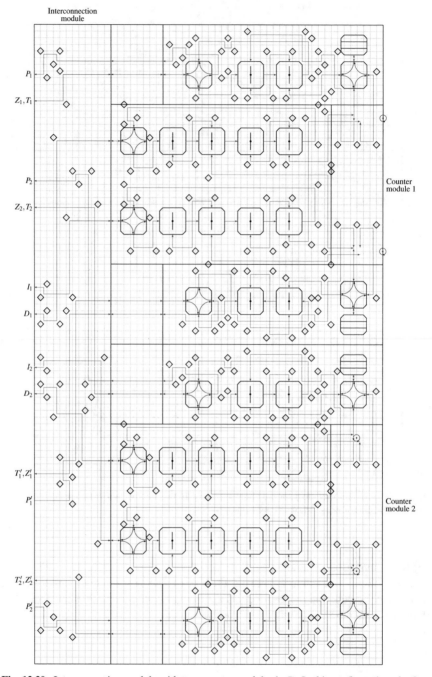

Fig. 12.30 Interconnection module with two counter modules in P_3. In this configuration, the first counter keeps 2, while the second keeps 0

(3) Inc/dec module

It controls increment and decrement operations of M. Here, we consider the RCM(2) M_1 in Example 9.1, which computes the function $f(x) = 2x + 2$, i.e., $(q_0, x, 0) \vdash^*_{M_1} (q_6, 0, 2x + 2)$ for all $x \in \mathbb{N}$.

$$M_1 = (2, \{q_0, q_1, q_2, q_3, q_4, q_5, q_6\}, \delta_1, q_0, \{q_6\})$$
$$\delta_1 = \{\ [q_0, 2, Z, q_1], [q_1, 2, +, q_2], [q_2, 2, +, q_3],$$
$$[q_3, 1, P, q_4], [q_3, 1, Z, q_6], [q_4, 1, -, q_5], [q_5, 2, P, q_1]\ \}$$

The lower part of Fig. 12.31 shows the inc/dec module for M_1. The size (height and width) of this module is $24 \times (8m + 4)$, where m is the number of non-halting states of M. The $(8i + 4)$-th column of this module corresponds to the state $q_i \in Q - \{q_m\}$ of M ($0 \leq i \leq m - 1$), while the fourth, eighth, 16th, and 20th rows correspond to the signal lines for I_1, D_1, I_2, and D_2, respectively.

Let Inc_j, Dec_j, Nop, Test_j, and Merge_j be the sets of states defined as follows ($j \in \{1, 2\}$).

$$\text{Inc}_j = \{q_i \mid \exists q_k \in Q\ ([q_i, j, +, q_k] \in \delta)\}$$
$$\text{Dec}_j = \{q_i \mid \exists q_k \in Q\ ([q_i, j, -, q_k] \in \delta)\}$$
$$\text{Nop} = \{q_i \mid \exists q_k \in Q, \exists j \in \{1, 2\}\ ([q_i, j, 0, q_k] \in \delta)\}$$
$$\text{Test}_j = \{q_i \mid \exists q_k \in Q, \exists s \in \{Z, P\}\ ([q_i, j, s, q_k] \in \delta)\}$$
$$\text{Merge}_j = \{q_k \mid \exists q_i, q_i' \in Q\ ([q_i, j, Z, q_k] \in \delta \wedge [q_i', j, P, q_k] \in \delta)\}$$

Note that the seven sets Inc_j, Dec_j, Nop, and Test_j are mutually disjoint since M is deterministic. Furthermore, $\text{Merge}_1 \cap \text{Merge}_2 = \emptyset$ since M is reversible.

If $q_i \in \text{Inc}_1$ (Dec_1, Inc_2, Dec_2, respectively), then put an RE of state H at the $(8i + 2)$-nd column of the second row (sixth, 14th, and 18th row, respectively). Here, the position of an element is referred by the upper-left corner of it. Consider the inc/dec module in Fig. 12.31. If the present state is, e.g., q_1, then a signal comes from the bottom of the 12th column. At the RE, the signal makes the rotatable bar turn vertical, and goes to the right to the port I_2 in order to execute an increment operation. Note that the signal goes straight through the RE at the 14th row of the 18th column without affecting the direction of the rotatable bar. When a signal comes back from the port I_2, it restores the rotatable bar to the horizontal direction, and then goes upward on the 12th column.

(4) Branch module

A branch module controls conditional branch operations for the counters. An example of this module is shown in the upper part of Fig. 12.31. The size of this module is $32 \times (8m + 4)$.

If $q_i \in \text{Test}_1$ (Test_2, respectively), then put an R-turn element at the $(8i + 2)$-nd column of the tenth row (26th row), an LR-turn element at the $(8i + 8)$-th column of the 12th row (28th row), and an RE of state H at the $(8i + 6)$-th column of the sixth row (22th row). The block consisting of these three elements is called a *counter-test submodule.* In addition, two LR-turn elements are put at the left end of the module as shown in Fig. 12.31.

On the bottom row of this module, the $(8i+4)$-th column is assigned to an input port for the state $q_i \in Q - \{q_m\}$ since it receives a signal from the inc/dec module. On the first row, the $(8i+4)$-th column is assigned to an output port for $q_i \in Q - (\text{Test}_1 \cup \text{Test}_2 \cup \{q_m\})$, and the $(8i+4)$-th and $(8i+8)$-th columns correspond to output ports for $q_i^{P_j}$ and $q_i^{Z_j}$ for $q_i \in \text{Test}_j$. The symbols $q_i^{P_j}$ and $q_i^{Z_j}$ mean that the present state is q_i and the test result of the j-th counter is positive and zero, respectively.

Consider the branch module for M_1 in Fig. 12.31. If the present state is, e.g., q_0, then a signal comes from the bottom row of the fourth column. By the counter-test submodule at the lower left corner, the signal goes to the port T_2. Then the response signal comes back from either Z_2 or P_2 port. Finally, it goes out from the port $q_0^{Z_2}$ or $q_0^{P_2}$ through the counter-test submodule.

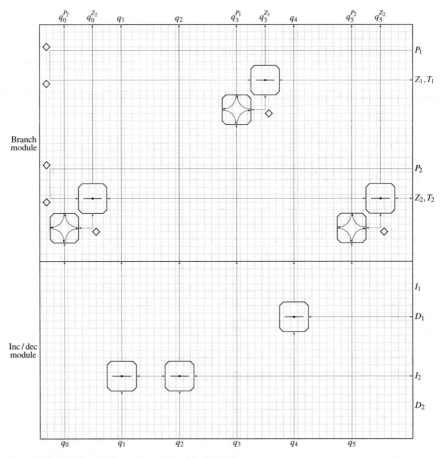

Fig. 12.31 Inc/dec and branch modules for M_1 in P_3

(5) State-transition module

A state-transition module is one that simulates the state-transition of M properly. Let Q_1 and Q_2 be the sets defined as follows.

$$Q_1 = \{q_i \mid q_i \in (Q - (\text{Test}_1 \cup \text{Test}_2) \cup \{q_m\}))\} \cup \{q_i^{Z_j}, q_i^{P_j} \mid q_i \in \text{Test}_j \ (j=1,2)\}$$
$$Q_2 = \{q_i \mid q_i \in (Q - (\text{Merge}_1 \cup \text{Merge}_2))\} \cup \{q_i^{Z_j}, q_i^{P_j} \mid q_i \in \text{Merge}_j \ (j=1,2)\}$$

Then, the size of this module is $(2|Q_2|+2) \times (8m+4)$.

This module computes a partial mapping $\delta' : Q_1 \to Q_2$ defined as follows from δ (it is described as a subset of $Q_1 \times Q_2$).

$$\begin{aligned}
\delta' = & \{(q_i, q_k) \mid \exists j \in \{1,2\}, \exists d \in \{-,0,+\} \ ([q_i, j, d, q_k] \in \delta)\} \\
& \cup \{(q_i^{X_j}, q_k^{X_j}) \mid [q_i, j, X, q_k] \in \delta \ \wedge \ X \in \{Z, P\} \ \wedge \ q_k \in \text{Merge}_j \ (j=1,2)\} \\
& \cup \{(q_i^{X_j}, q_k) \mid [q_i, j, X, q_k] \in \delta \ \wedge \ X \in \{Z, P\} \ \wedge \ q_k \notin \text{Merge}_j \ (j=1,2)\}
\end{aligned}$$

It is easily verified that δ' is a one-to-one mapping because M is reversible.

On the bottom row of this module, the correspondence between columns and the elements in Q_1 is the same as the first row of the branch module. Let $\hat{Q}_2$ be the ordered set obtained from Q_2 by ordering q_i's and $q_i^{X_j}$'s in the descending order of the subscript i and further assuming $q_i^{Z_j}$ precedes $q_i^{P_j}$. We now make a correspondence between the rows of the rightmost column and the elements in Q_2, i.e., we assign the $2n$-th row to the n-th element of $\hat{Q}_2$ $(n \in \{1, \cdots, |Q_2|\})$.

Once the assignment of columns and rows to the sets Q_1 and Q_2 are fixed, the mapping δ' is easily realized in P_3 space by appropriately putting LR-turn elements to turn a signal rightward. Figure 12.32 shows a state-transition module for M_1.

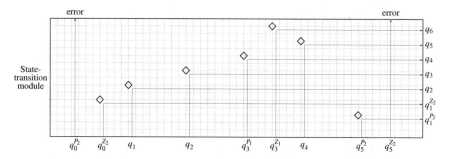

Fig. 12.32 State-transition module for M_1 in P_3

(6) Turn modules

Turn modules 1 and 2 simply make a signal turn right in order to feed it to a begin/end/turn module from a state-transition module. The size of the turn modules 1 and 2 are both $(2|Q_2|+2) \times (2|Q_2|+2)$. Figure 12.33 shows these modules for the example M_1.

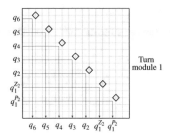 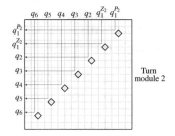

Fig. 12.33 Turn modules 1 and 2 for M_1 in P_3

(7) Begin/end/turn module

A begin/end/turn module also acts like turn modules 1 and 2 to feed a signal to a merge module. There are, however, small differences on the signal paths related to the initial state q_0 and the final state q_m. Also there are an additional input port "Begin" and an output port "End". A signal coming from the "Begin" port is fed to the output port q_0 of this module (this is in fact possible because M is in the normal form). By this, computation of an RCM(2) M is initiated by a signal given from outside. A signal coming from the port q_m is fed to the "End" port telling that the computation has terminated. The size of this module is $(2|Q_2|+2) \times (8m+4)$. The lower part of Fig. 12.34 shows the begin/end/turn module for M_1.

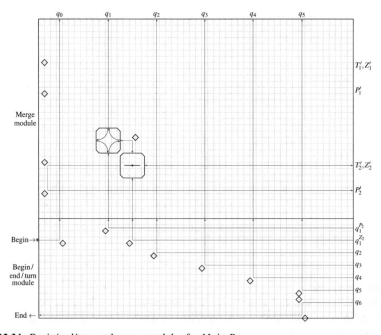

Fig. 12.34 Begin/end/turn and merge modules for M_1 in P_3

(8) Merge module

It is a circuit to reversibly merge every pairs of signal lines $q_i^{Z_j}$ and $q_i^{P_j}$ such that $q_i \in \text{Merge}_j$ into a single signal line q_i. The size of this module is $32 \times (8m+4)$. On the bottom row of the module, the $(8i+4)$-th column is assigned to each $q_i \in (Q - (\text{Merge}_1 \cup \text{Merge}_2 \cup \{q_m\}))$. For a state $q_i \in \text{Merge}_j$, the $(8i+4)$-th and $(8i+6)$-th columns are assigned to $q_i^{P_j}$ and $q_i^{Z_j}$, respectively. On the first row of this module, the $(8i+4)$-th column corresponds to $q_i \in Q - \{q_m\}$.

If $q_i \in \text{Merge}_1$ (Merge_2, respectively), then put an R-turn element at the $(8i+2)$-nd column of the tenth (18th) row, an LR-turn element at the $(8i+8)$-th column of the third (11th) row, and a rotary element at the $(8i+6)$-th column of of the 14th (22th) row. The block consisting of these three elements is called an *undo-test submodule*. In addition, two LR-turn elements are put at the left part of the module as in Fig. 12.34.

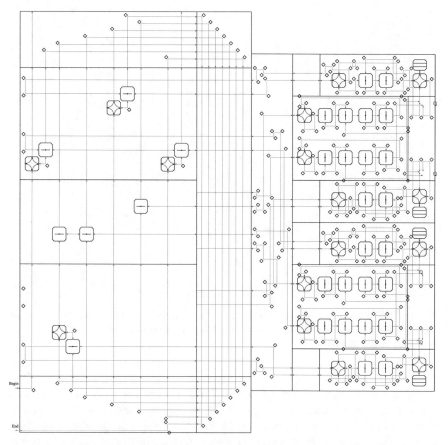

Fig. 12.35 Circuit diagram of the RCM(2) M_1 embedded in the cellular space of P_3

Consider the merge module shown in Fig. 12.34 for M_1. If a signal comes from $q_1^{P_2}$, it goes to the P_2' port through the undo-test submodule. Similarly, if a signal comes from $q_1^{Z_2}$, it goes to the Z_2' port. In either case, a response signal will be obtained from the T_2' port, and thus two signal lines are merged. It travels through the undo-test module again, and then goes out from q_1 port on the first row.

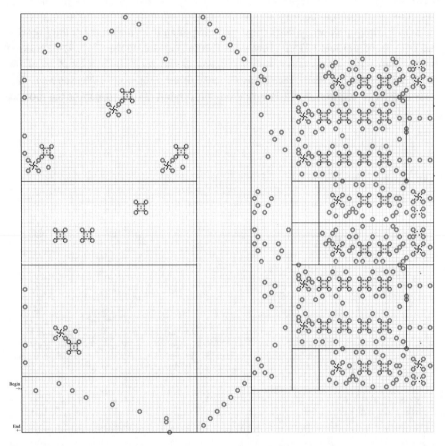

Fig. 12.36 The whole configuration that simulates the reversible two-counter machine M_1 in the cellular space of P_3 [8]. A computer simulation movie of the computing process starting from this configuration can be seen in [5]

By combining the modules described above, we can construct a configuration that simulates a given RCM(2). Figure 12.35 shows the symbolic representation of the circuit that simulates M_1, and Fig. 12.36 is the whole configuration embedded in the cellular space of P_3. If we give a signal from the input port "Begin", it starts to compute from the initial state q_0. When it halts in the final state q_6, a signal goes out from the output port "End" leaving the result of the computation in the counters.

It is easy to see that any deterministic RCM(2) can be constructed by the method described above.

12.4.4 Turing universality of the RPCA P_3

From Theorem 9.2, which states universality of RCM(2), and the above construction of RCM(2) in P_3, we have the following theorem.

Theorem 12.2. *The 81-state two-dimensional four-neighbor RPCA P_3 with finite configurations is Turing universal.*

Finally, we give some remarks on other two-dimensional RPCAs related to P_3. Before the 81-state RPCA model P_3, there was a 256-state four-neighbor RPCA P_4 [7], where each part of its cell has four states. Actually, P_3 is a revised version of P_4. In fact, they are designed based on essentially the same idea. There are also five basic elements in P_4, from which eight kinds of circuit modules are realized. Then, an RCM(2) is constructed out of them as in Fig. 12.28. Therefore, P_4 with finite configurations is Turing universal. The difference is that P_3 has fewer states, and adjustment of signal timing is more difficult than in P_4. The configuration size of an RCM(2) in P_3 is also larger than that in P_4, i.e., about four times larger in its area.

There is another 81-state four-neighbor RPCA P_3' [6] in which LR-turn element, R-turn element, reflector, and RE can be simulated (but it cannot simulate position marker). Hence, P_3' with ultimately periodic configurations is Turing universal. Though the number of states is the same, the sizes of the patterns of the basic elements are smaller than those in P_3.

12.5 Intrinsic Universality of Two-Dimensional RPCAs

Intrinsic universality is a property of a CA U such that any CA A in some large class $\mathscr{A}$ of CAs is simulated by U (see, e.g., [11]). It should be noted that U must be able to simulate any evolution process of configurations even if they are infinite configurations. In this section, after giving definitions related to it, we show the RPCAs given in the previous sections are intrinsically universal. We first make some preparations to define this notion.

Let $A_1 = (\mathbb{Z}^2, Q_1, N_1, f_1, \#)$ and $A_2 = (\mathbb{Z}^2, Q_2, N_2, f_2, \#)$ be two-dimensional CAs, $h, w \in \mathbb{Z}_+$, and $R = \{0, \ldots, w-1\} \times \{0, \ldots, h-1\}$. Let $c : Q_1 \to Q_2^R$ be an injection (hence h and w must be the ones such that $|Q_1| \le |Q_2^R|$ holds), and $d : Q_2^R \to (Q_1 \cup \{\perp\})$ be the function defined below.

$$\forall X \in Q_2^R : \left(d(X) = \begin{cases} q & \text{if } c(q) = X \\ \perp & \text{elsewhere} \end{cases} \right)$$

We can interpret c as a function that encodes a state in Q_1 by a rectangular array of states in Q_2 of size $h \times w$. On the other hand, d is a decoding function. The functions c and d are extended to $c^* : \mathrm{Conf}(A_1) \to \mathrm{Conf}(A_2)$ and $d^* : \mathrm{Conf}(A_2) \to (\mathrm{Conf}(A_1) \cup \{\bot\})$ as follows.

$$\forall \alpha_1 \in \mathrm{Conf}(A_1):$$
$$c^*(\alpha_1) = \alpha_2 \text{ such that } \forall(x_1, y_1) \in \mathbb{Z}^2, \ \forall(x_2, y_2) \in R:$$
$$(\alpha_2(wx_1 + x_2, hy_1 + y_2) = c(\alpha_1(x_1, y_1))(x_2, y_2))$$
$$\forall \alpha_2 \in \mathrm{Conf}(A_2):$$
$$d^*(\alpha_2) = \begin{cases} \alpha_1 & \text{if } \forall(x_1, y_1) \in \mathbb{Z}^2, \ \forall(x_2, y_2) \in R: \\ & (\alpha_2(wx_1 + x_2, hy_1 + y_2) = c(\alpha_1(x_1, y_1))(x_2, y_2)) \\ \bot & \text{elsewhere} \end{cases}$$

Figure 12.37 shows how the configuration α_1 of A_1 is encoded and embedded in α_2 of A_2 by the function c^*. By above, we can see that c^* and d^* are finitely defined based on c and d. Hereafter, c and c^* are called *encoding functions*, and d and d^* are called *decoding functions*.

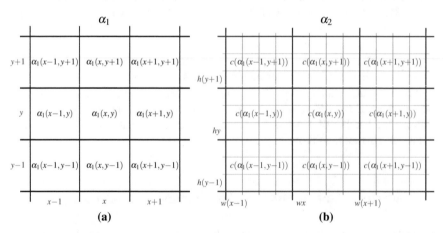

Fig. 12.37 Embedding a configuration α_1 of the CA A_1 into a configuration α_2 of the CA A_2 by the encoding function c^*. **(a)** The configuration α_1. **(b)** The configuration α_2, in which each cell's state of A_1 is represented by an array of states of A_2's cells of size $h \times w$ using the function c

Now, intrinsic universality is defined as follows.

Definition 12.5. Let $\mathscr{A}$ be a class of two-dimensional CAs. A two-dimensional CA U, whose set of states and global function are Q_U and F_U, is called *intrinsically universal* with respect to $\mathscr{A}$, if the following condition holds.

$\forall A \in \mathscr{A}$, whose set of states and global function are Q_A and F_A,
$\exists h, w \in \mathbb{Z}_+, \exists \tau \in \mathbb{Z}_+,$
$\exists c : Q_A \to Q_U^R, \exists d : Q_U^R \to (Q_A \cup \{\perp\})$, where $R = \{0, \dots, w-1\} \times \{0, \dots, h-1\}$,
$\forall \alpha, \alpha' \in \mathrm{Conf}(A) :$
$\quad (F_A(\alpha) = \alpha' \Rightarrow d^*(F_U^\tau(c^*(\alpha))) = \alpha')$

Lemma 12.2. *Let U be a two-dimensional RCA. If any reversible logic circuit composed of Fredkin gates (or rotary elements) and delay elements is simulated in U, then U is intrinsically universal with respect to the class of two-dimensional RPCAs.*

Proof. We give here only an outline of a proof, since precise descriptions of the coding and decoding functions c and d for each RPCA A will be very lengthy.

First, we consider the case that a Fredkin gate is simulated in U. In Sect. 10.6, a method of composing a circuit from Fredkin gates and delay elements that simulates one cell of a one-dimensional three-neighbor RPCA was given (Fig. 10.31). By modifying the method, it is also possible to construct a circuit that simulates a cell of a two-dimensional RPCA A with an arbitrary neighborhood size. It is done by adding decoder modules (Fig. 4.30) and inverse decoder modules to the circuit shown in Fig. 10.31. Placing infinitely many copies of the circuit two-dimensionally, and connecting them appropriately, the RPCA A can be simulated. Such an infinite circuit is further embedded in a configuration of U that satisfies the condition in Definition 12.5. Though the design details of the configurations will be very complex, it is clear that such configurations exist, since Fredkin gate, signal routing, and delay are all possible in U.

Next, we consider the case that a rotary element (RE) is simulated in U. In Sect. 10.6, a method of composing a circuit from RE that simulates decoder and inverse decoder modules is shown (Fig. 10.32). It is also explained in Sect. 10.6 that one cell of a two-dimensional RPCA A with an arbitrary neighborhood size can be implemented as an RE-circuit using these modules. Placing infinitely many copies of the circuit two-dimensionally, as in the first case, the RPCA A can be simulated. Such an infinite circuit can be further embedded in a configuration of U that satisfies the condition in Definition 12.5. By above, we have the theorem. □

Theorem 12.3. *The 16-state two-dimensional four-neighbor RPCAs S_1 and S_2, and the 81-state two-dimensional four-neighbor RPCA P_3 are intrinsically universal with respect to the class of two-dimensional RPCAs.*

Proof. In Sect. 12.3 it is shown that any reversible logic circuit composed of Fredkin gates and delay elements is simulated in the 16-state RPCAs S_1 and S_2. Also in Sect. 12.4, it is shown that any reversible logic circuit composed of rotary elements and delay elements is simulated in the 81-state RPCAs P_3. Hence, by Lemma 12.2, these three RPCAs are intrinsically universal. □

12.6 Concluding Remarks

In the past studies on universal irreversible two-dimensional CAs, methods of implementing logic circuits that simulate sequential machines have often been employed to show their universality [1, 3, 10]. Banks [1] gave a two-state CA with von Neumann neighborhood, in which any logic circuit realizing a Boolean function is embeddable. On the other hand, in the 29-state CA of von Neumann [10], any sequential machine can be implemented by a circuit that uses a "coded channel", but does not directly use logical functions such as AND, OR and NOT (see also [2]). Since each cell of a CA can be formalized as a sequential machine, the intrinsic universality of these CAs is also derived.

In this chapter, three models of simple two-dimensional Turing universal and intrinsically universal RPCAs that can simulate logic elements were given. In the first two models S_1 and S_2, it was shown that the Fredkin gate is realizable in them, from which any reversible sequential machine (RSM) can be constructed. On the other hand, in the third model P_3 the rotary element (RE) is realizable, and thus any RSM can be constructed.

The models S_1 and S_2 are 16-state RPCAs on the square grid. In these RPCAs, any reversible logic circuit composed of Fredkin gates and delay elements can be realized. Hence, any reversible TM is implemented as a horizontally ultimately periodic configuration in them. Also, for any two-dimensional RPCA, a configuration of a circuit that simulates its cell can be obtained. Hence, it is intrinsically universal.

The set of local rules of S_1 (Fig. 12.1) is isomorphic to that of the block CA of Margolus (Fig. 10.11 **(b)**), and thus S_1 is a reformulation of it in the framework of PCAs. However, the evolution processes of the configurations of a PCA are easier to understand than those of a block CA, since PCAs are a subclass of the standard CAs. In Chap. 13, we shall study RPCAs on the triangular tessellation. Although even such triangular RPCAs could be reformulated as block RCAs, it is much harder to understand how the triangular block RCAs evolve. Therefore, the framework of PCAs are particularly useful for designing reversible CAs on the triangular or some other tessellation.

The third model P_3 is an 81-state RPCA on the square grid, where each of the four parts of a cell has three states. Though its number of states is larger than those of the first two models, any reversible two-counter machine can be realized as a finite configuration concisely. It is also possible to simulate a reversible logic circuit composed of rotary elements in P_3. Hence, it is intrinsically universal, as well as Turing universal.

References

1. Banks, E.R.: Universality in cellular automata. In: Proc. Symposium on Switching and Automata Theory, IEEE, pp. 194–215 (1970). doi:10.1109/SWAT.1970.27

2. Burks, A.W.: Von Neumann's self-reproducing automata. In: Essays on Cellular Automata (ed. A.W. Burks), pp. 3–64. University of Illinois Press, Urbana (1970)
3. Codd, E.F.: Cellular Automata. Academic Press, New York (1968)
4. Margolus, N.: Physics-like model of computation. Physica D **10**, 81–95 (1984). doi:10.1016/0167-2789(84)90252-5
5. Morita, K.: Universal reversible cellular automata in which counter machines are concisely embedded. Hiroshima University Institutional Repository, http://ir.lib.hiroshima-u.ac.jp/00031367 (2011)
6. Morita, K., Ogiro, T.: Simple universal reversible cellular automata in which reversible logic elements can be embedded. IEICE Trans. Inf. & Syst. **E87-D**, 650–656 (2004)
7. Morita, K., Tojima, Y., Imai, K.: A simple computer embedded in a reversible and number-conserving two-dimensional cellular space. Multiple-Valued Logic **6**(5-6), 483–514 (2001)
8. Morita, K., Tojima, Y., Imai, K., Ogiro, T.: Universal computing in reversible and number-conserving two-dimensional cellular spaces. In: Collision-based Computing (ed. A. Adamatzky), pp. 161–199. Springer (2002). doi:10.1007/978-1-4471-0129-1_7
9. Morita, K., Ueno, S.: Computation-universal models of two-dimensional 16-state reversible cellular automata. IEICE Trans. Inf. & Syst. **E75-D**, 141–147 (1992)
10. von Neumann, J.: Theory of Self-reproducing Automata (ed. A.W. Burks). The University of Illinois Press, Urbana (1966)
11. Ollinger, N.: Universalities in cellular automata. In: Handbook of Natural Computing, pp. 189–229. Springer (2012). doi:10.1007/978-3-540-92910-9_6

Chapter 13
Reversible Elementary Triangular Partitioned Cellular Automata

Abstract A three-neighbor triangular partitioned cellular automaton (TPCA) is a CA such that each cell is triangular-shaped and has three parts. A TPCA is called an elementary TPCA (ETPCA), if it is rotation-symmetric, and each part of a cell has only two states. The class of ETPCAs is one of the simplest subclasses of two-dimensional CAs, since the local function of each ETPCA is described by only four local rules. Here, we investigate the universality of reversible ETPCAs (RETPCAs). First, nine kinds of conservative RETPCAs, in which the total number of particles is conserved in their evolution processes, are studied. It is proved that six conservative RETPCAs among nine are Turing universal and intrinsically universal by showing any reversible logic circuit composed of Fredkin gates can be simulated in them. It is also shown that three conservative RETPCAs among nine are non-universal. Next, we study a specific non-conservative RETPCA T_{0347}, where 0347 is its identification number in the class of 256 ETPCAs. In spite of its simplicity it exhibits complex behavior like the Game of Life CA. Using gliders to represent signals, Turing universality and intrinsic universality of T_{0347} are also proved.

Keywords elementary triangular partitioned cellular automaton, reversible cellular automaton, Fredkin gate, Turing universality, intrinsic universality

13.1 Elementary Triangular Partitioned Cellular Automata

A triangular cellular automaton (TCA) is a two-dimensional CA defined on the *triangular tessellation* shown in Fig. 13.3. Though a TCA is not a standard model in the study of CAs, its local function can be simpler than that of the usual CA on the square tessellation, if we consider a three-neighbor TCA. Hence, this model will be useful to investigate how computational universality and other complex phenomena appear from a very simple local function. Here, we study the class of three-neighbor triangular partitioned cellular automata such that each part of a cell has only two states, and they are rotation-symmetric (i.e., isotropic). They are called

367

the *elementary triangular partitioned cellular automata* (ETPCAs). As in the case of one-dimensional elementary cellular automata (ECAs) [13] (see Example 10.3), there are only 256 ETPCAs. As we shall see later, ETPCAs are particularly simple among all CAs, since each of their local functions is described by only four local rules. However, the class of ETPCAs contains various interesting CAs.

In this chapter, we investigate *reversible* ETPCAs (RETPCAs). In the class of one-dimensional ECAs, there are only six reversible ones, i.e., the ECAs of rule numbers 15, 51, 85, 170, 204, and 240 [13]. However, all the local functions of these ECAs are of one variable. For example, the ECA rule 15 has the local function $f_{15}(q_{-1}, q_0, q_1) = \overline{q_{-1}}$. Hence, these six are all trivial one-neighbor CAs. On the other hand, there are 36 RETPCAs, and most of them are nontrivial. In fact, as we shall see, at least ten RETPCAs among 36 are computationally universal.

In this section, we give definitions on ETPCAs and several notions related to it. In Sect. 13.2, we study universality of *conservative* RETPCAs, in which the total number of particles is conserved in each local rule. We shall show that, among nine conservative RETPCAs, six are Turing universal as well as intrinsically universal with respect to the class of two-dimensional RPCAs. We shall also show that the remaining three conservative RETPCAs are non-universal. In Sect. 13.3, we investigate a specific non-conservative RETPCA T_{0347}, where 0347 is an identification number among 256 ETPCAs. In spite of the simplicity of the local function and the constraint of reversibility, evolutions of configurations in T_{0347} have very rich varieties, and look like those in the Game of Life CA to some extent. In particular, a "glider" and "glider guns" exist in T_{0347}. Furthermore, using gliders to represent signals, we can implement universal reversible logic gates in it. By this, both Turing universality and intrinsic universality of T_{0347} are derived.

13.1.1 Triangular partitioned cellular automata (TPCAs)

A three-neighbor triangular partitioned cellular automaton (TPCA) is a PCA such that each cell has three parts, and the next state of a cell is determined by the states of the adjacent parts of the three neighbor cells. Figure 13.1 shows the cellular space of a TPCA, and a local rule.

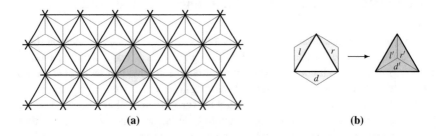

(a)   (b)

Fig. 13.1 A three-neighbor triangular PCA (TPCA). (a) Its cellular space, and (b) a local rule

All the cells of a TPCA are identical copies of a finite state machine as usual, and each cell has three parts, i.e., the left, downward, and right parts, whose state sets are L, D and R, respectively. However, the directions of the cells are not the same, i.e., there are *up-triangle cells* and *down-triangle cells* as in Fig. 13.2 (a) and (b). Here, we assume that a down-triangle cell is one obtained by rotating an up-triangle cell by 180°. Therefore, for an up-triangle cell whose state is $(l,d,r) \in L \times D \times R$ shown in Fig. 13.2 (a), there is a down-triangle cell such that its state is also (l,d,r), and the positions of the three parts are as shown in Fig. 13.2 (b).

(a)   (b)

Fig. 13.2 (a) An up-triangle cell, and (b) a down-triangle cell in the cellular space of a TPCA, whose states are $(l,d,r) \in L \times D \times R$

We now place cells of a TPCA on $\mathbb{Z}^2$ as shown in Fig. 13.3. We assume that if the coordinates of an up-triangle cell is (x,y), then $x+y$ must be even. It should be noted, if we define an TPCA on $\mathbb{Z}^2$, there arises a problem that the neighborhood is slightly non-uniform. Namely, for an up-triangle cell, its neighbors are the west, south and east adjacent cells, while for a down-triangle cell, its neighbors are the east, north and west adjacent cells. Although such non-uniformity can be dissolved by defining a TPCA on a Cayley graph (see e.g., [10]), here we define a TPCA on $\mathbb{Z}^2$ in order to give a similar formulation as in Definition 10.5. By this, we can specify a rectangular-like region in the cellular space of a TPCA, and define an ultimately periodic configuration relatively easily.

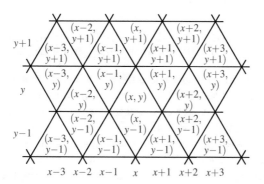

Fig. 13.3 The x-y coordinates in the cellular space of TPCA. If the cell at (x,y) is an up-triangle one, then $x+y$ must be even

Definition 13.1. A *deterministic triangular partitioned cellular automaton (TPCA)* is a system defined by

$$T = (\mathbb{Z}^2, (L, D, R), ((-1,0), (0,-1), (1,0)), ((1,0), (0,1), (-1,0)), f, (\#, \#, \#)).$$

Here, $\mathbb{Z}^2$ is the set of all two-dimensional points with integer coordinates at which cells are placed. Each cell has three parts, i.e., the left, downward and right parts, where L, D and R are non-empty finite set of states of these parts. The state set Q of each cell is thus given by $Q = L \times D \times R$. The triplet $((-1,0), (0,-1), (1,0))$ is a *neighborhood* for up-triangle cells, and $((1,0), (0,1), (-1,0))$ is a neighborhood for down-triangle cells. The item $f : Q \rightarrow Q$ is a *local function*, and $(\#, \#, \#) \in Q$ is a *quiescent state* that satisfies $f(\#, \#, \#) = (\#, \#, \#)$. We also allow a TPCA that has no quiescent state.

If $f(l, d, r) = (l', d', r')$ holds for $(l, d, r), (l', d', r') \in Q$, then this relation is called a *local rule* (or simply a *rule*) of the TPCA T.

Configurations of a TPCA, and the global function induced by the local function are defined as below.

Definition 13.2. Let

$$T = (\mathbb{Z}^2, (L, D, R), ((-1,0), (0,-1), (1,0)), ((1,0), (0,1), (-1,0)), f, (\#, \#, \#))$$

be a TPCA. A *configuration* of T is a function $\alpha : \mathbb{Z}^2 \rightarrow Q$. The set of all configurations of T is denoted by $\mathrm{Conf}(T)$, i.e., $\mathrm{Conf}(T) = \{\alpha \,|\, \alpha : \mathbb{Z}^2 \rightarrow Q\}$. Let $\mathrm{pr}_L : Q \rightarrow L$ be the *projection function* such that $\mathrm{pr}_L(l, d, r) = l$ for all $(l, d, r) \in Q$. The projection functions $\mathrm{pr}_D : Q \rightarrow D$ and $\mathrm{pr}_R : Q \rightarrow R$ are also defined similarly. The *global function* $F : \mathrm{Conf}(T) \rightarrow \mathrm{Conf}(T)$ of T is defined as the one that satisfies the following condition.

$$\forall \alpha \in \mathrm{Conf}(T), \forall (x, y) \in \mathbb{Z}^2 :$$
$$F(\alpha)(x, y)$$
$$= \begin{cases} f(\mathrm{pr}_L(\alpha(x-1, y)), \mathrm{pr}_D(\alpha(x, y-1)), \mathrm{pr}_R(\alpha(x+1, y))) & \text{if } x + y \text{ is even} \\ f(\mathrm{pr}_L(\alpha(x+1, y)), \mathrm{pr}_D(\alpha(x, y+1)), \mathrm{pr}_R(\alpha(x-1, y))) & \text{if } x + y \text{ is odd} \end{cases}$$

From this definition, we can see that the next state of the up-triangle cell is determined by the present states of the left part of the west neighbor cell, the downward part of the south neighbor cell, and the right part of the east neighbor cell. On the other hand, the next state of the down-triangle cell is determined by the present states of the left part of the east neighbor cell, the downward part of the north neighbor cell, and the right part of the west neighbor cell. Therefore, for a local rule $f(l, d, r) = (l', d', r')$, there are two kinds of pictorial representations as shown in Fig. 13.4 **(a)** and **(b)**. Namely, Fig. 13.4 **(a)** is for up-triangle cells, while Fig. 13.4 **(b)** is for down-triangle cells.

For a TPCA T that has a quiescent state, we can define a *finite* and an *infinite configurations* in a similar manner as in the standard CA (Sect. 10.2).

Fig. 13.4 Pictorial representations of the local rule $f(l,d,r) = (l',d',r')$. They are **(a)** for up-triangle cells, and **(b)** for down-triangle cells

13.1.1.1 Reversibility in TPCAs

As in the case of a PCA on the square tessellation, we can also show that injectivity of the global function is equivalent to injectivity of the local function in a TPCA. The following lemma is proved in a similar manner as in Lemma 10.3.

Lemma 13.1. *Let*

$$T = (\mathbb{Z}^2, (L,D,R), ((-1,0),(0,-1),(1,0)), ((1,0),(0,1),(-1,0)), f, (\#,\#,\#))$$

be a TPCA, and F be its global function. Then, F is injective iff f is injective.

Proof. We first prove if F is injective, then f is injective. Assume, on the contrary, f is not injective. Thus, there exist $(l_1,d_1,r_1),(l_2,d_2,r_2) \in Q = L \times D \times R$ such that $f(l_1,d_1,r_1) = f(l_2,d_2,r_2)$ and $(l_1,d_1,r_1) \neq (l_2,d_2,r_2)$. Let $(\hat{l},\hat{d},\hat{r})$ be an element arbitrarily chosen from Q. We define two configurations α_1 and α_2 as below.

$$\forall (x,y) \in \mathbb{Z}^2 :$$

$$\alpha_1(x,y) = \begin{cases} (l_1,\hat{d},\hat{r}) & \text{if } (x,y) = (-1,0) \\ (\hat{l},d_1,\hat{r}) & \text{if } (x,y) = (0,-1) \\ (\hat{l},\hat{d},r_1) & \text{if } (x,y) = (1,0) \\ (\hat{l},\hat{d},\hat{r}) & \text{elsewhere} \end{cases}$$

$$\alpha_2(x,y) = \begin{cases} (l_2,\hat{d},\hat{r}) & \text{if } (x,y) = (-1,0) \\ (\hat{l},d_2,\hat{r}) & \text{if } (x,y) = (0,-1) \\ (\hat{l},\hat{d},r_2) & \text{if } (x,y) = (1,0) \\ (\hat{l},\hat{d},\hat{r}) & \text{elsewhere} \end{cases}$$

Since $(l_1,d_1,r_1) \neq (l_2,d_2,r_2)$, $\alpha_1 \neq \alpha_2$ holds. By the definition of F, the following holds.

$\forall (x,y) \in \mathbb{Z}^2 :$
$F(\alpha_1)(x,y)$
$$= \begin{cases} f(\mathrm{pr}_L(\alpha_1(x-1,y)), \mathrm{pr}_D(\alpha_1(x,y-1)), \mathrm{pr}_R(\alpha_1(x+1,y))) & \text{if } x+y \text{ is even} \\ f(\mathrm{pr}_L(\alpha_1(x+1,y)), \mathrm{pr}_D(\alpha_1(x,y+1)), \mathrm{pr}_R(\alpha_1(x-1,y))) & \text{if } x+y \text{ is odd} \end{cases}$$
$$= \begin{cases} f(l_1,d_1,r_1) & \text{if } (x,y) = (0,0) \\ f(\hat{l},\hat{d},\hat{r}) & \text{if } (x,y) \neq (0,0) \end{cases}$$

$\forall (x,y) \in \mathbb{Z}^2 :$

$F(\alpha_2)(x,y)$

$= \begin{cases} f(\mathrm{pr}_L(\alpha_2(x-1,y)), \mathrm{pr}_D(\alpha_2(x,y-1)), \mathrm{pr}_R(\alpha_2(x+1,y))) & \text{if } x+y \text{ is even} \\ f(\mathrm{pr}_L(\alpha_2(x+1,y)), \mathrm{pr}_D(\alpha_2(x,y+1)), \mathrm{pr}_R(\alpha_2(x-1,y))) & \text{if } x+y \text{ is odd} \end{cases}$

$= \begin{cases} f(l_2,d_2,r_2) & \text{if } (x,y)=(0,0) \\ f(\hat{l},\hat{d},\hat{r}) & \text{if } (x,y) \neq (0,0) \end{cases}$

But, since $f(l_1,d_1,r_1) = f(l_2,d_2,r_2)$, $F(\alpha_1) = F(\alpha_2)$ holds. It contradicts the assumption that F is injective.

Next, we show if f is injective, then F is injective. We assume, on the contrary, F is not injective. Thus, there are configurations α_1 and α_2 such that $F(\alpha_1) = F(\alpha_2)$ and $\alpha_1 \neq \alpha_2$. Since $\alpha_1 \neq \alpha_2$, there exist $(x_0,y_0) \in \mathbb{Z}^2$ and $X \in \{L,D,R\}$ that satisfy $\mathrm{pr}_X(\alpha_1(x_0,y_0)) \neq \mathrm{pr}_X(\alpha_2(x_0,y_0))$. Below, we consider only the case x_0+y_0 is even, since it is similarly proved for the case x_0+y_0 is odd. Furthermore, we consider only the case $X = L$, since the cases $X = D$ and $X = R$ are similar. Thus, the following holds.

$F(\alpha_1)(x_0-1,y_0) = f(\mathrm{pr}_L(\alpha_1(x_0,y_0)), \mathrm{pr}_D(\alpha_1(x_0-1,y_0+1)), \mathrm{pr}_R(\alpha_1(x_0-2,y_0)))$

$F(\alpha_2)(x_0-1,y_0) = f(\mathrm{pr}_L(\alpha_2(x_0,y_0)), \mathrm{pr}_D(\alpha_2(x_0-1,y_0+1)), \mathrm{pr}_R(\alpha_2(x_0-2,y_0)))$

From $\mathrm{pr}_L(\alpha_1(x_0,y_0)) \neq \mathrm{pr}_L(\alpha_2(x_0,y_0))$, and the fact f is injective, $F(\alpha_1)(x_0-1,y_0) \neq F(\alpha_2)(x_0-1,y_0)$. But, it contradicts the assumption $F(\alpha_1) = F(\alpha_2)$. □

A reversible TPCA is defined as follows.

Definition 13.3. Let T be a TPCA. The TPCA T is called a *reversible TPCA* if its local (or equivalently global) function is injective.

13.1.1.2 Rotation-symmetry in TPCAs

We define the notion of rotation-symmetry for a TPCA as follows.

Definition 13.4. Let

$$T = (\mathbb{Z}^2, (L,D,R), ((-1,0),(0,-1),(1,0)), ((1,0),(0,1),(-1,0)), f, (\#,\#,\#))$$

be a TPCA. The TPCA T is called *rotation-symmetric* (or *isotropic*) if the following conditions (1) and (2) holds.

(1) $L = D = R$
(2) $\forall (l,d,r),(l',d',r') \in L \times D \times R \ \ (f(l,d,r)=(l',d',r') \ \Rightarrow \ f(d,r,l)=(d',r',l'))$

If a TPCA T is rotation-symmetric, then for each local rule in the pictorial form shown in Fig. 13.4 **(a)**, there are also two local rules obtained from it by rotating the both sides of it by $120°$ and $240°$. Furthermore, by Definition 13.2, for each local rule in the pictorial form shown in Fig. 13.4 **(a)**, there is a local rule in the pictorial form shown in Fig. 13.4 **(b)**, which is obtained by rotating the both sides of the former by $180°$. Hence, the local function f of a rotation-symmetric TPCA is uniform in all the six directions.

It is easy to show the next lemma.

Lemma 13.2. *Let*

$$T = (\mathbb{Z}^2, (S,S,S), ((-1,0),(0,-1),(1,0)), ((1,0),(0,1),(-1,0)), f, (\#,\#,\#))$$

be a rotation-symmetric TPCA. Then the following holds.

$$\forall s, s_1, s_2, s_3 \in S \ (f(s,s,s) = (s_1,s_2,s_3) \ \Rightarrow \ s_1 = s_2 = s_3)$$

Proof. Assume, on the contrary, there exist $s, s_1, s_2, s_3 \in S$ such that $f(s,s,s) = (s_1, s_2, s_3)$ and $(s_1 \neq s_2) \vee (s_2 \neq s_3) \vee (s_3 \neq s_1)$ hold. We consider only the case $s_1 \neq s_2$, since other cases are similar. By the condition (2) in Definition 13.4, $f(s,s,s) = (s_2, s_3, s_1) \neq (s_1, s_2, s_3)$ holds. Thus, it contradicts the fact f is a function such that $f : S^3 \to S^3$ (note that we consider only deterministic CAs here). □

13.1.1.3 Ultimately periodic configurations in TPCAs

Next, we define horizontally periodic, and horizontally ultimately periodic configurations of a TPCA, which are similarly given as in Definition 12.1.

Definition 13.5. Let

$$T = (\mathbb{Z}^2, (L,D,R), ((-1,0),(0,-1),(1,0)), ((1,0),(0,1),(-1,0)), f, (\#,\#,\#))$$

be a TPCA, and $Q = L \times D \times R$. A two-dimensional configuration $\alpha : \mathbb{Z}^2 \to Q$ is called *horizontally periodic* if there are $p \in \mathbb{Z}_+$ and $y_0, y_1 \in \mathbb{Z}$ such that $y_0 < y_1$ that satisfy the following.

$$\forall (x,y) \in \mathbb{Z}^2$$
$$((y_0 \leq y \leq y_1 \ \Rightarrow \ \alpha(x,y) = \alpha(x+2p,y)) \wedge$$
$$((y < y_0 \vee y > y_1) \ \Rightarrow \ \alpha(x,y) = \#))$$

Thus, the pattern in the *rectangular-like region* $\{(x,y) \mid 0 \leq x \leq 2p-1, \ y_0 \leq y \leq y_1\}$ in the triangular cellular space repeats infinitely to the right and to the left.

A configuration $\alpha : \mathbb{Z}^2 \to Q$ is called *horizontally ultimately periodic* if there are $p_L, p_R \in \mathbb{Z}_+$, $x_L, x_R \in \mathbb{Z}$ $(x_L < x_R)$, and $y_0, y_1 \in \mathbb{Z}$ $(y_0 < y_1)$ that satisfy the following.

$$\forall (x,y) \in \mathbb{Z}^2$$
$$(((y_0 \leq y \leq y_1) \wedge (x \leq x_L) \ \Rightarrow \ \alpha(x-2p_L,y) = \alpha(x,y)) \wedge$$
$$((y_0 \leq y \leq y_1) \wedge (x \geq x_R) \ \Rightarrow \ \alpha(x,y) = \alpha(x+2p_R,y)) \wedge$$
$$((y < y_0 \vee y > y_1) \ \Rightarrow \ \alpha(x,y) = \#))$$

The sets of all horizontally periodic configurations, and all horizontally ultimately periodic configurations of a TPCA T are denoted by $\mathrm{Conf}_{\mathrm{hp}}(T)$, and $\mathrm{Conf}_{\mathrm{hup}}(T)$, respectively.

In this definition, $2p$, $2p_L$, and $2p_R$ are called the *period*, the *left period*, and the *right period* of the configuration, respectively. Note that these periods must be even, since the same type of triangles appear with the period of 2 in a TPCA.

13.1.2 Elementary Triangular Partitioned Cellular Automata (ETPCAs) and reversible ETPCAs (RETPCAs)

Definition 13.6. Let

$$T = (\mathbb{Z}^2, (L,D,R), ((-1,0),(0,-1),(1,0)), ((1,0),(0,1),(-1,0)), f, (0,0,0))$$

be a TPCA. The TPCA T is called an *elementary triangular partitioned cellular automaton* (ETPCA), if $L = D = R = \{0,1\}$, and it is rotation-symmetric.

The set of states of a cell of an ETPCA is $L \times D \times R = \{0,1\}^3$, and thus a cell has eight states. When drawing figures of T's local rules and configurations, we indicate the states 0 and 1 of each part of a cell by a blank and a particle (i.e., ●), respectively.

Lemma 13.3. *The total number of ETPCAs is 256.*

Proof. Let T be an ETPCA, and f be its local function. Since any ETPCA is rotation-symmetric, the local function f is specified by giving only the four local rules $f(0,0,0) = (l_0,d_0,r_0)$, $f(0,1,0) = (l_1,d_1,r_1)$, $f(1,0,1) = (l_2,d_2,r_2)$, and $f(1,1,1) = (l_3,d_3,r_3)$. This is because $f(1,0,0) = (d_1,r_1,l_1)$, $f(0,0,1) = (r_1,l_1,d_1)$, $f(0,1,1) = (d_2,r_2,l_2)$, and $f(1,1,0) = (r_2,l_2,d_2)$ hold by rotation-symmetry. Here, (l_1,d_1,r_1) and (l_2,d_2,r_2) are elements in $\{0,1\}^3$. On the other hand, by Lemma 13.2, (l_0,d_0,r_0) and (l_3,d_3,r_3) are elements in $\{(0,0,0),(1,1,1)\}$. By above, there are $2 \times 8 \times 8 \times 2 = 256$ possibilities of local functions. □

Example 13.1. Let T be a TPCA such that $L = D = R = \{0,1\}$, and f be its local function defined as follows.

$$
\begin{array}{ll}
f(0,0,0) = (0,0,0) & f(0,1,1) = (0,0,1) \\
f(0,0,1) = (1,0,1) & f(1,0,1) = (1,0,0) \\
f(0,1,0) = (0,1,1) & f(1,1,0) = (0,1,0) \\
f(1,0,0) = (1,1,0) & f(1,1,1) = (1,1,1)
\end{array}
$$

It is easy to verify that f satisfies the condition (2) in Definition 13.4. Hence, T is rotation-symmetric, and thus it is an ETPCA. □

13.1.2.1 Identification number for ETPCAs

Next, we give an identification (ID) number to each ETPCA to specify an ET-PCA shortly. Since a local function f of an ETPCA is determined only by the four values of $f(0,0,0), f(0,1,0), f(1,0,1)$, and $f(1,1,1)$ as discussed in the proof of Lemma 13.3, the ID number of the ETPCA is given based on these values. We now make a preparation. Let octal $: \{0,1\}^3 \to \{0,\ldots,7\}$ be a function defined as follows: $\forall (s_2, s_1, s_0) \in \{0,1\}^3 (\text{octal}(s_2, s_1, s_0) = 2^2 s_2 + 2^1 s_1 + 2^0 s_0)$. Namely, the function "octal" converts a three-digit binary number into a one-digit octal number.

Definition 13.7. Let T be an ETPCA, and $f : \{0,1\}^3 \to \{0,1\}^3$ be its local function. Let $w = \text{octal}(f(0,0,0))$, $x = \text{octal}(f(0,1,0))$, $y = \text{octal}(f(1,0,1))$, and $z = \text{octal}(f(1,1,1))$. The four digit number $wxyz$ is called an *identification (ID) number* of the ETPCA T. Note that, here, $wxyz$ represents a concatenation of four symbols $w, x, y,$ and z. The ETPCA with the ID number $wxyz$ is indicated by "ETPCA $wxyz$". It is also denoted by T_{wxyz}.

As is explained in the proof of Lemma 13.3, if $wxyz$ is an ID number of some ETPCA, then $w, z \in \{0,7\}$ and $x, y \in \{0,1,\ldots,7\}$ must hold.

Example 13.2. Let T be a TPCA given in Example 13.1, and f be its local function. Then, we have the following.

$$
\begin{aligned}
w &= \text{octal}(f(0,0,0)) = \text{octal}(0,0,0) = 0 \\
x &= \text{octal}(f(0,1,0)) = \text{octal}(0,1,1) = 3 \\
y &= \text{octal}(f(1,0,1)) = \text{octal}(1,0,0) = 4 \\
z &= \text{octal}(f(1,1,1)) = \text{octal}(1,1,1) = 7
\end{aligned}
$$

Thus, T is the ETPCA 0347, and is denoted by T_{0347}. Figure 13.5 shows the pictorial representation of f, where f is specified by the four local rules $f(0,0,0) = (0,0,0)$, $f(0,1,0) = (0,1,1)$, $f(1,0,1) = (1,0,0)$, and $f(1,1,1) = (1,1,1)$.   □

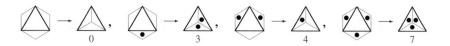

Fig. 13.5 Pictorial representation of the local function f of the ETPCA 0347 in Example 13.2

Figure 13.6 shows the correspondence between the ID number $wxyz$ of an ET-PCA and the pictorial representation of its local function. Here, $w, x, y,$ and z specify the local rules for the four cases such that the number of incoming particles is 0, 1, 2, and 3, respectively.

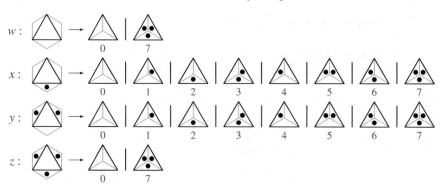

Fig. 13.6 Correspondence between the ID number $wxyz$ of an ETPCA and its local function specified by four local rules. Here, $w, z \in \{0, 7\}$, and $x, y \in \{0, 1, \ldots, 7\}$. Vertical bars indicate alternatives of a right-hand side of each local rule

13.1.2.2 Reversible ETPCAs (RETPCAs)

A *reversible ETPCA* (RETPCA) is an ETPCA whose local function is injective (Definition 13.3). It is easy to show the following.

Lemma 13.4. *Let T_{wxyz} be an ETPCA. It is reversible iff the following conditions (1) and (2) hold.*

(1) $(w, z) \in \{(0, 7), (7, 0)\}$
(2) $(x, y) \in \{1, 2, 4\} \times \{3, 5, 6\} \cup \{3, 5, 6\} \times \{1, 2, 4\}$

Proof. We first show that if T_{wxyz} is reversible, then the above conditions hold. Let f be the local function of T_{wxyz}. Since f is an injection, $f(l, d, r) \neq f(l', d', r')$ holds for all $(l, d, r), (l', d', r') \in \{0, 1\}^3$ such that $(l, d, r) \neq (l', d', r')$. Hence, it is necessary that w, x, y, and z are different each other. By Lemma 13.2, $w, z \in \{0, 7\}$ holds, and thus the condition (1) is derived. Now, x must be an element in $\{1, 2, 4\} \cup \{3, 5, 6\}$. Consider the case $x \in \{1, 2, 4\}$. Then

$$\{\text{octal}(f(0, 1, 0)), \text{octal}(f(1, 0, 0)), \text{octal}(f(0, 0, 1))\} = \{1, 2, 4\},$$

since T_{wxyz} is rotation-symmetric. Therefore, y must be in $\{3, 5, 6\}$. Similarly, if $x \in \{3, 5, 6\}$, then $y \in \{1, 2, 4\}$. Hence, the condition (2) holds.

Next, we show if the conditions (1) and (2) hold, then T_{wxyz} is reversible. In the condition (2), we consider only the case $(x, y) \in \{1, 2, 4\} \times \{3, 5, 6\}$, since the case $(x, y) \in \{3, 5, 6\} \times \{1, 2, 4\}$ is similarly proved. Then,

$$\{\text{octal}(f(0, 1, 0)), \text{octal}(f(1, 0, 0)), \text{octal}(f(0, 0, 1))\} = \{1, 2, 4\}, \text{ and}$$
$$\{\text{octal}(f(1, 0, 1)), \text{octal}(f(0, 1, 1)), \text{octal}(f(1, 1, 0))\} = \{3, 5, 6\}$$

hold, because T_{wxyz} is rotation-symmetric. Furthermore, since (1) holds,

$$\{\text{octal}(f(0, 0, 0)), \text{octal}(f(1, 1, 1))\} = \{0, 7\}.$$

Therefore, $\{\mathrm{octal}(f(l,d,r)) \mid (l,d,r) \in \{0,1\}^3\} = \{0,1,\ldots,7\}$, and thus f is an injection. □

13.1.2.3 Conservative ETPCAs

Next, we define a conservative ETPCA, in which the total number of particles (i.e., ●'s) is conserved in each local rule.

Definition 13.8. Let T_{wxyz} be an ETPCA. It is called a *conservative ETPCA* (or *bit-conserving ETPCA*) if the following condition holds.

$$w = 0 \,\wedge\, x \in \{1,2,4\} \,\wedge\, y \in \{3,5,6\} \,\wedge\, z = 7$$

From Lemma 13.4 and Definition 13.8, it is clear that the following lemma holds.

Lemma 13.5. *Let T be an ETPCA. If T is conservative, then it is reversible.*

By the above lemma, conservative ETPCAs are called *conservative RETPCAs* hereafter. We can see that there are 36 RETPCAS (by Lemma 13.4), and among them there are nine conservative RETPCAs (by Definition 13.8).

Example 13.3. The ETPCA T_{0157}, whose local function is shown in Fig. 13.7, is a conservative RETPCA. On the other hand, the ETPCA T_{0347} in Example 13.2 (see Fig. 13.5) is a non-conservative RETPCA. □

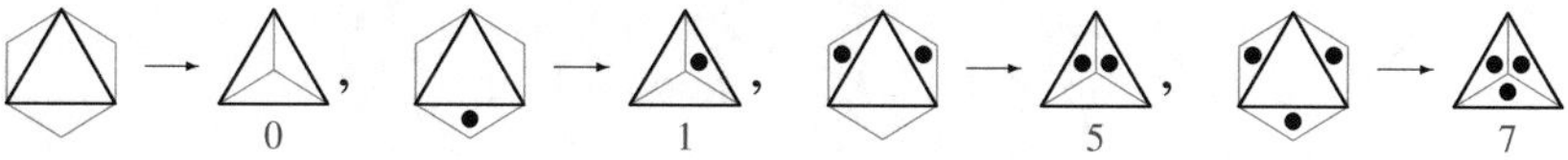

Fig. 13.7 The local function of the conservative RETPCA 0157

13.1.3 Dualities in ETPCAs

As shown in Lemma 13.3, there are 256 ETPCAs. However, there are some "equivalent" ETPCAs, and thus the number of essentially different ETPCAs is much smaller. In this subsection, we introduce three kinds of dualities on ETPCAs, and classify the ETPCAs based on them. They are dualities under reflection, complementation, and odd-step complementation. Note that the one-dimensional versions of the first two dualities on ECAs have been given in [12].

13.1.3.1 Duality under reflection

Definition 13.9. Let T and $\hat{T}$ be ETPCAs, and f and $\hat{f}$ be their local functions. We say T and $\hat{T}$ are *dual under reflection*, if the following holds.

$$\forall (l,d,r),(l',d',r') \in \{0,1\}^3 \ (f(l,d,r) = (l',d',r') \ \Leftrightarrow \ \hat{f}(r,d,l) = (r',d',l'))$$

It is written as $T \underset{\text{refl}}{\longleftrightarrow} \hat{T}$.

By this definition, we can see that the local rules of $\hat{T}$ are the mirror images of those of T. Therefore, an evolution process of T's configurations is simulated in a straightforward manner by the mirror images of the T's configurations in $\hat{T}$.

It is easily verified that if T is reversible (or conservative, respectively), then $\hat{T}$ is also reversible (conservative) by the definition. It is clear $\underset{\text{refl}}{\longleftrightarrow}$ is a symmetric relation by the definition, i.e., $T \underset{\text{refl}}{\longleftrightarrow} T'$ iff $T' \underset{\text{refl}}{\longleftrightarrow} T$.

Example 13.4. Consider the two ETPCAs T_{0137} and T_{0467}. Since their local functions f_{0137} and f_{0467} are as below (see also Fig. 13.8), they satisfy the condition in Definition 13.9.

$$
\begin{array}{ll}
f_{0137}(0,0,0) = (0,0,0) & f_{0467}(0,0,0) = (0,0,0) \\
f_{0137}(0,0,1) = (1,0,0) & f_{0467}(1,0,0) = (0,0,1) \\
f_{0137}(0,1,0) = (0,0,1) & f_{0467}(0,1,0) = (1,0,0) \\
f_{0137}(1,0,0) = (0,1,0) & f_{0467}(0,0,1) = (0,1,0) \\
f_{0137}(0,1,1) = (1,1,0) & f_{0467}(1,1,0) = (0,1,1) \\
f_{0137}(1,0,1) = (0,1,1) & f_{0467}(1,0,1) = (1,1,0) \\
f_{0137}(1,1,0) = (1,0,1) & f_{0467}(0,1,1) = (1,0,1) \\
f_{0137}(1,1,1) = (1,1,1) & f_{0467}(1,1,1) = (1,1,1)
\end{array}
$$

Therefore, $T_{0137} \underset{\text{refl}}{\longleftrightarrow} T_{0467}$.   □

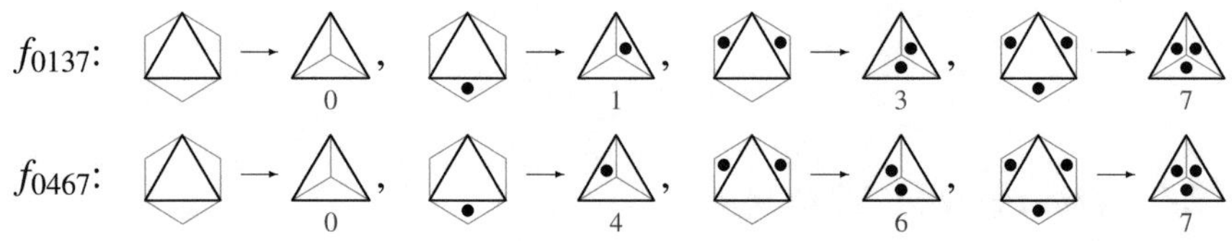

Fig. 13.8 The local functions of T_{0137} and T_{0467} that are dual under reflection

13.1.3.2 Duality under complementation

For $x \in \{0,1\}$, let $\bar{x}$ denote $1-x$, i.e., the complement of x.

Definition 13.10. Let T and $\overline{T}$ be ETPCAs, and f and $\bar{f}$ be their local functions. We say T and $\overline{T}$ are *dual under complementation*, if the following holds.

$$\forall (l,d,r), (l',d',r') \in \{0,1\}^3 \; (f(l,d,r) = (l',d',r') \; \Leftrightarrow \; \bar{f}(\bar{l},\bar{d},\bar{r}) = (\bar{l'},\bar{d'},\bar{r'}))$$

It is written as $T \underset{\text{comp}}{\longleftrightarrow} \overline{T}$.

By this definition, we can see that the local rules of $\overline{T}$ are the 0-1 exchange (i.e., taking their complements) of those of T. Therefore, an evolution process of T's configurations is simulated in a straightforward manner by the complemented images of the T's configurations in $\overline{T}$. However, it should be noted that, if T works on finite configurations, then the configurations of $\overline{T}$ that simulate T are not finite. Likewise, if T works on horizontally ultimately periodic configurations, then the configurations of $\overline{T}$ that simulate T are not horizontally ultimately periodic.

It is easily verified that if T is reversible (or conservative, respectively), then $\overline{T}$ is also reversible (conservative) by the definition. It is clear that $\underset{\text{comp}}{\longleftrightarrow}$ is a symmetric relation by the definition.

Example 13.5. Consider the two ETPCAs T_{0157} and T_{0267}. Since their local functions f_{0157} and f_{0267} are as below (see also Fig. 13.9), they satisfy the condition in Definition 13.10.

$$\begin{array}{ll}
f_{0157}(0,0,0) = (0,0,0) & f_{0267}(1,1,1) = (1,1,1) \\
f_{0157}(0,0,1) = (1,0,0) & f_{0267}(1,1,0) = (0,1,1) \\
f_{0157}(0,1,0) = (0,0,1) & f_{0267}(1,0,1) = (1,1,0) \\
f_{0157}(1,0,0) = (0,1,0) & f_{0267}(0,1,1) = (1,0,1) \\
f_{0157}(0,1,1) = (0,1,1) & f_{0267}(1,0,0) = (1,0,0) \\
f_{0157}(1,0,1) = (1,0,1) & f_{0267}(0,1,0) = (0,1,0) \\
f_{0157}(1,1,0) = (1,1,0) & f_{0267}(0,0,1) = (0,0,1) \\
f_{0157}(1,1,1) = (1,1,1) & f_{0267}(0,0,0) = (0,0,0)
\end{array}$$

Therefore, $T_{0157} \underset{\text{comp}}{\longleftrightarrow} T_{0267}$. □

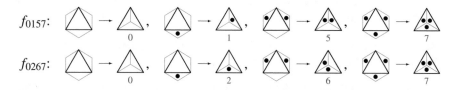

$f_{0157}:$ ... $f_{0267}:$ ...

Fig. 13.9 The local functions of T_{0157} and T_{0267} that are dual under complementation

13.1.3.3 Duality under odd-step complementation

Definition 13.11. Let T be an ETPCA such that its local function f satisfies the following.

(1) $\forall (l,d,r), (l',d',r') \in \{0,1\}^3 \ (f(l,d,r) = (l',d',r') \Rightarrow f(\bar{l},\bar{d},\bar{r}) = (\bar{l'},\bar{d'},\bar{r'}))$

Let $\tilde{T}$ be another ETPCA, and $\tilde{f}$ be its local function. We say T and $\tilde{T}$ are *dual under odd-step complementation*, if the following holds.

$$\forall (l,d,r), (l',d',r') \in \{0,1\}^3 \ (f(l,d,r) = (l',d',r') \Leftrightarrow \tilde{f}(l,d,r) = (\bar{l'},\bar{d'},\bar{r'}))$$

It is written as $T \underset{\text{osc}}{\longleftrightarrow} \tilde{T}$.

Since the ETPCA T satisfies the condition (1) in Definition 13.11, we can see that for each local rule $f(l,d,r) = (l',d',r')$ of T, there are two local rules $\tilde{f}(l,d,r) = (\bar{l'},\bar{d'},\bar{r'})$ and $\tilde{f}(\bar{l},\bar{d},\bar{r}) = (l',d',r')$ of $\tilde{T}$ (hence $\tilde{T}$ also satisfies (1)). Let F and $\tilde{F}$ be the global function of T and $\tilde{T}$, respectively. If the initial configuration of T is $\alpha : \mathbb{Z}^2 \to \{0,1\}^3$, then we assume α is also given to $\tilde{T}$ as its initial configuration. Since there is a local rule $\tilde{f}(l,d,r) = (\bar{l'},\bar{d'},\bar{r'})$ for each $f(l,d,r) = (l',d',r')$, the configuration $\tilde{F}(\alpha)$ is the complement of the configuration $F(\alpha)$. Furthermore, since there is a local rule $\tilde{f}(\bar{l},\bar{d},\bar{r}) = (l',d',r')$ for each $f(l,d,r) = (l',d',r')$, the configuration $\tilde{F}^2(\alpha)$ is the same as $F^2(\alpha)$. In this way, at an even step $\tilde{T}$ gives the same configuration as T, while at an odd step $\tilde{T}$ gives the complemented configuration of T.

It is easily verified that if T is reversible, then $\tilde{T}$ is also reversible by the definition. However, when T is conservative, $\tilde{T}$ is not conservative. It is clear that $\underset{\text{osc}}{\longleftrightarrow}$ is a symmetric relation by the definition.

Example 13.6. Consider the two ETPCAs T_{0347} and T_{7430}. Their local functions f_{0347} and f_{7430} are as below (see also Fig. 13.10).

$$
\begin{array}{ll}
f_{0347}(0,0,0) = (0,0,0) & f_{7430}(0,0,0) = (1,1,1) \\
f_{0347}(0,0,1) = (1,0,1) & f_{7430}(0,0,1) = (0,1,0) \\
f_{0347}(0,1,0) = (0,1,1) & f_{7430}(0,1,0) = (1,0,0) \\
f_{0347}(1,0,0) = (1,1,0) & f_{7430}(1,0,0) = (0,0,1) \\
f_{0347}(0,1,1) = (0,0,1) & f_{7430}(0,1,1) = (1,1,0) \\
f_{0347}(1,0,1) = (1,0,0) & f_{7430}(1,0,1) = (0,1,1) \\
f_{0347}(1,1,0) = (0,1,0) & f_{7430}(1,1,0) = (1,0,1) \\
f_{0347}(1,1,1) = (1,1,1) & f_{7430}(1,1,1) = (0,0,0)
\end{array}
$$

We can see they satisfy the condition in Definition 13.11. Therefore, $T_{0347} \underset{\text{osc}}{\longleftrightarrow} T_{7430}$. Figure 13.11 shows an example of their evolution processes.   □

Note that, in Definition 13.11, the ETPCA T must satisfy the condition (1). Therefore, the relation $\underset{\text{osc}}{\longleftrightarrow}$ is defined on the ETPCAs of the form T_{wxyz} such that $w + z = 7$ and $x + y = 7$. Hence, only the following 16 ETPCAs have their dual counterparts under odd-step complementation.

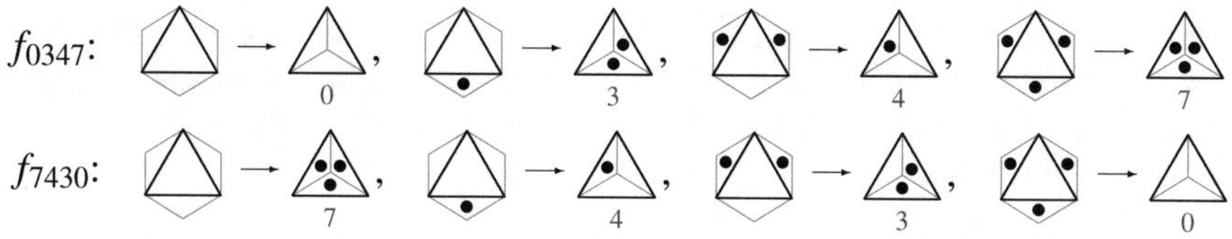

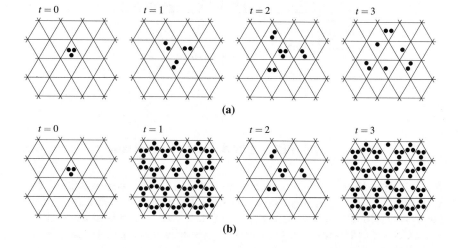

Fig. 13.10 The local functions of T_{0347} and T_{7430}, which are dual under odd-step complementation

$t = 0$ $t = 1$ $t = 2$ $t = 3$

(a)

$t = 0$ $t = 1$ $t = 2$ $t = 3$

(b)

Fig. 13.11 Example of evolution processes in **(a)** T_{0347}, and **(b)** T_{7430}, which are dual under odd-step complementation

$$T_{0077} \xleftrightarrow{\text{osc}} T_{7700}, \quad T_{0167} \xleftrightarrow{\text{osc}} T_{7610}, \quad T_{0257} \xleftrightarrow{\text{osc}} T_{7520}, \quad T_{0347} \xleftrightarrow{\text{osc}} T_{7430},$$
$$T_{0437} \xleftrightarrow{\text{osc}} T_{7340}, \quad T_{0527} \xleftrightarrow{\text{osc}} T_{7250}, \quad T_{0617} \xleftrightarrow{\text{osc}} T_{7160}, \quad T_{0707} \xleftrightarrow{\text{osc}} T_{7070}$$

13.1.3.4 Equivalence classes of ETPCAs

If ETPCAs T and T' are dual under reflection, complementation, or odd-step complementation, then they can be regarded as essentially the same ETPCAs. Here, we classify the 256 ETPCAs into equivalence classes based on these three kinds of dualities.

We define the relation $\longleftrightarrow$ as follows. For any ETPCAs T and T',

$$T \longleftrightarrow T' \;\Leftrightarrow\; (T \xleftrightarrow{\text{refl}} T' \;\vee\; T \xleftrightarrow{\text{comp}} T' \;\vee\; T \xleftrightarrow{\text{osc}} T')$$

holds. Now, let $\longleftrightarrow^*$ be the reflexive and transitive closure of $\longleftrightarrow$. Then, $\longleftrightarrow^*$ is an equivalence relation, since $\longleftrightarrow$ is symmetric. By this, 256 ETPCAs are classified into 82 equivalence classes (though we do not give the details of the 82 equivalence classes here, they were obtained by a computer program). Note that, if we use only the two dualities $\underset{\text{refl}}{\longleftrightarrow}$ and $\underset{\text{comp}}{\longleftrightarrow}$, then we have 88 equivalence classes, whose number is just the same as in one-dimensional ECAs [12]. Table 13.1 shows the total numbers and the numbers of equivalence classes of ETPCAs, RETPCAs, and conservative RETPCAs.

Table 13.1 Total numbers and numbers of equivalence classes of ETPCAs, RETPCAs, and conservative RETPCAs

	Total number	Equivalence classes
ETPCAs	256	82
RETPCAs	36	12
Conservative RETPCAs	9	4

13.2 Conservative RETPCAs and Their Universality

By Definition 13.8, there are nine conservative RETPCAs. They are T_{0137}, T_{0157}, T_{0167}, T_{0237}, T_{0257}, T_{0267}, T_{0437}, T_{0457} and T_{0467}. Here, we give "aliases" to the nine conservative RETPCAs for the later convenience. In a local rule of a conservative RETPCA, we can interpret that the incoming particles make left-, U-, or right-turn. Therefore, each local rule is represented by a turning direction L, U or R for the one- and two-particle cases as shown in Fig. 13.12. Note that in the three-particle case (i.e., the local rule (3)), any interpretation among left- U- and right-turn is possible. Based on it, we denote a conservative RETPCA by T_{XY}, if its local function f is given by the set of the local rules $\{(0), (1X), (2Y), (3)\}$, where $X, Y \in \{L, U, R\}$. Namely, the rule (1L) ((1U), and (1R), respectively) is interpreted as the one where an incoming particle makes left-turn (U-turn, and right-turn). The rules (2L), (2U), and (2R) are also interpreted similarly. Therefore nine conservative RETPCAs are represented as follows.

$$\begin{aligned}
T_{LL} &= T_{0437}, & T_{LU} &= T_{0457}, & T_{LR} &= T_{0467}, \\
T_{UL} &= T_{0237}, & T_{UU} &= T_{0257}, & T_{UR} &= T_{0267}, \\
T_{RL} &= T_{0137}, & T_{RU} &= T_{0157}, & T_{RR} &= T_{0167}
\end{aligned}$$

It is easy to show that the following pairs of conservative RETPCAs are dual under reflection.

$$T_{RU} \underset{\text{refl}}{\longleftrightarrow} T_{LU}, \quad T_{UR} \underset{\text{refl}}{\longleftrightarrow} T_{UL}, \quad T_{RL} \underset{\text{refl}}{\longleftrightarrow} T_{LR}, \quad T_{RR} \underset{\text{refl}}{\longleftrightarrow} T_{LL}, \quad T_{UU} \underset{\text{refl}}{\longleftrightarrow} T_{UU}$$

In this section, we shall prove that T_{RU}, T_{UR}, and T_{RL} with horizontally ultimately periodic configurations are Turing universal. Hence, by the duality under reflection, T_{LU}, T_{UL}, and T_{LR} with horizontally ultimately periodic configurations are also Turing universal. On the other hand, we shall prove that T_{RR}, T_{LL}, and T_{UU} are

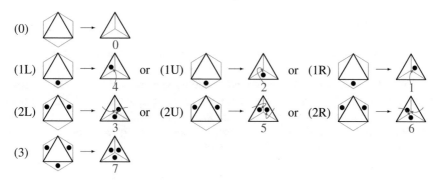

Fig. 13.12 Representing each local rule of a conservative RETPCA by a turning direction L, U or R of particles for the one- and two-particle cases

non-universal. By above, universality of all the nine conservative RETPCAs will be clarified.

Note that, although $T_{RU} \xleftrightarrow{\text{comp}} T_{UR}$ holds, Turing universality of T_{RU} with horizontally ultimately periodic configurations does not imply Turing universality of T_{UR} with horizontally ultimately periodic configurations. This is because horizontal ultimate periodicity of a configuration is not preserved under complementation (see Definition 13.5). Hence, in the following, we also consider the case of T_{UR} and show its universality besides T_{RU}.

The configurations of T_{RU}, T_{UR}, and T_{RL} that simulate switch gate, Fredkin gate and others are rather complex. Thus, there may be some difficulties to see how they works. Simulation movies given in [6] will be helpful to understand them.

13.2.1 Universality of the RETPCA T_{RU}

The conservative RETPCA T_{RU} has a local function shown in Fig. 13.13. In T_{RU}, if one particle comes, it makes right-turn, and if two come, they make U-turns. It was first investigated by Imai and Morita [4]. They showed any reversible logic circuit composed of Fredkin gates and delay elements can be simulated in it. Thus, it is Turing universal and intrinsically universal. In this subsection, we explain this result.

T_{RU}:

Fig. 13.13 The local function of the conservative RETPCA T_{RU} $(= T_{0157})$

13.2.1.1 Signal and transmission wire in T_{RU}

The pattern shown in Fig. 13.14 is called a *block* as in the case of S_1 and S_2 (Sect. 12.3). It is a stable pattern. Putting blocks in the space appropriately, we can compose several kinds of functional modules as explained below. On the other hand, a *signal* in T_{RU} consists of a single particle. If a signal exists alone, it simply rotates clockwise around some point (see the second local rule of Fig. 13.13), and thus it cannot go straight ahead. However, if there is a "wall" composed of blocks, then the signal can move along it (Fig. 13.15).

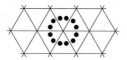

Fig. 13.14 A stable pattern called a block in T_{RU}

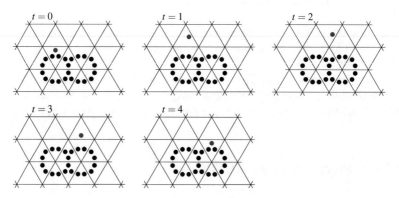

Fig. 13.15 In T_{RU}, a signal can move along a wall composed of blocks

Figure 13.16 is a straight *transmission wire* composed of five blocks. Here, adjacent blocks have two common particles. At $t = 0$ a signal is at the top of the leftmost block. It takes four steps for the signal to go to the next block. Such a type of wires can be rotated by a multiple of 60° in the triangular space. Therefore, there are wires with the slopes of 0°, 60°, 120°, 180°, 240°, and 300°.

Figure 13.17 shows a straight transmission wire with the slope of 30°. In this case there is a small gap between adjacent blocks. It takes eight steps for a signal to reach the next block. This type of wires can also be rotated by a multiple of 60°. Hence, those with the slopes of 30°, 90°, 150°, 210°, 270°, and 330° are possible.

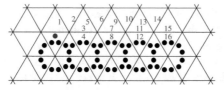

Fig. 13.16 A straight transmission wire in T_{RU}. The numbers in the figure show the position of the signal at time t $(1 \leq t \leq 16)$

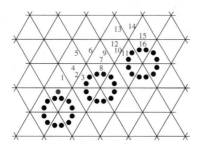

Fig. 13.17 A straight transmission wire with the slope of 30° in T_{RU}

We can bend a transmission wire relatively freely as shown in Fig. 13.18. The wire in this figure consists of five wire segments with the slopes of 0°, −60°, −30°, 0°, and 30°, respectively. Routing of a signal is performed in this way.

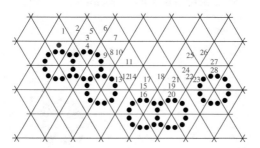

Fig. 13.18 A bent wire in T_{RU}

13.2.1.2 Adjusting signal timing in T_{RU}

Adjustment of signal timing (i.e., delay time of a signal) is often required when we want to interact two or more signals. In T_{RU}, it is rather complicated to do so. Below, we explain methods of adjusting the delay time of a signal.

We first give a method of obtaining an extra delay. If we make narrow gaps in the transmission wire of the type of Fig. 13.16, then it will have an additional delay of four steps for each gap. Figure 13.19 shows a wire with two gaps. Thus, its total delay is eight steps more than the delay of the wire without gap. Note that, in the case of a wire of the type of Fig. 13.17, it is not possible to have an extra delay by this method.

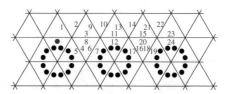

Fig. 13.19 A straight transmission wire with an additional delay of 8 steps in T_{RU}

Here, we give *signal control modules* shown in Fig. 13.20. Hitting a target signal with the control signal appropriately, trajectory of the target signal can be altered. The module shown in Fig. 13.20 (**a**) consists only of a single control signal. It is a periodic pattern of period 6, since the control signal rotates clockwise. It is used for fine adjustment of a signal timing. On the other hand, Fig. 13.20 (**b**) shows another type of a signal control module. It has a block and a control signal, and is a periodic pattern of period 30. It is used when we need a signal control module whose period is longer than 6. It may have two control signals for controlling two target signals. A signal crossing module explained later is composed of a signal control module of this type.

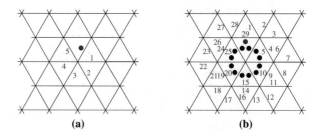

(a)   (b)

Fig. 13.20 Two kinds of signal control modules in T_{RU}. (**a**) A module consisting only of a control signal. (**b**) A module consisting of a block and a control signal

To make a delay of -2 steps (i.e., speed-up of 2 steps), we use the signal control module of Fig. 13.20 (**a**). Placing it near a transmission wire as in Fig. 13.21, we obtain a kind of *phase shifter*. At $t = 0$ an input signal is given to the wire, and at $t = 2$ the input signal interacts with the control signal. By this, at $t = 3$, the trajectory of the input signal is changed. Finally, at $t = 6$, the input signal reaches the rightmost block of the wire. Hence, a delay of -2 steps is realized. The trajectory of the control signal is not changed even if it interacts with the input signal. An input can be given every 6 steps.

Combining this method with the method of making the delay of multiple of 4 shown in Fig. 13.19, any delay of even steps is obtained. It should be noted that a delay of odd steps is not necessary by the following reason. Assume a signal is in an up-triangle at $t = 0$. At $t = 1$ it must be in a down-triangle, then at $t = 2$ it is in an up-triangle, and so on. Generally, the signal is in an up-triangle at even time step, and in a down-triangle at odd time step. Therefore, to interact two signals at some specific cell, they must be in the same type of triangles at $t = 0$. Therefore, if both of the signals visit the same cell, then the difference of their arriving time is always even. Hence, we only need delays of even steps. Actually, by the above consideration, extra delay of odd steps is impossible.

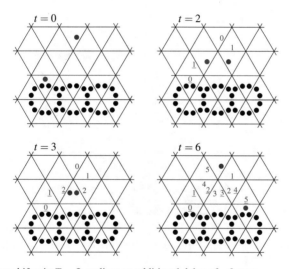

Fig. 13.21 Phase shifter in T_{RU}. It realizes an additional delay of -2 steps

13.2.1.3 Signal crossing in T_{RU}

A *signal crossing module* is for crossing two signals on the two-dimensional plane. It is realized using the signal control module of Fig. 13.20 **(b)**. Figures 13.22 and 13.23 show how it works. Here, the signal control module has two control signals. Assume two input signals are given to x and y at the same time. At $t = 15$, the signal from x first interacts with one of the control signals. By this, it goes along the wire that leads to the output x. At $t = 26$, the signal from the input y interacts with the other control signal, and then goes to the output y. It is easy to see that it works correctly for the cases other than the case of $x = y = 1$.

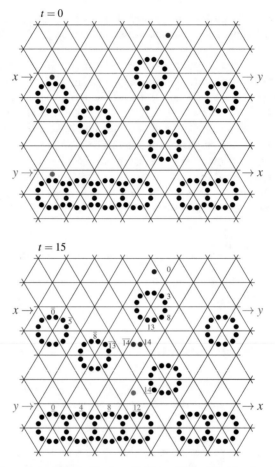

Fig. 13.22 Signal crossing module in T_{RU} (part 1). The position of the signal x at time t is indicated by $\bar{t}$, while that of y is by $\underline{t}$

13.2.1.4 Switch gate and inverse switch gate in T_{RU}

In T_{RU}, a switch gate and an inverse switch gate can be simulated by a single cell. Figure 13.24 **(a)** shows the input and output positions for implementing a switch gate. If $c = 1$ and $x = 1$ in the left-hand side of **(a)**, then at the next time step $c = 1$, $cx = 1$ and $\bar{c}x = 0$ are obtained in the right-hand side by the third local rule of T_{RU} (Fig. 13.13). If $c = 1$ and $x = 0$, then at the next time step $c = 1$, $cx = 0$ and $\bar{c}x = 0$ are obtained by the second local rule. Likewise, if $c = 0$ and $x = 1$, then at the next time step $c = 0$, $cx = 0$ and $\bar{c}x = 1$ are obtained by the second local rule. The case of Fig. 13.24 **(b)** of an inverse switch gate is also similar. Note that, here, a signal in T_{RU} does not correspond to a ball of BBM, since a cell of T_{RU} directly simulates a switch gate and an inverse switch gate.

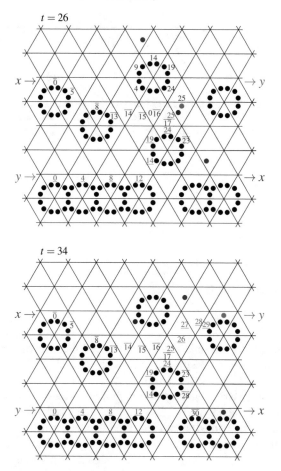

Fig. 13.23 Signal crossing module in T_{RU} (part 2)

However, since it is not convenient to use one cell as a building unit for a larger circuit, we design a switch gate module and an inverse switch gate module from it. A *gate module* in the standard form is a pattern embedded in a rectangular-like region in the cellular space that satisfies the following (see Fig. 13.25).

(1) It realizes a reversible logic gate.
(2) Input ports are at the left end.
(3) Output ports are at the right end.
(4) Delay between input and output is constant.

Figure 13.26 show a *switch gate module* implemented in T_{RU}, where input ports are placed at the left end, and output ports are at the right end. Here, the previous design of switch gate given in [4] was improved, and the size was reduced. It contains a signal crossing module in the upper left part, a phase shifter in the lower middle

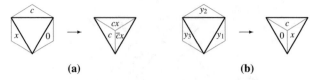

Fig. 13.24 In T_{RU}, a switch gate, and an inverse switch gate are realized by only one cell. **(a)** Input and output positions for a switch gate, and **(b)** those for an inverse switch gate. In **(b)**, $c = y_1$ and $x = y_2 + y_3$ hold under the assumption $(y_2 \Rightarrow y_1) \wedge (y_3 \Rightarrow \neg y_1)$. See also Figs. 4.7, 4.9, and Table 4.5

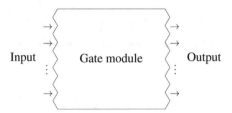

Fig. 13.25 Gate module in the standard form

part, and several signal transmission wires. The cell that acts as a switch gate (see Fig. 13.24) is placed around the middle of this pattern, and is indicated by bold lines. The signal crossing module is used to place the output port c at the right end. The phase shifter is for adjusting the output timing of $\overline{c}x$. Since there is a signal crossing module of period 30, inputs can be given only at time t such that $t \bmod 30 = 0$.

Figure 13.26 **(a)** shows the trajectories of the signals when $c = 1$ and $x = 1$. In this case, two signals from c and x interact at the switch gate cell at $t = 26$. Figure 13.26 **(b)** is the case $c = 0$ and $x = 1$. In this case, a signal from the input x simply goes out from the output port $\overline{c}x$ without interacting with any other signal at the switch gate cell. The case $c = 1$ and $x = 0$ is clear, and thus no figure is shown for it. In this case, the trajectory of the signal c is just the same as in Fig. 13.26 **(a)**. The total delay between inputs and outputs is 78 steps.

An *inverse switch gate module* implemented in T_{RU} is shown in Fig. 13.27. It is obtained by taking a mirror image of the switch gate pattern. But, the positions of control signals of a phase shifter and a signal crossing module are changed. The total delay between inputs and outputs is also 78 steps.

13.2.1.5 Fredkin gate in T_{RU}

Figure 13.28 gives the complete pattern that realizes a *Fredkin gate module*. Its size is smaller than the one given in [4]. It simulates the circuit shown in Fig. 4.19 composed of two switch gates and two inverse switch gates. Since many phase shifters

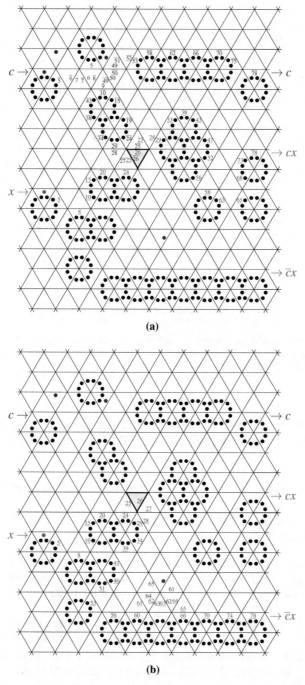

Fig. 13.26 Switch gate module in T_{RU}. **(a)** The case $c = 1$ and $x = 1$, and **(b)** the case $c = 0$ and $x = 1$. The cell that acts as a switch gate is indicated by bold lines

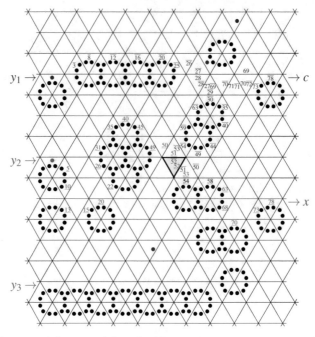

Fig. 13.27 Inverse switch gate module realized in T_{RU} (the case $y_1 = 1$, $y_2 = 1$ and $y_3 = 0$). The cell that acts as an inverse switch gate is indicated by bold lines. It is a mirror image of the switch gate pattern in Fig. 13.26 except the positions of control signals

and signal crossing modules are used, inputs can be given only at time t such that $t \bmod 30 = 0$. The total delay between inputs and outputs is 418 steps.

13.2.1.6 Turing universality and intrinsic universality of T_{RU} and T_{LU}

By above, and by the duality $T_{RU} \xleftrightarrow{\text{refl}} T_{LU}$, we have the following theorem on universality of T_{RU} and T_{LU}.

Theorem 13.1. *[4] The conservative RETPCAs T_{RU} and T_{LU} with horizontally ultimately periodic configurations are Turing universal. They are also intrinsically universal with respect to the class of two-dimensional RPCAs.*

Proof. As we have seen above, any finite reversible logic circuit composed of Fredkin gates and delay elements is simulated in T_{RU}. It is also easy to see that such a circuit can be embedded in a rectangular-like region of the triangular cellular space of T_{RU}. Thus, by Lemmas 12.1 and 12.2, and by the duality under reflection, we have the theorem.   □

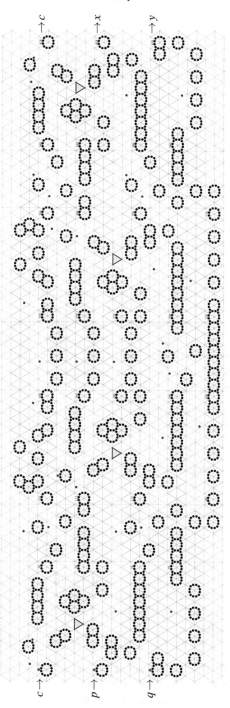

Fig. 13.28 Fredkin gate realized in T_{RU}. Here, $x = cp + \bar{c}q$, and $y = cq + \bar{c}p$

13.2.2 Universality of the RETPCA T_{UR}

Next, we investigate T_{UR}, whose local function is shown in Fig. 13.29. In T_{RL}, if one particle comes, it makes U-turn, and if two come, they make right-turns.

Fig. 13.29 The local function of the conservative RETPCA T_{UR} $(= T_{0267})$

13.2.2.1 Converting finite configurations of T_{RU} into finite ones of T_{UR}

Since T_{RU} $(= T_{0157})$ and T_{UR} $(= T_{0267})$ are dual under complementation as shown in Example 13.5, evolution of configurations in T_{RU} is simulated by the complemented configurations in T_{UR}. However, even if the configurations of T_{UR} are horizontally ultimately periodic, the complemented ones are not so by Definition 13.5.

In the following, we show that a finite configuration of T_{RU} can be converted into a finite configuration of T_{UR} that simulates the former using a special property of T_{UR}. By this, we shall have a result that T_{UR} with horizontally ultimately periodic configurations is universal.

The procedure of converting a finite configuration of T_{RU} consisting of transmission wires and signals into a finite configuration of T_{UR} that simulates the former is as follows (see Fig. 13.30).

(a) Assume a finite configuration of T_{RU} consisting of wires and signals is given.
(b) Mark the cells that are not visited by signals. Since signals can travel only near the wires, this can be done in finite steps.
(c) Take the complement of the configuration. Though the resulting configuration is an infinite one, it is finitely described since the original configuration is finite.
(d) Delete particles in the marked part of the configuration. By this, the configuration becomes finite again.
(e) Mend the cut edges by putting particles to stabilize the configuration. The configuration obtained in (d) collapses from the cut edges. But, if we put a particle at the cell adjacent to each of the cut edges as in Fig. 13.30 **(e)**, then the configuration does not collapse.
(f) By above, we have a finite configuration of T_{UR} that simulates the original.

Figure 13.31 gives a finite configuration of a transmission wire in T_{UR} obtained by the procedure shown in Fig. 13.30. In this configuration, a signal is a blank state, which is indicated by ○ here, and travels *on* the wire.

Figures 13.32 and 13.33 show a *switch gate module* and an *inverse switch gate module* obtained from those in Figs. 13.26 and 13.27 by the above method.

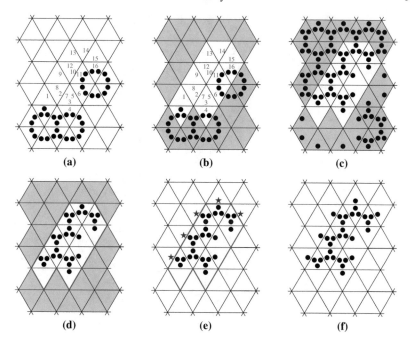

Fig. 13.30 Procedure for converting a finite configuration of T_{RU} into a finite configuration of T_{UR}. (**a**) A given configuration of T_{RU}. (**b**) Mark the cells that are not visited by signals. (**c**) Take the complement of the configuration. (**d**) Delete particles in the marked part. (**e**) Put patches at the positions of ★. (**f**) Resulting configuration of T_{UR}

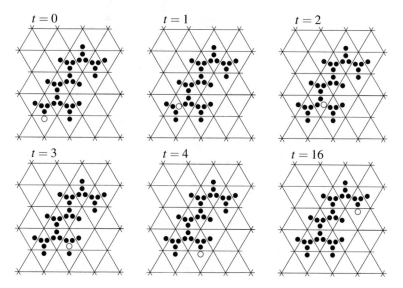

Fig. 13.31 Transmission wire in T_{UR} obtained by the procedure shown in Fig. 13.30. Here, a signal is represented by a "hole" indicated by ○, which is a blank state

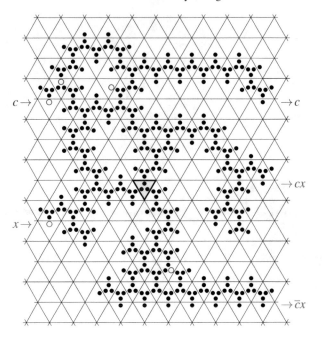

Fig. 13.32 Switch gate module in T_{UR}, which is obtained from the one shown in Fig. 13.26

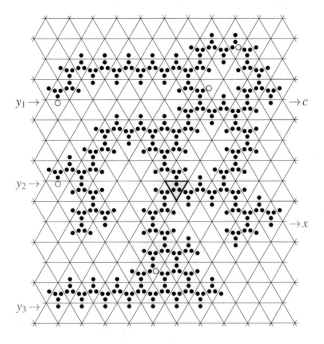

Fig. 13.33 Inverse switch gate module in T_{UR}, which is obtained from the one shown in Fig. 13.27

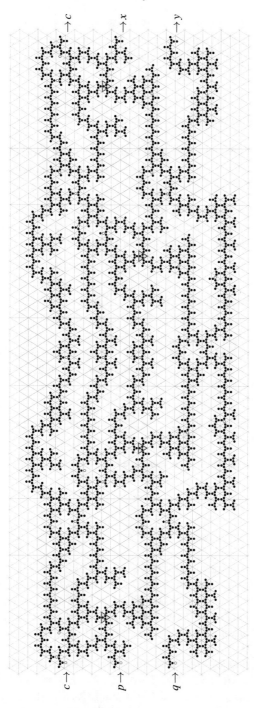

Fig. 13.34 Fredkin gate module in T_{UR}. Here, $x = cp + \bar{c}q$, and $y = cq + \bar{c}p$

Using switch gate and inverse switch gate modules, we can construct *Fredkin gate module* in T_{UR} shown in Fig. 13.34. It is also obtained from the Fredkin gate module in T_{RU} (Fig. 13.28) by the above conversion method. The delay between input and output is 418 steps, which is the same in the case of T_{RU}.

13.2.2.2 Turing universality and intrinsic universality of T_{UR} and T_{UL}

As we have seen above, any reversible logic circuit composed of Fredkin gates and delay elements can be simulated in T_{UR}. We also have $T_{UR} \xleftrightarrow{\text{refl}} T_{UL}$. Thus, we can prove the following as in Theorem 13.1.

Theorem 13.2. *The conservative RETPCAs T_{UR} and T_{UL} with horizontally ultimately periodic configurations are Turing universal. They are also intrinsically universal with respect to the class of two-dimensional RPCAs.*

13.2.3 Universality of the RETPCA T_{RL}

Here, we consider T_{RL}, whose local function is shown in Fig. 13.35. In T_{RL}, if one particle comes, it makes right-turn, and if two come, they make left-turns. Its universality was shown in [8]. In this subsection, we explain this result.

Fig. 13.35 The local function of the conservative RETPCA T_{RL} ($=T_{0137}$)

13.2.3.1 Basic modules in T_{RL}

Since the construction method of Fredkin gate and its circuit in T_{RL} has some similarity to the case of T_{RU}, only an outline of making basic modules is given below.

In T_{RL} a *signal* is represented by a single particle as in the case of T_{RU}. On the other hand, a *block* in T_{RL}, which is a stable pattern, consist of six particles as shown in Fig. 13.36. A *transmission wire* is composed of sequence of blocks, along which signals can travel (Fig. 13.36).

To implement a delay module and a signal crossing module, we use a *signal control module* shown in Fig. 13.37 (**a**). In this case, we need only one type of signal control module, which consists of a single particle that simply rotates. Since it is a pattern of period 6, a signal to be controlled must be given at a right timing.

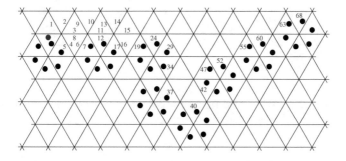

Fig. 13.36 A signal, and a transmission wire composed of blocks in T_{RL}. The signal travels along the wire. The number t ($1 \leq t \leq 68$) shows the position of the signal at time t

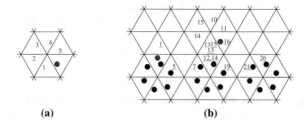

(a)   (b)

Fig. 13.37 (a) Signal control module, and (b) delay module of 2 steps in T_{RL}

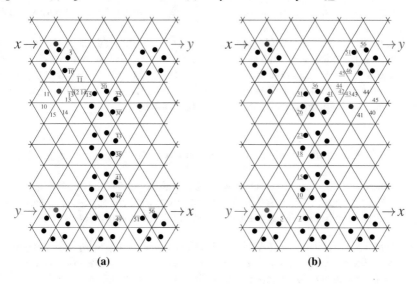

(a)   (b)

Fig. 13.38 Signal crossing module in T_{RL}. Trajectories of (a) signal x, and (b) signal y

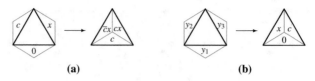

(a)   **(b)**

Fig. 13.39 A single cell of T_{RL} works as **(a)** a switch gate, and **(b)** an inverse switch gate. In **(b)**, $c = y_1$ and $x = y_2 + y_3$ hold under the assumption $(y_2 \Rightarrow y_1) \wedge (y_3 \Rightarrow \neg y_1)$

A *delay module* is a pattern for fine adjustment of signal timing. Putting a signal control module near a transmission wire as in Fig. 13.37 **(b)**, an extra delay of 2 steps is realized. Note that, in the case of T_{RU}, a delay of -2 steps was realized in such a method (Fig. 13.21). On the other hand, a large delay is implemented by appropriately bending a transmission wire. Again in this case, a delay of odd steps is not necessary by the same reason as in T_{RU}.

A *signal crossing module* consists of two signal control modules and transmission wires (Fig. 13.38). Since the signal control modules are of period 6, input signals can be given at time t such that $t \mod 6 = 0$.

Also in T_{RL}, a single cell works as a switch gate and an inverse switch gate as shown in Fig. 13.39. Figures 13.40 and 13.41 shows a *switch gate module*, and an *inverse switch gate module*, each of which contains a (modified) signal crossing module, and three delay modules. The cells that work as switch gate and inverse switch gate are indicated by bold lines. The delay between input and output is 126 steps.

Figure 13.42 shows *Fredkin gate module*. It is constructed by connecting two switch gate modules, two inverse switch gate modules, five signal crossing modules, and many delay modules as in Fig. 4.19. Its size is of 30×131, and the delay between input and output is 744 steps. Since it contains many signal control modules, input can be given only at time t such that $t \mod 6 = 0$.

13.2.3.2 Turing universality and intrinsic universality of T_{RL} and T_{LR}

As we have seen above, any reversible logic circuit composed of Fredkin gates and delay elements can be simulated in T_{RL}. In addition, we have $T_{RL} \xleftrightarrow{\text{refl}} T_{LR}$ (note that $T_{RL} \xleftrightarrow{\text{comp}} T_{LR}$ also holds). Thus, we can prove the following as in Theorem 13.1.

Theorem 13.3. *[8] The conservative RETPCAs T_{RL} and T_{LR} with horizontally ultimately periodic configurations are Turing universal. They are also intrinsically universal with respect to the class of two-dimensional RPCAs.*

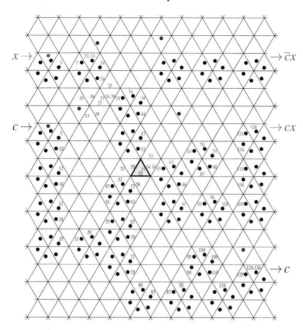

Fig. 13.40 Switch gate module in T_{RL}

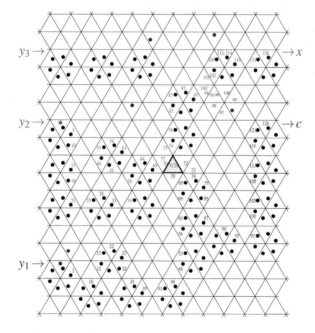

Fig. 13.41 Inverse switch gate module in T_{RL}

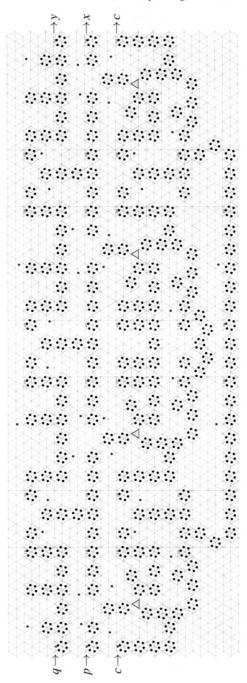

Fig. 13.42 Fredkin gate realized in T_{RL}. Here, $x = cp + \bar{c}q$, and $y = cq + \bar{c}p$

13.2.4 Non-universality of the RETPCAs T_{UU}, T_{RR} and T_{LL}

Here, we consider T_{UU}, T_{RR}, and T_{LL}, whose local functions are given in Fig. 13.43, and show that they are neither Turing universal nor intrinsically universal.

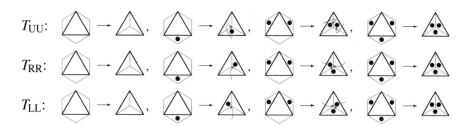

Fig. 13.43 The local functions of the conservative RETPCAs T_{UU} ($=T_{0257}$), T_{RR} ($=T_{0167}$), and T_{LL} ($=T_{0437}$)

We can see that, in T_{UU} all the coming particles make U-turns, in T_{RR} they make right-turns, and in T_{LL} they make left-turns. Therefore, *every* configuration of T_{UU} (T_{RR}, or T_{LL}, respectively) is of period 2 (period 6). Although this fact is intuitively clear, we give the following two lemmas.

Lemma 13.6. *Let F_{UU} be the global function of T_{UU}. Then the following holds.*

$$\forall \alpha \in \mathrm{Conf}(T_{UU}) \; (F_{UU}^2(\alpha) = \alpha)$$

Proof. Let f_{UU} be the local function of T_{UU}. It is easy to see the next relation holds.

$$\forall (l,d,r) \in \{0,1\}^3 \; (f_{UU}(l,d,r) = (l,d,r))$$

By Definition 13.2, the following holds for all $\alpha \in \mathrm{Conf}(T_{UU})$ and $(x,y) \in \mathbb{Z}^2$.

$$
\begin{aligned}
&F_{UU}(\alpha)(x,y) \\
&= \begin{cases} f_{UU}(\mathrm{pr}_L(\alpha(x-1,y)), \mathrm{pr}_D(\alpha(x,y-1)), \mathrm{pr}_R(\alpha(x+1,y))) & \text{if } x+y \text{ is even} \\ f_{UU}(\mathrm{pr}_L(\alpha(x+1,y)), \mathrm{pr}_D(\alpha(x,y+1)), \mathrm{pr}_R(\alpha(x-1,y))) & \text{if } x+y \text{ is odd} \end{cases}
\end{aligned}
$$

Therefore, we can see

$$
\begin{aligned}
\mathrm{pr}_L(F_{UU}(\alpha)(x,y)) &= \begin{cases} \mathrm{pr}_L(\alpha(x-1,y)) & \text{if } x+y \text{ is even} \\ \mathrm{pr}_L(\alpha(x+1,y)) & \text{if } x+y \text{ is odd} \end{cases} \\
\mathrm{pr}_D(F_{UU}(\alpha)(x,y)) &= \begin{cases} \mathrm{pr}_D(\alpha(x,y-1)) & \text{if } x+y \text{ is even} \\ \mathrm{pr}_D(\alpha(x,y+1)) & \text{if } x+y \text{ is odd} \end{cases} \\
\mathrm{pr}_R(F_{UU}(\alpha)(x,y)) &= \begin{cases} \mathrm{pr}_D(\alpha(x+1,y)) & \text{if } x+y \text{ is even} \\ \mathrm{pr}_D(\alpha(x-1,y)) & \text{if } x+y \text{ is odd} \end{cases}
\end{aligned}
$$

and thus we obtain the following.

$$\mathrm{pr}_L(F^2_{\mathrm{UU}}(\alpha)(x,y)) = \begin{cases} \mathrm{pr}_L(F_{\mathrm{UU}}(\alpha)(x-1,y)) & \text{if } x+y \text{ is even} \\ \mathrm{pr}_L(F_{\mathrm{UU}}(\alpha)(x+1,y)) & \text{if } x+y \text{ is odd} \end{cases}$$
$$= \mathrm{pr}_L(\alpha(x,y))$$
$$\mathrm{pr}_D(F^2_{\mathrm{UU}}(\alpha)(x,y)) = \begin{cases} \mathrm{pr}_D(F_{\mathrm{UU}}(\alpha)(x,y-1)) & \text{if } x+y \text{ is even} \\ \mathrm{pr}_D(F_{\mathrm{UU}}(\alpha)(x,y+1)) & \text{if } x+y \text{ is odd} \end{cases}$$
$$= \mathrm{pr}_D(\alpha(x,y))$$
$$\mathrm{pr}_R(F^2_{\mathrm{UU}}(\alpha)(x,y)) = \begin{cases} \mathrm{pr}_D(F_{\mathrm{UU}}(\alpha)(x+1,y)) & \text{if } x+y \text{ is even} \\ \mathrm{pr}_D(F_{\mathrm{UU}}(\alpha)(x-1,y)) & \text{if } x+y \text{ is odd} \end{cases}$$
$$= \mathrm{pr}_R(\alpha(x,y))$$

Therefore,

$$\forall \alpha \in \mathrm{Conf}(T_{\mathrm{UU}}), \; \forall (x,y) \in \mathbb{Z}^2 \; (F^2_{\mathrm{UU}}(\alpha)(x,y) = \alpha(x,y))$$

holds, and the lemma is proved.   □

The following lemma can be proved in a similar manner as in Lemma 13.6 using the fact that the local functions f_{RR} of T_{RR}, and f_{LL} of T_{LL} satisfy $f_{\mathrm{RR}}(l,d,r) = (r,l,d)$, and $f_{\mathrm{LL}}(l,d,r) = (d,r,l)$ for all $(l,d,r) \in \{0,1\}^3$. Since an exact description of the proof is lengthy, we omit its proof.

Lemma 13.7. *Let F_{RR} and F_{LL} be the global functions of T_{RR} and T_{RR}, respectively. Then the following holds.*

$$\forall \alpha \in \mathrm{Conf}(T_{\mathrm{RR}}) \; (F^6_{\mathrm{RR}}(\alpha) = \alpha)$$
$$\forall \alpha \in \mathrm{Conf}(T_{\mathrm{LL}}) \; (F^6_{\mathrm{LL}}(\alpha) = \alpha)$$

We now prove the following theorem that states non-universality of T_{UU}, T_{RR}, and T_{LL}. It is almost clear from the fact that all the configurations of T_{UU}, T_{RR}, or T_{LL} have the same fixed period (Lemmas 13.6 and 13.7).

Theorem 13.4. *[8] The conservative RETPCAs T_{UU}, T_{RR}, and T_{LL} are neither Turing universal, nor intrinsically universal with respect to the class of two-dimensional RPCAs.*

Proof. We consider only T_{RR}, since the cases of T_{UU} and T_{LL} are similar. We show T_{RR} is not Turing universal. Assume, on the contrary, T_{RR} is Turing universal. It is easy to find a TM T and its computing process $\alpha_0 \vdash_T \alpha_1 \vdash_T \cdots \vdash_T \alpha_m$, where $\alpha_0, \ldots, \alpha_m$ are distinct instantaneous descriptions (IDs) of T, and $m \geq 6$. Since T_{RR} can simulate T, there are a monotonically increasing total recursive function $\tau_{\alpha_0} : \mathbb{N} \rightarrow \mathbb{N}$, and two total recursive functions $c : \mathrm{ID}(T) \rightarrow \mathrm{Conf}(T_{\mathrm{RR}})$, and $d : \mathrm{Conf}(T_{\mathrm{RR}}) \rightarrow (\mathrm{ID}(T) \cup \{\perp\})$ that satisfy the following by Definition 12.2, where $\mathrm{ID}(T)$ is the set of all IDs of T and F_{RR} is the global function of T_{RR}.

$$\forall n \in \{0, \ldots, m\} \; (d(F^{\tau_{\alpha_0}(n)}_{\mathrm{RR}}(c(\alpha_0)))) = \alpha_n)$$

Note that, in Definition 12.2, encoding and decoding functions c and d are the ones such that $c : \mathrm{ID}(T) \rightarrow D(\mathrm{Conf}_{\mathrm{hup}}(T_{\mathrm{RR}}))$, and $d : D(\mathrm{Conf}_{\mathrm{hup}}(T_{\mathrm{RR}})) \rightarrow (\mathrm{ID}(T) \cup \{\perp\})$.

But, here, we can show the theorem even if configurations of T_{RR} are not limited to horizontally ultimately periodic ones.

By Lemma 13.7, there are $n_1, n_2 \in \{0, \ldots, 6\}$ such that $n_1 < n_2$, and they satisfy $F_{RR}^{\tau_{\alpha_0}(n_1)}(c(\alpha_0)) = F_{RR}^{\tau_{\alpha_0}(n_2)}(c(\alpha_0))$. Hence,

$$\alpha_{n_1} = d(F_{RR}^{\tau_{\alpha_0}(n_1)}(c(\alpha_0))) = d(F_{RR}^{\tau_{\alpha_0}(n_2)}(c(\alpha_0))) = \alpha_{n_2}$$

holds. Thus, the sequence of IDs $\alpha_{n_1}, \ldots, \alpha_{n_2-1}$ repeats indefinitely from the time $t = n_1$. This contradicts the assumption $\alpha_1, \ldots, \alpha_m$ are all different. Therefore, T_{RR} is not Turing universal.

We can show that T_{RR} is not intrinsically universal in a similar manner as above. Assume, on the contrary, T_{RR} is intrinsically universal. We can find an RPCA A and its distinct configurations $\alpha_0, \ldots, \alpha_m$ such that $m \geq 6$, and $F_A(\alpha_i) = \alpha_{i+1}$ for $i \in \{0, \ldots, m-1\}$, where F_A is the global function of A. Since T_{RR} can simulate A, by Definition 12.5, there are $\tau \in \mathbb{Z}_+$, an encoding function $c^* : \mathrm{Conf}(A) \to \mathrm{Conf}(T_{RR})$, and a decoding function $d^* : \mathrm{Conf}(T_{RR}) \to (\mathrm{Conf}(A) \cup \{\bot\})$ that satisfy the following for all $k \in \{0, \ldots, m\}$.

$$d^*(F_{RR}^{k\tau}(c^*(\alpha_0))) = \alpha_k$$

By Lemma 13.7, there are $n_1, n_2 \in \{0, \ldots, 6\}$ such that $n_1 < n_2$ and $F_{RR}^{n_1\tau}(c^*(\alpha_0)) = F_{RR}^{n_2\tau}(c^*(\alpha_0))$. Hence, $\alpha_{n_1} = d^*(F_{RR}^{\tau(n_1)}(c^*(\alpha_0))) = d^*(F_{RR}^{\tau(n_2)}(c^*(\alpha_0))) = \alpha_{n_2}$. Thus, the sequence of configurations $\alpha_{n_1}, \ldots, \alpha_{n_2-1}$ repeats indefinitely from the time $t = n_1$. This contradicts the assumption $\alpha_1, \ldots, \alpha_m$ are all different. Therefore, T_{RR} is not intrinsically universal. $\square$

13.3 Non-conservative RETPCA T_{0347} That Exhibits Complex Behavior

In this section, we focus on a specific non-conservative RETPCA T_{0347} [5], and investigate its properties. Its local function is given in Fig. 13.44. In spite of its extreme simplicity of the local function, it exhibits quite interesting behavior as in the case of the Game of Life CA [1, 2, 3] (see also Example 10.1). In particular, a glider, which is a space-moving pattern, and glider guns that generate gliders periodically exist. Reversible logical operations are also possible by colliding two gliders. Using these properties of T_{0347}, we shall see that T_{0347} is both Turing universal and intrinsically universal.

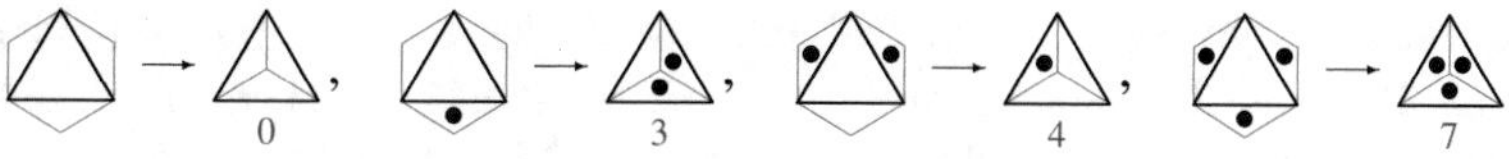

Fig. 13.44 The local function of the non-conservative RETPCA T_{0347}

13.3.1 Properties of the RETPCA T_{0347}

There are several useful patterns in T_{0347}. We first give four kinds of such patterns. They are a *glider*, a *block*, a *fin*, and a *rotator*. We shall see that various interesting phenomena are observed from the interactions of these patterns. In Sect. 13.3.3, some of these phenomena will be used to show its universality.

Although the local rule of T_{0347} is very simple (Fig. 13.44), its evolution processes are often very complex, and it is hard to follow them by hand. In [7], various examples of evolution processes of T_{0347} can be seen by movies. We also created an emulator of T_{0347} on a general purpose CA simulator Golly [11]. The file of the emulator (Reversible_World_v2.zip) is available at the Rule Table Repository of Golly (http://github.com/GollyGang/ruletablerepository) and in [9].

13.3.1.1 Useful patterns in T_{0347}

The most useful pattern in T_{0347} is a *glider* shown in Fig. 13.45. It swims in the cellular space like a fish (or an eel). It travels a unit distance, the side-length of a triangle, in 6 steps. By rotating it appropriately, it can move in any of the six directions. Later, it will be used to represent a *signal* to implement reversible logic circuits in T_{0347},

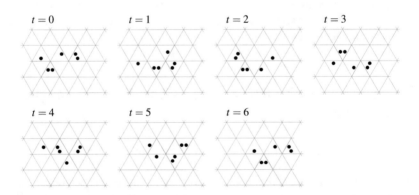

Fig. 13.45 Movement of a glider. The glider patterns at time $t = 0, \ldots, 5$, and 6 are said to be of phase $0, \ldots, 5$, and 0, respectively

A *block* is a pattern shown in Fig. 13.46 **(a)** or **(b)**. It does not change its pattern if no other pattern touches it. Therefore, it is a *stable* pattern. There are two kinds of blocks, i.e., type I (Fig. 13.46 **(a)**) and type II (Fig. 13.46 **(b)**). As will be explained in Sect. 13.3.1.2, an appropriate type of a block must be used when colliding a glider with it. Combining several blocks, right-turn, U-turn, and left-turn of a glider will be implemented.

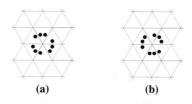

Fig. 13.46 Blocks of **(a)** type I and **(b)** type II. They are stable patterns

A *fin* is a pattern that simply rotates with period 6 as in Fig. 13.47. It can also travel around a block (Fig. 13.48), or a sequence of blocks (Fig. 13.49). As we shall see later, if we collide a glider to a sequence of blocks appropriately, then the glider is split into a rotator (Fig. 13.50) and a fin. Conversely, if a rotator and a fin interact properly, then they are combined to create a glider.

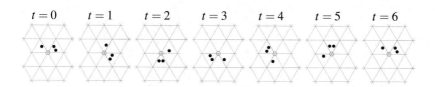

Fig. 13.47 A fin that rotates around the point indicated by ○

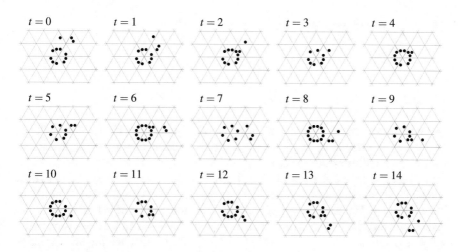

Fig. 13.48 A fin that travels around a block. It takes 42 steps to return to the initial position. Note that the block changes its pattern transiently, but it becomes the initial pattern again at $t = 14$

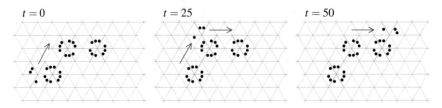

Fig. 13.49 A fin travelling along a sequence of blocks

A *rotator* is a pattern shown in Fig. 13.50. Like a fin, it rotates around some point, and its period is 42. As is already stated, a glider is decomposed into a fin and a rotator.

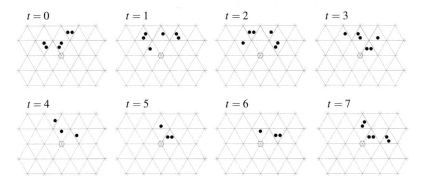

Fig. 13.50 A rotator that moves around the point indicated by ○

13.3.1.2 Controlling gliders in T_{0347}

We now make several experiments of colliding a glider with blocks. We shall see that the move direction of a glider is changed by such interactions of these objects.

First, we collide a glider with a single block. We put a glider that moves eastward, and a block of type I as shown in Fig. 13.51 ($t = 0$). At $t = 12$ they collide. Then, the glider is split into a fin and a rotator, where the latter is regarded as a "body" of the glider ($t = 16$). The body begins to rotate around the point indicated by ○. On the other hand, the fin travels around the block ($t = 38$). When it comes back to the original position, it interacts with the body ($t = 50$). By this, the rotation center of the body is shifted upward by two cells, and the fin travels around the block once more ($t = 61$). At $t = 94$, the body and the fin meet again, and the fin is attached to the body. Thus a glider is reconstructed, and it goes westward ($t = 97$). By above, a *backward-turn module* for a of glider is realized.

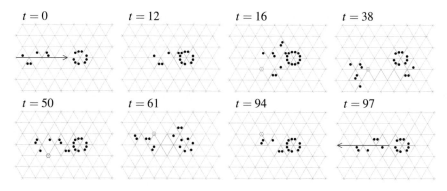

Fig. 13.51 Colliding a glider with a type I block. It works as a backward-turn module

In the above process, if we use a type II block instead of a type I block, then the glider goes to the north-east direction, but the block cannot be re-used, since some garbage remains (Fig. 13.52). Therefore, an appropriate type of block should be used depending on the coming direction of the glider. Figure 13.53 shows the allowed input positions of a glider in each type of a block.

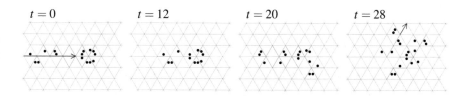

Fig. 13.52 If we collide a glider moving eastward with a type II block, then the block is broken and garbage remains

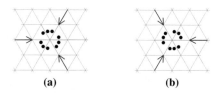

Fig. 13.53 Allowed input positions for (a) the type I block, and (b) the type II block

Next, we collide a glider with two blocks (Fig. 13.54). As in the case of one block (Fig. 13.51), the glider is split into a rotator and a fin ($t = 56$). The fin travels around the blocks three times without interacting with the rotator. At the end of the fourth round, they meet to form a glider, which goes to the south-west direction ($t = 334$). Hence, two blocks act as a 120°-*right-turn module*.

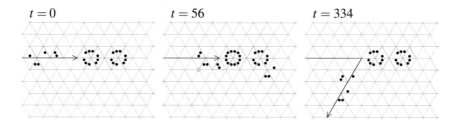

Fig. 13.54 Right-turn module composed of two blocks

Figures 13.55 and 13.56 show that three blocks and five blocks also act as right-turn modules. They have shorter delays than the case of two blocks. Note that, as in Fig. 13.56, blocks need not be placed in a straight line. More precisely, the sequence of blocks can be bent by ±60° at each point of a block. But, if we do so, the other type of a block must be used at the next position. Otherwise, blocks will be destroyed.

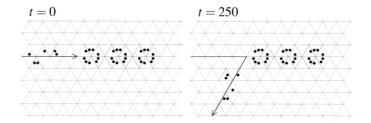

Fig. 13.55 Right-turn module composed of three blocks

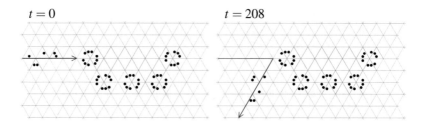

Fig. 13.56 Right-turn module composed of five blocks, which are not linearly placed

If we collide a glider with a sequence of four, six, or seven blocks, then they will be destroyed. On the other hand, a sequence of eight blocks acts as a backward-turn module like one block, and that of nine blocks acts as a right-turn module like two blocks. Generally, a sequence of $n + 7$ blocks ($n > 0$) shows a similar behavior as that of n blocks though the total delay is longer. The reason is as follows. The period that the fin goes around the $n + 7$ blocks is $36(n + 7) + 6$. Thus, when the fin comes back, the phase of the rotator becomes the same as in the case of n blocks, since the period of a rotator is 42, and 36×7 is a multiple of 42.

A U-turn module is given in Fig. 13.57. Also in this case, the glider is first split into a rotator and a fin ($t = 36$). But, slightly before the fin comes back to the start position, it meets the rotator, and a glider is reconstructed, which moves westward ($t = 113$). Note that, here the output path is different from the input path, while in the backward-turn module they are the same (Fig. 13.51).

$t = 0$ $t = 36$ $t = 113$

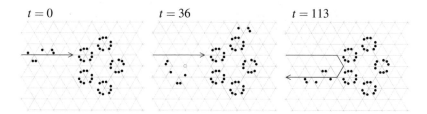

Fig. 13.57 U-turn module

Figure 13.58 shows a left-turn module. It is more sophisticated than the right-turn and U-turn modules. The glider is split into a rotator and a fin as before. The fin first travels outside of the module, and then inside. But, around the middle of the module it meets the rotator. A glider is reconstructed from them, and it moves to the north-west direction ($t = 366$).

$t = 0$ $t = 366$

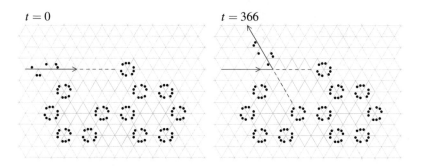

Fig. 13.58 $120°$-left-turn module

Table 13.2 shows the net delay and the phase shift of each of six turn modules. The *net delay d* of a turn module is the additional delay caused by the module. For example, consider the case of right-turn module with two blocks (Fig. 13.54). We can regard the travelling distance of the glider along the arrow line from $t = 0$ to 334 is 5 (note that the glider patterns at $t = 0$ and 334 are of phase 0, i.e., both standard ones). If a glider travels straight the distance of 5, then it takes $5/(1/6) = 30$ steps, since the speed of a glider is $1/6$. Therefore, the net delay for this module is $d = 334 - 30 = 304$. The *phase shift s* of a turn module is the shift value of the phase of a glider by the module. It is calculated by the equation $s = (-d) \bmod 6$. In the case of right-turn module with two blocks, $s = (-304) \bmod 6 = 2$.

Table 13.2 Net delay and phase shift of the six turn modules

Module	Net delay d	Phase shift s
Backward-turn	73	+5
Right-turn (120°) by 2 blocks	304	+2
Right-turn (120°) by 3 blocks	220	+2
Right-turn (120°) by 5 blocks	178	+2
U-turn	77	+1
Left-turn (120°)	342	0

It is possible to make a 60°-right-turn module by combining 120°-right-turn and backward-turn modules as in Fig. 13.59. First, the input glider makes 120°-right-turn by the module composed of three blocks ($t = 250$). Next, the glider is reflected by the backward-turn module. Finally, it makes 120°-right-turn again by the three-block module ($t = 585$). Note that, by replacing the three blocks by two or five blocks, we also obtain a 60°-right-turn module with a different time delay.

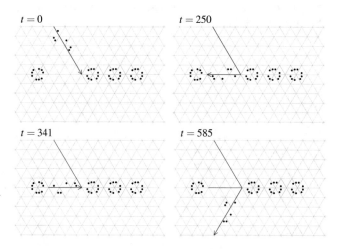

Fig. 13.59 60°-right-turn module composed of 120°-right-turn and backward-turn modules

This mechanism is also used as an interface between a *bidirectional signal path* and *unidirectional signal paths* as shown in Fig. 13.60.

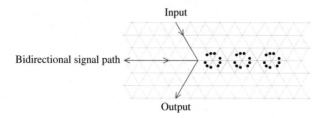

Fig. 13.60 Interface between a bidirectional signal path, and unidirectional signal paths

Combining the turn modules, we can change the direction of a glider to any of the six directions. Thus, when we use a glider as a signal, routing of signals is possible. Delay time of a signal is also adjusted by these modules. By modifying the signal route, and replacing right-turn modules by those with different numbers of blocks, any delay of a multiple of 6 steps is realized. Figure 13.61 shows how to make an additional delay of 6 steps, which is one cycle of a glider. It is also possible to shift the phase of a glider. For example, by making right-turn (120°) and then left-turn (120°), its phase is shifted by 2 keeping the moving direction the same (see Table 13.2).

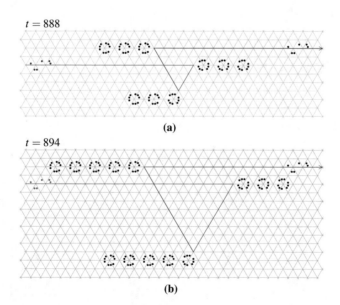

Fig. 13.61 Adjustment of delay. In **(b)** the delay of the glider is larger than that in **(a)** by 6 steps

13.3.2 Glider guns in T_{0347}

A *glider gun* is a pattern that generates gliders periodically as the one in the Game
of Life CA [3]. In the RETPCA T_{0347}, it is easy to create a three-way glider gun. As
shown in Fig. 13.62, it is obtained by colliding a glider with a fin. It generates three
gliders every 24 steps.

Interestingly, there is a *glider absorber* in T_{0347} (Fig. 13.63). It absorbs three
gliders every 24 steps, and finally produces a fin and a glider. It is considered as a
"backward glider gun" that generates gliders to the negative time direction. Combining the above two, it is also possible to obtain a gun that generates gliders in both
positive and negative time directions [7].

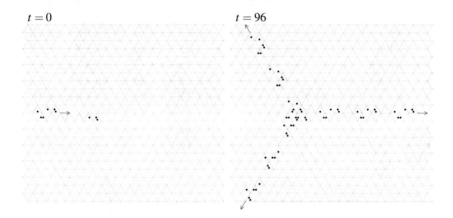

Fig. 13.62 Three-way glider gun

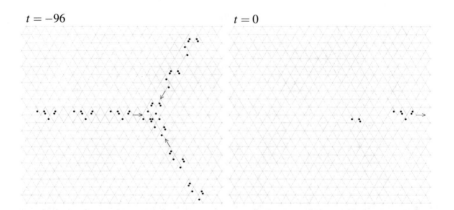

Fig. 13.63 Glider absorber. It is considered as a glider gun to the negative time direction

There is another way of composing a glider gun. Figure 13.64 shows that three gliders are generated by the head-on collision of two gliders. Based on this mechanism, we can design a one-way glider gun as shown in Fig. 13.65, where two of the three generated gliders (i.e., the two gliders that move to the east and to the south-west at $t = 30$ of Fig. 13.64) are circulated and re-used to generate the next three. This glider gun generates a glider every 1422 steps. Note that, in Fig. 13.64, the west-moving glider at $t = 0$ and the east-moving one at $t = 30$ take the same path. Therefore, the mechanism shown in Fig. 13.60 is used for managing this bidirectional signal path.

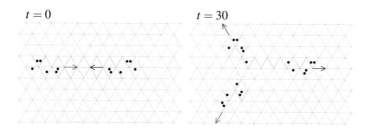

Fig. 13.64 Generating three gliders by the head-on collision of two gliders

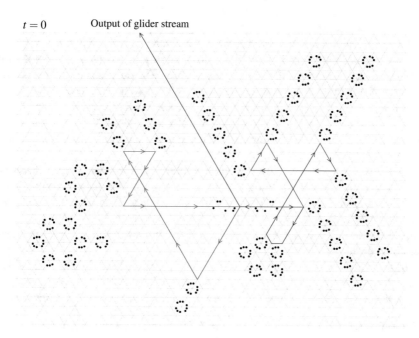

Fig. 13.65 One-way glider gun

13.3.3 Universality of the RETPCA T_{0347}

We first show a switch gate and an inverse switch gate can be implemented in T_{0347} using gliders as signals. The operation of a switch gate itself is realized by colliding two gliders as shown in Fig. 13.66. It is important that, in this collision, the glider from the input port c travels to the south-east direction *with no delay* even though it interacts with the glider from x (hence its phase is not shifted also).

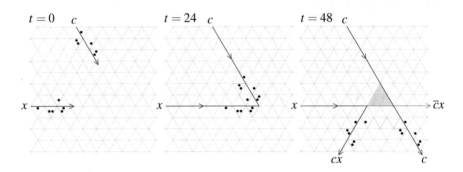

Fig. 13.66 Switch gate operation realized by collision of two gliders

As in the cases of the universal conservative RETPCAs in Sect. 13.2, we implement a switch gate and an inverse switch gate as gate modules (see Fig. 13.25). Figure 13.67 shows a *switch gate module*. The delay between input and output in this module is 2232 steps. Figure 13.68 shows an *inverse switch gate module*. It is a "quasi-mirror-image" of the switch gate module. The positions of the blocks are just the mirror images of those in the switch gate module. But, each block is replaced by the other type of the corresponding block (not by the mirror image of the block). The delay between input and output is also 2232 steps. A Fredkin gate module can be realized by connecting two switch gate modules and two inverse switch gate modules as in Fig. 4.19.

If we use only 120°-right-turn modules (Table 13.2) to connect gate modules, then there is no need of adjusting the phases of gliders. This is because the phase shift becomes 0, if we make 120°-right-turns three times. Therefore, we should adjust the delay time only by a multiples of 6 steps. It is done in a similar way as in Fig. 13.61. In this way, we can construct a larger circuit from these gate modules relatively easily.

In this way, any reversible logic circuit composed of Fredkin gates and delay elements can be simulated in T_{0347}. In addition, we have a relation $T_{0347} \xleftrightarrow[\text{refl}]{} T_{0617}$. Thus, we can prove the following theorem in a similar manner as in Theorem 13.1.

Theorem 13.5. *[5] The non-conservative RETPCAs T_{0347} and T_{0617} with horizontally ultimately periodic configurations are Turing universal. They are also intrinsically universal with respect to the class of two-dimensional RPCAs.*

$t = 2232$

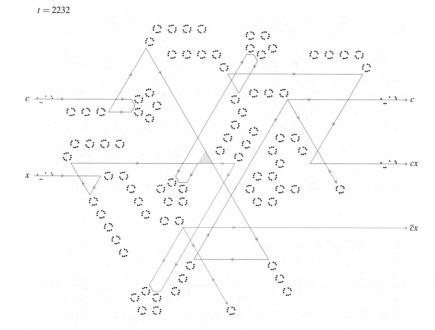

Fig. 13.67 Switch gate module implemented in T_{0347}

$t = 2232$

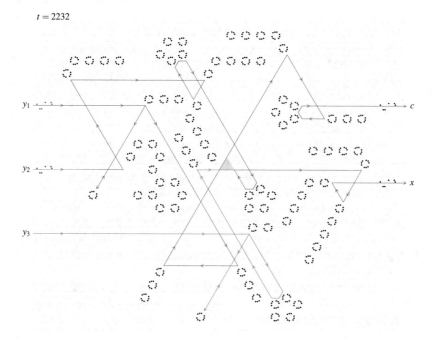

Fig. 13.68 Inverse switch gate module implemented in T_{0347}

Though $T_{0347} \xleftrightarrow[\text{comp}]{} T_{0347}$, we also have the relation $T_{0347} \xleftrightarrow[\text{osc}]{} T_{7430}$ (see Example 13.6). Hence, any evolution process of T_{0347} can be simulated by T_{7430} in such a manner that T_{0347}'s configurations of even time steps are simulated by the same ones, while those of odd time steps are simulated by the complemented ones. Thus, the configurations of T_{7430} to simulate T_{0347} are not horizontally ultimately periodic, even if those of T_{0347} are so. On the other hand, since T_{0347} is intrinsically universal (Theorem 13.5), T_{7430} is also intrinsically universal by Definition 12.5.

By above, and by the relation $T_{7430} \xleftrightarrow[\text{refl}]{} T_{7160}$, we have the following theorem.

Theorem 13.6. *The non-conservative RETPCAs T_{7430} and T_{7160} with infinite (but, finitely describable) configurations are Turing universal. They are also intrinsically universal with respect to the class of two-dimensional RPCAs.*

13.4 Concluding Remarks

In this chapter, we investigated reversible elementary triangular partitioned cellular automata (RETPCAs). First, nine conservative RETPCAs were studied, and it was shown that six among nine are Turing universal and intrinsically universal (Theorems 13.1, 13.2 and 13.3). In the RETPCAs T_{RU}, T_{LU}, T_{RL} and T_{LR}, a single particle (i.e., the state 1) acts as a signal, while in T_{UR} and T_{UL}, a single hole (i.e., the state 0) acts as a signal. Using such signals, it was shown that any reversible logic circuit is embeddable in these RETPCAs, and thus their universality was derived. On the other hand, T_{UU}, T_{RR}, and T_{LL} were shown to be non-universal (Theorem 13.4). Hence, the universality of all nine conservative RETPCAs was clarified.

Next, we studied a particular non-conservative RETPCA T_{0347}. This RETPCA shows interesting and complex behavior. As in the Game of Life CA, a glider, which is a space-moving pattern, and glider guns exist in it. We saw that trajectories of a glider can be controlled rather freely by colliding it with blocks, which are stable patterns, or with another glider. Using such properties it was shown that any reversible logic circuit can be simulated in T_{0347}, and thus the Turing universality and the intrinsic universality of T_{0347} were derived. Since RETPCAs T_{0617}, T_{7430} and T_{7160} are dual with T_{0347} under reflection and/or odd-step complementation, their universality was also derived (Theorems 13.5 and 13.6).

By the above, we have ten computationally universal RETPCAs. However, there are 256 ETPCAs in total, and thus investigation of other (R)ETPCAs, in particular universal ones, is left for future study. It is also an open problem whether there is a Turing universal RETPCA with *finite* configurations as in the RPCA P_3 on the square tessellation (Sect. 12.4).

In [6, 7] the evolution processes of configurations of T_{RU}, T_{UR}, T_{RL}, and T_{0347} can be seen by simulation movies. On T_{0347}, an emulator file for the CA simulator Golly [11] is also available in [9].

It is known that, besides the Fredkin gate, the reversible logic element with memory RLEM 4-31 (see Sect. 6.2) can be simulated in T_{0347} [9]. Therefore, we can construct a configuration of T_{0347} that simulates the circuit for the reversible Turing machine (RTM) T_{parity} shown in Fig. 6.10. Files of such configurations are also found in [9], and thus we can observe the whole simulation processes of RTMs in the cellular space of T_{0347} using Golly.

References

1. Berlekamp, E., Conway, J., Guy, R.: Winning Ways for Your Mathematical Plays, Vol. 2. Academic Press, New York (1982)
2. Gardner, M.: Mathematical games: The fantastic combinations of John Conway's new solitaire game "Life". Sci. Am. **223 (4)**, 120–123 (1970). doi:10.1038/scientificamerican1070-120
3. Gardner, M.: Mathematical games: On cellular automata, self-reproduction, the Garden of Eden and the game "Life".   Sci. Am. **224 (2)**, 112–117 (1971). doi:10.1038/scientificamerican0271-112
4. Imai, K., Morita, K.: A computation-universal two-dimensional 8-state triangular reversible cellular automaton.   Theoret. Comput. Sci. **231**, 181–191 (2000).   doi:10.1016/S0304-3975(99)00099-7
5. Morita, K.: An 8-state simple reversible triangular cellular automaton that exhibits complex behavior.   In: Automata 2016 (eds. M. Cook, T. Neary) LNCS 9664, pp. 170–184 (2016). doi:10.1007/978-3-319-39300-1_14
6. Morita, K.: Reversible and conservative elementary triangular partitioned cellular automata (slides with simulation movies).   Hiroshima University Institutional Repository, http://ir.lib.hiroshima-u.ac.jp/00039997 (2016)
7. Morita, K.: A reversible elementary triangular partitioned cellular automaton that exhibits complex behavior (slides with simulation movies). Hiroshima University Institutional Repository, http://ir.lib.hiroshima-u.ac.jp/00039321 (2016)
8. Morita, K.: Universality of 8-state reversible and conservative triangular partitioned cellular automaton.   In: ACRI 2016 (eds. S. El Yacoubi, et al.) LNCS 9863, pp. 45–54 (2016). doi:10.1007/978-3-319-44365-2_5
9. Morita, K.: Reversible world : Data set for simulating a reversible elementary triangular partitioned cellular automaton on Golly.   Hiroshima University Institutional Repository, http://ir.lib.hiroshima-u.ac.jp/00042655 (2017)
10. Róka, Z.: Simulations between cellular automata on Cayley graphs. Theoret. Comput. Sci. **225**, 81–111 (1999). doi:10.1016/S0304-3975(97)00213-2
11. Trevorrow, A., Rokicki, T., et al.: Golly: an open source, cross-platform application for exploring Conway's Game of Life and other cellular automata. http://golly.sourceforge.net/ (2005)
12. Wolfram, S.: Theory and Applications of Cellular Automata.   World Scientific Publishing (1986)
13. Wolfram, S.: A New Kind of Science. Wolfram Media Inc. (2002)

Chapter 14
Self-reproduction in Reversible Cellular Automata

Abstract J. von Neumann first showed that machine self-reproduction is possible using the framework of cellular automaton (CA). In his CA, self-reproducing objects have universality in both computing and construction, and thus they were very complex. Later, Langton relaxed this condition, and designed a simple self-reproducing automaton. In this chapter, we study how self-reproducing automata are constructed in a reversible environment. It is shown that there are two- and three-dimensional reversible cellular automata (RCAs), in which various objects called Worms and Loops can self-reproduce. Hence, Langton's type self-reproduction is possible in RCAs. There, conversion between a shape of an object and its description (or gene), and copying the description are done reversibly. Using these properties, self-reproducing automata are designed in RCAs. An additional advantage of them is that the "shape-encoding mechanism" is employed, i.e., the shape of a Worm or a Loop is encoded into its description in a reversible way. This makes the whole mechanism simple, and increases the variety of self-reproducing objects.

Keywords reversible cellular automaton, three-dimensional cellular automaton, self-reproduction, shape-encoding mechanism

14.1 Self-reproducing Cellular Automata

Self-reproducing cellular automaton was first studied by von Neumann [8]. In the cellular space of his famous *29-state cellular automaton*, he designed a pattern that has both capabilities of universal computing and self-reproduction. Figure 14.1 shows the structure of the self-reproducing automaton embedded in its cellular space. It consists of three components: a Turing machine (TM) T, a universal constructor (UC) U, and a tape.

In his model, the UC U plays an important role. It can construct *any* automaton M composed of "unexcited states" if a *description* $d(M)$ of M is given on the tape, where $d(M)$ can be regarded as a *gene* of M. Here, an "unexcited state" means that it

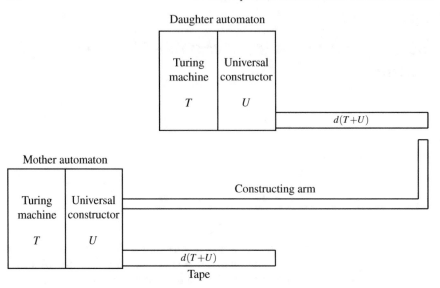

Fig. 14.1 Structure of von Neumann's self-reproducing automata [8]

has no active signal, and thus it does not change its state unless it is activated by the neighboring cells. It is known that any sequential machine (i.e., a finite automaton with both input and output ports), and a tape unit can be constructed out of ten kinds of unexcited states of the von Neumann's 29-state CA [1, 8]. Therefore, any TM can also be constructed using these states. The UC U is an automaton similar to a TM except that it has a constructing arm. The machine U reads the description $d(M)$ given on the tape, and moves its constructing arm appropriately to write a pattern of M in the cellular space. After creating M, the UC U can give an activation signal to start M. Since there exists such a universal constructor, von Neumann's 29-state CA is called *construction-universal*. It is also Turing universal, since any TM is embeddable in its cellular space.

The self-reproducing automaton designed by von Neumann has the description $d(T + U)$ of T and U on its tape. It performs the following operations. First, it constructs the body of a daughter automaton using $d(T + U)$. Second, it copies the tape containing $d(T + U)$, and attach it to the daughter automaton. Third, it activates the daughter automaton. By above, the daughter automaton starts to do the same operations as the mother automaton, i.e., it will produce grand-daughter automaton. After creating the daughter automaton, the mother automaton computes something as it likes using the function of the TM T.

Von Neumann supposed that a self-reproducing automaton must have both Turing universality and construction-universality. This condition is to exclude trivial self-replication of patterns like the growth of snow crystals. In fact, real living organisms have some ability of information processing besides the ability of self-reproduction. His self-reproducing automaton clearly satisfies this condition, while replication of patterns in Fredkin's CA in Example 10.2 does not. However, because of this constraint, von Neumann's model becomes very complex. In particular, the length of the description $d(T + U)$, and the number of steps to complete self-reproduction are very large.

After the work of von Neumann, various kinds of CA models that support self-reproduction appeared (see e.g., [9, 10] for the history). Codd [2] proposed a simpler CA with eight states that has essentially the same capabilities as von Neumann's model. Langton [4] showed that, if Turing universality and construction-universality are not supposed, a very simple self-reproducing object, which is called *Langton's Loop* (Fig. 14.2), can be designed in the modified eight-state CA model of Codd.

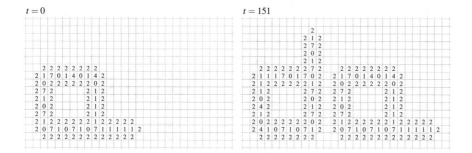

Fig. 14.2 Self-reproducing Loops in Langton's eight-state CA [4]

Langton also thought that replication of a pattern as in Fredkin's CA is not a true self-reproduction, since such a phenomenon is caused by the local function of the CA, but not by the property of the pattern. Therefore, he proposed the following *Langton's criterion* for self-reproducing automata: The construction of the copy (daughter automaton) should be *actively directed* by the configuration itself (mother automaton) properly using the information (description, or gene) of the configuration [4]. Langton's Loop (Fig. 14.2) has its own description inside its "sheath" made of the state 2's. More precisely, the signal sequence 70170170170170170170170140140 1401 in the sheath describes the shape of a quarter of the Loop. The mother Loop decodes the sequence, and creates a daughter Loop from it. Von Neumann's self-reproducing automaton, of course, satisfies the Langton's criterion. But, the Fredkin's CA does not, since any pattern replicates in its cellular space, and thus replication cannot be controlled by the mother pattern.

Note that, in some literatures "self-reproduction" and "self-replication" are sometimes used synonymously. But, here, by *self-reproduction* we mean a process of producing a daughter automaton from a mother one in von Neumann's or Langton's sense, and by *self-replication* we mean a creating process of copies of an initial pattern that does not satisfy the criterion of Langton.

14.2 Self-reproduction in Two- and Three-Dimensional RCAs

In this section, we show that Langton's type self-reproduction is possible even in a *reversible* CA. Since Turing universality is not required here, the main tasks for realizing self-reproduction are *conversion* between a description (i.e., genotype) and a shape of an object (i.e., phenotype), and *copying* the description. We shall show that these two tasks can be performed reversibly, and thus self-reproduction is possible in RCAs. In addition, in the following RCAs, conversion between a description and a shape is bi-directional. Namely, we use not only a mechanism of decoding a description to make a shape, but also a mechanism of encoding a shape of an object into a description. The latter is called a *shape-encoding mechanism*. By this, complexity of self-reproducing objects is greatly reduced. Furthermore, the variety of objects' also increases greatly. In fact, an object called a Worm of a Loop of almost arbitrary shape can self-reproduce in an RCA.

In Sect. 14.2.1, we explain a two-dimensional five-neighbor RPCA SR_{2D} in which Worms and Loops can self-reproduce [5]. Since each part of a cell has eight states, there are 8^5 states in total. Although the total number is large, only 765 states among 8^5 are actually used for self-reproduction. In addition, self-reproduction is carried out very simply by the shape-encoding mechanism.

In Sect. 14.2.2, three-dimensional seven-neighbor RPCA SR_{3D} [3] is explained. Since each part of a cell has nine states, there are 9^7 states per cell. Though basic methods for self-reproduction employed in SR_{3D} is similar to those in SR_{2D}, it is not a mere extension of the latter. This is because varieties of possible shapes and arrangements of Worms and Loops are much greater than in SR_{2D}.

14.2.1 Two-dimensional model SR_{2D}

We give a two-dimensional five-neighbor RPCA SR_{2D} in which various shapes of objects can reproduce themselves [5]. It is defined as follows.

$$SR_{2D} = (\mathbb{Z}^2, (C, U, R, D, L), ((0,0), (0,-1), (-1,0), (0,1), (1,0)), f, (\#, \#, \#, \#, \#))$$
$$C = U = R = D = L = \{\#, *, +, -, A, B, C, D\}$$

Each part of a cell of SR_{2D} has eight states, and thus a cell has 8^5 states. Though the total number of states of a cell is very large, the number of local rules that are actually used is rather small as we shall see below. The states A, B, C and D act as signals that are used to compose "commands", while the states $*, +$ and $-$ are used to control these signals. A basic object in SR_{2D} is a transmission wire, in which signals can travel. Self-reproducing objects in SR_{2D} are nothing but certain types of transmission wires. Hence, a transmission wire has various functions to support self-reproduction. In the following, each of the functions, as well as local rules that realize the functions, will be explained one by one.

We define SR_{2D} as a rotation symmetric PCA (see Definition 12.4), and thus each local rule is invariant under the rotation of 90, 180 and 270 degrees. Therefore, we write only one of the four rules and omit the other rotated ones. However, SR_{2D} is not reflection-symmetric (for example, the local rules (11) and (12) below violates the condition for reflection-symmetry in Definition 12.4).

14.2.1.1 Signal transmission

First, a rule for the quiescent state $(\#,\#,\#,\#,\#)$ is given in Fig. 14.3. In the following, the state $\#$ is indicated by a blank.

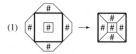

Fig. 14.3 Quiescent-state rule

A *transmission wire* (or simply *wire*) is a pattern to send a sequence of signals consisting of A, B and C. Note that, the signal D has a different function for self-reproduction of Loops, and it will be explained in Sect. 14.2.1.5. Figure 14.4 is an example of a part of a simple (i.e., non-branching) wire. The direction of signal transmission is determined by the control state $+$. Figure 14.5 shows the local rules for it. By the rules (2) – (4), signals x_i and y_i in Fig. 14.4 shift by one cell along the wire in two time steps. Note that, strictly speaking, each of (2) – (4) is a "rule scheme" that represents many rules. For example, (2) represents 36 rules since $x, y \in \{A,B,C\}$, and it is rotation-symmetric.

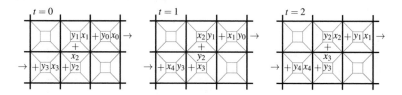

Fig. 14.4 Signal transmission on a simple wire $(x_i, y_i \in \{A,B,C\})$

A wire may contain two-way (i.e., bifurcating) or three-way (i.e., trifurcating) branches. Figure 14.6 is an example of a wire with a bifurcation. A branching point acts as a "fan-out", i.e., the signals are copied at this point. Rules (5) – (7) in Fig. 14.7 are for two-way branch, and rule (8) is for three-way one.

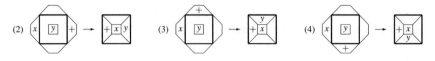

Fig. 14.5 Rules for signal transmission ($x, y \in \{A, B, C\}$)

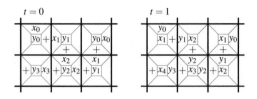

Fig. 14.6 Signal transmission on a wire with a bifurcation ($x_i, y_i \in \{A, B, C\}$)

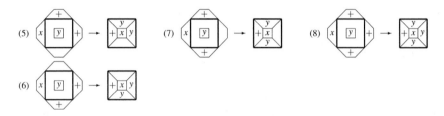

Fig. 14.7 Rules for signal transmission at a branching point ($x, y \in \{A, B, C\}$)

14.2.1.2 Commands and their execution

A *command* is a sequence composed of two signals. There are six commands consisting of signals A, B and C as shown in Table 14.1. These commands are used for extending or branching a wire (commands containing signal D will be explained in Sect. 14.2.1.5).

Table 14.1 Six commands composed of two signals from $\{A, B, C\}$

First signal	Second signal	Operation
A	A	Advance the head forward
A	B	Advance the head leftward
A	C	Advance the head rightward
B	A	Branch the wire in three ways
B	B	Branch the wire in two ways (making a leftward branch)
B	C	Branch the wire in two ways (making a rightward branch)

We assume that, at even time step, two signals of a command are in one cell of a wire. For example, the command sequence on the wire shown in Fig. 14.8 is AC, BB, AB, BC.

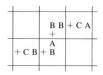

Fig. 14.8 Command sequence AC, BB, AB, BC travelling on a wire at even time step

A *head* is an end cell of a wire to which signals flow, and a *tail* is an end cell from which signals flow. Figure 14.9 shows a wire with two heads and a tail. At time $t = 0 \pmod 4$, heads have the state $*$ in its center, and a tail has $+$ in its center.

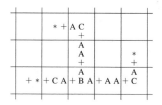

Fig. 14.9 A wire with two heads (with $*$ in the center part), and a tail (with $+$ in the center part)

Six commands shown in Table 14.1 are decoded and executed at the head of a wire. Here, we explain how the advance commands AA, AB, AC are executed (branch commands BA, BB, BC will be explained later). Rules (9) – (17) in Fig. 14.10 are for executing these commands. Since it takes four time steps to execute an advance command, these rules are classified into four groups (from Phase 0 to Phase 3) according to the phase of the execution. An example of this process is shown in Fig. 14.11, where "Phase t" rules in Fig. 14.10 are applied at time t.

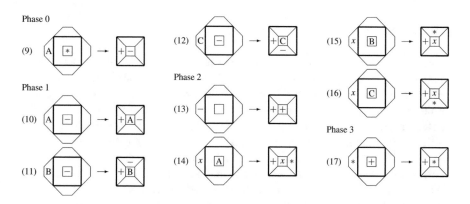

Fig. 14.10 Rules for advancing a head ($x \in \{A, B, C\}$)

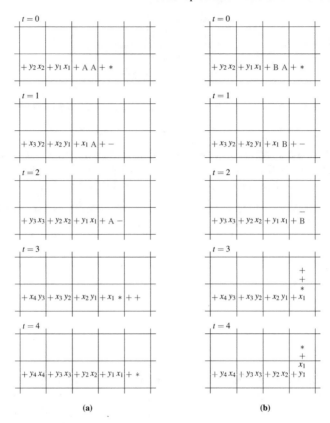

Fig. 14.11 Execution of an advance command. **(a)** The case of command AA, and **(b)** the case of command AB ($x_i, y_i \in \{A, B, C\}$)

14.2.1.3 Worms

A *Worm* is a simple wire with open ends, thus it has a head and a tail. It crawls in the space of SR_{2D}. As explained in Sect. 14.2.1.2, commands in Table 14.1 are decoded and executed at the head of a Worm. On the other hand, at the tail cell, the shape of the Worm is encoded into an advance command. That is, if the tail of the Worm is straight (or left-turning, right-turning, respectively) in its form, the command AA (AB, AC) is generated. The tail then retracts by one cell. These operations are done by rules (18) – (29) in Fig. 14.12. Note that in a reversible cellular space, simple retraction (or erasure) of a tail without leaving the shape information is impossible. Therefore, retraction must accompany some encoding process. Figure 14.13 shows an example of encoding and retracting processes. It takes four time steps to encode and retract a tail by one cell. The command sequence generated by the encoding process may be regarded as a "gene" of the Worm.

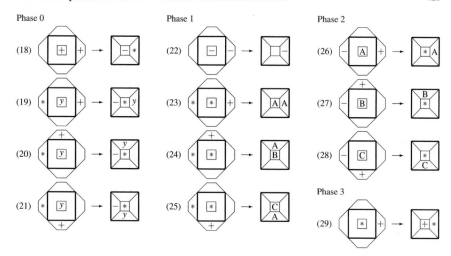

Fig. 14.12 Rules for retracting a tail ($y \in \{A, B, C\}$)

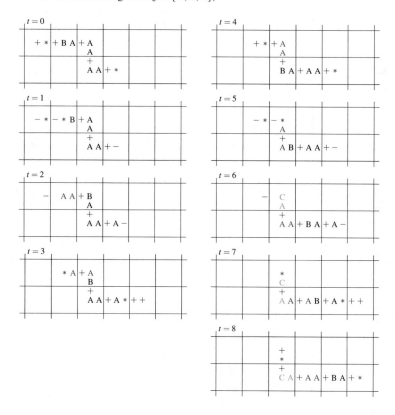

Fig. 14.13 Retracting process of a tail, where encoding the shape of the tail into advance commands is carried out at the same time. Here, the commands AA and AC are generated

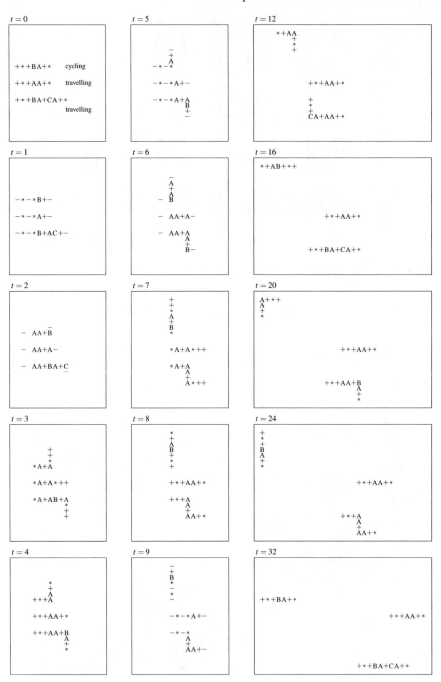

Fig. 14.14 Behavior of Worms in SR$_{2D}$

It is easy to see that the length of a Worm does not vary if it contains only advance commands and never touches itself. Hence, the same pattern appears infinitely many times. Thus, we can classify Worms into two categories: cycling Worms and travelling Worms. A Worm is called *cycling* if its pattern appears at the same position after some time steps. A Worm is called *travelling* if its pattern appears at a different position after some time steps, thus it moves away in some direction. Figure 14.14 show examples of cycling and travelling Worms.

14.2.1.4 Self-reproduction of Worms

We now explain branching and splitting processes of a Worm, and then show that a travelling Worm can self-reproduce indefinitely in the two-dimensional plane by giving a branch command. Rules (30) – (37) in Fig. 14.15 are for executing branch commands BA, BB, and BC. A branching process initiated by a command BA is shown in Fig. 14.16. In the case of a command BB or BC, a Worm branches in two-ways.

At the branching point, a command sequence (i.e., gene) is copied by the rules (5) – (8). Hence, these branches have the same shape, though they grow in different directions.

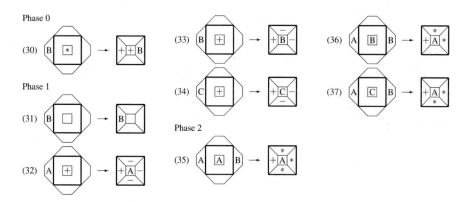

Fig. 14.15 Rules for branching a head

When a tail reaches a branching point, splitting rules (38) – (52) in Fig. 14.17 are applied. Figure 14.18 shows an example of splitting process caused by a command BA that finally produces three daughter Worms. These Worms also have branch commands, but they differ: The center daughter has a three-way branch command BA, while the left and right daughter have a leftward and rightward branch commands BB, BC, respectively by the rule (44). Figure 14.19 shows a splitting process caused by BB that produces two daughters. In this case, the left daughter has no branch command, while the center one has the leftward branch command BB by

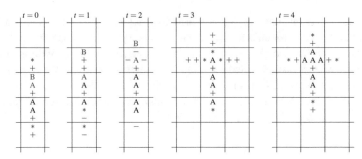

Fig. 14.16 Execution of a branch command BA

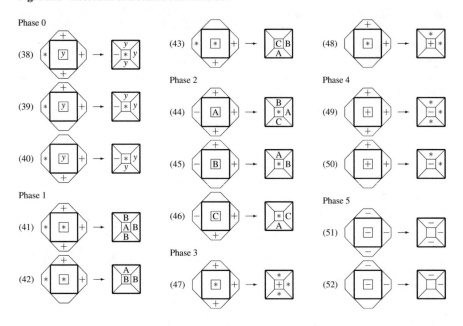

Fig. 14.17 Rules for splitting a tail ($y \in \{A,B,C\}$)

rule (45). As we shall see below, overcrowding of Worms can be avoided by this mechanism.

Using branching and splitting mechanism, a travelling Worm with a branch command can self-reproduce indefinitely provided that it does not touch itself in the branching process. Figures 14.21 and 14.22 show self-reproduction processes of Worms.

It is easy to see that a travelling Worm with no branch command of length n repeats its (translated) pattern every $8(n-2)$ steps. Assume at time 0 there is a pattern of a travelling Worm having only one branch command BA. It also takes $8(n-2)$ steps to produce a configuration containing three daughter Worms identical to the initial one except that they may have different branch command and may be

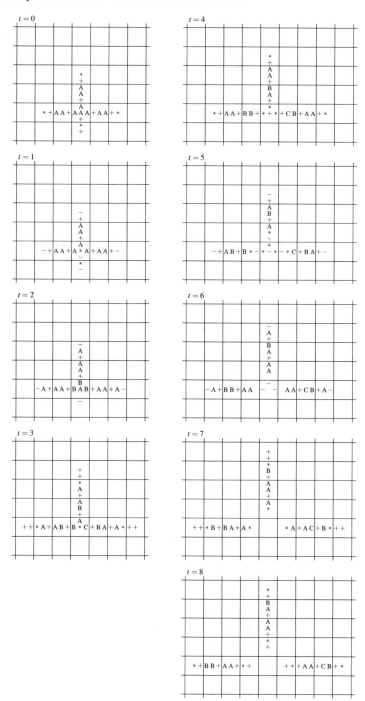

Fig. 14.18 A splitting process that produces three daughter Worms

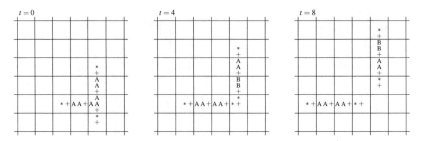

Fig. 14.19 A splitting process that produces two daughter Worms

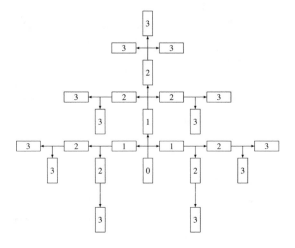

Fig. 14.20 Lineage of Worms. The number represents the generation of a Worm

rotated. The center daughter further produces three grand-daughters. Each of the left and right daughters produces two, and so on. Figure 14.20 shows a family of Worms and their positions.

Let $A(k), B(k), C(k)$ and $Z(k)$ be the total number of Worms having a branch command BA, BB, BC, and no branch command, respectively, at time $8(n-2)k$. Then the following equations hold for $k \in \{0, 1, 2, \cdots\}$.

$$
\begin{aligned}
A(k) &= 1 \\
B(0) &= 0, \quad B(k+1) = A(k) + B(k) \\
C(0) &= 0, \quad C(k+1) = A(k) + C(k) \\
Z(0) &= 0, \quad Z(k+1) = Z(k) + B(k) + C(k)
\end{aligned}
$$

By solving these equations we can obtain

$$
N(k) = A(k) + B(k) + C(k) + Z(k) = k^2 + k + 1,
$$

the total number of Worms at the k-th generation.

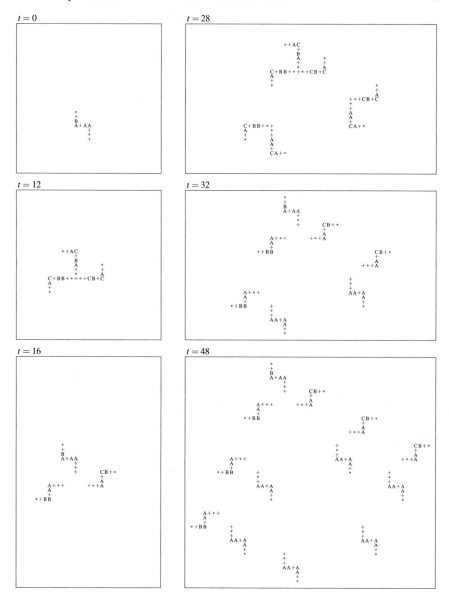

Fig. 14.21 Self-reproduction process of a small Worm

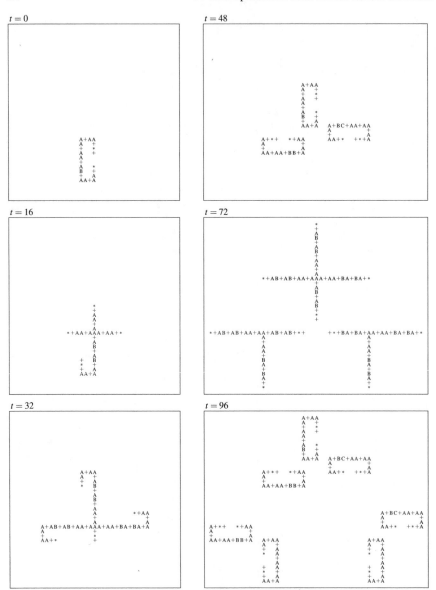

Fig. 14.22 Self-reproduction process of a curled Worm

14.2.1.5 Self-reproduction of Loops

A *Loop* is a simple closed wire, thus has neither a head nor a tail as shown in Fig. 14.23.

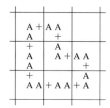

Fig. 14.23 An example of a Loop

If a Loop contains only advance or branch commands, these commands simply rotate in the Loop and self-reproduction does not occur. In order to make a Loop self-reproduce, commands in Table 14.2 are required.

Table 14.2 Commands DB and DC for self-reproduction of Loops

First signal	Second signal	Operation
D	B	Create an arm
D	C	Encode the shape of a Loop

A command DB is transmitted by rules (53) – (58) in Fig. 14.24. On a straight part of a wire, it propagates in the same way as other commands in Table 14.1 (rules (53) – (56)). But, at the corner of a wire, it starts to make an "arm" (rules (57) and (58)). An *arm* is a kind of branch to construct an offspring of a Loop. Rules (59) – (67) in Fig. 14.25 are for creating an arm.

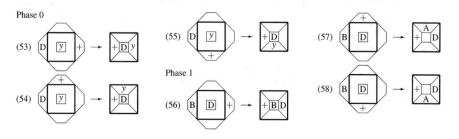

Fig. 14.24 Rules for transmitting a command DB ($y \in \{A, B, C\}$)

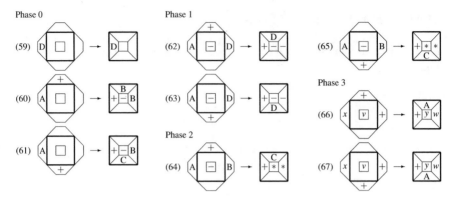

Fig. 14.25 Rules for creating an arm $((v,w) \in \{(*,A),(-,B),(+,C)\}, (x,y) \in \{(A,*),(B,-), (C,+)\})$

The root of an arm is a special kind of branching point. Signals reaching this cell are transmitted only to the arm, and signals A's are put into the mother Loop (rules (66) and (67)). Note that at the center part of this branching cell, the states $*, -$, and $+$ are used to represent the signals A, B, and C, respectively. Figure 14.26 shows a process of transmitting a command DB and creating an arm.

After creating an arm, the shape of the mother Loop is encoded into a sequence of advance commands. This process is controlled by a special command DC, which is generated when the arm is created (at time $t = 6$ and 7 in Fig. 14.26). Encoding is performed by rules (68) – (76) in Fig. 14.27. Generated sequence of advance commands travel through the Loop and then sent to the arm by rules (66) and (67). This command sequence is the gene of the mother Loop. Figure 14.28 shows an example of an encoding process.

If the command DC reaches the branching point, encoding process of the shape of the Loop terminates. Then the arm is cut off by rules (77) – (84) in Fig. 14.29. This process is shown in Fig. 14.30.

The arm cut off from the mother Loop acts just like a Worm. But, its head will eventually meet its tail, since the command sequence was created from the shape of the mother Loop. Thus, it will form a Loop identical to the mother Loop. Rules (85) – (92) in Fig. 14.31 are for making a daughter Loop, and Fig. 14.32 shows an example of its process.

Examples of entire self-reproduction processes of Loops are shown in Figs. 14.33 and 14.34. By putting a command DB at an appropriate position, *every* Loop having only AA commands in other cells can self-reproduce in this way.

14.2.1.6 Reversibility of SR_{2D}

In the previous subsubsections, we gave rule schemes (1) – (92) for the local function f of SR_{2D}. From them we can obtain 765 instances of local rules including

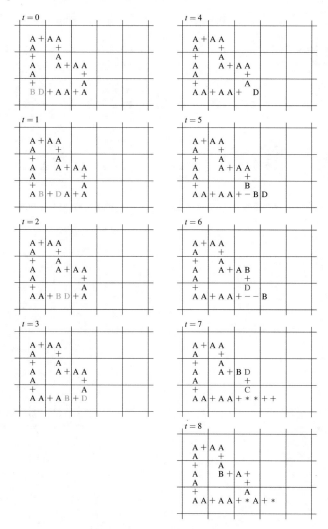

Fig. 14.26 Processes of transmitting a command DB ($0 \leq t \leq 4$), and creating an arm ($4 \leq t \leq 8$)

rotated ones (the complete list of them is given in [5]). We can verify that there is no pair of distinct rules whose right-hand sides are the same. Since it is a tedious task, it was done by a computer program. By Lemma 6.1 we can obtain a total injective function f, and thus SR$_{2D}$ is an RCA. Note that, though SR$_{2D}$ has 8^5 states in total, only 765 states are actually used for self-reproduction.

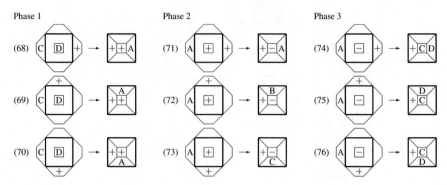

Fig. 14.27 Rules for encoding the shape of a Loop by a command DC. Note that the rules (53) – (55) are used in Phase 0

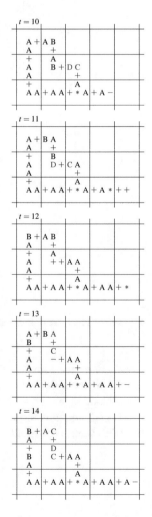

Fig. 14.28 Encoding the shape of a Loop into an advance command by a command DC. Here, an advance command AC is generated at $t = 14$

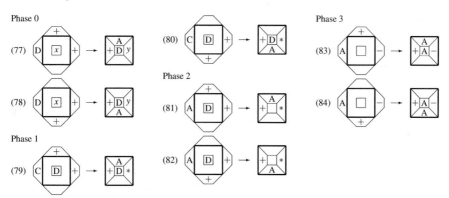

Fig. 14.29 Rules for cutting off an arm $((x,y) \in \{(*,A),(-,B),(+,C)\})$

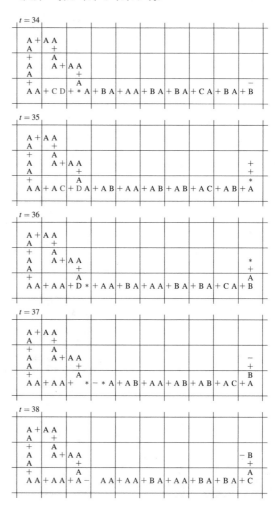

Fig. 14.30 A process of cutting off an arm

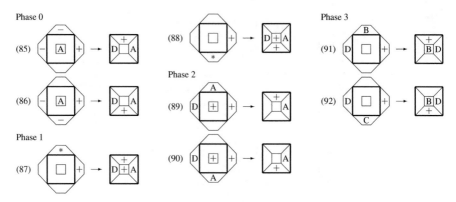

Fig. 14.31 Rules for making a daughter Loop

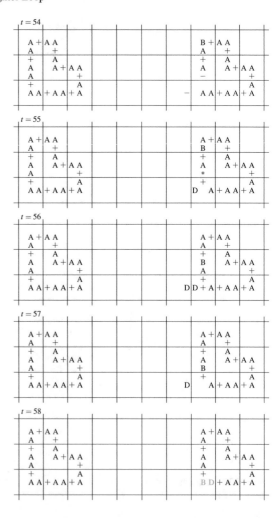

Fig. 14.32 A process of making a daughter Loop

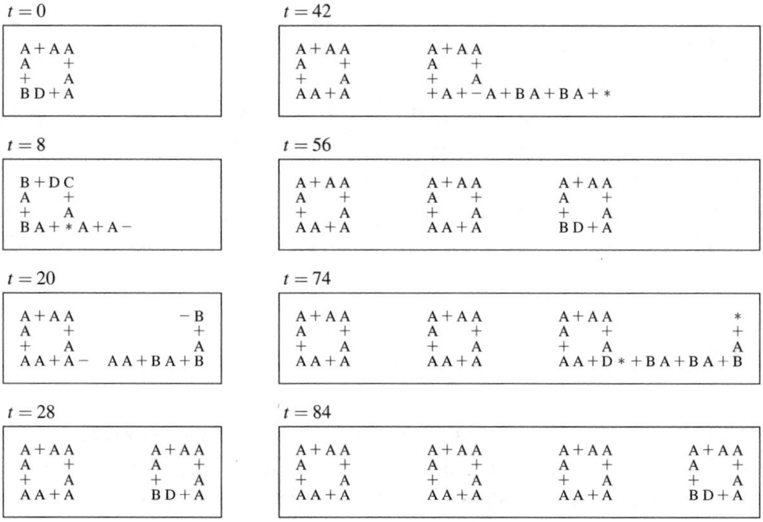

```
t = 0                              t = 42

 A + A A                            A + A A        A + A A
 A     +                            A     +        A     +
 +     A                            +     A        +     A
 B D + A                            A A + A        + A + − A + B A + B A + *


t = 8                              t = 56

 B + D C                            A + A A        A + A A        A + A A
 A     +                            A     +        A     +        A     +
 +     A                            +     A        +     A        +     A
 B A + * A + A −                    A A + A        A A + A        B D + A


t = 20                             t = 74

 A + A A           − B              A + A A        A + A A        A + A A              *
 A     +           +                A     +        A     +        A     +              +
 +     A           A                +     A        +     A        +     A              A
 A A + A −   A A + B A + B          A A + A        A A + A        A A + D * + B A + B A + B


t = 28                             t = 84

 A + A A       A + A A              A + A A        A + A A        A + A A        A + A A
 A     +       A     +              A     +        A     +        A     +        A     +
 +     A       +     A              +     A        +     A        +     A        +     A
 A A + A       B D + A              A A + A        A A + A        A A + A        B D + A
```

Fig. 14.33 Self-reproduction process of the smallest Loop

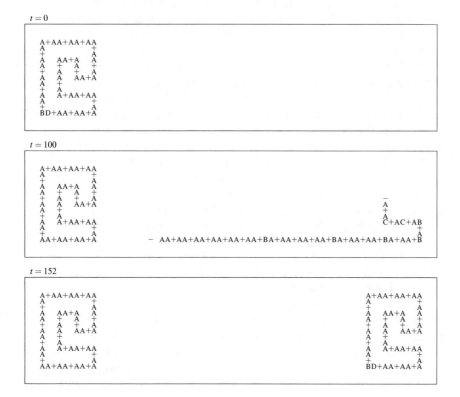

Fig. 14.34 Self-reproduction process of a larger Loop

Since SR_{2D} is reversible, there arises a naive question. Assume some self-reproducing configuration is given at $t = 0$. Then, how are the configurations at $t < 0$? If we use only the rules (1) – (92), we cannot go back the evolution process for $t < 0$, because undefined cases will occur. If we add rules "randomly" and make f be a total injective function, then we observe that random-like patterns appear and grow in the negative time direction. On the other hand, if we add some new states and rules to SR_{2D} appropriately, it is also possible to have an RPCA model in which self-reproduction occurs both in the positive and the negative directions of time.

14.2.2 Three-dimensional model SR_{3D}

It is possible to construct a three-dimensional model of self-reproduction by extending the RPCA SR_{2D}. Imai, Hori and Morita [3] designed a three-dimensional rotation-symmetric seven-neighbor RPCA in which Worms and Loops can reproduce themselves. It is written as SR_{3D} below. Each of seven parts of a cell has nine states, and thus a cell has 9^7 states in total. Although it is very large, the number of actually used states (i.e., the number of local rules) is 6886, which is rather small as in the case of SR_{2D}. The local rules that are actually used are described by 338 rule schemes [3]. In the following, only an outline of SR_{3D} is explained.

Basic mechanism of self-reproduction in SR_{3D} is similar to that in SR_{2D}, i.e., the shape of an object is represented by a command sequence, and encoding, decoding and copying operations are performed in a reversible way. However, it is not a mere extension of SR_{2D}, because varieties of possible shapes and arrangements of Worms and Loops are much greater than the two-dimensional case. For example, Fig. 14.35 shows a complex Loop having a knot. Even such a loop can self-reproduce.

In the three-dimensional case, Worms and Loops have a shape of a ribbon, which is of three-cell width as in Fig. 14.35. If the width is one, they cannot distinguish four directions, since SR_{3D} is rotation-symmetric. SR_{3D} has all the commands in SR_{2D}. In addition, it has two more commands. They are for twisting a head 90 degrees clockwise and counterclockwise, which are needed to make the head of a Worm turn upward or downward, besides the right and the left turn. The upward or the downward turn is performed by twisting the head of the Worm first, and then making the operation of the right or the left turn (Fig. 14.36). The branch commands for Worms, and the arm-creating and shape-encoding commands for Loops are also similar to the case of SR_{2D} (Tables 14.1 and 14.2)

Figure 14.37 shows simple self-reproduction of a straight Worm. Figure 14.38 shows self-reproduction of a Loop. In this case, the produced Loops form a semi-infinite chain. Adjustment of the position of a daughter Loop is made by controlling the head position by a command sequence contained in the mother Loop at time 0, which is also inherited by the daughter Loop. Self-reproduction of another type of a Loop is given in Fig. 14.39. Here, by creating four arms, reproduction is sped up. Several example movies of self-reproduction processes including the ones in Figs. 14.37 – 14.39 can be seen in [7].

Fig. 14.35 A three-dimensional complex Loop with a knot in the RPCA SR$_{3D}$ [3, 7]

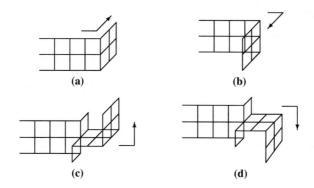

Fig. 14.36 Realizing four kinds of turns at the head of a Worm in SR$_{3D}$. **(a)** Left, **(b)** right, **(c)** upward, and **(d)** downward turns

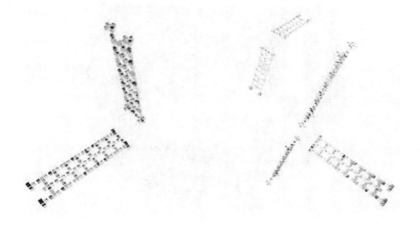

Fig. 14.37 Self-reproduction of a three-dimensional straight Worm in the RPCA SR$_{3D}$ [3, 7]

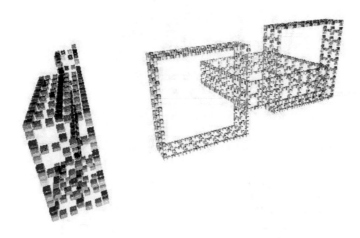

Fig. 14.38 Self-reproduction of a three-dimensional Loop in the RPCA SR$_{3D}$ [3, 7]. Here, the produced Loops form a chain

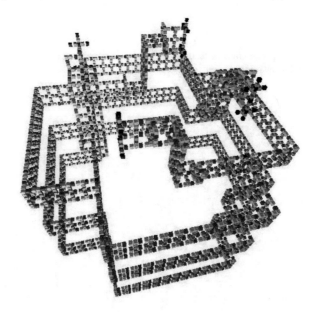

Fig. 14.39 Self-reproduction of another type of a three-dimensional Loop in the RPCA SR$_{3D}$ [3, 7]

14.3 Concluding Remarks

In this chapter, two kinds of self-reproducing RPCAs were designed. They are two- and three-dimensional RPCAs SR_{2D} and SR_{3D} in which Worms and Loops can reproduce themselves. These RPCAs are neither Turing universal nor construction-universal in the von Neumann sense. However, a self-reproduction process is carried out by a command sequence kept in a Worm or a Loop, which is a description of the object, and thus it satisfies the Langton's criterion for self-reproduction [4] (see Sect. 14.1). In these RPCAs, conversion between a command sequence and a shape of an object, and copying a command sequence are performed reversibly. By this, self-reproduction is realizable in RPCAs.

Another feature of SR_{2D} and SR_{3D} is that they use the shape-encoding mechanism. In these RPCAs, a shape of an object can be encoded into a command sequence, i.e., conversion from a shape to its description is possible. This makes the whole self-reproduction mechanism simple. Also, the variety of shapes of self-reproducing objects becomes large. Actually, almost all Worms and Loops can reproduce themselves provided that they do not touch themselves in the process of self-reproduction. The shape-encoding mechanism was also used for designing an irreversible CA in which Worms and Loops can self-reproduce in a simple way [6].

It will be possible to construct an RPCA that is both Turing universal and construction-universal in the von Neumann sense. But, it may become quite complex, and may need a very large number of states. It is left for future study to design such an RPCA in an *elegant way*.

References

1. Burks, A.W.: Von Neumann's self-reproducing automata. In: Essays on Cellular Automata (ed. A.W. Burks), pp. 3–64. University of Illinois Press, Urbana (1970)
2. Codd, E.F.: Cellular Automata. Academic Press, New York (1968)
3. Imai, K., Hori, T., Morita, K.: Self-reproduction in three-dimensional reversible cellular space. Artif. Life **8**, 155–174 (2002). doi:10.1162/106454602320184220
4. Langton, C.G.: Self-reproduction in cellular automata. Physica D **10**, 135–144 (1984). doi:10.1016/0167-2789(84)90256-2
5. Morita, K., Imai, K.: Self-reproduction in a reversible cellular space. Theoret. Comput. Sci. **168**, 337–366 (1996). doi:10.1016/S0304-3975(96)00083-7
6. Morita, K., Imai, K.: A simple self-reproducing cellular automaton with shape-encoding mechanism. In: Proc. Artificial Life V (eds. C.G. Langton, K. Shimohara), The MIT Press, pp. 489–496 (1997)
7. Morita, K., Imai, K.: Self-reproduction in two- and three-dimensional reversible cellular automata (slides with simulation movies). Hiroshima University Institutional Repository, http://ir.lib.hiroshima-u.ac.jp/00031368 (2011)
8. von Neumann, J.: Theory of Self-reproducing Automata (ed. A.W. Burks). The University of Illinois Press, Urbana (1966)
9. Sipper, M.: Fifty years of research on self-replication: An overview. Artif. Life **4**, 237–257 (1998). doi:10.1162/106454698568576
10. Tempesti, G.: Self-replicating loops: a survey. Int. J. General Systems **41**, 633–643 (2012). doi:10.1080/03081079.2012.695902

Index

Printed in the United States
By Bookmasters